BEGINNING VISUAL BASIC® 2015

BEGINNING

Visual Basic® 2015

BEGINNING

Visual Basic® 2015

Bryan Newsome

wrox™
A Wiley Brand

Beginning Visual Basic® 2015

Published by
John Wiley & Sons, Inc.
10475 Crosspoint Boulevard
Indianapolis, IN 46256
www.wiley.com

Copyright © 2016 by John Wiley & Sons, Inc., Indianapolis, Indiana

Published simultaneously in Canada

ISBN: 978-1-119-09211-7

ISBN: 978-1-119-09207-0 (ebk)

ISBN: 978-1-119-09208-7 (ebk)

10 9 8 7 6 5 4 3 2 1

For general information on our other products and services please contact our Customer Care Department within the United States at (877) 762-2974, outside the United States at (317) 572-3993 or fax (317) 572-4002.

Wiley publishes in a variety of print and electronic formats and by print-on-demand. Some material included with standard print versions of this book may not be included in e-books or in print-on-demand. If this book refers to media such as a CD or DVD that is not included in the version you purchased, you may download this material at http://booksupport.wiley.com. For more information about Wiley products, visit www.wiley.com.

Library of Congress Control Number: 2015953114

For my girls, Jennifer and Katelyn.

ABOUT THE AUTHOR

BRYAN NEWSOME leads a team of top developers specializing in Microsoft solutions. Since starting building Visual Basic 5 solutions, he has embraced each new version of Visual Basic and now creates all new solutions leveraging the .NET platform and VB.NET. He provides clients with solutions and mentoring on leading-edge Microsoft technologies. For VB.NET, Bryan is a Microsoft Certified Application Developer.

ABOUT THE TECHNICAL EDITOR

VALAN MONEY is a Microsoft Certified Solution Developer for Web and Windows applications. He has been using Visual Basic since 1996 and got his first certification in Visual Basic 4.0. Since then, he has also received certifications in newer versions of VB and VB.NET. He works as Technical Team Lead and Senior Consultant for projects using Microsoft technologies. He holds a Masters degree in Computer Science from St. Joseph's College, Tiruchirappalli, India.

CREDITS

Senior Acquisitions Editor
Kenyon Brown

Project Editor
Maureen S. Tullis

Technical Editor
Valan Money

Production Editor
Dassi Zeidel

Copy Editor
Scott D. Tullis

Manager of Content Development & Assembly
Mary Beth Wakefield

Marketing Director
David Mayhew

Marketing Manager
Carrie Sherrill

Professional Technology & Strategy Director
Barry Pruett

Business Manager
Amy Knies

Associate Publisher
Jim Minatel

Project Coordinator, Cover
Brent Savage

Proofreader
Nancy Carrasco

Indexer
Johnna VanHoose Dinse

Cover Designer
Wiley

Cover Image
©anasimin/iStockphoto

ACKNOWLEDGMENTS

Thanks to those who worked so hard to get this book on the shelves at Wiley and Wrox. Special thanks (again) to Maureen Tullis who went above and beyond to help me finish mostly on schedule.

CONTENTS

INTRODUCTION

VISUAL BASIC 2015 IS Microsoft's latest version of the highly popular Visual Basic .NET programming language, one of the many languages supported in Visual Studio 2015. Visual Basic 2015's strength lies in its ease of use and the speed at which you can create Windows Forms and Windows 8 applications, web applications, and mobile device applications.

In this book, we introduce you to programming with Visual Basic 2015 and show you how to create these types of applications and services. Along the way you'll also learn about object-oriented techniques and learn how to create your own business objects and Windows controls.

Microsoft's .NET Framework provides Visual Basic 2015 programmers with the capability to create full object-oriented programs, just like the ones created using C# or C++. The .NET Framework provides a set of base classes that are common to all programming languages in Visual Studio 2015, which provides you with the same capability to create object-oriented programs as a programmer using C# or C++.

This book will give you a thorough grounding in the basics of programming using Visual Basic 2015; from there the world is your oyster.

WHO THIS BOOK IS FOR

This book is designed to teach you how to write useful programs in Visual Basic 2015 as quickly and easily as possible.

There are two kinds of beginners for whom this book is ideal:

➤ You're a beginner to programming and you've chosen Visual Basic 2015 as the place to start. That's a great choice! Visual Basic 2015 is not only easy to learn, it's also fun to use and very powerful.

➤ You can program in another language but you're a beginner to .NET programming. Again, you've made a great choice! Whether you've come from Fortran or Cobol, you'll find that this book quickly gets you up to speed on what you need to know to get the most from Visual Basic 2015.

WHAT THIS BOOK COVERS

Visual Basic 2015 offers a great deal of functionality in both tools and language. No one book could ever cover Visual Basic 2015 in its entirety—you would need a library of books. What this book aims to do is to get you started as quickly and easily as possible. It shows you the roadmap, so to speak, of what there is and where to go. Once we've taught you the basics of creating working applications (creating the windows and controls, how your code should handle unexpected events, what object-oriented programming is, how to use it in your applications, and so on) we'll show you some of the areas you might want to try your hand at next:

- ➤ Chapters 1 through 8 provide an introduction to Visual Studio 2015 and Windows programming.
- ➤ Chapter 9 provides an introduction to application debugging and error handling.
- ➤ Chapter 10 provides an introduction to object-oriented programming and building objects.
- ➤ Chapter 11 provides an introduction to creating Windows Forms user controls.
- ➤ Chapters 12 and 13 provide an introduction to programming with databases and covers Structured Query Language, SQL Server, and ADO.NET.
- ➤ Chapter 14 provides an introduction to ASP.NET and shows you how to write applications for the web.
- ➤ Chapter 15 introduces you to deploying applications using ClickOnce technology.
- ➤ Chapter 16 show you how to build your first Windows 8 application and introduces you to design principles for touch interfaces.

WHAT YOU NEED TO USE THIS BOOK

Apart from a willingness to learn, all you'll need are a PC running Windows 8 (preferred), Windows 7, Windows Server 2008 R2, Windows Server 2015; Internet Explorer; and of course:

- ➤ Microsoft Visual Basic 2015Community Edition or higher

For the database chapters, you should install SQL Server 2014 Express, although, any edition you have should work with little to no changes required.

CONVENTIONS

To help you get the most from the text and keep track of what's happening, we've used a number of conventions throughout the book.

TRY IT OUT

The *Try It Out* is an exercise you should work through, following the text in the book.

1. They usually consist of a set of steps.
2. Each step has a number.
3. Follow the steps through with your copy of the database.

How It Works

After each *Try It Out*, the code you've typed will be explained in detail.

> **WARNING** *Boxes like this one hold important, not-to-be forgotten information that is directly relevant to the surrounding text.*

> **NOTE** *Tips, hints, tricks, and asides to the current discussion look like this.*

As for other conventions in the text:

➤ New terms and important words are *highlighted* in italics when first introduced.

➤ Keyboard combinations are treated like this: Ctrl+R.

➤ Filenames, URLs, and code within the text are treated like so: `persistence.properties`.

    ```
    This book uses monofont type with no highlighting for most code examples.
    This book uses bolding to emphasize code that is of particular
    importance in the present context.
    ```

SOURCE CODE

As you work through the examples in this book, you may choose either to type in all the code manually or to use the source-code files that accompany the book. All of the source code used in this book is available for download at `www.wrox.com`. Once at the site, simply locate the book's title (either by using the Search box or by using one of the title lists) and click the Download Code link on the book's detail page to obtain all the source code for the book.

> **NOTE** *Because many books have similar titles, you may find it easiest to search by ISBN; this book's ISBN is 978-1-119-09211-7*

Once you download the code, just decompress it with your favorite compression tool. Alternately, you can go to the main Wrox code download page at `www.wrox.com` to see the code available for this book and all other Wrox books.

ERRATA

We make every effort to ensure that there are no errors in the text or in the code. However, no one is perfect, and mistakes do occur. If you find an error in one of our books, like a spelling mistake or faulty piece of code, we would be very grateful for your feedback. By sending in errata, you may save another reader hours of frustration, and at the same time you will be helping us provide even higher-quality information.

To find the errata page for this book, go to www.wrox.com and locate the title using the Search box or one of the title lists. Then, on the book details page, click the Book Errata link. On this page you can view all errata that have been submitted for this book and posted by Wrox editors. A complete book list, including links to each book's errata, is also available at www.wrox.com/misc-pages/booklist.shtml.

If you don't spot "your" error on the Book Errata page, go to www.wrox.com/contact/techsupport .shtml and complete the form there to send us the error you have found. We'll check the information and, if appropriate, post a message to the book's errata page and fix the problem in subsequent editions of the book.

P2P.WROX.COM

For author and peer discussion, join the P2P forums at p2p.wrox.com. The forums are a web-based system on which you can post messages relating to Wrox books and related technologies and interact with other readers and technology users. The forums offer a subscription feature to email you topics of interest of your choosing when new posts are made to the forums. Wrox authors, editors, other industry experts, and your fellow readers are present on these forums.

At http://p2p.wrox.com you will find a number of different forums that will help you not only as you read this book, but also as you develop your own applications. To join the forums, just follow these steps:

1.   Go to p2p.wrox.com and click the Register link.

2.   Read the terms of use and click Agree.

3.   Complete the required information to join as well as any optional information you wish to provide, and click Submit.

4.   You will receive an email with information describing how to verify your account and complete the joining process.

> **NOTE** *You can read messages in the forums without joining P2P, but in order to post your own messages, you must join.*

Once you join, you can post new messages and respond to messages other users post. You can read messages at any time on the web. If you would like to have new messages from a particular forum emailed to you, click the Subscribe to this Forum icon by the forum name in the forum listing.

For more information about how to use the Wrox P2P, be sure to read the P2P FAQs for answers to questions about how the forum software works, as well as many common questions specific to P2P and Wrox books. To read the FAQs, click the FAQ link on any P2P page.

BEGINNING

Visual Basic® 2015

1

Welcome to Visual Basic 2015

WHAT YOU WILL LEARN IN THIS CHAPTER:

- ➤ Using event-driven programming

- ➤ Installing Visual Basic 2015

- ➤ Touring the Visual Basic 2015 integrated development environment (IDE)

- ➤ Creating a simple Windows program

- ➤ Using the integrated Help system

WROX.COM CODE DOWNLOADS FOR THIS CHAPTER

The wrox.com code downloads for this chapter are found at www.wrox.com/begvisualbasic2015 on the Download Code tab. The code is in the 092117 C01.zip download.

This is an exciting time to enter the world of programming with Visual Basic 2015 and Windows 8 and the new Windows 10. The new Windows operating systems represent the latest from Microsoft and are packed with a lot of new features to make Windows programming fun. Much has changed in the Windows user interface, and Visual Basic 2015 makes it easy to write professional-looking Windows applications as well as web applications and web services. Haven't upgraded to Windows 8 or 10 yet? No worries; Visual Basic 2015 also enables you to write professional-looking applications for previous versions of Windows as well.

The goal of this book is to help you use the Visual Basic 2015 programming language, even if you have never programmed before. You start slowly and build on what you have learned in subsequent chapters. So take a deep breath, let it out slowly, and tell yourself you can do this. No sweat! No kidding!

Programming a computer is a lot like teaching a child to tie his shoes. Until you find the correct way of giving the instructions, not much is accomplished. Visual Basic 2015 is a language you can use to tell your computer how to do things; but like a child, the computer will understand only if you explain things very clearly. If you have never programmed before, this sounds like an arduous task, and sometimes it can be. However, Visual Basic 2015 offers an easy-to-use language to explain some complex tasks. Although it never hurts to have an understanding of what is happening at the lowest levels, Visual Basic 2015 frees the programmer from having to deal with the mundane complexities of writing Windows applications. You are free to concentrate on solving real problems.

Visual Basic 2015 helps you create solutions that run on the Microsoft Windows operating systems, such as Windows 7, 8, or 10, Windows Server 2008, and Windows Phone. If you are looking at this book, you might have already felt the need or desire to create such programs. Even if you have never written a computer program before, as you progress through the Try It Out exercises in this book, you will become familiar with the various aspects of the Visual Basic 2015 language, as well as its foundations in the Microsoft .NET Framework. You will find that it is not nearly as difficult as you imagined. Before you know it, you will feel quite comfortable creating a variety of different types of programs with Visual Basic 2015.

Visual Basic 2015 can also be used to create web applications and web services, as well as mobile applications that can run on Tablet PCs or smartphones. However, you will begin by focusing on Windows applications before extending your boundaries to other platforms.

IMPLEMENTING EVENT-DRIVEN PROGRAMMING

A Windows program is quite different from yesteryear's MS-DOS program. A DOS program follows a relatively strict path from beginning to end. Although this does not necessarily limit the functionality of the program, it does limit the road the user has to take to get to it. A DOS program is like walking down a hallway; to get to the end you have to walk down the entire hallway, passing any obstacles that you may encounter. A DOS program would let you open only certain doors along your stroll.

Windows, on the other hand, opened up the world of *event-driven programming. Events* in this context include clicking a button, resizing a window, or changing an entry in a text box. The code that you write responds to these events. In terms of the hallway analogy: In a Windows program, to get to the end of the hall you just click the end of the hall. The hallway itself can be ignored. If you get to the end and realize that is not where you wanted to be, you can just set off for the new destination without returning to your starting point. The program reacts to your movements and takes the necessary actions to complete your desired tasks.

Another big advantage in a Windows program is the *abstraction of the hardware*, which means that Windows takes care of communicating with the hardware for you. You do not need to know the inner workings of every laser printer on the market just to create output. You do not need to study the schematics for graphics cards to write your own game. Windows wraps up this functionality by providing generic routines that communicate with the drivers written by hardware manufacturers. This is probably the main reason why Windows has been so successful. The generic routines are referred to as the Windows *application programming interface (API)*, and most of the classes in the .NET Framework take care of communicating with those APIs.

Before Visual Basic 1 was introduced to the world in 1991, developers had to be well versed in C and C++ programming, as well as the building blocks of the Windows system itself, the Windows

API. This complexity meant that only dedicated and properly trained individuals were capable of turning out software that could run on Windows. Visual Basic changed all that, and it has been estimated that there are now as many lines of production code written in Visual Basic as in any other language.

Visual Basic changed the face of Windows programming by removing the complex burden of writing code for the user interface (UI). By allowing programmers to *draw* their own UI, it freed them to concentrate on the business problems they were trying to solve. When the UI is drawn, the programmer can then add the code to react to events.

Visual Basic has also been *extensible* from the very beginning. Third-party vendors quickly saw the market for reusable modules to aid developers. These modules, or *controls*, were originally referred to as *VBXs* (named after their file extension). Prior to Visual Basic 5, if you did not like the way a button behaved, you could either buy or create your own, but those controls had to be written in C or C++. Database access utilities were some of the first controls available. Version 5 of Visual Basic introduced the concept of *ActiveX*, which enabled developers to create their own *ActiveX controls*.

When Microsoft introduced Visual Basic 3, the programming world changed significantly. You could build database applications directly accessible to users (so-called *front-end applications*) completely with Visual Basic. There was no need to rely on third-party controls. Microsoft accomplished this task with the introduction of *Data Access Objects* (*DAOs*), which enabled programmers to manipulate data with the same ease as manipulating the user interface.

Versions 4 and 5 extended the capabilities of version 3 to enable developers to target the new Windows 95 platform. They also made it easier for developers to write code, which could then be manipulated to make it usable to other language developers. Version 6 provided a new way to access databases with the integration of *ActiveX Data Objects* (*ADOs*). The ADO feature was developed by Microsoft to aid web developers using *Active Server Pages* (*ASP*) to access databases. All the improvements to Visual Basic over the years have ensured its dominant place in the programming world—it helps developers write robust and maintainable applications in record time.

INSTALLING VISUAL BASIC 2015

You may own Visual Basic 2015 in one of the following forms:

➤ **As part of Visual Studio 2015, a suite of tools and languages that also includes C# (pronounced "C-sharp") and Visual C++:** The Visual Studio 2015 product line includes Visual Studio Professional Edition or Visual Studio Tools Team Editions. The Team Edition versions come with progressively more tools for building and managing the development of larger, enterprise-wide applications.

➤ **As Visual Basic 2015 Express Edition:** This is a free edition for students and beginners, which includes the Visual Basic 2015 language and a smaller set of the tools and features available with Visual Studio 2015.

Both these products enable you to create your own applications for the Windows platform. The installation procedure is straightforward. In fact, the Visual Studio Installer is smart enough to figure out exactly what your computer requires to make it work.

The descriptions in the following Try It Out exercise are based on installing Visual Studio 2015 CTP 6. Most of the installation processes are straightforward, and you can accept the default installation options for most environments. Therefore, regardless of which edition you are installing, the installation process should be smooth when accepting the default installation options.

TRY IT OUT Installing Visual Basic 2015

There are two common ways to install Visual Studio. You can burn a DVD or attach a downloaded image (iso) or use the web installer. To use the web installer, just follow the on-screen prompts. If you choose to download the iso, follow these steps:

1. After downloading vs2015.ctp_ult_enu.iso, right-click the file and select Mount for the context menu. The Visual Studio 2015 DVD will open in a new Explorer Window. You need to run `vs_ultimate.exe` from the root directory of the DVD. Then click OK to start the setup program. After the setup program initializes, you see the initial screen, as shown in Figure 1-1. This dialog displays the location and size of the installation.

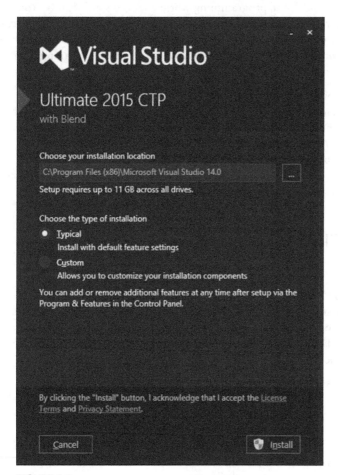

FIGURE 1-1

2. You need to select the type of installation on this screen. You should select Typical. After selecting the option, click Install to begin.

> **NOTE** *If you are a Windows Vista, Windows 7, or Windows 8 user, you may be prompted that the setup program needs to run, in which case you will need to grant permission to let it continue. After the setup program continues, you can sit back and relax while all the features are being installed. This process can take 20 minutes or more depending on the installation features chosen and the speed of your computer.*

3. Once the installation is complete, you are presented with a dialog informing you of the status of the installation, after which you will most likely have to restart.

Now the real fun can begin—so get comfortable, relax, and enter the world of Visual Basic 2015.

THE VISUAL STUDIO 2015 IDE

You don't need Visual Basic 2015 to write applications in the Visual Basic .NET language. The capability to run Visual Basic .NET code is included with the .NET Framework. You could write all your Visual Basic .NET code using a text editor such as Notepad. You could also hammer nails using your shoe as a hammer, but that slick pneumatic nailer sitting there is a lot more efficient. In the same way, by far the easiest way to write in Visual Basic .NET code is by using the Visual Studio 2015 Integrated Development Framework, known as the *IDE*. This is what you see when working with Visual Basic 2015: the windows, boxes, and so on. The IDE provides a wealth of features unavailable in ordinary text editors—such as code checking, visual representations of the finished application, and an explorer that displays all the files that make up your project.

The Profile Setup Page

An IDE is a way of bringing together a suite of tools that makes developing software a lot easier. If Visual Studio is not running, fire it up and see what you've got. If you used the default installation, go to your Windows Apps or Search Menu and then select Visual Studio 2015 CTP. A splash screen appears briefly so you can sign in. Because you will work offline for this book, you should choose Not Now, Maybe Later. When you create an account for free, your settings are saved and all your computers are synced to the same settings as far as Visual Studio is concerned. You will have more direct access to some online resources.

Then you see the Choose Default Environment Settings dialog. Select the Visual Basic Development Settings option and your choice for color theme; then click Start Visual Studio, as shown in Figure 1-2.

FIGURE 1-2

After Visual Studio configures the environment based on the chosen settings, the Microsoft Development Environment appears, as shown in Figure 1-3.

The Menu

By now, you might be eager to start writing some code; but hold off and begin your exploration of the IDE by looking at the menu and toolbar, which are not really all that different from the toolbars and menus available in other Windows applications (although they differ from the Ribbon in Microsoft Office 2007 and some of the newer Windows applications).

The Visual Studio 2015 menu is dynamic, which means items are added or removed depending on what you are trying to do. When looking at the blank IDE, the menu bar consists only of the File, Edit, View, Build, Debug, Team, SQL, Data, Format, Tools, Unit Test, Analyze, Window, and Help menus. When you start working on a project, however, the full Visual Studio 2015 menu appears, as shown in Figure 1-4.

At this point, there is no need to cover each menu topic in detail. You will become familiar with each of them as you progress through the book. Here is a quick rundown of what activities each menu item pertains to:

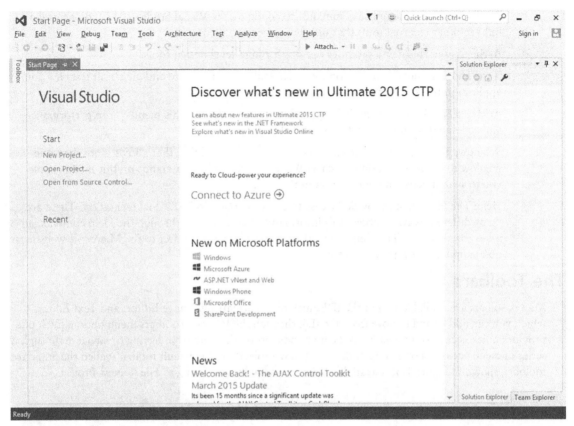

FIGURE 1-3

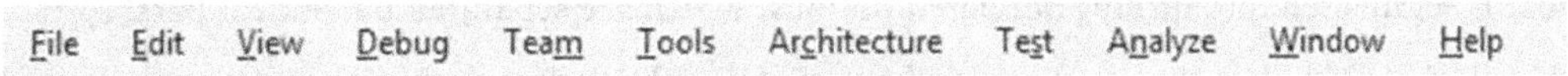

File   Edit   View   Debug   Team   Tools   Architecture   Test   Analyze   Window   Help

FIGURE 1-4

➤ **File:** Most software programs have a File menu. It has become the standard where you should find, if nothing else, a way to exit the application. In this case, you can also find ways of opening and closing single files and whole projects.

➤ **Edit:** The Edit menu provides access to the common items you would expect: Undo, Redo, Cut, Copy, Paste, and Delete.

➤ **View:** The View menu provides quick access to the windows that exist in the IDE, such as the Solution Explorer, Properties window, Output window, Toolbox, and so on.

➤ **Debug:** The Debug menu enables you to start and stop running your application within the Visual Basic 2015 IDE. It also gives you access to the Visual Studio 2015 debugger. The debugger enables you to step through your code while it is running to see how it is behaving.

➤ **Team:** This menu connects to Team Foundation Server. You use this when working with a team to build software.

➤ **Tools:** The Tools menu has commands to configure the Visual Studio 2015 IDE, as well as links to other external tools that may have been installed.

➤ **Architecture:** This menu provides options for high-level design tools.

➤ **Test:** The Test menu provides options that enable you to create and view unit tests for your application to exercise the source code in various scenarios.

➤ **Analyze:** The Analyze menu helps you check your code. Use this menu to run performance- and code-analysis tools to help you write better code.

➤ **Window:** This menu has become standard for any application that allows more than one window to be open at a time, such as Word or Excel. The commands on this menu enable you to switch between the windows in the IDE.

➤ **Help:** The Help menu provides access to the Visual Studio 2015 documentation. There are many different ways to access this information (for example, through the Help contents, an index, or a search). The Help menu also has options that connect to the Microsoft website to obtain updates or report problems.

The Toolbars

Many toolbars are available within the IDE, including Formatting, Image Editor, and Text Editor, which you can add to and remove from the IDE through the View ➪ Toolbars menu option. Each one provides quick access to frequently used commands, preventing you from having to navigate through a series of menu options. For example, the icon (New Project) on the default toolbar (called the Standard toolbar), shown in Figure 1-5, is available from the menu by navigating to File ➪ New Project.

FIGURE 1-5

The toolbar is segmented into groups of related options, which are separated by vertical bars:

➤ **Navigation:** The first group of icons is for navigating through code. Use these to go backward and forward as you move through your code.

➤ **Project and file options:** The next four icons provide access to the commonly used project- and file-manipulation options available through the File and Project menus, such as opening and saving files.

➤ **Code commenting:** The third group of icons is for commenting out and un-commenting sections of code. This process can be useful in debugging when you want to comment out a section of code to determine what results the program might produce by not executing those lines of code.

➤ **Managing code edits:** The fourth group of icons is for undoing and redoing edits and for navigating through your code.

➤ **Code step through:** The fifth group of icons provides the ability to start (via the green triangle), pause, and stop your application. You can also use three icons in this group to step into your code line by line, step over entire sections of code, and step out of a procedure. The solution configuration is used to build your project so you can debug and step into your code or so you can produce a build that you can release to customers. These icons will be covered in depth in Chapter 8.

➤ **Find in files dialog:** The final icon gives you access to the Find in Files dialog. This is an important feature that you will use often. You can also access this dialog by the shortcut keys Ctrl+F.

If you forget what a particular icon does, you can hover your mouse pointer over it so that a tool tip appears displaying the name of the toolbar option.

You could continue to look at each of the windows in the IDE by clicking the View menu and choosing the appropriate window; but as you can see, they are all empty at this stage and therefore not very revealing. The best way to look at the capabilities of the IDE is to use it while writing some code.

CREATING A SIMPLE APPLICATION

To finish your exploration of the IDE, you need to create a project so that the windows shown earlier in Figure 1-3 have some interesting content for you to look at.

TRY IT OUT   Creating a Hello User Project

In this Try It Out exercise, you will create a very simple application called Hello User that allows you to enter a person's name and display a greeting to that person in a message box:

1.   Click the New Project button on the toolbar.

2.   In the New Project dialog, select Visual Basic in the Installed Templates tree-view box to the left. The Templates pane on the right will display all the available templates for the project type chosen. Select the Windows Forms Application template.

3.   Type **Hello User** in the Name text box and click OK. Your New Project dialog should look like Figure 1-6.

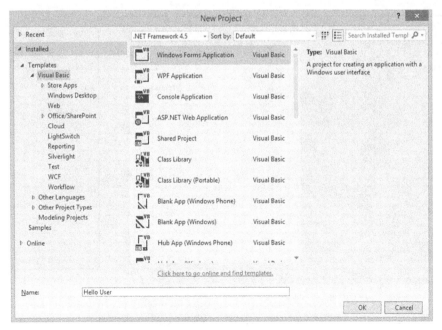

FIGURE 1-6

Visual Studio 2015 allows you to target your application to a specific version of the Microsoft .NET Framework. The combo box at the top of the Templates pane in the New Project dialog has version 4.5 selected, but you can target your application to earlier versions of the .NET Framework.

The IDE then creates an empty Windows application for you. So far, your Hello User program consists of one blank window, called a Windows Form (or sometimes just a form), with the default name of Form1.vb, as shown in Figure 1-7.

Whenever Visual Studio 2015 creates a new file, either as part of the project creation process or when you create a new file, it uses a name that describes what it is (in this case, a form) followed by a number.

Windows in the Visual Studio 2015 IDE

At this point, you can see that the various windows in the IDE are beginning to show their purposes, and you should take a brief look at them now before you come back to the Try It Out exercise.

> **NOTE** *If any of these windows are not visible on your screen, you can use the View menu to show them. Also, if you do not like the location of any particular window, you can move it by clicking its title bar and dragging it to a new location. The windows in the IDE can float (stand out on their own) or be docked (as they appear in Figure 1-7).*

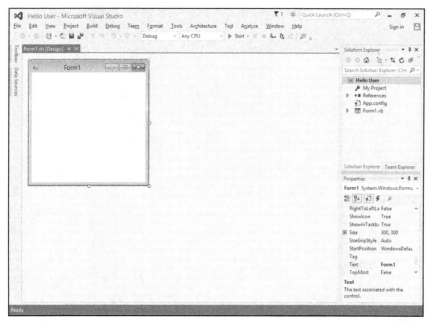

FIGURE 1-7

The following list introduces the most common windows:

➤ **Toolbox:** This contains reusable controls and components that can be added to your application. These range from buttons to data connectors to customized controls that you have either purchased or developed.

➤ **Design window:** This window is where a lot of the action takes place. This is where you draw your user interface on your forms. This window is sometimes referred to as *the Designer*.

➤ **Solution Explorer:** This window contains a hierarchical view of your solution. A *solution* can contain many projects, whereas a *project* contains forms, classes, modules, and components that solve a particular problem.

➤ **Properties:** This window shows what *properties* the selected object makes available. Although you can set these properties in your code, sometimes it is much easier to set them while you are designing your application (for example, drawing the controls on your form). You will notice that the `File Name` property has the value `Form1.vb`. This is the physical filename for the form's code and layout information.

TRY IT OUT Creating a Hello User Project (continued)

Next, you'll give your form a name and set a few properties for it:

1. Change the name of your form to something more indicative of your application. Click `Form1.vb` in the Solution Explorer window. Then, in the Properties window, change the `File Name` property from `Form1.vb` to `HelloUser.vb` and press Enter, as shown in Figure 1-8.

FIGURE 1-8

2. When changing properties you must either press Enter or click another property for it to take effect. Note that the form's filename has also been updated in the Solution Explorer to read `HelloUser.vb`.

3. Click the form displayed in the Design window. The Properties window changes to display the form's `Form` properties (rather than the `File` properties, which you have just been looking at).

> **NOTE** *The Properties window is dramatically different. This difference is the result of two different views of the same file. When the form name is highlighted in the Solution Explorer window, the physical file properties of the form are shown. When the form in the Design window is highlighted, the visual properties and logical properties of the form are shown.*

The Properties window allows you to set a control's properties easily. *Properties* are a particular object's set of internal data; they usually describe appearance or behavior. In Figure 1-9 you can see that properties appear alphabetically. The properties can also be grouped together in categories: Accessibility, Appearance, Behavior, Data, Design, Focus, Layout, Misc, and Window Style.

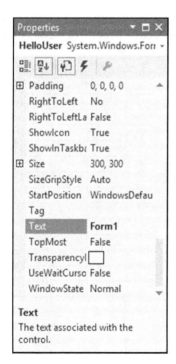

FIGURE 1-9

4. Right now, the title (Text property) of your form (displayed in the bar at the top of the form) is Form1. This is not very descriptive, so change it to reflect the purpose of this application. Locate the Text property in the Properties window. Change the Text property's value to **Hello from Visual Basic 2015** and press Enter. Note that the form's title has been updated to reflect the change.

> **NOTE** *If you have trouble finding properties, click the little AZ icon on the toolbar toward the top of the Properties window. This changes the property listing from being ordered by category to being ordered by name.*

5. You are now finished with this procedure. Click the Start button on the Visual Studio 2015 toolbar (the green triangle) to run the application. As you work through the book, whenever we say "run the project" or "start the project," just click the Start button. An empty window with the title Hello from Visual Basic 2015 appears.

That was simple, but your little application isn't doing much at the moment. Let's make it a little more interactive. To do this, you will add some controls—a label, a text box, and two buttons—to the form. This will enable you to see how the Toolbox makes adding functionality quite simple. You may be wondering at this point when you will actually look at some code. Soon! The great thing about Visual Basic 2015 is that you can develop a fair amount of your application without writing any code. Sure, the code is still there, behind the scenes, but as you will see, Visual Basic 2015 writes a lot of it for you.

The Toolbox

The Toolbox is accessed through the View ⇨ Toolbox menu option, by clicking the Toolbox icon on the Standard menu bar, or by pressing Ctrl+Alt+X. Alternatively, the Toolbox tab appears on the left of the IDE; hovering your mouse over this tab causes the Toolbox window to fly out, partially covering your form.

The Toolbox contains a node-type view of the various controls and components that can be placed onto your form. Controls such as text boxes, buttons, radio buttons, and combo boxes can be selected and then *drawn* onto your form. For the HelloUser application, you'll use only the controls in the Common Controls node. Figure 1-10 shows a listing of common controls for Windows forms.

Controls can be added to your forms in any order, so it doesn't matter whether you add the label control after the text box or the buttons before the label.

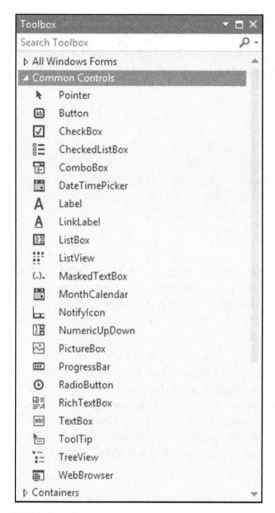

FIGURE 1-10

TRY IT OUT Adding Controls to the HelloUser Application

In the following Try It Out exercise, you start adding controls.

1. Stop the project if it is still running because you now want to add some controls to your form. The simplest way to stop your project is to click the close (X) button in the top right corner of the form. Alternatively, you can click the blue square on the toolbar (which displays a tool tip that says "Stop Debugging" if you hover over it with your mouse pointer).

2. Add a Label control to the form. Click Label in the Toolbox, drag it over to the form's Designer, and drop it in the desired location. (You can also place controls on your form by double-clicking the required control in the Toolbox or clicking the control in the Toolbox and then drawing it on the form.)

3. If the Label control you have just drawn is not in the desired location, no problem. When the control is on the form, you can resize it or move it around. Figure 1-11 shows what the control looks like after you place it on the form. To move it, click the control and drag it to the desired location. The label automatically resizes itself to fit the text that you enter in the Text property.

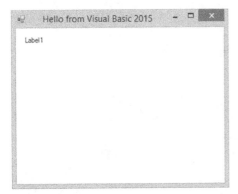

FIGURE 1-11

4. After drawing a control on the form, you should at least configure its name and the text that it will display. You will see that the Properties window to the right of the Designer has changed to Label1, telling you that you are currently examining the properties for the label. In the Properties window, set your new label's Text property to **Enter Your Name**. Note that after you press Enter or click another property, the label on the form has automatically resized itself to fit the text in the Text property. Now set the Name property to **lblName**.

5. Directly beneath the label, you want to add a text box so that you can enter a name. You will repeat the procedure you followed for adding the label, but this time make sure you select the TextBox control from the toolbar. After you have dragged and dropped (or double-clicked) the control into the appropriate position as shown in Figure 1-12, use the Properties window to set its Name property to **txtName**. Notice the sizing handles on the left and right side of the control. You can use these handles to resize the text box horizontally.

FIGURE 1-12

6. In the bottom left corner of the form, add a Button control in exactly the same manner as you added the label and text box. Set its Name property to **btnOK** and its Text property to **&OK**. Your form should now look similar to the one shown in Figure 1-13.

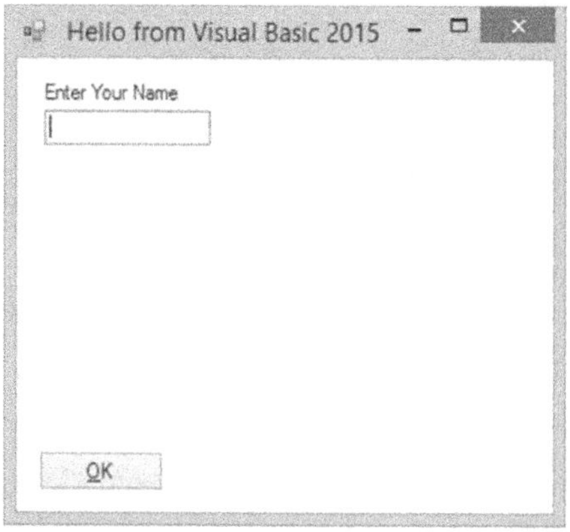

FIGURE 1-13

The ampersand (&) is used in the Text property of buttons to create a keyboard shortcut (known as a hot key). The letter with the & sign placed in front of it becomes underlined (as shown in Figure 1-13) to signal users that they can select that button by pressing the Alt+letter key combination, rather than using the mouse (on some configurations the underline doesn't appear until the user presses Alt). In this particular instance, pressing Alt+O would be the same as clicking the OK button. There is no need to write code to accomplish this.

7. Now add a second Button control to the bottom right corner of the form by dragging the Button control from the Toolbox onto your form. Notice that as you get close to the bottom right of the form, a blue snap line appears, as shown in Figure 1-14. This snap line enables you to align

FIGURE 1-14

this new Button control with the existing Button control on the form. The snap lines assist you in aligning controls to the left, right, top, or bottom of each other, depending on where you are trying to position the new control. The light blue line provides you with a consistent margin between the edge of your control and the edge of the form. Set the Name property to **btnExit** and the Text property to **E&xit**. Your form should look similar to Figure 1-15.

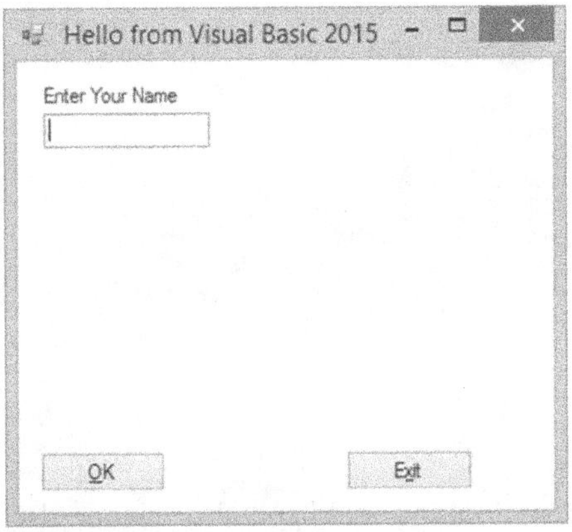

FIGURE 1-15

Now, before you finish your sample application, the following section briefly discusses some coding practices that you should be using.

Modified Hungarian Notation

You might have noticed that the names given to the controls look a little funny. Each name is prefixed with a shorthand identifier describing the type of control it is. This makes it much easier to understand what type of control you are working with as you look through the code. For example, say you had a control called simply Name, without a prefix of lbl or txt. You would not know whether you were working with a text box that accepted a name or with a label that displayed a name. Imagine if, in the previous Try It Out exercise, you had named your label Name1 and your text box Name2—you would very quickly become confused. What if you left your application for a month or two and then came back to it to make some changes?

When working with other developers, it is very important to keep the coding style consistent. One of the most commonly used styles for control names within application development in many languages was designed by Dr. Charles Simonyi, who worked for the Xerox Palo Alto Research Center (XPARC) before joining Microsoft. He came up with short prefix mnemonics that allowed programmers to easily identify the type of information a variable might contain. Because Simonyi is from Hungary, and the prefixes make the names look a little foreign, this naming system became known as *Hungarian Notation*. The original notation was used in C/C++ development, so the notation for Visual Basic 2015 is termed *Modified Hungarian Notation*. Table 1-1 shows some of the commonly used prefixes that you'll utilize in this book.

TABLE 1-1: Common Prefixes in Visual Basic 2015

CONTROL	PREFIX
Button	btn
ComboBox	cbo
CheckBox	chk
Label	lbl
ListBox	lst
MainMenu	mnu
RadioButton	rdb
PictureBox	pic
TextBox	txt

Hungarian Notation can be a real timesaver when you are looking at either code someone else wrote or code that you wrote months earlier. However, by far the most important thing is to be consistent in your naming. When you start coding, choose a convention for your naming. You will see many different types of naming styles; they go in and out of style constantly. Don't get stuck on one because when you go onto other projects you will be forced to use the style they use. After you pick a convention, stick to it for that project. When modifying others' code, use theirs. A standard naming convention followed throughout a project will save countless hours when the application is maintained. Now let's get back to the application. It's time to write some code.

The Code Editor

Now that you have the HelloUser form defined, you have to add some code to make it actually do something interesting. You have already seen how easy it is to add controls to a form. Providing the functionality behind those on-screen elements is no more difficult. To add the code for a control, you just double-click the control in question. This opens the Code Editor in the main window, shown in Figure 1-16.

Note that an additional tab has been created in the main window. Now you have the Design tab and the Code tab, each containing the name of the form you are working on. You draw the controls on your form in the Design tab, and you write code for your form in the Code tab. One thing to note here is that Visual Studio 2015 has created a separate file for the code. The visual definition and the code behind it exist in separate files: HelloUser.vb [Design] and HelloUser.vb. This is actually the reason why building applications with Visual Basic 2015 is so slick and easy. Using the design mode you can visually lay out your application; then, using Code view, you add just the bits of code to implement your desired functionality.

Note also the two combo boxes at the top of the window. They provide shortcuts to the various parts of your code. The combo box on the left is the Class Name combo box. If you expand this combo box, you see a list of all the objects within your form. The combo box on the right is the

Method Name combo box. If you expand this combo box, you see a list of all defined functions and events for the object selected in the Class Name combo box. If this particular form had a lot of code behind it, these combo boxes would make navigating to the desired code area very quick—jumping to the selected area in your code. However, all the code for this project so far fits in the window, so there aren't a lot of places to get lost.

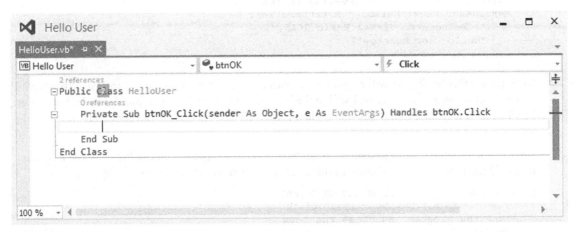

FIGURE 1-16

TRY IT OUT Adding Code to the Hello User Project

1. To begin adding the necessary code, click the Design tab to show the form again. Then double-click the OK button. The code window opens with the following code. This is the shell of the button's `Click` event and the place where you enter the code that you want to run when you click the button. This code is known as an *event handler*, sometimes also referred to as an *event procedure*:

```
Private Sub btnOK_Click(sender As Object, e As EventArgs)
    Handles btnOK.Click

End Sub
```

As a result of the typographic constraints in publishing, it may not be possible to put the `Sub` declaration on one line. Visual Basic 2015 allows you to break up lines of code by using the underscore character (_) to signify a line continuation. The space before the underscore is required. Any whitespace preceding the code on the following line is ignored. In some cases, you can break a line of code without the underscore as shown in the code that follows. You will learn more about the rules of breaking lines later.

```
Private Sub btnOK_Click(sender As Object,
    e As EventArgs) Handles btnOK.Click

End Sub
```

`Sub` is an example of a keyword. In programming terms, a *keyword* is a special word that is used to tell Visual Basic 2015 to do something special. In this case, it tells Visual Basic 2015 that this is a *subroutine*, a procedure that does not return a value. Anything that you type between the lines `Private Sub` and `End Sub` makes up the event procedure for the OK button.

2. Now add the bolded code to the procedure:

```
Private Sub btnOK_Click(ByVal sender As System.Object, _
    ByVal e As System.EventArgs) Handles btnOK.Click
    'Display a message box greeting to the user
    MessageBox.Show("Hello, " & txtName.Text & _
        "! Welcome to Visual Basic 2015.", _
        "Hello User Message")
End Sub
```

Throughout this book, you will be presented with code that you should enter into your program if you are following along. Usually, I will make it pretty obvious where you put the code, but as I go, I will explain anything that looks out of the ordinary. The bold code is the code that you should enter.

3. After you have added the preceding code, go back to the Design tab and double-click the Exit button. Add the following bolded code to the `btnExit_Click` event procedure:

```
Private Sub btnExit_Click(sender As Object,
    e As EventArgs) Handles btnExit.Click
    'End the program and close the form
    Me.Close()
End Sub
```

4. Now that the code is finished, the moment of truth has arrived and you can see your creation. First, however, save your work by using File ⇨ Save All from the menu or by clicking the Save All button on the toolbar. The Save Project dialog appears, prompting you for a name and location for saving the project.

    By default, a project is saved in a folder with the project name; in this case, Hello User. Because this is the only project in the solution, there is no need to create a separate folder for the solution, which contains the same name as the project, thus the "Create directory for solution" check box is unselected.

5. Now click the Start button on the toolbar. At this point, Visual Studio 2015 compiles the code. *Compiling* is the activity of taking the Visual Basic 2015 source code that you have written and translating it into a form that the computer understands. After the compilation is complete, Visual Studio 2015 *runs* (also known as *executes*) the program, and you'll be able to see the results.

    Any errors that Visual Basic 2015 encounters appear as tasks in the Error List window. Double-clicking a task transports you to the offending line of code. You will learn more about how to debug the errors in your code in Chapter 9.

6. When the application loads, you see the main form. Enter a name and click OK or press the Alt+O key combination (see Figure 1-17).

FIGURE 1-17

A window known as a *message box* appears as shown in Figure 1-18, welcoming the person whose name was entered in the text box on the form—in this case, Chris.

7. After you close the message box by clicking OK, click the Exit button on your form. The application closes and you are returned to the Visual Studio 2015 IDE.

How It Works

The code that you added to the Click event for the OK button takes the name that was entered in the text box and uses it as part of the message displayed in Figure 1-18.

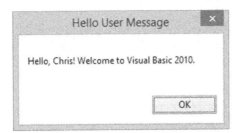

FIGURE 1-18

The first line of text you entered in this procedure ('Display a message box greeting to the user) is actually a *comment*, text that is meant to be read by the human programmer who is writing or maintaining the code, not by the computer. Comments in Visual Basic 2015 begin with a single quote ('), and everything following on that line is considered a comment and ignored by the compiler. Comments are discussed in detail in Chapter 3.

The MessageBox.Show method displays a message box that accepts various parameters. As used in your code, you have passed the string text to be displayed in the message box. This is accomplished through the *concatenation* of string constants defined by text enclosed in quotes. Concatenation of strings into one long string is performed through the use of the ampersand (&) character.

The code that follows concatenates a string constant of "Hello," followed by the value contained in the Text property of the txtName text box control, followed by a string constant of "! Welcome to Visual Basic 2015." The second parameter passed to the MessageBox.Show method is the caption to be used in the title bar of the Message Box dialog.

Finally, the underscore (_) character used at the end of the lines in the following code enables you to split your code onto separate lines. This tells the compiler that the rest of the code for the parameter is continued on the next line. This is very useful when building long strings because it enables you to view the entire code fragment in the Code Editor without having to scroll the Code Editor window to the right to view the entire line of code.

```
Private Sub btnOK_Click(sender As Object,
    e As EventArgs) Handles btnOK.Click
    'Display a message box greeting to the user
    MessageBox.Show("Hello, " & txtName.Text & _
        "! Welcome to Visual Basic 2015.", _
        "Hello User Message")
End Sub
```

The next procedure that you added code for was the Exit button's Click event. Here you simply enter this code: Me.Close(). The Me keyword refers to the form itself. The Close method of the form closes the form and releases all resources associated with it, thus ending the program:

```
Private Sub btnExit_Click(sender As Object,
    e As EventArgs) Handles btnExit.Click
    'End the program and close the form
    Me.Close()
End Sub
```

USING THE HELP SYSTEM

The Help system included in Visual Basic 2015 is an improvement over the Help systems in the earliest versions of Visual Basic. As you begin to learn Visual Basic 2015, you will probably become very familiar with the Help system. However, a brief overview would be useful, just to help speed your searches for information.

The Help menu contains the items shown in Figure 1-19.

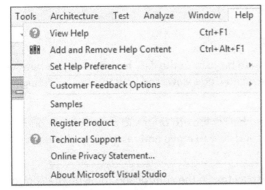

FIGURE 1-19

As you can see, this menu contains a few more items than the typical Windows application. The main reason for this is the vastness of the documentation. Few people could keep it all in their heads—but luckily that is not a problem, because you can always quickly and easily refer to the Help system or search the forums for people who are experiencing or have experienced a similar programming task. Think of it as a safety net for your brain.

You can also quickly access the Help documentation for a particular subject by simply clicking on a keyword in the Code Editor and pressing the F1 key.

SUMMARY

Hopefully, you are beginning to see that developing basic applications with Visual Basic 2015 is a breeze. You have taken a look at the IDE and have seen how it can help you put together software very quickly. The Toolbox enables you to add controls to your form and design a user interface very quickly and easily. The Properties window makes configuring those controls a snap, whereas the Solution Explorer gives you a bird's-eye view of the files that make up your project. You even wrote a little code.

In the coming chapters, you will go into even more detail and get comfortable writing code. Before you get too far into Visual Basic 2015 itself, however, the next chapter provides an introduction to the Microsoft .NET Framework, which is what gives all the .NET languages their ease of use, ease of interoperability, and simplicity in learning.

EXERCISES

The answers for this exercise and those at the end of each chapter in this book can be found in Appendix A.

1. Create a Windows application with a Textbox control and a Button control that displays whatever is typed in the text box when the user clicks the button.

▶ **WHAT YOU LEARNED IN THIS CHAPTER**

TOPIC	CONCEPTS
The integrated development environment (IDE)	How to create projects in the IDE, how to navigate between Design view and Code view, and how to run and debug projects.
Adding controls to your form in the Designer	How to use the Toolbox to drag and drop controls onto your form, and how to move and resize controls on your form.
Setting the properties of your controls	How to display text in the control and to name the controls something meaningful.
Adding code to your form in the code window	How to add code to control what your program does.

2

The Microsoft .NET Framework

WHAT YOU WILL LEARN IN THIS CHAPTER:

➤ What the .NET Framework is

➤ Using the .NET vision

➤ Common Language Runtime

➤ Common Type System

The .NET Framework provides an unprecedented platform for building Windows, web, and mobile applications with one or more programming languages. It is a definitive guide, encompassing and encapsulating where we have come from as a development community and, of course, where we are going.

.NET has been a success in many respects. Within the .NET Framework, languages (C# and F#) have been born, and the well-established Visual Basic language has been reborn. The .NET Framework even supports legacy languages such as C++.

The .NET Framework provides the base for all development using Visual Studio 2015. It provides base classes, available to all Visual Studio 2015 languages, for such functions as accessing databases, parsing XML, displaying and processing Windows and web forms, and providing security for your applications. All languages in Visual Studio 2015 share and use the same base classes, making your choice of a programming language in Visual Studio 2015 a matter of personal preference and syntax style.

THE .NET VISION

To understand .NET, you have to ignore the marketing hype from Microsoft and really think about what it is doing. With the first version of the .NET Framework and indeed even now, Microsoft appears to be pushing .NET as a platform for building web services and large-scale enterprise systems. Web services is a tiny, tiny part of what .NET is all about. In simple terms,

.NET splits an operating system's platform (be it Windows, Linux, Mac OS, or any other OS) into two layers: a programming layer and an execution layer.

All computer platforms are trying to achieve roughly the same effect: to provide applications to the user. If you wanted to write a book, you would have the choice of using the word processor in StarOffice under Linux or Word under Windows. However, you would use the computer in the same way; in other words, the application remains the same, irrespective of the platform.

It is a common understanding that software support is a large part of any platform's success. Typically, the more high quality the available software is for a given platform, the larger the consumer adoption of that platform will be. The PC is the dominant platform because it was the predominant target for software writers back in the early 1980s. That trend has continued to this day, and people are writing applications that run on Windows, which targets the 32-bit and 64-bit Intel processors. The Intel processor harks back to the introduction of the Intel 8086 processor in 1979 and today includes the Intel Core and Xeon family of processors. It also includes competitors such as AMD's FX and A-Series.

Without .NET, developers are still reliant on Windows, and Windows is still reliant on Intel. Although the relationship between Microsoft and Intel is thought to be fairly symbiotic, it is reasonable to assume that the strategists at Microsoft, who are feeling (rightly) paranoid about the future, might want to lessen the dependence on a single family of chips, too.

The Windows/Intel combination (sometimes known as *Wintel*) is also known as the *execution layer*. This layer takes the code and runs it—simple as that.

Although .NET originally targeted and still targets only the Windows platform, you are seeing development communities using open-source projects to convert .NET to run on other platforms such as Linux and Unix. This means that a program written by a .NET developer on Windows could run unchanged on Linux. In fact, the Mono project (`www.mono-project.com`) has already released several versions of its product. This project has developed an open-source version of a C# and VB.NET compiler, a runtime for the Common Language Infrastructure (CLI, also known as the Common Intermediate Language, or CIL), a subset of the .NET classes, and other .NET goodies independent of Microsoft's involvement.

.NET is a *programming layer*. It is totally owned and controlled by Microsoft. By turning all developers into .NET programmers instead of Windows programmers, software is written as .NET software, not Windows software.

To understand the significance of this, imagine that a new platform is launched and starts eating up market share like crazy. Imagine that, like the Internet, this new platform offers a revolutionary way of working and living that offers real advantages. With the .NET vision in place, all Microsoft has to do to gain a foothold on this platform is develop a version of .NET that works on it. All the .NET software now runs on the new platform, lessening the chance that the new platform will usurp Microsoft's market share.

This Sounds Like Java

Some of this does sound a lot like Java. In fact, Java's mantra of "write once, run anywhere" fits nicely into the .NET doctrine. However, .NET is not a Java clone. Microsoft has a different approach.

To write in Java, developers were expected to learn a new language. This language was based on C++. Whereas Java is "one language, many platforms," .NET is "many languages, one platform—for now." Microsoft wants to remove the barrier to entry for .NET by making it accessible to anyone who has used pretty much any language. The two primary languages for .NET are Visual Basic 2015 and C#. Visual Studio 2015 comes supplied with both of these. Although C# is not C++, developers of C++ applications should be able to migrate to C# with about the same amount of relearning that a Visual Basic 6 developer will have to do in order to move to Visual Basic 2015. Of course, the .NET Framework supports developers using C++ and allows them to write C++ applications using the .NET Framework.

With Java, Sun attempted to build from the ground up something so abstracted from the operating system that when you compare an application written natively in something like Visual C++ with a Java equivalent, it becomes fairly obvious that the Java version will run slower and not look as good in terms of user interface. Sun tried to take too big a bite out of the problem by attempting to support everything, so in the end it did not support one single thing completely. That's probably why Java developers have so many third-party and open-source tools, such as Eclipse and Ruby.

Where Now?

Microsoft has bet its future on .NET and rightly so, with its ever-increasing adoption by developers and businesses alike. With developers writing software for the programming layer rather than an execution layer, it really doesn't matter whether Windows or Linux or some other software is the dominant platform in 2020. The remainder of this chapter drills into the mechanics of .NET and takes a detailed look at how the whole thing works.

WRITING SOFTWARE FOR WINDOWS

To understand how .NET works, you need to look at how developers used to write software for Windows. The general principle was the same as with .NET, only they had to do things in different ways to work with different technologies—the Component Object Model (COM), ActiveX Data Objects (ADO), and so forth.

Any software that you write has to interact with various parts of the operating system to do its job. If the software needs a block of memory to store data in, it interacts with the memory manager subsystem. To read a file from disk, you use the disk subsystem. To request a file from the network, you use the network subsystem. To draw a window on the screen, you use the graphics subsystem, and so on.

This *subsystems* approach breaks down as far as .NET is concerned because there is no commonality between the ways you use the subsystems on different platforms, despite the fact that platforms tend to have things in common. For example, if you are writing an application for Linux, you might still need to use the network, disk, and screen subsystems. However, because different organizations developed these platforms, the way you open a file using the Linux platform is different from the way you do it on Windows. If you want to move code that depends on one platform to another, you will probably have to rewrite portions of the code. You will also have to test the code to ensure that it still works as intended.

Windows software communicates with the operating system and various subsystems using something called the *Windows 32-bit application programming interface (Win32 API)*. Although object orientation in programming was around at the time, this API was designed to be an evolution of the original Windows API, which predates the massive adoption of object-oriented techniques, which are discussed in Chapter 10.

It is not easy to port the Win32 API to other platforms, which is why there is no version of the Win32 API for Linux, even though Linux has been around for more than a decade. There is a cut-down version of the Win32 API for the Mac, but this has never received much of an industry following.

The Win32 API provides all basic functionality, but now and again, Microsoft extends the capabilities of Windows with a new API. A classic example is the Windows Internet API, also known as the *WinInet API*. This API enables an application to download resources from a web server, upload files to an FTP server, discover proxy settings, and so on. Again, it is not object-oriented, but it does work. Another example of this is the Win32 API that is part of the Windows 7 operating system. Because so many of the core components of the operating system have changed, a new version of the Win32 API had to be developed for this operating system.

A large factor in the success of early versions of Visual Basic is that it took the tricky-to-understand Win32 API calls and packaged them in a way that could be easily understood. Using the native Win32 API, it takes about 100 lines of code to draw a window on the screen. The same effect can be achieved in Visual Basic with a few gestures of the mouse. Visual Basic represents an abstraction layer on top of the Win32 API that makes it easier for developers to use.

A long-time frustration for C++ developers was that a lot of the things that were very easy to do in Visual Basic remained not so much hard as laborious in C++. Developers like C++ because it gives them an amazing amount of control over how a program works, but their programs take longer to write. Microsoft introduced the Microsoft Foundation Classes (MFC) because of this overhead, which, along with the IDE of Visual Studio, brought the ease of Visual C++ development closer to that of Visual Basic.

The .NET Framework Classes

Unlike the Win32 API, .NET is totally object-oriented. Anything you want to do in .NET, you are going to be doing with an object. If you want to open a file, you create an object that knows how to do this. If you want to draw a window on the screen, you create an object that knows how to do this. When you get to Chapter 10 you will discover that this is called *encapsulation*; the functionality is encapsulated in an object, and you don't really care how it's done behind the scenes.

Although the concept of subsystems still exists in .NET, these subsystems are never accessed directly—instead, they are abstracted away by the Framework classes. Either way, your .NET application never has to talk directly to the subsystem (although you can do so if you really need or want to). Rather, you talk to objects, which then talk to the subsystem. In Figure 2-1, the box marked System.IO.File is a class defined in the .NET Framework.

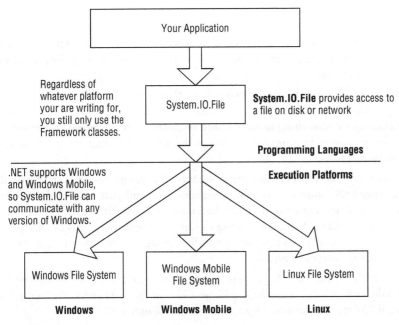

Your Application

Regardless of whatever platform your are writing for, you still only use the Framework classes.

System.IO.File

System.IO.File provides access to a file on disk or network

Programming Languages

.NET supports Windows and Windows Mobile, so System.IO.File can communicate with any version of Windows.

Execution Platforms

Windows File System

Windows Mobile File System

Linux File System

Windows

Windows Mobile

Linux

FIGURE 2-1

If you are talking to objects that talk to subsystems, do you really care what the subsystem looks like? Thankfully, the answer is no, and this is how Microsoft removes your reliance on Windows. If you know the name of a file, you use the same objects to open it whether you are running on a Windows 8 machine, a Windows Phone, a tablet, or even the Mono Project version of the .NET Framework, Linux. Likewise, if you need to display a window on the screen, you don't care whether it is on a Windows operating system or a Mac.

The .NET Framework is actually a set of classes called *base classes*. The base classes in the .NET Framework are rather extensive and provide the functionality for just about anything that you need to do in a Windows or web environment, from working with files to working with data to working with forms and controls.

The class library is vast, containing several thousand objects available to developers, although in your daily development you need to understand only a handful of them to create powerful applications.

Another really nice thing about the base classes in the .NET Framework is that they are the same irrespective of the language used, so if you are writing a Visual Basic 2015 application, you use the same object you would use from within a C# application. That object will have the same methods, properties, and events, meaning there is very little difference in capabilities between the languages, because they all rely on the Framework.

Executing Code

The base class library is only half the equation. After you have written the code that interacts with the classes, you still need to run it. This poses a tricky problem: To remove the reliance on the platform is to remove the reliance on the processor.

Whenever you write software for Windows, you are guaranteed that this code will run on an Intel chip. With .NET, Microsoft does not want to make this guarantee. It might be that the dominant chip in 2020 is a Transmeta chip or something never yet seen or heard of. What needs to be done is to abstract .NET from the processor, in a similar fashion to the way .NET is abstracted from the underlying subsystem implementations.

Programming languages are somewhere in between the languages that people speak every day and the language that the computer itself understands. The language that a computer uses is the *machine code* (sometimes called *machine instructions* or *machine language*) and consists entirely of zeros and ones, each corresponding to electrical current flowing or not flowing through this or that part of the chip. When you are using a PC with an Intel or compatible processor, this language is more specifically known as ×86 *machine instructions*.

If you wrote an application with Visual Basic 6, you had to *compile* it into a set of ×86 machine instructions before you could deploy it. This machine code would then be installed and executed on any machine that supported ×86 instructions and was also running Windows.

If you write an application with Visual Basic 2015, you still have to compile the code. However, you don't compile the Visual Basic 2015 code directly into ×86 machine instructions because that would mean that the resulting program would run only on processors that support this language—in other words, the program would run only on Intel chips and their compatible competitors. Instead, compilation creates something called *Microsoft Intermediate Language* (*MSIL*). This language is not dependent on any processor. It is a layer above the traditional machine code.

MSIL code will not just run on any processor because processors don't understand MSIL. To run the code, it has to be further compiled, as shown in Figure 2-2, from MSIL code into the native code that the processor understands.

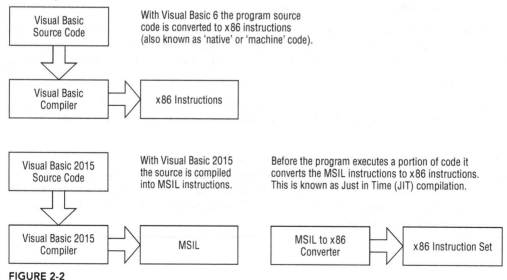

FIGURE 2-2

However, this approach also provides the industry with a subtle problem. In a world in which .NET is extremely popular (some might say dominant), who is responsible for developing an MSIL-to-native compiler when a new processor is released? Is the new processor at the mercy of Microsoft's willingness to port .NET to the chip? Time will tell.

The next section describes what makes .NET work: the Common Language Runtime.

COMMON LANGUAGE RUNTIME

The *Common Language Runtime (CLR)* is the heart of .NET. CLR takes your .NET application, compiles it into native processor code, and runs it. It provides an extensive range of functionalities to help applications run properly:

➤ Code loading and execution

➤ Application isolation

➤ Memory management

➤ Security

➤ Exception handling

➤ Interoperability

Don't worry if you don't understand what all these functionalities are—the following sections discuss all of them except for memory management. Memory management is quite a complex subject and is discussed in Chapter 11.

Code Loading and Execution

The code loading and execution part of the CLR deals with reading the MSIL code from the disk and running it. It compiles the code from MSIL into the native code (machine code) that the processor understands.

Java also has a concept similar to MSIL, known as *byte code*, which the Java runtime loads and executes.

Application Isolation

One important premise of modern operating systems such as Windows and Linux is that applications are isolated from one another. This is critically important from the standpoint of both security and stability.

Imagine that you have a badly written program and it crashes the PC. This shouldn't happen; only the badly behaved program should crash. You don't want other applications or the operating system itself to be affected by a program running on it. For example, if your email program crashes, you don't want to lose any unsaved changes in your word processor. With proper application isolation, one application crashing should not cause others to crash.

In some instances, even under Windows XP, a badly behaved program can do something so horrendous that the entire machine crashes. This is commonly known as the *Blue Screen of Death*

(*BSOD*), so called because your attractive Windows desktop is replaced with a stark blue screen with a smattering of white text explaining the problem. This problem should be alleviated in .NET, but it is unlikely to be completely solved.

The other aspect to application isolation is one of security. Imagine that you are writing a personal and sensitive email. You don't want other applications running on your computer to be able to grab or even stumble across the contents of the email and pass it on to someone else. Applications running in an isolated model can't just take what they want. Instead, they have to ask whether they can have something, and they are given it only if the operating system permits it.

This level of application isolation is already available in Windows. .NET extends and enhances this functionality by further improving it.

Security

.NET has powerful support for the concept of code security. The Framework was designed to give system administrators, users, and software developers a fine level of control over what a program can and can't do.

Imagine you have a program that scans your computer's hard disk looking for Word documents. You might think this is a useful program if it is the one that you run to find missing documents. Now imagine that this program is delivered through email and it automatically runs and emails copies of any "interesting" documents to someone else. You are less likely to find that useful.

This is the situation you find yourself in today with old-school Windows development. To all intents and purposes, Windows applications have unrestricted access to your computer and can do pretty much anything they want. That is why the Melissa- and I Love You–type viruses are possible—Windows does not understand the difference between a benign script file you write that looks through your address book and sends emails to everyone, for example, and those written by others and delivered as viruses.

Windows solves this problem by locking down the security aspects of Windows applications. If an application is not properly signed, Windows will prompt you for permission to let the program run. Likewise, Windows will prompt you for any program needing administrative permission to do operating system tasks. You then have the option to let these programs run or to cancel them, thus protecting your computer from rogue viruses.

With .NET this situation changes because of the security features built into the CLR. Under the CLR, code requires *evidence* to run. This evidence can consist of policies set by you and your system administrator, as well as the origin of the code (for example, whether it came off your local machine, off a machine on your office network, or over the Internet).

> **NOTE** *Security is a very involved topic and beyond the scope of this book. However, you can find many books that cover only the topic of .NET security, and it is worthwhile to find the book that best meets your needs.*

Interoperability

Interoperability in the .NET Framework is achieved on various levels not covered here. However, we must point out some of the types of interoperation that it provides. One kind of interoperation is at the core of the Framework, where data types are shared by all managed languages. This is known as the *Common Type System* (CTS). This is a great improvement for language interoperability (see the section "The Common Type System and Common Language Specification," later in this chapter).

The other type of interoperation is that of communicating with existing COM interfaces. Because a large application-software base is written in COM, it was inevitable that .NET should be able to communicate with existing COM libraries. This is also known as *COM interop*.

Exception Handling

Exception handling is the concept of dealing with exceptional happenings when you are running the code. Imagine that you have written a program that opens a file on disk. What if that file is not there? Well, the fact that the file is not there is exceptional, and you need to handle it in some way. It could be that you crash or you could display a window asking the user to supply a new filename. Either way, you have a fine level of control over what happens when an error does occur.

.NET provides a powerful exception handler that can catch exceptions when they occur and give your programs the opportunity to react and deal with the problem in some way. Chapter 9 talks about exception handling in more detail, but for now, think of exception handling as something provided by the CLR to all applications.

THE COMMON TYPE SYSTEM AND COMMON LANGUAGE SPECIFICATION

One of the most important aspects of .NET that Microsoft had to get right is interlanguage operation. Remember, Microsoft's motivation was to get any developer using any language to use .NET; and for this to happen, all languages had to be treated equally. Likewise, applications created in one language have to be understood by other languages. For example, if you create a class in Visual Basic 2015, a C# developer should be able to use and extend that class. Alternatively, you might need to define a string in C#, pass that string to an object built in Visual Basic 2015, and make that object understand and manipulate the string successfully.

The CTS enables software written in different languages to work together. Before .NET, Visual Basic and C++ handled strings completely differently, and you had to go through a conversion process each time you went from one to the other. With the CTS in place, all .NET languages use strings, integers, and so on in the same way, so no conversion needs to take place.

In addition, the Common Language Specification (CLS) was introduced by Microsoft to make it easier for language developers to adapt their languages to be compatible with .NET.

The CTS and CLS are the foundation for this interoperation, but detailed discussion is, unfortunately, beyond the scope of this book.

When talking to other .NET developers, you will likely hear the term *managed code*. This simply describes code that runs inside the CLR. In other words, you get all the advantages of the CLR, such as the memory management and all the language interoperability features previously mentioned.

Code written in Visual Basic 2015 and C# is automatically created as managed code. C++ code is not automatically created as managed code because C++ does not fit well into the memory management scheme implemented by the CLR. You can, if you are interested, turn on an option to create managed code from within C++, in which case you use the term *managed C++*.

Hand-in-hand with managed code is *managed data*. As you can probably guess, this is data managed by the CLR, although in nearly all cases this data actually consists of objects. Objects managed by the CLR can easily be passed between languages.

SUMMARY

This chapter introduced the Microsoft .NET Framework and explained why Microsoft chose to radically change the way programs were written for Windows. You also learned that part of Microsoft's motivation for this was to move the dependence of developers from the execution platform (Windows, Linux, or whatever) over to a new programming platform that it would always own.

After learning why Microsoft developed .NET, you saw how writing for it is similar, in some ways, to Windows using APIs. You still have a layer that you program against; but now, instead of being flat like the Win32 API, it is a rich set of classes that enables you to write true object-oriented programs no matter what .NET language you choose to develop in. As you will see in this book, using the .NET Framework is much easier than using Windows APIs. This chapter also discussed how these classes could be ported to other platforms and how your applications could transfer across.

Finally, you looked at some of the more technical aspects of the .NET Framework, specifically the Common Language Runtime.

To summarize, you should now understand:

➤   Microsoft's new business venture

➤   Goals of the .NET Framework

➤   Abstractions provided by the .NET Framework

➤   The core of the .NET Framework

▶ **WHAT YOU LEARNED IN THIS CHAPTER**

TOPIC	CONCEPTS
The .NET Vision	A set of .NET Framework classes that isolates the operating system details from the developer and provides a set of classes that can be used by any .NET programming language.
Object-Oriented Programming	The .NET Framework base classes provide objects that every other class in the framework derives from. Thus developers write object-oriented code consuming the .NET Framework objects.
Common Language Runtime	The CLR takes .NET code written in any .NET language (for example, Visual Basic or C#) and compiles that code into a native processor code targeted for the processor your computer is using.

3

Writing Software

WHAT YOU WILL LEARN IN THIS CHAPTER:

➤ Understanding algorithms

➤ Using variables

➤ Exploring different data types, including integers, floating-point numbers, strings, and dates

➤ Studying code scope

➤ Understanding debugging applications basics

➤ Understanding how computers store data in memory

WROX.COM CODE DOWNLOADS FOR THIS CHAPTER

The wrox.com code downloads for this chapter are found at www.wrox.com/begvisualbasic2015 on the Download Code tab. The code is in the 092117 C03.zip download and individually named according to the names given throughout the chapter.

Now that you have Visual Basic 2015 up and running and have even written a simple program, you're going to look at the fundamentals behind the process of writing software and start putting together some exciting programs of your own.

INFORMATION AND DATA

Information describes facts and can be presented or found in any format, whether that format is optimized for humans or computers. For example, if you send four people to different intersections to manually survey traffic, at the end of the process you will end up with four hand-written tallies of the number of cars that went past (say, a tally for each hour).

The term *data* is used to describe information that has been collated, ordered, and formatted so it can be used by a piece of computer software. The information you have (several notebooks full of handwritten tallies) cannot be directly used by a piece of software. Instead, someone has to work with it to convert it into usable data that the computer can understand. For example, the tallies can be transferred to an Excel spreadsheet that can be directly used by a piece of software designed to read that Excel spreadsheet and analyze the results.

Algorithms

The computer industry changes at an incredible speed. Most professionals retrain and reeducate themselves on an ongoing basis to keep their skills sharp and up to date. However, some aspects of computing haven't really changed since they were first invented and perhaps won't change within our lifetimes. The process and discipline of software development is a good example of an aspect of computer technology whose essential nature hasn't changed since its inception.

For software to work, you need to have some data to work with. The software then takes that data and manipulates it into another form. For example, software can take your customer database, stored as ones and zeroes on your computer's hard drive, and make it available for you to read on your computer's monitor. The on-board computer in your car constantly examines the environmental and performance information, adjusting the fuel mix to make your car run at maximum efficiency. For every call you make or receive, your cell phone provider records the phone number and the length of the call in order to generate a bill based on this information.

The base underpinning of all software is the *algorithm*. Before you can write software to solve a problem, you have to break it down into a step-by-step description of how the problem will be solved. An algorithm is independent of the programming language, so, if you want, you can describe it to yourself either as a spoken language with diagrams, or with whatever helps you visualize the problem. Imagine that you work for a wireless telephone company and need to produce bills based on calls that your customers make. Here's an algorithm that describes a possible solution:

1. On the first day of the month, produce a bill for each customer.
2. For each customer, list the calls that the customer has made in the previous month.
3. Determine the cost of each call based on the time and day of week.
4. For each bill, you total the cost of each call.
5. If a customer exceeds a preset time limit, charge the customer a certain rate for each minute that exceeds the allotted time.
6. You apply sales tax to each bill.
7. After you have the final bill, you need to print and mail it.

These seven steps describe, fairly completely, an algorithm for a piece of software that generates bills for a wireless telephone company for outgoing calls made by a customer. At the end of the day, it doesn't matter whether you build this solution in C++, Visual Basic, C#, Java, and so on—the basic algorithms of the software never change. However, it's important to realize that each of those seven parts of the algorithm may well be made up of smaller, more detailed algorithms.

The good news for a newcomer to programming is that algorithms are usually easy to construct. There shouldn't be anything in the preceding algorithm that you don't understand. Algorithms always follow common-sense reasoning, although you may have to code algorithms that contain complex mathematical or scientific reasoning. It may not seem like common sense to you, but it will to someone else! The bad news is that the process of turning the algorithm into code can be arduous. As a programmer, learning how to construct algorithms is the most important skill you will ever obtain.

All good programmers respect the fact that the preferred language of the programmer is largely irrelevant. Different languages are good at doing different things. C++ gives developers a lot of control over the way a program works; however, it's harder to write software in C++ than it is in Visual Basic. Likewise, building the user interface for desktop applications is far easier to do in Visual Basic than it is in C++. (Some of these issues are eliminated when you use managed C++ with .NET, so this statement is less true today than it was years ago.) What you need to learn to do as a programmer is adapt different languages to achieve solutions to a problem in the best possible way. Although when you begin programming you'll be hooked on one language, remember that different languages are focused on developing different kinds of solutions. At some point, you may have to take your basic skills as an algorithm designer and coder to a new language.

What Is a Programming Language?

A *programming language* is anything capable of making a decision. Computers are very good at making decisions, but the problems or questions they need to answer have to be fairly basic, such as, "Is this number greater than 3?" or, "Is this car blue?"

If you have a complicated decision to make, the process of making that decision has to be broken down into simple parts that the computer can understand. You use algorithms to determine how to break down a complicated decision into simpler ones.

A good example of a problem that's hard for a computer to solve is recognizing peoples' faces. You can't just say to a computer, "Is this a picture of Dave?" Instead, you have to break the question down into a series of simpler questions that the computer can understand.

The decisions that you ask computers to make must have one of two possible answers: yes or no. These possibilities are also referred to as true and false, or 1 and 0. In software terms, you cannot make a decision based on the question, "How much bigger is 10 compared with 4?" Instead, you have to make a decision based on the question, "Is 10 bigger than 4?" The difference is subtle, yet important—the first question does not yield an answer of yes or no, whereas the second question does. Of course, a computer is more than capable of answering the first question, but this is actually done through an operation; in other words, you have to actually subtract 4 from 10 to use the result in some other part of your algorithm.

You might be looking at the requirement for yes/no answers as a limitation, but it isn't really. Even in our everyday lives, the decisions we make are of the same kind. Whenever you decide something, you accept (yes, true, 1) something and reject (no, false, 0) something else.

You are using Visual Basic for a language, but the important aspects of programming are largely independent of the language. The key is to understand that any software, no matter how flashy it is, or which language it is written in, is made up of *methods* (functions and subroutines, the lines of code that actually implement the algorithm) and *variables* (placeholders for the data that the methods manipulate).

WORKING WITH VARIABLES

A variable is something that you store a value in as you work through your algorithm. You can then make a decision based on that value (for example, "Is it equal to 7?" or, "Is it more than 4?"), or you can perform operations on that value to change it into something else (for example, "Add 2 to the value," "Multiply it by 6," and so on).

Before you get bogged down in code, take a moment to look at another algorithm:

1. Create a variable called `intNumber` and store in it the value 27.

2. Add 1 to the value of the variable called `intNumber` and store the new value in the same variable.

3. Display the value of the variable called `intNumber` to the user.

This algorithm creates a variable called `intNumber` and stores in it the value 27. This means that a part of the computer's memory is being used by the program to store the value 27. That piece of memory keeps storing that value until you change it or tell the program that you don't need it anymore.

In the second step, an add operation is performed. You're taking the value contained in `intNumber` and adding 1 to its value. After you've performed this operation, the piece of memory given over to storing `intNumber` contains the value 28.

In the final step, you want to tell the user the value of `intNumber`, so you read the current value from memory and write it out to the screen.

Again, there's nothing about the algorithm there that you can't understand. It's just common sense! However, the Visual Basic code looks a little more cryptic.

> **NOTE** *The use of Hungarian notation for variable names is not as prominent as it once was. Many now think that getting teams to use the same style is easier when variables are just names. So,* `intNumberOfDoors` *would just be* `NumberOfDoors`. *You will see both styles in your coding future (as well as others) and just remember that the best style is based on the team that is working on the project. Try and make your code readable so that few comments are needed to understand what you're doing.*

TRY IT OUT Working with Variables

In the following Try It Out, you learn more about working with variables. All the code for this Try It Out is in folder Variables in the Zip file for this chapter.

1. Create a new project in Visual Studio 2015 by selecting File ➪ New Project from the menu bar. In the New Project dialog, select Windows Forms Application from the right pane, enter the project name as **Variables**, and click OK (see Figure 3-1).

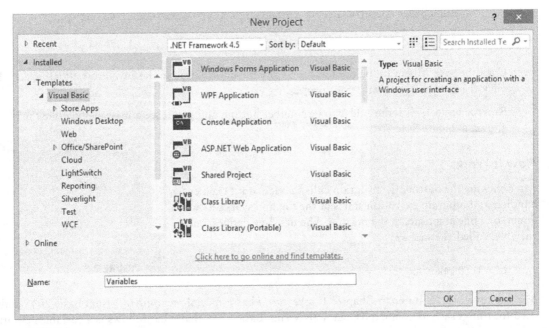

FIGURE 3-1

2. Make Form1 a little smaller and add a Button control from the Toolbox to it. Set the button's Text property to **Add 1 to intNumber** and its Name property to **btnAdd.** Your form should look similar to Figure 3-2.

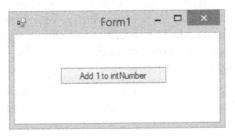

FIGURE 3-2

3. Double-click the button to open the btnAdd_Click event handler. Add the following bold code to it:

```
Private Sub btnAdd_Click(sender As Object,
        e As EventArgs) Handles btnAdd.Click
    Dim intNumber As Integer
    intNumber = 27
    intNumber = intNumber + 1
```

```
MessageBox.Show("Value of intNumber + 1 = " & intNumber.ToString,
    "Variables")
End Sub
```

4. Click the Save All button on the toolbar, verify the information in the Save Project dialog, and then click the Save button to save your project.

5. Run the project, click the Add 1 to intNumber button, and you'll see a message box like the one shown in Figure 3-3.

How It Works

After clicking the button, the program calls the btnAdd_Click event handler, and program execution starts at the top and works its way down, one line at a time, to the bottom. The first line defines a new variable, called intNumber:

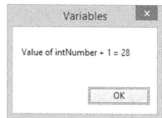

FIGURE 3-3

```
Dim intNumber As Integer
```

Dim is a keyword. As stated in Chapter 1, a *keyword* has a special meaning in Visual Basic 2015 and is used for things such as commands. Dim tells Visual Basic 2015 that what follows is a variable definition:

> *Its curious name harkens back to the original versions of the BASIC language. BASIC has always needed to know how much space to reserve for an array (arrays are discussed in Chapter 5), so it had a command to indicate the dimensions of the array—Dim for short. Visual Basic extends that command to all other kinds of variables as well to mean "make some space for" in general.*

The variable name, intNumber, comes next. Note that the variable name uses the Modified Hungarian Notation discussed in Chapter 1. In this case the prefix int is short for integer, which represents the data type for this variable, as described in the following paragraph. Then a name was chosen for this variable; in this case, the name is Number. Whenever you see this variable throughout your code, you know that this variable will represent a number that is of the Integer data type.

An Integer tells Visual Basic 2015 what kind of value you want to store in the variable. This is known as the *data type*. For now, all you need to know is that this is used to tell Visual Basic 2015 that you expect to store an integer (whole number) value in the variable.

The next line sets the value of intNumber:

```
intNumber = 27
```

In other words, it stores the value 27 in the variable intNumber.

The next statement simply adds 1 to the variable intNumber:

```
intNumber = intNumber + 1
```

What this line actually means is this: Keep the current value of intNumber and add 1 to it.

The final line displays a message box with the text `Value of intNumber + 1 =` and the current value of `intNumber`. You also set the title of the message box to `Variables` to match the project name. When using numeric variables in text, it is a good idea to use the `ToString` method to cast the numeric value to a string. This makes the code easier to read and understand because you know that you are working with strings at this:

```
MessageBox.Show("Value of intNumber + 1 = " & intNumber.ToString,
    "Variables")
```

COMMENTS AND WHITESPACE

When writing software code, you must be aware that you or someone else might have to change that code in the future. Therefore, you should try to make it as easy to understand and legible as possible. Comments and whitespace are the two primary means of doing this.

Comments

Comments are parts of a program that are ignored by the Visual Basic 2015 compiler, which means you can write whatever you want in them, be it English, C#, Perl, FORTRAN, Chinese, or whatever. What they're supposed to do is help the human developer reading the code understand what each part of the code is supposed to be doing.

All languages support comments, not just Visual Basic 2015. If you're looking at C# code, for example, you'll find that comments start with a double forward slash (//).

How do you know when you need a comment? It varies from one case to another, but a good rule of thumb is to think about the algorithm involved. The program in the previous Try It Out exercise had the following algorithm:

1. Define a value for `intNumber`.

2. Add 1 to the value of `intNumber`.

3. Display the new value of `intNumber` to the user.

You can add comments to the code from that example to match the steps in the algorithm:

```
'Define a variable for intNumber
Dim intNumber As Integer

'Set the initial value
intNumber = 27

'Add 1 to the value of intNumber
intNumber = intNumber + 1

'Display the new value of intNumber
MessageBox.Show("Value of intNumber + 1 = " & intNumber.ToString,
    "Variables")
```

In Visual Basic 2015, you begin your comments with an apostrophe (`'`). Anything on the same line following that apostrophe is your comment. You can also add comments onto a line that already has code, like this:

```
intNumber = intNumber + 1 'Add 1 to the value of intNumber
```

This works just as well because only comments (not code) follow the apostrophe. Note that the comments in the preceding code, more or less, match the algorithm. A good technique for adding comments is to write a few words explaining the stage of the algorithm that's being expressed as software code.

> **NOTE** Normally, you would place comments above the code or at the end of a line of code. You cannot place a comment in the middle of a line of code even if it is on a continued line.

You can also use the built-in XML Documentation Comment feature of Visual Studio 2015 to create comment blocks for your methods. To use this feature, place your cursor on the blank line preceding your method definition and type three consecutive apostrophes. The comment block is automatically inserted, as shown in the code here:

```
'" <summary>
'"
'" </summary>
'" <param name="sender"></param>
'" <param name="e"></param>
    Private Sub btnAdd_Click(sender As Object,
        e As EventArgs) Handles btnAdd.Click
```

What's really cool about this feature is that Visual Studio 2015 automatically fills in the name values of the parameters in the comment block based on the parameters defined in your method. If your method does not have any parameters, the `<param>` tag will not be inserted into the comment block.

Once a comment block has been inserted, you can provide a summary of what the method does and any special comments that may need to be noted before this method is called or any other special requirements of the method. If the method returns a value, a `<returns>` tag will also be inserted, and you can insert the return value and description. When you use IntelliSense your documentation will improve the information another developer will see. Also, you can generate documentation based on the XML comments you enter.

Comments are primarily used to make the code easier to understand, either to a new developer who's never seen your code before or to you when you haven't reviewed your code for a while. The purpose of a comment is to point out something that might not be immediately obvious or to summarize code to enable the developer to understand what's going on without having to ponder each and every line.

You'll find that programmers have their own guidelines about how to write comments. If you work for a larger software company, or your manager/mentor is hot on coding standards, they'll dictate which formats your comments should take and where you should and should not add comments to the code.

Whitespace

Another important aspect of writing readable code is to leave a lot of whitespace. *Whitespace* (space on the screen or page not occupied by characters) makes code easier to read, just as spaces do in English. In the previous example, there is a blank line before each comment. This implies to anyone reading the code that each block is a unit of work, which it is.

You'll be coming back to the idea of whitespace in the next chapter, which discusses controlling the flow through your programs using special code blocks, but you'll find that the use of whitespace varies between developers. For now, remember not to be afraid to space out your code—it will greatly improve the readability of your programs, especially as you write long chunks of code.

The compiler ignores whitespace and comments, so there are no performance differences between code with a lot of whitespace and comments, and code with none.

DATA TYPES

When you use variables, it's a good idea to know ahead of time the things that you want to store in them. So far in this chapter, you've seen a variable that holds an integer number.

When you define a variable, you must tell Visual Basic 2015 the type of data that should be stored in it. As you might have guessed, this is known as the *data type*, and all meaningful programming languages have a vast array of different data types from which to choose. The data type of a variable has a great impact on how the computer runs your code. In this section, you'll take a deeper look at how variables work and how their types affect the performance of your program.

Working with Numbers

When you work with numbers in Visual Basic 2015, you work with two kinds of numbers: integers and floating-point numbers. Both have very specific uses. *Integers* are usually not very useful for calculations of quantities—for example, calculating how much money you have left on your mortgage or calculating how long it would take to fill a swimming pool with water. For these kinds of calculations, you're more likely to use *floating-point* variables, which can be used to represent numbers with fractional parts, whereas integer variables can hold only whole numbers.

On the other hand, oddly, you'll find that in your day-to-day activities you're far more likely to use integer variables than floating-point variables. Most of the software that you write will use numbers to keep track of what is going on by counting rather than calculating quantities.

For example, suppose that you are writing a program that displays customer details on the screen. Furthermore, suppose that you have 100 customers in your database. When the program starts, you'll display the first customer on the screen. You also need to keep track of which customer is being displayed, so that when the user says, "Next, please," you'll actually know which one is next.

Because a computer is more comfortable working with numbers than with anything else, you'll usually find that each customer has been given a unique number. In most cases, this unique number will be an integer. What this means is that each of your customers will be assigned a unique integer number between 1 and 100. In your program, you'll also have a variable that stores the ID of the customer you're currently looking at. When the user asks to see the next customer, you add one to that ID (also called *incrementing by one*) and display the new customer.

You'll see how this works as you move on to more advanced topics, but for now, rest assured that you're more likely to use integers than floating-point numbers. Take a look now at some common operations.

Common Integer Math Operations

In this section, you create a new project for your math operations. In the Try It Out exercise that follows, you'll see how to add, subtract, multiply, and divide integer numbers.

TRY IT OUT   Common Integer Math

All the code in this Try It Out is in the folder Integer Math in the Zip file for this chapter.

1. Create a new project in Visual Studio 2015 by selecting File ⇨ New Project from the menu. In the New Project dialog, select Windows Forms Application from the right pane (refer to Figure 3-1), enter the project name as **Integer Math**, and click OK.

2. Using the Toolbox, add a new Button control to Form1 as before. Set its Name property to **btnIntMath** and its Text property to **Math Test**. Double-click it and add the following bolded code to the new Click event handler that will be created:

```
Private Sub btnIntMath_Click(sender As Object,
                e As EventArgs) Handles btnIntMath.Click
    'Declare variable
    Dim intNumber As Integer

    'Set number, add numbers, and display results
    intNumber = 16
    intNumber = intNumber + 8
    MessageBox.Show("Addition test. " & intNumber.ToString,
      "Integer Math")

    'Set number, subtract numbers, and display results
    intNumber = 24
    intNumber = intNumber-2
    MessageBox.Show("Subtraction test. " & intNumber.ToString,
      "Integer Math")

    'Set number, multiply numbers, and display results
    intNumber = 6
    intNumber = intNumber * 10
    MessageBox.Show("Multiplication test. " & intNumber.ToString,
      "Integer Math")

    'Set number, divide numbers, and display results
    intNumber = 12
    intNumber = CType(intNumber / 6, Integer)
    MessageBox.Show("Division test. " & intNumber.ToString,
      "Integer Math")
End Sub
```

3. Save your project by clicking the Save All button on the toolbar.

4. Run the project and click the Math Test button. You'll be able to click through four message box dialogs, as shown in Figure 3-4.

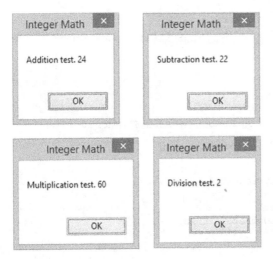

FIGURE 3-4

How It Works

None of the code should be too baffling. You've already seen the addition operator. Here it is again:

```
'Set number, add numbers, and display results
intNumber = 16
intNumber = intNumber + 8
MessageBox.Show("Addition test. " & intNumber.ToString,
    "Integer Math")
```

Let intNumber be equal to the value of 16.

Then, let intNumber be equal to the current value of intNumber (which is 16) plus 8.

As shown in the first message dialog in Figure 3-4, you get a result of 24, which is correct.

The subtraction operator is a minus (–) sign. Here it is in action:

```
'Set number, subtract numbers, and display results
intNumber = 24
intNumber = intNumber - 2
MessageBox.Show("Subtraction test. " & intNumber.ToString,
    "Integer Math")
```

Again, the same deal as before:

Let intNumber be equal to the value 24.

Let `intNumber` be equal to the current value of `intNumber` (which is 24) minus 2.

The multiplication operator is an asterisk (*). Here it is in action:

```
'Set number, multiply numbers, and display results
intNumber = 6
intNumber = intNumber * 10
MessageBox.Show("Multiplication test. " & intNumber.ToString,
    "Integer Math")
```

Here your algorithm states the following:

Let `intNumber` be equal to the value 6.

Let `intNumber` be equal to the current value of `intNumber` (which is 6) times 10.

Finally, the division operator is a forward slash (/). Here it is in action:

```
'Set number, divide numbers, and display results
intNumber = 12
intNumber = CType(intNumber / 6, Integer)
MessageBox.Show("Division test. " & intNumber.ToString,
    "Integer Math")
```

Again, all you're saying is this:

Let `intNumber` be equal to the value of 12.

Let `intNumber` be equal to the current value of `intNumber` (which is 12) divided by 6.

The division of `intNumber` by the value of 6 has been enclosed in the `CType` function. The `CType` function returns the result of explicitly converting an expression to a specified data type, which in this case is an integer number as indicated by the `Integer` type name. Because the division of two numbers can result in a floating-point number, you should use the `CType` function to force the results to an integer number.

This explicit conversion is not necessary when the Option Strict setting is set to Off, but is required when this setting is set to On. The Option Strict setting ensures compile-time notification of narrowing conversion of numeric operations so they can be avoided and prevent runtime errors.

To access the settings for Option Strict, click the Tools ⇨ Options menu item in Visual Studio 2015. In the Options dialog, expand the Projects and Solutions node and then click VB Defaults. From here you can turn the Option Strict setting on and off.

While you are in the dialog, notice that two other options are on by default.

➤ **Option Explicit:** This is best to leave set to On and ensures that you declare each variable. This may not sound important, but if you misspell a variable, you will see an error. If you turn Option Explicit off, your code compiles and runs but your results will be wrong. This will be hard to troubleshoot; therefore, leave this set to On unless you have a specific reason to change it.

➤ **Option Infer:** This is also set to On. This means that the compiler will infer the data type when it can. You can type **Dim x = 5** and x becomes an integer or **Dim y = "a string of characters"** and y becomes a string data type. If you turn Option Infer to Off, the previous statements result in an error.

Integer Math Shorthand

In the next Try It Out, you'll see how you can perform the same operations without having to write as much code by using *shorthand operators* (assignment operators). Although they look a little less logical than their more verbose counterparts, you'll soon learn to love them.

TRY IT OUT Using Shorthand Operators

In this Try It Out exercise, you'll modify the code from the last Try It Out exercise and use integer shorthand operators to add, subtract, and multiply integer numbers:

1. Go back to Visual Studio 2015 and open the code for `Form1.vb` again. Change the following bolded lines:

```
Private Sub btnIntMath_Click(sender As Object,
        e As EventArgs) Handles btnIntMath.Click
    'Declare variable
    Dim intNumber As Integer
    'Set number, add numbers, and display results
    intNumber = 16
    intNumber += 8
    MessageBox.Show("Addition test. " & intNumber.ToString,
        "Integer Math")
    'Set number, subtract numbers, and display results
    intNumber = 24
    intNumber -= 2
    MessageBox.Show("Subtraction test. " & intNumber.ToString,
        "Integer Math")
    'Set number, multiply numbers, and display results
    intNumber = 6
    intNumber *= 10
    MessageBox.Show("Multiplication test. " & intNumber.ToString,
        "Integer Math")
    'Set number, divide numbers, and display results
    intNumber = 12
    intNumber = CType(intNumber / 6, Integer)
    MessageBox.Show("Division test. " & intNumber.ToString,
        "Integer Math")
End Sub
```

2. Run the project and click the Math Test button. You'll get the same results as in the previous Try It Out exercise.

How It Works

To use the shorthand version, you just drop the last `intNumber` variable and move the operator to the left of the equals sign. Here is the old version:

```
intNumber = intNumber + 8
```

Here's the new version:

```
intNumber += 8
```

Integer shorthand math works well for adding, subtracting, and multiplying integer numbers. However, it cannot be used when dividing numbers because the results could return a number that contains a remainder. You could type intNumber \= 3 to divide intNumber by 3, but the result would be truncated because it can only store an integer.

The Problem with Integer Math

The main problem with integer math is that you can't do anything that involves a number with a fractional part. For example, you can't do this:

```
'Try multiplying numbers.
intNumber = 6
intNumber = intNumber * 10.23
```

Or, rather, you can actually run that code, but you won't get the result you were expecting. Because intNumber has been defined as a variable designed to accept an integer only, the result is rounded up or down to the nearest integer. In this case, although the actual answer is 61.38, intNumber will be set to the value 61. If the answer were 61.73, intNumber would be set to 62.

> **NOTE** With the Option Strict setting set to On, the preceding code would produce an error in the IDE, and the program would not compile. With the Option Strict setting set to Off, this code is allowed.

A similar problem occurs with division. Here's another piece of code:

```
'Try dividing numbers.
intNumber = 12
intNumber = intNumber / 7
```

This time the answer is 1.71. However, because the result has to be rounded up in order for it to be stored in intNumber, you end up with intNumber being set equal to 2. As you can imagine, if you were trying to write programs that actually calculated some form of value, you'd be in big trouble because every step in the calculation would be subject to rounding errors.

In the next section, you'll look at how you can do these kinds of operations with floating-point numbers.

Floating-Point Math

You know that integers are not good for most mathematical calculations because most calculations of these types involve a fractional component of some quantity. Later in this chapter, you'll see how to use floating-point numbers to calculate the area of a circle. The following Try It Out introduces the concepts.

TRY IT OUT Floating-Point Math

All the code for this Try It Out is in the folder Floating Point Math in the Zip file for this chapter.

In this Try it Out exercise, you will create a project that multiplies and divides floating-point numbers:

1. Create a new Windows Forms Application project in Visual Studio 2015 called Floating Point Math. As before, place a button on the form, setting its Name property to **btnFloatMath** and its Text property to **Double Test**.

2. Double-click btnFloatMath and add the following bolded code:

```
Private Sub btnFloatMath_Click(sender As Object,
           e As EventArgs) Handles btnFloatMath.Click
       'Declare variable
       Dim dblNumber As Double

       'Set number, multiply numbers, and display results
       dblNumber = 45.34
       dblNumber *= 4.333
       MessageBox.Show("Multiplication test. " & dblNumber.ToString,
           "Floating Points")

       'Set number, divide numbers, and display results
       dblNumber = 12
       dblNumber /= 7
       MessageBox.Show("Division test. " & dblNumber.ToString,
           "Floating Points")
    End Sub
```

3. Save your project by clicking the Save All button on the toolbar.

4. Run the project. You should see the results shown in Figure 3-5.

FIGURE 3-5

How It Works

Perhaps the most important change in this code is the way you're defining your variable:

```
'Declare variable
Dim dblNumber As Double
```

Rather than saying "As Integer" at the end, you're saying "As Double." This tells Visual Basic 2015 that you want to create a variable that holds a double-precision floating-point number instead of an integer number. This means that any operation performed on dblNumber will be a floating-point operation rather than an integer operation. Also note that you have used a different Modified Hungarian Notation prefix to signify that this variable contains a number that is of the Double data type.

However, there's no difference in the way either of these operations is performed. Here, you set dblNumber to be a decimal number and then multiply it by another decimal number:

```
'Set number, multiply numbers, and display results
dblNumber = 45.34
dblNumber *= 4.333
MessageBox.Show("Multiplication test. " & dblNumber.ToString,
    "Floating Points")
```

When you run this, you get a result of 196.45822 that, as you can see, has a decimal component, so you can use it in calculations.

Of course, floating-point numbers don't have to have an explicit decimal component:

```
'Set number, divide numbers, and display results
dblNumber = 12
dblNumber /= 7
MessageBox.Show("Division test. " & dblNumber.ToString,
    "Floating Points")
```

This result still yields a floating-point result because dblNumber has been set up to hold such a result. You can see this by your result of 1.71428571428571, which is the same result you were looking for when you were examining integer math.

This time, the code allows you to use the math shorthand to divide two numbers because the variable that holds the results accepts a floating-point number. Thus, you do not have to use the CType function to convert the results to an integer value.

A floating-point number gets its name because it is stored like a number written in scientific notation on paper. In scientific notation, the number is given as a power of 10 and a number between 1 and 10 that is multiplied by that power of 10 to get the original number. For example, 10,001 is written 1.0001×10^4, and 0.0010001 is written 1.0001×10^{-3}. The decimal point *floats* to the position after the first digit in both cases. The advantage is that large numbers and small numbers are represented with the same degree of precision (in this example, one part in 10,000). A floating-point variable is stored in the same way inside the computer, but in base-2 instead of base-10 (see the section "Storing Variables," later in this chapter).

Other States

Floating-point variables can hold a few other values besides decimal numbers. Specifically, these are:

➤ NaN, which means *not a number*

➤ Positive infinity, positive numbers without end

➤ Negative infinity, negative numbers without end

We won't show how to get all of the results here, but the mathematicians among you will recognize that .NET caters to your advanced math needs.

Single-Precision Floating-Point Numbers

We've been saying *double-precision floating-point*. In .NET, there are two main ways to represent floating-point numbers, depending on your needs. In certain cases, the decimal fractional component of numbers can zoom off to infinity (pi being a particularly obvious example), but the computer does not have an infinite amount of space to hold digits, so there has to be some limit at which the computer stops keeping track of the digits to the right of the decimal point. This limit is related to the size of the variable, which is a subject discussed in much more detail toward the end of this chapter. There are also limits on how large the component to the left of the decimal point can be.

A double-precision floating-point number can hold any value between -1.7×10^{308} and $+1.7 \times 10^{308}$ to a great level of accuracy (one penny in \$45 trillion). A single-precision floating-point number can hold only between -3.4×10^{38} and $+3.4 \times 10^{38}$. Again, this is still a pretty huge number, but it holds decimal components to a lesser degree of accuracy (one penny in only \$330,000)—the benefits being that single-precision floating-point numbers require less memory, and calculations involving them are faster on some computers.

You should avoid using double-precision numbers unless you actually require more accuracy than the single-precision type allows. This is especially important in very large applications, in which using double-precision numbers for variables that require only single-precision numbers could slow your program significantly.

The calculations you're trying to perform will dictate which type of floating-point number you should use. If you want to use a single-precision number, use As `Single` rather than As `Double`, like this:

```
Dim sngNumber As Single
```

Working with Strings

A *string* is a sequence of characters, and you use double quotes to mark its beginning and end. You've seen how to use strings to display the results of simple programs on the screen. Strings are commonly used for exactly this function—telling the user what happened and what needs to happen next. Another common use is storing a piece of text for later use in an algorithm. You'll see a lot of strings throughout the rest of the book. So far, you've used strings like this:

```
MessageBox.Show("Multiplication test." & dblNumber.ToString,
    "Floating Points")
```

`"Multiplication test."` and `"Floating Points"` are strings; you can tell because of the double quotes (`"`). However, what about `dblNumber`? The value contained within `dblNumber` is being converted to a string value that can be displayed on the screen by use of the `ToString` method of the `Double` structure, which defines the variable type. For example, if `dblNumber` represents the value 27, to display it on the screen it has to be converted into a quoted string two characters in length, and this is what the `ToString` method does.

TRY IT OUT Using Strings

All the code for this Try It Out is in the folder `Strings` in the Zip file for this chapter.

This Try It Out demonstrates some of the things you can do with strings:

1. Create a new Windows Forms Application using the File ⇨ New Project menu option. Call it **Strings**.

2. Using the Toolbox, draw a button with the `Name` property **btnStrings** on the form and set its `Text` property to **Using Strings**. Double-click it and then add the following bolded code:

```
Private Sub btnStrings_Click(sender As Object,
                             e As EventArgs) Handles btnStrings.Click
        'Declare variable
        Dim strResults As String

        'Set the string value
        strResults = "Hello World!"

        'Display the results
        MessageBox.Show(strResults, "Strings")
    End Sub
```

3. Save your project by clicking the Save All button on the toolbar.

4. Run the project and click the Using Strings button. You'll see a message like the one shown in Figure 3-6.

How It Works

You can define a variable that holds a string using a notation similar to that used with the number variables, but this time using `As String`:

```
'Declare variable
Dim strResults As String
```

FIGURE 3-6

You can also set that string to have a value, again as before:

```
'Set the string value
strResults = "Hello World!"
```

You need to use double quotes around the string value to *delimit* the string, which means marking where the string begins and ends. This is an important point because these double quotes tell the Visual Basic 2015 compiler not to try to compile the text contained within the string. If you don't include the quotes, Visual Basic 2015 treats the value stored in the variable as part of the program's code and tries to compile it (it can't), which causes the whole program to fail to compile.

With the value `Hello World!` stored in a string variable called `strResults`, you can pass that variable to the message box whose job it is to extract the value from the variable and display it. Therefore, you can see that strings can be defined and used in the same way as the numeric values shown earlier. The next section looks at how to perform operations on strings.

Concatenation

Concatenation means linking things together in a chain or series to join them. If you have two strings that you join together, one after the other, you say they are concatenated.

Concatenation

You can think of concatenation as addition for strings. In the next Try It Out, you work with concatenation:

1. Using the same Strings project, view the Designer for Form1 and add a new button. Set its Name property to **btnConcatenation** and its Text property to **Concatenation**. Double-click the button and add the following bolded code:

```
Private Sub btnConcatenation_Click(sender As Object,
          e As EventArgs) Handles btnConcatenation.Click
    'Declare variables
    Dim strResults As String
    Dim strOne As String
    Dim strTwo As String

    'Set the string values
    strOne = "Hello"
    strTwo = " World!"

    'Concatenate the strings
    strResults = strOne & strTwo

    'Display the results
    MessageBox.Show(strResults, "Strings")
End Sub
```

2. Run the project and click the Concatenation button. You'll see the same results that were shown in Figure 3-6.

How It Works

In this Try It Out, you started by declaring three variables that are String data types:

```
'Declare variables
Dim strOne As String
Dim strTwo As String
Dim strResults As String
```

Then you set the values of the first two strings:

```
'Set the string values
strOne = "Hello"
strTwo = " World!"
```

After you set the values of the first two strings, you use the & operator to concatenate the two previous strings, setting the results of the concatenation in a new string variable called `strResults`:

```
'Concatenate the strings
strResults = strOne & strTwo
```

Using the Concatenation Operator Inline

You don't have to define variables to use the concatenation operator. You can use it on the fly, as shown in the Floating-Point Math, Integer Math, and Variables projects. You've already seen the concatenation operator being used like this in previous examples. What this is actually doing is converting the value stored in `dblNumber` to a string so that it can be displayed on the screen. Consider the following code:

```
MessageBox.Show("Division test. " & dblNumber.ToString,
    "Floating Points")
```

The portion that reads `"Division test."` is actually a string, but you don't have to define it as a string variable. In Visual Basic 2015 parlance, this is called a *string literal*, meaning that it's exactly as shown in the code and doesn't change. When you use the concatenation operator on this string together with `dblNumber.ToString`, the value contained in the `dblNumber` variable is converted into a string and tacked onto the end of `"Division test"`. Remember that the `ToString` method converts the value contained in a variable to a string value. The result is one string that is passed to `MessageBox.Show` and that contains both the base text and the current value of `dblNumber`.

More String Operations

You can do plenty more with strings! Take a look at some examples in the next Try It Out.

TRY IT OUT   Returning the Length of a String

The first thing you'll do is look at a property of the string that can be used to return its length.

1.   Using the Strings project, return to the Designer for Form1. Add a TextBox control to the form and set its Name property to **txtString**. Add another Button control and set its Name property to **btnLength** and its Text property to **Length**. Rearrange the controls so that they look like Figure 3-7.

FIGURE 3-7

2. Double-click the Length button to open its Click event handler. Add the following bolded code:

```
Private Sub btnLength_Click(sender As Object,
                e As EventArgs) Handles btnLength.Click
        'Declare variable
        Dim strResults As String
        'Get the text from the TextBox
        strResults = txtString.Text
        'Display the length of the string
        MessageBox.Show(strResults.Length.ToString & " characters(s)",
            "Strings")
    End Sub
```

3. Run the project and enter some text into the text box.

4. Click the Length button. You'll see results similar to those shown in Figure 3-8.

FIGURE 3-8

How It Works

The first thing you do is declare a variable to contain string data. Then you extract the text from the text box and store it in your string variable called strResults:

```
'Declare variable
Dim strResults As String
'Get the text from the TextBox
strResults = txtString.Text
```

When you have the string, you can use the Length property to get an integer value that represents the number of characters in it. Remember that as far as a computer is concerned, characters include things like spaces and other punctuation marks. Because the Length property returns the number of characters as an Integer data type, you want to convert that number to a string using the ToString method:

```
'Display the length of the string
MessageBox.Show(strResults.Length.ToString & " characters(s)",
    "Strings")
```

Substrings

Common ways to manipulate strings in a program include using a set of characters that appears at the start, a set that appears at the end, or a set that appears somewhere in between. These are known as *substrings*.

TRY IT OUT   Working with Substrings

In the following Try It Out, you build on your previous application in order to have it display the first-three, middle-three, and last-three characters.

1. Using the Strings project, return to the Designer for Form1. Add another Button control to Form1 and set its Name property to **btnSubStrings** and its Text property to **SubStrings**. Double-click the button and add the bolded code that follows:

```
Private Sub btnSubStrings_Click(sender As Object,
              e As EventArgs) Handles btnSubStrings.Click
        'Declare variable
        Dim strResults As String

        'Get the text from the TextBox
        strResults = txtString.Text

        'Display the first three characters
        MessageBox.Show(strResults.Substring(0, 3), "Strings")

        'Display the middle three characters
        MessageBox.Show(strResults.Substring(3, 3), "Strings")

        'Display the last three characters
        MessageBox.Show(strResults.Substring(strResults.Length-3), "Strings")
    End Sub
```

2. Run the project. Enter the word **Concatenation** in the text box.

3. Click the SubStrings button and you'll see three message boxes, one after another, as shown in Figure 3-9.

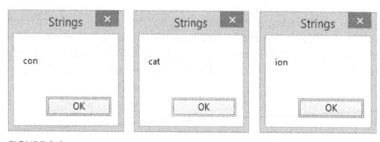

FIGURE 3-9

How It Works

The Substring method lets you grab a set of characters from any position in the string. The method can be used in one of two ways. The first way is to give it a starting point and a number of characters to grab. In the first instance, you're telling it to start at character position 0—the beginning of the string— and grab three characters:

```
'Display the first three characters
MessageBox.Show(strResults.Substring(0, 3), "Strings")
```

In the next instance, you start three characters in from the start and grab three characters:

```
'Display the middle three characters
MessageBox.Show(strResults.Substring(3, 3), "Strings")
```

In the final instance, you're providing only one parameter. This tells the Substring method to start at the given position and grab everything right up to the end. In this case, you're using the Substring method in combination with the Length method, so you're saying, "Grab everything from three characters in from the right of the string to the end":

```
'Display the last three characters
MessageBox.Show(strResults.Substring(strResults.Length-3), "Strings")
```

Formatting Strings

Often when working with numbers, you'll need to alter the way they are displayed as a string. Figure 3-5 shows how a division operator works. In this case, you don't really need to see 14 decimal places—2 or 3 would be fine! What you need is to format the string so that you see everything to the left of the decimal point, but only 3 digits to the right, which is what you do in the next Try It Out.

TRY IT OUT Formatting Strings

In this Try It Out exercise, you'll modify the Floating Point Math project you created earlier to display numbers in various string formats:

1. Open the Floating Point Math project that you created earlier in this chapter.

2. Open the Code Editor for Form1 and make the following bolded changes to the btnFloatMath_ Click procedure:

```
'Set number, divide numbers, and display results
     dblNumber = 12
     dblNumber /= 7

     'Display the results without formatting
     MessageBox.Show("Division test without formatting. " &
```

```
        dblNumber.ToString, "Floating Points")

    'Display the results with formatting
    MessageBox.Show("Division test with formatting. " &
        String.Format("{0:n3}", dblNumber), "Floating Points")
End Sub
```

3. Run the project. After the message box dialog for the multiplication test is displayed, you'll see two more message boxes, as shown in Figure 3-10.

FIGURE 3-10

How It Works

The magic here is in the call to `String.Format`. This powerful method allows the formatting of numbers. The key is all in the first parameter because this defines the format the final string will take:

```
MessageBox.Show("Division test with formatting. " &
    String.Format("{0:n3}", dblNumber), "Floating Points")
```

You passed `String.Format` two parameters. The first parameter, `"{0:n3}"`, is the format that you want. The second parameter, `dblNumber`, is the value that you want to format. Note that because you are formatting a number to a string representation, you do not need to provide the `ToString` method after `dblNumber`, as in the previous call to the `Show` method of the `MessageBox` class. This is because the `String.Format` method is looking for a number, not a string.

The 0 in the format tells `String.Format` to work with the zeroth data parameter, which is just a cute way of saying "the second parameter" or `dblNumber`. What follows the colon is how you want `dblNumber` to be formatted. In this case, it is `n3`, which means "floating-point number, 3 decimal places." You could have said `n2` for "floating-point number, 2 decimal places."

Localized Formatting

When building .NET applications, it's important to realize that the user may be familiar with cultural conventions that are uncommon to you. For example, if you live in the United States, you're used to seeing the decimal separator as a period (.). However, if you live in France, the decimal separator is actually a comma (,).

Windows can deal with such problems for you, based on the locale settings of the computer. If you use the .NET Framework in the correct way, by and large you'll never need to worry about this problem.

Here's an example: If you use a formatting string of n3 again, you are telling .NET that you want to format the number with thousands separators and that you want the number displayed to three decimal places (1,714.286).

> **NOTE** *The equation changed from 12 / 7 to 12000 / 7 to allow the display of the thousands separator (,).*

Now, if you tell your computer that you want to use the French locale settings, and you run the *same code* (making no changes whatsoever to the application itself), you'll see 1 714,286.

> **NOTE** *You can change your language options by going to the Control Panel and clicking the Regional and Language Options icon and changing the language to French.*

In France, the thousands separator is a space, not a comma; whereas the decimal separator is a comma, not a period. By using String.Format appropriately, you can write one application that works properly regardless of how the user has configured the locale settings on the computer.

Replacing Substrings

Another common string manipulation replaces occurrences of one string with another.

TRY IT OUT Replacing Substrings

To demonstrate replacing a substring, in this Try It Out you'll modify your Strings application to replace the string "Hello" with the string "Goodbye":

1. Open the Strings project that you were working with earlier.

2. Return to the Forms Designer for Form1, add another Button control, and set its Name property to **btnReplace** and its Text property to **Replace**. Double-click the button and add the following bolded code to its Click event handler:

```
Private Sub btnReplace_Click(sender As Object,
                 e As EventArgs) Handles btnReplace.Click
        'Declare variables
        Dim strData As String
        Dim strResults As String

        'Get the text from the TextBox
```

```
      strData = txtString.Text

      'Replace the string occurrence
      strResults = strData.Replace("Hello", "Goodbye")

      'Display the new string
      MessageBox.Show(strResults, "Strings")

   End Sub
```

3. Run the project and enter **Hello World!** into the text box (using this exact capitalization).

4. Click the Replace button. You should see a message box that says Goodbye World!

How It Works

The Replace method works by taking the substring to look for as the first parameter and the new substring to replace it with as the second parameter. After the replacement is made, a new string is returned that you can display in the usual way:

```
      'Replace the string occurrence
      strResults = strData.Replace("Hello", "Goodbye")
```

You're not limited to a single search and replace within this code. If you enter **Hello** twice into the text box and click the button, you'll notice two Goodbye returns. However, case is important—if you enter **hello**, it will not be replaced. You'll take a look at case-insensitive string comparisons in the next chapter.

Using Dates

Another data type that you'll often use is Date. This data type holds, not surprisingly, a date value.

TRY IT OUT   Displaying the Current Date

You learn to display the current date in the next Try It Out. All the code in this Try It Out is in the folder Date Demo in the Zip file for this chapter.

1. Create a new Windows Forms Application project called **Date Demo**.

2. In the usual way, use the Toolbox to draw a new Button control on the form. Call it **btnShowDate** and set its Text property to **Show Date.**

3. Double-click the button to open its Click event handler and add the following bolded code:

```
Private Sub btnShowDate_Click(sender As Object,
    e As EventArgs) Handles btnShowDate.Click

    'Declare variable
```

```
    Dim dteResults As Date

    'Get the current date and time
    dteResults = Now

    'Display the results
    MessageBox.Show(dteResults.ToString, "Date Demo")
End Sub
```

4. Save your project by clicking the Save All button on the toolbar.

5. Run the project and click the button. You should see something like what is shown in Figure 3-11, depending on the locale settings on your machine.

How It Works

You can use the Date data type to hold a value that represents any date and time. After creating the variable, you initialize it to the current date and time using the Now property. Then you display the date in a message box dialog. Note that because you want to display a Date data type as a string, you once again use the ToString method to convert the results to a string format:

```
'Declare variable
Dim dteResults As Date

'Get the current date and time
dteResults = Now

'Display the results
MessageBox.Show(dteResults.ToString, "Date Demo")
```

Date data types aren't any different from other data types, although you can do more with them. The next couple of sections demonstrate ways to manipulate dates and control how they are displayed on the screen.

Formatting Date Strings

You've already seen one way in which dates can be formatted. By default, if you pass a Date variable to MessageBox.Show, the date and time are displayed as shown in Figure 3-11.

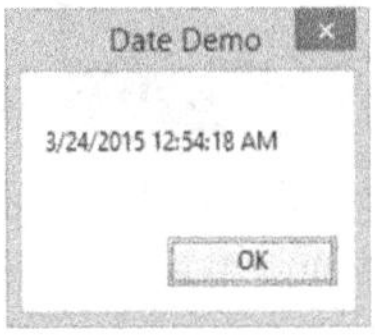

Because this machine is in the United States, the date is shown in *m/d/yyyy* format, and the time is shown using the 12-hour clock. This is another example of how the computer's locale setting affects the formatting of different data types. For example, if you set your computer to the United Kingdom locale, the date is in *dd/mm/yyyy* format, and the time is displayed using the 24-hour clock—for example, 03/29/2012 9:36:30.

FIGURE 3-11

Although you can control the date format to the nth degree, it's best to rely on .NET to ascertain how the user wants strings to look and then automatically display them in their preferred format.

Formatting Dates

In this Try It Out, you'll look at four useful methods that enable you to format dates:

1. Return to the Code Editor for Form1, find the `Click` event handler for the button, and add the following bolded code:

```
'Display the results
MessageBox.Show(dteResults.ToString, "Date Demo")

'Display dates
MessageBox.Show(dteResults.ToLongDateString, "Date Demo")
MessageBox.Show(dteResults.ToShortDateString, "Date Demo")

'Display times
MessageBox.Show(dteResults.ToLongTimeString, "Date Demo")
MessageBox.Show(dteResults.ToShortTimeString, "Date Demo")
```

2. Run the project. You'll be able to click through five message boxes. You have already seen the first message box dialog; it displays the date and time according to your computer's locale settings. The next message box dialog displays the long date, and the next one displays the short date. The fourth message box displays the long time, and the last one displays the short time.

How It Works

This demonstrates the four basic ways that you can display dates and times in Windows applications—namely, long date, short date, long time, and short time. The names of the formats are self-explanatory:

```
'Display dates
MessageBox.Show(dteResults.ToLongDateString, "Date Demo")
MessageBox.Show(dteResults.ToShortDateString, "Date Demo")

'Display times
MessageBox.Show(dteResults.ToLongTimeString, "Date Demo")
MessageBox.Show(dteResults.ToShortTimeString, "Date Demo")
```

Extracting Date Properties

When you have a variable of type `Date`, there are several properties that you can call to learn more about the date; let's look at them.

Extracting Date Properties

In this Try It Out exercise, you'll see how to extract portions of the date and portions of the time contained in a `Date` variable.

1. Return to the Forms Designer for the Date Demo project and add another Button control to Form1. Set its `Name` property to **btnDateProperties** and its `Text` property to **Date Properties**. Double-click the button and add the following bolded code to the `Click` event:

```
Private Sub btnDateProperties_Click(sender As Object,
        e As EventArgs) Handles btnDateProperties.Click
```

```
'Declare variable
Dim dteResults As Date

'Get the current date and time
dteResults = Now

'Display the various date properties
MessageBox.Show("Month: " & dteResults.Month, "Date Demo")
MessageBox.Show("Day: " & dteResults.Day, "Date Demo")
MessageBox.Show("Year: " & dteResults.Year, "Date Demo")
MessageBox.Show("Hour: " & dteResults.Hour, "Date Demo")
MessageBox.Show("Minute: " & dteResults.Minute, "Date Demo")
MessageBox.Show("Second: " & dteResults.Second, "Date Demo")
MessageBox.Show("Day of week: " & dteResults.DayOfWeek, "Date Demo")
MessageBox.Show("Day of year: " & dteResults.DayOfYear, "Date Demo")
End Sub
```

2. Run the project. If you click the button, you'll see a set of fairly self-explanatory message boxes.

How It Works

Again, there's nothing here that's rocket science. If you want to know the hour, use the `Hour` property. Note, the hour is based on a 24-hour clock. To get the year, use `Year`, and so on.

Date Constants

In the preceding Try It Out, when you called the `DayOfWeek` property, you were actually given an integer value, as shown in Figure 3-12.

The date that we're working with, July 6, 2015, is a Monday, and although it may not be immediately obvious, Monday is represented as 2. Because the first day of the week is Sunday in the United States, you start counting from Sunday, with Sunday being 0. However, there is a possibility that you're working on a computer whose locale setting starts the calendar on a Monday, in which case `DayOfWeek` would return 3. Complicated? Perhaps, but just remember that you can't guarantee that what you think is `"Day 2"` is always going to be Monday. Likewise, what's Wednesday in English is *Mittwoch* in German.

FIGURE 3-12

TRY IT OUT   Getting the Names of the Weekday and the Month

If you need to know the name of the day or the month in your application, a better approach is to have .NET get the name for you, again from the particular locale settings of the computer, as demonstrated in the next Try It Out.

1. Return to the Forms Designer in the Date Demo project and add a new Button control. Set its `Name` property to **btnDateNames** and its `Text` property to **Date Names**. Double-click the button and add the following bolded code to the `Click` event handler:

```
Private Sub btnDateNames_Click(sender As Object,
              e As EventArgs) Handles btnDateNames.Click
```

```
'Declare variable
Dim dteResults As Date

'Get the current date and time
dteResults = Now

MessageBox.Show("Weekday name: " & dteResults.ToString("dddd"),
    "Date Demo")
MessageBox.Show("Month name: " & dteResults.ToString("MMMM"),
    "Date Demo")
    End Sub
```

2. Run the project and click the button. You will see a message box indicating the weekday name (for
    example, Monday), and a second one indicating the month (for example, September).

How It Works

When you used your `ToLongDateString` method and its siblings, you were basically allowing .NET
to look in the locale settings for the computer for the date format the user preferred. In this example,
you're using the `ToString` method but supplying your own format string:

```
MessageBox.Show("Weekday name: " & dteResults.ToString("dddd"),
    "Date Demo")
MessageBox.Show("Month name: " & dteResults.ToString("MMMM"),
    "Date Demo")
```

Usually, it is best practice not to use the `ToString` method to format dates to different string values
because you should rely on the built-in formats in .NET, but here you're using the `"dddd"` string to
get the weekday name, and `"MMMM"` to get the month name. (Note that case is important here: `"mmmm"`
won't work.)

To show how this works, if the computer is set to use Italian locale settings, you get one message box
telling you the weekday name is `Lunedi` and another telling you the month name is `Settembre`.

You can use some built-in functions to retrieve date information as well. Functions, such as
`WeekDayName()` and `MonthName()`, return the string representing the month or day-of-week integer
values.

Defining Date Literals

You know that if you want to use a string literal in your code, you can do this:

```
Dim strResults As String
strResults = "Woobie"
```

Date literals work in more or less the same way. However, you use the pound sign (#) to delimit the
start and end of the date.

TRY IT OUT   Defining Date Literals

You learn to define date literals in this Try It Out:

1.   Return to the Forms Designer for the Date Demo project and add another Button control to the
form. Set its `Name` property to **btnDateLiterals** and its `Text` property to **Date Literals**.
Double-click the button and add the following bolded code to the `Click` event handler:

```
Private Sub btnDateLiterals_Click(sender As Object,
            e As EventArgs) Handles btnDateLiterals.Click
        'Declare variable
        Dim dteResults As Date

        'Set a date and time
        dteResults = #1/1/2010 8:01:00 AM#

        'Display the date and time
        MessageBox.Show(dteResults.ToLongDateString & " " &
            dteResults.ToLongTimeString, "Date Demo")
    End Sub
```

2.   Run the project and click the button. You should see the message box shown in Figure 3-13.

How It Works

When defining a date literal, it must be defined in the *mm/dd/yyyy* format, regardless of the actual locale settings of the computer. You may
or may not see an error if you try to define the date in the format *dd/
mm/yyyy*. This is because you could enter a date in the format *dd/mm/
yyyy* (for example, 06/07/2010) that is also a valid date in the required
mm/dd/yyyy format. This requirement reduces ambiguity: Does
6/7/2010 mean July 6 or June 7?

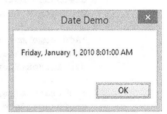

FIGURE 3-13

> **NOTE** *In fact, this is a general truth of programming as a whole: There are no such
> things as dialects when writing software. It's usually best to conform to United
> States standards. As you'll see throughout the rest of this book, they include vari-
> ables and method names—for example,* `GetColor` *rather than* `GetColour`.

It's also worth noting that you don't have to supply both a date and a time. You can supply one, the
other, or both.

Manipulating Dates

One thing that's always been pretty tricky for programmers to do is manipulate dates. Most of you
will remember New Year's Eve 1999, waiting to see whether computers could deal with tipping into
a new century. Also, dealing with leap years has always been a bit of a problem.

The next turn of the century that also features a leap year will be 2399 to 2400. In the next Try It Out, you'll take a look at how you can use some of the methods available on the Date data type to adjust the date around that particular leap year.

TRY IT OUT Manipulating Dates

1. Return to the Forms Designer for the Date Demo project and add another Button control to the form. Set its Name property to **btnDateManipulation** and its Text property to **Date Manipulation**. Double-click the button and add the following bolded code to the Click event handler:

```
Private Sub btnDateManipulation_Click(sender As Object,
                e As EventArgs) Handles btnDateManipulation.Click
        'Declare variables
        Dim dteStartDate As Date
        Dim dteChangedDate As Date

        'Start in the year 2400
        dteStartDate = #2/28/2400#

        'Add a day and display the results
        dteChangedDate = dteStartDate.AddDays(1)
        MessageBox.Show(dteChangedDate.ToLongDateString, "Date Demo")

        'Add some months and display the results
        dteChangedDate = dteStartDate.AddMonths(6)
        MessageBox.Show(dteChangedDate.ToLongDateString, "Date Demo")

        'Subtract a year and display the results
        dteChangedDate = dteStartDate.AddYears(-1)
        MessageBox.Show(dteChangedDate.ToLongDateString, "Date Demo")
    End Sub
```

2. Run the project and click the button. You'll see three message boxes, one after another. The first message box displays the long date for 2/29/2400, whereas the second message box displays the long date for 8/28/2400. The final message box displays the long date for 2/28/2399.

How It Works

The Date data type supports several methods for manipulating dates. Here are three of them:

```
'Add a day and display the results
dteChangedDate = dteStartDate.AddDays(1)
MessageBox.Show(dteChangedDate.ToLongDateString, "Date Demo")

'Add some months and display the results
dteChangedDate = dteStartDate.AddMonths(6)
MessageBox.Show(dteChangedDate.ToLongDateString, "Date Demo")

'Subtract a year and display the results
dteChangedDate = dteStartDate.AddYears(-1)
MessageBox.Show(dteChangedDate.ToLongDateString, "Date Demo")
```

It's worth noting that when you supply a negative number to any of the Add methods when working with Date variables, the effect is subtraction (demonstrated by going from 2400 back to 2399). The other important Add methods are AddHours, AddMinutes, AddSeconds, and AddMilliseconds.

Boolean

So far, you've seen the Integer, Double, Single, String, and Date data types. The other one you need to look at is Boolean. After you've done that, you've seen all the simple data types that you're most likely to use in your programs.

A Boolean variable can be either True or False; it can never be anything else. Boolean values are extremely important when it's time for your programs to start making decisions, which is something you look at in more detail in Chapter 4.

STORING VARIABLES

The most limited resource on your computer is typically its memory. It is important that you try to get the most out of the available memory. Whenever you create a variable, you are using a piece of memory, so you must strive to use as few variables as possible and use the variables that you do have in the most efficient manner.

Today, absolute optimization of variables is not something you need to go into a deep level of detail about, for two reasons. First, computers have far more memory these days, so the days when programmers tried to cram payroll systems into 32KB of memory are long gone. Second, these days, compilers have a great deal of intelligence built into them to help generate the most optimized code possible.

Binary

Computers use binary to represent everything, which means that whatever you store in a computer must be expressed as a binary pattern of ones and zeros. Take a simple integer: 27. In binary code, this number is actually 11011, each digit referring to a power of two. The diagram in Figure 3-14 shows how you represent 27 in the more familiar base-10 format and then in binary (base-2).

10^7	10^6	10^5	10^4	10^3	10^2	10^1	10^0
10,000,000	1,000,000	100,000	10,000	1,000	100	10	1
0	0	0	0	0	0	2	7

In base-10, each digit represents a power of ten. To find what number the "pattern of base-10 digits" represents, you multiply the relevant number by the power of ten that the digit represents and add the results.

$$2 \times 10 + 7 \times 1 = 27$$

2^7	2^6	2^5	2^4	2^3	2^2	2^1	2^0
128	64	32	16	8	4	2	1
0	0	0	1	1	0	1	1

In base-2, or binary, each digit represents a power of two. To find what number the "pattern of binary" represents, you multiply the relevant number by the power of two that the digit represents and add the results.

$$1 \times 16 + 1 \times 8 + 1 \times 2 + 1 \times 1 = 27$$

FIGURE 3-14

Although this may appear to be a bit obscure, note what is happening. In base-10, the decimal system that you're familiar with, each digit fits into a *slot*. This slot represents a power of 10—the first representing 10 to the power 0, the second 10 to the power 1, and so on. If you want to know what number the pattern represents, you take each slot in turn, multiply it by the value it represents, and add the results.

The same applies to binary—it's just that you're not familiar with dealing with base-2. To convert the number back to base-10, you take the digit in each slot in turn and multiply that power of 2 by the number that the slot represents (0 or 1). Add all the results together and you get the number.

Bits and Bytes

In computer terms, a binary slot is called a *bit*. It is the smallest possible unit of information, the answer to a single yes/no question, represented by a part of the computer's circuitry that either has electricity flowing in it or not. The reason why there are 8 slots/bits in the diagram in Figure 3-14 is that there are 8 bits in a byte:

➤ A *byte* is the unit of measurement that you use when talking about computer memory.

➤ A *kilobyte*, or *KB*, is 1,024 bytes. You use 1,024 rather than 1,000 because 1,024 is the 10th power of 2, so as far as the computer is concerned it is a round number. Computers don't tend to think of things in terms of 10s like you do, so 1,024 is more natural to a computer than 1,000 is.

➤ A *megabyte* is 1,024 kilobytes, or 1,048,576 bytes. Again, that is another round number because this is the 20th power of 2.

➤ A *gigabyte* is 1,024 megabytes, or 1,073,741,824 bytes. (Again, think 2 to the power of 30 and you're on the right track.) A *terabyte* is 2 to the 40th power.

➤ A *petabyte* is 2 to the 50th power.

So what's the point of all this? Well, having an understanding of how computers store variables helps you design your programs better. Suppose that your computer has 256MB of memory. That's 262,144KB or 268,435,456 bytes or (multiply by 8) 2,147,483,648 bits. As you write your software, you have to make the best possible use of this available memory.

Representing Values

Most desktop computers in use today are 32-bit, which means that they're optimized for dealing with integer values that are 32 bits in length. The number shown in the last example was an 8-bit number. With an 8-bit number, the largest value you can store is as follows:

```
1x128 + 1x64 + 1x32 + 1x16 + 1x8 + 1x4 + 1x2 + 1x1 = 255
```

A 32-bit number can represent any value between –2,147,483,648 and 2,147,483,647. Now, if you define a variable like this, you want to store an integer:

```
Dim intNumber As Integer
```

In response, .NET allocates a 32-bit block of memory in which you can store any number between 0 and 2,147,483,647. Also, remember you have only a finite amount of memory; and on your 256MB computer, you can store only a maximum of 67,108,864 long numbers. It sounds like a lot, but remember that memory is for sharing. You shouldn't write software that deliberately tries to use as much memory as possible. Be frugal!

You also defined variables that were double-precision floating-point numbers, like this:

```
Dim dblNumber As Double
```

To represent a double-precision floating-point number, you need 64 bits of memory. That means you can store only a maximum of 33,554,432 double-precision floating-point numbers.

> **NOTE** *Single-precision floating-point numbers take up 32 bits of memory—in other words, half as much as a double-precision number and the same as an integer value.*

If you do define an integer, whether you store 1, 3, 249, or 2,147,483,647, you're always using exactly the same amount of memory: 32 bits. The size of the number has no bearing on the amount of memory required to store it. This might seem incredibly wasteful, but the computer relies on numbers of the same type taking the same amount of storage. Without this, it would be unable to work at a decent speed.

Now look at how you define a string:

```
Dim strResults As String
strResults = "Hello World!"
```

Unlike integers and doubles, strings do not have a fixed length. Each character in the string takes up 2 bytes, or 16 bits. Therefore, to represent this 12-character string, you need 24 bytes, or 192 bits. That means your computer can store only a little more than 2 million strings of that length. Obviously, if the string is twice as long, you can hold half as many, and so on.

A common mistake that new programmers make is not taking into consideration what impact the data type has on storage. Suppose that you have a variable that's supposed to hold a string and you try to hold a numeric value in it, like this:

```
Dim strData As String
strData = "65536"
```

You're using 10 bytes (or 80 bits) to store it. That's less efficient than storing the value in an `Integer` data type. To store this numerical value in a string, each character in the string has to be converted into a numerical representation. This is done according to something called *Unicode*, which is a standard way of defining the way computers store characters. Each character has a unique number between 0 and 65,535; and it's this value that is stored in each byte allocated to the string.

Here are the Unicode codes for each character in the string:

➤   **6:** Unicode 54, binary 0000000000110110

➤   **5:** Unicode 53, binary 0000000000110101

➤   **5:** Unicode 53, binary 0000000000110101

➤   **3:** Unicode 51, binary 0000000000110011

➤   **6:** Unicode 54, binary 0000000000110110

Each character requires 16 bits, so storing a 5-digit number in a string requires 80 bits—five 16-bit numbers. What you should do is this:

```
Dim intNumber As Integer
intNumber = 65536
```

This stores the value as a single number binary pattern. An `Integer` uses 32 bits, so the binary representation will be 00000000000000010000000000000000, far smaller than the space needed to store it as a string.

Converting Values

Although strings seem natural to us, they're unnatural to a computer. A computer wants to take two numbers and perform some simple mathematical operation on them. However, a computer can perform such a vast number of these simple operations each second that you, as a human, get the results you want.

Let's imagine that a computer wants to add 1 to the value 27. You already know that you can represent 27 in binary as 11011. Figure 3-15 shows what happens when you want to add 1 to the value 27.

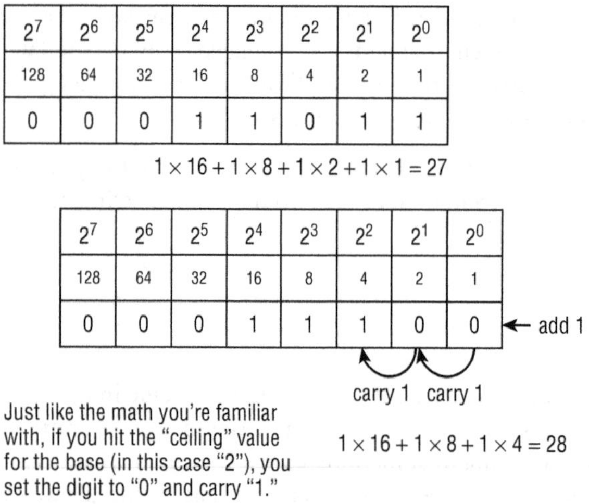

2^7	2^6	2^5	2^4	2^3	2^2	2^1	2^0
128	64	32	16	8	4	2	1
0	0	0	1	1	0	1	1

$$1 \times 16 + 1 \times 8 + 1 \times 2 + 1 \times 1 = 27$$

2^7	2^6	2^5	2^4	2^3	2^2	2^1	2^0
128	64	32	16	8	4	2	1
0	0	0	1	1	1	0	0

← add 1

carry 1   carry 1

Just like the math you're familiar with, if you hit the "ceiling" value for the base (in this case "2"), you set the digit to "0" and carry "1."

$$1 \times 16 + 1 \times 8 + 1 \times 4 = 28$$

FIGURE 3-15

As you can see, binary math is no different from decimal (base-10) math. If you try to add one to the first bit, it won't fit, so you revert it to 0 and carry the 1 to the next bit. The same happens, and you carry the 1 to the third bit. At this point, you've finished, and if you add up the value you get 28, as intended.

Any value that you have in your program ultimately has to be converted to simple numbers in order for the computer to do anything with them. To make the program run more efficiently, you have to keep the number of conversions to a minimum. Here's an example:

```
Dim strResults As String
strResults = "27"
strResults = strResults + 1
MessageBox.Show(strResults)
```

Let's look at what's happening:

1. You create a string variable called strResults.

2. You assign the value 27 to that string. This uses 4 bytes of memory.

3. To add 1 to the value, the computer has to convert 27 to an internal, hidden Integer variable that contains the value 27. This uses an additional 4 bytes of memory, taking the total to 8. However, more important, this conversion takes time!

4. When the string is converted to an integer, 1 is added to it.

5. The new value then has to be converted into a string.

6. The string containing the new value is displayed on the screen.

To write an efficient program, you don't want to be constantly converting variables between different types. You want to perform the conversion only when it's absolutely necessary.

Here's some more code that has the same effect:

```
Dim intNumber As Integer
intNumber = 27
intNumber += 1
MessageBox.Show(intNumber.ToString)
```

1. You create an integer variable called intNumber.

2. You assign the value 27 to the variable.

3. You add 1 to the variable.

4. You convert the variable to a string and display it on the screen.

In this case, you have to do only one conversion, and it's a logical one: Use the ToString method on the Integer data type. MessageBox.Show works in terms of strings and characters, so that's what it is most comfortable with.

What you have done is reduce the number of conversions from two (string to integer, integer to string) to one. This makes your program run more efficiently and use less memory. Again, it's a small improvement, but imagine this improvement occurring hundreds of thousands of times each minute—you'll get an improvement in the performance of the system as a whole.

> **NOTE** It is absolutely vital that you work with the correct data type for your needs. In simple applications like the ones you've created in this chapter, a performance penalty is not really noticeable. However, when you write more complex and sophisticated applications, you want to optimize your code by using the right data type.

METHODS

A *method* is a self-contained block of code that does something. Methods, also called *procedures* or *subroutines*, are essential for two reasons. First, they break a program up and make it more understandable. Second, they promote code *reuse*—a topic you'll be spending most of your time on throughout the rest of this book.

As you know, when you write code, you start with a high-level algorithm and keep refining the detail of that algorithm until you have the software code that expresses all the algorithms up to and including the high-level one. A method describes a line in one of those algorithms—for example, "open a file," "display text on screen," "print a document," and so on.

Knowing how to break up a program into methods is something that comes with experience. To add to the frustration, it's far easier to understand why you need to use methods when you're working on far more complex programs than the ones you've seen so far. In the rest of this section, we'll endeavor to show you why and how to use methods.

Why Use Methods?

In day-to-day use, you need to pass information to a method for it to produce the expected results. This might be a single integer value, a set of string values, or a combination of both. These are known as *input values*. However, some methods don't take input values, so having input values is not a requirement of a method. The method uses these input values and a combination of environmental information (for instance, facts about the current state of the program that the method knows about) to do something useful.

When you give information to a method, you are said to *pass* it data. You can also refer to that data as *parameters*. Finally, when you want to use a method, you *call* it.

> **NOTE** To summarize, you call a method, passing data in through parameters.

The reason for using methods is to promote this idea of code reuse. The principle behind using a method makes sense if you consider the program from a fairly high level. If you have an understanding of all the algorithms involved in a program, you can find commonality. If you need to do the same thing more than once, you should wrap it up into a method that you can reuse.

Imagine that you have a program that comprises many algorithms, and some of those algorithms call for the area of a circle to be calculated. Because *some* of those algorithms need to know how to calculate the area of a circle, it's a good candidate for a method. You write code that knows how to find the area of a circle given its radius, and *encapsulate* it (wrap it up) into a method, which you can reuse when you're coding the other algorithms. This means you don't have to keep writing code that does the same thing—you do it once and reuse it as often as needed.

It might be the case that one algorithm needs to work out the area of a circle with 100 for its radius, and another needs to work out one with a radius of 200. By building the method so that it takes the radius as a parameter, you can use the method from wherever you want.

> **NOTE** With Visual Basic 2015, you can define a method using the Sub keyword or the Function keyword. Sub, short for subroutine, is used when the method doesn't return a value, as mentioned in Chapter 1. Function is used when the method returns a value.

Methods You've Already Seen

The good news is that you've been using methods already. Consider the following bolded code that you wrote at the beginning of this chapter:

```
Private Sub btnAdd_Click(sender As Object,
                         e As EventArgs) Handles btnAdd.Click

    'Define a variable for intNumber
    Dim intNumber As Integer

    'Set the initial value
    intNumber = 27

    'Add 1 to the value of intNumber
    intNumber = intNumber + 1

    'Display the new value of intNumber
    MessageBox.Show("Value of intNumber + 1 = " & intNumber.ToString,
        "Variables")
End Sub
```

That code is a method—it is a self-contained block of code that does something. In this case, it adds 1 to the value of intNumber and displays the result in a message box.

This method does not return a value (that is, it's a subroutine, so it starts with the Sub keyword and ends with the End Sub statement). Anything between these two statements is the code assigned to the method. Let's take a look at how the method is defined (this code was automatically created by Visual Basic 2015):

```
Private Sub btnAdd_Click(sender As Object,
        e As EventArgs) Handles btnAdd.Click
```

1. You have the word `Private`. The meaning of this keyword is discussed in later chapters. For now, think of it as ensuring that this method cannot be called by any code outside of this class.

2. The keyword `Sub` tells Visual Basic 2015 that you want to define a subroutine.

3. Next is `btnAdd_Click`. This is the name of the subroutine.

4. Then you have `sender As Object, e As EventArgs`.

   This tells Visual Basic 2015 that the method takes two parameters: `sender` and `e`. We'll talk about this more later.

5. Finally, you have `Handles btnAdd.Click`. This tells Visual Basic 2015 that this method should be called whenever the `Click` event on the control `btnAdd` is fired.

TRY IT OUT Using Methods

This Try It Out takes a look at how you can build a method that displays a message box and calls the same method from three separate buttons. All the code for this Try It Out is in the Three Buttons folder in the Zip file for this chapter.

1. Create a new Windows Forms Application project called Three Buttons.

2. Use the Toolbox to draw three buttons on the form.

3. Double-click the first button (Button1) to create a new `Click` event handler. Add the following bolded code:

```
Private Sub Button1_Click(sender As Object,
        e As EventArgs) Handles Button1.Click
    'Call your method
    SayHello()
End Sub

Private Sub SayHello()
    'Display a message box
    MessageBox.Show("Hello World!", "Three Buttons")
End Sub
```

4. Save your project by clicking the Save All button on the toolbar.

5. Run the project. You'll see the form with three buttons appear. Click the topmost button to see "Hello World!" displayed in a message box.

How It Works

As you know now, when you double-click a Button control in the Designer, a new method is automatically created:

```
Private Sub Button1_Click(sender As Object,
        e As EventArgs) Handles Button1.Click
End Sub
```

The `Handles Button1.Click` statement at the end tells Visual Basic 2015 that this method should automatically be called when the `Click` event on the button is fired. As part of this, Visual Basic 2015 provides two parameters, which you don't have to worry about for now. Outside of this method, you've defined a new method:

```
Private Sub SayHello()
    'Display a message box
    MessageBox.Show("Hello World!", "Three Buttons")
End Sub
```

The new method is called `SayHello`. Anything that appears between the `Sub` and `End Sub` keywords is part of the method and when that method is called, the code is executed. In this case, you've asked it to display a message box.

So you know that when the button is clicked, Visual Basic 2015 will call the `Button1_Click` method. You then call the `SayHello` method. The upshot of all this is that when the button is clicked, the message box is displayed:

```
Private Sub Button1_Click(sender As Object,
        e As EventArgs) Handles Button1.Click

    'Call your method
    SayHello()
End Sub
```

That should make the general premise behind methods a little clearer, but why did you need to break the code into a separate method to display the message box? You learn more about that in the next Try It Out.

TRY IT OUT   Reusing the Method

In this exercise, you'll see how you can reuse a method by calling it from other areas of your code:

1. If your project is still running, stop it.

2. Return to the Forms Designer, double-click the second button, and add the following bold code to the new event handler:

```
Private Sub Button2_Click(sender As Object,
        e As EventArgs) Handles Button2.Click
    'Call your method
    SayHello()
End Sub
```

3. Switch back to the Forms Designer, double-click the third button, and add the bold code:

```
Private Sub Button3_Click(sender As Object,
        e As EventArgs) Handles Button3.Click
    'Call your method
    SayHello()
End Sub
```

4. Now run the project. You'll notice that when you click each of the buttons, they all open the same message box.

5. Stop the project and find the `SayHello` method definition. Change the text to be displayed, like this:

```
Private Sub SayHello()
    'Display a message box
    MessageBox.Show("I have changed!", "Three Buttons")
End Sub
```

6. Run the project again and click each of the three buttons. You'll notice that the text displayed on the message boxes has changed.

How It Works

Each of the event handlers calls the same `SayHello()` method:

```
Private Sub Button1_Click(sender As Object,
        e As EventArgs) Handles Button1.Click
    'Call your method
    SayHello()
End Sub

Private Sub Button2_Click(sender As Object,
        e As EventArgs) Handles Button2.Click
    'Call your method
    SayHello()
End Sub

Private Sub Button3_Click(sender As Object,
        e As EventArgs) Handles Button3.Click
    'Call your method
    SayHello()
End Sub
```

You'll also notice that the `Handles` keyword on each of the methods ties the method to a different control—Button1, Button2, or Button3.

What's really important (and clever) here is that when you change the way that `SayHello` works, the effect you see on each button is the same. This is a really important programming concept. You can centralize code in your application so that when you change it in one place, the effect is felt throughout the application, enabling you to avoid entering the same or very similar code repeatedly.

Building a Method

In the last Try It Out exercise, you built a method that simply displayed static text. Methods are most useful when they accept data and then actually do something useful with that data. Sometimes you'll want a method to return a value, as you'll see in the next Try It Out exercise.

TRY IT OUT   Building a Method

In the next Try It Out, you'll build a method that's capable of returning a value. Specifically, you'll build a method that can return the area of a circle if its radius is provided. You can do this with the following algorithm:

➤   Square the radius.

➤   Multiply it by pi.

To try out this exercise, reuse the Three Buttons project and return to the Code Editor.

1. Add the following code to define a new method (which will be a function because it returns a value):

```
'CalculateAreaFromRadius-find the area of a circle
Private Function CalculateAreaFromRadius(ByVal radius As Double) As Double
    'Declare variables

    Dim dblRadiusSquared As Double
    Dim dblResult As Double

    'Square the radius
    dblRadiusSquared = radius * radius

    'Multiply it by pi
    dblResult = dblRadiusSquared * Math.PI

    'Return the result
    Return dblResult
End Function
```

2. Now delete the existing code from the Button1_Click event handler, and add the following bolded code:

```
Private Sub Button1_Click(sender As Object,
        e As EventArgs) Handles Button1.Click
    'Declare variable
    Dim dblArea As Double

    'Calculate the area of a circle with a radius of 100
    dblArea = CalculateAreaFromRadius(100)

    'Display the results
    MessageBox.Show(dblArea.ToString, "Area of 100")
End Sub
```

3. Run the project and click Button1. You'll see a result similar to the one shown in Figure 3-16.

FIGURE 3-16

How It Works

In this exercise, you first build a separate method called `CalculateAreaFromRadius`. You do this by using the `Private Function ... End Function` block:

```
Private Function CalculateAreaFromRadius(ByVal radius As Double) As Double

End Function
```

Anything between `Function` and `End Function` is the *body* of the method and will be executed only when the method is called.

The `ByVal radius As Double` portion defines a parameter for the method. When a parameter is passed by value, as indicated here by the keyword `ByVal`, .NET in effect creates a new variable and stores the passed parameter information in it. Even if the method is called with a variable given for the parameter, the contents of that original variable are not modified by the method. In this case, you're telling .NET that you want to pass a parameter into the method called `radius`. In effect, this statement creates a variable called `radius`, just as if you had done this:

```
Dim radius As Double
```

In fact, there's a little more. The variable is automatically set to the value passed through as a parameter, so if you pass `200` through as the value of the parameter, what you're effectively doing is this:

```
Dim radius As Double = 200
```

If you passed `999` as the value of the parameter, you'd have this:

```
Dim radius As Double = 999
```

> **NOTE** Another way of passing a parameter is by reference, using the keyword `ByRef` instead of `ByVal`. When a parameter is passed by reference, the parameter name used within the method body effectively becomes another name for the variable specified when the method is called, so anything the method does that modifies the parameter value modifies the original variable value as well.

The `As Double` sitting at the end of the method declaration tells Visual Basic 2015 that this method will return a double-precision floating-point number back to whomever called it:

```
Private Function CalculateAreaFromRadius(ByVal radius As Double)_
    As Double
```

Now you can look at the method properly. First, you know that to find the area of a circle you have this algorithm:

1. Get a number that represents the radius of a circle.

2. Square the number.

3. Multiply it by pi.

And that's precisely what you've done:

```
'Declare variables
Dim dblRadiusSquared As Double
Dim dblResult As Double

'Square the radius
dblRadiusSquared = radius * radius

'Multiply it by pi
dblResult = dblRadiusSquared * Math.PI
```

The `Math.PI` in the previous code is a constant defined in .NET that defines the value of pi for us. After the last line, you need to return the result to whatever code called the method. That's done with the following statement:

```
'Return the result
Return dblResult
```

The code you added in `Button1_Click` calls the method and tells the user the results:

```
'Declare variable
Dim dblArea As Double

'Calculate the area of a circle with a radius of 100
dblArea = CalculateAreaFromRadius(100)

'Display the results
MessageBox.Show(dblArea.ToString, "Area of 100")
```

The first thing to do is define a variable called `dblArea` that will contain the area of the circle. You set this variable to whatever value `CalculateAreaFromRadius` returns. Using parentheses at the end of a method name is how you send the parameters. In this case, you're passing just one parameter, and you're passing the value 100.

After you call the method, you wait for the method to finish calculating the area. This area is returned from the method (the `Return result` line defined within `CalculateAreaFromRadius`) and stored in the variable `dblArea`. You can then display this on the screen in the usual way.

Choosing Method Names

The .NET Framework has a few standards for how things should be named. These conventions help developers move between languages—a topic discussed in Chapter 2. We recommend that whenever you create a method, you use *Pascal casing*. This is a practice in which the first letter in each word in the method is uppercase, but nothing else is. This is merely a suggestion for best coding practices and is not a requirement of Visual Basic 2015. Examples of this are as follows:

➤ `CalculateAreaFromRadius`

➤ `OpenXmlFile`

➤ `GetEnvironmentValue`

Note that even when an abbreviation is used (in this case, XML), it *isn't* written in uppercase. This alleviates confusion for developers, who might or might not know how something should be capitalized.

We recommend that you always write parameter and variable names in camel casing. (If you've ever seen Java code, you'll be familiar with this.) To get camel casing, you do the same as Pascal casing, but you don't capitalize the very first letter:

➤   `myAccount`

➤   `customerDetails`

➤   `updatedDnsRecord`

Again, abbreviations (such as DNS) are not treated as a special case, so they appear as a mix of uppercase and lowercase letters, just like in Pascal casing.

> **NOTE** *The name camel casing comes from the fact that the identifier has a hump in the middle—for example,* `camelCasing`*. Pascal casing is so called because the convention was invented for use with the programming language Pascal.*

In Chapter 2, you saw that .NET isn't tied to a particular language. Because some languages are case sensitive and others are not, it's important that you define standards to make life easier for programmers who may be coming from different programming language backgrounds.

The term *case sensitive* means that the positions of uppercase and lowercase letters are important. In a case-sensitive language, `MYACCOUNT` is not the same as `myAccount`. However, Visual Basic 2015 is *not* a case-sensitive language, meaning that for all intents and purposes you can do whatever you want with respect to capitalization; in other words, `MYACCOUNT` would be the same as `mYacCounT`. Actually, if you type a variable name in the wrong case, Visual Studio corrects it for you in the code.

> **NOTE** *Note that languages such as Java, C#, and C++ are case sensitive.*

Scope

When introducing the concept of methods, we described them as *self-contained*. This has an important effect on the way that variables are used and defined in methods. Imagine you have the following two methods, both of which define a variable called `strName`:

```
Private Sub DisplaySebastiansName()
    'Declare variable and set value
    Dim strName As String
```

```
        strName = "Sebastian Blackwood"

        'Display results
        MessageBox.Show(strName, "Scope Demo")
    End Sub

    Private Sub DisplayBalthazarsName()
        'Declare variable and set value
        Dim strName As String
        strName = "Balthazar Keech"

        'Display results
        MessageBox.Show(strName, "Scope Demo")
    End Sub
```

Even though both of these methods use a variable with the same name (strName), the self-contained feature of methods means that this is perfectly practicable and the variable names won't affect each other. Try it out next.

TRY IT OUT   Scope

In this exercise, you'll start exploring the scope of variables by using the same variable name in two different methods. All the code in this Try It Out is in the folder Scope Demo in the Zip file for this chapter.

1.   Create a new Windows Forms Application project called Scope Demo.

2.   Add a Button control to the form, setting its Name property to **btnScope** and its Text property to **Scope**. Double-click the button and add the following bolded code to the Click event handler, and add the other two methods:

```
Private Sub btnScope_Click(sender As Object,
        e As EventArgs) Handles btnScope.Click
    'Call a method
    DisplayBalthazarsName()
End Sub

Private Sub DisplaySebastiansName()
    'Declare variable and set value
    Dim strName As String
    strName = "Sebastian Blackwood"

    'Display results
    MessageBox.Show(strName, "Scope Demo")
End Sub

Private Sub DisplayBalthazarsName()
    'Declare variable and set value
    Dim strName As String
    strName = "Balthazar Keech"

    'Display results
    MessageBox.Show(strName, "Scope Demo")
End Sub
```

3. Save your project by clicking the Save All button on the toolbar.

4. Run the project. You'll see the message box displaying the name Balthazar Keech when you click the button.

How It Works

This exercise illustrates that even if you use the same variable name in two separate places, the program still works as intended:

```
Private Sub DisplaySebastiansName()
    'Declare variable and set value
    Dim strName As String
    strName = "Sebastian Blackwood"

    'Display results
    MessageBox.Show(strName, "Scope Demo")
End Sub

Private Sub DisplayBalthazarsName()
    'Declare variable and set value
    Dim strName As String
    strName = "Balthazar Keech"

    'Display results
    MessageBox.Show(strName, "Scope Demo")
End Sub
```

When a method starts running, the variables defined within that method (in other words, between Sub and End Sub, or between Function and End Function) are given *local scope*. The *scope* defines which parts of the program can see the variable, and *local* specifically means *within the current method*.

The strName variable technically doesn't exist until the method starts running. At this point, .NET and Windows allocate memory to the variable so that it can be used in the code. First you set the value and then you display the message box. Therefore, in this case, as you're calling the method DisplayBalthazarsName, the variable is created the moment the method is called; you run the code in the method that alters the newly created version of strName; and when the method has finished, the variable is deleted.

> **NOTE** *You will see in Chapter 4 that scope can even be limited to loops within your subroutines and functions.*

SUMMARY

This chapter introduced the concept of writing software not just for Visual Basic 2015 but also for all programming languages. We started by introducing the concept of an algorithm—the underpinning of all computer software. We then introduced the concept of variables, and looked closely at the most commonly used data types: Integer, Double, String, Date, and Boolean. You saw how you could use these data types to perform operations such as mathematical operations, concatenating strings, returning the length of a string, splitting text into substrings, retrieving the current date, and extracting date properties. You then looked at how variables are stored in the computer.

After this, you looked at methods—what they are, why you need them, how to create them, and how the variables you declare within your methods have local scope within that method and do not apply outside of it. We also described the difference between a function and a subroutine.

EXERCISES

1. Create a Windows application with two button controls. In the Click event for the first button, declare two Integer variables and set their values to any number you want. Perform any math operation on these variables and display the results in a message box. In the Click event for the second button, declare two String variables and set their values to anything you want. Perform a string concatenation on these variables and display the results in a message box.

2. Create a Windows application with a text box and a button control. In the button's Click event, display three message boxes. The first message box should display the length of the string that was entered into the text box, the second message box should display the first half of the string, and the third message box should display the last half of the string.

▶ **WHAT YOU LEARNED IN THIS CHAPTER**

TOPIC	CONCEPTS
Algorithms	What an algorithm is and how it applies to software development.
Variables	How to declare and use the most common types of variables.
String functions	How to use the most common string functions when working with the `String` data type.
Date data type	How to use the `Date` data type and display dates and times so that they are automatically localized to the user's computer settings.
Methods	How to create and use simple methods that either accept parameters or not and either return a value or not.

Controlling the Flow

WROX.COM CODE DOWNLOADS FOR THIS CHAPTER

The `wrox.com` code downloads for this chapter are found at www.wrox.com/begvisualbasic2015 on the Download Code tab. The code is in the `092117 C04.zip` download and individually named according to the names given throughout the chapter.

In Chapter 3, you learned about algorithms and their role in programming. In this chapter, you will look at how you can control the flow through your algorithms so that you can make decisions like "If X is the case, go and do A; otherwise do B." This ability to make decisions is known as *branching*. You'll also see how you can repeat a section of code (a process known as *looping*) a specified number of times, or while a certain condition applies.

MAKING DECISIONS

Algorithms often include decisions. It's this decision-making ability that makes computers do what they do so well. When you're writing code, you make two kinds of decisions. The first kind is used to find out what part of an algorithm you're currently working on or to cope with problems. For example, imagine that you have a list of 10 people and need to write a piece of code to send an email to each of them. To do this, after sending each email, you ask, "Have I finished?" If so, you quit the algorithm; otherwise, you get the next person in the list. As another example, you might need to open a file, so you ask, "Does the file exist?" You have to deal with both possible answers to that question.

The second kind of decision is used to perform a different part of the algorithm depending on one or more facts. Imagine you're going through your list of 10 people so that you can send an email to those who own a computer, but telephone those who don't. As you look at each person, you use the fact that the person does or doesn't own a computer to choose what you should do.

These decisions are all made in the same way, and it doesn't matter whether you have more of the first kind, more of the second kind, or whatever. Now, let's take a look at how to make a decision using the If statement.

THE IF STATEMENT

The simplest way to make a decision in a Visual Basic 2015 program is to use the If...Then statement. You learn to use an If...Then statement in the following Try It Out exercise.

TRY IT OUT A Simple If...Then Statement

Let's look at the If...Then statement. All the code for this Try It Out is in the Simple If folder in the Zip file for this chapter.

1. Create a Windows Forms Application project called **Simple If**. Add a Button control, setting its Name property to **btnIf**, and its Text property to **If**. Double-click the button and add the following bolded code:

```
Private Sub btnIf_Click(sender As Object,
        e As EventArgs) Handles btnIf.Click
    'Declare and set a variable
    Dim intNumber As Integer = 27

    'Here's where you make a decision,
    'and tell the user what happened
    If intNumber = 27 Then
        MessageBox.Show("'intNumber' is, indeed, 27!", "Simple If")
    End If
End Sub
```

2. Save your project and then run it. Click the If button and you'll see the message box shown in Figure 4-1.

How It Works

In this example, first you declare an Integer variable called **intNumber** and set its value to **27**, all in the same line of code, as shown here:

```
'Declare and set a variable
Dim intNumber As Integer = 27
```

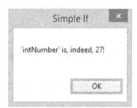

FIGURE 4-1

Then you use an If...Then statement to determine what you should do next. In this case, you say, "If intNumber is equal to 27...":

```
'Here's where you make a decision,
'and tell the user what happened
```

```
If intNumber = 27 Then
    MessageBox.Show("'intNumber' is, indeed, 27!", "Simple If")
End If
```

The code block that follows the If...Then executes only if intNumber equals 27. You end the code block with End If. Anything between If and End If is called only if the expression you're testing for is true.

So, as you walk through the code, you get to the If statement, and it's true. You drop into the code block that runs if the expression is true, and the text is displayed in a message box.

> **NOTE** *Notice that the code within the* If...End If *block is automatically indented for you. This is to increase readability so that you can tell what code will run in the event that the condition is true. It's also good to add some whitespace before the* If...Then *statement and after the* End If *statement to enhance readability further.*
>
> *A simple* If *block like the previous one can also be written on one line, without an* End If *statement:*
>
> ```
> If intNumber = 2 Then MessageBox.Show("Equals 27","Simple If")
> ```
>
> *This works equally well—although you are limited to only one line of code within the* If *statement. Now you know what happens if your condition is* true; *but what happens if you fail the test and the result is* false? *You find out in the next Try It Out.*

TRY IT OUT   Failing the Test

In this example, you see how to code for when the If statement is not true. All the code in this Try It Out is in the folder Simple If in the Zip file for this chapter.

1. Return to the Forms Designer for the Simple If program. Add another Button control to the form and set its Name property to **btnAnotherIf** and its Text property to **Another If**. Double-click the button and add the following bolded code:

```
Private Sub btnAnotherIf_Click(sender As Object,
        e As EventArgs) Handles btnAnotherIf.Click

        'Declare and set a variable
        Dim intNumber As Integer = 27

        'Here's where you make a decision,
        'and tell the user what happened
        If intNumber = 1000 Then
            MessageBox.Show("'intNumber' is, indeed, 1000!", "Simple If")
        End If
End Sub
```

2. Run your project and click the Another If button; nothing happens.

How It Works

In this case, the question "Is `intNumber` equal to 1000?" comes out `false`. The code block executes only if the statement is `true`, so it's skipped. If the statement were `true`, the line between the `If` and `End If` lines would have executed. However, in this instance the statement was `false`, so the next line to be executed was the first line directly following the `End If` line (which is `End Sub`). In effect, the true code block is skipped.

The Else Statement

If you want to run one piece of code if the condition is `true` and another piece if the condition is `false`, then you use the `Else` statement. This expands on the previous Try It Out.

TRY IT OUT **The Else Statement**

This Try It Out builds on the previous Try It Out to show how the `Else` statement works. All the code in this Try It Out is in the folder `Simple If` in the Zip file for this chapter.

1. Return to the Code Editor in the Simple If project and modify the code in the `btnAnotherIf_Click` procedure so that it looks like this:

```
Private Sub btnAnotherIf_Click(sender As Object,
                e As EventArgs) Handles btnAnotherIf.Click

    'Declare and set a variable
    Dim intNumber As Integer = 27

    'Here's where you make a decision,
    'and tell the user what happened
    If intNumber = 1000 Then
        MessageBox.Show("'intNumber' is, indeed, 1000!", "Simple If")
    Else
        MessageBox.Show("'intNumber' is not 1000!", "Simple If")
    End If
End Sub
```

2. Run the project and click `btnAnotherIf`. You'll see the message box shown in Figure 4-2.

How It Works

Here, the code following the `Else` statement runs if the condition in the `If` statement is not met. In this case, the value of `intNumber` is 27, but the condition being tested for is `intNumber = 1000`, so the code after the `Else` statement is run:

```
MessageBox.Show("'intNumber' is not 1000!", "Simple If")
```

FIGURE 4-2

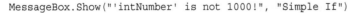

Allowing Multiple Alternatives with ElseIf

If you want to test for more than one condition, you need to make use of the `ElseIf` statement.

The ElseIf Statement

In this Try It Out, you'll use your Simple If program to see how you can test for the value of intNumber being 27 and 1000. All the code in this Try It Out is in the Simple If folder in the Zip file for this chapter.

1. Return to the Code Editor and change the code in the btnAnotherIf_Click procedure so that it looks like this:

```
Private Sub btnAnotherIf_Click(sender As Object,
                e As EventArgs) Handles btnAnotherIf.Click

    'Declare and set a variable
    Dim intNumber As Integer = 27

    'Here's where you make a decision,
    'and tell the user what happened
    If intNumber = 1000 Then
        MessageBox.Show("'intNumber' is, indeed, 1000!", "Simple If")
    ElseIf intNumber = 27 Then
        MessageBox.Show("'intNumber' is 27!", "Simple If")
    Else
        MessageBox.Show("'intNumber' is neither 1000 nor 27!", "Simple If")
    End If
End Sub
```

2. Run the project and click the Another If button. You'll see the message box shown in Figure 4-3.

FIGURE 4-3

How It Works

This time, the code in the ElseIf statement ran because intNumber met the condition intNumber = 27. Note that you can still include the Else statement at the end to catch instances where intNumber is neither 27 nor 1000, but something else entirely:

```
ElseIf intNumber = 27 Then
    MessageBox.Show("'intNumber' is 27!", "Simple If")
Else
    MessageBox.Show("'intNumber' is neither 1000 nor 27!", "Simple If")
End If
```

> **NOTE** You can add as many ElseIf statements as you need to test for conditions. However, bear in mind that each ElseIf statement is executed as Visual Basic 2015 attempts to discover whether the condition is true. This slows your program if you have a lot of conditions to be tested. If this is the case, you should try to put the statements in the order they are most likely to be executed, with the most common one at the top. This is faster as the code exits after finding the first true test. Alternatively, you should use a Select Case block, which is discussed later in the chapter.

Nested If Statements

It's possible to nest an `If` statement inside another:

```
If intX = 3 Then
    MessageBox.Show("intX = 3")

    If intY = 6 Then
        MessageBox.Show("intY = 6")
    End If

End If
```

There's no real limit to how far you can nest your `If` statements. However, the more levels of nesting you have, the harder it is to follow what's happening in your code, so try to keep the nesting of `If` statements to a minimum.

Single-Line If Statement

The single-line form of the `If` statement is typically used for short, simple tests, and it saves space in the Code Editor. However, it doesn't provide the structure and flexibility of the multiline form and is usually harder to read:

```
If intX = 3 Then MessageBox.Show("intX = 3") Else MessageBox.Show("intX is not 3")
```

You don't need an `End If` at the end of a single-line `If...Then` statement.

Multiple statements can also be executed within a single-line `If...Then` statement. All statements must be on the same line and must be separated by colons, as in the following example:

```
If intX = 3 Then MessageBox.Show("intX = 3"): intX = intX + 1: Total += intX
```

Comparison Operators

You know how to check whether a particular variable is equal to some value and execute code if this is the case. In fact, `If` is far more flexible than this. You can ask questions such as these, all of which have yes/no answers:

> ➤   Is `intNumber` greater than `49`?

> ➤   Is `intNumber` less than `49`?

> ➤   Is `intNumber` greater than or equal to `49`?

> ➤   Is `intNumber` less than or equal to `49`?

> ➤   Is `strName` not equal to `Ben`?

When working with string values, most of the time you'll use the Equal To or Not Equal To operator. When working with numeric values (both integer and floating-point), you can use all the arithmetic operators discussed in the previous chapter.

Using Not Equal To

You have not used Not Equal To yet, so test the Not Equal To operator with strings.

TRY IT OUT   Using Not Equal To

The Not Equal To (<>) operator will be `false` when Equal To (=) is true, and it will be `true` when Equal To is `false`. Let's try it out. All the code for this Try It Out is in the folder If Demo in the Zip file for this chapter.

1. Create a Windows Forms Application project called **If Demo**. Add a `TextBox` control and a Button control. Set the `Name` property for TextBox1 to **txtName** and the `Text` property to **Stephanie**. Set the `Name` property for Button1 to **btnCheck** and the `Text` property to **Check**.

2. Double-click the Button control to create its `Click` event handler. Add the bolded code:

```
Private Sub btnCheck_Click(sender As Object,
                e As EventArgs) Handles btnCheck.Click

    'Declare a variable and get the name from the text box
    Dim strName As String
    strName = txtName.Text

    'Is the name Wendy?
    If strName <> "Wendy" Then
        MessageBox.Show("The name is *not* Wendy.", "If Demo")
    End If
End Sub
```

3. Save your project and then run it. When the form is displayed, click the Check button and you will see a message box indicating that the name is not Wendy.

How It Works

The Not Equal To operator looks like this: <>. When the button is clicked, the first thing you do is retrieve the name from the text box by looking at its `Text` property:

```
'Declare a variable and get the name from the text box
Dim strName As String
strName = txtName.Text
```

After you have the name, you use an `If` statement. This time, however, you use the Not Equal To operator, rather than the Equal To operator. Also note that you are comparing two string values:

```
'Is the name Wendy?
If strName <> "Wendy" Then
    MessageBox.Show("The name is *not* Wendy.", "If Demo")
End If
```

The code between `Then` and `End If` executes only if the answer to the question asked in the `If` statement is `True`. You might find this to be a bit of a heady principle because the question you're asking is this: "Is strName not equal to Wendy?" to which the answer is, "Yes, the strName is *not* equal to Wendy." Because the answer to this question is yes, or `True`, the code runs and the message box displays. However, if you enter Wendy into the text box and click Check, nothing happens because the answer to the question is, "No, the strName *is* equal to Wendy." Therefore, you have a no, or `False`, answer.

NOTE *If you try this, be sure to type* **Wendy** *with an uppercase* **W** *and the rest of the letters in lowercase; otherwise, the application won't work properly. You'll see why later.*

An alternative way of checking that something does not *equal something else is to use the* Not *keyword. The condition in the* If *statement could have been written as follows:*

```
If Not strName = "Wendy" Then
```

Using the Numeric Operators

In this section, you take a look at the four other comparison operators you can use. These are all fairly basic, so you'll go through this quite fast.

TRY IT OUT **Using Less Than**

In this Try It Out, you will work with greater than, less than, greater than or equal to, and less than or equal to. All the code in this Try It Out is in the If Demo folder in the Zip file for this chapter.

1. Return to the Forms Designer for the If Demo project. Add another TextBox control and set its Name property to **txtValue**. Add another Button control and set its Name property to **btnCheckNumbers** and its Text property to **Check Numbers**.

2. Double-click the Check Numbers button and add the following bolded code to its Click event handler:

```
Private Sub btnCheckNumbers_Click(sender As Object,
    e As EventArgs) Handles btnCheckNumbers.Click


    'Declare variable
    Dim intNumber As Integer

    Try
        'Get the number from the text box
        intNumber = CType(txtValue.Text, Integer)
    Catch
        Exit Sub
    End Try

    'Is intNumber less than 27?
    If intNumber < 27 Then
        MessageBox.Show("Is 'intNumber' less than 27? Yes!", "If Demo")
    Else
        MessageBox.Show("Is 'intNumber' less than 27? No!", "If Demo")
    End If
End Sub
```

3. Run the project. Enter **14** into the text box and click the Check Numbers button. You'll be told whether the number entered is less than or greater than 27, as shown in Figure 4-4.

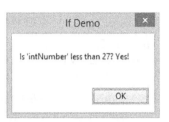

How It Works

First, you get the value back from the text box. However, there is a slight wrinkle. Because this is a text box, end users are free to enter anything they want into it, and if a series of characters that cannot be

FIGURE 4-4

converted into an integer is entered, the program crashes. Therefore, you add an *exception handler* to ensure that you always get a value back. Also, with the Option Strict option turned on, you'll need to convert the string value in the text box to an `Integer` data type using the `CType` function as you did in the last chapter. If the user enters something invalid, `intNumber` remains 0 (the default value); otherwise, it will be whatever is entered:

```
'Declare variable
Dim intNumber As Integer

Try
    'Get the number from the text box
    intNumber = CType(txtValue.Text, Integer)
Catch
    Exit Sub
End Try
```

> **NOTE** *You'll be introduced to exception handling properly in Chapter 9. For now, you can safely ignore it!*
>
> *The Less Than operator looks like this: <. Here, you test to determine whether the number entered was less than 27, and if it is, you say so in a message box; otherwise, you say No:*
>
> ```
> 'Is intNumber less than 27?
> If intNumber < 27 Then
>   MessageBox.Show("Is 'intNumber' less than 27? Yes!", "If Demo")
> Else
>   MessageBox.Show("Is 'intNumber' less than 27? No!", "If Demo")
> End If
> ```
>
> *Here's something interesting, though. If you actually enter **27** into the text box and click the button, you'll see a message box that tells you* `intNumber` *is not less than 27. The* `If` *statement said No, and it's right;* `intNumber` *is actually equal to 27, and the cutoff point for this operator is anything up to but not including the value itself. You can get around this problem with a different operator, as you'll see in the next Try It Out.*

Using the Less Than Or Equal To Operator

The Less Than Or Equal To operator will be true when the tested value is less than the comparison value and also when the two values are equal. You will see this next. All the code for this Try It Out is in the code folder If Demo in the Zip file for this chapter.

1. Return to the Code Editor and change the If statement in the btnCheckNumbers_Click event handler, as shown here:

```
Try
    'Get the number from the text box
    intNumber = CType(txtValue.Text, Integer)
Catch
    Exit Sub
End Try

 'Is intNumber less than or equal to 27?
If intNumber <= 27 Then
    MessageBox.Show("Is 'intNumber' less than or equal to 27? Yes!", _
        "If Demo")
Else
    MessageBox.Show("Is 'intNumber' less than or equal to 27? No!", _
        "If Demo")
End If
```

2. Now run the project and enter **27** into the text box. Click the Check Numbers button, and you should see the results shown in Figure 4-5.

How It Works

In this example, the Less Than Or Equal To operator looks like this: <=. In this situation, you're extending the possible range of values up to and including the value you're checking. Therefore, in this case when you enter **27**, you get the answer Yes, n is less than or equal to 27. This type of operator is known as an *inclusive operator*.

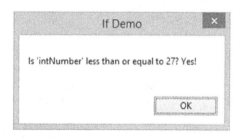

FIGURE 4-5

The final two operators look very similar to this, so let's look at them now.

Using Greater Than and Greater Than Or Equal To

In this example, you see how to use the Greater Than and Greater Than Or Equal To operators. All the code for this Try It Out is in the code folder If Demo in the Zip file for this chapter.

1. Return to the Code Editor and add two additional If statements in the btnCheckNumbers_Click event handler, as shown here:

```
'Is intNumber less than or equal to 27?
    If intNumber <= 27 Then
        MessageBox.Show("Is 'intNumber' less than or equal to 27? Yes!",
```

```
        "If Demo")
    Else
        MessageBox.Show("Is 'intNumber' less than or equal to 27? No!",
            "If Demo")
    End If

    'Is intNumber greater than 27?
    If intNumber > 27 Then
        MessageBox.Show("Is 'intNumber' greater than 27? Yes!",
            "If Demo")
    Else
        MessageBox.Show("Is 'intNumber' greater than 27? No!",
            "If Demo")
    End If

    'Is intNumber greater than or equal to 27?
    If intNumber >= 27 Then
        MessageBox.Show("Is 'intNumber' greater than or equal to 27? Yes!",
            "If Demo")
    Else
        MessageBox.Show("Is 'intNumber' greater than or equal to 27? No!",
            "If Demo")
    End If
End Sub
```

2. Run the program. This time, enter a value of **99** and click the Check Numbers button. You'll see three message boxes, one after the other. The first message box indicates that intNumber is not less than or equal to 27, whereas the second message box indicates that intNumber is greater than 27. The final message box indicates that intNumber is greater than or equal to 27.

How It Works

The Greater Than and Greater Than Or Equal To operators are basically the opposite of their Less Than counterparts. This time, you're asking, "Is intNumber greater than 27?" and, "Is intNumber greater than or equal to 27?" The results speak for themselves.

The And and Or Operators

What happens when you need your If statement to test more than one condition? For example, suppose that you want to ensure that intNumber is less than 27 *and* greater than 10. Or, how about checking that strName is "Wendy" or "Stephanie"? You can combine operators used with an If statement with the And and Or operators, as you do in the next Try It Out.

TRY IT OUT Using the Or Operator

All the code for this Try It Out is in the code folder And Or Demo in the Zip file for this chapter.

1. Create a new Windows Forms Application called **And Or Demo**.

2. In the Forms Designer for Form1, add two TextBox controls and a Button control. Set the Name properties of the text boxes to **txtName1** and **txtName2** and the Name property of the button to **btnOrCheck**.

3. Set the Text property for txtName1 to **Wendy** and the Text
    property for txtName2 to **Stephanie**. Finally, set the Text
    property for btnOrCheck to **Or Check**. Your completed form
    should look similar to the one shown in Figure 4-6.

4. Double-click the Or Check button and add the following code to
    its Click event handler:

```
Private Sub btnOrCheck_Click(sender As Object,
        e As EventArgs) Handles btnOrCheck.Click

    'Declare variables
    Dim strName1 As String, strName2 As String

    'Get the names
    strName1 = txtName1.Text
    strName2 = txtName2.Text

    'Is one of the names Wendy?
    If strName1 = "Wendy" Or strName2 = "Wendy" Then
        MessageBox.Show("One of the names is Wendy.",
            "And Or Demo")
    Else
        MessageBox.Show("Neither of the names is Wendy.",
            "And Or Demo")
    End If
End Sub
```

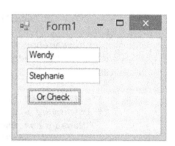

FIGURE 4-6

5. Run the project and click the button. You should see the results
    shown in Figure 4-7.

6. Click OK to dismiss the message box dialog and flip the names
    around so that the top one (txtName1) is Stephanie and the
    bottom one (txtName2) is Wendy. Click the button again. You'll
    see a message box indicating that one of the names is Wendy.

7. Click OK to dismiss the message box again and this time change
    the names so that neither of them is Wendy. Click the button, and
    you should see a message box indicating that neither of the names
    is Wendy.

FIGURE 4-7

How It Works

This example shows that the Or operator is a great way of building If statements that compare two
different values in a single hit. In your Click event handler, you first declare your variables and then
retrieve both names and store them in variables strName1 and strName2:

```
'Declare variables
Dim strName1 As String, strName2 As String

'Get the names
strName1 = txtName1.Text
strName2 = txtName2.Text
```

Notice that you've defined two variables on the same line. This is a perfectly legitimate coding practice, although it can sometimes make the code look congested. The variables are separated with commas; note that it's still important to use the As keyword to tell Visual Basic 2015 the data type of each variable.

Once you have both names, you use the Or operator to combine two separate If statements. The question you're asking here is this: "Is strName1 equal to Wendy or is strName2 equal to Wendy?" The answer to this question (provided that one of the text boxes contains the name Wendy) is, "Yes, either strName1 is equal to Wendy, or strName2 is equal to Wendy." Again, it's a yes/no or true/false answer, even though the question is seemingly more complex:

```
'Is one of the names Wendy?
If strName1 = "Wendy" Or strName2 = "Wendy" Then
    MessageBox.Show("One of the names is Wendy.",
        "And Or Demo")
Else
    MessageBox.Show("Neither of the names is Wendy.",
        "And Or Demo")
End If
```

Using the And Operator

The And operator is conceptually similar to Or, except that both parts of the condition need to be satisfied, as you will see in the next Try It Out.

TRY IT OUT   Using the And Operator

Let's see how to use the And operator. All the code for this Try It Out is in the folder And Or Demo in the Zip file for this chapter.

1. Return to the Forms Designer in the And Or Demo project. Add another Button control to the form. Set its Name property to **btnAndCheck** and its Text property to **And Check**. Double-click the button and add the following bolded code to its Click event handler:

```
Private Sub btnAndCheck_Click(sender As Object,
                e As EventArgs) Handles btnAndCheck.Click

    'Declare variables
    Dim strName1 As String, strName2 As String

    'Get the names
    strName1 = txtName1.Text
    strName2 = txtName2.Text

    'Are both names Wendy?
    If strName1 = "Wendy" And strName2 = "Wendy" Then
        MessageBox.Show("Both names are Wendy.",
            "And Or Demo")
    Else
        MessageBox.Show("One of the names is not Wendy.",
            "And Or Demo")
    End If
End Sub
```

2. Run the program and click the And Check button. A message box tells you that one of the names is not Wendy.

3. Change both names so that they are both Wendy and click the button. You'll see the results shown in Figure 4-8.

How It Works

Let's review why this works. After you retrieve both names from the text boxes, you compare them. In this case, you're asking the question, "Is strName1 equal to Wendy, *and* is strName2 equal to Wendy?" In this case, both parts of the If statement must be satisfied in order for the "Both names are Wendy" message box to be displayed:

FIGURE 4-8

```
'Are both names Wendy?
If strName1 = "Wendy" And strName2 = "Wendy" Then
    MessageBox.Show("Both names are Wendy.",
        "And Or Demo")
Else
    MessageBox.Show("One of the names is not
        Wendy.",
        "And Or Demo")
End If
```

More on And and Or

You've seen And and Or used with strings. They can also be used with numeric values, like this:

```
If intX = 2 And intY = 3 Then
    MessageBox.Show("Hello, both of the conditions have been satisfied!")
End If
```

or

```
If intX = 2 Or intY = 3 Then
    MessageBox.Show("Hello, one of the conditions has been satisfied!")
End If
```

In Visual Basic 2015, there's no realistic limit to the number of And operators or Or operators that you can include in a statement. It's perfectly possible to do the following, although it's unlikely you'd want to do so:

```
If intA = 1 And intB = 2 And intC = 3 And intD = 4 And intE = 5 And
    intF = 6 And intG = 7 And intH = 1 And intI = 2 And intJ = 3 And
    intK = 4 And intL = 5 And intM = 6 And intN = 7 And intO = 1 And
    intP = 2 And intQ = 3 And intR = 4 And intS = 5 And intT = 6 And
    intU = 7 And intV = 1 And intW = 2 And intX = 3 And intY = 4 And
    intZ = 5 Then
    MessageBox.Show("That's quite an If statement!")
End If
```

Finally, it's possible to use parentheses to group operators and look for a value within a range. For example, say you want to determine whether the value of intX is between 12 and 20 exclusive or between 22 and 25 exclusive. You can use the following If...Then statement:

```
If (intX > 12 And intX < 20) Or (intX > 22 And intX < 25) Then
```

There are many other combinations of operators, far more than we have room to go into here. Rest assured that if you want to check for a condition, there is a combination to suit your needs.

String Comparison

When working with strings and If statements, you often run into the problem of uppercase and lowercase letters. A computer treats the characters A and a as separate entities, even though people consider them to be similar. This is known as *case sensitivity*—meaning that the case of the letters does matter when comparing strings. For example, if you run the following code, the message box would *not* be displayed:

```
Dim strName As String
strName = "Winston"
If strName = "WINSTON" Then
    MessageBox.Show("Aha! You are Winston.")
End If
```

Because WINSTON is not, strictly speaking, the same as Winston, this If statement does not return a message. However, in many cases you don't actually care about case, so you have to find a way of comparing strings and ignoring the case of the characters.

TRY IT OUT   Using Case-Insensitive String Comparisons

In this Try It Out, you work with case-insensitive strings. All the code for this Try It Out is in the code folder And Or Demo in the Zip file for this chapter.

1. Return to the Forms Designer in the And Or Demo project and add another TextBox and Button control to the form.

2. Set the Name property of the TextBox to **txtName3** and the Text property to **Bryan**. Set the Name property of the Button to **btnStringCompare** and the Text property to **String Compare**.

3. Double-click the **String Compare** button to open its Click event handler and add the following bolded code:

```
Private Sub btnStringCompare_Click(sender As Object,
                     e As EventArgs) Handles btnStringCompare.Click

    'Declare variable
    Dim strName As String

    'Get the name
    strName = txtName3.Text

    'Compare the name
    If String.Compare(strName, "BRYAN", True) = 0 Then
        MessageBox.Show("Hello, Bryan!", "And Or Demo")
    End If
End Sub
```

4. Run the project and click btnStringCompare. You should see a result like the one shown in Figure 4-9.

5. Dismiss the message box and enter the name in the last text box as **BrYaN**, or some other combination of uppercase and lowercase letters, and click the button. You should still see a message box that says, "Hello, Bryan!"

6. However, if you enter a name that isn't Bryan, the message box will not be displayed when you click the button.

FIGURE 4-9

How It Works

After you get the name back from the text box, you have to use a function to compare the two values, rather than use the basic Equal To operator. In this instance, you're using the Compare method on System.String, passing it the two strings you want to compare. The first string is the value stored in strName (which is the value entered into the text box), with the second string being "BRYAN". The last parameter that you supply is True, which tells Compare to perform a case-insensitive match; in other words, it should ignore the differences in case. If you supplied False for this parameter, the comparison would be case sensitive, in which case you would be no better off than using the vanilla Equal To operator:

```
'Compare the name
If String.Compare(strName, "BRYAN", True) = 0 Then
    MessageBox.Show("Hello, Bryan!", "And Or Demo")
End If
```

String.Compare returns a fairly curious result. It actually returns an integer rather than a True or False value because String.Compare can be used to determine *how* two strings differ, rather than just a straightforward, "Yes, they are," or "No, they're not." If the method returns 0, the strings match. If the method returns a value that is not 0, the strings do not match.

> **NOTE** String.Compare *returns an indication of the difference between two strings in order to help you build sorting algorithms.*

SELECT CASE

On occasion, you need to make a set of decisions such as these:

➤ Is the customer called Bryan? If so, do this.

➤ Is the customer called Stephanie? If so, do this.

➤ Is the customer called Cathy? If so, do this.

➤ Is the customer called Betty? If so, do this.

➤ Is the customer called Edward? If so, do this.

You can obviously do this with a set of If...Then statements. In fact, it would look a little like this:

```
If Customer.Name = "Bryan" Then
    (<i>do something</i>)
ElseIf Customer.Name = "Stephanie" Then
    (<i>do something</i>)
ElseIf Customer.Name = "Cathy" Then
    (<i>do something</i>)
ElseIf Customer.Name = "Betty" Then
    (<i>do something</i>)
ElseIf Customer.Name = "Edward" Then
    (<i>do something</i>)
End If
```

What happens if you decide you want to check `Customer.FirstName` rather than `Customer.Name`? You'd have to change every `If` statement, which is a pain. In addition, if `Customer.Name` turns out to be `"Edward"`, you still have to go through the other four `If` statements, which is very inefficient. In the next Try It Out, you learn a better way.

TRY IT OUT Using Select Case

All the code for this Try It Out is in the code folder `Select Demo` in the Zip file for this chapter.

1. Create a new Windows Forms Application project. Call it **Select Demo**. Set the `Text` property of the form to **Select Case**.

2. From the Toolbox, add a ListBox control to the form and set its `Name` property to **lstData**, its `IntegralHeight` property to **False**, and its `Dock` property to **Fill**.

> **NOTE** To set the `Dock` property, click the center box in the dropdown to set the property or type **Fill**.

3. With lstData selected in the Forms Designer, look at the Properties window and select the `Items` property. Click the ellipsis button to the right of the property, and in the String Collection Editor that appears, add the five names on separate lines (as shown in Figure 4-10).

4. Click OK to save the changes. The names will be added to your list box.

5. Now double-click lstData to create a new `SelectedIndexChanged` event handler and add the following bolded code:

FIGURE 4-10

```
Private Sub lstData_SelectedIndexChanged(sender As Object,
    e As EventArgs) Handles lstData.SelectedIndexChanged

    'Declare variables
    Dim strName As String
    Dim strFavoriteColor As String

    'Get the selected name
    strName = lstData.Items(lstData.SelectedIndex).ToString
    'Use a Select Case statement to get the favorite color
    'of the selected name
    Select Case strName
        Case "Bryan"
            strFavoriteColor = "Madras Yellow"

      Case "Ashley"
            strFavoriteColor = "Sea Blue"

        Case "Jennifer"
            strFavoriteColor = "Morning Mist"

        Case "Eddie"
            strFavoriteColor = "Passionate Purple"

        Case "Katelyn"
            strFavoriteColor = "Red"
    End Select

    'Display the favorite color of the selected name
    MessageBox.Show(strName & "'s favorite color is " &
        strFavoriteColor, "Select Demo")
End Sub
```

6. Save your project and then run it. Whenever you click one of the names, a message box like the one shown in Figure 4-11 appears.

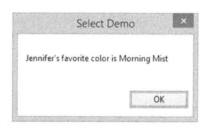

FIGURE 4-11

How It Works

In this Try It Out, the first thing you need to do in the SelectedIndexChanged event handler is to declare your variables and determine which name was selected. You do this by finding the item in the list that matches the current value of the SelectedIndex property. The Items collection of the ListBox class returns an Object data type, so you use the ToString method to convert the object to a String data type for the strName variable:

```
'Declare variables
Dim strName As String
Dim strFavoriteColor As String

'Get the selected name
strName = lstData.Items(lstData.SelectedIndex).ToString
```

When you have that, you start a Select Case...End Select block. To do this, you need to supply the variable that you're matching against; in this case, you're using the name that was selected in the list.

Inside the `Select Case...End Select` block, you define separate `Case` statements for each condition to be checked against. In this example, you have five, and each is set to respond to a different name. If a match can be found, Visual Basic 2015 executes the code immediately following the relevant `Case` statement.

For example, if you clicked Katelyn, the message box would display Red as her favorite color because Visual Basic 2015 would execute the line `strFavoriteColor = "Red"`. If you clicked Ashley, the message box would display Sea Blue as her favorite color, because Visual Basic 2015 would execute `strFavoriteColor = "Sea Blue"`.

```
'Use a Select Case statement to get the favorite color
'of the selected name
Select Case strName
    Case "Bryan"
        strFavoriteColor = "Madras Yellow"

    Case "Ashley"
        strFavoriteColor = "Sea Blue"

    Case "Jennifer"
        strFavoriteColor = "Morning Mist"

    Case "Eddie"
        strFavoriteColor = "Passionate Purple"

    Case "Katelyn"
        strFavoriteColor = "Red"
End Select
```

After the `Select Case...End Select` block, you display a message box:

```
'Display the favorite color of the selected name
MessageBox.Show(strName & "'s favorite color is " &
    strFavoriteColor, "Select Demo")
```

How do you get out of a `Select Case...End Select` block? As you're processing code that's beneath a `Case` statement, if you meet another `Case` statement, Visual Basic 2015 jumps out of the block and down to the line immediately following the block. Here's an illustration:

1. The user clicks Katelyn. The `SelectedIndexChanged` event is activated, and you store `"Katelyn"` in `strName`.

2. You reach the `Select Case` statement, which is set to compare the value in `strName` with one of the five supplied names. The names are tested in order like the `If` statement.

3. Visual Basic 2015 finds a `Case` statement that satisfies the request and immediately moves to `strFavoriteColor = "Red"`.

4. Visual Basic 2015 moves to the next line. This is the first line after the `Select Case...End Select` and it displays the message box.

`Select Case` is a powerful and easy-to-use technique for making a choice from several options. However, you must leave the block as soon as another `Case` statement or `End Select` is reached.

Case-Insensitive Select Case

Just like `If`, `Select Case` is case sensitive; prove it in the next Try It Out.

TRY IT OUT Using Case-Sensitive Select Case

In this Try It Out, you will prove that case matters when using `Select Case` to compare strings. All the code for this Try It Out is in the code folder `Select Demo` in the Zip file for this chapter.

1. Return to the Select Demo project and open the Forms Designer. Locate the `Items` property for the list box and open the String Collection Editor again.

2. Change all the names so that they appear in all uppercase letters, as shown in Figure 4-12.

3. Click OK to save your changes and then run the project. You'll notice that when you click a name, the message box doesn't specify a favorite color (see Figure 4-13).

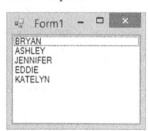

FIGURE 4-12

How It Works

`Select Case` performs a case-sensitive match, just like `If`. This means that if you provide the name `BRYAN` or `EDDIE` to the statement, there won't be a corresponding `Case` statement because you're trying to say:

```
If "EDDIE" = "Eddie"
```

or

```
If "BRYAN" = "Bryan"
```

FIGURE 4-13

Earlier in this chapter, you learned how to use the `String.Compare` method to perform case-insensitive comparisons with `If` statements. With `Select Case`, you can't use this method, so if you want to be insensitive toward case, you need to employ a different technique—the one you learn in the next Try It Out.

TRY IT OUT Case-Insensitive Select Case

In this example, you will learn another way to compare strings using `Select Case`. All the code for this Try It Out is in the code folder `Select Demo` in the Zip file for this chapter.

1. Return to the Select Demo project, open the Code Editor for Form1, and make the following changes to the event handler for `SelectedIndexChanged`. Pay special attention to the `Case` statements—the name that you're trying to match *must* be supplied in all lowercase letters:

```
Private Sub lstData_SelectedIndexChanged(sender As Object,
    e As EventArgs) Handles lstData.SelectedIndexChanged

    'Declare variables
    Dim strName As String
```

```
Dim strFavoriteColor As String

'Get the selected name
strName = lstData.Items(lstData.SelectedIndex).ToString

'Use a Select Case statement to get the favorite color
'of the selected name
Select Case strName.ToLower
    Case "bryan"
        strFavoriteColor = "Madras Yellow"

    Case "ashley"
        strFavoriteColor = "Sea Blue"

    Case "jennifer"
        strFavoriteColor = "Morning Mist"

    Case "eddie"
        strFavoriteColor = "Passionate Purple"

    Case "katelyn"
        strFavoriteColor = "Red"
End Select

'Display the favorite color of the selected name
MessageBox.Show(strName & "'s favorite color is " & strFavoriteColor,
    "Select Demo")
End Sub
```

2. Run the project and try selecting a name again. This time you will
    see that the message box includes the favorite color of the person
    you clicked, as shown in Figure 4-14.

How It Works

To make the selection case insensitive in this example, you have to
convert the strName variable into all lowercase letters. This is done using the ToLower method:

FIGURE 4-14

```
Select Case strName.ToLower
```

This means that whatever string you're given (whether it's "BRYAN" or "Bryan"), you always convert
it to all lowercase ("bryan"). However, when you do this, you have to ensure that you're comparing apples to apples (and not to Apples), which is why you had to convert the values you're checking
against in the Case statements to all lowercase, too. Therefore, when given "BRYAN", you convert this to
"bryan" and then try to find the Case that matches "bryan":

```
Case "bryan"
        strFavoriteColor = "Madras Yellow"

    Case "ashley"
        strFavoriteColor = "Sea Blue"

    Case "jennifer"
```

```
                strFavoriteColor = "Morning Mist"

        Case "eddie"
            strFavoriteColor = "Passionate Purple"

        Case "katelyn"
            strFavoriteColor = "Red"
    End Select
```

Finally, once you have the favorite color, you display a message box as usual.

> **NOTE** *You could have done the opposite of this and converted all the names to uppercase and used* `strName.ToUpper` *rather than* `strName.ToLower`.

Multiple Selections

You're not limited to matching one value inside a `Select Case ... End Select` block. You can also match multiple items.

TRY IT OUT   Multiple Selections

In this Try It Out, you'll modify the application so that you also report the gender of the person you click. All the code for this Try It Out is in the code folder `Select Demo` in the Zip file for this chapter.

1. Return to the Select Demo project, open the Code Editor for Form1, and add the bolded code in the `SelectedIndexChanged` handler:

```
'Display the favorite color of the selected name
    MessageBox.Show(strName & "'s favorite color is " & strFavoriteColor,
        "Select Demo")

    'Use a Select Case statement to display a person's gender
    Select Case strName.ToLower
        Case "bryan", "eddie", "ashley"
            MessageBox.Show("This person's gender is male.", "Select Demo")
        Case "jennifer", "katelyn"
            MessageBox.Show("This person's gender is female.", "Select Demo")
    End Select
End Sub
```

2. Run the project and click one of the female names. You will see results as shown in Figure 4-15, following the message box indicating the person's favorite color.

How It Works

OK, now let's look at how multiple selections work. The code you use to get back the name and initialize the `Select Case` block remains the same. However, in each `Case` statement you can provide a list of

FIGURE 4-15

possible values, separated by commas. In the first one, you look for `bryan` or `edward` or `ashley`. If any of these matches, you run the code under the `Case` statement:

```
Case "bryan", "eddie", "ashley"
    MessageBox.Show("This person's gender is male.", "Select Demo")
```

In the second statement, you look for `jennifer` or `katelyn`. If any of these two matches, you again run the code under the `Case` statement:

```
Case "jennifer", "katelyn"
    MessageBox.Show("This person's gender is female.", "Select Demo")
```

It's important to realize that these are all *or* matches. You're saying, "one *or* the other," not, "one *and* the other."

The Case Else Statement

What happens if none of the `Case` statements that you've included is matched? You saw this before in the demonstration of the case-sensitive nature of `Select Case`. In the next Try It Out, you see it with the `Case Else` statement.

TRY IT OUT   Using Case Else

All the code for this Try It Out is in the code folder `Select Demo` in the Zip file for this chapter.

1. Return to the Forms Designer, locate the `Items` property for the list box, and open the String Collection Editor again. Add another name in all uppercase letters to the collection and then click the OK button.

2. In the `lstData_SelectedIndexChanged` event handler, add the following bolded code:

```
'Use a Select Case statement to display a person's gender
    Select Case strName.ToLower
        Case "bryan", "edward"
            MessageBox.Show("This person's gender is male.", "Select Demo")
        Case "stephanie", "cathy", "betty"
            MessageBox.Show("This person's gender is female.", "Select Demo")
        Case Else
            MessageBox.Show("I don't know this person's gender.",
                "Select Demo")
    End Select
End Sub
```

3. Run the project and click the last name that you just added. You will see results similar to those shown in Figure 4-16.

How It Works

The `Case Else` statement is used if none of the other supplied `Case` statements matches what you're looking for. There isn't a `Case "tony"` defined within the block, so you default to using whatever is underneath

FIGURE 4-16

the `Case Else` statement. In this instance, you display a message box indicating that you do not know the gender of the person who's been selected.

Different Data Types with Select Case

In this chapter, you used `Select Case` with variables of type `String`. However, you can use `Select Case` with all basic data types in Visual Basic 2015, such as `Integer`, `Double`, and `Boolean`.

In day-to-day work, the most common types of `Select Case` are based on `String` and `Integer` data types. However, as a general rule, if a data type can be used in an `If` statement with the Equals (=) operator, it will work with `Select Case`.

LOOPS

When writing computer software, you often need to perform the same task several times to get the effect you want. For example, you might need to create a telephone bill for *all* customers or read in ten files from your computer's disk.

To accomplish this, you use a *loop*, and in this section you'll take a look at the two main types of loops available in Visual Basic 2015:

➤ **For loops:** These loops occur a certain number of times (for example, exactly ten times).

➤ **Do loops:** These loops keep running until a certain condition is reached (for example, until all the data is processed).

The For...Next Loop

The simplest loop to understand is the `For...Next` loop.

TRY IT OUT **Building a For...Next Loop**

You will learn to build a `For...Next` Loop in this Try It Out. All the code for this Try It Out is in the code folder `Loops` in the Zip file for this chapter.

1. Create a new Windows Forms Application project called **Loops**.

2. Add a ListBox and a Button control to the form.

3. Change the `Name` property of the ListBox to `lstData` and its `IntegralHeight` property to **False.**

4. Change the `Name` property of the button to **btnForNextLoop**. Set its Text property to **For NextLoop**. You'll be adding more buttons later, so make this button a little wider, as shown in Figure 4-17.

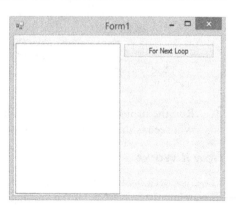

FIGURE 4-17

5. Double-click the button to create its `Click` event handler and add the following bolded code:

```
Private Sub btnForNextLoop_Click(sender As Object,
                    e As EventArgs) Handles btnForNextLoop.Click

    'Declare variable
    Dim intCount As Integer

    'Clear the list
    ClearList()

    'Perform a loop
    For intCount = 1 To 5
        'Add the item to the list
        lstData.Items.Add("I'm item " & intCount.ToString &
            " in the list!")
    Next
End Sub
```

6. Now create the following method:

```
Private Sub ClearList()
    'Clear the list
    lstData.Items.Clear()
End Sub
```

7. Save and run the project and then click the For Next Loop button. You should see results like those in Figure 4-18.

How It Works

First, inside the `Click` event handler, you define a variable:

```
'Declare variable
Dim intCount As Integer
```

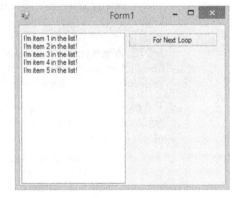

FIGURE 4-18

Next, you clear the list box by calling the `ClearList` method. Although the list is empty at this point, you'll be adding more buttons to this project in the following Try It Out exercises and you might want to compare the results of each of the buttons.

```
'Clear the list
ClearList()
```

You start the loop by using the `For` keyword. This tells Visual Basic 2015 that you want to create a loop. Everything that follows the `For` keyword is used to define how the loop should act. In this case, you're giving it the variable you just created and then telling it to count *from 1 to 5*:

```
'Perform a loop
For intCount = 1 To 5
```

The variable that you give the loop (in this case `intCount`) is known as the *control variable*. When you first enter the loop, Visual Basic 2015 sets the control variable to the initial count value—in this case, 1.

After the loop starts, Visual Basic 2015 moves to the first line within the `For` loop—in this case, the line that adds a string to the list box:

```
'Add the item to the list
lstData.Items.Add("I'm item " & intCount.ToString &
    " in the list!")
```

This time, this line of code adds `I'm item 1 in the list!` to the list box. Visual Basic 2015 then hits the `Next` statement, and that's where things start to get interesting:

```
Next
```

When the `Next` statement is executed, Visual Basic 2015 increments the control variable by one. The first time `Next` is executed, the value in `intCount` changes from 1 to 2. Provided that the value of the control variable is less than or equal to the "stop" value (in this case 5), Visual Basic 2015 moves back to the first line after the `For` statement, in this case:

```
'Add the item to the list
lstData.Items.Add("I'm item " & intCount.ToString &
    " in the list!")
```

This time, this line of code adds `I'm item 2 in the list!` to the list box. Again, after this line is executed, you run the `Next` statement. The value of `intCount` is now incremented from 2 to 3, and because 3 is less than or equal to 5, you move back to the line that adds the item to the list. This happens until `intCount` is incremented from 5 to 6. Because 6 is greater than the stop value for the loop, the loop stops.

> **NOTE** When you're talking about loops, you use the term iteration. One iteration includes one movement from the `For` statement to the `Next` statement. Your loop has five iterations.
>
> The method you define contains only one line of code, but its reuse becomes apparent in the next Try It Out. This method merely clears the Items collection of the list box:
>
> ```
> Private Sub ClearList()
>     'Clear the list
>     lstData.Items.Clear()
> End Sub
> ```

Using the Step Keyword

You don't have to start your loop at 1; you can pick any value you want. Nor do you have to increment the control value by 1 on each iteration; again, you can increment by any value you want.

TRY IT OUT Using Step

In this Try It Out, you learn about the flexibility of the `Step` keyword. All the code for this Try It Out is in the code folder `Loops` in the Zip file for this chapter.

1. Return to the Forms Designer for the Loops project. Add a Button control to your form. Set its Name property to **btnForNextLoopWithStep** and its Text property to **For Next Loop w/ Step**.

2. Double-click the button and add the following bolded code in the Click event handler:

```
Private Sub btnForNextLoopWithStep_Click(sender As Object,
    e As EventArgs) Handles btnForNextLoopWithStep.Click

    'Clear the list
    ClearList()

    'Perform a loop
    For intCount As Integer = 4 To 62 Step 7
        'Add the item to the list
        lstData.Items.Add(intCount.ToString)
    Next
End Sub
```

3. Run the project and click the For Next Loop w/Step button. You will see results like those in Figure 4-19.

How It Works

The magic in this example all happens with this statement:

```
'Perform a loop
For intCount As Integer = 4 To 62 Step 7
```

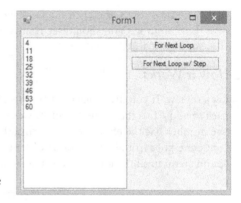

FIGURE 4-19

First, note that you didn't declare the intCount variable using a Dim statement. This has been done as part of the For statement and makes this variable local to this loop. Using the As keyword and the data type for the variable (in this case, Integer), you have effectively declared an inline variable.

Next, instead of using 1 as the start value, you're using 4. This means that on the first iteration of the loop, intCount is set to 4, which you can see because the first item added to the list is indeed 4. You've used the Step keyword to tell the loop to increment the control value by 7 on each iteration rather than by the default of 1. This is why intCount is set to 11, not 5 by the time you start running the second iteration of the loop.

Although you gave For a stop value of 62, the loop has actually stopped at 60 because the stop value is a *maximum*. After the ninth iteration, intCount is actually 67, which is more than 62, so the loop stops.

Looping Backward

By using a Step value that's less than 0 (or a negative number), you can make the loop go backward, rather than forward, as demonstrated in the next Try It Out.

TRY IT OUT Looping Backward

In this example, you will make a loop go backward. All the code for this Try It Out is in the code folder Loops in the Zip file for this chapter.

1. Return to the Forms Designer and add another Button control to your form, setting its Name property to **btnBackwardsForNextLoop** and its Text property to **Backwards For Next Loop**.

2. Double-click the button and add the following bolded code in the Click event handler:

```
Private Sub btnBackwardsForNextLoop_Click(sender As Object,
    e As EventArgs) Handles btnBackwardsForNextLoop.Click

    'Clear the list
    ClearList()

    'Perform a loop
    For intCount As Integer = 10 To 1 Step -1
        'Add the item to the list
        lstData.Items.Add(intCount.ToString)
    Next
End Sub
```

3. Run the project and click the Backwards For Next Loop button. You should see results like those shown in Figure 4-20.

How It Works

Let's review. If you use a negative number, like -1, For tries to add -1 to the current control value. Adding a negative number has the effect of subtracting the number, so intCount goes from its start value of 10 to its new value of 9, and so on until the stop value is reached.

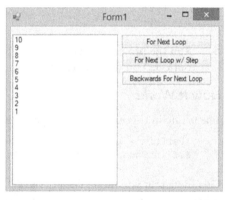

FIGURE 4-20

The For Each...Next Loop

In practical, day-to-day work, it's unlikely that you'll use For...Next loops as illustrated here. Because of the way the .NET Framework typically works, you'll usually use a derivative of the For...Next loop called the For Each...Next loop.

In the algorithms you design, whenever a loop is necessary, you'll have a collection of things to work through, and sometimes this set is expressed as an *array*. For example, you might want to look through all the files in a folder, looking for those that are larger than a particular size. When you ask the .NET Framework for a list of files, you are returned an array of strings, with each string in that array describing a single file.

TRY IT OUT For Each Loop

In this Try It Out, you'll modify your Loops application so that it returns a list of folders contained at the root of your C drive. All the code for this Try It Out is in the code folder Loops in the Zip file for this chapter.

1. Return to the Forms Designer, add another Button control to your form, and set its Name property to **btnForEachLoop** and its Text property to **For Each Loop**.

2. Double-click the button and add the following bolded code to the `Click` event handler:

```
Private Sub btnForEachLoop_Click(sender As Object,
    e As EventArgs) Handles btnForEachLoop.Click

    'Clear the list
    ClearList()

    'List each folder at the root of your C drive
    For Each strFolder As String In
        My.Computer.FileSystem.GetDirectories("C:\")

        'Add the item to the list
        lstData.Items.Add(strFolder)
    Next
End Sub
```

3. Run the project and click the For Each Loop button. You should see a list of folders that are at the root of your C drive.

How It Works

In the For Each Loop example, the `My` namespace in the .NET Framework exposes several classes that make it easy to find the information that you'll use on a daily basis. In particular, the `Computer` class provides several other classes related to the computer on which your program is running. Because you want to find out about files and folders, you use the `FileSystem` class, which provides methods and properties for working with files and folders.

The `GetDirectories` method returns a *collection* of strings representing names of directories (or folders) on your computer. In this case, you use it to return a collection of folder names in the root of the computer's C drive.

The concept with a `For Each...Next` loop is that for each iteration, you'll be given the "thing" that you're supposed to be working with. You need to provide a source of things (in this case, a collection of strings representing folder names) and a control variable into which the current thing can be put. The `GetDirectories` method provides the collection, and the inline variable `strFolder` provides the control variable:

```
'List each folder at the root of your C drive
For Each strFolder As String In
    My.Computer.FileSystem.GetDirectories("C:\")
Next
```

This means that on the first iteration, `strFolder` is equal to the first item in the string collection (in this case, `"C:\$Recycle.Bin"`). You then add that item to the list box:

```
'Add the item to the list
lstData.Items.Add(strFolder)
```

For every iteration of the loop, you're given a string containing a folder name, and you add that string to the list. When there are no more folders to be returned, execution automatically drops out of the loop.

The Do...Loop Loops

The other kind of loop you can use is one that keeps happening until a certain condition is met. This is known as a `Do...Loop`, and there are a number of variations.

The first one you'll learn about is the `Do Until...Loop`. This kind of loop keeps going until something happens.

TRY IT OUT   Using the Do Until...Loop

For this Try It Out, you're going to use the random number generator that's built into the .NET Framework and create a loop that will keep generating random numbers *until* it produces the number 10. When you get the number 10, you'll stop the loop.

1. Return to the Forms Designer in the Loops project, add another Button control to your form, and set its `Name` property to **btnDoUntilLoop** and its `Text` property to **Do Until Loop**.

2. Double-click the button and add the following bolded code to its `Click` event handler:

```
Private Sub btnDoUntilLoop_Click(sender As Object,
    e As EventArgs) Handles btnDoUntilLoop.Click

    'Declare variables
    Dim objRandom As New Random
    Dim intRandomNumber As Integer = 0

    'Clear the list
    ClearList()

    'Process the loop until intRandomNumber = 10
    Do Until intRandomNumber = 10
        'Get a random number between 0 and 24
        intRandomNumber = objRandom.Next(25)
        'Add the number to the list
        lstData.Items.Add(intRandomNumber.ToString)
    Loop
End Sub
```

3. Run the project and click the Do Until Loop button. You'll see results similar to the results shown in Figure 4-21. Keep clicking the button. The number of elements in the list is different each time.

How It Works

A `Do Until...Loop` keeps running the loop until the given condition is met. When you use this type of loop, there isn't a control variable *per se*; instead you have to keep track of the current position of the loop. You begin by declaring a variable (also known as an object) for the `Random` class, which provides methods for generating random numbers. This object has been prefixed with `obj` to specify that this

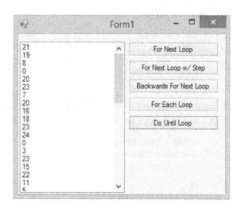

FIGURE 4-21

is an object derived from a class. The next variable that you declare is the `intRandomNumber`, which is used to receive the random number generated by your `objRandom` object:

```
'Declare variables
Dim objRandom As New Random()
Dim intRandomNumber As Integer = 0
```

Then you clear the list of any previous items that might have been added:

```
'Clear the list
ClearList()
```

Next, you set up the loop, indicating that you want to keep running the loop until `intRandomNumber` is equal to 10:

```
'Process the loop until intRandomNumber = 10
Do Until intRandomNumber = 10
```

With each iteration of the loop, you ask the random number generator for a new random number and store it in `intRandomNumber` by calling the `Next` method of `objRandom`. In this case, you passed 25 as a parameter to `Next`, meaning that any number returned should be between 0 and 24 inclusive—that is, the number you supply must be one larger than the biggest number you ever want to get. In other words, the bounds that you ask for are noninclusive. You then add the number that you got to the list:

```
'Get a random number between 0 and 24
    intRandomNumber = objRandom.Next(25)
    'Add the number to the list
    lstData.Items.Add(intRandomNumber.ToString)
Loop
```

The magic happens when you get to the `Loop` statement. At this point, Visual Basic 2015 returns not to the first line within the loop, but instead to the `Do Until` line. When execution returns to `Do Until`, the expression is evaluated. Provided it returns `False`, the execution pointer moves to the first line within the loop. However, if `intRandomNumber` is 10, the expression returns `True`, and instead of moving to the first line within the loop, you continue at the first line immediately after `Loop`. In effect, the loop is stopped.

Do While...Loop

The conceptual opposite of a `Do Until...Loop` is a `Do While...Loop`. This kind of loop keeps iterating while a particular condition is `True`. Let's see it in action.

TRY IT OUT   Using the Do While...Loop

In this Try It Out, you will use a `Do While...Loop` to continue while a random number is less than 15. All the code for this Try It Out is in the code folder `Loops` in the Zip file for this chapter.

1.   Return to the Forms Designer and add another Button control to your form. Set its `Name` property to **btnDoWhileLoop** and its `Text` property to **Do While Loop**.

2. Double-click the button and add the following bolded code to the `Click` event handler:

```
Private Sub btnDoWhileLoop_Click(sender As Object,
    e As EventArgs) Handles btnDoWhileLoop.Click

    'Declare variables
    Dim objRandom As New Random
    Dim intRandomNumber As Integer = 0

    'Clear the list
    ClearList()

    'Process the loop while intRandomNumber < 15
    Do While intRandomNumber < 15
        'Get a random number between 0 and 24
        intRandomNumber = objRandom.Next(25)
        'Add the number to the list
        lstData.Items.Add(intRandomNumber.ToString)
    Loop
End Sub
```

3. Run the project and click the Do While Loop button. You'll see something similar to the results shown in Figure 4-22.

How It Works

Every time you press the button, the loop executes as long as the random number generator produces a number less than 15.

A `Do While...Loop` keeps running as long as the given expression remains `True`. As soon as the expression becomes `False`, the loop quits. When you start the loop, you check to ensure that `intRandomNumber` is less than 15. If it is, the expression returns `True`, and you can run the code within the loop:

FIGURE 4-22

```
'Process the loop while intRandomNumber < 15
Do While intRandomNumber < 15
    'Get a random number between 0 and 24
    intRandomNumber = objRandom.Next(25)
    'Add the number to the list
    lstData.Items.Add(intRandomNumber.ToString)
Loop
```

Again, when you get to the `Loop` statement, Visual Basic 2015 moves back up to the `Do While` statement. When it gets there, it evaluates the expression again. If it's `True`, you run the code inside the loop once more. If it's `False` (because `intRandomNumber` is greater than or equal to 15), you continue with the first line after `Loop`, effectively quitting the loop.

Acceptable Expressions for a Do...Loop

You might be wondering what kind of expressions you can use with the two variations of Do...Loop. If you can use it with an If statement, you can use it with a Do...Loop. For example, you can write this:

```
Do While intX > 10 And intX < 100
```

or this:

```
Do Until (intX > 10 And intX < 100) Or intY = True
```

or this:

```
Do While String.Compare(strA, strB) > 0
```

In short, it's a pretty powerful loop!

Other Versions of the Do...Loop

It's possible to put the Until or While statements after Loop, rather than after Do. Consider these two loops:

```
Do While intX < 3
    intX += 1
Loop
```

and

```
Do
    intX += 1
Loop While intX < 3
```

At first glance, it looks like the While intX < 3 has just been moved around. You might think that these two loops are equivalent—but there's a subtle difference. Suppose that the value of intX is greater than 3 (for example, 4) when these two Do loops start. The first loop does not run at all. However, the second loop does run *once*. When the Loop While intX < 3 line is executed, the loop will be exited. This happens despite the condition saying that intX must be less than 3.

Now consider these two Do Until loops:

```
Do Until intX = 3
    intX += 1
Loop
```

and

```
Do
    intX += 1
Loop Until intX = 3
```

Again, although at first glance it looks like these two loops are equivalent, they're not; they behave slightly differently. Let's say that intX is 3 this time. The first loop doesn't run because intX already meets the exit condition for this loop. However, the second loop does run *once*. Then, when you execute `Loop Until intX = 3` the first time, `intX` is now 4, so you go back to the start of the loop and increment `intX` to 5, and so on. In fact, this is a classic example of an *infinite loop* (discussed later in this chapter) that will not stop.

> **NOTE** *When you use* `Loop While` *or* `Loop Until`, *you are saying that you want the loop to execute at least once, no matter what. In general, it's best to stick with* `Do While` *and* `Do Until`, *rather than use* `Loop While` *and* `Loop Until`.

You might also come across a variation of `Do While...Loop` called `While...End While`. This convention is a throwback to previous versions of Visual Basic, but old-school developers might still use it with .NET code, so it's important that you can recognize it. These two are equivalent, but you should use the first one:

```
Do While intX < 3
    intX += 1
Loop
```

and

```
While intX < 3
    intX += 1
End While
```

Nested Loops

You might need to start a loop even if you're already working through another loop. This is known as *nesting*, and it's similar in theory to the nesting demonstrated when you looked at `If` statements.

TRY IT OUT Using Nested Loops

In this Try It Out, you'll see how you can create and run through a loop, even if you're already working through another one. All the code for this Try It Out is in the code folder `Loops` in the Zip file for this chapter.

1. In the Forms Designer, add another Button control to your form and set its `Name` property to **btnNestedLoops** and its `Text` property to **Nested Loops**.

2. Double-click the button and add the following bolded code to its `Click` event handler:

```
Private Sub btnNestedLoops_Click(sender As Object,
    e As EventArgs) Handles btnNestedLoops.Click

    'Clear the list
    ClearList()

    'Process an outer loop
    For intOuterLoop As Integer = 1 To 2
        'Process a nested (inner) loop
        For intInnerLoop As Integer = 1 To 3
```

```
        lstData.Items.Add(intOuterLoop.ToString &
            ", " & intInnerLoop.ToString)
        Next
    Next
End Sub
```

3. Run the program and click the Nested Loops button.
    You should see results that look like those shown in
    Figure 4-23.

How It Works

This code is really quite simple. Your first loop (outer loop)
iterates intOuterLoop from 1 to 2, and the nested loop
(inner loop) iterates intInnerLoop from 1 to 3. Within the
nested loop, you have a line of code to display the current
values of intOuterLoop and intInnerLoop:

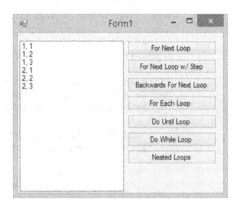

```
'Process an outer loop
For intOuterLoop As Integer = 1 To 2
    'Process a nested (inner) loop
    For intInnerLoop As Integer = 1 To 3
        lstData.Items.Add(intOuterLoop.ToString &
            ", " & intInnerLoop.ToString)
    Next
Next
```

FIGURE 4-23

Each For statement must be paired with a Next statement, and each Next statement that you reach
always "belongs" to the last created For statement. In this case, the first Next statement you reach is for
the 1 To 3 loop, which results in intInnerLoop being incremented. When the value of intInnerLoop
gets to be 4, you exit the inner loop.

After you quit the inner loop, you hit another Next statement. This statement belongs to the first
For statement, so intOuterLoop is set to 2 and you move back to the first line within the first,
outer loop—in this case, the other For statement. Once there, the inner loop starts once more.
Although in this Try It Out you've seen two For...Next loops nested together, you can nest
Do...While loops and even mix them, so you can have two Do...Loop statements nested inside a
For loop, and vice versa.

Quitting Early

Sometimes you don't want to see a loop through to its natural conclusion. For example, you might
be looking through a list for something specific, and when you find it, there's no need to go through
the remainder of the list.

TRY IT OUT   Quitting a Loop Early

In this Try It Out, you'll look through folders on your local drive, but this time, when you get to
c:\Program Files, you'll display a message and quit. All the code for this Try It Out is in the code
folder Loops in the Zip file for this chapter.

1. Return to the Forms Designer, add another Button control to your form, and set its Name property to **btnQuittingAForLoop** and its Text property to **Quitting A For Loop**.

2. Double-click the button and add the following bolded code to the Click event handler:

```
Private Sub btnQuittingAForLoop_Click(sender As Object,
    e As EventArgs) Handles btnQuittingAForLoop.Click

    'Clear the list
    ClearList()

    'List each folder at the root of your C drive
    For Each strFolder As String In
        My.Computer.FileSystem.GetDirectories("C:\")

        'Add the item to the list
        lstData.Items.Add(strFolder)

        'Do you have the folder C:\Program Files?
        If String.Compare(strFolder, "c:\program files", True) = 0 Then

            'Tell the user
            MessageBox.Show("Found it, exiting the loop now.", "Loops")

            'Quit the loop early
            Exit For

        End If
    Next
End Sub
```

3. Run the program and click the Quitting A For Loop button. You'll see something similar to the results shown in Figure 4-24.

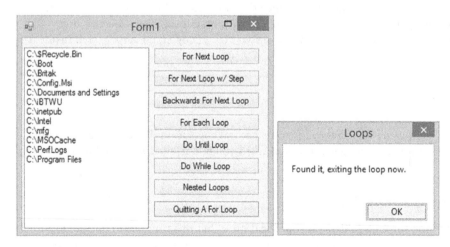

FIGURE 4-24

How It Works

This time, with each iteration you use the `String.Compare` method that was discussed earlier to check the name of the folder to see whether it matches `C:\Program Files`:

```
'Do you have the folder C:\Program Files?
If String.Compare(strFolder, "c:\program files", True) = 0 Then
```

If it does, the first thing you do is display a message box:

```
'Tell the user
MessageBox.Show("Found it, exiting the loop now.", "Loops")
```

After the user has clicked OK to dismiss the message box, you use the `Exit For` statement to quit the loop. In this instance, the loop is short-circuited, and Visual Basic 2015 moves to the first line after the `Next` statement:

```
'Quit the loop early
Exit For
```

Of course, if the name of the folder doesn't match the one you're looking for, you keep looping. Using loops to find an item in a list is one of their most common uses. Once you've found the item you're looking for, using the `Exit For` statement to short-circuit the loop is a very easy way to improve the performance of your application. The `Exit For` statement exits only one loop at a time, so if you are nesting loops be sure to exit the correct one.

Imagine you have a list of 1,000 items to look through. You find the item you're looking for on the tenth iteration. If you don't quit the loop after you've found the item, you're effectively asking the computer to look through another 990 useless items. If, however, you do quit the loop early, you can move on and start running another part of the algorithm.

Quitting Do...Loops

As you might have guessed, you can quit a `Do...Loop` in more or less the same way, as you see in the next Try It Out.

TRY IT OUT Quitting a Do...Loop

In this example, you will use `Exit Do` to quit a `Do...Loop`. All the code for this Try It Out is in the code folder `Loops` in the Zip file for this chapter.

1. Return to the Forms Designer one last time and add another Button control to your form. Set its `Name` property to **btnQuittingADoLoop** and its `Text` property to **Quitting a Do Loop**.

2. Double-click the button and add the following bolded code to the `Click` event handler:

```
Private Sub btnQuittingADoLoop_Click(sender As Object,
    e As EventArgs) Handles btnQuittingADoLoop.Click

    'Declare variable
    Dim intCount As Integer = 0

    'Clear the list
```

```
    ClearList()

    'Process the loop
    Do While intCount < 10

        'Add the item to the list
        lstData.Items.Add(intCount.ToString)

        'Increment the count by 1
        intCount += 1

        'Should you quit the loop
        If intCount = 3 Then

            Exit Do
        End If

    Loop
End Sub
```

3.   Run the project and click the Quitting a Do Loop button. You'll see a list containing the values 0, 1, and 2.

How It Works

In this case, because you're in a Do...Loop, you have to use Exit Do, rather than Exit For. However, the principle is exactly the same. Exit Do works with both the Do While...Loop and Do Until...Loop loops.

Infinite Loops

When building loops, you can create something called an *infinite loop*. This is a loop that, once started, never finishes. Consider this code:

```
Dim intX As Integer = 0
Do
    intX += 1
Loop Until intX = 0
```

This loop starts and runs through the first iteration. Then, when you execute Loop Until intX = 0 the first time, intX is 1. Therefore, you return to the start of the loop and increment intX to 2, and so on. What's important here is that it will never get to 0. The loop becomes infinite, and the program won't crash (at least not instantly), but it might well become unresponsive.

When you suspect a program has dropped into an infinite loop, you need to force the program to stop. If you are running your program in Visual Studio 2015, flip over to it, and select Debug ⇨ Stop Debugging from the menu. This immediately stops the program. If you are running your compiled program, you'll need to use the Windows Task Manager. Press Ctrl+Alt+Del and select Task Manager. Your program should appear as Not Responding. Select your program in the Task Manager and click End Task. Eventually this opens a dialog indicating that the program is not responding (which you knew already) and asking whether you want to kill the program stone dead. Click End Task again.

In some extreme cases, the loop can take up so much processing power or other system resources that you won't be able to open Task Manager or flip over to Visual Studio. In these cases, you can persevere and try to use either of these methods; or you can reset your computer and chalk it up to experience.

Visual Studio 2015 does not automatically save your project before running the application the first time, so you're likely to lose all your program code if you have to reset. Therefore, it is wise to save your project before you start running your code.

SUMMARY

This chapter took a detailed look at the various ways that programs can make decisions and loop through code. You first saw the alternative operators that can be used with If statements and examined how multiple operators can be combined by using the And and Or keywords. Additionally, you examined how case-insensitive string comparisons could be performed.

You then looked at Select Case, an efficient technique for choosing one outcome out of a group of possibilities. Next you examined the concept of looping within a program and were introduced to the two main types of loops: For loops and Do loops. For loops iterate a given number of times, and the derivative For Each loop can be used to loop automatically through a list of items in a collection. Do While loops iterate while a given condition remains True, whereas Do Until loops iterate until a given condition becomes True.

In summary, you should know how to use the following:

➤ If, ElseIf, and Else statements to test for multiple conditions

➤ Nested If statements

➤ Comparison operators and the String.Compare method

➤ The Select Case statement to perform multiple comparisons

➤ For...Next and For...Each loops

➤ Do...Loop and Do While...Loop statements

EXERCISES

1. When using a Select Case statement, how do you allow for multiple items in the Case statement?

2. What is the difference between a Do Until and a Loop Until Do loop?

3. Is "Bryan" and "BRYAN" the same string as Visual Basic sees it?

4. When you use the string.compare method, what is the last parameter (a Boolean parameter) used for?

5. In a Select Case statement, how do you put in a catch-all case for items that do not have a match?

6. When writing a For Each loop, how do you have the loop iterate backward?

7. What keyword do you use to exit a loop early?

► **WHAT YOU HAVE LEARNED IN THIS CHAPTER**

TOPIC	CONCEPTS
Comparison operators	To compare items, you can use the following operators: `>`, `>=`, `<`, `<=`, `=`, `<>`, `And`, `Or`.
Using If	Use `If` statements to make decisions. For multiple decisions, you can also use `If...Else` or `ElseIf`. You can nest `If...Else` statements for more complex decisions. For simple decisions, you can even use a single-line `If` statement.
Using Select Case	Use `Select Case` to test an item for one of many possible values. To make sure you find a match, use the `Case Else` statement.
Using For loops	Use `For loops` to execute tasks for a certain number of times. The statement `Exit For` is used to quit a `For loop`.
Using Do loops	Use `Do loops` to execute tasks while or until a condition is reached. The statement `Exit Do` is used to quit a `Do loop`.

5

Working with Data Structures

- ➤ Using arrays
- ➤ Working with enumerations
- ➤ Using constants
- ➤ Working with structures
- ➤ Working with and using an `ArrayList`
- ➤ Creating and adding items to a collection
- ➤ Understanding and building lookup tables with `Hashtables`
- ➤ Manipulating arrays using redimensioning and preserver

WROX.COM CODE DOWNLOADS FOR THIS CHAPTER

The `wrox.com` code downloads for this chapter are found at www.wrox.com/begvisualbasic2015 on the Download Code tab. The code is in the `092117 C05.zip` download and individually named according to the names given throughout the chapter.

> **WARNING** *Note that the Try It Outs in this chapter build on each other and the download version of the code provided is the final version and therefore may look slightly different from the versions you see in the previous chapter.*

In the previous chapters, you worked with simple data types—namely, `Integer` and `String` variables. Although these data types are useful in their own right, more complex programs call for working with *data structures*—groups of data elements that are organized in a single unit. In this chapter, you learn about the various data structures available in Visual Basic 2015. You also will see some ways in which you can work with complex sets of data. Finally, you learn how you can build powerful collection classes for working with, maintaining, and manipulating lists of complex data.

UNDERSTANDING ARRAYS

A fairly common requirement in writing software is the need to hold lists of similar or related data. You can provide this functionality by using an *array*. Arrays are just lists of data that have a single data type. For example, you might want to store a list of your friends' ages in an integer array or their names in a string array.

This section explains how to define, populate, and use arrays in your applications.

Defining and Using Arrays

When you define an array, you're actually creating a variable that has one or more dimensions. For example, if you define a variable as a string, you can hold only a single string value in it:

```
Dim strName As String
```

However, with an array you create a kind of multiplier effect with a variable, so you can hold more than one value in a single variable. An array is defined by entering the size of the array after the variable name. For example, if you wanted to define a string array with 10 elements, you'd do this:

```
Dim strName(9) As String
```

> **NOTE** *The reason why you use* (9) *instead of* (10) *to get an array with 10 elements is explained in detail later. The basic explanation is simply that because numbering in an array starts at 0, the first element in an array is 0, the second element is 1, and so on.*

When you have an array, you can access individual elements in it by providing an index value between 0 and a maximum possible value—this maximum possible value happens to be one less than the total size of the array.

For example, to set the element with index 2 in the array, you'd do this:

```
strName(2) = "Katie"
```

To get that same element back again, you'd do this:

```
MessageBox.Show(strName(2))
```

What's important is that other elements in the array are unaffected when you set their siblings, so if you do this, `strName(2)` remains set to `"Katie"`:

```
strName(3) = "Betty"
```

TRY IT OUT Defining and Using a Simple Array

Perhaps the easiest way to understand what an array looks like and how it works is to write some code. All the code for this Try It Out is in the code folder Array Demo in the Zip file for this chapter.

1. In Visual Studio 2015, click File ⇨ New Project. In the New Project dialog, create a new Windows Forms Application called **Array Demo**.

2. When the Designer for Form1 appears, add a ListBox control to the form. Using the Properties window set its Name property to **lstFriends** and its IntegralHeight property to **False**.

3. Add a Button control to the form. Set its Name property to **btnArrayElement** and set its Text property to **Array Element**. Arrange your controls so that your form looks similar to Figure 5-1 because you'll be adding more Button controls to this project later.

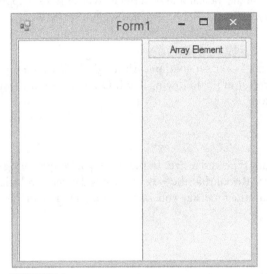

FIGURE 5-1

4. Double-click the button and add the following bolded code to its Click event handler. You'll receive an error message that the ClearList procedure is not defined. You can ignore this error because you'll be adding that procedure in the next step:

```
Private Sub btnArrayElement_Click(sender As Object,
                e As EventArgs) Handles btnArrayElement.Click

        'Clear the list
        ClearList()

        'Declare an array
        Dim strFriends(4) As String

        'Populate the array
        strFriends(0) = "Wendy"
        strFriends(1) = "Harriet"
```

```
        strFriends(2) = "Jay"
        strFriends(3) = "Michelle"
        strFriends(4) = "Richard"

        'Add the first array item to the list
        lstFriends.Items.Add(strFriends(0))
    End Sub
```

5. Now create the following procedure:

```
Private Sub ClearList()
    'Clear the list
    lstFriends.Items.Clear()
End Sub
```

6. Save your project by clicking the Save All button on the toolbar and then run it. When the form appears, click the Array Element button. The ListBox on your form will be *populated* with the name Wendy.

How It Works

In this example, you clear the ListBox by calling the ClearList method. Although the list is empty at this point, you'll be adding more buttons to this project in the following Try It Out exercises and might want to compare the results of the each of the buttons:

```
'Clear the list
ClearList()
```

When you define an array, you have to specify a data type and a size. In this case, you're specifying an array of type String and defining an array size of 5. Recall that the way the size is defined is a little quirky. You have to specify a number one fewer than the final size you want (more on that shortly). Therefore, here you have used the following line:

```
'Declare an array
Dim strFriends(4) As String
```

This way, you end up with an array of size 5. Another way of expressing this is to say that you have an array consisting of five *elements*.

When you are done, you have your array, and you can access each item in the array by using an *index*. The index is given as a number in parentheses after the name of the array. Indexes begin at 0 and go up to one fewer than the number of items in the array. The following example sets all five possible items in the array to the names:

```
'Populate the array
strFriends(0) = "Wendy"
strFriends(1) = "Harriet"
strFriends(2) = "Jay"
strFriends(3) = "Michelle"
strFriends(4) = "Richard"
```

Just as you can use an index to set the items in an array, you can use an index to get items back out. In this case, you're asking for the item at position 0, which returns the first item in the array—namely, Wendy:

```
'Add the first array item to the list
lstFriends.Items.Add(strFriends(0))
```

The reason why the indexes and sizes seem skewed is that the indexes are zero-based, whereas humans tend to number things beginning at 1. When putting items into or retrieving items from an array, you have to adjust the position you want down by 1 to get the actual index; for example, the fifth item is actually at position 4, the first item is at position 0, and so on. When you define an array, you do not actually specify the size of the array but rather the upper *index bound*—that is, the highest possible value of the index that the array will support.

> **NOTE** *Why should the indexes be zero-based? Remember that to the computer, a variable represents the address of a location in the computer's memory. Given an array index, Visual Basic 2015 just multiplies the index by the size of one element and adds the product to the address of the array as a whole to get the address of the specified element. The starting address of the array is also the starting address of the first element in it. That is, the first element is 0 times the size of an element away from the start of the whole array; the second element is 1 times the size of an element away from the start of the whole array; and so on.*
>
> *The method you define contains only one line of code, but its reuse becomes apparent in the next Try It Out. This method merely clears the Items collection of the ListBox.*
>
> ```
> Private Sub ClearList()
>     'Clear the list
>     lstFriends.Items.Clear()
> End Sub
> ```

Using For Each...Next

One common way to work with arrays is by using a `For Each...Next` loop. This loop was introduced in Chapter 4 when you used it with a string collection returned from the `My.Computer.FileSystem.GetDirectories` method.

TRY IT OUT   Using For Each...Next with an Array

This Try It Out demonstrates how you use `For Each...Next` with an array. All the code for this Try It Out is in the code folder `Array Demo` in the Zip file for this chapter.

1. Close your program if it is still running and open the Code Editor for Form1. Add the following bolded variable declaration at the top of your form class:

    ```
    Public Class Form1
        'Declare a form level array
        Private strFriends(4) As String
    ```

2. In the Class Name combo box at the top left of your Code Editor, select `(Form1 Events)`. In the Method Name combo box at the top right of your Code Editor, select the `Load` event. This causes

the `Form1_Load` event handler to be inserted into your code. Add the following bolded code to this procedure:

```
Private Sub Form1_Load(sender As Object, e As EventArgs) Handles Me.Load

    'Populate the array
    strFriends(0) = "Wendy"
    strFriends(1) = "Harriet"
    strFriends(2) = "Jay"
    strFriends(3) = "Michelle"
    strFriends(4) = "Richard"
End Sub
```

3.   Switch to the Forms Designer and add another Button control. Set its `Name` property to **btnEnumerateArray** and its `Text` property to **Enumerate Array**.

4.   Double-click this new button and add the following bolded code to its `Click` event handler:

```
Private Sub btnEnumerateArray_Click(sender As Object,
                e As EventArgs) Handles btnEnumerateArray.Click

    'Clear the list
    ClearList()

    'Enumerate the array
    For Each strName As String In strFriends
        'Add the array item to the list
        lstFriends.Items.Add(strName)
    Next
End Sub
```

5.   Run the project and click the button. You'll see results like those in Figure 5-2.

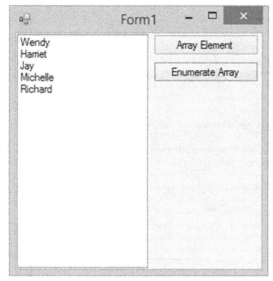

FIGURE 5-2

How It Works

You start this exercise by declaring an array variable that is local to the form, meaning that the variable is available to all procedures in the form class. Whenever variables are declared outside a method in the form class, they are available to all methods in the form:

```
'Declare a form level array
Private strFriends(4) As String
```

Next you added the Load event handler for the form and then added code to populate the array. This procedure will be called whenever the form loads, ensuring that your array always gets populated:

```
Private Sub Form1_Load(sender As Object, e As EventArgs) Handles Me.Load

    'Populate the array
    strFriends(0) = "Wendy"
    strFriends(1) = "Harriet"
    strFriends(2) = "Jay"
    strFriends(3) = "Michelle"
    strFriends(4) = "Richard"
End Sub
```

Chapter 4 shows the For Each...Next loop iterate through a string collection; in this example, it is used in an array. The principle is similar; you create a control variable of the same type as an element in the array and give this to the loop when it starts. This has all been done in one line of code. The control variable, strName, is declared and used in the For Each statement by using the As String keyword.

The internals behind the loop move through the array starting at element 0 until reaching the last element. For each iteration, you can examine the value of the control variable and do something with it; in this case, you add the name to the list:

```
'Enumerate the array
For Each strName As String In strFriends
    'Add the array item to the list
    lstFriends.Items.Add(strName)
Next
```

Note that the items are added to the list in the same order that they appear in the array. You can also add more than one item to a ListBox using the AddRange method. That's because For Each...Next proceeds from the first item to the last item as each item is defined.

Passing Arrays as Parameters

It's extremely useful to be able to pass an array (which could be a list of values) to a function as a parameter.

TRY IT OUT   Passing Arrays as Parameters

In this Try It Out, you'll look at how to pass an array to a function as a parameter. All the code for this Try It Out is in the code folder Array Demo in the Zip file for this chapter.

1. Return to the Forms Designer in the Array Demo project and add another Button control. Set its
    Name property to **btnArraysAsParameters** and its Text property to **Arrays as Parameters**.

2. Double-click the button and add the following bolded code to its Click event handler. You'll
    receive an error message that the AddItemsToList procedure is not defined. You can ignore this
    error because you'll be adding that procedure in the next step:

```
Private Sub btnArraysAsParameters_Click(sender As Object,
                e As EventArgs) Handles btnArraysAsParameters.Click


    'Clear the list
    ClearList()

    'List your friends
    AddItemsToList(strFriends)
End Sub
```

3. Add the AddItemsToList procedure as follows:

```
Private Sub AddItemsToList(ByVal arrayList As String())
    'Enumerate the array
    For Each strName As String In arrayList
        'Add the array item to the list
        lstFriends.Items.Add(strName)
    Next
End Sub
```

4. Run the project and click the button. You'll see the same results that were shown in Figure 5-2.

How It Works

The trick here is to tell the AddItemsToList method that the parameter it's expecting is an array of
type String. You do this by using empty parentheses, like this:

```
Private Sub AddItemsToList(ByVal arrayList() As String)
```

If you specify an array but don't define a size (or upper-bound value), you're telling Visual Basic 2015 that
you don't know or care how big the array is. That means you can pass an array of any size through to
AddItemsToList. In the btnArraysAsParameters_Click procedure, you're sending your original array:

```
'List your friends
AddItemsToList(strFriends)
```

TRY IT OUT   Adding More Friends

What happens if you define another array of a different size? In this Try It Out, you'll see. All the code
for this Try It Out is in the code folder Array Demo in the Zip file for this chapter.

1. Return to the Forms Designer of the Array Demo project. Add another Button control
    and set its Name property to **btnMoreArrayParameters** and its Text property to
    More Array Parameters.

2. Double-click the button and to its `Click` event handler add:

```
Private Sub btnMoreArrayParameters_Click(sender As Object,
                e As EventArgs) Handles btnMoreArrayParameters.Click

    'Clear the list
    ClearList()

    'Declare an array
    Dim strMoreFriends(1) As String

    'Populate the array
    strMoreFriends(0) = "Elaine"
    strMoreFriends(1) = "Debra"

    'List your friends
    AddItemsToList(strFriends)
    AddItemsToList(strMoreFriends)
End Sub
```

3. Run the project and click the button. You will see the form shown in Figure 5-3.

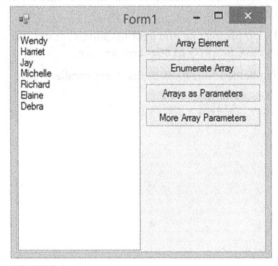

FIGURE 5-3

How It Works

What you have done here is prove that the array you pass as a parameter does not have to be of a fixed size. You created a new array of size 2 and passed it through to the same `AddItemsToList` function.

As you're writing code, you can tell whether a parameter is an array type by looking for empty parentheses in the IntelliSense pop-up box, as illustrated in Figure 5-4.

> **Note** *Not only are you informed that* `arrayList` *is an array type but you also see that the data type of the array is* `String`.
>
> ```
> 'List your friends
> AddItemsToList(strFriends)
> AddItemsToList(strMoreFriends)|
> ```
> ```
>    Sub Form1.AddItemsToList(arrayList As String())
> ```
>
> **FIGURE 5-4**

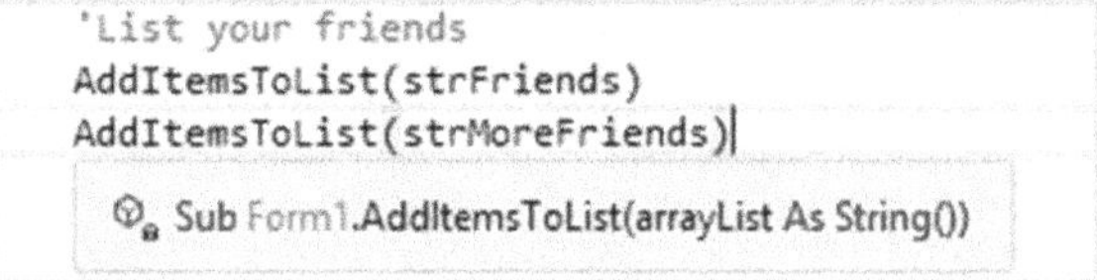

Sorting Arrays

It is sometimes useful to be able to sort an array. You might find this useful when you display data to users in a manner they can easily search or when you need to evaluate data logically.

TRY IT OUT Sorting Arrays

This Try It Out demonstrates how you can sort an array alphabetically. All the code for this Try It Out is in the code folder `Array Demo` in the Zip file for this chapter.

1. Return to the Forms Designer in the Array Demo project and add another Button control. Set its `Name` property to **btnSortingArrays** and its `Text` property to **Sorting Arrays**.

2. Double-click the button and add the following bolded code to its `Click` event handler:

```
Private Sub btnSortingArrays_Click(sender As Object,
            e As EventArgs) Handles btnSortingArrays.Click

    'Clear the list
    ClearList()

    'Sort the array
    Array.Sort(strFriends)

    'List your friends
    AddItemsToList(strFriends)
End Sub
```

3. Run the project and click the button. You'll see the ListBox on your form populated with the **names** from your array sorted alphabetically.

How It Works

All arrays are internally implemented in a class called `System.Array`. In this case, you use a method called `Sort` on that class. The `Sort` method takes a single parameter—namely, the array you want to sort. The method then does what its name suggests: sorts it for you into an order appropriate to the data type of the array elements. In this case, you are using a string array, so you get an alphanumeric sort. If you were to attempt to use this technique on an array containing integer or floating-point values, the array would be sorted in numeric order:

```
'Sort the array
Array.Sort(strFriends)
```

The capability to pass different parameter types in different calls to the same method name and to get behavior that is appropriate to the parameter types and parameter numbers actually passed is called *method overloading.* Sort is referred to as an overloaded method.

Going Backward

For Each Next goes through an array in only one direction. It starts at position 0 and loops through to the end of the array. If you want to go through an array backward (from the length –1 position to 0), you have two options.

One, you can step through the loop backward by using a standard For Next loop to start at the upper index bound of the first dimension in the array and work your way to 0 using the Step -1 keyword, as shown in the following example:

```
For intIndex As Integer = strFriends.GetUpperBound(0) To 0 Step -1
    'Add the array item to the list
    lstFriends.Items.Add(strFriends(intIndex))
Next
```

Alternately, you can call the Reverse method on the Array class to reverse the order of the array and then use your For Each Next loop.

TRY IT OUT   Reversing an Array

This Try It Out shows you how to call the Reverse method on the Array class to reverse the order of an array. All the code for this Try It Out is in the code folder Array Demo in the Zip file for this chapter.

1. Return to the Forms Designer and add another Button control. Set its Name property to **btnReversingAnArray** and its Text property to **Reversing an Array**.

2. Double-click the button and add the following bolded code to its Click event handler:

```
Private Sub btnReversingAnArray_Click(sender As Object,
        e As EventArgs) Handles btnReversingAnArray.Click

    'Clear the list
    ClearList()

    'Reverse the order—elements will be in descending order
    Array.Reverse(strFriends)

    'List your friends
    AddItemsToList(strFriends)
End Sub
```

3. Run the project and click the button. You'll see the friends listed in reverse order, as shown in Figure 5-5.

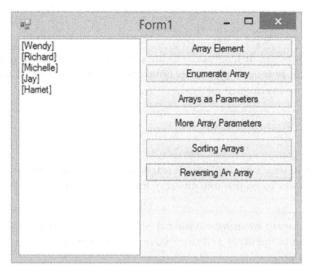

FIGURE 5-5

How It Works

The Reverse method reverses the order of elements in a one-dimensional array, which is what you are working with here. By passing the strFriends array to the Reverse method, you are asking the Reverse method to re-sequence the array from bottom to top:

```
'Reverse the order—elements will be in descending order
Array.Reverse(strFriends)
```

After the items in your array have been reversed, you simply call the AddItemsToList procedure to have the items listed:

```
'List your friends
AddItemsToList(strFriends)
```

> **NOTE** *If you want to list your array in descending sorted order, you would call the* Sort *method on the* Array *class to have the items sorted in ascending order, and then call the* Reverse *method to have the sorted array reversed, putting it into descending order.*

Initializing Arrays with Values

It is possible to create an array in Visual Basic 2015 and populate it in one line of code, rather than having to write multiple lines of code to declare and populate the array, as shown here:

```
'Declare an array
Dim strFriends(4) As String

'Populate the array
```

```
strFriends(0) = "Wendy"
strFriends(1) = "Harriet"
strFriends(2) = "Jay"
strFriends(3) = "Michelle"
strFriends(4) = "Richard"
```

TRY IT OUT Initializing Arrays with Values

You learn more about initializing arrays with values in this Try It Out. All the code for this Try It Out is in the code folder `Array Demo` in the Zip file for this chapter.

1. Return to the Forms Designer in the Array Demo project and add one last Button control. Set its `Name` property to **btnInitializingArraysWithValues** and its `Text` property to **Initializing Arrays with Values.**

2. Double-click the button and add the following bolded code to its `Click` event handler:

```
Private Sub btnInitializingArraysWithValues_Click(sender As Object,
            e As EventArgs) Handles btnInitializingArraysWithValues.Click

    'Clear the list
    ClearList()

    'Declare and populate an array
    Dim strMyFriends() As String = {"Elaine", "Richard", "Debra",
        "Wendy", "Harriet"}
    'List your friends
    AddItemsToList(strMyFriends)
End Sub
```

3. Run the project and click the button. Your ListBox will be populated with the friends listed in this array.

How It Works

The pair of braces ({}) allows you to set the values that should be held in an array directly. In this instance, you have five values to enter into the array, separated with commas. Note that when you do this, you don't specify an upper bound for the array; instead, you use empty parentheses. Visual Basic 2015 prefers to calculate the upper bound for you based on the values you supply:

```
'Declare and populate an array
Dim strMyFriends() As String = {"Elaine", "Richard", "Debra",
    "Wendy", "Harriet"}
```

This technique can be quite awkward to use when populating large arrays. If your program relies on populating large arrays, you might want to use the method illustrated earlier: Specify the positions and the values. This is especially true when populating an array with values that change at run time.

UNDERSTANDING ENUMERATIONS

So far, the variables you've seen had virtually no limitations on the kinds of data you can store in them. Technical limits notwithstanding, if you have a variable defined `As Integer`, you can put any number you want in it. The same holds true for `String` and `Double`. You have seen another variable type, however, that has only two possible values: `Boolean` variables can be either `True` or `False` and nothing else.

Often, when writing code, you want to limit the possible values that can be stored in a variable.

Using Enumerations

Enumerations enable you to build a new type of variable, based on one of these data types: `Integer`, `Long`, `Short`, or `Byte`. This variable can be set to one value of a set of possible values that you define, ideally preventing someone from supplying invalid values. It is used to provide clarity in the code because it can describe a particular value.

TRY IT OUT Using Enumerations

In this Try It Out, you'll look at how to build an application that checks the time of day and, based on that, can record a `DayAction` of one of the following possible values:

- ➤ Asleep
- ➤ Getting ready for work
- ➤ Traveling to work
- ➤ At work
- ➤ At lunch
- ➤ Traveling from work
- ➤ Relaxing with friends
- ➤ Getting ready for bed

1. Create a new Windows Forms application in Visual Studio 2015 called **Enum Demo**.

2. Set the `Text` property of Form1 to **What's Richard Doing?**

3. Now add a DateTimePicker control and set the following properties:

    - ➤ Set `Name` to **dtpHour**.
    - ➤ Set `Format` to **Time**.
    - ➤ Set `ShowUpDown` to **True**.
    - ➤ Set `Value` to **01:00 am**. VS will add the current date in the property to the time.

4. Add a Label control to the form, setting its `Name` property to **lblState** and its `Text` **property to** **State Not Initialized**. Resize your form so it looks similar to Figure 5-6.

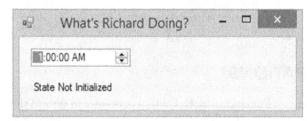

FIGURE 5-6

5. View the Code Editor for the form by right-clicking the form and choosing View Code from the context menu or by pressing F7 while on the form. At the top of the class, add the following bolded enumeration:

```
Public Class Form1

    'DayAction Enumeration
    Private Enum DayAction As Integer
        Asleep = 0
        GettingReadyForWork = 1
        TravelingToWork = 2
        AtWork = 3
        AtLunch = 4
        TravelingFromWork = 5
        RelaxingWithFriends = 6
        GettingReadyForBed = 7
    End Enum
```

6. With an enumeration defined, you can create new member variables that use the enumeration as their data type. Add this member:

```
'Declare variable
Private CurrentState As DayAction
```

7. Add the following code below the variable you just added:

```
'Hour property
Private Property Hour() As Integer
    Get
        'Return the current hour displayed
        Return dtpHour.Value.Hour
    End Get
    Set(value As Integer)
        'Set the date using the hour passed to this property
        dtpHour.Value =
            New Date(Now.Year, Now.Month, Now.Day, value, 0, 0)
        'Set the display text
        lblState.Text = "At " & value & ":00, Richard is "
    End Set
End Property
```

8. In the Class Name combo box at the top of the Code Editor, select (Form1 Events), and in the Method Name combo box, select the Load event. Add the following bolded code to the event handler:

```
Private Sub Form1_Load(sender As Object, e As EventArgs) Handles Me.Load

    'Set the Hour property to the current hour
    Me.Hour = Now.Hour
End Sub
```

9. In the Class Name combo box at the top of the Code Editor, select dtpHour, and in the Method Name combo box, select the ValueChanged event. Add the following bolded code to the event handler:

```
Private Sub dtpHour_ValueChanged(sender As Object,
```

```
                     e As EventArgs) Handles dtpHour.ValueChanged

           'Update the Hour property
           Me.Hour = dtpHour.Value.Hour
       End Sub
```

10. Save your project and then run it. You will be able to click the up-and-down arrows in the DateTimePicker control and see the text updated to reflect the hour selected, as shown in Figure 5-7.

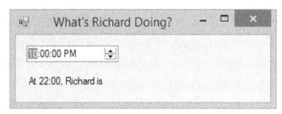

FIGURE 5-7

How It Works

In this application, the user will be able to use the DateTimePicker to choose the hour. The program then looks at the hour and determines which one of the eight states Richard is in at the given time. To achieve this, you have to keep the hour around somehow. To store the hour, you have created a property for the form in addition to the properties it already has, such as Name and Text. The new property is called Hour, and it is used to set the current hour in the DateTimePicker control and the Label control. The property is defined with a Property...End Property statement:

```
       Private Property Hour() As Integer
           Get
               'Return the current hour displayed
               Return dtpHour.Value.Hour
           End Get
           Set(value As Integer)
               'Set the date using the hour passed to this property
               dtpHour.Value =
                   New Date(Now.Year, Now.Month, Now.Day, value, 0, 0)
               'Set the display text
               lblState.Text = "At " & value & ":00, Richard is "
           End Set
       End Property
```

Note the Get...End Get and Set...End Set blocks inside the Property...End Property statement. The Get block contains a Return statement and is called automatically to return the property value when the property name appears in an expression. The data type to be returned is not specified in the Get statement because it was already declared As Integer in the Property statement. The Set block is called automatically when the value is set, such as by putting the property name to the left of an equal sign.

When the application starts, you set the Hour property to the current hour on your computer. You get this information from Now, a Date variable containing the current date and time:

```
       Private Sub Form1_Load(sender As Object, e As EventArgs) Handles Me.Load

           'Set the Hour property to the current hour
           Me.Hour = Now.Hour
       End Sub
```

You also set the `Hour` property when the `Value` property changes in the DateTimePicker control:

```
Private Sub dtpHour_ValueChanged(sender As Object,
            e As EventArgs) Handles dtpHour.ValueChanged
    'Update the Hour property
    Me.Hour = dtpHour.Value.Hour
End Sub
```

When the `Hour` property is set, you have to update the value of the DateTimePicker control to show the new hour value, and you have to update the label on the form as well. The code to perform these actions is put inside the `Set` block for the `Hour` property.

The first update that you perform is to update the `Value` property of the DateTimePicker control. The `Value` property of the date-time picker is a `Date` data type; thus, you cannot simply set the hour in this control, although you can retrieve just the hour from this property. To update this property, you must pass it a `Date` data type.

You do this by calling `New` (see Chapter 10) for the `Date` class, passing it the different date and time parts as shown in the code: year, month, day, hour, minute, second. You get the year, month, and day by extracting them from the `Now` variable. The hour is passed using the `value` parameter that was passed to this `Hour` property, and the minutes and seconds are passed as 0 because you do not want to update the specific minutes or seconds:

```
'Set the date using the hour passed to this property
dtpHour.Value =
    New Date(Now.Year, Now.Month, Now.Day, value, 0, 0)
```

The second update performed by this `Hour` property is to update the label on the form using some static text and the hour that is being set in this property:

```
'Set the display text
lblState.Text = "At " & value & ":00, Richard is "
```

You have not evaluated the `Hour` property to determine the state using the `DayAction` enumeration, but you do that next.

Determining the State

In the next Try It Out, you look at determining the state when the `Hour` property is set. You can take the hour returned by the DateTimePicker control and use it to determine which value in your enumeration it matches.

TRY IT OUT Determining State

This exercise demonstrates this and displays the value on your form. All the code for this Try It Out is in the code folder Enum Demo in the Zip file for this chapter.

1. Open the Code Editor for Form1 and modify the `Hour` property as follows:

```
Set(value As Integer)
    'Set the date using the hour passed to this property
    dtpHour.Value =
```

```
    New Date(Now.Year, Now.Month, Now.Day, value, 0, 0)

    'Determine the state
    If value >= 6 And value < 7 Then
        CurrentState = DayAction.GettingReadyForWork
    ElseIf value >= 7 And value < 8 Then
        CurrentState = DayAction.TravelingToWork
    ElseIf value >= 8 And value < 13 Then
        CurrentState = DayAction.AtWork
    ElseIf value >= 13 And value < 14 Then
        CurrentState = DayAction.AtLunch
    ElseIf value >= 14 And value < 17 Then
        CurrentState = DayAction.AtWork
    ElseIf value >= 17 And value < 18 Then
        CurrentState = DayAction.TravelingFromWork
    ElseIf value >= 18 And value < 22 Then
        CurrentState = DayAction.RelaxingWithFriends
    ElseIf value >= 22 And value < 23 Then
        CurrentState = DayAction.GettingReadyForBed
    Else
        CurrentState = DayAction.Asleep
    End If

    'Set the display text
    lblState.Text = "At " & value & ":00, Richard is " &
        CurrentState
End Set
```

2. Run the project. You'll see something like Figure 5-8.

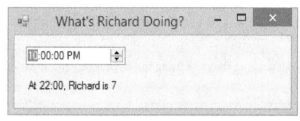

FIGURE 5-8

3. Here's the problem: The user doesn't know what 7means. Close the project and find the following section of code at the end of the Hour property:

```
'Set the display text
    lblState.Text = "At " & value & ":00, Richard is " &
        CurrentState
End Set
```

4. Change the last line to read as follows:

```
'Set the display text
    lblState.Text = "At " & value & ":00, Richard is " &
        CurrentState.ToString()
End Set
```

5. Now run the project and you'll see something like Figure 5-9.

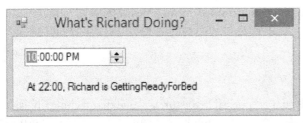

FIGURE 5-9

How It Works

As you typed the code in this example, you might have noticed that whenever you tried to set a value against `CurrentState`, you were presented with an enumerated list of possibilities, as shown in Figure 5-10.

```
'Determine the state
If value >= 6 And value < 7 Then
    CurrentState = DayAction.
ElseIf value    DayAction.Asleep = 0  ᵃ⁼ Asleep
    CurrentS                          ᵃ⁼ AtLunch
ElseIf value >= 8 And value <         ᵃ⁼ AtWork
    CurrentState = DayAction.         ᵃ⁼ GettingReadyForBed
ElseIf value >= 13 And value          ᵃ⁼ GettingReadyForWork
    CurrentState = DayAction.         ᵃ⁼ RelaxingWithFriends
ElseIf value >= 14 And value          ᵃ⁼ TravelingFromWork
    CurrentState = DayAction.         ᵃ⁼ TravelingToWork
ElseIf value >= 17 And value
    CurrentState = DayAction.
ElseIf value >= 18 And value < 22 Then
    CurrentState = DayAction.RelaxingWithFriends
ElseIf value >= 22 And value < 23 Then
    CurrentState = DayAction.GettingReadyForBed
Else
    CurrentState = DayAction.Asleep
End If
```

FIGURE 5-10

Visual Studio 2015 knows that `CurrentState` is of type `DayAction`. It also knows that `DayAction` is an enumeration and that it defines eight possible values, each of which is displayed in the IntelliSense pop-up box. Clicking an item in the enumerated list causes a ToolTip to be displayed with the actual value of the item; for example, clicking `DayAction.RelaxingWithFriends` will display a ToolTip with a value of 6.

Fundamentally, however, because `DayAction` is based on an integer, `CurrentState` is an integer value. That's why the first time you ran the project with the state determination code in place, you saw an integer at the end of the status string. At 7:00 A.M., you know that Richard is traveling to work, or rather `CurrentState` equals `DayAction.TravelingToWork`. You defined this as 2, which is why 2 is displayed at the end of the string.

What you've done in this Try It Out is to tack a call to the `ToString` method onto the end of the `CurrentState` variable. This results in a string representation of `DayAction` being used, rather than the integer representation.

Enumerations are incredibly useful when you want to store one of a possible set of values in a variable. As you start to drill into more complex objects in the Framework, you'll find that they are used all over the place!

Setting Invalid Values

One of the limitations of enumerations is that it is possible to store a value that technically isn't one of the possible defined values of the enumeration. For example, you can change the Hour property so that instead of setting CurrentState to Asleep, you can set it to 999:

```
ElseIf value >= 22 And value < 23 Then
    CurrentState = DayAction.GettingReadyForBed
Else
    CurrentState = 999
End If
```

If you build the project, you'll notice that Visual Basic 2015 doesn't flag this as an error if you have the Option Strict option turned off. When you run the project, you'll see that the value for CurrentState is shown on the form as 999.

So, you can set a variable that references an enumeration to a value that is not defined in that enumeration and the application will still "work" (as long as the value is of the same type as the enumeration). If you build classes that use enumerations, you have to rely on the consumer of that class being well behaved. One technique to solve this problem would be to disallow invalid values in any properties that used the enumeration as their data type.

UNDERSTANDING CONSTANTS

Another good programming practice to be aware of is the *constant*. Imagine you have the following two methods, each of which does something with a given file on the computer's disk (obviously, we're omitting the code here that actually manipulates the file):

```
Public Sub DoSomething()
    'What's the filename?
    Dim strFileName As String = "c:\Temp\Demo.txt"
    'Open the file
    ..
End Sub
Public Sub DoSomethingElse()
    'What's the filename?
    Dim strFileName As String = "c:\Temp\Demo.txt"
    'Do something with the file
    ..
End Sub
```

Using Constants

The code defining a string literal gives the name of a file twice. This is poor programming practice because if both methods are supposed to access the same file, and if that filename changes, this change has to be made in two separate places.

In this instance, both methods are next to each other and the program itself is small. However, imagine you have a massive program in which a separate string literal pointing to the file is defined in 10, 50, or even 1,000 places. If you needed to change the filename, you'd have to change it many times. This is exactly the kind of thing that leads to serious problems for maintaining software code.

What you need to do instead is define the filename globally and then use that global symbol for the filename in the code, rather than use a string literal. This is what a constant is. It is, in effect, a special kind of variable that cannot be varied when the program is running.

TRY IT OUT   Using Constants

In this Try It Out, you learn to use constants. All the code for this Try It Out is in the code folder
`Constants Demo` in the Zip file for this chapter.

1. Create a new Windows Forms application in Visual Studio 2015 called **Constants Demo**.

2. When the Forms Designer appears, add three Button controls. Set the Name property of the first button to **btnOne**, the second to **btnTwo**, and the third to **btnThree**. Change the Text property of each to **One**, **Two**, and **Three**, respectively. Arrange the controls on your form so it looks similar to Figure 5-11.

3. View the Code Editor for the form by right-clicking the form and choosing View Code from the context menu. At the top of the class definition, add the following bolded code:

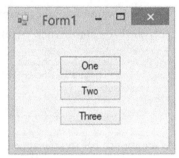

FIGURE 5-11

```
Public Class Form1

    'File name constant
    Private Const strFileName As String = "C:\Temp\Hello.txt"
```

4. In the Class Name combo box at the top of the editor, select btnOne, and in the Method Name combo box, select the Click event. Add the following bolded code to the Click event handler:

```
Private Sub btnOne_Click(sender As Object, e As EventArgs) Handles btnOne.Click

    'Using a constant
    MessageBox.Show("1: " & strFileName, "Constants Demo")
End Sub
```

5. Select btnTwo in the Class Name combo box and select its Click event in the Method Name combo box. Add the bolded code here:

```
Private Sub btnTwo_Click(sender As Object, e As EventArgs) Handles btnTwo.Click

    'Using the constant again
    MessageBox.Show("2: " & strFileName, "Constants Demo")
End Sub
```

6. Select btnThree in the Class Name combo box and the Click event in the Method Name combo box. Add this code to the Click event handler:

```
Private Sub btnThree_Click(sender As Object,
    e As EventArgs) Handles btnThree.Click

    'Reusing the constant one more time
    MessageBox.Show("3: " & strFileName, "Constants Demo")
End Sub
```

7. Save and run your project and then click button One. You'll see the message box shown in Figure 5-12.

Likewise, you'll see the same filename when you click buttons Two and Three.

FIGURE 5-12

How It Works

This example demonstrates that a constant is actually a type of value that cannot be changed when the program is running. It is defined as a variable, but you add Const to the definition, indicating that this variable is constant and cannot change:

```
'File name constant
Private Const strFileName As String = "C:\Temp\Hello.txt"
```

You'll notice that it has a data type, just like a variable, and you have to give it a value when it's defined—which makes sense because you can't change it later.

When you want to use the constant, you refer to it just as you would refer to any variable:

```
Private Sub btnOne_Click(sender As Object, e As EventArgs) Handles btnOne.Click

    'Using a constant
    MessageBox.Show("1: " & strFileName, "Constants Demo")
End Sub
```

As mentioned before, the appeal of a constant is that it enables you to change a value that's used multiple times by altering a single piece of code. However, note that you can change constants only at design time; you cannot change their values at run time. Look at how this works.

Different Constant Types

You've seen how to use a string constant, but in this section, you can use other types of variables as constants. Basically, a constant must not be able to change, so you should not store an object data type (which we will discuss in Chapter 10) in a constant.

Integers are very common types of constants. They can be defined like this:

```
Public Const intHoursAsleepPerDay As Integer = 8
```

Also, it's fairly common to see constants used with enumerations, like this:

```
Public Const intRichardsTypicalState As DayAction = DayAction.AtWork
```

STRUCTURES

Applications commonly need to store several pieces of information of different data types that all relate to one thing and must be kept together in a group, such as a customer's name and address (strings) and balance (a number). Usually, an object of a class is used to hold such a group of variables, as you'll discover in Chapter 10, but you can also use a *structure*.

Building Structures

Structures are similar to class objects but are somewhat simpler, so they're discussed here.

Later, as you design applications, you need to be able to decide whether a structure or a class is appropriate. As a rule of thumb, we suggest that if you end up putting a lot of methods on a structure, it should probably be a class. In today's programming, you most commonly see classes used over structures. If you are working on older code, you may see structures used more often. It's also relatively tricky to convert from a structure to a class later because structures and objects are created using different syntax rules, and sometimes the same syntax produces different results between structures and objects. Therefore, choose once and choose wisely, and if you have doubts, go with a class!

TRY IT OUT Building a Structure

Take a look at how you can build a structure. All the code for this Try It Out is in the code folder Structure Demo in the Zip file for this chapter.

1. Create a new Windows Forms application in Visual Studio 2015 called **Structure Demo**.

2. When the Forms Designer appears, add four Label controls, four TextBox controls, and a Button control. Arrange your controls so that they look similar to Figure 5-13.

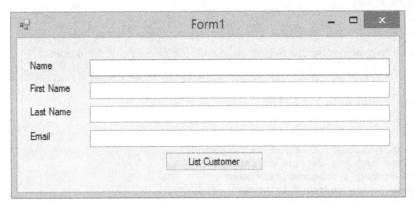

FIGURE 5-13

3. Set the Name properties as follows:

   ➤ Set Label1 to **lblName**.

   ➤ Set TextBox1 to **txtName**.

   ➤ Set Label2 to **lblFirstName**.

   ➤ Set TextBox2 to **txtFirstName**.

   ➤ Set Label3 to **lblLastName**.

   ➤ Set TextBox3 to **txtLastName**.

   ➤ Set Label4 to **lblEmail**.

➤ Set `TextBox4` to **`txtEmail`**.

➤ Set `Button1` to **`btnListCustomer`**.

4. Set the `Text` properties of the following controls:

➤ Set `lblName` to **Name**.

➤ Set `lblFirstName` to **First Name**.

➤ Set `lblLastName` to **Last Name**.

➤ Set `lblEmail` to **Email**.

➤ Set `btnListCustomer` to **List Customer**.

5. Right-click the project name in the Solution Explorer, choose the Add menu item from the context menu, and then choose the Class submenu item. In the Add New Item – Structure Demo dialog, enter **Customer** in the Name field, and then click the Add button to have this item added to your project.

6. When the Code Editor appears, replace all existing code with the following code:

```
Public Structure Customer

    'Public members
    Public FirstName As String
    Public LastName As String
    Public Email As String
End Structure
```

> **NOTE** Be sure to replace the `Class` definition with the `Structure` definition!

7. View the Code Editor for the form and add this procedure:

```
Public Class Form1

    Public Sub DisplayCustomer(customer As Customer)
        'Display the customer details on the form
        txtFirstName.Text = customer.FirstName
        txtLastName.Text = customer.LastName
        txtEmail.Text = customer.Email
    End Sub
```

8. In the Class Name combo box at the top of the editor, select `btnListCustomer`, and in the Method Name combo box select the `Click` event. Add the following bolded code to the `Click` event handler:

```
Private Sub btnListCustomer_Click(sender As Object,
            e As EventArgs) Handles btnListCustomer.Click

    'Create a new customer
    Dim objCustomer As Customer
    objCustomer.FirstName = "Michael"
```

```
        objCustomer.LastName = "Dell"
        objCustomer.Email = "mdell@somecompany.com"

        'Display the customer
        DisplayCustomer(objCustomer)
    End Sub
```

9. Save and run your project. When the form appears, click the List Customer button and you should see results similar to those shown in Figure 5-14.

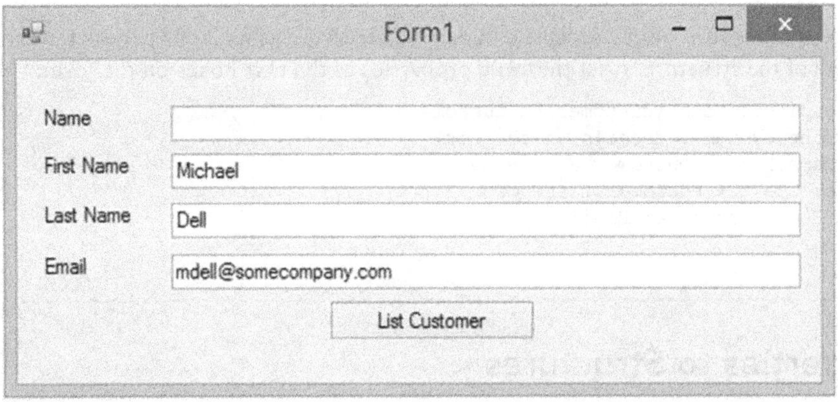

FIGURE 5-14

How It Works

In this example, you define a structure using a `Structure...End Structure` statement. Inside this block, the variables that make up the structure are declared by name and type. These variables are called *members* of the structure:

```
Public Structure Customer
    'Public members
    Public FirstName As String
    Public LastName As String
    Public Email As String
End Structure
```

Notice the keyword `Public` in front of each variable declaration, as well as in front of the `Structure` statement. You have frequently seen `Private` used in similar positions. The `Public` keyword means that you can refer to the member (such as `FirstName`) outside of the definition of the `Customer` structure.

In the `btnListCustomer_Click` procedure, you define a variable of type `Customer` using the `Dim` statement. (If `Customer` were a class, you would also have to initialize the variable by setting `objCustomer` equal to `New Customer`, as discussed in Chapter 10.)

```
Private Sub btnListCustomer_Click(sender As Object,
        e As EventArgs) Handles btnListCustomer.Click

    'Create a new customer
    Dim objCustomer As Customer
```

Then you can access each of the member variables inside the `Customer` structure `objCustomer` by giving the name of the structure variable, followed by a dot, followed by the name of the member:

```
objCustomer.FirstName = "Michael"
    objCustomer.LastName = "Dell"
    objCustomer.Email = "mdell@somecompany.com"

    'Display the customer
    DisplayCustomer(objCustomer)
End Sub
```

The `DisplayCustomer` procedure simply accepts a `Customer` structure as its input parameter and then accesses the members of the structure to set the `Text` properties of the text boxes on the form:

```
Public Sub DisplayCustomer(customer As Customer)
    'Display the customer details on the form
    txtFirstName.Text = customer.FirstName
    txtLastName.Text = customer.LastName
    txtEmail.Text = customer.Email
End Sub
```

Adding Properties to Structures

When you need to store basic information, you can add properties to a structure just as you did to the form in the `Enum Demo` project earlier in the chapter. You learn how in the next Try It Out.

TRY IT OUT Adding a Name Property

In this Try It Out, you add a `ReadOnly Name` property. All the code for this Try It Out is in the code folder `Structure Demo` in the Zip file for this chapter.

1. Open the Code Editor for `Customer` and add this bolded code to create a read-only property Name:

```
'Public members
Public FirstName As String
Public LastName As String
Public Email As String

'Name property
Public ReadOnly Property Name() As String
    Get
        Return FirstName & " " & LastName
    End Get
End Property
```

2. Open the Code Editor for Form1. Modify the `DisplayCustomer` method with the bolded code:

```
Public Sub DisplayCustomer(customer As Customer)
    'Display the customer details on the form
    txtName.Text = customer.Name
    txtFirstName.Text = customer.FirstName
    txtLastName.Text = customer.LastName
    txtEmail.Text = customer.Email
End Sub
```

3. Run the project and click the List Customer button. You'll see that the Name text box, which was empty in Figure 5-14, is now populated with the customer's first name and last name.

How It Works

First, you create the property and mark it as **ReadOnly** so it cannot be changed.

```
'Name property

Public ReadOnly Property Name() As String
    Get
        Return FirstName & " " & LastName
    End Get
End Property
```

Next, you use the new name property to populate the textbox for Name.

```
txtName.Text = customer.Name
```

WORKING WITH ARRAYLISTS

Suppose you need to store a set of Customer structures. You could use an array, but in some cases the array might not be so easy to use:

➤ If you need to add a new Customer to the array, you need to change the size of the array and insert the new item in the new last position in the array. (You'll learn how to change the size of an array later in this chapter.)

➤ If you need to remove a Customer from the array, you need to look at each item in the array in turn. When you find the one you want, you have to create another version of the array one element smaller than the original array and copy every item except the one you want to delete into the new array.

➤ If you need to replace a Customer in the array with another Customer, you need to look at each item in turn until you find the one you want and then replace it manually.

The ArrayList provides a way to create an array that can be easily manipulated as you run your program.

Using an ArrayList

ArrayLists allow for a collection of objects that is dynamically sized. You can add and remove items at any point. When you are not sure how many items your collection will contain, the ArrayList is a good option. Look at using an ArrayList in this next Try It Out.

TRY IT OUT Using an ArrayList

In this Try It Out, you see how to use an ArrayList. All the code for this Try It Out is in the code folder Structure Demo in the Zip file for this chapter.

1. Return to the Structure Demo project in Visual Studio 2015. Make the form larger, move the existing controls down, and then add a new ListBox control as shown in Figure 5-15. Set the Name property of the ListBox to **lstCustomers** and its IntegralHeight property to **False**.

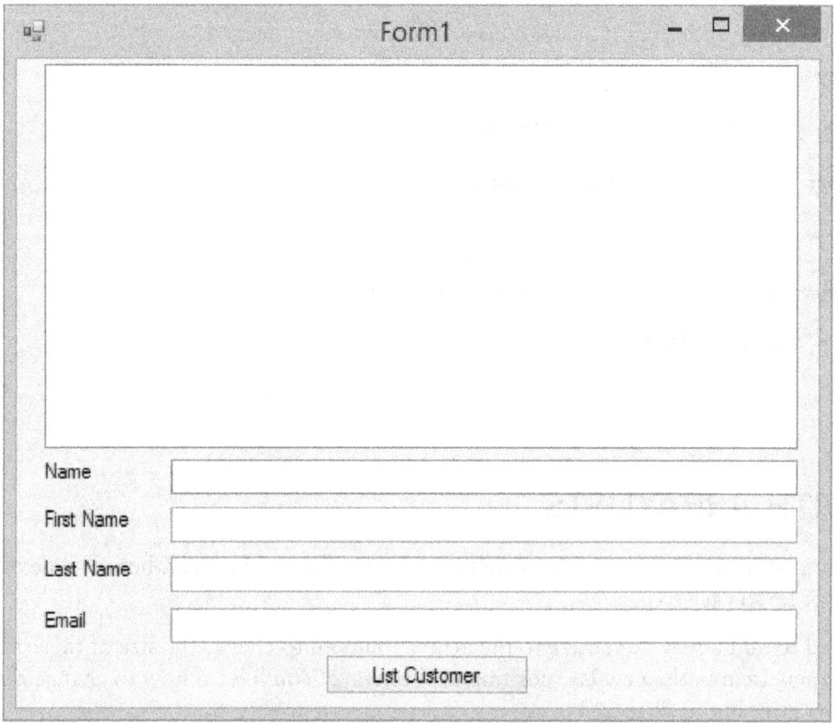

FIGURE 5-15

> **NOTE** You can click the form and press Ctrl+A to select all the controls and then drag them to their new location. Once highlighted, you can also move them with the keyboard arrows in tiny increments or by pressing Ctrl and the arrows for larger movements.

2. Open the Code Editor for Form1 and add the member bolded here to the top of the class definition:

```
Public Class Form1

    'Form level members
    Private objCustomers As New ArrayList
```

3. Add this method to Form1 to create a new customer:

```
Public Sub CreateCustomer(firstName As String,
    lastName As String, email As String)

    'Declare a Customer object
```

```
    Dim objNewCustomer As Customer

    'Create the new customer
    objNewCustomer.FirstName = firstName
    objNewCustomer.LastName = lastName
    objNewCustomer.Email = email

    'Add the new customer to the list
    objCustomers.Add(objNewCustomer)

    'Add the new customer to the ListBox control
    lstCustomers.Items.Add(objNewCustomer)
End Sub
```

4. Modify the `btnListCustomer_Click` method next by making these code changes. The code below was broken and continued to two lines to fit the formatting of the book. You can put each line of code on one line.

```
Private Sub btnListCustomer_Click(sender As Object,
        e As EventArgs) Handles btnListCustomer.Click

    'Create some customers
    CreateCustomer("Darrel", "Hilton", "dhilton@somecompany.com")
    CreateCustomer("Frank", "Peoples", "fpeoples@somecompany.com")
    CreateCustomer("Bill", "Scott","bscott@somecompany.com")
End Sub
```

5. Run the project and click the List Customer button. You'll see results like those shown in Figure 5-16.

FIGURE 5-16

How It Works

You are adding Customer structures to the list, but they are being displayed by the list as Structure_ Demo.Customer; this is the full name of the structure. The ListBox control accepts string values, so by specifying that you wanted to add the Customer structure to the ListBox, Visual Basic 2015 called the ToString method of the Customer structure. By default, the ToString method for a structure returns the structure name, which is not the content that you wanted to see. Therefore, you need to tweak the Customer structure so that it can display something more meaningful.

TRY IT OUT   Overriding ToString

In this Try It Out, when you tweak the Customer structure, you'll see how the ArrayList works. All the code for this Try It Out is in the code folder Structure Demo in the Zip file for this chapter.

1. Return to the Structure Demo project, open the Code Editor for Customer, and add the following method to the structure, ensuring that it is below the member declarations. Remember from Chapter 3 that to insert an XML Document Comment block, you type three apostrophes above the method name:

    ```
    ''' <summary>
    ''' Overrides the default ToString method
    ''' </summary>
    Public Overrides Function ToString() As String
        Return Name & " (" & Email & ")"
    End Function
    End Structure
    ```

2. Run the project and click the List Customer button. You'll see the results shown in Figure 5-17.

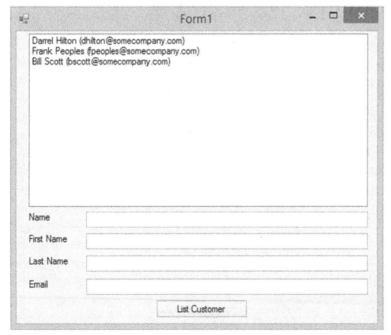

FIGURE 5-17

How It Works

Whenever a `Customer` structure is added to the list, the ListBox calls the `ToString` method on the structure to get a string representation of that structure. With this code, you *override* the default functionality of the `ToString` method so that instead of returning just the name of the structure, you get some useful text:

```
''' <summary>
''' Overrides the default ToString method
''' </summary>

Public Overrides Function ToString() As String
    Return Name & " (" & Email & ")"
End Function
```

An `ArrayList` can be used to store a list of objects/structures of any type (in contrast to a regular array). In fact, you can mix the types within an `ArrayList`—a topic we'll be talking about in a little while. In this example, you created a method called `CreateCustomer` that initializes a new `Customer` structure based on parameters that were passed to the method:

```
Public Sub CreateCustomer(firstName As String,
    lastName As String, email As String)

    'Declare a Customer object
    Dim objNewCustomer As Customer

    'Create the new customer
    objNewCustomer.FirstName = firstName
    objNewCustomer.LastName = lastName
    objNewCustomer.Email = email
```

After the structure has been initialized, you add it to the `ArrayList` stored in `objCustomers`:

```
    'Add the new customer to the list
    objCustomers.Add(objNewCustomer)
```

You also add it to the ListBox like this:

```
    'Add the new customer to the ListBox control
    lstCustomers.Items.Add(objNewCustomer)
```

With `CreateCustomer` defined, you can call it to add new members to the `ArrayList` and to the ListBox control when the user clicks the List Customer button:

```
Private Sub btnListCustomer_Click(sender As Object,
            e As EventArgs) Handles btnListCustomer.Click

    'Create some customers
    CreateCustomer("Darrel", "Hilton", "dhilton@somecompany.com")
    CreateCustomer("Frank", "Peoples", "fpeoples@somecompany.com")
    CreateCustomer("Bill", "Scott", "bscott@somecompany.com")
End Sub
```

Deleting from an ArrayList

OK, so now you know the principle behind an `ArrayList`. You use it to do something that's traditionally hard to do with arrays but is pretty easy to do with an `ArrayList`, such as dynamically add new values.

TRY IT OUT   Deleting from an ArrayList

This Try It Out shows you how easy it is to delete items from an `ArrayList`. All the code for this Try It Out is in the code folder `Structure Demo` in the Zip file for this chapter.

1.   Return to the Code Editor in the Structure Demo project and add the `SelectedCustomer` property to the form as follows:

```
Public ReadOnly Property SelectedCustomer() As Customer
    Get
        If lstCustomers.SelectedIndex <> -1 Then
            'Return the selected customer
            Return CType(objCustomers(lstCustomers.SelectedIndex), Customer)
        End If
    End Get
End Property
```

> **NOTE** Because the `If` statement does not have an else, the code would throw a `null` reference error warning. Just disregard the warning.

2.   Now switch to the Forms Designer and add a new Button control to the bottom of the form, and set its `Name` property to **btnDeleteCustomer** and its `Text` property to **Delete Customer**.

3.   Double-click the button and add this bolded code:

```
Private Sub btnDeleteCustomer_Click(sender As Object,
            e As EventArgs) Handles btnDeleteCustomer.Click

    'If no customer is selected in the ListBox then.
    If lstCustomers.SelectedIndex = -1 Then

        'Display a message
        MessageBox.Show("You must select a customer to delete.",
            "Structure Demo")

        'Exit this method
        Exit Sub
    End If

    'Prompt the user to delete the selected customer
    If MessageBox.Show("Are you sure you want to delete " &
        SelectedCustomer.Name & "?", "Structure Demo",
        MessageBoxButtons.YesNo, MessageBoxIcon.Question) =
        DialogResult.Yes Then

        'Get the customer to be deleted
```

```
        Dim objCustomerToDelete As Customer = SelectedCustomer

        'Remove the customer from the ArrayList
        objCustomers.Remove(objCustomerToDelete)

        'Remove the customer from the ListBox
        lstCustomers.Items.Remove(objCustomerToDelete)
    End If
End Sub
```

4. Run the project and click the List Customer button. *Do not* select a customer in the ListBox and then click the Delete Customer button. You'll see a message box indicating that you must select a customer.

5. Now select a customer and click Delete Customer. You'll see a confirmation dialog similar to the one shown in Figure 5-18.

6. Click Yes, and the customer you selected will be removed from the list.

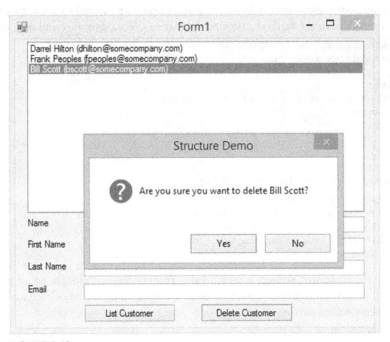

FIGURE 5-18

How It Works

The trick here is to build a read-only property that returns the Customer structure selected in the ListBox back to the caller on demand. The SelectedIndex property of the ListBox returns a value of -1 if no selection has been made. Otherwise, it returns the zero-based index of the selected customer. Because the Items collection of the ListBox contains a collection of Object data types, you must convert the object returned to a Customer object, which you do by using the CType function:

```
Public ReadOnly Property SelectedCustomer() As Customer
    Get
        If lstCustomers.SelectedIndex <> -1 Then
            'Return the selected customer
            Return CType(objCustomers(lstCustomers.SelectedIndex), Customer)
        End If
    End Get
End Property
```

Because there is no else statement for the If, you will see a warning about a non-returning code path. Be aware of these when you are writing your code. To correct this, you could add an else statement for the situation.

Like the Name property that you added to the Customer structure, this property is identified as read-only by the keyword ReadOnly. It contains a Get block but no Set block. The reason for making it read-only is that it constructs the value it returns from other information (the contents of the Customer structures in the list) that can be set and changed by other means.

Inside the Click event handler for the Delete Customer button, you first test to see whether a customer has been selected in the ListBox. If no customer has been selected, then you display a message box indicating that a customer must be selected. Then you exit the method, allowing the user to select a customer and try again:

```
'If no customer is selected in the ListBox then.
If lstCustomers.SelectedIndex = -1 Then

    'Display a message
    MessageBox.Show("You must select a customer to delete.",
        "Structure Demo")
    'Exit this method
    Exit Sub
End If
```

If a customer has been selected, you prompt the user to confirm the deletion:

```
'Prompt the user to delete the selected customer
If MessageBox.Show("Are you sure you want to delete " &
    SelectedCustomer.Name & "?", "Structure Demo",
    MessageBoxButtons.YesNo, MessageBoxIcon.Question) =
    DialogResult.Yes Then
```

If the user does want to delete the customer, you get a return value from MessageBox.Show equal to DialogResult.Yes. Then you declare a customer structure to save the customer to be deleted and populate that structure with the selected customer:

```
'Get the customer to be deleted
Dim objCustomerToDelete As Customer = SelectedCustomer
```

The Remove method of the ArrayList can then be used to remove the selected customer:

```
'Remove the customer from the ArrayList
objCustomers.Remove(objCustomerToDelete)
```

You also use a similar technique to remove the customer from the ListBox:

```
'Remove the customer from the ListBox
lstCustomers.Items.Remove(objCustomerToDelete)
```

Showing Items in the ArrayList

For completeness, you'll want to add one more piece of functionality to enhance the user interface of your application.

Showing Details of the Selected Item

In this Try It Out, you add code in the `SelectedIndexChanged` event for the Customers ListBox. Every time a new customer is selected, the customer's details will be displayed in the text boxes on the form. All the code for this Try It Out is in the code folder `Structure Demo` in the Zip file for this chapter.

1. Return to the Forms Designer in the Structure Demo project and double-click the ListBox. This creates a new `SelectedIndexChanged` event handler. Add the bolded code:

```
Private Sub lstCustomers_SelectedIndexChanged(sender As Object,
            e As EventArgs) Handles lstCustomers.SelectedIndexChanged

    'Display the customer details
    DisplayCustomer(SelectedCustomer)
End Sub
```

2. Run the project and click the List Customer button to populate the ListBox. Now when you select a customer in the ListBox, that customer's information will appear in the fields at the bottom of the form, as shown in Figure 5-19.

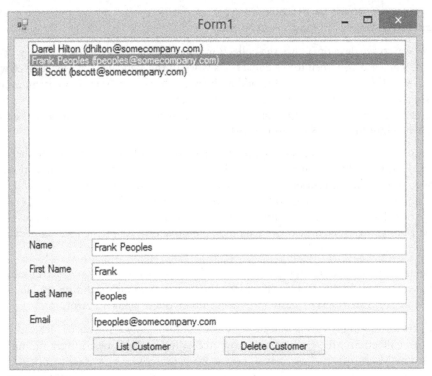

FIGURE 5-19

How It Works

In this example, you hook up the `SelectedIndexChanged` event so the new selected customer is displayed when the event fires.

```
DisplayCustomer(SelectedCustomer)
```

WORKING WITH COLLECTIONS

The `ArrayList` is a kind of *collection* that the .NET Framework uses extensively. A collection is a way of easily creating *ad hoc* groups of similar or related items. If you refer to your Structure Demo code and peek into the `CreateCustomer` method, you'll notice that when adding items to the `ArrayList` and to the ListBox, you use a method called `Add`:

```
'Add the new customer to the list
objCustomers.Add(objNewCustomer)

'Add the new customer to the ListBox control
lstCustomers.Items.Add(objNewCustomer)
```

The code that deletes a customer uses a method called `Remove` on both objects:

```
'Remove the customer from the ArrayList
objCustomers.Remove(objCustomerToDelete)

'Remove the customer from the ListBox
lstCustomers.Items.Remove(objCustomerToDelete)
```

Microsoft is very keen to see developers use the collection paradigm whenever they need to work with a list of items. They are also keen to see collections work in the same way, irrespective of what they actually hold, which is why you use `Add` to add an item and `Remove` to remove an item, even though you're using a `System.Collections.ArrayList` object in one case and a `System.Windows`
`.Forms.ListBox.ObjectCollection` object in another. Microsoft has taken a great deal of care with this feature when building the .NET Framework.

Consistency is good—it enables developers to map an understanding of one thing and use that same understanding with a similar thing. When designing data structures for use in your application, you should take steps to follow the conventions that Microsoft has laid down. For example, if you have a collection class and want to create a method that removes an item, call it `Remove`, not `Delete`. Developers using your class will have an intuitive understanding of what `Remove` does because they're familiar with it. Conversely, developers would do a double take on seeing `Delete` because that term has a different connotation.

One of the problems with using an `ArrayList` is that the developer who has an `ArrayList` cannot guarantee that every item in the list is of the same type. For this reason, each time an item is extracted from the `ArrayList`, the type should be checked to avoid causing an error.

The solution is to create a *strongly typed* collection, which contains only elements of a particular type. Strongly typed collections are very easy to create. According to .NET best-programming practices as defined by Microsoft, the best way to create one is to derive a new class from `System`
`.Collections.CollectionBase` (discussed in the explanation for the next two Try It Outs) and add two methods (`Add` and `Remove`) and one property (`Item`):

➤ `Add` adds a new item to the collection.

➤ `Remove` removes an item from the collection.

➤ `Item` returns the item at the given index in the collection.

Creating CustomerCollection

Sometimes, you will need to store many of your structures together. You can do that using a collection.

TRY IT OUT Creating CustomerCollection

In this Try It Out, you create a `CustomerCollection` designed to hold a collection of `Customer` structures. All the code for this Try It Out is in the code folder `Structure Demo` in the Zip file for this chapter.

1. Return to the Structure Demo project in Visual Studio 2015 and in the Solution Explorer, right-click the project and choose Add from the context menu; then choose the Class submenu item. In the Add New Item – Structure Demo dialog, enter `CustomerCollection` in the `Name` field and then click the Add button to have the class added to your project.

2. Add the following bolded line in the Code Editor:

```
Public Class CustomerCollection
    Inherits CollectionBase

End Class
```

3. You need to add an `Add` method to add a customer to the collection. Add the following code:

```
'Add a customer to the collection
Public Sub Add(newCustomer As Customer)
    Me.List.Add(newCustomer)
End Sub
```

4. You also need to add a `Remove` method to remove a customer from the collection, so add this method:

```
'Remove a customer from the collection
Public Sub Remove(oldCustomer As Customer)
    Me.List.Remove(oldCustomer)
End Sub
```

5. Open the Code Editor for the form and find the definition for the `objCustomers` member. Change its type from `ArrayList` to `CustomerCollection` as bolded here:

```
Public Class Form1

    'Form level members
    Private objCustomers As New CustomerCollection
```

6. Finally, run the project. You'll notice that the application works as before.

How It Works

Now, your `CustomerCollection` class is the first occasion for you to create a *class* explicitly (although you have been using them implicitly from the beginning). Classes and objects are discussed in Chapter 10 and subsequent chapters. For now, note that, like a structure, a class represents a data type that groups one or more members that can be of different data types, and it can have properties and methods associated with it. Unlike a structure, a class can be *derived* from another class, in which case it *inherits* the members, properties, and methods of that other class (which is known as the *base class*); and it can have more members, properties, and methods of its own.

Your `CustomerCollection` class inherits from the `System.Collections.CollectionBase` class, which contains a basic implementation of a collection that can hold any object. In that respect, it's very similar to an `ArrayList`. The advantage comes when you add your own methods to this class.

Because you provided a version of the `Add` method that has a parameter type of `Customer`, it can accept and add only a `Customer` structure. Therefore, it's impossible to put anything into the collection that isn't a `Customer`. You can see there that IntelliSense is telling you that the only thing you can pass through to `Add` is a `Structure_Demo.Customer` structure. See Chapter 9 for more on IntelliSense.

Internally, `CollectionBase` provides you with a property called `List`, which in turn has `Add` and `Remove` methods that you can use to store items. That's precisely what you use when you need to add or remove items from the list:

```
'Add a customer to the collection
Public Sub Add(newCustomer As Customer)
    Me.List.Add(newCustomer)
End Sub
'Remove a customer from the collection
Public Sub Remove(oldCustomer As Customer)
    Me.List.Remove(oldCustomer)
End Sub
```

Building collections this way is a .NET best practice. As a newcomer to .NET programming, you might not appreciate just how useful this is, but trust us—it is. Whenever you need to use a collection of classes, this technique is the right way to go and one that you'll be familiar with.

Adding an Item Property

At the beginning of this section, you read that you were supposed to add two methods and one property. You've seen the methods but not the property, so take a look at it in the next Try It Out.

TRY IT OUT Adding an Item Property

In this Try It Out, you will add an `Item` property and make it the default property of the class. All the code for this Try It Out is in the code folder `Structure Demo` in the Zip file for this chapter.

1. Return to Visual Studio 2015, open the Code Editor for the `CustomerCollection` class, and add this code:

```
'Item property to read or update a customer at a given position
'in the list
Default Public Property Item(index As Integer) As Customer
    Get
        Return CType(Me.List.Item(index), Customer)
    End Get
    Set(value As Customer)
        Me.List.Item(index) = value
    End Set
End Property
```

2. To verify that this works, open the Code Editor for Form1. Modify the `SelectedCustomer` property with this code:

```
Public ReadOnly Property SelectedCustomer() As Customer
    Get
        If lstCustomers.SelectedIndex <> -1 Then
            'Return the selected customer
            Return objCustomers(lstCustomers.SelectedIndex)
        End If
    End Get
End Property
```

3. Run the project. Click the List Customer button and note that when you select items in the list, the details are shown in the fields as they were before.

How It Works

The `Item` property is actually very important; it gives the developer direct access to the data stored in the list but maintains the strongly typed nature of the collection.

If you look at the code for `SelectedCustomer` again, you'll notice that when you wanted to return the given item from within `objCustomers`, you didn't have to provide the property name of `Item`. Instead, `objCustomers` behaved as if it were an array:

```
If lstCustomers.SelectedIndex <> -1 Then
    'Return the selected customer
    Return objCustomers(lstCustomers.SelectedIndex)
End If
```

IntelliSense tells you to enter the index of the item that you require and that you should expect to get a `Customer` structure in return.

You don't have to specify the property name of `Item` because you marked the property as the default by using the `Default` keyword:

```
'Item property to read or update a customer at a given position
'in the list
Default Public Property Item(index As Integer) As Customer
    Get
        Return CType(Me.List.Item(index), Customer)
    End Get
    Set(value As Customer)
        Me.List.Item(index) = value
    End Set
End Property
```

A given class can have only a single default property, and that property must take a parameter of some kind. This parameter must be an index or search term of some description. The one used here provides an index to an element in a collection list. You can have multiple overloaded versions of the same property so that, for example, you could provide an email address rather than an index. This provides a great deal of flexibility, further enhancing your class.

What you have at this point is the following:

➤ A way to store a list of `Customer` structures, and just `Customer` structures

➤ A way to add new items to the collection on demand

➤   A way to remove existing items from the collection on demand

➤   A way to access members in the collection as if it were an `ArrayList`

BUILDING LOOKUP TABLES WITH HASHTABLE

So far, whenever you want to find something in an array or in a collection, you have to provide an integer index representing the position of the item. It's common to end up needing a way to look up an item in a collection when you have something other than an index. For example, you might want to find a customer when you provide an email address.

In this section you'll take a look at the `Hashtable`. This is a special kind of collection that works on a *key-value* principle.

Using Hashtables

A `Hashtable` is a collection in which each item is given a *key*. This key can be used at a later time to unlock the value. For example, if you add Darrel's `Customer` structure to the `Hashtable`, you would give it a key that matches his email address of `dhilton@somecompany.com`. If later you come along with that key, you'll be able to find his record quickly.

Whenever you add an object to the `Hashtable`, it calls a `System.Object.GetHashCode` method, which provides a unique integer value for that object that is the same every time it is called, and internally uses this integer ID as the key. Likewise, whenever you want to retrieve an object from the `Hashtable`, it calls `GetHashCode` on the object to get a lookup key and matches that key against the ones it has in the list. When it finds it, it returns the related value to you.

Lookups from a `Hashtable` are very, very fast. Regardless of the object you pass in, you're only matching on a relatively small integer ID. An integer ID takes up 4 bytes of memory, so if you pass in a 100-character string (which is 200 bytes long), the lookup code needs to compare only 4 bytes, which makes everything run very quickly.

TRY IT OUT   Using a Hashtable

You learn to use a `Hashtable` in this Try It Out. All the code for this Try It Out is in the code folder `Structure Demo` in the Zip file for this chapter.

1.   Return to Visual Studio 2015 and open the Code Editor for the `CustomerCollection` class. Add the bolded member to the top of the class definition:

```
Public Class CustomerCollection
    Inherits CollectionBase

    'Private member
    Private objEmailHashtable As New Hashtable
```

2.   Add the following read-only property to the class:

```
'EmailHashtable property to return the Email Hashtable
Public ReadOnly Property EmailHashtable() As Hashtable
    Get
```

```
        Return objEmailHashtable
    End Get
End Property
```

3. Now make this change to the Add method:

```
'Add a customer to the collection
Public Sub Add(newCustomer As Customer)
    Me.List.Add(newCustomer)

    'Add the email address to the Hashtable
    EmailHashtable.Add(newCustomer.Email, newCustomer)
End Sub
```

4. Next, add this overloaded version of the Item property that allows you to find a customer by email address:

```
'Overload Item property to find a customer by email address
 Default Public ReadOnly Property Item(email As String) As Customer
     Get
         Return CType(EmailHashtable.Item(email), Customer)
     End Get
 End Property
```

5. Open the Forms Designer for Form1, resize the controls on your form, and add a new Button control next to the Email text box, as shown in Figure 5-20. Set the Name property of the button to **btnLookup** and the Text property to **Lookup**.

FIGURE 5-20

6. Double-click the Lookup button and add the following bolded code to its `Click` event handler:

```
Private Sub btnLookup_Click(sender As Object,
            e As EventArgs) Handles btnLookup.Click

    'Declare a customer object and set it to the customer
    'with the email address to be found
    Dim objFoundCustomer As Customer = objCustomers(txtEmail.Text)

    If Not IsNothing(objFoundCustomer.Email) Then
        'Display the customers name
        MessageBox.Show("The customers name is: " &
            objFoundCustomer.Name, "Structure Demo")
    Else
        'Display an error
        MessageBox.Show("There is no customer with the e-mail
            address " & txtEmail.Text & " .", "Structure Demo")
    End If
End Sub
```

7. Run the project and click the List Customer button to populate the list of customers. If you enter an email address that does not exist into the Email text box and then click the Lookup button, you'll see a message box similar to the one shown in Figure 5-21.

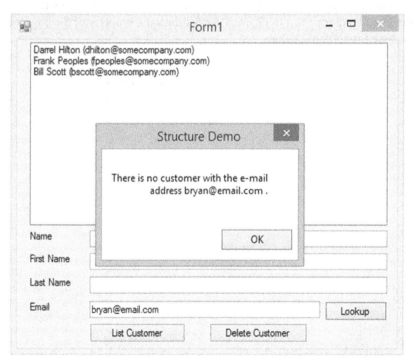

FIGURE 5-21

If you enter an email address that does exist—for example, `dhilton@somecompany.com`—the name of the customer is shown in the message box.

How It Works

In this example, you added a new member to the `CustomerCollection` class that can be used to hold a `Hashtable`:

```
'Private member
Private objEmailHashtable As New Hashtable
```

Whenever you add a new `Customer` to the collection, you also add it to the `Hashtable`:

```
'Add a customer to the collection
Public Sub Add(newCustomer As Customer)
    Me.List.Add(newCustomer)
    'Add the email address to the Hashtable
    EmailHashtable.Add(newCustomer.Email, newCustomer)
End Sub
```

However, unlike the kinds of `Add` methods shown earlier, the `EmailHashtable.Add` method takes two parameters. The first is the key, and you're using the email address as the key. The key can be any object you want, but it must be unique. You cannot supply the same key twice. (If you do, an exception will be thrown.) The second parameter is the value that you want to link the key to, so whenever you give that key to the `Hashtable`, you get that object back.

The next trick is to create an overloaded version of the default `Item` property. This one, however, takes a string as its only parameter. IntelliSense displays the overloaded method as items 1 and 2 when you access it from your code.

This time you can provide either an index or an email address. If you use an email address, you end up using the overloaded version of the `Item` property, and this defers to the `Item` property of the `Hashtable` object. This takes a key and returns the related item, provided that the key can be found:

```
'Overload Item property to find a customer by email address
Default Public ReadOnly Property Item(email As String) As Customer
    Get
            Return EmailHashtable.Item(email)
    End Get
End Property
```

At this point, you have a collection class that not only enables you to look up items by index but also allows you to look up customers by email address.

Cleaning Up: Remove, RemoveAt, and Clear

Because it isn't possible to use the same key twice in a `Hashtable`, you have to take steps to ensure that what's in the `Hashtable` matches whatever is in the list itself.

Although you implemented the `Remove` method in your `CustomerCollection` class, the `CollectionBase` class also provides the `RemoveAt` and `Clear` methods. Whereas `Remove` takes an object, `RemoveAt` takes an index.

TRY IT OUT   Cleaning Up the List

In this Try It Out, you need to provide new implementations of these methods to adjust the `Hashtable`. All the code for this Try It Out is in the code folder `Structure Demo` in the Zip file for this chapter.

1. Return to Visual Studio 2015 and open the Code Editor for Form1. Locate the `btnListCustomer_Click` method and add the bolded code to clear the two lists:

```
Private Sub btnListCustomer_Click(sender As Object,
    e As EventArgs) Handles btnListCustomer.Click

    'Clear the lists
    objCustomers.Clear()
    lstCustomers.Items.Clear()

    'Create some customers
    CreateCustomer("Darrel", "Hilton", "dhilton@somecompany.com")
    CreateCustomer("Frank", "Peoples", "fpeoples@somecompany.com")
    CreateCustomer("Bill", "Scott", "bscott@somecompany.com")
End Sub
```

2. To demonstrate how a `Hashtable` cannot use the same key twice, run your project and click the List Customer button to have the customer list loaded. Now click the List Customer button again and you'll see the error message shown in Figure 5-22.

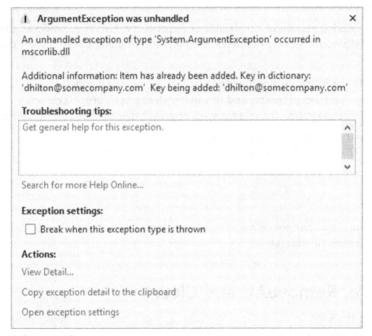

FIGURE 5-22

3. Click the Stop Debugging button on the toolbar in Visual Studio 2015 to stop the program.

4. Add the following method to the `CustomerCollection` class:

```
'Provide a new implementation of the Clear method
Public Shadows Sub Clear()
    'Clear the CollectionBase
```

```
    MyBase.Clear()
    'Clear your hashtable
    EmailHashtable.Clear()
End Sub
```

5. Modify the `Remove` method as follows:

```
'Remove a customer from the collection
Public Sub Remove(oldCustomer As Customer)
    Me.List.Remove(oldCustomer)

    'Remove customer from the Hashtable
    EmailHashtable.Remove(oldCustomer.Email.ToLower)
End Sub
```

6. Add the `RemoveAt` method to override the default method defined in the `CollectionBase` class:

```
'Provide a new implementation of the RemoveAt method
Public Shadows Sub RemoveAt(index As Integer)
    Remove(Item(index))
End Sub
```

7. Run the project and click the List Customer button to load the customers. Click the List Customer button again to have the existing list of customers cleared before the customers are added again. Note that no exception is thrown this time.

How It Works

With these changes, the exception isn't thrown the second time around because you have ensured that the `Hashtable` and the internal list maintained by `CollectionBase` are properly synchronized. Specifically, whenever your `CustomerCollection` list is cleared using the `Clear` method, you ensure that the `Hashtable` is also cleared.

To clear the internal list maintained by `CollectionBase`, you ask the base class to use its own `Clear` implementation, rather than try to provide your own implementation. You do this by calling `MyBase` `.Clear`. Right after that, you call `Clear` on the `Hashtable`:

```
'Provide a new implementation of the Clear method
Public Shadows Sub Clear()
    'Clear the CollectionBase
    MyBase.Clear()
    'Clear your hashtable
    EmailHashtable.Clear()
End Sub
```

You'll also find that when you delete items from the collection by using `Remove`, the corresponding entry is also removed from the `Hashtable` because of the modification to the `Remove` method:

```
'Provide a new implementation of the RemoveAt method
Public Shadows Sub RemoveAt(index As Integer)
    Remove(Item(index))
End Sub

EmailHashtable.Remove(oldCustomer.Email.ToLower)
```

The Shadows keyword indicates that this Clear procedure and RemoveAt procedure should be used rather than the Clear procedure and RemoveAt procedure in the base class. The arguments and the return type do not have to match those in the base class procedure, even though they do here.

> **NOTE** *You don't need to worry too much about the details of Shadows and Overrides at this point because they are discussed in detail in Chapter 10.*

Case Sensitivity

It's about this time that case sensitivity rears its ugly head again. If you run your project and click the List Customer button and then enter a valid email address in all uppercase letters, you'll see a message box indicating that there is no customer with that email address.

TRY IT OUT   Try It Out Case Sensitivity

You need to get the collection to ignore case sensitivity on the key. In this Try It Out, you do this by ensuring that whenever you save a key, you transform the email address into all lowercase characters. Whenever you perform a lookup based on a key, you transform whatever you search for into lowercase characters, too. All the code for this Try It Out is in the code folder Structure Demo in the Zip file for this chapter.

1. Return to Visual Studio 2015, open the Code Editor for the CustomerCollection class and make the bolded change to the Add method:

```
'Add a customer to the collection
Public Sub Add(newCustomer As Customer)
    Me.List.Add(newCustomer)
    'Add the email address to the Hashtable
    EmailHashtable.Add(newCustomer.Email.ToLower, newCustomer)
End Sub
```

2. Find the overloaded Item property that takes an email address and modify the code as shown here:

```
'Overload Item property to find a customer by email address
Default Public ReadOnly Property Item(email As String) As Customer
    Get
        Return CType(EmailHashtable.Item(email.ToLower), Customer)
    End Get
End Property
```

3. Find the Remove method and modify the code as shown here:

```
'Remove a customer from the collection
Public Sub Remove(oldCustomer As Customer)
    Me.List.Remove(oldCustomer)

    'Remove customer from the Hashtable
    EmailHashtable.Remove(oldCustomer.Email.ToLower)
End Sub
```

4. Run the project and click the List Customer button. Now if you enter a valid email address in all uppercase characters, the lookup will still work.

How It Works

In Chapter 4 you saw how you could perform case-insensitive string comparisons using the `String` `.Compare` method.

You can use the `ToLower` method available on strings. This creates a new string in which all the characters are transformed into their lowercase equivalents, so whether you pass DHILTON@SOMECOMPANY.COM or DHilton@SomeCompany.com in, you always get dhilton@somecompany.com out.

When you add an item to the collection, you can get `ToLower` to convert the email address stored in the `Customer` structure so that it is always in lowercase:

```
'Add the email address to the Hashtable
EmailHashtable.Add(newCustomer.Email.ToLower, newCustomer)
```

Likewise, when you actually do the lookup, you also turn whatever value is passed in as a parameter into all lowercase characters:

```
Return CType(EmailHashtable.Item(email.ToLower), Customer)
```

When you're consistent with it, this action makes uppercase characters "go away"—in other words, you'll never end up with uppercase characters being stored in the key or being checked against the key.

> **NOTE** *This technique for removing the problem of uppercase characters can be used for normal string comparisons, but String.Compare is more efficient.*

ADVANCED ARRAY MANIPULATION

Being able to manipulate the size of an array from code and store complex sets of data in an array is important, but with .NET it's far easier to achieve both of them using the collection functionality that the majority of this chapter has discussed. The following two sections are included for completeness and to enable you to compare the two for yourself.

Dynamic Arrays

When using an array, if you want to change its size in order to add items, or clean up space when you remove items, you need to use the `ReDim` keyword to make it a dynamic array. This is a short form of, not surprisingly, *redimension*.

TRY IT OUT   Using the ReDim Keyword

In this Try It Out, you'll reuse the Array Demo project you created at the beginning of the chapter and tweak it so that you can add new friends to the array after the initial array has been created. All the code for this Try It Out is in the code folder `Array Demo` in the Zip file for this chapter.

1. Find and open the Array Demo project in Visual Studio 2015. Open the Code Editor for Form1 and modify the code in the `AddItemsToList` method so that it looks like this:

```
Private Sub AddItemsToList(arrayList() As String)
    'Enumerate the array
```

```
      For Each strName As String In arrayList
          'Add the array item to the list
          lstFriends.Items.Add("[" & strName & "]")
      Next
End Sub
```

2. Run the project and click the Initializing Arrays With Values button. Your form should look like Figure 5-23; note the square brackets around each name.

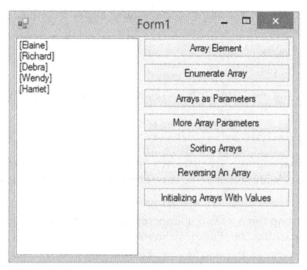

FIGURE 5-23

3. Stop the project and make the bolded change to the btnInitializingArraysWithValues_Click method:

```
Private Sub btnInitializingArraysWithValues_Click(sender As Object,
                e As EventArgs) Handles btnInitializingArraysWithValues.Click

    'Clear the list
    ClearList()

    'Declare and populate an array
    Dim strMyFriends() As String = {"Elaine", "Richard", "Debra",
        "Wendy", "Harriet"}

    'Make the strMyFriends array larger
    ReDim strMyFriends(6)
    strMyFriends(5) = "Lane"
    strMyFriends(6) = "Joel"

    'List your friends
    AddItemsToList(strMyFriends)
End Sub
```

4. Run the project again and click the Initializing Arrays With Values button. Your form should look like the one shown in Figure 5-24.

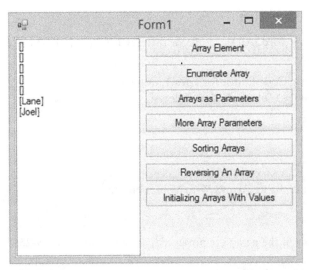

FIGURE 5-24

How It Works

After defining an array of five items, you use the ReDim keyword to redimension the array to have an upper boundary of 6, which, as you know, gives it a size of 7. After you do that, you have two new items in the array to play with—items 5 and 6:

```
'Make the strMyFriends array larger
ReDim strMyFriends(6)

strMyFriends(5) = "Lane"
strMyFriends(6) = "Joel"
```

Then, you can pass the resized array through to AddItemsToList:

```
'List your friends
AddItemsToList(strMyFriends)
```

However, as shown in the results, the values for the first five items have been lost. (This is why you wrapped brackets around the results—if the name stored in the array is blank, you still see something appear in the list.) ReDim does indeed resize the array, but when an array is redimensioned, by default all the values in the array are cleared, losing the values you defined when you initialized the array in the first place.

You can solve this problem by using the Preserve keyword.

Using Preserve

By including the Preserve keyword with the ReDim keyword, you can instruct Visual Basic 2015 to not clear the existing items. One thing to remember is that if you make an array smaller than it originally was, data will be lost from the eliminated elements even if you use Preserve.

Using the Preserve Keyword

In this Try It Out, you use the `Preserve` keyword. All the code for this Try It Out is in the code folder `Array Demo` in the Zip file for this chapter.

1. Return to Visual Studio 2015, open the Code Editor for Form1, and modify the `btnInitializingArraysWithValues_Click` method as follows:

```
'Make the strMyFriends array larger
ReDim Preserve strMyFriends(6)
strMyFriends(5) = "Lane"
strMyFriends(6) = "Joel"
```

2. Run the project again and click the Initializing Arrays With Values button.

How It Works

You should now find that the existing items in the array are preserved, as shown in Figure 5-25.

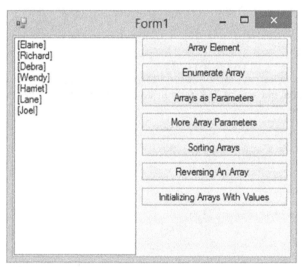

FIGURE 5-25

SUMMARY

In this chapter, you saw some ways in which you can manage complex groups of data. You started by looking at the concept of an array, or rather, defining a special type of variable that's configured to hold a one-dimensional list of similar items instead of a single item.

You then looked at the concepts behind enumerations and constants. Both of them can be used to great effect in making more readable and manageable code. An enumeration enables you to define human-readable, common-sense titles for basic variable types. For example, rather than say `"CurrentState = 2"`, you can say `"CurrentState = DayAction.TravelingToWork"`. Constants enable you to define literal values globally and use them elsewhere in your code.

You then looked at structures, which are similar to classes and are well suited for storing groups of items of information that all pertain to a particular thing or person. After looking at these, you learned about various types of collections, including the basic ArrayList, and then you saw how you can build your own powerful collection classes inherited from CollectionBase. Finally, you looked at the Hashtable class and some of the less commonly used array functionality.

To summarize, you should know how to:

➤ Define and redimension fixed and dynamic string arrays.

➤ Enumerate through arrays and find their upper dimension.

➤ Define an enumeration of values using the Enum class.

➤ Create and use structures to manipulate sets of related data.

➤ Use an ArrayList to hold any type of object.

➤ Use collections to manage sets of related data.

EXERCISES

1. What keyword do you use to keep the values in an array that you ReDim? Where do you insert it?

2. How do you order an array?

3. Are arrays zero-based or one-based?

4. Why would you use an enumeration in code?

5. When initializing an array with values, what characters do you use to enclose the values?

6. How does a constant differ from a normal variable?

7. Structures are simpler and similar to what object?

8. Hashtables provide a fast mechanism for what?

▶ **WHAT YOU LEARNED IN THIS CHAPTER**

TOPIC	CONCEPTS
Arrays	Lists of a single data type. Sorting can be done using `Array.Sort`. `Array.Reverse` can reverse the order of the array. `ReDim` and `Preserve` the values in an `Array`.
Enumerations	Used to prevent invalid values from being used and to add clarity to your code.
Constants	Variables that cannot be changed. They are typically global in scope.
Structures	Allow you to store different types of data together. Similar to a class but typically simpler in design.

6

Building Windows Applications

WHAT YOU WILL LEARN IN THIS CHAPTER:

➤   How to add more features using buttons, text boxes, and radio buttons

➤   How to create a simple toolbar and toolbar buttons to respond to events

➤   How to create additional forms and windows in your applications

WROX.COM CODE DOWNLOADS FOR THIS CHAPTER

The wrox.com code downloads for this chapter are found at www.wrox.com/begvisualbasic2015 on the Download Code tab. The code is in the 092117 C06.zip download and individually named according to the names given throughout the chapter.

When Microsoft first released Visual Basic 1.0, developers fell in love with it because it made building the user interface components of an application very simple. Instead of having to write thousands of lines of code to display windows—the very staple of a Windows application— developers could simply draw the window on the screen.

In Visual Basic (any version), a window is known as a *form*. With the .NET Framework, this form design capability has been brought to all the managed languages—as *Windows Forms* in Windows Forms applications. You've been using Windows Forms over the course of the previous chapters. However, you haven't really given that much thought to them—focusing instead on the code that you've written inside them.

In this chapter, you'll look in detail at Windows Forms and learn how you can use Visual Basic 2015 to put together fully featured Windows applications using Windows Forms Application projects.

RESPONDING TO EVENTS

Building a user interface using Windows Forms or Windows is all about responding to *events* (such as the Click event), so programming for Windows is commonly known as *event-driven programming*. To build a form, you paint controls onto a blank window called the Designer using the mouse. Each of these controls can tell you when an event happens. For example, if you run your program and click a button that's been painted onto a form, that button will say, "Hey, I've been clicked!" and give you an opportunity to execute some code that you provide to respond to that event. You have already been using this feature.

Event-driven programming has two basic objects: a sender and a handler. In the next example, you will use a Button as a sender and a procedure (button_click) as a handler. When you click the button, it will raise or broadcast the event of clicking the Button, and that event will be handled by the click event procedure you create. Once the handler receives the event notification, the code you write inside of the procedure will be executed. Your click event has sender and EventArgs parameters. The sender will be the object that raised the event, which in this case is a Button object. The EventArgs may be nothing or a class derived from EventArgs such as MouseEventArgs. The EventArgs will contain information on what caused the event, and in the case of MouseEventArgs it will have information such as which button was clicked.

A good way to illustrate the event philosophy is to wire up a button to an event. An example is the Click event, which is *fired* or *raised* whenever the button is clicked. You have more events than just the Click event, although in day-to-day practice it's unlikely you'll use more than a handful of these. Even though you've already seen the Click event in action, this next Try It Out goes into some of the details of the Code Editor and new Button events that you have not seen up until this point.

TRY IT OUT   Using Button Events

In this Try It Out, you'll work on a Windows Forms Application project. This will enable you to see firsthand how button events are handled in Windows applications. All the code in this Try It Out is in the Windows Form Button Events folder in the Zip file for this chapter.

1.   Start Visual Studio 2015. Select File ⇨ New Project from the menu. In the New Project dialog, select Visual Basic as the Project type and Windows Forms Application as the Templates type. Enter a project name, **Windows Forms Button Events**, in the Name field and then click the OK button.

2.   Click the form in the Forms Designer. In the Properties window, change the Text property from Form1 to **Windows Button Events**.

3.   From the Toolbox, drag a Button control onto the form. Change its Text property to **Hello World!** and its Name property to **btnSayHello**. Resize your button and form so that it looks similar to the one shown in Figure 6-1.

FIGURE 6-1

4. Save your project by clicking the Save All button on the toolbar.

5. Double-click the button and add the following bolded code to the `Click` event handler:

```
Private Sub btnSayHello_Click(sender As Object,
            e As EventArgs) Handles btnSayHello.Click

    MessageBox.Show("Hello World!", Me.Text)
End Sub
```

6. Drop down the list in the Class Name combo box at the top of the code window. You'll see the options shown in the top portion of Figure 6-2.

> **NOTE** Visual Basic 2015 shows a small icon to the left of everything it displays in these lists. These can tell you what the item in the list actually is. A small purple box represents a method, a small blue box represents a member, four books stacked together represent a library, three squares joined together with lines represent a class, and a yellow lightning bolt represents an event.

Visual Studio may also decorate these icons with other icons to indicate the way they are defined. For example, next to Finalize in Figure 6-3 you'll see an asterisk, which tells you the method is protected. The padlock icon tells you the item is private. It's not really important to memorize all these now, but Visual Basic 2015 is fairly consistent with its representations, so if you do learn them over time they will help you understand what's going on.

Notice that the last two items in the list are slightly indented. This tells you that (Form1 Events) and btnSayHello are all related to Form1. That is, the btnSayHello class is a member of Form1. As you add more members to the form, they will appear in this list.

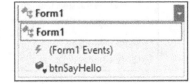

FIGURE 6-2

Now select Form1 in this list.

7. Open the drop-down list from the Method Name combo box to the right of the Class Name combo box and you'll see the options shown in Figure 6-3; the top portion of the figure lists the events in the Windows Form Button Events project, and the bottom portion of the figure lists the events in the WPF Button Events project. These options are described in the list that accompanies the figure.

> ➤ The contents of the Method Name combo box vary according to the item selected in the Class Name combo box. This list lets you navigate through the methods related to the selected class. In this case, its main job is to show you the methods and properties related to the class.

FIGURE 6-3

> ➤ The (Declarations) entry takes you to the top of the class, where you can change the definition of the class and add member variables.

> ➤ The New method creates a new constructor for the class that you are working with. The constructor should contain any initialization code that needs to be executed for the class.

➤ The `Finalize` method creates a new method called `Finalize` and adds it to the class. It will be called when your program ends, to release any unmanaged resources.

➤ The `Dispose` method takes you to the `Dispose` method for the class that you are working with and allows you to add any additional clean-up code for your class.

➤ The `InitializeComponent` method takes you to the code that initializes the controls for the class you are working with. You should not modify this method directly. Instead, use the Forms Designer to modify the properties of your form's controls.

8. Select `btnSayHello` in the Class Name combo box. Now, drop down the Method Name combo box, as shown in Figure 6-4.

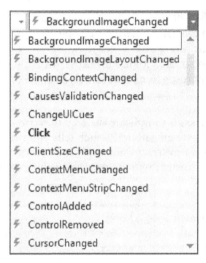

FIGURE 6-4

Because you selected `btnSayHello` in the Class Name combo box, the Method Name combo box now contains items that are exclusively related to that control. In this case, you have a huge list of events. One of those events, `Click`, is shown in bold because you provided a definition for that event. If you select `Click`, you'll be taken to the method in the form that provides an event handler for this method.

9. Now add another event handler to the Button control in the Windows Forms app. With `btnSayHello` still selected in the Class Name combo box, select the `MouseEnter` event in the Method Name combo box. A new event handler method will be created, to which you need to add the following bolded code:

```
Private Sub btnSayHello_MouseEnter(sender As Object,
            e As EventArgs) Handles btnSayHello.MouseEnter

    'Change the Button text
    btnSayHello.Text = "The mouse is here!"
End Sub
```

The `MouseEnter` event will be fired whenever the mouse pointer enters the control—in other words, crosses its boundary.

10. To complete this exercise, you need to add another event handler. With `btnSayHello` still selected in the Class Name combo box, select the `MouseLeave` event in the Method Name combo box. Again, a new event will be created, so add the bolded code here:

```
Private Sub btnSayHello_MouseLeave(sender As Object,
              e As EventArgs) Handles btnSayHello.MouseLeave

    'Change the Button text
    btnSayHello.Text = "The mouse has gone!"
End Sub
```

The `MouseLeave` event will be fired whenever the mouse pointer moves back outside of the control.

11. Run the project to see new events in action. As the mouse enters or leaves the button, you see the button text change.

How It Works

Most of the controls that you use will have a dazzling array of events, although in day-to-day programming only a few of them will be consistently useful. For the Button control, the most useful event is usually the `Click` event.

Visual Basic 2015 knows enough about the control to create the event handlers for you automatically when you select them. This makes your life a lot easier and saves on typing!

You've seen the `Click` event handler for buttons in Windows forms in Chapters 1, 3, 4, and 5. The one parameter that I want to point out in the `btnSayHello_Click` method is the parameter defined as an `EventArgs`. The `EventArgs` class is defined in the `System` namespace and is used for the most common controls in Windows Forms applications.

The `EventArgs` class will contain various data depending on the event being raised. For example, when the button is clicked and the `Click` event is raised, `EventArgs` will contain `MouseEventArgs`, enabling you to determine which mouse button was clicked and the X and Y coordinates of the mouse within the button:

```
Private Sub btnSayHello_Click(sender As Object,
              e As EventArgs) Handles btnSayHello.Click

    MessageBox.Show("Hello World!", Me.Text)
End Sub
```

If you look at the end of the `btnSayHello_MouseEnter` method definition, you'll notice the `Handles` keyword. This ties the method definition into the `btnSayHello.MouseEnter` event. When the button fires this event, your code will be executed:

```
Private Sub btnSayHello_MouseEnter(sender As Object,
              e As EventArgs) Handles btnSayHello.MouseEnter

    'Change the Button text
    btnSayHello.Text = "The mouse is here!"
End Sub
```

Although you set the button's `Text` property at design time using the Properties window, here you can see that you can change those properties at runtime, too.

> **NOTE** As a quick reminder here, design time *is the term used to define the* period of time when you are actually writing the program—in other words, working with the Designer or adding code. Runtime is the term used to define the period of time when the program is running.

Likewise, the `MouseLeave` event works in a similar way to `MouseEnter`:

```
Private Sub btnSayHello_MouseLeave(sender As Object,
            e As EventArgs) Handles btnSayHello.MouseLeave

    'Change the Button text
    btnSayHello.Text = "The mouse has gone!"
End Sub
```

COUNTING CHARACTERS

Visual Studio 2015 comes with a comprehensive set of controls that you can use in your projects. For the most part, you'll be able to build all your applications using just these controls, but you can create your own controls when a special need arises.

In this section, you use some of the provided controls to put together a basic application.

The first job in creating your application is to start a new project and build a form. This form will contain a multiline text box in which text can be entered. It will also contain two radio buttons that give you the option of counting either the words or the number of characters in the text box.

TRY IT OUT   Building the Form

In this Try It Out, you build a basic Windows Forms application that enables users to enter text into a form. The application will count the number of words and letters in the block of text that is entered. All the code in this Try It Out is in code folder `Word Counter` in the Zip file for this chapter.

1. Select File ⇨ New Project from the Visual Studio 2015 menu and create a new Windows Forms Application project. Enter the project name **Word Counter** and click OK.

2. Click Form1 in the Forms Designer and in the Properties window, set the `StartPosition` property to **CenterScreen**, and the `Text` property to **Word Counter**.

3. To instruct users what to do with the form, add a label. Select the Label control from the Toolbox and drag it to the top left corner of the form. Change the `Text` property to **Enter some text for counting**.

    Strictly speaking, unless you have to talk to the control from your code, you don't need to change its `Name` property. With a text box, you need to use its properties and methods in code to make the application work. However, a label is just there for aesthetics, so you don't need to change the name for Label1 all the time.

> **NOTE** *When you are referring to a control from code, it's a good coding practice to give the control a name. Other developers should be able to determine what the control represents based on its name, even if they've never seen your code before. Refer to Chapter 1 for prefixes to use with your control names.*

4. Drag a TextBox control from the Toolbox under the Label. Use Figure 6-5 to design the form.

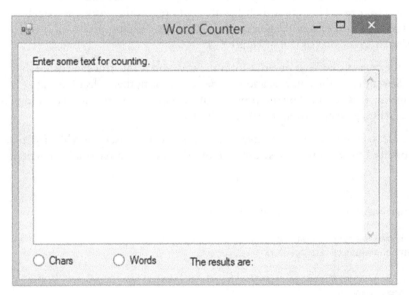

FIGURE 6-5

Now change the properties of the text box as follows:

Set Name to **txtWords**.

Set Multiline to **True**.

Set ScrollBars to **Vertical**.

5. Your application will be capable of counting either the characters the user entered or the number of words. To allow users to select the preferred count method, you use two *radio buttons*. Draw two RadioButton controls onto the form next to each other below the text box. You need to refer to the radio buttons from your code, so change the properties as follows:

For the first radio button:

> Set Name to **radCountChars**.
>
> Set Checked to **True**.
>
> Set Text to **Chars**.

For the second radio button:

> Set Name to **radCountWords**.
>
> Set Text to **Words**.

6. As the user types, the characters or words that the user enters will be counted as appropriate. You want to pass your results to the user, so add two new Label controls next to the RadioButton controls that you just added.

7. The first Label control is just for aesthetics, so leave the Name property as is and change its Text property to **The results are:**. The second Label control will report the results, so you need to give it a name. Set the Name property as **lblResults** and clear the Text property. Your completed form should look similar to the one shown in Figure 6-5.

8. Now that you have the controls laid out on your form the way you want, you can ensure that they stay that way. Select one of the controls and not the actual form; then select Format ➪ Lock Controls from the menu. This sets the Locked property of each of the controls to True and prevents them from accidentally being moved, resized, or deleted.

9. Add the following code to count characters (remember that in order to insert an XML Document Comment block, you need to type three apostrophes above the function after you have written the code):

```
''' <summary>
''' Count the characters in a block of text
''' </summary>
''' <param name="text">The string containing the text
''' to count characters in</param>

Private Function CountCharacters(ByVal text As String) As Integer
    Return text.Length
End Function
```

10. Now you need to build an event handler for the text box. Select txtWords in the Class Name combo box and select the TextChanged event in the Method Name combo box. Add the following bolded code to the event handler:

```
Private Sub txtWords_TextChanged(sender As Object,
            e As EventArgs) Handles txtWords.TextChanged

        'Count the number of characters
        Dim intChars As Integer =
```

```
                CountCharacters(txtWords.Text)

            'Display the results
            lblResults.Text = intChars & " characters"
        End Sub
```

11. Run the project. Enter some text into the text box and you'll see a screen like the one in Figure 6-6.

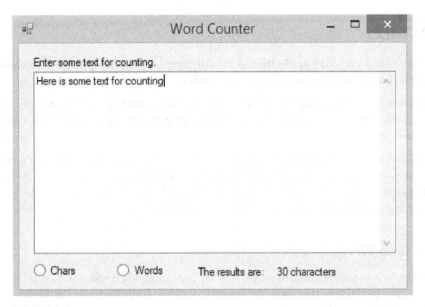

FIGURE 6-6

How It Works

Whenever a character is typed into the text box, the label at the bottom of the form reports the current number of characters. That's because the TextChanged event is fired whenever the user changes the text in the box. This happens when new text is entered, when changes are made to existing text, and when old text is deleted. The application is listening for this event, and whenever you hear it (or rather receive it), you call CountCharacters and pass in the block of text from the text box. As the user types text into the txtWords text box, the Text property is updated to reflect the text that has been entered. You can get the value for this property (in other words, the block of text) and pass it to CountCharacters:

```
    'Count the number of characters
    Dim intChars As Integer = CountCharacters(txtWords.Text)
```

The CountCharacters function in return counts the characters and passes back an integer representing the number of characters that it has counted:

```
    Return text.Length
```

After the number of characters is known, the `lblResults` control for your Windows form can be updated using this:

```
'Display the results
lblResults.Text = intChars & " characters"
```

COUNTING WORDS

Although building a Visual Basic 2015 application is actually very easy, building an elegant solution to a problem requires a combination of thought and experience.

Take your application, for example. When the Words radio button is checked, you want to count the number of words; whereas when Chars is checked, you want to count the number of characters. This has two implications.

First, when you respond to the `TextChanged` event, you need to call a different method that counts the words rather than your existing method for counting characters. This isn't too difficult. Second, whenever a different radio button is selected, you need to change the text in the results from "characters" to "words," or back again. Again, this isn't that difficult.

TRY IT OUT   Counting Words

In this Try It Out, you'll add some more event handlers to your code, and when you finish, you'll examine the logic behind the techniques you used. All the code for this Try It Out is in the folder Word Counter in the Zip file for this chapter.

1. Return to the Word Counter project and stop it if is still running. The first thing you want to do is add another function that counts the number of words in a block of text. Add this code to create the `CountWords` function:

```
'" <summary>
'" Count the number of words in a block of text
'" </summary>
'" <param name="text">The string containing the text to count</param>
'" <returns>The number of words in the string</returns>
'" <remarks></remarks>
Private Function CountWords(text As String) As Integer
    'Is the text empty?
    If text.Trim.Length = 0 Then Return 0

    'Split the words
    Dim strWords() As String = text.Split(" "c)

    'Return the number of words
    Return strWords.Length
End Function
```

2. The `UpdateDisplay` procedure handles getting the text from the text box and updating the display. It also understands whether it's supposed to find the number of words or number of characters by looking at the `Checked` property on the `radCountWords` radio button. Add this code to create the procedure:

```
Private Sub UpdateDisplay()
    'Do we want to count words?
    If radCountWords.Checked Then
        'Update the results with words
        lblResults.Text = CountWords(txtWords.Text) & " words"
    Else
        'Update the results with characters
        lblResults.Text = CountCharacters(txtWords.Text) & " characters"
    End If
End Sub
```

3. Now instead of calling `CountCharacters` from within your `TextChanged` handler, you want to call `UpdateDisplay`. Make the following change:

```
Private Sub txtWords_TextChanged(sender As Object,
            e As EventArgs) Handles txtWords.TextChanged

    'Something changed so display the results
    UpdateDisplay()
End Sub
```

4. You want the display to change when you change the radio button from Chars to Words and vice versa. To add the `CheckedChanged` event, select `radCountWords` in the Class Name combo box at the top of the code window and the `CheckedChanged` event in the Method Name combo box. Add the following bolded code to the event handler procedure:

```
Private Sub radCountWords_CheckedChanged(sender As Object,
            e As EventArgs) Handles radCountWords.CheckedChanged

    'Something changed so display the results
    UpdateDisplay()
End Sub
```

5. Repeat the previous step for the `radCountChars` radio button:

```
Private Sub radCountChars_CheckedChanged(sender As Object,
            e As EventArgs) Handles radCountChars.CheckedChanged

    'Something changed so display the results
    UpdateDisplay()
End Sub
```

6. Run the project, enter some text, and then check the Words radio button. Notice that the display changes to show the number of words, as shown in Figure 6-7.

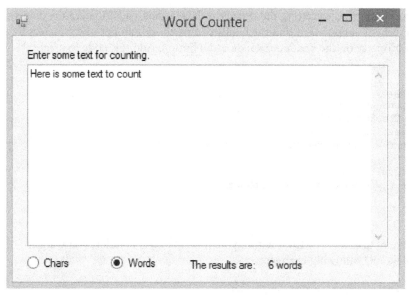

FIGURE 6-7

How It Works

Before you look at the technique that you used to put the form together, take a quick look at the CountWords function:

```
'" <summary>
'" Count the number of words in a block of text
'" </summary>
'" <param name="text">The string containing the text to count</param>
'" <returns>The number of words in the string</returns>
'" <remarks></remarks>
Private Function CountWords(text As String) As Integer
    'Is the text empty?
    If text.Trim.Length = 0 Then Return 0

    'Split the words
    Dim strWords() As String = text.Split(" "c)

    'Return the number of words
    Return strWords.Length
End Function
```

You start by checking to see whether the string passed to this function is empty by first trimming the blank spaces from the end of the string using the Trim method of the String class and then comparing the Length property of the String class to a value of 0. If no text has been passed to this procedure, you immediately return from the function with a value of 0, indicating that zero words were counted.

The Split method of the String class is used to take a string and turn it into an array of string objects. There are several overloaded methods of the Split method, and the parameter you passed here is a Char data type. You want to split the string using the space character, so you specify a space in double quotes and add a lowercase *c* following the quotes to let the compiler know that this is a Char data type, enabling the compiler to convert the space. This means that Split returns an array containing each of the words in the string. You then return the length of this array—in other words, the number of words—back to the caller.

> **NOTE** *Because this code uses a single space character to split the text into words, you'll get unexpected behavior if you separate your words with more than one space character or use the Return key to start a new line.*

One of the golden rules of programming is to never write more code than you absolutely have to. In particular, when you find yourself in a position in which you are going to write the same piece of code twice, try to find a workaround that requires that you write it only once. In this example, you have to change the value displayed in lblResults from different places. The most sensible way to do this is to split the code that updates the label into a separate method: UpdateDisplay. You can then easily set up the TextChanged and CheckedChanged event handlers to call this method in your project.

The upshot of this is that you have to write only the tricky routine to get the text, find the results, and update them once. This technique also creates code that is easier to change in the future and easier to debug when a problem is found. Here is the code for the UpdateDisplay method:

```
Private Sub UpdateDisplay()
    'Do we want to count words?
    If radCountWords.Checked Then
        'Update the results with words
        lblResults.Text = CountWords(txtWords.Text) & " words"
    Else
        'Update the results with characters
        lblResults.Text = CountCharacters(txtWords.Text) &
          " characters"
    End If
End Sub
```

CREATING MORE COMPLEX APPLICATIONS

Normal applications generally have a number of common elements. Among these elements are toolbars and status bars. Putting together an application that has these features is a fairly trivial task in Visual Basic 2015.

In the next Try It Out, you build an application that enables you to make changes to the text entered into a text box, such as changing its color and making it all uppercase or lowercase. You'll be using a ToolBar control to change both the color of the text in your text box and the case of the text to either all uppercase letters or all lowercase letters.

The StatusBar control will also be used in your project to display the status of your actions as a result of clicking a button on the toolbar.

Your first step on the road to building your application is to create a new project.

Creating the Text Editor Project

You will be building the Text Editor project. All the code in this Try It Out is in the folder `Text Editor` in the Zip file for this chapter.

1. Create a new Windows Forms Application project and name it **Text Editor**.

2. Right-click the form in the Solution Explorer, select Rename, and change its name to **TextEditor.vb**. Then press Enter to save the changes.

3. Click the form in the Forms Designer, and in the Properties window change the `Text` property to `Text Editor`.

4. To save paper, the screenshots show the design window as quite small. Using the Properties window of the form, you should explicitly set the size of the form by setting the `Size` property to `600, 460`.

5. Save your project by clicking the Save All button on the toolbar.

In the next section, you start building the user interface part of the application.

CREATING THE TOOLBAR

The toolbar you are building will contain a collection of buttons like the toolbar in Visual Studio 2015.

Adding the Toolbar

In this Try It Out, you will create the toolbar and add the buttons to it. All the code in this Try It Out is in the `Text Editor` folder in the Zip file for this chapter.

1. Return to the Forms Designer in the Text Editor project. Select the ToolStrip control from the Toolbox and then drag and drop it on the form. It will automatically dock at the top of the form. Set the `Stretch` property to **True** to cause the toolbar to stretch across the entire form at runtime.

2. To add buttons to the toolbar you use a built-in editor. Find the `Items` property in the Properties window, select it, and left-click the collection button to the right of (Collection)(look for . . .).

3. You're going to add six buttons to the toolbar: Clear, Red, Blue, Uppercase, Lowercase, and About. To add the first button, click the Add button in the Items Collection Editor. The Items Collection Editor displays a properties palette much like the one that you're used to using. For each button you need to change its name, change its display style, give it an icon, clear its text, and provide some explanatory ToolTip text. Change the `Name` property to **tbrClear** as shown in Figure 6-8.

4. Download the Visual Studio Image Library from `https://msdn.microsoft.com/en-us/library/vstudio/ms246582(v=vs.140).aspx` and extract the files. At the time of writing, the

2013 version was the newest version available (VS2013 Image Library.zip).Locate the Image property and select it. Then click the ellipsis button for this property to invoke the Select Resource Editor. In the Select Resource editor, click the Import button. In the Open dialog, browse to the installation folder where you downloaded the Image Library and locate the following folder:

```
VS2013 Image Library\Visual Studio 2013 Image Library\2013_VS Icon Refresh\
```

From this folder, browse to the \Actions\BMP folder. Select the NewFile_6276_32.bmp file and then click Open to import the resource. Next, click OK in the Select Resource editor and you'll be returned to the Items Collection Editor. You can choose any images if you cannot find the ones noted.

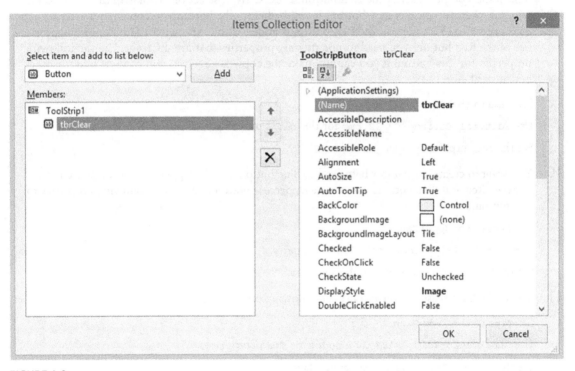

FIGURE 6-8

5. The background color of the bitmap is black, so you need to adjust the image transparency color so the image displays correctly in the toolbar. Locate the ImageTransparentColor property and click the drop-down arrow next to the text "Magenta." Then locate the color black near the top of the list and select it.

6. Set the ToolTipText property to New. This completes the steps necessary to create the first button.

7. You want to create a Separator between the Clear button and the Red button. Add this control using the Add ToolStripButton tool. Select the ToolStrip at the top of the form. You will see the drop-down to add a new item. Open the drop-down and select Separator. A Separator will be added to the ToolStrip. You can accept all the default properties for this button.

8. Repeat steps 3 to 6 to create the Red button and use the following properties for this button. Use the image library you used for Clear for all the images you import unless instructed to use another folder.

Set Name to **tbrRed** and clear the Text property.

Use FontColor_11146_32.bmp for the Image property.

Set ImageTransparentColor to **Black.**

Set the ToolTipText property to **Red.**

9. Next is the Blue button. For this button and the others, you will copy and paste the Red button. In the ToolStrip, select the Red button. Press Ctrl+C, select the ToolStrip (if the button is selected when you paste a new button, it will be before the button you copied, not after it) and then press Ctrl+V. A copy of the Red button is added with a new name. This copies the properties of the Red button; you need to update only properties that are different. Use the following properties for this button; if you cannot make the copy/paste work, you can just add the other buttons as before:

Set Name to **tbrBlue.**

Use EditTitleString_357_32.bmp for the Image property.

Set the ToolTipText property to **Blue.**

10. You want to create a separator between the Blue button and the Uppercase button as well as between Red and Blue buttons. Create the Uppercase button and use the following properties for this button:

Set Name to **tbrUpperCase.**

Use **Compile_191_32.bmp**for the Image property.

Set the ToolTipText property to **Upper Case.**

11. Create the Lowercase button and use the following properties for it:

Set Name to **tbrLowerCase.**

Use **CheckOutforEdit_13187_32.bmp** for the Image property.

Set the ToolTipText property to **Lower Case.**

12. You want to create a separator between the Lowercase button and the Help button.

13. Create the Help button and use the following properties for it. Note the different image path for the help image:

Set Name to **tbrHelpAbout.**

Use **Help_6522_32.bmp** for the Image property.

Set the ToolTipText property to **About.**

14. Click the OK button in the Items Collection Editor to close it.

15. Save your project by clicking the Save All button on the toolbar.

How It Works

For Windows Forms Application projects, the ToolStrip control docks to a particular position on the form. In this case, it docks itself to the top edge of the form.

The six buttons and three separators that you added to the toolbar actually appear as full members of the TextEditor class and have the usual events that you are accustomed to seeing. Later, you'll see how you can respond to the Click event for the various buttons.

A toolbar button can display text only, an image only, or both text and an image. Your project displays an image that is the default display style for toolbar buttons. Normally you would create your own images or have a graphics designer create the images, but for this Try It Out you used images from Visual Studio. At this point, your toolbar should look similar to the one shown in Figure 6-9.

The ToolTipText property enables Visual Basic 2015 to display a ToolTip for the button whenever the user hovers the mouse over it. You don't need to worry about actually creating or showing a ToolTip; Visual Basic 2015 does this for you.

FIGURE 6-9

CREATING THE STATUS BAR

The status bar is a panel that sits at the bottom of an application window and tells the user what's going on.

TRY IT OUT Adding a Status Bar

All the code for this Try It Out is in the code folder Text Editor in the Zip file for this chapter.

1. Return to your Text Editor project, drag a StatusStrip control from the Toolbox and drop it onto your form. You'll notice that it automatically docks itself to the bottom edge of the form, and you'll only be able to change the height portion of its Size property if desired.

2. You need to add one StatusStripLabel to the Items collection of the StatusStrip so that you can display text on the status bar. Use the drop-down in the StatusStrip and select StatusLabel to add one.

3. Set the following properties for the StatusStripLabel:

    Set Name to **sslStatus**.

    Set DisplayStyle to **Text**.

    Set Text to **Ready**.

4. You can also use the Items Collection Editor dialog for the StatusStripLabel.

5. Open the Code Editor for the form and add the following code. You can quickly view the Code Editor by right-clicking the form and choosing View Code from the context menu or pressing F7:

```
'Get or set the text on the status bar
Public Property StatusText() As String
```

```
    Get
        Return sslStatus.Text
    End Get
    Set(value As String)
        sslStatus.Text = value
    End Set
End Property
```

How It Works

There's no need to run the projects at this point, so let's just talk about what you've done here.

Visual Studio 2015 has some neat features for making form design easier. One thing that was always laborious in previous versions of Visual Basic was creating a form that would automatically adjust itself when the user changed its size.

In Visual Studio 2015, controls have the capability to dock themselves to the edges of the form. By default, the StatusStrip control is set to dock to the bottom of the form, but you can change the docking location if so desired. That way, when someone resizes the form, either at design time or at runtime, the status bar (StatusStrip control) stays where you put it.

CREATING AN EDIT BOX

The first thing you do in the next Try It Out is create a text box that can be used to edit the text entered. The text box has a MultiLine property, which by default is set to False. This property determines whether the text box should have only one line or can contain multiple lines. When you change this property to True, the text box control can be resized to any size that you want, and you can enter multiple lines of text in this control.

TRY IT OUT Creating an Edit Box

In this Try It Out, you will create an edit text box. All the code for this Try It Out is in the folder Text Editor in the Zip file for this chapter.

1. Return to the Forms Designer in the Windows Forms Text Editor project. Drag a TextBox control from the Toolbox and drop it onto your form.

2. Change the following properties of the TextBox control:

    Set Name to **txtEdit**.

    Set Dock to **Fill**.

    Set MultiLine to **True.**

    Set ScrollBars to **Vertical.**

    Set Margin for the bottom to **20**.

    Your form should now look like Figure 6-10.

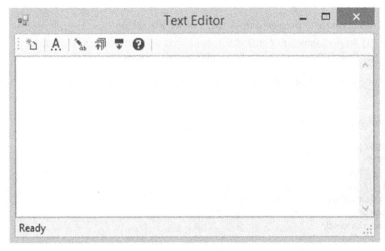

FIGURE 6-10

How It Works

By adding a text box and changing a few properties, you now have an edit text box.

For the Windows Application, you turned on the vertical scrollbars by setting ScrollBars to **Vertical**. Setting Dock to **Fill** allows the text box to resize with the form. The Multiline property set to **True** allows the user to type in and view multiple lines and text.

CLEARING THE EDIT BOX

To clear a text box, you just need to set the text to **""** or **String.Empty**. You will do this next.

TRY IT OUT Clearing txtEdit

In the following Try It Out, you're going to create a property called EditText that will get or set the text you're going to edit. Then, clearing the edit box will simply be a matter of setting the EditText property to an empty string. All the code in this Try It Out is in the folder Text Editor in the Zip file for this chapter.

1. Switch to the Code Editor in your Text Editor project and add this code:

```
'Gets or sets the text that you're editing
Public Property EditText() As String
    Get
        Return txtEdit.Text
    End Get
    Set(value As String)
        txtEdit.Text = value
    End Set
End Property
```

As you have done earlier, when you created a property to abstract away the action of setting the status bar text, you created this property to give developers using the TextEditor form the ability to get or set the text of the document regardless of how you actually implement the editor.

2. You can now build ClearEditBox, the method that actually clears your text box. Add the following code:

```
'Clears the txtEdit control
Public Sub ClearEditBox()
    'Set the EditText property
    EditText = String.Empty

    'Reset the font color
    txtEdit.ForeColor = Color.Black
    'Set the status bar text
    StatusText = "Text box cleared"
End Sub
```

3. Select txtEdit in the Class Name combo box and the TextChanged event in the Method Name combo box at the top of the Code Editor. Add this code:

```
Private Sub txtEdit_TextChanged(sender As Object,
            e As EventArgs) Handles txtEdit.TextChanged

    'Reset the status bar text
    StatusText = "Ready"
End Sub
```

How It Works

The first thing you want to do is clear your text box. In the next Try It Out, you see how you can call ClearEditBox from the toolbar.

All this procedure does is set the EditText property to an empty string. Then it sets the ForeColor property of the text box (which is the color of the actual text) to black and places the text "Text box cleared" in the status bar:

```
'Clears the txtEdit control
Public Sub ClearEditBox()
    'Set the EditText property
    EditText = String.Empty
    'Reset the font color
    txtEdit.ForeColor = Color.Black
    'Set the status bar text
    StatusText = "Text box cleared"
End Sub
```

As mentioned, EditText abstracts the action of getting and setting the text in the box away from your actual implementation. This makes it easier for other developers down the line to use your TextEditor form class in their own applications.

```
'Gets or sets the text that you're editing
Public Property EditText() As String
```

```
Get
    Return txtEdit.Text
End Get
Set(value As String)
    txtEdit.Text = value
End Set
End Property
```

As you type, the `TextChanged` event handler will be repeatedly called.

Changing the status bar text at this point resets any message that might have been set in the status bar. For example, if users have to type a lot of text and look down to see "Text box cleared," they may be a little concerned. Setting it to "Ready" is a pretty standard way of informing the user that the computer is doing something or waiting. It does not mean anything specific.

RESPONDING TO TOOLBAR BUTTONS

In the following Try It Out, you'll start implementing the `Click` events for the various toolbar buttons on your toolbar. When you look at building application menus in Chapter 8, you'll notice that most menus provide the same functionality as your toolbar buttons, so you'll want to implement the code in your menu item `Click` event procedures and have the corresponding toolbar button procedures call the menu item `Click` event procedures.

TRY IT OUT Responding to Toolbar Button Click Events

All the code in this Try It Out is in the `Text Editor` folder in the Zip file for this chapter.

1. Return to the Code Editor in your Windows Forms Text Editor project and select `tbrClear` from the Class Name combo box; and in the Method Name combo box, select the `Click` event. Add the following bolded code to the `Click` event handler:

```
Private Sub tbrClear_Click(sender As Object,
        e As EventArgs) Handles tbrClear.Click

    'Clear the edit box
    ClearEditBox()
End Sub
```

2. You need to create a procedure that changes the text in the edit box to red and updates the status bar. Add the following code:

```
Public Sub RedText()
    'Make the text red
    txtEdit.ForeColor = Color.Red

    'Update the status bar text
    StatusText = "The text is red"
End Sub
```

3. Select `tbrRed` in the Class Name combo box, select the `Click` event in the Method Name combo box, and add the following bolded code to the `Click` event handler:

```
Private Sub tbrRed_Click(sender As Object,
              e As EventArgs) Handles tbrRed.Click

    'Make the text red
    RedText()
End Sub
```

4. Run the project and enter some text. Click the Red button; the text color will change from black to red. Note that if you continue typing in the edit box, the new text will also be red. Click the Clear button to remove the text and revert the color of any new text to black.

5. Return to the Code Editor in the Windows Forms Text Editor project and add the following `BlueText` procedure to change the text in the edit box to blue:

```
Public Sub BlueText()
    'Make the text blue
    txtEdit.ForeColor = Color.Blue

    'Update the status bar text
    StatusText = "The text is blue"
End Sub
```

6. Select `tbrBlue` in the Class Name combo box and the `Click` event in the Method Name combo box. Add the following bolded code to the `Click` event handler:

```
Private Sub tbrBlue_Click(sender As Object,
              e As EventArgs) Handles tbrBlue.Click

    'Make the text blue
    BlueText()
End Sub
```

7. You now need to create a procedure to change the text in the edit box to all uppercase. Add the following code to your project:

```
Public Sub UpperCaseText()
    'Make the text uppercase
    EditText = EditText.ToUpper

    'Update the status bar text
    StatusText = "The text is all uppercase"
End Sub
```

8. Select `tbrUpperCase` in the Class Name combo box and the `Click` event in the Method Name combo box. Add the following bolded code to the `Click` event handler:

```
Private Sub tbrUpperCase_Click(sender As Object,
              e As EventArgs) Handles tbrUpperCase.Click

    'Make the text uppercase
    UpperCaseText()
End Sub
```

9. Add the following procedure to change the text to all lowercase:

```
Public Sub LowerCaseText()
    'Make the text lowercase
    EditText = EditText.ToLower

    'Update the status bar text
    StatusText = "The text is all lowercase"
End Sub
```

10. Select tbrLowerCase in the Class Name combo box and the Click event in the Method Name combo box. Add the following code to the Click event handler:

```
Private Sub tbrLowerCase_Click(sender As Object,
            e As EventArgs) Handles tbrLowerCase.Click

    'Make the text lowercase
    LowerCaseText()
End Sub
```

11. Run the project and enter some text into the box in a mixture of lowercase and uppercase. Then click the Uppercase button to make the text all uppercase. Clicking the Lowercase button will convert the text to all lowercase, and clicking the Red or Blue buttons will cause the text to change color. Finally, clicking the Clear button will cause all text to be cleared and the color and case to be restored to the default.

How It Works

This Try It Out was quite simple. By this time, you are quite adept at creating the Click event handler for buttons on your form; creating the Click event handler for a toolbar button is no different. The first thing you did was create the Click event handler for the Clear toolbar button and add the code to call the ClearEditBox procedure:

```
Private Sub tbrClear_Click(sender As Object,
        e AsEventArgs) Handles tbrClear.Click

    'Clear the edit box
    ClearEditBox()
End Sub
```

Next, you created the RedText procedure to change the text in the edit box to red and to update the status bar with the appropriate information. To change the color of the text in the edit box, you set the ForeColor property of the edit box using the Red constant from the Color enumeration. (The Color enumeration contains an extensive list of named colors.) The ForeColor property remains red until you set it to something else, so clicking the Clear button turns it back to black:

```
Public Sub RedText()
    'Make the text red
    txtEdit.ForeColor = Color.Red

    'Update the status bar text
    StatusText = "The text is red"
End Sub
```

In order to call the RedText procedure, you added code to the Click event for the Red button on the toolbar:

```
'Make the text red
RedText()
```

The code for the Blue button on the toolbar works in the same manner. You create the BlueText procedure to set the ForeColor property of the edit box to Blue in your Windows Forms Text Editor project, and then update the status bar with the appropriate message. You then call the BlueText procedure from the Click event of the Blue toolbar button.

If the user clicks the Uppercase button on the toolbar, you call UppercaseText, which uses the ToUpper method to convert all the text held in EditText to uppercase text:

```
'Make the text uppercase
EditText = EditText.ToUpper
```

Likewise, if the user clicks the Lowercase button, you call LowercaseText, which uses the ToLower method to convert all the text held in EditText to lowercase text:

```
'Make the text lowercase
EditText = EditText.ToLower
```

Each of these procedures is called from the Click event of the appropriate toolbar buttons; and these procedures also update the message in the status bar to reflect whether the text has been changed to red, blue, uppercase, or lowercase.

USING MULTIPLE FORMS

All Windows applications have two types of windows: normal windows and dialog boxes, or *dialogs*. A normal window provides the main user interface for an application. For example, if you use Microsoft Word, you use a normal window for editing your documents.

On occasion, the application will display a dialog when you want to access a special feature. This type of window hijacks the application and forces the user to use just that window. For example, when you select the Print option in Word, a dialog appears; and from that point on, until you close the dialog by clicking OK, Cancel, or the close box, you can't go back and change the document—the only thing you can use is the Print dialog itself. Forms that do this are called *modal*. While they're up, you're in that mode.

Dialogs are discussed in more detail in Chapter 7. For now, you can focus on adding additional forms to your application. The form that you add in the next exercise is a simple modal form.

ABOUT DIALOG

Most applications have an About dialog that describes the application's name and copyright information. Because you already have a toolbar button for this feature, you'll want to create this form now.

TRY IT OUT Adding an About Dialog

All the code in this Try It Out is in the Text Editor folder in the Zip file for this chapter.

1. To add a new form to the project, you can use the Solution Explorer. Right-click the Windows Forms Text Editor project and select Add Windows Form. In the Add New Item–Windows Forms Text Editor dialog, shown in Figure 6-11, select the About Box in the Templates pane, enter **About.vb** in the Name field, and click the Add button to create the new form.

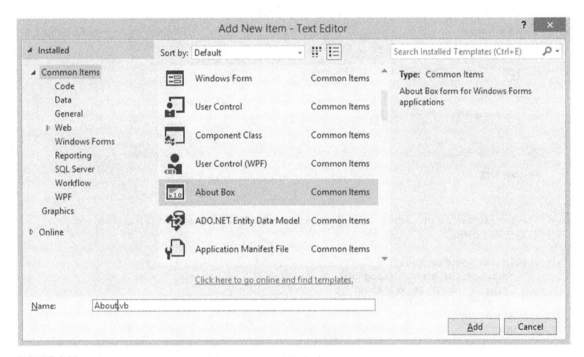

FIGURE 6-11

2. When the Form's Designer appears, you'll notice that all the normal details that are shown in an About dialog are already on the form. These details include product name, version number, copyright information, and so on.

3. Right-click the form and choose View Code from the context menu. You'll notice that the Load event for the form already contains a significant amount of code to populate the details on the About form. There is a TODO comment in the code that informs you that you need to update the assembly information for the application.

4. In the Solution Explorer, double-click My Project. Click the Assembly Information button in the Application pane of the Windows Forms Text Editor properties to display the Assembly Information dialog. Edit the information in this dialog, as shown in Figure 6-12, and then click OK to close the dialog.

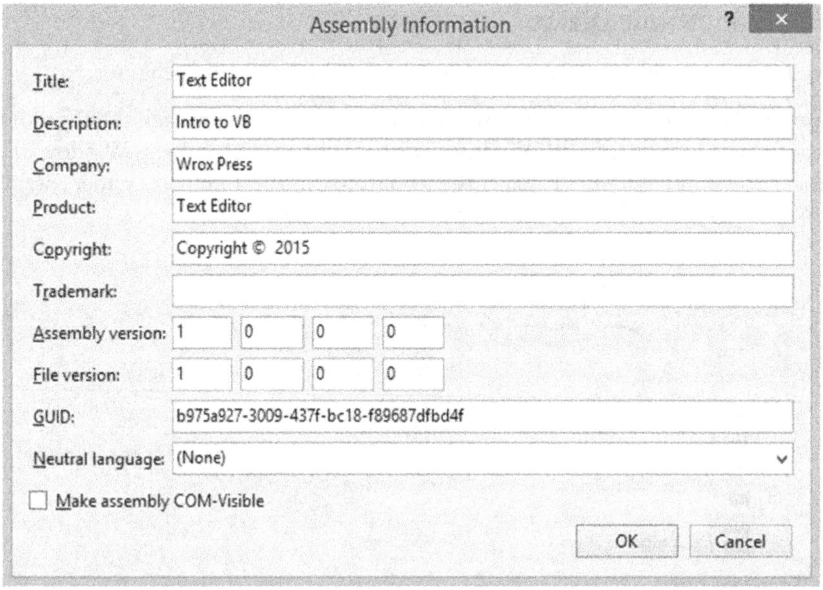

FIGURE 6-12

5.   You need to write a procedure that will display the About dialog, so add this code to the TextEditor form:

```
Public Sub ShowAboutBox()
    'Display the About dialog box
    Using objAbout As New About
        objAbout.ShowDialog(Me)
    End Using
End Sub
```

6.   Finally, you need to call ShowAboutBox when the Help About button on the toolbar is clicked. In the Class Name combo box at the top of the Code Editor, select tbrHelpAbout; and in the Method Name combo box, select the Click event. Add the following bolded code to the Click event handler:

```
Private Sub tbrHelpAbout_Click(sender As Object,
    e As EventArgs) Handles tbrHelpAbout.Click

    'Display the About dialog box
        ShowAboutBox()
    End Sub
```

7.   Run the project and click the Help About button. You should see the dialog shown in Figure 6-13.

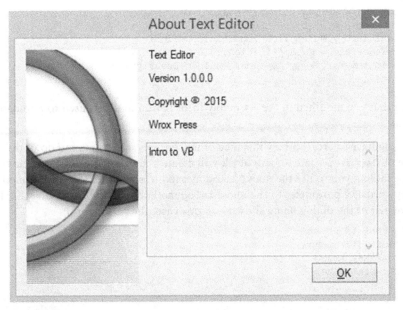

FIGURE 6-13

How It Works

A variety of prebuilt forms are provided in Visual Studio 2015, as shown in Figure 6-11. You can choose to add the About Box form to your project to display an About dialog from your application.

When the About form starts, it fires the Load event, and this event already has the appropriate code written to load the fields on the form. You'll notice that this code makes efficient use of the My.Application.AssemblyInfo namespace to retrieve the appropriate information from your application's assembly for the About form:

```
Private Sub About_Load(sender As Object, e As EventArgs)  Handles MyBase.Load
    ' Set the title of the form.
    Dim ApplicationTitle As String
    If My.Application.Info.Title <> "" Then
        ApplicationTitle = My.Application.Info.Title
    Else
        ApplicationTitle = System.IO.Path.GetFileNameWithoutExtension(
          My.Application.Info.AssemblyName)
    End If
    Me.Text = String.Format("About {0}", ApplicationTitle)
    ' Initialize all of the text displayed on the About Box.
    ' TODO: Customize the application's assembly information in the
      "Application" pane        of the project
    '    properties dialog (under the "Project" menu).
    Me.LabelProductName.Text = My.Application.Info.ProductName
```

```
      Me.LabelVersion.Text = String.Format("Version {0}",
       My.Application.Info. Version.ToString)
      Me.LabelCopyright.Text = My.Application.Info.Copyright
      Me.LabelCompanyName.Text = My.Application.Info.CompanyName
      Me.TextBoxDescription.Text = My.Application.Info.Description
   End Sub
```

The assembly information that you modified in the Assembly Information dialog is used to populate the fields on your About form.

To display another form, you have to create a new instance of it. That's exactly what you do in the `ShowAboutBox` procedure. A `Using. . .End Using` block will create a new instance of an object (the `About` form in this case), enabling you to use the `ShowDialog` method to show the About form modally. When you pass the `Me` keyword as a parameter to the `ShowDialog` method, you are specifying that the `TextEditor` form is the owner of the dialog being shown—in this case, the `About` form:

```
Public Sub ShowAboutBox()
    'Display the About dialog box
    Using objAbout As New About
        objAbout.ShowDialog(Me)
    End Using
End Sub
```

To call the `ShowAboutBox` procedure, you had to add code to the `Click` event of the HelpAbout button on the toolbar:

```
Private Sub tbrHelpAbout_Click(sender As Object,
    e AsEventArgs) Handles tbrHelp.Click

    'Display the About dialog box
    ShowAboutBox()
End Sub
```

With very little effort and a minimal amount of code, you have added a lot of functionality to your Windows Form Text Editor project. You can see firsthand how Visual Studio 2015 provides productivity and time-saving features such as prebuilt forms.

SUMMARY

This chapter discussed some of the more advanced features of Windows forms, as well as the commonly used controls. It discussed the event-driven nature of Windows and showed three events that can happen to a button: `Click`, `MouseEnter`, and `MouseLeave`.

You created a simple application that enables you to enter some text and then, using radio buttons, choose between counting the number of characters and counting the number of words.

You then turned your attention to building a more complex application that enables you to edit text by changing its color or its case. This application demonstrated how easy it is to build an application with toolbars and status bars. You even added an About dialog to display basic information about your application, such as the application title, description, version number, and copyright information.

To summarize, you should now know how to:

➤ Write code to respond to control events.

➤ Set properties on controls to customize their look and behavior.

➤ Use the ToolStrip and StatusStrip controls.

➤ Display other forms in your application.

EXERCISES

1. Name two controls you can use when adding a toolbar to your form.

2. What property do you set to display text to users when they hover over a button on a toolbar?

3. To work with a text box so a user can add many lines of text, what property must be set to True in a Windows Forms application?

4. Why would you want to show a form using the ShowDialog method?

▶ **WHAT YOU LEARNED IN THIS CHAPTER**

TOPIC	CONCEPTS
Handling Click Events	You can create procedures that act as event handlers for control events. To do this, just double-click a button and add your code to the procedure. The button is called the sender, and the procedure is known as the handler.
Creating a Basic Menu	In a Windows Forms or WinForm application, you just need to add a ToolStrip control to your form and then add controls to it. You can add controls like Button, Separator, Label, TextBox, ComboBox, and others. Next, you can add the controls you want on your menu.
Adding a Status Bar	To provide feedback to the user, you can use a status bar. In a WinForm application, you can add a StatusStrip control to the bottom of the form. Next you can add a StatusStripLabel and other controls to provide feedback.
About Box (Built-in Forms)	You can save a lot of time by using prebuilt common forms like the About Box. You can quickly have an About the Program form using this form.

7

Displaying Dialogs

WHAT YOU WILL LEARN IN THIS CHAPTER:

➤ Creating a message box using different buttons and icons

➤ Creating an Open dialog that enables you to open files

➤ Creating a Save dialog that enables you to save files

➤ Creating a Font dialog that enables you to apply the selected font to text

➤ Creating a Color dialog that enables you to define and select custom colors

➤ Creating a Print dialog that prints text from your application

➤ Creating a Browse dialog that enables you to browse for folders

WROX.COM CODE DOWNLOADS FOR THIS CHAPTER

The wrox.com code downloads for this chapter are found at www.wrox.com/begvisualbasic2015 on the Download Code tab. The code is in the 092117 C07.zip download and individually named according to the names given throughout the chapter.

Visual Basic 2015 provides several built-in dialogs that help you provide a rich user interface in your front-end applications. These dialogs provide the same common user interface found in most Windows applications. They also provide many properties and methods that enable you to customize them to suit your needs while still maintaining the standard look of Windows Forms applications.

This chapter explores these dialogs in depth and shows how you can use them in your Visual Basic 2015 applications to help you build more professional-looking applications for your users.

THE MESSAGEBOX

`MessageBox` is one of those dialogs that you will use often as a developer. This dialog enables you to display custom messages to your users and accept their input regarding the choice that they have made. This dialog is very versatile; you can customize it to display a variety of icons with your messages and choose which buttons to display.

In your day-to-day operation of a computer, you have seen message boxes that display each of the icons shown in Figure 7-1. In this section, you learn how to create and display message boxes that use these icons.

The first icon in Figure 7-1 has two names: Asterisk and Information. The second icon also has two names: Exclamation and Warning. The third icon has three names: Error, Hand, and Stop. The final icon in Figure 7-1 has only one name: Question.

FIGURE 7-1

When building a Windows application, at times you need to prompt the user for information or display a warning that something expected did not happen or that something unexpected did. For example, suppose that the user of your application modified some data and tried to close the application without saving the data. You could display a message box that carries an information or warning icon and an appropriate message—that all unsaved data will be lost. You could also provide OK and Cancel buttons to enable users to continue or cancel the operation.

This is where the `MessageBox` dialog comes in: It enables you to quickly build custom dialogs that prompt the user for a decision while displaying your custom message, choice of icons, and choice of buttons. All this functionality also enables you to display a message box informing users of validation errors and to display formatted system errors that are trapped by error handling.

Before you jump into some code, take a look at the `MessageBox` class. The `Show` method is called to display the `MessageBox`. The title, message, icons, and buttons displayed are determined by the parameters you pass to this method. This may seem complicated, but actually using `MessageBox` is very simple—as you have seen and will see in the following sections.

Available Icons for MessageBox

You saw the four available icons in Figure 7-1. Table 7-1 outlines these standard icons that you can display in a message box. The actual graphic displayed is a function of the operating system constants, so there are four unique symbols with multiple field names assigned to them.

TABLE 7-1: Message Box Icon Enumeration

MEMBER NAME	DESCRIPTION
Asterisk	Specifies that the message box displays an information icon
Information	Specifies that the message box displays an information icon
Error	Specifies that the message box displays an error icon
Hand	Specifies that the message box displays an error icon

continues

TABLE 7-1 *(continued)*

MEMBER NAME	DESCRIPTION
Stop	Specifies that the message box displays an error icon
Exclamation	Specifies that the message box displays an exclamation icon
Warning	Specifies that the message box displays an exclamation icon
Question	Specifies that the message box displays a question-mark icon
None	Specifies that the message box will not display any icon

Available Buttons for MessageBox

Table 7-2 outlines the several combinations of buttons that you can display in a message box.

TABLE 7-2: Message Box Button Enumeration

MEMBER NAME	DESCRIPTION
AbortRetryIgnore	Specifies that the message box displays Abort, Retry, and Ignore buttons
OK	Specifies that the message box displays an OK button
OKCancel	Specifies that the message box displays OK and Cancel buttons
RetryCancel	Specifies that the message box displays Retry and Cancel buttons
YesNo	Specifies that the message box displays Yes and No buttons
YesNoCancel	Specifies that the message box displays Yes, No, and Cancel buttons

Setting the Default Button

Along with displaying the appropriate buttons, you can instruct the message box to set a default button for you. This enables users to read the message and press the Enter key to invoke the action for the default button without having to click the button itself with the mouse. Table 7-3 outlines the available default button options.

TABLE 7-3: Default Message Box Button Enumeration

MEMBER NAME	DESCRIPTION
Button1	Specifies that the first button in the message box should be the default button
Button2	Specifies that the second button in the message box should be the default button
Button3	Specifies that the third button in the message box should be the default button

You set the default button relative to the `MessageBox` buttons, from left to right. Therefore, if you have the Yes, No, and Cancel buttons displayed and you choose the third button to be the default, Cancel will be the default button. Likewise, if you choose the third button to be the default and you have only OK and Cancel buttons, the first button becomes the default. The default button will be highlighted until you hover your mouse over another button.

Miscellaneous Options

A couple of other options are available in the `MessageBoxOptions` enumeration and can be used with the message box. These are shown in Table 7-4.

TABLE 7-4: Other Message Box Options

MEMBER NAME	DESCRIPTION
DefaultDesktopOnly	Specifies that the message box be displayed on the active desktop.
RightAlign	Specifies that the text in a message box be right-aligned instead of left-aligned, which is the default.
RtlReading	Specifies that the text in a message box be displayed with the right-to-left (RTL) reading order; it applies only to languages that are read from right to left.
ServiceNotification	Specifies that the message box be displayed on the active desktop. The caller is a Windows service notifying the user of an event.

The Show Method Syntax

You call the `Show` method to display the message box. The following code example displays the message box shown in Figure 7-2. Notice that the code specifies the text displayed in the message box as the first argument, followed by the text displayed in the title bar. Then you specify the buttons that should be displayed, followed by the type of icon that should be displayed beside the text. Finally, you specify the button that you want to set as the default button—in this case, `Button1`.

> **NOTE** *If you want to run this code, start a new Windows Application project, double-click the form in the Designer to generate the* `Form1_Load` *event, and place the following code inside that method:*
>
> ```
> MessageBox.Show("My Text", "My Caption",
>     MessageBoxButtons.OKCancel, MessageBoxIcon.Information,
>     MessageBoxDefaultButton.Button1)
> ```

FIGURE 7-2

Now that you have seen the available icons, buttons, and default button fields, take a look at the Show method of the MessageBox class. You can specify the Show method in several ways; the more common syntaxes are shown in the following list:

➤ MessageBox.Show(*message text*)

➤ MessageBox.Show(*message text, caption*)

➤ MessageBox.Show(*message text, caption, buttons*)

➤ MessageBox.Show(*message text, caption, buttons, icon*)

➤ MessageBox.Show(*message text, caption, buttons, icon, default button*)

In the previous examples, *message text* represents the message that is displayed in the message box. This text can be static text (a literal string value) or supplied in the form of a string variable. The other parameters are optional:

➤ **caption:** Represents either static text or a string variable that will be used to display text in the title bar of the message box. If this parameter is omitted, no text is displayed in the title bar.

➤ **buttons:** Represents a value from the MessageBoxButtons enumeration. This parameter enables you to specify which of the available buttons to display in the message box. If you omit this parameter, the OK button is the only displayed button in the box.

➤ **icon:** Represents a value from the MessageBoxIcon enumeration. This parameter enables you to specify which of the available icons displays in the message box. If you omit this parameter, no icon is displayed.

➤ **default button:** Represents a value from the MessageBoxDefaultButton enumeration. This parameter enables you to specify which of the buttons is set as the default button in the message box. If you omit this parameter, the first button displayed becomes the default button.

All the syntax examples shown in the previous section return a value from the DialogResult enumeration, which indicates which button in the message box was chosen. Table 7-5 shows the available members in the DialogResult enumeration.

TABLE 7-5: DialogResult Enumeration Members

MEMBER NAME	DESCRIPTION
Abort	The return value is Abort and is the result of clicking the Abort button.
Cancel	The return value is Cancel and is the result of clicking the Cancel button.
Ignore	The return value is Ignore and is the result of clicking the Ignore button.
No	The return value is No and is the result of clicking the No button.
None	Nothing is returned, which means the dialog continues running until a button is clicked.
OK	The return value is OK and is the result of clicking the OK button.
Retry	The return value is Retry and is the result of clicking the Retry button.
Yes	The return value is Yes and is the result of clicking the Yes button.

Example Message Boxes

Because multiple buttons can be displayed in a message box, there are multiple ways to display a dialog and check the results. Of course, if you were displaying only one button using the message box for notification, you would not have to check the results at all and could use a very simple syntax.

TRY IT OUT   Creating a Two-Button Message Box

This Try It Out demonstrates how to display two buttons in a message box and then check for the results from the message box to determine which button was clicked. All the code for this Try It Out is in the code folder MessageBox Buttons in the Zip file for this chapter.

1. Start Visual Studio 2015 and select File ➪ New Project from the menu. In the New Project dialog, select Windows Forms Application in the Templates pane and enter a project name of **MessageBox Buttons** in the Name field. Click OK to create this project.

2. Click the form in the Forms Designer and then set its Text property to MessageBox Buttons.

3. Add a Label control to the form to display results regarding which button in the message box a user clicks. Set the Name property to **lblResults** and the Text property to **Nothing Clicked**.

4. Now add a Button control from the Toolbox to the form that will display a message box. Set its Name property to **btn2Buttons** and its Text property to **2 Buttons**.

5. Double-click the button and add the bolded code in the Click event handler:

```
Private Sub btn2Buttons_Click(sender As Object,
e As EventArgs) Handles btn2Buttons.Click
If MessageBox.Show("Your Internet connection will now be closed.",
    "Network Notification", MessageBoxButtons.OKCancel,
    MessageBoxIcon.Information, MessageBoxDefaultButton.Button1) _
```

```
                     = Windows.Forms.DialogResult.OK Then

              lblResults.Text = "OK Clicked"
              'Call some method here
          Else
              lblResults.Text = "Cancel Clicked"
              'Call some method here
          End If
       End Sub
```

6. Save your project by clicking the Save All button on the toolbar.

7. Run the project and then click the 2 Buttons button. You should see a message box dialog like the one shown in Figure 7-3.

FIGURE 7-3

How It Works

The code uses the Show method of the MessageBox class and uses an If...End If statement to determine whether the user clicked the OK button:

```
If MessageBox.Show("Your Internet connection will now be closed.",
    "Network Notification", MessageBoxButtons.OKCancel,
    MessageBoxIcon.Information, MessageBoxDefaultButton.Button1) _
    = Windows.Forms.DialogResult.OK Then
```

The code specifies that the OK and Cancel buttons are to be displayed in the dialog and that the OK button is to be the default button.

You have to specify something for the icon parameter because this is required when you want to set the default button parameter. If you did not want to display an icon, you could use the Nothing keyword for that parameter.

Also notice that you check the results returned from MessageBox using Windows.Forms.DialogResult.OK. You could have just as easily checked for Windows.Forms.DialogResult.Cancel and written the If...End If statement around that.

This is great if you want to test the results of only one or two buttons, but what if you want to test the results from a message box that contains three buttons? The following Try It Out demonstrates just that.

TRY IT OUT   Testing a Three-Button MessageBox

This Try It Out demonstrates how to display three buttons in a message box and then find out which button is clicked. All the code for this Try It Out is in the code folder `MessageBox Buttons` in the Zip file for this chapter.

1. Stop your project if it is still running and open the Forms Designer for Form1.

2. Add another Button control and set its `Name` property to **btn3Buttons** and its `Text` property to **3 Buttons**. Double-click the button and add the bolded code to its `Click` event handler:

```
Private Sub btn3Buttons_Click(sender As Object,
    e As EventArgs) Handles btn3Buttons.Click
    'Declare local variable
    Dim intResult As DialogResult

    'Get the results of the button clicked
    intResult =
        MessageBox.Show("Do you want to save changes to New Document?",
        "My Word Processor", MessageBoxButtons.YesNoCancel,
        MessageBoxIcon.Warning, MessageBoxDefaultButton.Button3)

    'Process the results of the button clicked
    Select Case intResult
        Case Windows.Forms.DialogResult.Yes
            lblResults.Text = "Yes Clicked"
            'Do yes processing here
        Case Windows.Forms.DialogResult.No
            lblResults.Text = "No Clicked"
            'Do no processing here
        Case Windows.Forms.DialogResult.Cancel
            lblResults.Text = "Cancel Clicked"
            'Do cancel processing here
    End Select
End Sub
```

3. Run the project and click the 3 Buttons button. The message box dialog shown in Figure 7-4 appears, showing an icon and three buttons. Note that the third button is the default now.

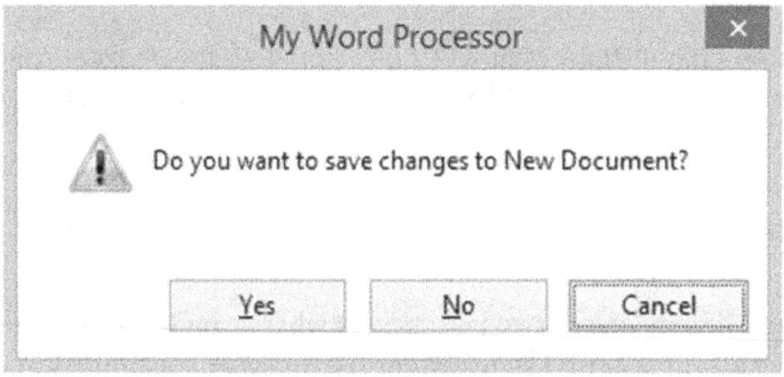

FIGURE 7-4

How It Works

The Show method returns a DialogResult, which is an Integer value. What you need to do when there are three buttons is capture the DialogResult in a variable and then test that variable.

In the following code, the first thing you do is declare a variable as a DialogResult to capture the DialogResult returned from the message box. Remember that the results returned from the dialog are nothing more than an enumeration of Integer values. Next, you set the DialogResult in the variable:

```
'Declare local variable
    Dim intResult As DialogResult
    'Get the results of the button clicked
    intResult =
        MessageBox.Show("Do you want to save changes to New Document?",
        "My Word Processor", MessageBoxButtons.YesNoCancel,
        MessageBoxIcon.Warning, MessageBoxDefaultButton.Button3)
```

Finally, you test the value of the intResult in a Select Case statement and act on it accordingly:

```
'Process the results of the button clicked
    Select Case intResult
        Case Windows.Forms.DialogResult.Yes
            lblResults.Text = "Yes Clicked"
            'Do yes processing here
        Case Windows.Forms.DialogResult.No
            lblResults.Text = "No Clicked"
            'Do no processing here
        Case Windows.Forms.DialogResult.Cancel
            lblResults.Text = "Cancel Clicked"
            'Do cancel processing here
    End Select
```

In each of the Case statements, you write the name of the button selected in the label to indicate which button was clicked.

Now you have a better understanding of how the MessageBox dialog works and you have a point of reference for the syntax. To become more familiar with the MessageBox, try altering the values of the message text, caption, buttons, icon, and default button parameters in the previous examples.

> **WARNING** Be careful not to overuse the MessageBox and display a message box for every little event. This can be a real annoyance to users. Use common sense and good judgment when deciding whether a message box is appropriate. You should display a MessageBox dialog only when you absolutely need to inform users that some type of error has occurred or when you need to warn users that an action that they have requested is potentially damaging. An example of the latter is shutting down the application without saving their work. In this case, you want to let users know that if they continue they will lose all unsaved work; then give them an option to continue or cancel the action of shutting down the application.

THE OPENFILEDIALOG CONTROL

Many Windows applications process data from files, so you need an interface to select files to open and save. The .NET Framework provides the OpenFileDialog and SaveFileDialog classes to do just that. In this section you'll take a look at the OpenFileDialog control, and in the next section you'll look at the SaveFileDialog control.

When you use Windows applications, such as Microsoft Word or Paint, you see the same basic Open dialog. This does not happen by accident. Available to all developers is a standard set of application programming interfaces (APIs) that enable the provision of this type of standard interface; however, using the APIs can be cumbersome and difficult for a beginner. Fortunately, all this functionality is already built into the .NET Framework, so you can use it as you develop with Visual Basic 2015.

The OpenFileDialog Control

You can use OpenFileDialog as a .NET class by declaring a variable of that type in your code and modifying its properties in code, or as a control by dragging the control from the Toolbox onto the form at design time. In either case, the resulting objects will have the same methods, properties, and events.

You can find the OpenFileDialog control in the Toolbox under the Dialogs tab, where you can drag and drop it onto your form. Then, all you need to do is set the properties and execute the appropriate method. To use OpenFileDialog as a class, you declare your own objects of this type in order to use the dialog. Then you have control over the scope of the dialog and can declare an object for it when needed, use it, and then destroy it, thereby using fewer resources.

This section focuses on using OpenFileDialog as a control. Once you have a better understanding of this dialog and feel comfortable using it, you can then expand your skills and use OpenFileDialog as a class by declaring your own objects for it. Using classes and objects is discussed in greater detail in Chapter 10.

You can use OpenFileDialog by simply invoking its ShowDialog method, producing results similar to those shown in Figure 7-5.

The Properties of OpenFileDialog

The dialog shown in Figure 7-5 is the standard Open dialog displayed in Windows 8. It provides filtering. Not all file types are listed in the window. This is where the properties of OpenFileDialog come in. You can set some of the properties before the Open dialog is displayed, thereby customizing the dialog to your needs.

Table 7-6 lists some of the available properties for the OpenFileDialog control.

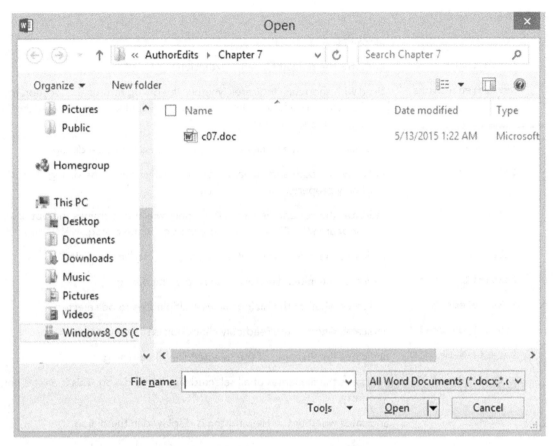

FIGURE 7-5

TABLE 7-6: Common OpenFileDialog Control Properties

PROPERTY	DESCRIPTION
AddExtension	Indicates whether an extension is automatically added to a filename if the user omits the extension. This is mainly used in the SaveFileDialog, described in the next section.
AutoUpgradeEnabled	Indicates whether this dialog should automatically upgrade its appearance and behavior when running on different versions of Windows. When false, it will appear with XP styles.
CheckFileExists	Indicates whether the dialog displays a warning if the user specifies a filename that does not exist.
CheckPathExists	Indicates whether the dialog displays a warning if the user specifies a path that does not exist.

continues

TABLE 7-6 *(continued)*

PROPERTY	DESCRIPTION
DefaultExt	Indicates the default filename extension.
DereferenceLinks	Used with shortcuts. Indicates whether the dialog returns the location of the file referenced by the shortcut (True) or whether it returns only the location of the shortcut (False).
FileName	Indicates the path and filename of the selected file in the dialog.
FileNames	Indicates the path and filenames of all selected files in the dialog. This is a read-only property.
Filter	Indicates the current filename filter string, which determines the options that appear in the Files of Type: combo box in the dialog.
FilterIndex	Indicates the index of the filter currently selected in the dialog.
InitialDirectory	Indicates the initial directory displayed in the dialog.
Multiselect	Indicates whether the dialog allows multiple files to be selected.
ReadOnlyChecked	Indicates whether the read-only check box is selected.
SafeFileName	Indicates the filename of the selected file in the dialog.
SafeFileNames	Indicates the filenames of all selected files in the dialog. This is a read-only property.
ShowHelp	Indicates whether the Help button is displayed in the dialog.
ShowReadOnly	Indicates whether the dialog contains a read-only check box.
SupportMultiDotted Extensions	Indicates whether the dialog supports displaying and saving files that have multiple filename extensions.
Title	Indicates the title that is displayed in the title bar of the dialog.
ValidateNames	Indicates whether the dialog should accept only valid Win32 filenames.

OpenFileDialog Methods

Although many methods are available in the OpenFileDialog class, you will be concentrating on the ShowDialog method in these examples. The following list contains some of the other available methods in OpenFileDialog:

➤ **Dispose:** Releases the resources used by the Open dialog. You should only call the dispose method if you create an OpenFileDialog at run time. In this chapter, you will create them at design time.

➤ **OpenFile:** Opens the file selected by the user with read-only permission. The file is specified by the FileName property.

➤ **Reset:** Resets all properties of the Open dialog to their default values.

➤ **ShowDialog:** Shows the dialog.

The `ShowDialog` method is straightforward because it accepts either no parameters or the owner of the dialog in the form of the `Me` keyword. Therefore, before calling the `ShowDialog` method, you must set all the properties that you want to set. After the dialog returns, you can query the properties to determine which file was selected, the directory, and the type of file selected. An example of the `ShowDialog` method is shown in the following code fragment:

```
OpenFileDialog1.ShowDialog()
```

The OpenFileDialog control returns a `DialogResult` of `OK` or `Cancel`, with `OK` corresponding to the Open button on the dialog. This control does not actually open and read a file for you; it is merely a common interface that enables users to locate and specify the file or files to be opened by the application. You need to query the `OpenFileDialog` properties that have been set by the control after the user clicks the Open button to determine which file or files should be opened.

Using the OpenFileDialog Control

Now that you have had a look at the OpenFileDialog control, you can put this knowledge to use by writing a program that uses this control.

TRY IT OUT Working with OpenFileDialog

The program in the next Try It Out uses the OpenFileDialog control to display the Open File dialog. You use the dialog to locate and select a text file, and then you'll read the contents of the file into a text box on your form using the `My.Computer.FileSystem` namespace. All the code for this Try It Out is in the code folder `Windows Forms Dialogs` in the Zip file for this chapter.

1. Create a new Windows Forms Application project called `Windows Forms Dialogs`.

2. To give your form a new name, in the Solution Explorer, right-click Form1.vb and choose Rename from the context menu. Then enter a new name of **Dialogs.vb**. Set the properties of the form as shown in the following list:

   Set `Size` to **460, 300.**

   Set `StartPosition` to **CenterScreen.**

   Set `Text` to **Dialogs.**

3. Because you will read the contents of a file into a text box, you want to add a text box to the form. You also want to add a button to the form so that you can invoke the Open File dialog at will. Add these two controls to the form and set their properties according to the following list:

   ➤ Name the text box **txtFile** and set the following properties:
   ```
   Anchor = Top,Bottom,Left,Right; Location = 13, 13; MultiLine = True;
   ScrollBars = Vertical; Size = 330, 232.
   ```

   ➤ Name the Button control **btnOpen** and set the following properties:
   ```
   Anchor = Top, Right; Location = 349, 13; Text = Open.
   ```

4. When you have finished placing the controls on your form and setting their properties, the form should look similar to Figure 7-6.

> **NOTE** *You anchored your controls in this example because when you resize or maximize your form, the text box is resized appropriately to the size of the form, and the button stays in the upper right corner. You can test it at this point by running your project and resizing the form.*

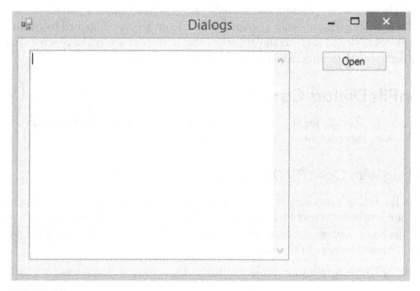

FIGURE 7-6

5. In the Toolbox, scroll down until you see the OpenFileDialog control in the Dialogs tab and then drag it onto your form and drop it. The control will actually be added to the bottom of the workspace in the integrated development environment (IDE).

At this point, you could click the control in the workspace and then set the various properties for this control in the Properties window. However, accept the default name and properties for this control for now because you'll set the various properties in code later.

6. Switch to the Code Editor for the form. Declare a string variable that will contain a filename. You set this variable later in your code to the actual path and filename from the Open File dialog:

```
Public Class Dialogs
    'Declare variable
    Private strFileName As String
```

7. Now you need to write some code in the Click event for the btnOpen button. In the Class Name combo box at the top of the Code Editor, select btnOpen, and in the Method Name combo box select the Click event. Add the following bolded code to the Click event handler:

```
Private Sub btnOpen_Click(sender As Object,
    e As EventArgs) Handles btnOpen.Click
    'Set the Open dialog properties
        OpenFileDialog1.Filter = "Text Documents
            (*.txt)|*.txt|All Files (*.*)|*.*"
        OpenFileDialog1.FilterIndex = 1
        OpenFileDialog1.Title = "Demo Open File Dialog"
    'Show the Open dialog if the user clicks the Open button,
    'load the file
    If OpenFileDialog1.ShowDialog =
        Windows.Forms.DialogResult.OK Then
        Try
          'Save the file path and name
          strFileName = OpenFileDialog1.FileName

        Catch ex As Exception
          MessageBox.Show(ex.Message,
            My.Application.Info.Title,
            MessageBoxButtons.OK, MessageBoxIcon.Error)
        End Try
    End If
End Sub
```

8. Now it's time to use some of the prebuilt code snippets that come with Visual Studio 2015. Right-click in the blank space inside the Try block statement right before the Catch block statement and choose Insert Snippet from the context menu. In the drop-down menu that appears, double-click Fundamentals-Collections, Data Types, File System, Math; and then in the new list, double-click File System-Processing Drives, Folders, and Files. Finally, scroll down the list and double-click Read Text from a File. Your code should now look like this, and you'll notice that the filename C:\Test.txt is bolded, indicating that this code needs to be changed:

```
Try
    'Save the file path and name
    strFileName = OpenFileDialog1.FileName

    Dim fileContents As String
    fileContents =
        My.Computer.FileSystem.ReadAllText("C:\Test.txt")
Catch ex As Exception
```

9. Modify the code in the Try block as shown here. Replace "C:Test.txt" with strFileName and add the following code to display the contents of the text file:

```
Try
    'Save the file path and name
    strFileName = OpenFileDialog1.FileName

    Dim fileContents As String
    fileContents =
```

```
        My.Computer.FileSystem.ReadAllText(strFileName)

    'Display the file contents in the text box
    txtFile.Text = fileContents
Catch ex As Exception
```

10. Save your project by clicking the Save All button on the toolbar.

11. Run your project. When your form appears, click the Open button to have the Open File dialog displayed. Notice the custom caption in the title bar of the dialog; you specified this in your code. If you click the File filter combo box, you will see two filters. Click the second filter to see all the files in the current directory.

12. Now locate a text file on your computer and select it. Then click the Open button to have the file opened and the contents of that file placed in the text box on the form, as shown in Figure 7-7.

13. For the final test, close your application and then start it again. Click the Open button on the form and notice that the Open File dialog has opened in the same directory from which you selected the last file. You didn't need to write any code to have the Open File dialog do this.

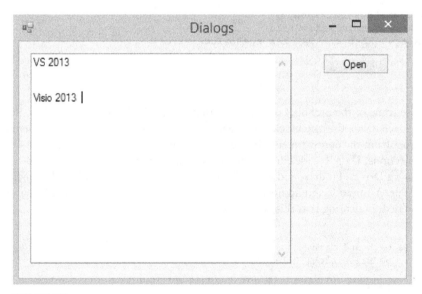

FIGURE 7-7

How It Works

Before displaying the Open File dialog, you need to set some properties of OpenFileDialog1 so that the dialog is customized for your application.

The first property that you set is the Filter property. This property enables you to define the filters that are displayed in the File filter combo box in the bottom right corner of the dialog. When you define a file-extension filter, you specify the filter description followed by a vertical bar (|) followed by the file extension. When you want the Filter property to contain multiple file extensions, as shown in the following code, you separate each file filter with a vertical bar as follows:

```
OpenFileDialog1.Filter =
    "Text Documents (*.txt)|*.txt|All Files (*.*)|*.*"
```

The next property that you set is `FilterIndex`. This property determines which filter is shown in the File filter combo box. This property is one of only a few that have a one-based index instead of a zero-based index. The default value for this property is 1, which is the first filter:

```
OpenFileDialog1.FilterIndex = 1
```

Finally, you set the `Title` property. This is the caption displayed in the title bar of the dialog:

```
OpenFileDialog1.Title = "Demo Open File Dialog"
```

To show the Open File dialog, you use the `ShowDialog` method. Remember that this method returns a `DialogResult` value, there are only two possible results, and you can compare the results from the `ShowDialog` method to `Windows.Forms.DialogResult.OK` and `Windows.Forms.DialogResult.Cancel`. If the user clicks the Open button in the dialog, the `ShowDialog` method returns a value of `OK`; if the user clicks the Cancel button, the `ShowDialog` method returns `Cancel`:

```
If OpenFileDialog1.ShowDialog = Windows.Forms.DialogResult.OK Then
```

Next, you add a `Try.Catch` block to handle any errors that may occur while opening a file. Inside the `Try` block you retrieve the path and filename that the user has chosen in the Open File dialog and set it in your `strFileName` variable. The path and filename are contained in the `FileName` property of the OpenFileDialog control:

```
'Save the file name
strFileName = OpenFileDialog1.FileName
```

Next, you use the built-in code snippets provided by Visual Studio 2015 to simplify your programming tasks by using the Read Text from a File code snippet. This code snippet contains the necessary code to read the contents from a text file and to place those contents in a string variable.

Then, you modify the code from the code snippet, supplying the `strFileName` variable in the bolded section of code. This code will read the entire contents of the text file into the `fileContents` variable:

```
Dim fileContents As String
fileContents = My.Computer.FileSystem.ReadAllText(strFileName)
```

The final line of code that you wrote takes the contents of the `allText` variable and sets it in the `Text` property of the TextBox control, thereby populating the text box with the contents of your text file:

```
'Display the file contents in the text box
txtFile.Text = fileContents
```

The code in the `Catch` block uses the `MessageBox` class to display the contents of the `Message` property of the exception thrown should an error occur. The `caption` parameter of the `MessageBox` class retrieves the title of your application from the `Title` property of the `My.Application.Info` object:

```
Catch ex As Exception
    MessageBox.Show(ex.Message, My.Application.Info.Title,
        MessageBoxButtons.OK, MessageBoxIcon.Error)
End Try
```

Many other properties in the OpenFileDialog control haven't been covered in this chapter, and you should feel free to experiment on your own to see all the possibilities that this dialog has to offer.

THE SAVEDIALOG CONTROL

Now that you can open a file with the OpenFileDialog control, take a look at the SaveFileDialog control so that you can save a file. Like the OpenFileDialog, the SaveFileDialog can be used as a control or a class. Once you have mastered the SaveFileDialog as a control, you will not have any problems using `SaveFileDialog` as a class.

After you open a file, you may need to make some modifications to it and then save it. The SaveFileDialog control provides the same functionality as the OpenFileDialog control, except in reverse. It enables you to choose the location and filename as you save a file. It is important to note that the SaveFileDialog control does not actually save your file; it merely provides a dialog that enables the user to locate where the file should be saved and to provide a name for the file.

The Properties of SaveFileDialog

Table 7-7 lists some of the properties available in the SaveFileDialog control. As you can see, this control, or class if you will, contains a wealth of properties that can be used to customize how the dialog behaves.

TABLE 7-7: Common SaveFileDialog Control Properties

PROPERTY	DESCRIPTION
AddExtension	Indicates whether an extension is automatically added to a filename if the user omits the extension.
AutoUpgradeEnabled	Indicates whether this dialog should automatically upgrade its appearance and behavior when running on different versions of Windows. When `false`, it will appear with XP styles.
CheckFileExists	Indicates whether the dialog displays a warning if the user specifies a filename that does not exist. This is useful when you want the user to save a file to an existing name.
CheckPathExists	Indicates whether the dialog displays a warning if the user specifies a path that does not exist.
CreatePrompt	Indicates whether the dialog prompts the user for permission to create a file if the user specifies a file that does not exist.
DefaultExt	Indicates the default file extension.
DereferenceLinks	Indicates whether the dialog returns the location of the *file* referenced by the shortcut or whether it returns the location of the *shortcut itself*.

continues

TABLE 7-7 *(continued)*

PROPERTY	DESCRIPTION
FileName	Indicates the filename of the selected file in the dialog. This is a read-only property.
FileNames	Indicates the filenames of all selected files in the dialog. This is a read-only property that is returned as a string array.
Filter	Indicates the current filename filter string, which determines the options that appear in the Files of Type: combo box in the dialog.
FilterIndex	Indicates the index of the filter currently selected in the dialog.
InitialDirectory	Indicates the initial directory displayed in the dialog.
OverwritePrompt	Indicates whether the dialog displays a warning if the user specifies a filename that already exists.
ShowHelp	Indicates whether the Help button is displayed in the dialog.
SupportMultiDottedExtensions	Indicates whether the dialog supports displaying and saving files that have multiple filename extensions.
Title	Indicates the title displayed in the title bar of the dialog.
ValidateNames	Indicates whether the dialog should accept only valid Win32 filenames.

SaveFileDialog Methods

The SaveFileDialog control exposes the same methods as the OpenFileDialog. If you want to review these methods, go back to the section entitled "OpenFileDialog Methods." All the examples use the ShowDialog method to show the Save File dialog.

Using the SaveFileDialog Control

In this exercise, you want to save the contents of the text box to a file.

You use the SaveFileDialog control to display a Save File dialog that enables you to specify the location and name of the file. Then you write the contents of the text box on your form to the specified file, again using a built-in code snippet provided by Visual Studio 2015.

TRY IT OUT Working with SaveFileDialog

To see how to include the SaveFileDialog control in your project, you begin with the Windows Forms Dialogs project from the previous Try It Out as a starting point and build upon it. All the code for this Try It Out is in the code folder Windows Forms Dialogs in the Zip file for this chapter.

1. Return to the Forms Designer in the Windows Forms Dialogs project.

2. Drag another Button control from the Toolbox and drop it beneath the Open button and set its properties as follows:

Set Name to **btnSave**.

Set Anchor to **Top, Right**.

Set Location to **349, 43**.

Set Text to **Save**.

3. In the Toolbox, scroll down until you see the SaveFileDialog control and then drag and drop it onto your form. The control will be added to the bottom of the workspace in the IDE.

4. Double-click the Save button to open its Click event and add the bolded code:

```
Private Sub btnSave_Click(sender As Object,
        e As EventArgs) Handles btnSave.Click
    'Set the Save dialog properties
    With SaveFileDialog1
        .DefaultExt = "txt"
        .FileName = strFileName
        .Filter = "Text Documents (*.txt)|*.txt|All Files (*.*)|*.*"
        .FilterIndex = 1
        .OverwritePrompt = True
        .Title = "Demo Save File Dialog"
    End With

    'Show the Save dialog and if the user clicks the Save button,
    'save the file
    If SaveFileDialog1.ShowDialog = Windows.Forms.DialogResult.OK Then
        Try
            'Save the file path and name
            strFileName = SaveFileDialog1.FileName

        Catch ex As Exception
            MessageBox.Show(ex.Message, My.Application.Info.Title,
                MessageBoxButtons.OK, MessageBoxIcon.Error)
        End Try
    End If
End Sub
```

5. Right-click in the blank space inside the Try block statement right before the Catch block statement and choose Insert Snippet from the context menu. In the drop-down menu that appears, double-click Fundamentals-Collections, Data Types, File System, Math, and then in the new list double-click File System-Processing Drives, Folders, and Files. Finally, scroll down the list and double-click Write Text to a File. Your code should now look as follows, and you'll notice that the filename C:\Test.txt is bolded, as is the text string Text, indicating that this code needs to be changed:

```
Try
        'Save the file path and name
        strFileName = SaveFileDialog1.FileName

        My.Computer.FileSystem.WriteAllText("C:\Test.txt", "Text", True)
Catch ex As Exception
```

6. Modify the code in the `Try` block as shown here:

```
Try
    'Save the file path and name
    strFileName = SaveFileDialog1.FileName
    My.Computer.FileSystem.WriteAllText(strFileName, txtFile.Text, False)
Catch ex As Exception
```

7. At this point, you are ready to test this code, so run your project. Start with a simple test. Type some text into the text box on the form and then click the Save button. The Save dialog appears. Notice that the File name combo box already has the complete path and filename in it. This is the path filename that was set in the `strFileName` variable when you declared it in the previous Try It Out.

8. Enter a new filename, but don't put a file extension on it. Then click the Save button, and the file will be saved. To verify this, click the Open button on the form to invoke the Open File dialog; you will see your new file.

9. To test the `OverwritePrompt` property of the SaveFileDialog control, enter some more text in the text box on the form and then click the Save button. In the Save File dialog, choose an existing filename and then click the Save button. You will be prompted to confirm replacement of the existing file, as shown in Figure 7-8. If you choose Yes, the dialog returns a `DialogResult` of `OK`, and the code inside your `If...End If` statement will be executed. If you choose No, you will be returned to the Save File dialog so that you can enter another filename.

> **NOTE** When the Open File or Save File dialog is displayed, the context menu is fully functional and you can cut, copy, and paste files, as well as rename and delete them. Other options may appear in the context menu depending on what software you have installed. For example, if you have WinZip installed, you will see the WinZip options on the context menu.

FIGURE 7-8

How It Works

Before displaying the Save File dialog, you need to set some properties to customize the dialog to your application. To write less code, you can use `With...End` to make repeated statements on one object. The first property you set is the `DefaultExt` property. This property automatically sets the file extension if one has not been specified. For example, if you specify a filename of NewFile with no extension, the dialog will automatically add .txt to the filename when it returns, so that you end up with a file-name of NewFile.txt.

```
.DefaultExt = "txt"
```

The FileName property is set to the same path and filename as that returned from the Open File dialog. This enables you to open a file, edit it, and then display the same filename when you show the Save File dialog. Of course, you can override this filename in the application's Save File dialog.

```
.FileName = strFileName
```

The next two properties are the same as in the OpenFileDialog control. They set the file extension filters to be displayed in the Save as Type: combo box and set the initial filter:

```
.Filter = "Text Documents (*.txt)|*.txt|All Files (*.*)|*.*"
.FilterIndex = 1
```

The OverwritePrompt property accepts a Boolean value of True or False. When set to True, this property prompts you with a MessageBox dialog if you choose an existing filename. If you select Yes, the Save File dialog returns a DialogResult of OK; if you select No, you are returned to the Save File dialog to choose another filename. When the OverwritePrompt property is set to False, the Save File dialog does not prompt you to overwrite an existing file, and your code will overwrite it without asking for the user's permission.

```
.OverwritePrompt = True
```

The Title property sets the caption in the title bar of the Save File dialog:

```
.Title = "Demo Save File Dialog"
```

After you have the properties set, you want to show the dialog. The ShowDialog method of the SaveFileDialog control also returns a DialogResult, so you can use the SaveFileDialog control in an If...End If statement to test the return value.

If the user clicks the Save button in the Save File dialog, the dialog returns a DialogResult of OK. If the user clicks the Cancel button in the dialog, the dialog returns a DialogResult of Cancel. The following code tests for Windows.Forms.DialogResult.OK:

```
If SaveFileDialog1.ShowDialog = Windows.Forms.DialogResult.OK Then
```

The first thing that you do here is save the path and filename chosen by the user in your strFileName variable. This is done in case the user has chosen a new filename in the dialog:

```
Try
    'Save the file path and name
    strFileName = SaveFileDialog1.FileName
```

Then you modify the code snippet generated by Visual Studio 2015 by replacing the bolded text with your variables. First, you replace the text "C:\Test.txt" with your variable, strFileName. This part of the code opens the file for output. Then you replace the text "Text" with the Text property of the text box on your form. This part of the code reads the contents of your text box and writes it to the file. The False parameter at the end of this line of code indicates whether text should be appended to the file. A value of False indicates that the file contents should be overwritten.

```
My.Computer.FileSystem.WriteAllText(strFileName,
    txtFile.Text, False)
```

The final bit of code in this If...End If block merely wraps up the Try.Catch block and the If...End If statement:

```
Catch ex As Exception
        MessageBox.Show(ex.Message, My.Application.Info.Title,
            MessageBoxButtons.OK, MessageBoxIcon.Error)
    End Try
End If
```

THE FONTDIALOG CONTROL

Sometimes you may need to write an application that allows users to choose the font in which they want their data to be displayed or entered. Or perhaps you may want to see all available fonts installed on a particular system. This is where the FontDialog control comes in; it displays a list of all available fonts installed on your computer in a standard dialog that your users have become accustomed to seeing.

Like the OpenFileDialog and SaveFileDialog controls, the FontDialog class can be used as a control by dragging it onto a form, or as a class by declaring it in code.

The FontDialog control is very easy to use; you just set some properties, show the dialog, and then query the properties that you need.

The Properties of FontDialog

Table 7-8 lists some of its available properties.

TABLE 7-8: Common FontDialog Control Properties

PROPERTY	DESCRIPTION
AllowScriptChange	Indicates whether the user can change the character set specified in the Script drop-down box to display a character set other than the one currently displayed
Color	Indicates the selected font color
Font	Indicates the selected font
FontMustExist	Indicates whether the dialog specifies an error condition if the user attempts to enter a font or style that does not exist
MaxSize	Indicates the maximum size (in points) a user can select
MinSize	Indicates the minimum size (in points) a user can select
ShowApply	Indicates whether the dialog contains an Apply button
ShowColor	Indicates whether the dialog displays the color choice
ShowEffects	Indicates whether the dialog contains controls that allow the user to specify strikethrough, underline, and text color options
ShowHelp	Indicates whether the dialog displays a Help button

The Methods of FontDialog

You will be using only one method (`ShowDialog`) of FontDialog in the following Try It Out. Other methods available include `Reset`, which enables you to reset all the properties to their default values.

Using the FontDialog Control

You can display the FontDialog control without setting any properties:

```
FontDialog1.ShowDialog()
```

The dialog would then look like Figure 7-9.

Note that the Font dialog contains an Effects section that enables you to check the options for Strikeout and Underline. However, color selection of the font is not provided by default. If you want this, you must set the `ShowColor` property before calling the `ShowDialog` method on the dialog:

```
FontDialog1.ShowColor = True
FontDialog1.ShowDialog()
```

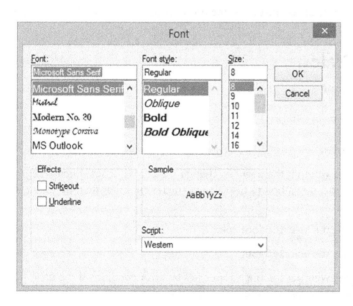

FIGURE 7-9

The `ShowDialog` method of this dialog, like all the ones that you have examined thus far, returns a `DialogResult`. This will be either `DialogResult.OK` or `DialogResult.Cancel`.

When the dialog returns, you can query for the `Font` and `Color` properties to see what font and color the user has chosen. You can then apply these properties to a control on your form or store them to a variable for later use.

Working with FontDialog

Now that you know what the Font dialog looks like and how to call it, you can use it in a Try It Out. Using the program from the last two Try It Outs to open a file, you will have the contents of the file read into the text box on the form. You then use the FontDialog control to display the Font dialog, which enables you to select a font. Then you change the font in the text box to the font that you have chosen. All the code for this Try It Out is in the code folder `Windows Forms Dialogs` in the Zip file for this chapter.

1. Return to the Forms Designer in the Windows Forms Dialogs project.

2. Add another button from the Toolbox and set its properties according to the values shown in this list:

   Set Name to **btnFont**.

   Set Anchor to **Top, Right**.

   Set Location to **349, 73**.

   Set Text to **Font**.

3. You now need to add the FontDialog control to your project, so locate this control in the Toolbox and drag and drop it onto the form or in the workspace below the form; the control will be automatically placed in the workspace below the form if dragged onto the form. Accept all default properties for this control.

4. You want to add code to the `Click` event of the Font button, so double-click it and add the following bolded code:

```
Private Sub btnFont_Click(sender As Object,
    e As EventArgs) Handles btnFont.Click

    'Set the Font dialog properties
    FontDialog1.ShowColor = True

    'Show the Font dialog and if the user clicks the OK button,
    'update the font and color in the text box
    If FontDialog1.ShowDialog = Windows.Forms.DialogResult.OK Then
        txtFile.Font = FontDialog1.Font
        txtFile.ForeColor = FontDialog1.Color
    End If
End Sub
```

5. Run your project. Once your form has been displayed, click the Font button to display the Font dialog as shown in Figure 7-10. Choose a new font and color and then click OK.

6. Add some text in the text box on your form. The text will appear with the new font and color that you have chosen.

7. This same font and color will also be applied to the text that is loaded from a file. To demonstrate this, click the Open button on the form and open a text file. The text from the file is displayed in the same font and color that you chose in the Font dialog.

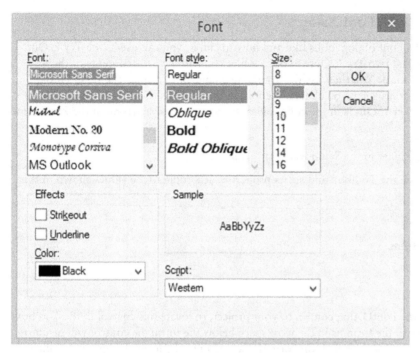

FIGURE 7-10

How It Works

You know that the Font dialog does not show a Color box by default, so you begin by setting the ShowColor property of the FontDialog control to **True** so that the Color box is displayed:

```
'Set the Font dialog properties
FontDialog1.ShowColor = True
```

Next, you actually show the Font dialog. Remember that the DialogResult returns a value of OK or Cancel, so that you can compare the return value from the FontDialog control to Windows.Forms.DialogResult.OK. If the button that the user clicked was OK, you execute the code within the If...End If statement:

```
'Show the Font dialog and if the user clicks the OK button,
'update the font and color in the text box
If FontDialog1.ShowDialog = Windows.Forms.DialogResult.OK Then
    txtFile.Font = FontDialog1.Font
    txtFile.ForeColor = FontDialog1.Color
End If
```

You set the Font property of the text box (txtFile) equal to the Font property of the FontDialog control. This is the font that the user has chosen. Then you set the ForeColor property of the text box equal to the Color property of the FontDialog control, because this will be the color that the user has chosen. After these properties have been changed for the text box, the existing text in the text box is automatically updated to reflect the new font and color. If the text box does not contain any text, any new text that is typed or loaded into the text box will appear in the new font and color.

THE COLORDIALOG CONTROL

Sometimes you may need to allow users to customize the colors on their form. This may be the color of the form itself, a control, or text in a text box. Visual Basic 2015 provides the ColorDialog control for all such requirements. Once again, the ColorDialog control can also be used as a class—declared in code without dragging a control onto the Forms Designer.

The ColorDialog control, shown in Figure 7-11, allows the user to choose from 48 basic colors.

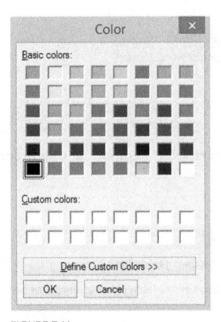

FIGURE 7-11

Note that users can also define their own custom colors, adding more flexibility to your applications. When the users click the Define Custom Colors button in the Color dialog, they can adjust the color to suit their needs (see Figure 7-12).

Having this opportunity for customization and flexibility in your applications gives them a more professional appearance, plus your users are happy because they are allowed to customize the application to suit their own personal tastes.

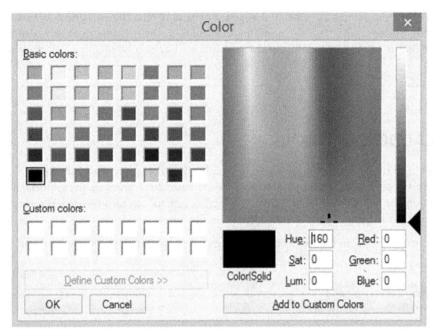

FIGURE 7-12

The Properties of ColorDialog

Before you dive into more code, take a look at some of the available properties for the ColorDialog control, shown in Table 7-9.

TABLE 7-9: Common ColorDialog Control Properties

PROPERTY	DESCRIPTION
AllowFullOpen	Indicates whether users can use the dialog to define custom colors
AnyColor	Indicates whether the dialog displays all available colors in the set of basic colors
Color	Indicates the color selected by the user
CustomColors	Indicates the set of custom colors shown in the dialog
FullOpen	Indicates whether the controls used to create custom colors are visible when the dialog is opened
ShowHelp	Indicates whether a Help button appears in the dialog
SolidColorOnly	Indicates whether the dialog will restrict users to selecting solid colors only

There aren't many properties that you need to worry about for this dialog, which makes it even simpler to use than the other dialogs you have examined so far.

As with the other dialog controls, ColorDialog contains a ShowDialog method. Because you have already seen this method in the previous examples, it is not discussed again.

Using the ColorDialog Control

All you need to do to display the Color dialog is to execute its ShowDialog method:

```
ColorDialog1.ShowDialog()
```

The ColorDialog control will return a DialogResult of OK or Cancel. Hence, you can use the previous statement in an If...End If statement and test for a DialogResult of OK, as you have done in the previous examples that you coded.

To retrieve the color that the user has chosen, you simply retrieve the value set in the Color property and assign it to a variable or any property of a control that supports colors, such as the ForeColor property of a text box:

```
txtFile.ForeColor = ColorDialog1.Color
```

TRY IT OUT Working with the ColorDialog Control

In this Try It Out, you continue using the same project and make the ColorDialog control display the Color dialog. Then, if the dialog returns a DialogResult of OK, you change the background color of the form. All the code for this Try It Out is in the code folder Windows Forms Dialogs in the Zip file for this chapter.

1. Return to the Forms Designer in the Windows Forms Dialogs project.

2. On the form, add another Button control from the Toolbox and set its properties according to the values shown:

   Set Name to **btnColor**.

   Set Anchor to **Top, Right**.

   Set Location to **349, 103**.

   Set Text to **Color**.

3. Add a ColorDialog control to your project from the Toolbox. It will be added to the workspace below the form. Accept all default properties for this control.

4. Double-click the Color button to open its Click event handler and add the following bolded code:

```
Private Sub btnColor_Click(sender As Object,
    e As EventArgs) Handles btnColor.Click
    'Show the Color dialog and if the user clicks the OK button,
    'update the background color of the form
```

```
      If ColorDialog1.ShowDialog = Windows.Forms.DialogResult.OK Then
          Me.BackColor = ColorDialog1.Color
      End If
End Sub
```

5. That's all the code you need to add. Start your project to test your changes.

6. Once the form is displayed, click the Color button to display the Color dialog. Choose any color that you want or create a custom color by clicking the Define Custom Colors button. After you have chosen a color, click the OK button in the Color dialog. The background color of the form will be set to the color that you selected.

7. As with the Font dialog, you do not have to set the Color property of the ColorDialog control before displaying the Color dialog again. It automatically remembers the color chosen, and this will be the color that is selected when the dialog is displayed again. To test this, click the Color button again; the color that you chose will be selected.

How It Works

This time you did not need to set any properties of the ColorDialog control, so you jumped right in and displayed it in an If...End If statement to check the DialogResult returned by the ShowDialog method of this dialog:

```
If ColorDialog1.ShowDialog = Windows.Forms.DialogResult.OK Then
```

Within the If...End If statement, you added the code necessary to change the BackColor property of the form. If the user clicks OK in the Color dialog, the background color of the form is changed with the following line of code:

```
Me.BackColor = ColorDialog1.Color
```

THE PRINTDIALOG CONTROL

Any application worth its salt will incorporate some kind of printing capabilities, whether it is basic printing or more sophisticated printing, such as allowing a user to print only selected text or a range of pages. In this section you explore basic printing, looking at several classes that help you to print text from a file.

Visual Basic 2015 provides the PrintDialog control. It does not actually do any printing, but enables you to select the printer that you want to use and set the printer properties such as page orientation and print quality. It also enables you to specify the print range. You will not be using these features in this next example, but it is worth noting that this functionality is available in the PrintDialog control, as shown in Figure 7-13.

Like the previous dialogs that you have examined, the Print dialog provides Print (corresponding to the OK buttons in the other dialogs) and Cancel buttons; thus, its ShowDialog method returns a DialogResult of OK or Cancel. You can then use this result in an If...End If statement and test for the DialogResult. The Apply button merely applies changes made in the Print dialog but does not close the dialog.

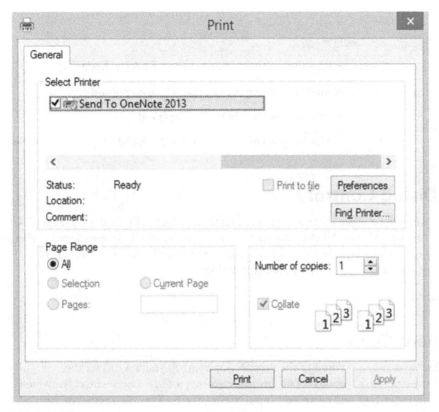

FIGURE 7-13

The Properties of PrintDialog

Table 7-10 shows some of the properties provided in PrintDialog. Just like the other dialogs, PrintDialog exposes a ShowDialog method.

TABLE 7-10: Common PrintDialog Control Properties

PROPERTY	DESCRIPTION
AllowCurrentPage	Indicates whether the Current Page option button is enabled
AllowPrintToFile	Indicates whether the Print to File check box is enabled
AllowSelection	Indicates whether the Selection option button is enabled
AllowSomePages	Indicates whether the Pages option button is enabled
Document	Indicates the print document used to obtain the printer settings

continues

TABLE 7-10 *(continued)*

PROPERTY	DESCRIPTION
PrinterSettings	Indicates the printer settings that the dialog will be modifying
PrintToFile	Indicates whether the Print to File check box is checked
ShowHelp	Indicates whether the Help button is displayed
ShowNetwork	Indicates whether the Network button is displayed

Using the PrintDialog Control

The only method that you will be using is the ShowDialog method, which will display the Print dialog shown in Figure 7-13 with only the All Page Range Option button enabled. As mentioned earlier, the PrintDialog control merely displays the Print dialog; it does not actually do any printing. The following code fragment shows how you display the Print dialog:

```
PrintDialog1.ShowDialog()
```

The PrintDocument Class

Before you can call the ShowDialog method of the PrintDialog control, you have to set the Document property of the PrintDialog class. This property accepts a PrintDocument class, which is used to obtain the printer settings and can send output to the printer. This class requires the System.Drawing.Printing namespace, so you must include this namespace before attempting to define an object that uses the PrintDocument class.

The Properties of the PrintDocument Class

Before continuing, take a look at some of the important properties of the PrintDocument class, listed in Table 7-11.

TABLE 7-11: Common PrintDocument Class Properties

PROPERTY	DESCRIPTION
DefaultPageSettings	Indicates the default page settings for the document.
DocumentName	Indicates the document name that is displayed while printing the document. This is also the name that appears in the Print Status dialog and printer queue.
PrintController	Indicates the print controller that guides the printing process.
PrinterSettings	Indicates the printer that prints the document.

Printing a Document

The `Print` method of the `PrintDocument` class prints a document to the printer specified in the `PrinterSettings` property. When you call the `Print` method of the `PrintDocument` class, the `PrintPage` event is raised for each page as it prints. Therefore, you need to create a method for that event and add an event handler for it. The method that you would create for the `PrintPage` event does the actual reading of the data to be printed.

Printing using the `PrintDocument` class requires a lot of coding and knowledge of how actual printing works. Fortunately, the help documentation provides some sample code in the `PrintDocument` class. This can be used as a starting point to help you gain an understanding of the basics of printing. Note that the sample code in the help documentation assumes that a single line in the file to be printed does not exceed the width of a printed page.

The sample code in the help documentation demonstrates how to print from a file.

TRY IT OUT   Working with the PrintDialog Control

In this Try It Out, you'll examine how to print the contents of a text box. All the code for this Try It Out is in the code folder `Windows Forms Dialogs` in the Zip file for this chapter.

1. Return to the Forms Designer in the Windows Forms Dialogs project.

2. Drag a Button control from the Toolbox. Position it beneath the Color button and set the following properties of the new button:

   Set `Name` to **btnPrint**.

   Set `Anchor` to **Top, Right**.

   Set `Location` to **349, 133**.

   Set `Text` to **Print**.

3. Add a PrintDialog control to the project, dragging and dropping it from the Toolbox onto the form. It will be added to the workspace below the form. Accept all default properties for this control. You will find it under the Printing tab.

4. Switch to the Code Editor so that you can add the required namespace for printing. Add this namespace to the top of your class:

```
Imports System.Drawing.Printing

Public Class Dialogs
```

5. Add the following variable declarations to the top of your class:

```
'Declare variables and objects
Private strFileName As String
Private strPrintRecord As String

Private WithEvents DialogsPrintDocument As PrintDocument
```

6. Select `DialogsPrintDocument` in the Class Name combo box and the `PrintPage` event in the Method Name combo box. Add the following bolded code to the `DialogsPrintDocument_PrintPage` event handler:

```
Private Sub DialogsPrintDocument_PrintPage(sender As Object,
    e As PrintPageEventArgs) Handles DialogsPrintDocument.PrintPage
    'Declare variables
    Dim intCharactersToPrint As Integer
    Dim intLinesPerPage As Integer
    Dim strPrintData As String
    Dim objStringFormat As New StringFormat
    Dim objPrintFont As New Font("Arial", 10)
    Dim objPageBoundaries As RectangleF
    Dim objPrintArea As SizeF

    'Get the page boundaries
    objPageBoundaries = New RectangleF(e.MarginBounds.Left,
        e.MarginBounds.Top, e.MarginBounds.Width,
        e.MarginBounds.Height)

    'Get the print area based on page margins and font used
    objPrintArea = New SizeF(e.MarginBounds.Width,
        e.MarginBounds.Height—objPrintFont.GetHeight(e.Graphics))

    'Break in between words on a line
    objStringFormat.Trimming = StringTrimming.Word

    'Get the number of characters to print
    e.Graphics.MeasureString(strPrintRecord, objPrintFont, objPrintArea,
        objStringFormat, intCharactersToPrint, intLinesPerPage)

    'Get the print data from the print record
    strPrintData = strPrintRecord.Substring(0, intCharactersToPrint)

    'Print the page
       e.Graphics.DrawString(strPrintData, objPrintFont, Brushes.Black,
        objPageBoundaries, objStringFormat)
    'If more lines exist, print another page
    If intCharactersToPrint < strPrintRecord.Length Then
        'Remove printed text from print record
        strPrintRecord = strPrintRecord.Remove(0, intCharactersToPrint)
        e.HasMorePages = True
    Else
        e.HasMorePages = False
    End If
End Sub
```

7. Select `btnPrint` in the Class Name combo box and the `Click` event in the Method Name combo box. Add the following bolded code to the `btnPrint_Click` event handler:

```
Private Sub btnPrint_Click(sender As Object,
    e As EventArgs) Handles btnPrint.Click
    'Instantiate a new instance of the PrintDocument
```

```
DialogsPrintDocument = New PrintDocument

'Set the PrintDialog properties
With PrintDialog1
    .AllowCurrentPage = False
    .AllowPrintToFile = False
    .AllowSelection = False
    .AllowSomePages = False
    .Document = DialogsPrintDocument
    .PrinterSettings.DefaultPageSettings.Margins.Top = 25
    .PrinterSettings.DefaultPageSettings.Margins.Bottom = 25
    .PrinterSettings.DefaultPageSettings.Margins.Left = 25
    .PrinterSettings.DefaultPageSettings.Margins.Right = 25
End With

If PrintDialog1.ShowDialog = DialogResult.OK Then
    'Set the selected printer settings in the PrintDocument
    DialogsPrintDocument.PrinterSettings =
        PrintDialog1.PrinterSettings

    'Get the print data
    strPrintRecord = txtFile.Text

    'Invoke the Print method on the PrintDocument
    DialogsPrintDocument.Print()
End If
End Sub
```

8. You are now ready to test your code, so run the project.

9. Click the Open button to open a file and then click the Print button to display the Print dialog shown in Figure 7-14.

> **NOTE** *The Print to File check box is disabled, as well as the Selection, Current Page, and Pages radio buttons. This is because you set the* AllowCurrentPage, AllowPrintToFile, AllowSelection, *and* AllowSomePages *properties in the PrintDialog control to* False.

If you have more than one printer installed (see Figure 7-14), you can choose the printer name that you want from the list.

10. Click the Print button in the Print dialog to have your text printed.

How It Works

You begin by importing the System.Drawing.Printing namespace, which is needed to support printing. This is the namespace in which the PrintDocument class is defined.

You then declare a variable and object needed for printing. The strPrintRecord variable is a string variable that will contain the data from the text box to be printed. The DialogsPrintDocument object is actually responsible for printing the text.

FIGURE 7-14

Notice the WithEvents keyword. This keyword is used to refer to a class that can raise events, and will cause Visual Studio 2015 to list those events in the Method Name combo box at the top of the Code Editor:

```
Private strPrintRecord As String

Private WithEvents DialogsPrintDocument As PrintDocument
```

The DialogsPrintDocument_PrintPage event handler handles printing a page of output. This event is initially called after you call the Print method on the object defined as the PrintDocument class—in this case, the DialogsPrintDocument.

This event handler is where you have to provide the code for actually printing a document, and you must determine whether more pages exist to be printed. This method starts off with a number of variable declarations. The first two variables are Integer data types and contain the number of characters to print to a page and the number of lines that can be printed on a page.

The strPrintData variable is a String data type that contains all the data to be printed on a single page. The objStringFormat variable is declared as a StringFormat class, and this class encapsulates text layout information used to format the data to be printed. The StringFormat class is used to trim the data on word boundaries so that the text does not overflow the print area of a page.

The `objPrintFont` object is defined as a `Font` class and sets the font used for the printed text, whereas the `objPageBoundaries` object is defined as a `RectangleF` structure. The `RectangleF` structure contains four floating-point numbers defining the location and size of a rectangle and is used to define the top and left coordinates of a page, as well as its width and height. The `objPrintArea` object is defined as a `SizeF` structure and contains the height and width of the print area of a page. This is the actual area that you can print in, not the actual size of the page:

```
Private Sub DialogsPrintDocument_PrintPage(sender As Object,
    e As PrintPageEventArgs) Handles DialogsPrintDocument.PrintPage

    'Declare variables
    Dim intCharactersToPrint As Integer
    Dim intLinesPerPage As Integer
    Dim strPrintData As String
    Dim objStringFormat As New StringFormat
    Dim objPrintFont As New Font("Arial", 10)
    Dim objPageBoundaries As RectangleF
    Dim objPrintArea As SizeF
```

The code in this method starts off by getting the page boundaries. The `PrintPageEventArgs` passed to this method in the e parameter contains the top and left coordinates of the page as well as the height and width of the page. These values are used to set the data in the `objPageBoundaries` object.

The print area of the page is contained in the `Width` and `Height` properties of the `PrintPageEventArgs`. The actual height of the page is calculated using the `GetHeight` method of the `Font` class in the `objPrintFont` object, as each font size requires more or less vertical space on a page:

```
'Get the page boundaries
objPageBoundaries = New RectangleF(e.MarginBounds.Left,
    e.MarginBounds.Top, e.MarginBounds.Width,
    e.MarginBounds.Height)

'Get the print area based on page margins and font used
objPrintArea = New SizeF(e.MarginBounds.Width,
    e.MarginBounds.Height—objPrintFont.GetHeight(e.Graphics))
```

You now set the `Trimming` property of the `objStringFormat` object to instruct it to break the data on a single line using word boundaries. This is done using the `StringTrimming` enumeration, which contains the `Word` constant. This ensures that a print line does not exceed the margins of a printed page.

You then need to determine the number of characters that will fit on a page based on the print area of the page, the font size used, and the data to be printed. This is done using the `MeasureString` method of the `Graphics` class. This method takes the data to be printed, the font used on the page, the print area of the page, and the formatting to be applied, and then determines the number of characters that can be printed and the number of lines that will fit on a printed page. The number of print characters and the number of lines is set in the `intCharactersToPrint` and `intLinesPerPage` variables, which are passed to the `MeasureString` method.

Once you know the number of characters that will fit on a page, you get that data from the `strPrintRecord` variable and set the data to be printed in the `strPrintData` variable. This is the variable that will contain the data to actually be printed:

```
'Break in between words on a line
objStringFormat.Trimming = StringTrimming.Word

'Get the number of characters to print
e.Graphics.MeasureString(strPrintRecord, objPrintFont,
    objPrintArea, objStringFormat,
    intCharactersToPrint, intLinesPerPage)

'Get the print data from the print record
strPrintData = strPrintRecord.Substring(0, intCharactersToPrint)
```

Now that you have the appropriate data to be printed in the `strPrintData` variable, you are ready to actually send the data to be printed to the printer. This time you are going to use the `DrawString` method of the `Graphics` class. This method actually formats and sends the data to the printer.

The parameters that you pass to the `DrawString` method are the data to be printed, the font to be used in printing, a `Brushes` object representing the font color of the text to print, the page boundaries, and a `StringFormat` object used to format the printed output:

```
'Print the page
e.Graphics.DrawString(strPrintData, objPrintFont, Brushes.Black,
    objPageBoundaries, objStringFormat)
```

The last section of code in this method determines whether more data exists to be printed. You want to compare the value contained in the `intCharactersToPrint` variable to the length of the `strPrintRecord` variable using the `Length` property of the `String` class. The `Length` property returns the number of characters in the string.

If the value contained in the `intCharactersToPrint` variable is less than the length of the `strPrintRecord` variable, more data exists to be printed. In this case, you first want to remove the data from the `strPrintRecord` that has already been printed using the `Remove` method of the `String` class. The `Remove` method accepts the starting position from which to remove data and the amount of data to remove. The amount of data to be removed is contained in the `intCharactersToPrint` variable, the data that has already been printed.

Finally, you set the `HasMorePages` property of the `PrintPageEventArgs` parameter to `True`, indicating more data exists to be printed. Setting this property to `True` will cause the `PrintPage` event of the `DialogsPrintDocument` object to be raised once more, and this event handler will be executed again to continue printing until all data has been printed.

If no more data exists to be printed, you set the `HasMorePages` property to `False`:

```
'If more lines exist, print another page
If intCharactersToPrint < strPrintRecord.Length Then
  'Remove printed text from print record
  strPrintRecord = strPrintRecord.Remove(0, intCharactersToPrint)
  e.HasMorePages = True
Else
  e.HasMorePages = False
End If
```

The code in the `Click` event of the Print button is less complicated than the code in the `DialogsPrint Document_PrintPage` event handler. This method starts out by instantiating a new instance of the `PrintDocument` class in the `DialogsPrintDocument` object.

You then want to set the properties of the PrintDialog control before showing it. Since you have only a simple method to print all pages in a document, you want to disable the features that allow printing only the current page, printing to a file, printing a selection of text, and printing specific pages. This is all done by setting the first four properties in the following code to False.

Next, you need to set the Document property of the PrintDialog to your PrintDocument object so that the dialog can obtain the printer settings. The printer settings are set and retrieved in the PrintDocument object and can be changed through the PrintDialog through its PrinterSettings property.

Finally, you set the default margins to be used when printing a document in the PrinterSettings property. This can be set before the PrintDialog is shown, to initially set the print margins for the printer:

```
'Instantiate a new instance of the PrintDocument
DialogsPrintDocument = New PrintDocument

'Set the PrintDialog properties
With PrintDialog1
    .AllowCurrentPage = False
    .AllowPrintToFile = False
    .AllowSelection = False
    .AllowSomePages = False
    .Document = DialogsPrintDocument
    .PrinterSettings.DefaultPageSettings.Margins.Top = 25
    .PrinterSettings.DefaultPageSettings.Margins.Bottom = 25
    .PrinterSettings.DefaultPageSettings.Margins.Left = 25
    .PrinterSettings.DefaultPageSettings.Margins.Right = 25
End With
```

The last thing you want to do in this method is actually display the PrintDialog and check for a DialogResult of OK. If the user clicks the Print button, the PrintDialog will return a DialogResult of OK, and you want to actually invoke the printing of the data.

The first thing that you do in the IfThen block is capture the printer settings from the PrintDialog and set them in the DialogsPrintDocument. If the user changed any of the margins or other printer settings, you want to pass them on to the PrintDocument that is used to print the data.

You also want to set the data to be printed from the text box in the strPrintRecord variable. Finally, you call the Print method on the DialogsPrintDocument object to start the printing process. Calling the Print method will raise the PrintPage event on the DialogsPrintDocument object, thus causing your code in the DialogsPrintDocument_PrintPage event handler to be executed:

```
If PrintDialog1.ShowDialog = DialogResult.OK Then
    'Set the selected printer settings in the PrintDocument
    DialogsPrintDocument.PrinterSettings =
        PrintDialog1.PrinterSettings

    'Get the print data
    strPrintRecord = txtFile.Text

    'Invoke the Print method on the PrintDocument
    DialogsPrintDocument.Print()
End If
```

THE FOLDERBROWSERDIALOG CONTROL

Occasionally, you'll need to allow your users to select a folder instead of a file. Perhaps your application performs backups, or perhaps you need a folder to save temporary files. The FolderBrowserDialog control displays the Browse For Folder dialog, which enables users to select a folder. This dialog does not display files—only folders, which provide an obvious way to allow users to select a folder needed by your application.

Like the other dialogs that you have examined thus far, the FolderBrowserDialog control can also be used as a class declared in code. The Browse For Folder dialog, shown in Figure 7-15 without any customization, enables users to browse for and select a folder.

FIGURE 7-15

The Properties of FolderBrowserDialog

Before you dive into some code, take a look at some of the available properties for the FolderBrowserDialog control, shown in Table 7-12.

TABLE 7-12: Common FolderBrowserDialog Control Properties

PROPERTY	DESCRIPTION
Description	Provides a descriptive message in the dialog.
RootFolder	Indicates the root folder from which the dialog should start browsing. Here you provide SpecialFolders like Desktop, Programs, or MyDocuments.
SelectedPath	Indicates the folder selected by the user.
ShowNewFolderButton	Indicates whether the Make New Folder button is shown in the dialog.

This is one dialog control for which you'll want to use all the most common properties, as shown in the preceding table, to customize the dialog displayed.

As with the other dialog controls, the FolderBrowserDialog contains a ShowDialog method. You have already seen this method in the previous examples, and because it is the same it does not need to be discussed again.

Using the FolderBrowserDialog Control

Before showing the Browse For Folder dialog, you'll want to set some basic properties. The three main properties that you are most likely to set are shown in the following code snippet. The first of these properties is the Description property. This property enables you to provide a description or instructions for your users.

The next property is RootFolder, which specifies the starting folder for the Browse For Folder dialog. This property uses one of the constants from the Environment.SpecialFolder enumeration. Typically, you would use the MyComputer constant to specify that browsing should start at the My Computer level, or sometimes you may want to use the MyDocuments constant to start browsing at the My Documents level.

The final property shown in the code snippet is the ShowNewFolderButton property. This property has a default value of True, which indicates that the Make New Folder button should be displayed. However, if you do not want this button displayed, you need to specify this property and set it to a value of False:

```
With FolderBrowserDialog1
    .Description = "Select a backup folder"
    .RootFolder = Environment.SpecialFolder.MyComputer
    .ShowNewFolderButton = False
End With
```

After you have set the necessary properties, you execute the ShowDialog method to display the dialog:

```
FolderBrowserDialog1.ShowDialog()
```

The FolderBrowserDialog control will return a `DialogResult` of `OK` or `Cancel`. Hence, you can use the previous statement in an `If...End If` statement and test for a `DialogResult` of `OK`, as you have done in the previous examples that you have coded.

To retrieve the folder that the user has chosen, you simply retrieve the value set in the `SelectedPath` property and assign it to a variable. The folder that is returned is a fully qualified path name. For example, if you chose a folder named `Temp` at the root of your C: drive, the path returned would be

```
C:\Temp: strFolder = FolderBrowserDialog1.SelectedPath
```

TRY IT OUT **Try It Out Working with the FolderBrowserDialog Control**

In this Try It Out, you continue using the same Windows Forms Dialogs project and have the FolderBrowserDialog control display the Browse For Folder dialog. Then, if the dialog returns a `DialogResult` of `OK`, you'll display the selected folder in the text box on your form. All the code for this Try It Out is in the code folder `Windows Forms Dialogs` in the Zip file for this chapter.

1. Return to the Forms Designer in the Windows Forms Dialog project.

2. Add another Button control from the Toolbox to the form beneath the Print button and set its properties as follows:

   Set `Name` to **btnBrowse**.

   Set `Anchor` to **Top, Right**.

   Set `Location` to **349, 163**.

   Set `Text` to **Browse**.

3. Add a FolderBrowserDialog control to your project from the Toolbox. It will be added to the workspace below the form. Accept all default properties for this control because you'll set the necessary properties in your code.

4. Double-click the Browse button to open its `Click` event handler and add the following bolded code:

```
Private Sub btnBrowse_Click(sender As Object,
        e As EventArgs) Handles btnBrowse.Click
    'Set the FolderBrowser dialog properties
    With FolderBrowserDialog1
        .Description = "Select a backup folder"
        .RootFolder = Environment.SpecialFolder.MyComputer
        .ShowNewFolderButton = False
    End With

    'Show the FolderBrowser dialog and if the user clicks the
    'OK button, display the selected folder
    If FolderBrowserDialog1.ShowDialog = Windows.Forms.DialogResult.OK Then
        txtFile.Text = FolderBrowserDialog1.SelectedPath
    End If
End Sub
```

5. That's all the code you need to add. To test your changes to your project, click the Start button on the toolbar.

6. When your form displays, click the Browse button, and you'll see a Browse For Folder dialog similar to the one shown in Figure 7-16.

7. Now browse your computer and select a folder. When you click the OK button, the selected folder will be displayed in the text box on your form. Notice that the folder returned contains a fully qualified path name.

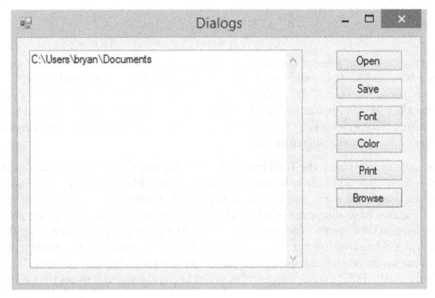

FIGURE 7-16

How It Works

Before displaying the Browse For Folder dialog, you needed to set some basic properties of the FolderBrowserDialog control to customize the look for this dialog. You start by setting the Description property to provide some basic instructions for the user. Then you select the root folder at which the Browse For Folder dialog should start browsing. In this instance, you use the MyComputer constant, which displayed all drives on your computer (refer to Figure 7-16). Finally, you set the ShowNewFolderButton property to False in order to not display the Make New Folder button:

```
'Set the FolderBrowser dialog properties
With FolderBrowserDialog1
    .Description = "Select a backup folder"
    .RootFolder = Environment.SpecialFolder.MyComputer
    .ShowNewFolderButton = False
End With
```

You display the dialog in an `If...End If` statement to check the `DialogResult` returned by the `ShowDialog` method of the FolderBrowserDialog control. Within the `If...End If` statement, you add the code necessary to display the folder selected in the text box on your form, using the `SelectedPath` property:

```
'Show the FolderBrowser dialog and if the user clicks the
'OK button, display the selected folder
If FolderBrowserDialog1.ShowDialog = Windows.Forms.DialogResult.OK Then
    txtFile.Text = FolderBrowserDialog1.SelectedPath
End If
```

SUMMARY

This chapter has taken a look at some of the dialogs that are provided in Visual Basic 2015. You examined the MessageBox dialog and the OpenFileDialog, SaveFileDialog, FontDialog, ColorDialog, PrintDialog, and FolderBrowserDialog controls. Each of these dialogs help you provide a common interface in your applications for their respective functions. They also hide a lot of the complexities required to perform their tasks, enabling you to concentrate on the logic needed to make your application functional and feature-rich.

Although you used the controls from the Toolbox for all these dialogs, except the MessageBox dialog, remember that these controls can also be used as normal classes. This means that the classes that these dialogs expose are the same properties and methods that you've seen, whether you are selecting a control visually or writing code using the class. You can define your own objects and set them to these classes, and then use the objects to perform the tasks that you performed using the controls. This provides better control over the scope of the objects. For example, you could define an object, set it to the `OpenDialog` class, use it, and then destroy it all in the same method. This uses resources only in the method that defines and uses the `OpenDialog` class, and reduces the size of your executable.

To summarize, you should now know:

- ➤ How to use the MessageBox dialog to display messages
- ➤ How to display icons and buttons in the MessageBox dialog
- ➤ How to use the OpenFileDialog control and read the contents of a file
- ➤ How to use the SaveFileDialog control and save the contents of a text box to a file
- ➤ How to use the FontDialog control to set the font and color of text in a text box
- ➤ How to use the ColorDialog control to set the background color of your form
- ➤ How to use the PrintDialog control to print text
- ➤ How to use the FolderBrowserDialog control to get a selected folder

1. To display a dialog to the user, what method do you use?

2. What method do you call to display a message box?

3. Name the five different ways to display an icon to the user on a message box.

4. How do you determine which button was pressed on a message box?

5. If you need to write basic code, where should you look for a simple example inside of Visual Studio?

▶ **WHAT YOU LEARNED IN THIS CHAPTER**

TOPIC	CONCEPTS
`MessageBox`	How to display and determine the button clicked on a message box
`OpenFileDialog`	How to use the OpenFileDialog control to find a file to open and read the text contents
`SaveFileDialog`	How to use the `SaveFileDialog` control to save text to a file
`FontDialog`	How to display the `FontDialog` and use the selected font to change the font in a program
`ColorDialog`	How to display the `ColorDialog` and use the selected font to change the color in a program
`PrintDialog`	What classes to use and how to use them to print text
`FolderBrowserDialog`	How to set up the control to be shown and determine which folder was selected

8

Creating Menus

WHAT YOU WILL LEARN IN THIS CHAPTER:

➤ Creating menus

➤ Creating submenus

➤ Creating context menus

WROX.COM CODE DOWNLOADS FOR THIS CHAPTER

The wrox.com code downloads for this chapter are found at www.wrox.com/begvisualbasic2015 on the Download Code tab. The code is in the 092117 C08.zip download and individually named according to the names given throughout the chapter.

Menus are a part of every good application and provide not only an easy way to navigate within an application but also useful tools for working with that application. Take, for example, Visual Studio 2015. It provides menus for navigating the various windows that it displays and useful tools for making the job of development easier through menus and context menus (also called pop-up menus) for cutting, copying, and pasting code. It also provides menu items for searching through code.

This chapter takes a look at creating menus in your Visual Basic 2015 applications. You explore how to create and manage menus and submenus and how to create context menus and override the default context menus. Visual Studio 2015 provides two menu controls in the Toolbox, and you will explore both of these.

UNDERSTANDING MENU FEATURES

The MenuStrip control in Visual Studio 2015 provides several key features. First and foremost, it provides a quick and easy way to add menus, menu items, and submenu items to your application. It also provides a built-in editor that enables you to add, edit, and delete menu items at the drop of a hat.

The menu items that you create may contain images, access keys, shortcut keys, and check marks as well as text labels.

Images

Nearly everyone is familiar with the images on the menus in applications such as Microsoft Outlook or Visual Studio 2015. In earlier versions of Visual Basic, developers were unable to create menu items with images without doing some custom programming or purchasing a third-party control. Visual Basic has come a long way and now provides an Image property for a menu item that makes adding an image to your menu items a breeze.

Access Keys

An *access key* (also known as an *accelerator key*) enables you to navigate the menus using the Alt key and a letter that is underlined in the menu item. When the access key is pressed, the menu appears on the screen, and the user can navigate through it using the arrow keys or the mouse.

Shortcut Keys

Shortcut keys enable you to invoke the menu item without displaying the menus at all. Shortcut keys usually consist of a control key and a letter, such as Ctrl+X to cut text.

Check Marks

A *check mark* symbol can be placed next to a menu item in lieu of an image, typically to indicate that the menu item is being used. For example, if you click the View menu in Visual Studio 2015 and then select the Toolbars menu item, you see a submenu that has many other submenu items, some of which have check marks. The submenu items that have check marks indicate the toolbars that are currently displayed.

Figure 8-1 shows many of the available features that you can incorporate into your menus. As you can see, this sample menu provides all the features that were just mentioned plus a *separator*. A separator looks like a raised ridge and provides a logical separation between groups of menu items.

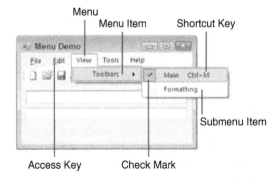

FIGURE 8-1

Figure 8-1 shows the menu the way it looks when the project is being run. Figure 8-2 shows how the menu looks in design mode.

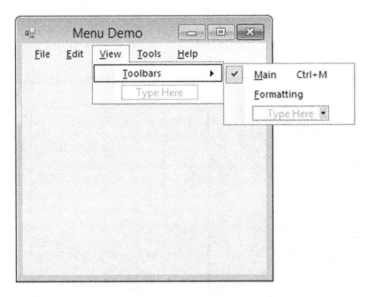

FIGURE 8-2

The first thing you'll notice when using the MenuStrip control is that it provides a means to add another menu, menu item, or submenu item quickly. Each time you add one of these, another blank text area is added.

The Properties Window

While you are creating or editing a menu, the Properties window displays the available properties that can be set for the menu being edited, as shown in Figure 8-3, which shows the properties for the Toolbars menu item.

You can create as many menus, menu items, and submenu items as you need. You can even go as deep as you need to when creating submenu items by creating another submenu within a submenu.

> **NOTE** Keep in mind that if the menus are hard to navigate, or if it is hard for users to find the items they are looking for, they will rapidly lose interest in your application.

You should stick with the standard format for menus that you see in most Windows applications today. These are the menus that you see in Visual Studio 2015. For example, you always have a File menu, and an Exit menu item in the File menu to exit from the application. If your application provides cut, copy, and paste functionality, you would place these menu items in the Edit menu, and so on.

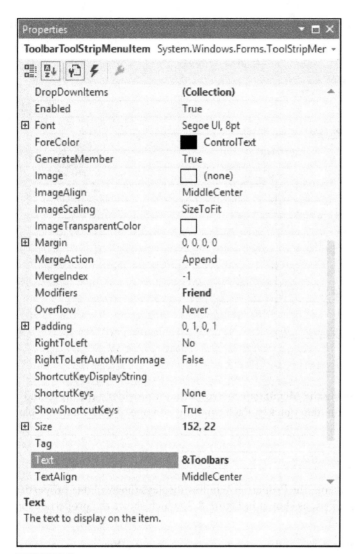

FIGURE 8-3

NOTE *The MSDN library contains a section on Windows User Experience Interaction Guidelines. A search for this on Google returns a link to* `http://msdn.microsoft.com/library/aa511258.aspx`. *You can find the menu guidelines at* `https://msdn.microsoft.com/en-us/library/dn742392.aspx`. *This section contains many topics that address the user interface and the Windows user interface. There is a lot of information about touch screen design as well. This chapter focuses on standard displays that do not support touch. You can explore these topics for more details on Windows UI design-related topics.*

The key is to make your menus look and feel like the menus in other Windows applications so that users feel comfortable using your application. This way, they don't feel like they have to learn the basics of Windows all over again. Some menu items will be specific to your application, but the key to incorporating them is to ensure that they fall into a general menu category that users are familiar with or to place them in your own menu category. You would then place this new menu in the appropriate place in the menu bar, generally in the middle.

CREATING MENUS

This section demonstrates how easy it is to create menus in your applications. In the following Try It Out, you'll create a form that contains a menu bar, two toolbars, and two text boxes. The menu bar will contain five menus: File, Edit, View, Tools, and Help, and a few menu items and submenu items. This enables you to fully exercise the features of the menu controls. Because several steps are involved in building this application, the process is broken down into several sections.

Designing the Menus

You will be implementing code behind the menu items to demonstrate the menu and how to add code to your menu items, so let's get started.

TRY IT OUT Creating Menus

In the first example, you will learn how to create menus and submenus. All the code in this chapter is in the folder Windows Forms Menus in the Zip file for this chapter.

1. Start Visual Studio 2015 and click File ⇨ New Project. In the New Project dialog, select Windows Forms Application in the Templates pane and enter the project name **Windows Forms Menus** in the Name field. Click the OK button to have the project created.

2. Click the form in the Forms Designer and set the Text property to **Menu Demo**.

3. Drag a MenuStrip control from the Toolbox and drop it on your form. It is automatically positioned at the top of your form. The control is also added to the bottom of the development environment, just like the dialog controls discussed in Chapter 7.

4. In the Properties window, set Font Size to **8**.

5. Right-click the MenuStrip1 control on the form and select the **Insert Standard Items** context menu item to have the standard menu items automatically inserted. If you don't see it, make sure you are right-clicking the control and not the type-here area that represents an item. This will insert the File, Edit, Tools, and Help menus.

6. Select the MenuStrip and then in the Properties window, click the items button with the ellipsis next to the Items property or right-click the MenuStrip control in your form and then choose Edit Items from the context menu. In the Items Collection Editor dialog, click the Add button to add a new menu item.

    To be consistent with the current naming standard already in use with the other menu items, set the Name property for this new menu item to **ViewToolStripMenuItem**.

Now set the `Text` property to **&View**. An ampersand (&) in the menu name provides an access key for the menu or menu item. The letter before which the ampersand appears is the letter used to access this menu item in combination with the Alt key, so for this menu you can access and expand the View menu by pressing Alt+V. You'll see this when you run your project later.

You want to position this menu between the Edit and Tools menus, so click the up arrow to the right of the menu items until the View menu is positioned between `EditToolStripMenuItem` and `ToolsToolStripMenuItem` in the list.

7. Now locate the `DropDownItems` property and click the ellipsis button next to it so that you can add menu items beneath the View menu. A second Items Collection Editor appears; its caption reads "Items Collection Editor (ViewToolStripMenuItem.DropDownItems)."

    There is only one menu item, Toolbars, under the View menu. Click the Add button in the Item Collections Editor to add a MenuItem.

    Again, you want to be consistent with the naming standard already being used, so set the `Name` property to **ToolbarToolStripMenuItem**. Then set the `Text` property to **&Toolbars**.

8. To add two submenu items under the Toolbars menu item, locate the `DropDownItems` property and click the button next to it to add items.

    In the Item Collections Editor, click the Add button to add a new menu item. Set the Name property for this submenu item to **MainToolStripMenuItem** and the `Text` property to **&Main**. Set the `ShortcutKeys` property to **Ctrl+M**. To do this, check the box for **Ctrl** and then select **M** from the Key drop-down list. Next, make sure the `ShowShortcutKeys` property is set to `True`.

    When you add the Main toolbar to this project in the next example, it is displayed by default, so this submenu item should be checked to indicate that the toolbar is displayed. Set the `Checked` property to **True** to cause this submenu item to be checked by default, and set the `CheckOnClick` property to **True** to allow the check mark next to this submenu item to be toggled on and off.

9. The next submenu item that you add is Formatting. Click the Add button to add a new menu item and set the `Name` property for this submenu item to **FormattingToolStripMenuItem** and the `Text` property to **&Formatting**.

    Because the Formatting menu you add in the next example will not be shown by default, you need to leave the `Checked` property set to **False**. You do, however, need to set the `CheckOnClick` property to **True** so that the submenu item can toggle the check mark on and off.

    Keep clicking the OK button in the Items Collection Editors until all the editors are closed.

10. Save your project by clicking the Save All button on the toolbar.

11. If you run your project at this point and then enter Alt+V and Alt+T (without releasing the Alt key), you will see the submenu items, as shown in Figure 8-4. You can also click the other menus and see their menu items.

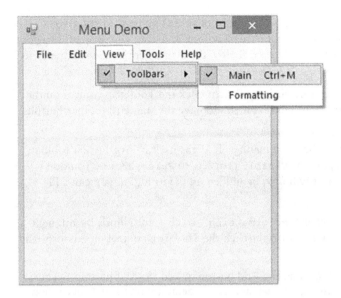

FIGURE 8-4

How It Works

Visual Studio 2015 takes care of a lot details for you by providing the Insert Standard Items context menu item in the MenuStrip control. You click this menu item to have Visual Studio 2015 create the standard menus and menu items found in most common applications. This enables you to concentrate on only the menus and menu items that are custom to your application, which is what you did by adding the View menu, Toolbars menu item, and Main and Formatting submenu items.

Adding Toolbars and Controls

In this section you add the toolbars and buttons for the toolbars that the application needs. The menus created in the previous section will control the displaying and hiding of these toolbars. You also add a couple of TextBox controls that are used in the application to cut, copy, and paste text using the toolbar buttons and menu items.

TRY IT OUT Adding Toolbars and Controls

You have certainly worked with toolbars before. In MS Word, you probably click the Print toolbar button when you need to print. In the next example, you will create similar toolbars. All the code in this chapter is in the folder `Windows Forms Menus` in the Zip file for this chapter.

To complete this Try It Out, you will need to download the Visual Studio Image Library from `http://go.microsoft.com/fwlink/p/?LinkId=275090`. Download this file and unzip on your computer because you will be using images from this library in this example. At the time of writing, only the 2013 Image Library was available. That library will work for this example.

1. Return to the Forms Designer in your Windows Forms Menus project. You need to add two toolbars to the form, so locate the ToolStrip control in the Toolbox and drag and drop it onto your form; it automatically aligns itself to the top of the form below the menu. Set the Name property to **tspMain**.

2. The default toolbar buttons will be fine for this project, so right-click the ToolStrip control on the form and select Insert Standard Items from the context menu to have the standard toolbar buttons added.

3. Next, add a second toolbar to the form in the same manner. It aligns itself below the first toolbar. Set its Name property to **tspFormatting** and its Visible property to **False**, because you don't want this toolbar to be shown by default. It will now be hidden on the form, but you can still access it on the bottom of the form.

4. You want to add three buttons to this toolbar (tspFormatting), so click the ellipsis button next to the Items property in the Properties window or right-click the ToolStrip control on the form and select Edit Items from the context menu.

    In the Items Collection Editor dialog, click the Add button to add the first button. Because you really won't be using these buttons, you can accept the default name and ToolTip text for these buttons. Ensure that the DisplayStyle property is set to Image, and then click the button next to the Image property.

    In the Select Resource dialog, click the Import button and browse to the location where you downloaded the Image Library. In the Open dialog, select AlignTableCellMiddleLeftJustHS.PNG and then click the Open button. Next, click the OK button in the Select Resource dialog to close it. Navigate the library by clicking the Archive folder, then the Actions folder, png_format, and finally Office and VS. Instead of browsing, you can always go to the main library folder and enter the filename in the search box.

5. In the Items Collection Editor dialog, click the Add button again to add the second button. Ensure that the DisplayStyle property is set to **Image** and then set the Image property to the **AlignTableCellMiddleCenterHS.png** file.

6. In the Items Collection Editor dialog, click the Add button again to add the next button. Ensure that the DisplayStyle property is set to **Image** and then set the Image property to the **AlignTableCellMiddleRightHS.png** file.

7. Click the OK button in the Items Collection Editor dialog to close it.

8. Add a Panel control from the Toolbox to your form and set its Dock property to **Fill**.

9. Add two TextBox controls to the Panel control and accept their default properties. Their location and size are not important, but they should be wide enough to contain text. Your completed form should look similar to the one shown in Figure 8-5. Notice that your second toolbar is not visible, because you set its Visible property to False.

If you run your project at this point you will see the menus, the main toolbar, and two text boxes. The formatting toolbar is not visible at this point because the Visible property is set to False.

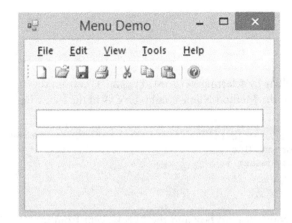

FIGURE 8-5

How It Works

You took a look at toolbars in Chapter 6, so review the Text Editor project for details on how the ToolStrip control works. The ToolStrip control, like the MenuStrip control, provides the Insert Standard Items context menu item, which does a lot of the grunt work for you by inserting the standard toolbar buttons, as was shown in Figure 8-5. This provides the most efficient means of having the standard toolbar buttons added to the ToolStrip control. You can, of course, rearrange the buttons that have been added and even add new buttons and delete existing buttons.

Because you set the Visible property to False for the tspFormatting ToolStrip control, that control does not take up any space on your form at design time after the control loses focus.

Coding Menus

Now that you have finally added all of your controls to the form, it's time to start writing some code to make these controls work. First, you have to add functionality to make the menus work. Then you add code to make some of the buttons on the main toolbar work.

TRY IT OUT Coding the File Menu

Next, you will put the code behind the menus so they actually do something. All the code in this chapter is in the folder Windows Forms Menus in the Zip file for this chapter.

1. Start by switching to the Code Editor for the form. In the Class Name combo box at the top of the Code Editor, select NewToolStripMenuItem and select the Click event in the Method Name combo box. Add the following bolded code to the Click event handler:

```
Private Sub NewToolStripMenuItem_Click(sender As Object,
    e As EventArgs) Handles NewToolStripMenuItem.Click
    'Clear the text boxes
    TextBox1.Text = String.Empty
```

```
        TextBox2.Text = String.Empty
        'Set focus to the first text box
        TextBox1.Focus()
    End Sub
```

2. Add the procedure for the New button on the toolbar by selecting `NewToolStripButton` from the Class Name combo box and the `Click` event from the Method Name combo box. Add the following bolded code to this procedure:

```
Private Sub NewToolStripButton_Click(sender As Object,
    e As EventArgs) Handles NewToolStripButton.Click
    'Call the NewToolStripMenuItem_Click procedure
    NewToolStripMenuItem_Click(sender, e)
End Sub
```

3. Select `ExitToolStripMenuItem` from the Class Name combo box and the `Click` event from the Method Name combo box and add the following bolded code to the procedure:

```
Private Sub ExitToolStripMenuItem_Click(sender As Object,
    e As EventArgs) Handles ExitToolStripMenuItem.Click
    'Close the form and end
    Me.Close()
End Sub
```

How It Works

To clear the text boxes on the form in the `NewToolStripMenuItem_Click` procedure, add the following code. All you are doing here is setting the `Text` property of the text boxes to an empty string. The next line of code sets the focus to the first text box by calling the `Focus` method of that text box:

```
'Clear the text boxes
TextBox1.Text = String.Empty
TextBox2.Text = String.Empty

'Set focus to the first text box
TextBox1.Focus()
```

When you click the New menu item under the File menu, the text boxes on the form are cleared of all text, and TextBox1 has the focus and is ready to accept text.

The New button on the toolbar should perform the same function, but you don't want to write the same code twice. You could put the text in the previous procedure in a separate procedure and call that procedure from both the `newToolStripMenuItem_Click` and `newToolStripButton_Click` procedures. Instead, you have the code in the `newToolStripMenuItem_Click` procedure and simply call that procedure from within the `newToolStripButton_Click` procedure. Because both procedures accept the same parameters, you simply pass the parameters received in this procedure to the procedure you are calling:

```
'Call the newToolStripMenuItem_Click procedure
newToolStripMenuItem_Click(sender, e)
```

Now you can click the New button on the toolbar or click the New menu item on the File menu and have the same results, clearing the text boxes on your form.

When you click the Exit menu item, you want the program to end. In the `exitToolStripMenuItem_Click` procedure, you added the following code. The `Me` keyword refers to the class where the code is executing, and in this case refers to the form class. The `Close` method closes the form, releases all resources, and ends the program:

```
'Close the form and end
Me.Close()
```

That takes care of the code for the File menu and its corresponding toolbar button. Now you can move on to the Edit menu and add the code for those menu items.

TRY IT OUT   **Coding the Edit Menu**

In this example, you add code to make the Edit menu and toolbar buttons work. All the code in this chapter is in the folder `Windows Forms Menus` in the Zip file for this chapter.

1.   The first menu item in the Edit menu is the Undo menu item. Select `UndoToolStripMenuItem` in the Class Name combo box and select the `Click` event in the Method Name combo box. Add the following bolded code to the `Click` event handler:

```
Private Sub UndoToolStripMenuItem_Click(sender As Object,
    e As EventArgs) Handles UndoToolStripMenuItem.Click
    'Undo the last operation
    If TypeOf Me.ActiveControl Is TextBox Then
        CType(Me.ActiveControl, TextBox).Undo()
    End If
End Sub
```

2.   The next menu item that you want to add code for is the Cut menu item. Select `CutToolStripMenuItem` in the Class Name combo box and the `Click` event in the Method Name combo box. Add the bolded code here:

```
Private Sub CutToolStripMenuItem_Click(sender As Object,
    e As EventArgs) Handles CutToolStripMenuItem.Click
    'Copy the text to the clipboard and clear the field
    If TypeOf Me.ActiveControl Is TextBox Then
        CType(Me.ActiveControl, TextBox).Cut()
    End If
End Sub
```

3.   You'll want the Cut button on the toolbar to call the code for the Cut menu item. Select `CutToolStripButton` in the Class Name combo box and the `Click` event in the Method Name combo box. Add the following bolded code:

```
Private Sub CutToolStripButton_Click(sender As Object,
    e As EventArgs) Handles CutToolStripButton.Click
    'Call the CutToolStripMenuItem_Click procedure
    CutToolStripMenuItem_Click(sender, e)
End Sub
```

4. The next menu item that you need to code is the Copy menu item. Select `CopyToolStripMenuItem` in the Class Name combo box and the `Click` event in the Method Name combo box and then add the following bolded code:

```
Private Sub CopyToolStripMenuItem_Click(sender As Object,
    e As EventArgs) Handles CopyToolStripMenuItem.Click
    'Copy the text to the clipboard
    If TypeOf Me.ActiveControl Is TextBox Then
        CType(Me.ActiveControl, TextBox).Copy()
    End If
End Sub
```

5. You want the Copy button on the toolbar to call the procedure you just added. Select `CopyToolStripButton` in the Class Name combo box and the `Click` event in the Method Name combo box and then add the following bolded code:

```
Private Sub CopyToolStripButton_Click(sender As Object,
    e As EventArgs) Handles CopyToolStripButton.Click
    'Call the CopyToolStripMenuItem_Click procedure
    CopyToolStripMenuItem_Click(sender, e)
End Sub
```

6. The Paste menu item is next, so select `PasteToolStripMenuItem` in the Class Name combo box and the `Click` event in the Method Name combo box. Add the following bolded code to the `Click` event handler:

```
Private Sub PasteToolStripMenuItem_Click(sender As Object,
    e As EventArgs) Handles PasteToolStripMenuItem.Click
    'Copy the text from the clipboard to the text box
    If TypeOf Me.ActiveControl Is TextBox Then
        CType(Me.ActiveControl, TextBox).Paste()
    End If
End Sub
```

7. The Paste toolbar button should execute the code in the `PasteToolStripMenuItem_Click` procedure. Select `PasteToolStripButton` in the Class Name combo box and the `Click` event in the Method Name combo box and add the following bolded code:

```
Private Sub PasteToolStripButton_Click(sender As Object,
    e As EventArgs) Handles PasteToolStripButton.Click
    'Call the PasteToolStripMenuItem_Click procedure
    PasteToolStripMenuItem_Click(sender, e)
End Sub
```

8. The last menu item under the Edit menu that you'll write code for is the Select All menu item. Select `SelectAllToolStripMenuItem` in the Class Name combo box and the `Click` event in the Method Name combo box and add the following bolded code:

```
Private Sub SelectAllToolStripMenuItem_Click(sender As Object,
    e As EventArgs) Handles SelectAllToolStripMenuItem.Click
    'Select all the text in the text box
    If TypeOf Me.ActiveControl Is TextBox Then
        CType(Me.ActiveControl, TextBox).SelectAll()
    End If
End Sub
```

How It Works

You added the code for the Edit menu starting with the Undo menu item. Because you have two text boxes on your form, you need a way to determine which text box you are dealing with or a generic way of handling an undo operation for both text boxes. In this example, you go with the latter option and provide a generic way to handle both text boxes.

You do this by first determining whether the active control you are dealing with is a TextBox control. The ActiveControl property of the Form class returns a reference to the active control on the form, the control that has focus.

Then you want to check the active control to see if it is a TextBox control. This is done using the TypeOf operator. This operator compares an object reference to a data type, and in the following code you are comparing the object reference returned in the ActiveControl property to a data type of TextBox.

When you know you are dealing with a TextBox control, you use the CType function to convert the object contained in the ActiveControl property to a TextBox control. This exposes the properties and methods of the TextBox control in IntelliSense, allowing you to choose the Undo method:

```
If TypeOf Me.ActiveControl Is TextBox Then
        CType(Me.ActiveControl, TextBox).Undo()
    End If
```

The menu and toolbar are never set as the active control. This enables you to use the menus and toolbar buttons and always reference the active control.

> **NOTE** *The ActiveControl property works fine in this small example because you are dealing with only two text boxes. However, in a real-world application, you would need to test the active control to see whether it supports the method you were using (for example, Undo).*
>
> *You use the same logic for the rest of the menu item procedures as the Undo menu item, checking the type of active control to see whether it is a TextBox control. Then you call the appropriate method on the TextBox control to cut, copy, paste, and select all text.*

Coding the View Menu and Toolbars

Now that you have added the code to make the Edit menu items and the corresponding toolbar buttons functional, the next step is to make the menu items under the View menu functional.

TRY IT OUT Coding the View Menu

Next, add the code to hide and show the toolbars. All the code in this chapter is in the folder Windows Forms Menus in the Zip file for this chapter.

1. Return to the Code Editor in the Windows Forms Menus project and in the Class Name combo box, select `MainToolStripMenuItem`. In the Method Name combo box, select the `Click` event. Add the following bolded code to the `Click` event handler:

```
Private Sub MainToolStripMenuItem_Click(sender As Object,
    e As EventArgs) Handles MainToolStripMenuItem.Click
    'Toggle the visibility of the Main toolbar
    'based on the menu item's Checked property
    If MainToolStripMenuItem.Checked Then
        tspMain.Visible = True
    Else
        tspMain.Visible = False
    End If
End Sub
```

2. You need to add the same type of code that you just added to the Formatting submenu item. Select `FormattingToolStripMenuItem` in the Class Name combo box and the `Click` event in the Method Name combo box and add the following bolded code:

```
Private Sub FormattingToolStripMenuItem_Click(sender As Object,
    e As EventArgs) Handles FormattingToolStripMenuItem.Click
    'Toggle the visibility of the Formatting toolbar
    'based on the menu item's Checked property
    If FormattingToolStripMenuItem.Checked Then
        tspFormatting.Visible = True
    Else
        tspFormatting.Visible = False
    End If
End Sub
```

How It Works

When the Main submenu item under the View menu item is clicked, the submenu item either displays a check mark or removes it based on the current state of the `Checked` property of the submenu item. You add code in the `Click` event of this submenu item to either hide or show the Main toolbar by setting its `Visible` property to **True** or **False**:

```
'Toggle the visibility of the Main toolbar
'based on this menu item's Checked property
If MainToolStripMenuItem.Checked Then
    tspMain.Visible = True
Else
    tspMain.Visible = False
End If
```

The same principle works for the Formatting submenu item, and its code is very similar to that of the Main submenu item:

```
'Toggle the visibility of the Formatting toolbar
'based on this menu item's Checked property
If FormattingToolStripMenuItem.Checked Then
    tspFormatting.Visible = True
Else
```

```
        tspFormatting.Visible = False
    End If
```

Testing Your Code

As your applications become more complex, testing your code becomes increasingly important. The more errors that you find and fix during your testing, the better able you will be to implement an application that is both stable and reliable for your users. This translates into satisfied users and earns you a good reputation for delivering a quality product.

You need to test not only the functionality of your application, but also various scenarios that a user might encounter or perform. For example, suppose you have a database application that gathers user input from a form and inserts it into a database. A good application validates all user input before trying to insert the data into the database, and a good test plan tries to break the data validation code. This ensures that your validation code handles all possible scenarios and functions properly.

TRY IT OUT Testing Your Code

You can treat this Try It Out as your test plan. Follow these steps to test your code. All the code in this chapter is in the folder Windows Forms Menus in the Zip file for this chapter.

1. It's time to test your code. Click the Run toolbar button. When your form loads, the only toolbar that you should see is the main toolbar, as shown in Figure 8-6.

FIGURE 8-6

2. Click the View menu and then click the Toolbars menu item. Note that the Main submenu item is selected and the main toolbar is visible. Go ahead and click the Formatting submenu item. The Formatting toolbar is displayed along with the main toolbar.

   Note also that the controls on your form shifted down when the Formatting toolbar was displayed. This happened because you placed a Panel control on your form, set its Dock property to **Fill,** and then placed your TextBox controls on the Panel control. Doing this allows the controls on your form to be repositioned, either to take up the space when a toolbar is hidden or to make room for the toolbar when it is shown; much like the behavior in Microsoft Outlook or Visual Studio 2015.

3. If you click the View menu again and then click the Toolbars menu item, you will see that both the Main and Formatting submenu items are checked. The selected submenu items indicate that the toolbar is visible, and an unchecked submenu item indicates that the toolbar is not visible.

4. Now test the functionality of the Edit menu. Click in the first text box and type some text. Then click the Edit menu and select the Select All menu item. Once you select the Select All menu item, the text in the text box is highlighted.

5. You now want to copy the text in the first text box while the text is highlighted. Hover your mouse over the Copy button on the toolbar to view the ToolTip. Now either click the Copy button on the toolbar or select the Edit ➪ Copy menu item.

   Place your cursor in the second text box and then either click the Paste button on the toolbar or select Edit ➪ Paste. The text is pasted into the second text box, as shown in Figure 8-7.

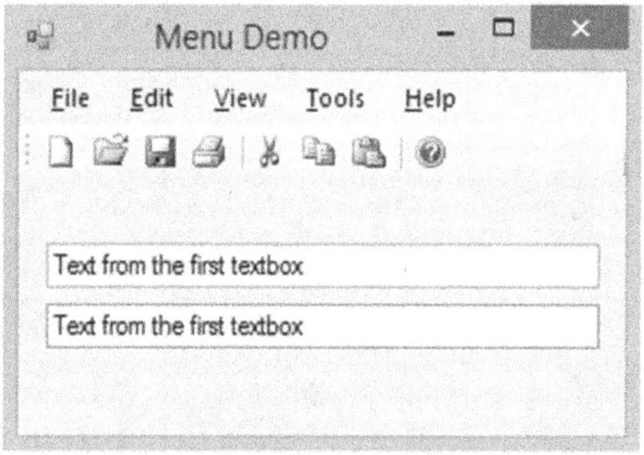

FIGURE 8-7

6. Click the first text box and then click Edit ➪ Undo. Note that the changes you made to the first text box have been undone. You might have expected that the text in the second text box would be removed, but Windows keeps track of the cut, copy, and paste operations for each control individually, so there's nothing you need to code to make this happen.

7. The last item on the Edit menu to test is the Cut menu item. Type some more text in the first text box, and then highlight the text in the first text box by clicking the Edit menu and selecting the Select All menu item. Then either click the Cut icon on the toolbar or select Edit ⇨ Cut. The text is copied to the Clipboard and is then removed from the text box.

Place your cursor in the second text box at the end of the text there. Then paste the text in this text box using the Paste shortcut key, Ctrl+V. The text has been placed at the end of the existing text in the text box. This is how Windows' cut, copy, and paste operations work, and, as you can see, there was very little code required to implement this functionality in your program.

8. Now click the File menu and choose the New menu item. The text in the text boxes is cleared. The only menu item left to test is the Exit menu item under the File menu.

9. Before testing the Exit menu item, take a quick look at context menus. Type some text in one of the text boxes. Now, right-click in that text box, and you will see a context menu pop up, similar to what is shown in Figure 8-8. Notice that this context menu appeared automatically; you didn't need to add any code to accomplish this. This is a feature of the Windows operating system, and Visual Studio 2015 provides a way to override the default context menus, as you will see in the next section.

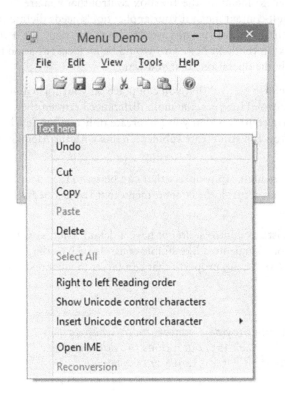

FIGURE 8-8

10. To test the last bit of functionality of your program, select File ⇨ Exit, and your program ends.

How It Works

This example showed you how to walk through a test plan to test your code. You should create test plans similar to this to be followed during testing of your code.

CONTEXT MENUS

Context menus are menus that pop up when a user clicks the right mouse button on a control or window. They provide users with quick access to the most commonly used commands for the control that they are working with. As you just saw in the preceding section, the context menu that appeared provides you with a way to manage the text in a text box.

Context menus are customized for the control that you are working with; and in more complex applications, such as Visual Studio 2015 or Microsoft Word, they provide quick access to the commands for the task being performed.

You saw that Windows provides a default context menu for the TextBox control that you are working with, and you can override the default context menu if your application's needs dictate that. For example, suppose you have an application in which you want users to be able to copy the text in a text box but not actually cut or paste text in that text box. This would be an ideal situation to provide your own context menu to allow only the operations that you want.

Visual Studio 2015 provides a ContextMenuStrip control that you can place on your form and customize, just as you did the MenuStrip control. However, the main difference between the MenuStrip control and the ContextMenuStrip control is that you can create only one top-level menu with the ContextMenuStrip control. You can still create submenu items with the MenuStrip if needed.

Most controls in the Toolbox have a `ContextMenuStrip` property that can be set to the context menu that you define. When you right-click that control, the context menu that you defined is displayed instead of the default context menu.

Some controls, such as the ComboBox and ListBox controls, do not have a default context menu because they contain a collection of items, not a single item like simple controls such as the TextBox. They do, however, have a `ContextMenuStrip` property that can be set to a context menu that you define.

> **NOTE** *The ComboBox control does not provide a context menu when its* `DropDownStyle` *property is set to* `DropDownList`, *but it does provide a context menu when its* `DropDownStyle` *property is set to* `Simple` *or* `DropDown`.

Creating Context Menus

Now that you know what context menus are, you are ready to learn how to create and use them in your Visual Basic 2015 applications.

TRY IT OUT Creating Context Menus

In this Try It Out, you expand the code from the previous Try It Out example by adding a context menu to work with your text boxes. You add one context menu and use it for both text boxes. You could just as easily create two context menus, one for each text box, and have the context menus perform different functions. All the code in this chapter is in the folder Windows Forms Menus in the Zip file for this chapter.

1. Return to the Forms Designer in your Windows Forms Menus project and then click the Toolbox to locate the ContextMenuStrip control. Drag and drop it onto your form, where it is added at the bottom of the development environment just as the MenuStrip control was.

2. In the Properties window, click the button next to the Items property. You'll be adding five menu items in your context menu in the next several steps.

3. Click the Add button in the Items Collection Editor dialog to add the first menu item and set the Name property to **ContextUndoToolStripMenuItem**. Click the ellipsis button next to the Image property and then click the Import button in the Select Resource dialog. Locate an Undo bitmap or portable network graphics (png) file on your computer and click the Open button. Click OK in the Select Resource dialog to close it and to return to the Items Collection Editor. Locate the Text property and set it to **Undo**.

4. You want to add a separator between the Undo menu item and the next menu item. Select Separator in the List combo box in the Items Collection Editor dialog and then click the Add button. Accept all default properties for the separator.

5. Select MenuItem in the combo box and click the Add button again to add the next menu item. Set the Name property to **ContextCutToolStripMenuItem**. Click the button next to the Image property and, in the Select Resource dialog, locate a Cut bitmap or png file. Finally, set the Text property to **Cut**.

6. Click the Add button again to add the next menu item and set the Name property to **ContextCopyToolStripMenuItem**. Click the ellipsis button next to the Image property and, in the Select Resource dialog, locate a Copy bitmap or icon file. Finally, set the Text property to **Copy**.

7. Click the Add button once again to add the next menu item and set the Name property to **ContextPasteToolStripMenuItem**. Click the ellipsis button next to the Image property and in the Select Resource dialog, import a file to use for Paste. Then set the Text property to **Paste**.

8. Now you want to add a separator between the Paste menu item and the next menu item. Select Separator in the combo box in the Items Collection Editor dialog and then click the Add button. Again, accept all default properties for the separator.

9. Select MenuItem in the combo box and click the Add button to add the final menu item. Set the Name property to **ContextSelectAllToolStripMenuItem** and the Text property to **Select All**. There is no image for this menu item. Finally, click OK in the Items Collection Editor dialog to close it.

10. When you are done, click any part of the form to make the context menu disappear. (You can always make it reappear by clicking the ContextMenuStrip control at the bottom of the development environment.)

11. Click the first text box on your form. In the Properties window, select ContextMenuStrip in the drop-down list for the ContextMenuStrip property. Repeat the same action for the second text box to assign a context menu in the ContextMenuStrip property.

12. Test your context menu for look and feel. At this point, you haven't added any code to it, but you can ensure that it looks visually correct. Run the application and then right-click in the first text box; you will see the context menu that you have just added, shown in Figure 8-9. The same context menu appears if you also right-click in the second text box.

13. Stop your program and switch to the Code Editor for your form so that you can add the code for the context menus. The first procedure that you want to add is that for the Undo context menu item. Select ContextUndoToolStripMenuItem in the Class Name combo box and the Click event in the Method Name combo box and add the following bolded code:

```
Private Sub ContextUndoToolStripMenuItem_Click(sender As Object,
    e As EventArgs) Handles ContextUndoToolStripMenuItem.Click
    'Call the UndoToolStripMenuItem_Click procedure
    UndoToolStripMenuItem_Click(sender, e)
End Sub
```

14. Select ContextCutToolStripMenuItem in the Class Name combo box and the Click event in the Method Name combo box. Add the following bolded code to the Click event handler:

```
Private Sub ContextCutToolStripMenuItem_Click(sender As Object,
    e As EventArgs) Handles ContextCutToolStripMenuItem.Click
    'Call the CutToolStripMenuItem_Click procedure
    CutToolStripMenuItem_Click(sender, e)
End Sub
```

15. For the Copy context menu item, select ContextCopyToolStripMenuItem in the Class Name combo box and the Click event in the Method Name combo box and then add the following bolded code:

```
Private Sub ContextCopyToolStripMenuItem_Click(sender As Object,
    e As EventArgs) Handles ContextCopyToolStripMenuItem.Click
    'Call the CopyToolStripMenuItem_Click procedure
    CopyToolStripMenuItem_Click(sender, e)
End Sub
```

16. Select ContextPasteToolStripMenuItem in the Class Name combo box for the Paste context menu item and the Click event in the Method Name combo box. Then add the following bolded code:

```
Private Sub ContextPasteToolStripMenuItem_Click(sender As Object,
    e As EventArgs) Handles ContextPasteToolStripMenuItem.Click
    'Call the PasteToolStripMenuItem_Click procedure
    PasteToolStripMenuItem_Click(sender, e)
End Sub
```

17. The last procedure that you need to perform is for the Select All context menu item. Select ContextSelectAllToolStripMenuItem in the Class Name combo box and the Click event in the Method Name combo box and then add the following bolded code:

```
Private Sub ContextSelectAllToolStripMenuItem_Click(sender As Object,
    e As EventArgs) _
    Handles ContextSelectAllToolStripMenuItem.Click
    'Call the SelectAllToolStripMenuItem_Click procedure
    SelectAllToolStripMenuItem_Click(sender, e)
End Sub
```

18. That's all the code that you need to add to implement your own context menu. Pretty simple, no? Now run your project to see your context menu in action and test it (see Figure 8-9). You can test the context menu by clicking each of the context menu items shown. They perform the same functions as their counterparts in the toolbar and Edit menu.

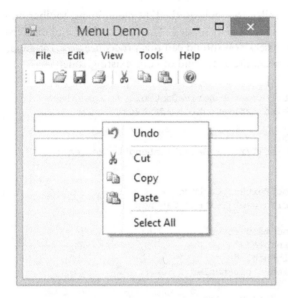

FIGURE 8-9

Do you see the difference in your context menu from the one shown in Figure 8-8? Your context menu has a cleaner look and shows the icons for the various menu items. There is one other subtle difference: Your menu items are all enabled, although some of them shouldn't be. You'll rectify this in the next Try It Out.

How It Works

The ContextMenuStrip works in the same manner as the MenuStrip, and you should have been able to follow along and create a context menu with ease. You may have noticed that you use a prefix of Context for your context menu names in this exercise. This distinguishes these menu items as context menu items, and groups these menu items in the Class Name combo box in the Code Editor.

The code you added here was a no-brainer because you have already written the code to perform undo, cut, copy, paste, and select all operations. In this exercise, you merely call the corresponding menu item procedures in your Click event handlers for the context menu items.

Enabling and Disabling Menu Items and Toolbar Buttons

Now that you have implemented a context menu and have it functioning, you are ready to write some code to complete the functionality in your application.

Enabling and Disabling Menu Items and Toolbar Buttons

In this Try It Out, you implement the necessary code to enable and disable menu items, context menu items, and toolbar buttons. All the code in this chapter is in the folder `Windows Forms Menus` in the Zip file for this chapter.

1. You need to create a procedure that can be called to toggle all the Edit menu items, toolbar buttons, and context menu items, enabling and disabling them as needed. They are enabled and disabled based upon what should be available to the user. You should call this procedure `ToggleMenus`, so stop your program and add the following procedure at the end of your existing code:

```
Private Sub ToggleMenus()
    'Declare a TextBox object and set it to the ActiveControl
    Dim objTextBox As TextBox = CType(Me.ActiveControl, TextBox)

    'Declare and set a Boolean variable
    Dim blnEnabled As Boolean = CType(objTextBox.SelectionLength, Boolean)

    'Toggle the Undo menu items
    UndoToolStripMenuItem.Enabled = objTextBox.CanUndo
    ContextUndoToolStripMenuItem.Enabled = objTextBox.CanUndo

    'Toggle the Cut toolbar button and menu items
    CutToolStripButton.Enabled = blnEnabled
    CutToolStripMenuItem.Enabled = blnEnabled
    ContextCutToolStripMenuItem.Enabled = blnEnabled

    'Toggle the Copy toolbar button and menu items
    CopyToolStripButton.Enabled = blnEnabled
    CopyToolStripMenuItem.Enabled = blnEnabled
    ContextCopyToolStripMenuItem.Enabled = blnEnabled

    'Reset the blnEnabled variable
    blnEnabled = My.Computer.Clipboard.ContainsText

    'Toggle the Paste toolbar button and menu items
    PasteToolStripButton.Enabled = blnEnabled
    PasteToolStripMenuItem.Enabled = blnEnabled
    ContextPasteToolStripMenuItem.Enabled = blnEnabled

    'Reset the blnEnabled variable
    If objTextBox.SelectionLength < objTextBox.TextLength Then
        blnEnabled = True
    Else
        blnEnabled = False
    End If

    'Toggle the Select All menu items
    SelectAllToolStripMenuItem.Enabled = blnEnabled
    ContextSelectAllToolStripMenuItem.Enabled = blnEnabled
End Sub
```

That's it! All of that code will toggle the Edit menu items, the context menu items, and the toolbar buttons. Now you need to figure out when and where to call this procedure.

2. Return to the Forms Designer and locate the Timer control in the Toolbox. Drag this control onto your form, where it is positioned at the bottom of the IDE. In the Properties window, set the `Enabled` property to **True** and the `Interval` property to **250**.

3. Double-click the Timer control at the bottom of the Integrated Development Environment (IDE) to create the `Tick` event handler and add this code:

```
Private Sub Timer1_Tick(sender As Object,
     e As EventArgs) Handles Timer1.Tick
    'Toggle toolbar and menu items
    ToggleMenus()
End Sub
```

4. Run your project again. After the form has been displayed, click in the first text box and enter some text. Then, right-click in the text box to display your context menu. Now the context menu has the appropriate menu items enabled, as shown in Figure 8-10, as do the toolbar buttons and Edit menu items.

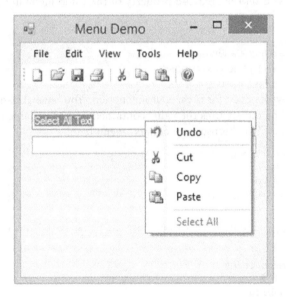

FIGURE 8-10

How It Works

The first thing that you do in the `ToggleMenus` procedure is declare an object and set it equal to the active TextBox control. You saw the `ActiveControl` property in the "Coding the Edit Menu" Try It Out exercise:

```
'Declare a TextBox object and set it to the ActiveControl
Dim objTextBox As TextBox = CType(Me.ActiveControl, TextBox)
```

Next you declare a `Boolean` variable that will be used to determine whether a property should set to `True` or `False`, and initially set it based on the `SelectionLength` property of the active text box. The `SelectionLength` property returns the number of characters selected in a text box. You can use this number to act as a `True` or `False` value because a value of `False` in Visual Basic 2015 is zero and a value of `True` is one. Because the value of `False` is always evaluated first, any number other than zero evaluates to `True`.

In order to make this happen, you need to convert the `SelectionLength` property from an `Integer` data type to a `Boolean` data type using the `CType` function, as shown here:

```
'Declare and set a Boolean variable
Dim blnEnabled As Boolean = CType(objTextBox.SelectionLength, Boolean)
```

The first Edit menu item is Undo, so you start with that one. The `TextBox` class has a property called `CanUndo`, which returns a `True` or `False` value indicating whether or not the last operation performed in the text box can be undone.

You use the `CanUndo` property to set the `Enabled` property of the Edit menu item. The `Enabled` property is set using a `Boolean` value, which works out great because the `CanUndo` property returns a `Boolean` value. The following code shows how you set the `Enabled` property of the Undo menu item and context menu item:

```
'Toggle the Undo menu items
undoToolStripMenuItem.Enabled = objTextBox.CanUndo
contextUndoToolStripMenuItem.Enabled = objTextBox.CanUndo
```

The next menu item in the Edit menu that you wrote code for is the Cut menu item. You have already set the `blnEnabled` variable, so the following code merely uses the value contained in that variable to set the `Enabled` property of the Cut menu item, toolbar button, and context menu item:

```
'Toggle the Cut toolbar button and menu items
CutToolStripButton.Enabled = blnEnabled
CutToolStripMenuItem.Enabled = blnEnabled
ContextCutToolStripMenuItem.Enabled = blnEnabled
```

The next menu item in the Edit menu is the Copy menu item. Again, you use the `blnEnabled` variable to set the `Enabled` property appropriately:

```
'Toggle the Copy toolbar button and menu items
CopyToolStripButton.Enabled = blnEnabled
CopyToolStripMenuItem.Enabled = blnEnabled
ContextCopyToolStripMenuItem.Enabled = blnEnabled
```

The next menu item in the Edit menu is the Paste menu item. Setting the `Enabled` property of this menu item requires a little more work. You query the `ContainsText` property of the `My.Computer` `.Clipboard` object to receive a `Boolean` value indicating whether the Clipboard contains any text. You then set that `Boolean` value in the `blnEnabled` variable, which is used to set the `Enabled` property of the Paste toolbar button, Paste menu item, and context menu item, as shown in the following code:

```
'Reset the blnEnabled variable
blnEnabled = My.Computer.Clipboard.ContainsText
'Toggle the Paste toolbar button and menu items
PasteToolStripButton.Enabled = blnEnabled
PasteToolStripMenuItem.Enabled = blnEnabled
ContextPasteToolStripMenuItem.Enabled = blnEnabled
```

The last Edit menu item is the Select All menu item. You again use the `SelectionLength` property to determine whether any or all text has been selected. If the `SelectionLength` property is less than the `TextLength` property, you set the `blnEnabled` variable to **True** because not all text in the text box has been selected; otherwise, you set it to **False**. After the `blnEnabled` variable has been appropriately set, you use that variable to set the `Enabled` property of the Select All menu item and context menu item:

```
'Reset the blnEnabled variable
If objTextBox.SelectionLength < objTextBox.TextLength Then
    blnEnabled = True
Else
    blnEnabled = False
End If

'Toggle the Select All menu items
SelectAllToolStripMenuItem.Enabled = blnEnabled
ContextSelectAllToolStripMenuItem.Enabled = blnEnabled
```

To enable and disable the menu items, context menu items, and toolbar buttons, you have to call the `ToggleMenus` procedure. The place to do this is in the `Tick` event of the Timer control that you placed on your form. The `Tick` event is fired using the `Interval` property that you set to a value of 250. The `Interval` property is expressed in milliseconds, where 1,000 milliseconds equals 1 second—so basically the `Tick` event of the Timer control is fired every quarter-second:

```
Private Sub Timer1_Tick(sender As Object,
    e As EventArgs) Handles Timer1.Tick

    'Toggle toolbar and menu items
    ToggleMenus()
End Sub
```

> **NOTE** *This example shows you how to use the timer control in another way. Using the timer control to call other methods is not always the best place. You can call the* `ToggleMenus` *events when the user clicks other objects as well.*

SUMMARY

This chapter explained how to implement menus, menu items, and submenu items. You also learned how to implement multiple toolbars, although that was not the focus of the chapter. Through practical hands-on exercises, you have seen how to create menus, menu items, and submenu items. You have also seen how to add access keys, shortcut keys, and images to these menu items.

Because you used the Edit menu in the Try It Outs, you have also seen how easy it is to implement basic editing techniques in your application by using the properties of the TextBox control and the `Clipboard` object. Now you know how easy it is to provide this functionality to your users—something users have come to expect in every good Windows application.

You also explored how to create and implement context menus and how to override the default context menus provided by Windows. Because you already coded the procedure to implement undo, cut, copy, and paste operations, you simply reused that code in your context menus.

Now that you have completed this chapter, you should know how to do the following:

➤ Add a MenuStrip control to your form and add menus, menu items, and submenu items.

➤ Customize the menu items with a check mark.

➤ Add access keys and shortcut keys to your menu items.

➤ Add a ContextMenuStrip control to your form and add menu items.

➤ Use the properties of the TextBox control to toggle the Enabled property of menu items.

EXERCISES

1. How do you add the commonly used menus and toolbars to either a MenuStrip or ToolStrip control?

2. How do you add a custom context menu to a TextBox control?

3. How do you add a shortcut or accelerator to a menu item, such as Alt+F?

4. How do you add a shortcut to a menu item, such as Ctrl+C?

▶ **WHAT YOU HAVE LEARNED IN THIS CHAPTER**

TOPIC	CONCEPTS
Work with menus and submenus	Add images, access keys, shortcut keys, and checkboxes to menus. When needed, you should disable menu items that cannot be used.
Add toolbars	Add custom buttons and images or choose standard items to have common buttons inserted for you.
Use context menus	Add a custom context menu to a control.

Debugging and Error Handling

WHAT YOU WILL LEARN IN THIS CHAPTER:

➤   How to correct the major types of errors you may encounter

➤   How to debug a program

➤   How to implement error handling in a program

WROX.COM CODE DOWNLOADS FOR THIS CHAPTER

The wrox.com code downloads for this chapter are found at www.wrox.com/begvisualbasic2015 on the Download Code tab. The code is in the 311813 c09.zip download and individually named according to the names given throughout the chapter.

Debugging is an essential part of any development project because it helps you find errors both in your code and in your logic. Visual Studio 2015 has a sophisticated debugger built right into the development environment. This debugger is the same for all languages that Visual Studio 2015 supports. When you have mastered debugging in one language, you can debug in any language that you can write in Visual Studio 2015.

No matter how good your code is, there are always going to be some unexpected circumstances that will cause your code to fail. If you do not anticipate and handle errors, your users will see a default error message about an unhandled exception, which is provided by the Common Language Runtime package. This is not a user-friendly message and usually does not clearly inform the user about what is going on or how to correct it.

This is where error handling comes in. Visual Studio 2015 also provides common structured error-handling functions that are used across all languages. These functions enable you to test a block of code and catch any errors that may occur. If an error does occur, you can display your own user-friendly message that informs the user of what happened and how to correct it, or you can simply handle the error and continue processing.

This chapter looks at some of the debugging features available in Visual Studio 2015 and provides a walkthrough of debugging a program. You examine how to set breakpoints in your code to stop execution at any given point, how to watch the value of a variable change, and how to control the number of times a loop can execute before stopping. All of these can help you determine just what is going on inside your code. Finally, this chapter takes a look at the structured error-handling functions provided by Visual Studio 2015.

MAJOR ERROR TYPES

Error types can be broken down into three major categories: syntax, execution, and logic. This section shows you the important differences among these three types of errors and how to correct them.

> **NOTE** Knowing what type of errors are possible and how to correct them will significantly speed up the development process. Of course, sometimes you just can't find the error on your own. Don't waste too much time trying to find errors in your code by yourself in these situations. Coming back to a nagging problem after a short coffee break can often help you crack it. Otherwise, ask a colleague to have a look at your code with you; two pairs of eyes are often better than one in these cases.

Syntax Errors

Syntax errors, the easiest type of errors to spot and fix, occur when the code you have written cannot be understood by the compiler because instructions are incomplete, supplied in unexpected order, or cannot be processed at all. An example of this would be declaring a variable of one name and misspelling this name in your code when you set or query the variable. This is hard to find if you turn off Option Explicit.

The development environment in Visual Studio 2015 has a very sophisticated syntax-checking mechanism, making it hard, but not impossible, to have syntax errors in your code. It provides instant syntax checking of variables and objects and lets you know immediately when you have a syntax error.

Suppose you try to set a variable that is not declared in a procedure. Visual Studio 2015 underlines the variable with a red wavy line, indicating that the declaration is in error as shown in Figure 9-1.

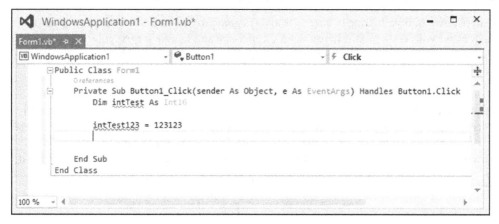

FIGURE 9-1

If the integrated development environment (IDE) can automatically correct the syntax error, you'll see a little yellow light bulb when you hover over the red underline or have your cursor on that line of code, as shown in Figure 9-2 (minus the color), indicating that the IDE has potential fixes available for this syntax error. This is a feature of Visual Studio 2015 that provides error-correction options that the IDE will suggest to correct the error using quick actions and a light bulb. Green underlines indicate a warning.

When you hover your mouse over the code in error, you'll receive a ToolTip, telling you what the error is, and a small gray box with a red circle and a white exclamation point. If you then move your mouse into the gray box, a down arrow appears, as shown in Figure 9-2, to let you know that a dialog box is available with some suggested error-correction options.

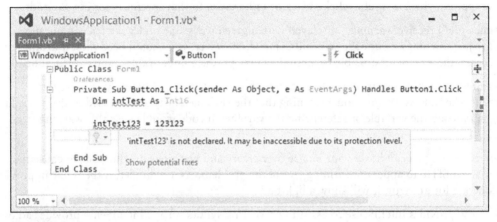

FIGURE 9-2

Clicking the down arrow or pressing Shift+Alt+F10 causes the Error Correction Options dialog to appear, as shown in Figure 9-3. This dialog presents one or more options for correcting the error.

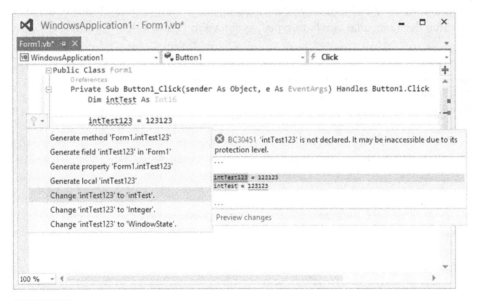

FIGURE 9-3

Note that the dialog box shows you how your code can be corrected: by generating things that would represent your undeclared item or by changing the name. In this case, you would change the name to the correct variable name intTest and click this link to apply the fix to your code.

Another option available for reviewing all the errors in your code is the Error List window. This window displays a grid with all the errors' descriptions, the files they exist in, and the line numbers and column numbers of the error. If your solution contains multiple projects, it also displays the project in which each error occurs.

You can access the Error List by clicking the Error List tab at the bottom of the IDE if it is already displayed in the IDE or by clicking the Error List item on the View menu. When the Error List window appears, you can double-click any error to be taken to that specific error in your code.

Sometimes you'll receive warnings, displayed with a green wavy line under the code in question. These are just warnings; your code will still compile. However, you should heed these warnings and try to correct these errors if possible because they may produce undesirable results at run time.

For example, a warning occurs in the line of code shown in Figure 9-3 before you make the correction. The IDE would give you a warning that the variable intTest is unused in the procedure. Simply initializing the variable or referencing the variable in code would cause this warning to go away.

Keep in mind that you can hover your mouse over errors and warnings in your code to cause the appropriate ToolTip to appear, informing you of the problem. As a reminder, if the IDE can provide a quick action for an error, it will show a lightbulb.

The IDE also provides IntelliSense to assist in preventing syntax errors. IntelliSense provides a host of features such as providing a drop-down list of members for classes, structures, and namespaces, as shown in Figure 9-4. This enables you to choose the correct member for the class, structure, or namespace that you are working with. It also provides ToolTip information for the selected member or method, also shown in Figure 9-4. IntelliSense initially displays a list of all members for the object being worked with; and as soon as you start typing one or more letters, the list of members is shortened to match the letters that you have typed, as shown in Figure 9-4.

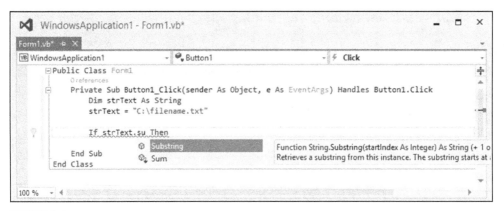

FIGURE 9-4

These IntelliSense features provide two major benefits. First, you do not have to remember all the available members for the class. You simply scroll through the list to find the member that you want to work with, or you type the first letter or two of the member to see a list reduced to the relevant members. To select the member in the list that you want to work with, you press the Tab or Enter key or double-click the member. Second, the features help you prevent syntax errors because you are less likely to misspell member names or try to use members that do not exist in the given class.

Another great feature of IntelliSense is that it provides a parameter list for the method you are working with. IntelliSense lists the number, names, and types of the parameters required by the function, as shown in Figure 9-4. This is also a timesaver because you do not have to remember the required parameters for every class member that you work with, or indeed search the product documentation for what you need.

If the method is overloaded—that is, there are several methods with the same name but different parameters—the ToolTip indicates this, as shown in Figure 9-4 with the text "(+ 1 overloads)." Also, when you start to work with the member, a pop-up list enables you to scroll through the different overloaded methods, as shown in Figure 9-5 for the Substring method of the String class, by simply clicking the up and down arrows to view the different overloaded methods.

FIGURE 9-5

Another IntelliSense list appears for the parameter you are working with, and this large list of all classes and members is also reduced to only those that might be relevant after you start typing one or more letters, as indicated in Figure 9-5. In this case, I started typing the letters **my** to have the list of available classes and namespaces reduced to only those that begin with the letters my.

Plenty of built-in features in the development environment can help prevent syntax errors. All you need to do is be aware of these features and take advantage of them to help prevent syntax errors in your code.

Execution Errors

Execution errors (or *runtime errors*) occur while your program is executing. These errors are often caused because something outside of the application, such as a user, database, or hard disk, does not behave as expected. In .NET, you will read about error handling or exception handling. If you talk to a programmer who has not worked in prior languages, they will use the term exception versus error. For programmers who have worked in earlier versions of VB, they will likely use error versus exception. You should treat them as the same. In this chapter, you will see both used.

Developers need to anticipate the possibility of execution errors and build appropriate error-handling logic. Implementing the appropriate error handling does not prevent execution errors, but it does enable you to handle them by either gracefully shutting down your application or bypassing the code that failed and giving the user the opportunity to perform that action again. Error handling is covered later in this chapter.

One way to prevent execution errors is to anticipate the error before it occurs, and then use error handling to trap and handle it. You must also thoroughly test your code before deploying it.

Most execution errors can be found while you are testing your code in the development environment. This enables you to handle the errors and debug your code at the same time. You can then see what type of errors may occur and implement the appropriate error-handling logic. Debugging, whereby you find and handle any execution errors that may crop up, is covered later in the "Debugging" section.

Logic Errors

Logic errors (or *semantic errors*) lead to unexpected or unwanted results because you did not fully understand what the code you were writing would do. A common logic error is an infinite loop:

```
Private Sub PerformLoopExample()
      Dim intIndex As Integer
      Do While intIndex < 10
          ..perform some logic
      Loop
   End Sub
```

If the code inside the loop does not set `intIndex` to `10` or above, this loop just keeps going forever. This is a very simple example, but even experienced developers find themselves writing and executing loops whose exit condition can never be satisfied.

Logic errors can be the most difficult to find and troubleshoot, because it is very difficult to be sure that your program is completely free of them.

Another type of logic error occurs when a comparison fails to give the result you expect. Say you made a comparison between a string variable, set by your code from a database field or from the text in a file, and the text entered by the user. You do not want the comparison to be case sensitive, so you might write code like this:

```
If strFileName = txtInput.Text Then
      ..perform some logic
    End If
```

However, if `strFileName` is set to `Index.HTML` and `txtInput.Text` is set to `index.html`, the comparison fails. One way to prevent this logic error is to convert both fields being compared to either uppercase or lowercase. This way, the results of the comparison would be `True` if the user entered the same text as that contained in the variable, even if the case were different. The next code fragment shows how you can accomplish this:

```
If strFileName.ToUpper = txtInput.Text.ToUpper Then
    ..perform some logic
End If
```

The `ToUpper` method of the `String` class converts the characters in the string to all uppercase and returns the converted results. Because the `Text` property of a text box is also a string, you can use the same method to convert the text to all uppercase. This would make the comparison in the previous example equal.

An alternative to using either the `ToUpper` or `ToLower` methods of the `String` class is to use the `Compare` method of the `String` class, as shown in the next example. This enables you to compare the two strings while ignoring the case of the strings. This is covered in Chapter 4.

```
If String.Compare(strFileName, txtInput.Text, True) Then
    ..perform some logic
End If
```

> **NOTE** Because logic errors are the hardest errors to troubleshoot and can cause applications to fail or give unexpected and unwanted results, you must check the logic carefully as you code and try to plan for all possible errors that may be encountered by a user. As you become more experienced, you will encounter and learn from the common errors that you and your users make.

One of the best ways to identify and fix logic errors is to use the debugging features of Visual Studio 2015. Using these features, you can find loops that execute too many times or comparisons that do not provide the expected result.

DEBUGGING

Debugging code is a part of life—even experienced developers make mistakes and need to debug their code. Knowing how to efficiently debug your code can make the difference between enjoying your job as a developer and hating it.

In the following sections, you'll create and debug a sample project while learning about the Exception Assistant, breakpoints, and how to step through your code and use the Watch, Autos, and Locals windows to examine variables and objects.

Creating a Sample Project

In this section, you take a look at some of the built-in debugging features in the Visual Studio 2015 development environment through various Try It Out exercises. You write a simple program and learn how to use the most common and useful debugging features available.

TRY IT OUT   Creating a Sample Project to Debug

You begin the debugging process by creating a program that uses three classes that you create. Classes and objects are covered in greater detail in the next chapter, but by creating and using these classes, you'll learn about some of the other features in Visual Basic 2015, as well as how to debug your programs. These classes are used to provide data to be displayed in a list box on your form. The classes introduce two powerful concepts in particular: the generic class with type constraints and the interface. These concepts are explained after the example in the How It Works section. All the code in this Try It Out is in the Debugging folder in the Zip file for this chapter.

1. Create a new Windows Forms Application project and name it **Debugging**.

2. In the Solution Explorer window, rename the form to **Debug.vb** by right-clicking the form and choosing Rename from the context menu. Click the form in the Forms Designer and then set the form's Text to **Debug Demo**.

3. Add some basic controls to the form and set their properties as shown in the following list:

   ➤ Create a Button control named **btnStart** and set Text to **Start**. Place it at the top left of the form.

   ➤ Create a ListBox control named **lstData** under the text box that takes up most of the form.

4. Right-click the Debugging project in the Solution Explorer, choose Add from the context menu, and then choose the Class submenu item. In the Add New Item—Debugging dialog box, enter a class name of **Customer** in the Name field and then click the Add button. Add the following bolded code to the class:

```
Public Class Customer
    Private intCustomerID As Integer
    Private strName As String

    Public Sub New(customerID As Integer, name As String)
        intCustomerID = customerID
        strName = name
    End Sub

    Public ReadOnly Property CustomerID() As Integer
        Get
            Return intCustomerID
        End Get
    End Property

    Public Property CustomerName() As String
        Get
            Return strName
        End Get
        Set(value As String)
            strName = value
        End Set
    End Property
End Class
```

5. Before moving on to create the next class, take a quick look at the AutoCorrect option in Visual Studio 2015 so that you can get firsthand experience with this feature. The CustomerName property

that you just created should really be a `ReadOnly` property. Insert the `ReadOnly` keyword between `Public` and `Property` and then click the next line of code.

6. You'll notice that the `Set` statement in this property has a red wavy line underneath it, indicating an error. If you hover your mouse over the line of code in error, you get a ToolTip informing you that a `ReadOnly` property cannot have a `Set` statement.

7. Open the Error List window, shown in Figure 9-6. You can use Ctrl+W, Ctrl+E or look under the View menu.

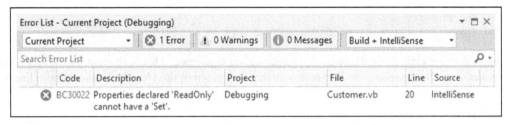

FIGURE 9-6

8. Remove the `Set` statement from this property.

9. Add another class to the Debugging project, called **Generics**. Then modify the `Class` statement as bolded here:

```
Public Class Generics(Of elementType)

End Class
```

10. Add the following bolded code to the `Generics` class:

```
Public Class Generics(Of elementType)
    'This class provides a demonstration of Generics

    'Declare Private variables
    Private strKey() As String
    Private elmValue() As elementType

    Public Sub Add(key As String, value As elementType)
        'Check to see if the objects have been initialized
        If strKey IsNot Nothing Then
            'Objects have been initialized
            ReDim Preserve strKey(strKey.GetUpperBound(0) + 1)
            ReDim Preserve elmValue(elmValue.GetUpperBound(0) + 1)
        Else
            'Initialize the objects
            ReDim strKey(0)
            ReDim elmValue(0)
        End If
        'Set the values
        strKey(strKey.GetUpperBound(0)) = key
        elmValue(elmValue.GetUpperBound(0)) = value
```

```
      End Sub

      Public ReadOnly Property Key(Index As Integer) As String
          Get
              Return strKey(index)
          End Get
      End Property

      Public ReadOnly Property Value(Index As Integer) As elementType
          Get
              Return elmValue(index)
          End Get
      End Property
  End Class
```

11. Add one more class to the Debugging project, called **Computer**. This is an example of a class that *implements* the IDisposable interface, which is explained in the How It Works section. Enter the following bolded code:

```
Public Class Computer
          Implements IDisposable
```

Once you press the Enter key, Visual Studio 2015 inserts the remaining code listed here automatically. Be sure to press Enter when IntelliSense has IDisposable highlighted. If you click or tab first, the code will not be added.

```
#Region "IDisposable Support"
Private disposedValue As Boolean ' To detect redundant calls

' IDisposable
Protected Overridable Sub Dispose(disposing As Boolean)
    If Not disposedValue Then
        If disposing Then
            ' TODO: dispose managed state (managed objects).
        End If

        'TODO: free unmanaged resources (unmanaged objects)
        'and override Finalize() below.

        ' TODO: set large fields to null.
    End If
    disposedValue = True
End Sub

' TODO: override Finalize() only if Dispose(disposing As Boolean)
' above has code to free unmanaged resources.
' Protected Overrides Sub Finalize()
'     ' Do not change this code.
'     Put cleanup code in Dispose(disposing As Boolean) above.
'     Dispose(False)
'     MyBase.Finalize()
'End Sub

' This code added by Visual Basic to correctly
' implement the disposable pattern.
Public Sub Dispose() Implements IDisposable.Dispose
```

```
    ' Do not change this code.  Put cleanup code
    '    in Dispose(disposing As Boolean) above.
    Dispose(True)
    ' TODO: uncomment the following line if Finalize() is overridden above.
    ' GC.SuppressFinalize(Me)
  End Sub
#End Region
```

12. Add the following two properties to the end of the Computer class:

```
Public ReadOnly Property FreeMemory() As String
      Get
          'Using the My namespace
          Return Format(
              My.Computer.Info.AvailablePhysicalMemory.ToString \ 1024,
              "#,###,##0") & " K"
      End Get
   End Property

   Public ReadOnly Property TotalMemory() As String
      Get
          'Using the My namespace
          Return Format(
              My.Computer.Info.TotalPhysicalMemory.ToString \ 1024,
              "#,###,##0") & " K"
      End Get
   End Property
```

13. Switch to the code for the Debug form and add the following highlighted Imports statement:

```
Imports System.Collections.Generic

Public Class Debug
```

14. You need to add a few private variable declarations next. Add the following code:

```
Public Class Debug
    'Using the Generics class
    Private objStringValues As New Generics(Of String)
    Private objIntegerValues As New Generics(Of Integer)

    'Using the List(Of T)(Of T) class
    Private objCustomerList As New List(Of Customer)
```

15. Add the following ListCustomer procedure to add customers to the list box on your form:

```
Private Sub ListCustomer(ByVal customerToList As Customer)
        lstData.Items.Add(customerToList.CustomerID &
              "-" & customerToList.CustomerName)
    End Sub
```

16. Next, you need to add the rest of the code to the Start button Click event handler. Select btnStart in the Class Name combo box at the top of the Code Editor and then select the Click event in the Method Name combo box. Add the following bolded code to the Click event handler.

```vb
Private Sub btnStart_Click(sender As Object,
    e As EventArgs) Handles btnStart.Click
  'Declare variables
  Dim strData As String

  lstData.Items.Add("String variable data:")
  If strData.Length > 0 Then
      lstData.Items.Add(strData)
  End If

  'Add an empty string to the ListBox
  lstData.Items.Add(String.Empty)

  'Demonstrates the use of the List(Of T) class
  lstData.Items.Add("Customers in the Customer Class:")
  objCustomerList.Add(New Customer(1001, "Henry For"))
  objCustomerList.Add(New Customer(1002, "Orville Wright"))
  For Each objCustomer As Customer In objCustomerList
      ListCustomer(objCustomer)
  Next

  'Add an empty string to the ListBox
  lstData.Items.Add(String.Empty)

  'Demonstrates the use of Generics
  lstData.Items.Add("Generics Class Key/Value Pairs using String Values:")
  objStringValues.Add("1001", "Henry Ford")
  lstData.Items.Add(objStringValues.Key(0) & " = " &
      objStringValues.Value(0))

  'Add an empty string to the ListBox
  lstData.Items.Add(String.Empty)

  'Demonstrates the use of Generics
  lstData.Items.Add("Generics Class Key/Value Pairs using Integer Values:")
  objIntegerValues.Add("Henry Ford", 1001)
  lstData.Items.Add(objIntegerValues.Key(0) & " = " &
    objIntegerValues.Value(0))

  'Add an empty string to the ListBox
  lstData.Items.Add(String.Empty)

  'Demonstrates the use of the Using statement
  'Allows acquisition, usage and disposal of the resource
  lstData.Items.Add("Computer Class Properties:")
  Using objMemory As New Computer
      lstData.Items.Add("FreeMemory = " & objMemory.FreeMemory)
      lstData.Items.Add("TotalMemory = " & objMemory.TotalMemory)
  End Using

  'Add an empty string to the ListBox
  lstData.Items.Add(String.Empty)

  'Demonstrates the use of the Continue statement
  Dim strPassword As String = "POpPassword"
```

```
        Dim strLowerCaseLetters As String = String.Empty
        'Extract lowercase characters from string
        For intIndex As Integer = 0 To strPassword.Length-1
            'Demonstrates the use of the Continue statement
            'If no uppercase character is found, continue the loop
            If Not strPassword.Substring(intIndex, 1) Like "[a-z]" Then
                'No upper case character found, continue loop
                Continue For
            End If
            'Lowercase character found, save it
            strLowerCaseLetters &= strPassword.Substring(intIndex, 1)
        Next

        'Display lowercase characters
        lstData.Items.Add("Password lower case characters:")
        lstData.Items.Add(strLowerCaseLetters)
    End Sub
```

17. Before examining how the code works, hover your mouse over the Error List tab at the bottom of the IDE so that the Error List window appears (see Figure 9-7). If the Error List tab is not visible, select View Error List from the menu bar. You have one warning about a potential error in your code. The line in question causes an error when you run your project; however, this is deliberate and is intended to demonstrate some of the debugging capabilities of Visual Studio 2015. You can ignore this warning for now because you'll be correcting it shortly.

18. Save your project by clicking the Save All button on the toolbar.

FIGURE 9-7

How It Works

After building the user interface for the Debugging project, you add the Customer class. This class is also straightforward and contains two private variables, a constructor, and two properties.

The two variables in the Customer class are declared as Private, which means that these variables are accessible only to the procedures in the class:

```
Public Class Customer
    Private intCustomerID As Integer
    Private strName As String
```

The *constructor* for this class—a method called whenever a new object of this class is to be created—is defined as a Public procedure with a procedure name of New. In VB, all constructors for classes in the .NET Framework must be declared with a procedure name of New.

This constructor accepts two input parameters: customerID and name. The parameters are used to set the values in the private variables defined for this class:

```
Public Sub New(customerID As Integer, name As String)
    intCustomerID = customerID
    strName = name
End Sub
```

Two properties are defined: CustomerID and CustomerName. These are read-only properties, meaning that the consumer of this class can use these properties only to read the customer ID and customer name; consumers cannot change them:

```
Public ReadOnly Property CustomerID() As Integer
    Get
        Return intCustomerID
    End Get
End Property

    Public Property CustomerName() As String
        Get
            Return strName
        End Get
    End Property
End Class
```

The next class that you added to the Debugging project is the Generics class. This class is used to demonstrate the use of generics in Visual Basic 2015.

The Collections class in the .NET Framework enables you to store data in the collection in a key/value pair. The key is always a string value that identifies the value, also known as an *item*. The item is defined as an object, which allows you to use the Collection class to store any data type that you want in the item. For example, you can use the Collection class to store Integer values or you can use it to store String values. No type-checking is performed. This lack of specificity can lead to performance problems as well as runtime problems.

Suppose you intend to use the Collection class to store Integer values. If (through poor coding practices) you allowed a String value to be added to the collection, you would not receive a runtime error when adding the item, but you could receive one when you tried to access the item.

The performance problems that you will encounter are the conversion of the data going into the collection and the data coming out of the collection. When you add an item to the collection, the data must be converted from its native data type to an Object data type, because that is how the Item property is defined. Likewise, when you retrieve an item from the collection, the item must be converted from an Object data type to the data type that you are using.

In Chapter 5, when working with ArrayLists (which are a kind of collection), you solved the problem of being able to store items of the wrong type by creating a strongly typed collection class. This did not solve the performance problem. Both problems are solved through generics and through the introduction of *type constraints*. A type constraint is specified on a class such as Collection by using the Of keyword followed by a list of type-name placeholders that are replaced by actual type names when an object of the class is created. This provides type safety by not allowing you to add an item that is not of the same data type that was defined for the class. It also improves performance because the item does not have to be converted to and from the Object data type. The data type for the item is defined using the data type that was defined for the class. You'll see how all this works in more detail as you explore the rest of the code and as you go through the debugging process.

After adding the Generics class, you modify the class by adding a type constraint using the Of keyword and defining a type list, which in this case contains only one type. This type name is a placeholder that will be used throughout the class to represent the data type that this class is working with. The actual data type is defined when an object of the class is created, as you'll see later in your code:

```
Public Class Generics(Of elementType)

End Class
```

You add two private variables to this class, with both of these variables being defined as arrays. The first variable is defined as a String data type, whereas the second variable is defined as a generic data type, which is set when an object of the class is created. Note that you have used the type name elementType, which was defined at the class level. This type name is replaced automatically by the data type that is used to create the Generics object:

```
Public Class Generics(Of elementType)
    'This class provides a demonstration of Generics

    'Declare Private variables
    Private strKey() As String
    Private elmValue() As elementType
```

The Add method enables you to add items to your collection. This method accepts two parameters: one for the key and the other for the value, making a key/value pair. The key parameter is always a string value, and the value parameter is defined using the data type used when a Generics object is created.

The first thing that you want to do in this procedure is see whether the variable arrays have been initialized. You do this by using the IsNot operator and comparing the strKey array to a value of Nothing. If the array is not equal to a value of Nothing, the array has already been initialized, and you simply need to increment the array dimension by 1. This is done by first getting the current upper bounds of the array and then adding 1 to it.

If the variable arrays have not been initialized, you need to initialize them using the ReDim statement as shown in the Else statement in the code that follows. After the arrays have been expanded or initialized, you add the key and value to the arrays:

```
Public Sub Add(key As String, value As elementType)
    'Check to see if the objects have been initialized
    If strKey IsNot Nothing Then
        'Objects have been initialized
        ReDim Preserve strKey(strKey.GetUpperBound(0) + 1)
        ReDim Preserve elmValue(elmValue.GetUpperBound(0) + 1)
    Else
        'Initialize the objects
        ReDim strKey(0)
        ReDim elmValue(0)
    End If

    'Set the values
    strKey(strKey.GetUpperBound(0)) = key
    elmValue(elmValue.GetUpperBound(0)) = value
End Sub
```

You add two read-only properties to this class to return the key and the value for a key/value pair. Notice that the Value property is defined to return the data type that will be used when a Generics object is created:

```
Public ReadOnly Property Key(index As Integer) As String
        Get
                Return strKey(Index)
        End Get
    End Property

    Public ReadOnly Property Value(index As Integer) As elementType
        Get
                Return elmValue(Index)
        End Get
    End Property
End Class
```

The final class that you added was the Computer class. This class implements the IDisposable interface. An interface in this sense is a set of methods and properties common to all classes that implement it. In this case, the IDisposable interface contains methods for releasing memory resources when an object of the class is disposed of. Methods that use this class should call the Dispose method when they are through with a Computer object.

To implement the interface, you add the Implements statement and specify the IDisposable interface. When you press the Enter key, Visual Studio 2015 adds the code from the IDisposable interface to your class, as shown in the following code:

```
Public Class Computer
Implements IDisposable

#Region "IDisposable Support"
Private disposedValue As Boolean ' To detect redundant calls

' IDisposable
Protected Overridable Sub Dispose(disposing As Boolean)
    If Not disposedValue Then
        If disposing Then
            ' TODO: dispose managed state (managed objects).
        End If

        'TODO: free unmanaged resources (unmanaged objects)
            'and override Finalize() below.

        ' TODO: set large fields to null.
    End If
    disposedValue = True
End Sub

' TODO: override Finalize() only if Dispose(disposing As Boolean)
'above has code to free unmanaged resources.
'Protected Overrides Sub Finalize()
'      ' Do not change this code.
'      Put cleanup code in Dispose(disposing As Boolean) above.
'      Dispose(False)
```

```
'    MyBase.Finalize()
'End Sub

' This code added by Visual Basic to correctly implement the disposable pattern.
Public Sub Dispose() Implements IDisposable.Dispose
  ' Do not change this code.  Put cleanup code
  '    in Dispose(disposing As Boolean) above.
  Dispose(True)
  ' TODO: uncomment the following line if Finalize() is overridden above.
  ' GC.SuppressFinalize(Me)
End Sub
#End Region

End Class
```

You add two read-only properties to this class: FreeMemory and TotalMemory. These properties return the available memory on your computer as well as the total amount of memory on your computer. These properties use the My.Computer.Info namespace to access the amount of available memory and the total amount of memory.

The AvailablePhysicalMemory and TotalPhysicalMemory properties of the My.Computer.Info namespace return the available and total memory in bytes. However, as users we are used to seeing these numbers in kilobytes. Therefore, you convert the number of bytes into kilobytes and then have that number formatted using commas.

> **NOTE** Remember that there are 1,024 bytes to a kilobyte, 1,024 kilobytes to a megabyte, and so on. The number that you pass to the Format function will be in kilobytes after you divide the number of bytes by 1,024.

You then add a space to the formatted number and then the letter K, indicating that the available and total memory figures are in kilobytes:

```
Public ReadOnly Property FreeMemory() As String
  Get
     'Using the My namespace
     Return Format(
       My.Computer.Info.AvailablePhysicalMemory.ToString \ 1024,
       "#,###,##0") & " K"
   End Get
End Property

Public ReadOnly Property TotalMemory() As String
  Get
     'Using the My namespace
     Return Format(
       My.Computer.Info.TotalPhysicalMemory.ToString \ 1024,
       "#,###,##0") & " K"
   End Get
End Property
```

You add code to the Debug form class next. This class uses a generic list class, List(Of T). You'll be using this class to hold a list of Customer objects created from your Customer class. The List(Of T) class uses a collection to hold the objects of the type that you specify: You need to import the System.Collections.Generic namespace in order to access the List(Of T) class. You accomplish that requirement by using an Imports statement:

```
Imports System.Collections.Generic
```

Next you define three private objects at the class level; these objects are available to all procedures in this class. The first two objects use your Generics class. Remember that the Generics class used the Of keyword to define a type list. In the declaration of your objects, you use similar Of clauses to specify that the Generics class should be using a String data type in the type list for the first object and an Integer data type for the second object. The data type specified here will be applied throughout the Generics class. Even when you compile your code, any instances where you try and add the wrong type to the collection gives you a message from the compiler.

The last object that you define here is an object that holds an array of Customer objects created from your Customer class:

```
'Using the Generics class
Private objStringValues As New Generics(Of String)
Private objIntegerValues As New Generics(Of Integer)

'Using the List(Of T) class
Private objCustomerList As New List(Of Customer)
```

The ListCustomer procedure simply accepts a Customer object as input and adds the CustomerID and CustomerName to the list box on your form:

```
Private Sub ListCustomer(customerToList As Customer)
    lstData.Items.Add(customerToList.CustomerID &
        "-" & customerToList.CustomerName)
End Sub
```

The Click event handler for the Start button contains the rest of the code for your project. You start this procedure by declaring a local String variable that will be used to demonstrate checking to see whether a variable has been initialized.

The code following the variable declaration checks the length of the variable and then adds the contents of the variable to the list box on the form:

```
Private Sub btnStart_Click(sender As Object,
    e As EventArgs) Handles btnStart.Click
'Declare variables
Dim strData As String

lstData.Items.Add("String variable data:")
If strData.Length > 0 Then
    lstData.Items.Add(strData)
End If
```

Because you will be writing the various results of your processing to the list box on your form, you'll want to add a blank entry to the list box to separate your results for aesthetic reasons, which is what the next line of code does. Here you simply use the Empty method of the String class to return an empty string to be added to the list box:

```
'Add an empty string to the ListBox
lstData.Items.Add(String.Empty)
```

This next section of code demonstrates the use of the List(Of T) class, as the comment in the code indicates. You add two new Customer objects to the objCustomerList object and then display those customers in the list box. Using a For Each. . .Next loop to iterate through the collection of Customer objects, you add each customer to the list box by calling the ListCustomer function, passing that function the Customer object:

```
'Demonstrates the use of the List(Of T) class
lstData.Items.Add("Customers in the Customer Class:")
objCustomerList.Add(New Customer(1001, "Henry For"))
objCustomerList.Add(New Customer(1002, "Orville Wright"))
For Each objCustomer As Customer In objCustomerList
    ListCustomer(objCustomer)
Next
```

Again you add a blank entry to the list box and use the objects that were defined using your Generics class. The first object, objStringValues, uses the Generics class with a String data type, as the object name indicates. Remember that the Add method in this class accepts a key/value pair and that the key parameter is always a String value. The value parameter uses the data type that was used to initialize this class, which in this case is also a String.

When you add a key/value pair to your objStringValues object, you want to display that data in the list box on your form. You do this by accessing the Key and Value properties in the Generics class from which this object was derived:

```
'Add an empty string to the ListBox
lstData.Items.Add(String.Empty)

'Demonstrates the use of Generics
lstData.Items.Add("Generics Class Key/Value Pairs" &
    " using String Values:")
objStringValues.Add("1001", "Henry Ford")
lstData.Items.Add(objStringValues.Key(0) & " = " &
    objStringValues.Value(0))
```

Again you add another blank line to the list box and then add a key/value pair that uses an Integer data type for the value parameter to the objIntegerValues object. Then you add that key/value pair to the list box:

```
'Add an empty string to the ListBox
lstData.Items.Add(String.Empty)

'Demonstrates the use of Generics
lstData.Items.Add("Generics Class Key/Value Pairs" &
    " using Integer Values:")
objIntegerValues.Add("Henry Ford", 1001)
lstData.Items.Add(objIntegerValues.Key(0) & " = " &
    objIntegerValues.Value(0))
```

After you add another blank line to the list box, you use a Using. . .End Using block to create a new object of the Computer class, add the free memory and total memory of your computer to the list box, and then dispose of the Computer class.

When you use a class, you typically instantiate it using the New keyword as you did with your Generics class, use the class, and then dispose of the class by calling its Dispose method if it implements one. The problem with that scenario is that when an exception occurs, the resource may or may not be disposed of. Even if you implement the code using structured error handling, a topic discussed later in this chapter, you are not always guaranteed to be able to dispose of the class.

The Using statement is an efficient means of acquiring a resource, using it, and then disposing of it, regardless of whether an exception occurs. There is one caveat to this: The class that you use in a Using. . .End Using block must implement the IDisposable interface, which is why you added this interface to your Computer class.

In the following code, the object name objMemory has not been defined anywhere except in the Using statement. The Using statement takes care of declaring this object for you and sets it to a new instance of the class that you specify, which in this case is the Computer class. Keep in mind that the object objMemory is local to the Using. . .End Using block and you can reference it only within this block.

When the End Using statement is reached, the Common Language Runtime (CLR) automatically calls the Dispose method on the Computer class, thereby releasing its reference to it, and the Computer class executes any cleanup code that has been implemented in the Dispose method:

```
'Add an empty string to the ListBox
lstData.Items.Add(String.Empty)

'Demonstrates the use of the Using statement
'Allows acquisition, usage and disposal of the resource
lstData.Items.Add("Computer Class Properties:")
Using objMemory As New Computer
    lstData.Items.Add("FreeMemory = " & objMemory.FreeMemory)
    lstData.Items.Add("TotalMemory = " & objMemory.TotalMemory)
End Using
```

Once again you add another blank line to the list box, and then you get to the final bit of code in this procedure. In this section of code, we wanted to demonstrate the use of the Continue statement. The Continue statement is an efficient means of immediately transferring control to the next iteration of a loop. Instead of coding a lot of If. . .Then statements in a loop, you can merely test to see whether a condition is what you want and if it is not, you can call the Continue statement to pass control to the next iteration of a Do, For, or While loop.

Take a look at the code that you have here. First you declare a couple of variables and set their values. The first variable, strPassword, is declared and set to a password that contains uppercase and lowercase letters. The second variable, strLowerCaseLetters, is declared and set to an empty string so that the variable is initialized.

Next, you set up a For. . .Next loop to check each character in the strPassword variable. The If. . .Then statement uses the Like operator to compare a character in the password variable to a pattern of letters. If a match is found, the Like operator returns a value of True. However, you are using a negative comparison here because you have included the Not keyword in the If. . .Then statement; so if the character in the password variable is not like one of the letters in the pattern [a-z], you execute the next statement, which is the Continue statement.

If the character in the password variable is a lowercase letter, then you concatenate the character to the `strLowerCaseLetters` variable, which is why you needed to initialize this variable to an empty string when you declared it.

Finally, after all lowercase letters have been extracted from the password variable, you display the results of the `strLowerCaseLetters` variable in the list box on your form:

```
'Add an empty string to the ListBox
  lstData.Items.Add(String.Empty)

  'Demonstrates the use of the Continue statement
  Dim strPassword As String = "POpPassword"
  Dim strLowerCaseLetters As String = String.Empty
  'Extract lowercase characters from string
  For intIndex As Integer = 0 To strPassword.Length-1
     'Demonstrates the use of the Continue statement
     'If no uppercase character is found, continue the loop
     If Not strPassword.Substring(intIndex, 1) Like "[a-z]" Then
        'No uppercase character found, continue loop
        Continue For
     End If
     'Lowercase character found, save it
     strLowerCaseLetters &= strPassword.Substring(intIndex, 1)
  Next

  'Display lowercase characters
  lstData.Items.Add("Password lower case characters:")
  lstData.Items.Add(strLowerCaseLetters)
End Sub
```

At this point, you are probably pretty eager to run your project and test your code.

TRY IT OUT   Using the Exception Assistant

In this Try It Out, you examine the Exception Assistant in Visual Studio 2015. This useful assistant provides help when an unhandled exception occurs in your code. All the code in this Try It Out is in the `Debugging` folder in the Zip file for this chapter.

1. Start your project by clicking the Start button on the toolbar or by clicking the Debug menu and choosing the Start menu item.

2. When your form appears, click the Start button on your form to have your code in the `Click` event handler for the Start button executed. You'll immediately see the Exception Assistant, shown in Figure 9-8.

> **NOTE** *The Exception Assistant dialog's title bar displays the type of exception that occurred. It also provides links to some basic troubleshooting tips and a link at the bottom that provides details about the exception.*

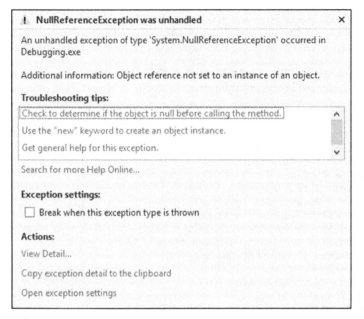

FIGURE 9-8

3. Click the View Detail link in the Exception Assistant dialog box to view the View Detail dialog box shown in Figure 9-9. You are mainly interested in the exception message, and, as you can see, it informs you that the object reference has not been set to an instance of an object. Basically, you have not initialized the variable strData. This is also a warning during compilation.

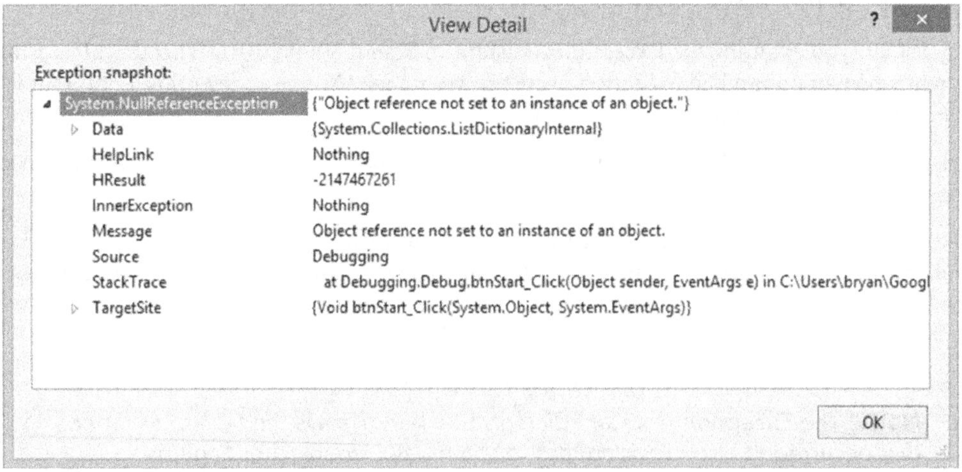

Exception snapshot:	
▲ System.NullReferenceException	{"Object reference not set to an instance of an object."}
▷ Data	{System.Collections.ListDictionaryInternal}
HelpLink	Nothing
HResult	-2147467261
InnerException	Nothing
Message	Object reference not set to an instance of an object.
Source	Debugging
StackTrace	at Debugging.Debug.btnStart_Click(Object sender, EventArgs e) in C:\Users\bryan\Googl
▷ TargetSite	{Void btnStart_Click(System.Object, System.EventArgs)}

View Detail

OK

FIGURE 9-9

4. Click the OK button to close the View Detail dialog box and then click the Close button in the upper right-hand corner of the Exception Assistant dialog box to close it.

5. Now click the Stop Debugging button on the toolbar or click the Debug menu and select the Stop Debugging menu item.

6. Locate the following section of code at the beginning of the btnStart_Click procedure:

```
If strData.Length > 0 Then
    lstData.Items.Add(strData)
End If
```

7. Modify that code as shown here:

```
If strData IsNot Nothing Then
    If strData.Length > 0 Then
        lstData.Items.Add(strData)
    End If
Else
    strData = "String now initialized"
    lstData.Items.Add(strData)
End If
```

8. Now run your project and click the Start button on your form after it appears. All of your code should have executed, and the list box should be populated with the various results of the processing that took place in the btnStart_Click procedure.

How It Works

When an unhandled error occurs in your code while debugging, the Exception Assistant dialog box appears and provides troubleshooting tips for the exception, as well as a link to view the details of the exception as shown in Figure 9-8. Figure 9-9 displayed the View Detail dialog, which provides detailed information about the exception, which can also be an invaluable tool for determining its exact cause.

You modified the code that caused the error as shown here. Because the string variable strData was declared but never initialized, the variable is Nothing. This means that it has not been set to an instance of the String class, and therefore the properties and methods of the variable cannot be referenced without causing a NullReferenceException (refer to Figure 9-8).

To rectify this problem, you first test the strData variable to see if it is not equal to Nothing by using the IsNot operator, as shown in the first line of the code that follows. If the variable has been initialized, then you can execute the code in the If statement. Otherwise, processing falls through to the Else statement, where you set the variable to a String constant and then display the contents of the variable in the list box:

```
If strData IsNot Nothing Then
    If strData.Length > 0 Then
        lstData.Items.Add(strData)
    End If
Else
    strData = "String now initialized"
    lstData.Items.Add(strData)
End If
```

An alternative to the previous code example would be to use a `Try. . .Catch` block to handle the exception. This technique is demonstrated later in this chapter.

Setting Breakpoints

When trying to debug a large program, you may find that you want to debug only a section of code; that is, you want your code to run up to a certain point and then stop. This is where *breakpoints* come in handy; they cause execution of your code to stop anywhere they are set. You can set breakpoints anywhere in your code and your code executes to that point and stops.

Execution of the code stops *before* executing the code on which the breakpoint is set.

You can set breakpoints when you write your code, or you can set them at run time by switching to your code and setting the breakpoint at the desired location. You cannot set a breakpoint while your program is actually executing a section of code such as the code in a loop, but you can do so when the program is idle and waiting for user input.

When the development environment encounters a breakpoint, execution of your code halts, and your program is considered to be in *break mode*. While your program is in break mode, a lot of debugging features are available. In fact, a lot of debugging features are available to you only when your program is in break mode.

You can set breakpoints by clicking the gray margin next to the line of code on which you want to set the breakpoint or by pressing F9 while on the line you want to set a breakpoint on or take one off. When the breakpoint is set, you can see a solid red circle in the gray margin, and the line is highlighted in red. When you are done with a particular breakpoint, you can remove it by clicking the solid red circle. You see more of this in the Try It Out exercise in this section.

Sometimes you'll want to debug code in a loop, such as one that reads data from a file. You know that the first x number of records are good, and it is time-consuming to step through all the code repetitively until you get to what you suspect is the bad record. A breakpoint can be set inside the loop and you can set a hit counter on it. The code inside the loop executes the number of times that you specified in the hit counter and then stops and places you in break mode. This can be a real timesaver, and you will take a look at breakpoint hit counts later in this section.

You can also set a condition on a breakpoint, such as when a variable contains a certain value or when the value of a variable changes. This is also examined later in this section.

TRY IT OUT   **Working with Breakpoints**

In this example, you begin with some breakpoint work. Next, some discussion on the IDE, and then finally you complete the example. All the code in this Try It Out is in the `Debugging` folder in the Zip file for this chapter.

1. The first thing you want to do is set a breakpoint in your code. Using Figure 9-10 as a guide, set the breakpoint in your code by clicking the gray margin to the left of the line of code shown.

2. Run the project.

3. To get to the code where the breakpoint is set, click the Start button on your form. The code executes up to the breakpoint, and the development environment window receives focus, making it the topmost window. The entire line should be highlighted in yellow and the breakpoint circle in the margin should now contain a yellow arrow in it pointing to the line of code where execution has been paused, which in this case is the End If statement shown in Figure 9-10.

> **NOTE** *A few new windows appear at the bottom of the development environment. What you see will vary depending on which windows you have specified to be shown—you can choose different ones using the tabs at the bottom.*

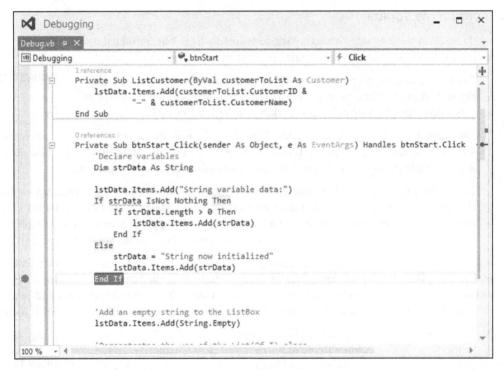

FIGURE 9-10

This Try It Out pauses at this point so you can learn about some of the features of the IDE in debug mode. The Try It Out picks up again with step 4.

The Breakpoints Window

You can display the Breakpoints window, if the tab is not shown, in the bottom right corner of the IDE by clicking the Breakpoints icon on the Debug toolbar, pressing Ctrl+Alt+B, or by selecting Debug Windows Breakpoints. The Breakpoints window shows at what line of code the current breakpoint is located, any conditions it has, and the hit count if applicable, as shown in Figure 9-11.

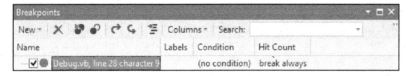

FIGURE 9-11

The Breakpoints window shows all the breakpoints you have set in your code. When a breakpoint is encountered, it is highlighted in both the code and the Breakpoints window, as shown in Figure 9-11. In this window, you can set new breakpoints, delete existing breakpoints, and change the properties of the breakpoints. You will see more of this later in the chapter.

Useful Icons on the Toolbar

In this Try It Out, you want to step through your code line by line. The Standard toolbar in the IDE contains three icons of particular interest to you, shown in Figure 9-12.

FIGURE 9-12

➤ The first icon is the Step Into icon. When you click this icon, you can step through your code line by line. This includes stepping into any function or procedure that the code calls and working through it line by line.

➤ The second icon is the Step Over icon. This works in a similar way to Step Into, but you pass straight over the procedures and functions—they still execute, but all in one go. You then move straight on to the next line in the block of code that called the procedure.

➤ Last is the Step Out icon. This icon enables you to jump to the end of the procedure or function that you are currently in and to move to the line of code *after* the line that called the procedure or function. This is handy when you step into a long procedure and want to get out of it. The rest of the code in the procedure is still executed, but you do not step through it.

There is one more really useful button worth adding to the toolbar: Run To Cursor. The Run To Cursor icon enables you to place your cursor anywhere in the code following the current breakpoint where execution has been paused and then click this icon. The code between the current breakpoint and where the cursor is positioned is executed, and execution stops on the line of code where the cursor is located.

To add this button to the Standard toolbar, click the Standard Toolbar Options at the end of the toolbar. Choose Add or Remove Buttons and then Customize. In the Customize dialog box, click the Add Command button in the Commands tab, and then select Debug in the Categories list. In the Commands list, select Run To Cursor and then click OK. Move the icon down in the Controls list to form a group of icons as shown in Figure 9-13, and then click the Close button to close the Customize dialog box.

FIGURE 9-13

You can add a button to a toolbar by clicking the options button on the right of each toolbar, represented by a down arrow with a line over it. Then click Add or Remove Buttons.

TRY IT OUT   Working with Breakpoints

4. You ended the last step of the Try It Out at the breakpoint. Before continuing, you want to examine the contents of the string variable, strData. Hover your mouse over the variable to view a Data Tip, as shown in Figure 9-14. Notice that the variable name is listed along with its contents, a magnifying glass, and a down arrow.

```
Else
        strData = "String now initialized"
        lstData.Items.Add(strData)
    End If                        ● strData Q ▾ "String now initialized" ▭
```

FIGURE 9-14

5. Clicking the contents of the variable in the Data Tip puts you in edit mode for the variable, and you can actually change the contents of that variable. Clicking the magnifying glass causes the contents of the variable to be displayed automatically in the Text Visualizer dialog box, which is a useful tool for displaying the data for string variables that contain a significant amount of data. Clicking the down arrow provides you with a drop-down list of options for viewing the contents of the variable, including options for Text Visualizer, XML Visualizer, HTML Visualizer, and JSON Visualizer.

6. At this point, you'll want to test the debugging icons on the toolbar, starting with the Run To Cursor icon first. Place your cursor on the line of code that calls the ListCustomer procedure.

    Click the Run To Cursor icon on the toolbar. The code between the breakpoint at the End If statement shown in Figure 9-14, and the line of code that calls the ListCustomer procedure is executed. Your project stops execution on the line of code on which you have your cursor, as shown in Figure 9-15.

```
'Demonstrates the use of the List(Of T) class
lstData.Items.Add("Customers in the Customer Class:")
objCustomerList.Add(New Customer(1001, "Henry For"))
objCustomerList.Add(New Customer(1002, "Orville Wright"))
For Each objCustomer As Customer In objCustomerList
    ListCustomer(objCustomer)  ≤3ms elapsed
Next
```

FIGURE 9-15

7. Click the Step Into icon next, and you should now be at the beginning of the ListCustomer procedure. Data Tips can be displayed for objects that contain multiple values as well as variables that contain only a single value.

    Hover your mouse over the customerToList parameter for this procedure to display the Data Tip for this object. You'll see a plus sign next to the object name in the Data Tip. Click the plus sign, or simply hover your mouse over it, and the contents of the object appear, as shown in Figure 9-16.

> **NOTE** This Data Tip displays not only the properties in the Customer class, the class from which the customerToList object is derived, but also the private variables in that class. You also have the same options for viewing the contents of string variables, which is indicated by the presence of the magnifying glass and down-arrow icons.

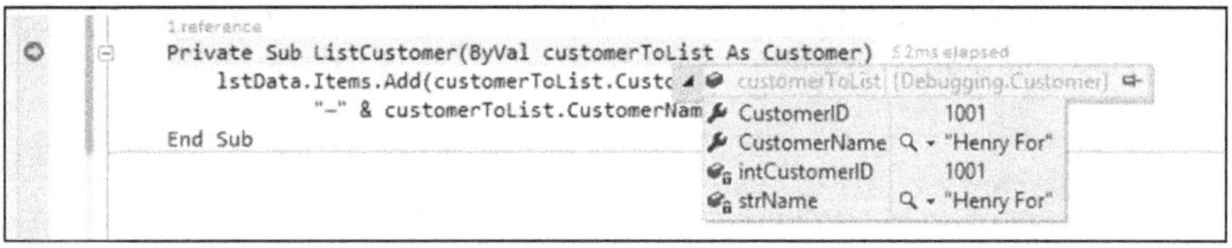

FIGURE 9-16

Because the text, which is supposed to read `"Henry Ford"`, is misspelled, you want to correct it in the Data Tip. This can be done by editing the `strName` variable in the Data Tip. Click the text `"Henry For"` in the Data Tip to put it into edit mode. Correct the text by adding the letter *d* at the end of the text and then click the name or variable name in the Data Tip. Note that the text for both the property and variable has been updated with your corrections. In addition, note that you can change the contents of `Integer` data types in the Data Tip as well.

8. Click the Step Into icon once more and you should be at the first line of code in the `ListCustomer` procedure.

9. Because you do not want to see any of this code at this time, you are going to step out of this procedure. This places you back at the line of code that called the procedure. Click the Step Out icon. Note that you are taken out of the `ListCustomer` procedure and back to where the call originated.

10. Now click the Step Into icon twice more so that you are back at the call to the `ListCustomer` procedure once again.

11. The final icon to be tested is the Step Over icon. Click this icon now and note that you have totally stepped over the execution of the `ListCustomer` procedure. The procedure was actually executed, but because you chose to step over it, the debugger does not indicate that the procedure was executed.

12. Continue processing as normal and execute the rest of the code without interruption. If you hover your mouse over the Start icon on the toolbar, you will notice that the ToolTip has been changed from Start to Continue. Click this icon to let the rest of the code run or press F5. You should now see your completed form as shown in Figure 9-17.

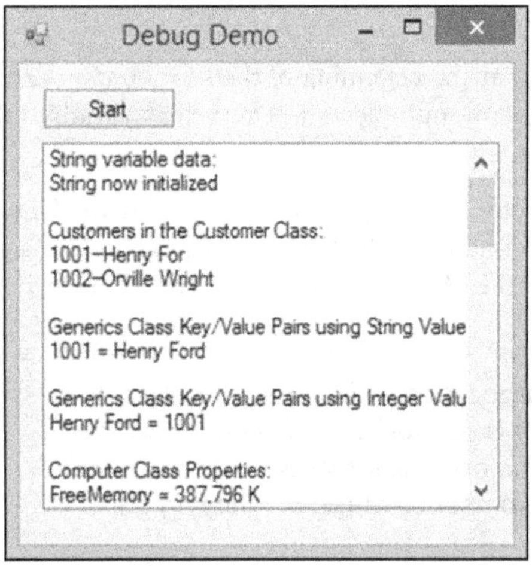

FIGURE 9-17

TRY IT OUT Using the Breakpoint's Hit Count

In this Try It Out, you examine the Breakpoint Hit Count dialog box. The Breakpoint Hit Count dialog box allows you to define the number of executions of a loop that should be performed before the IDE stops execution of your code and puts it into break mode. As previously described, this is useful for processing loops because you can specify how many iterations the loop should make before you encounter a breakpoint. All the code in this Try It Out is in the Debugging folder in the Zip file for this chapter.

1. Stop your project and set a breakpoint in the For loop as shown in Figure 9-18. Remember that to set a breakpoint, you need to click in the gray margin on the line of code where the breakpoint should be. You can also right-click the line and choose Breakpoint and then Insert Breakpoint.

2. Start your project again by clicking the Start icon on the toolbar.

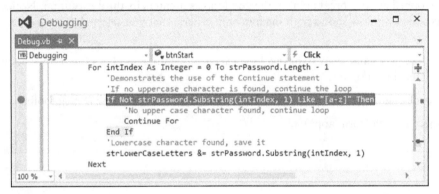

FIGURE 9-18

3. In the Breakpoints window, right-click the second breakpoint and choose Hit Count from the context menu to invoke the Breakpoint Hit Count dialog box.

4. The breakpoint that you currently have set halts execution every time it is encountered. Change it to break only when the loop enters its third execution. You do this by hovering over the breakpoint and clicking the Settings cog. Then check Conditions in the Breakpoint Settings and choose Hit Count greater than or equal to 3, as shown in Figure 9-19.

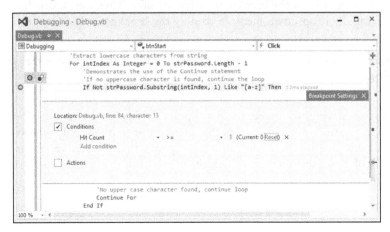

FIGURE 9-19

Click the X button to close this Settings box. Notice the Hit Count column in the Breakpoints window in the IDE. The second breakpoint now displays the Hit Count condition that you just defined. The red circle will now have a white plus sign in the center of it for this breakpoint.

5. At this point, click the Start button on the form. By clicking the Start button you are again stopped at your first breakpoint.

6. This breakpoint is highlighted in the Breakpoints window. You no longer need this breakpoint, so click it and then click the Delete icon in the Breakpoints window; the breakpoint will be deleted. Your code is still paused at this point, so click the Continue button on the Debug toolbar.

7. You are now stopped at your breakpoint in the For loop as it enters its third execution. Notice that the Breakpoints window shows both the hit count criteria that you selected and the current hit count.

As you can see, this is a handy way to have a loop execute a definite number of iterations before breaking at a defined breakpoint.

8. Now let your code continue executing by clicking the Continue button on the Debug toolbar.

9. Stop your project after the form appears.

TRY IT OUT Changing Breakpoint Properties

In this Try It Out, you modify the properties of the only breakpoint that you have left. All the code in this Try It Out is in the Debugging folder in the Zip file for this chapter.

1. In the previous Try It Out, you modified the breakpoint while the project was running. This time you will modify the breakpoint while the project is stopped. To view the Breakpoints window, select Debug ➪ Windows ➪ Breakpoints.

2. In the Breakpoints window, right-click the breakpoint click settings. Then check Conditions and choose Hit Count from the drop-down menu to display the Breakpoint Hit Count dialog box.

3. Change the hit count back to its original setting by unchecking condition and then click the OK button to close this dialog.

4. To set a specific condition for this breakpoint, right-click the breakpoint and choose Conditions after clicking on settings to invoke the Breakpoint Condition dialog box. Enter the condition as shown in Figure 9-20. This causes this breakpoint to break only when the variable intIndex is equal to 3. Note that you could also specify that the breakpoint be activated when the value of a variable changes. Click the OK button to close the dialog box and then start your project.

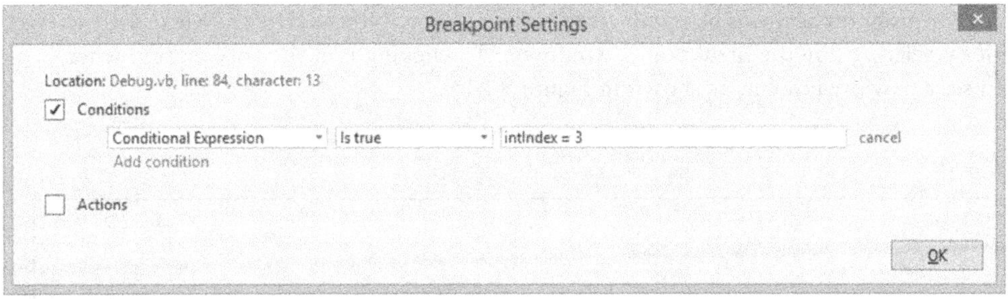

FIGURE 9-20

5. Click the Start button on your form. Once the intIndex variable is equal to 3, the breakpoint is activated and execution of the code is paused at the line where the breakpoint is specified. This is actually your fourth time into the loop because the For...Next loop specifies a starting index of 0 for the variable intIndex.

6. Finally, let your code finish executing by clicking the Continue button on the Debug toolbar. Once your form appears, stop your project.

Debugging Using the Watch Window and QuickWatch Dialog Box

The Watch window provides a method for you to observe variables and expressions easily while the code is executing—this can be invaluable when you are trying to debug unwanted results in a variable. You can even change the values of variables in the Watch window. You can also add as many variables and expressions as needed to debug your program. This provides a mechanism for watching the values of your variables change without any intervention on your part. This is an easy place to watch many variables.

The QuickWatch dialog box is best for watching a single variable or expression. You can add or delete variables or expressions in the QuickWatch dialog box only when your program is in break mode. Therefore, before you run your program, you need to set a breakpoint before the variable or expression that you want to watch. When the breakpoint has been reached, you can add as many Watch variables or expressions as needed.

TRY IT OUT Using QuickWatch

In this Try It Out, you add the intIndex variable to the Watch window and add an expression using the intIndex variable. This enables you to observe this variable and expression as you step through your code. All the code in this Try It Out is in the Debugging folder in the Zip file for this chapter.

1. Start your program again. When your form appears, switch to the IDE and clear the current break-point by deleting it in the Breakpoints window or by clicking it in the gray margin where it is set. Then set a new breakpoint, as shown in Figure 9-21.

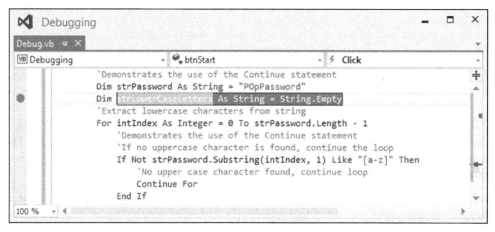

FIGURE 9-21

2. You can add a QuickWatch variable or expression only while your program is paused. Click the Start button on the form so the breakpoint will be encountered and your program paused.

3. When the breakpoint has been encountered, right-click the `intIndex` variable in the `For. . .Next` loop and choose Expression: 'intIndex' and then QuickWatch from the context menu to invoke the QuickWatch dialog box. Note that this variable has not only been added to the Expression drop-down box but has also been placed in the current value grid in the dialog, as shown in Figure 9-22. Click the Add Watch button to add this variable to the Watch window.

> **NOTE** Because the variable is declared in the `For. . .Next` loop, you see an error here. You can safely ignore this error because once the loop has started processing, the variable will be declared.

4. While you have the QuickWatch dialog open, set an expression to be evaluated. Type the expression **intIndex = 1** in the Expression drop-down box. Then click the Add Watch button to have this expression added to the Watch window. Close the QuickWatch dialog by clicking the Close button.

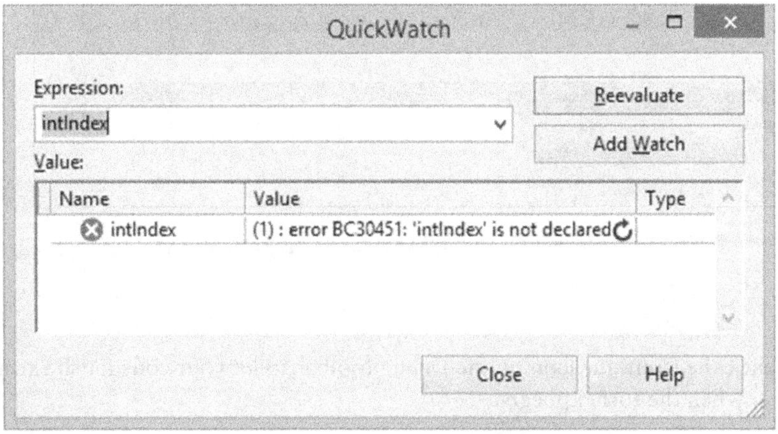

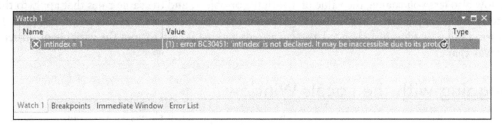

FIGURE 9-22

5. If you do not see the Watch window at the bottom of the IDE, select Debug ➪ Windows ➪ Watch ➪ Watch 1. You should see a variable and an expression in the Watch window, as shown in Figure 9-23.

FIGURE 9-23

The second watch expression that you added here returns a value of True when the intIndex variable equals 1, so Visual Studio 2015 sets the type to Boolean after you enter the For. . .Next loop.

6. Step through your code line by line so that you can watch the value of the variable and expression change. Click the Step Into icon on the Debug toolbar to step to the next line of code. Keep clicking the Step Into icon to see the values of the variable and expression in the Watch window change.

> **NOTE** As you step through the loop in your code, you continue to see the value for the intIndex variable change in the Watch window. When the value of the variable in the Watch window turns red, as shown in Figure 9-24 (although you will not see it in the black-and-white image well), the value has just been changed. You can manually change the value at any time by entering a new value in the Value column in the Watch window.

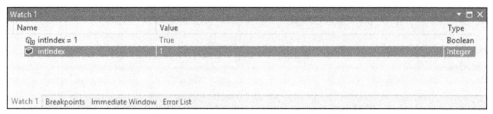

FIGURE 9-24

7. When you are done, click the Continue icon on the Debug toolbar to let your code finish executing. Then stop your project when the form appears.

Debugging with the Autos Window

The Autos window is similar to the Watch window, except that it shows all variables and objects, the current statement, and the three statements before and after the current statement. The Autos window also lets you change the value of a variable or object, and the same rules that apply to the Watch window apply here (that is, the program must be paused before a value can be changed). The text for a value that has just changed also turns red, making it easy to spot the variable or object that was changed.

Debugging with the Locals Window

The Locals window is similar to the Watch window, except that it shows all variables and objects for the current function or procedure. The Locals window also lets you change the value of a variable or object, and the same rules that apply to the Watch window apply here (that is, the program must be paused before a value can be changed). The text for a value that has just changed also turns red, making it easy to spot the variable or object that was changed.

The Locals window is great if you want a quick glance at everything that is going on in a function or procedure, but it is not very useful for watching the values of one or two variables or expressions. That's because the Locals window contains all variables and objects in a procedure or function. Therefore, if you have a lot of variables and objects, you have to scroll through the window constantly to view them. This is where the Locals window comes in handy; it enables you to observe just the variables that you need. You learned about the Watch window in the previous example.

TRY IT OUT Using the Locals Window

In this Try It Out, you examine the contents of the Locals window in two different procedures. This demonstrates how the contents of the Locals window changes from one procedure to the next. All the code in this Try It Out is in the Debugging folder in the Zip file for this chapter.

1. To prepare for this exercise, you need to have the current breakpoint set and set a new breakpoint in the `ListCustomer` procedure. Locate the `ListCustomer` procedure and set a breakpoint on the one line of code in that procedure:

```
lstData.Items.Add(customerToList.CustomerID &
    "-" & customerToList.CustomerName)
```

2. Now start your program.

3. If you do not see the Locals window at the bottom of the IDE, select Debug ➪ Windows ➪ Locals. Notice that at this point the Locals window contains no variables or objects. This is because you have not entered a procedure or function. Click the Start button on the form. Your breakpoint in the `ListCustomer` procedure is encountered first and execution is paused.

4. Notice the various objects and their types listed in the Locals window. The first item in the list is `Me`, which is the form itself. If you expand this item, you see all the objects and controls associated with your form. If you expand the `customerToList` object, you'll see the properties and variables defined in the `Customer` class, as shown in Figure 9-25.

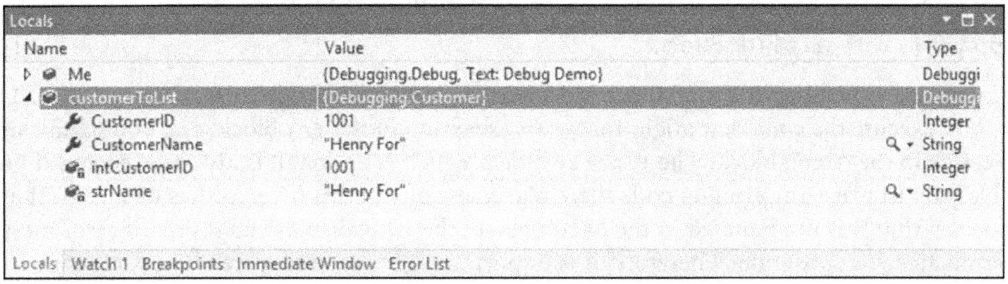

FIGURE 9-25

5. Click the Continue icon on the Debug toolbar until you encounter your second breakpoint.

6. Take a look at the Locals window. You should see a different set of objects and variables. The one constant item in both procedures is `Me`, which is associated with the form.

7. If you step through a couple of lines of code in the loop where the breakpoint has paused your program, you see the values in the Locals window change. You can continue to step through your code, or you can click the Continue icon on the Debug toolbar to let your program run to completion.

> **NOTE** *After you change your build configuration from Debug to Release, debugging is no longer available; even if you have breakpoints set in your code, they will not be encountered.*

8. To clear all breakpoints in your code, you can delete each breakpoint in the Breakpoints window or you can click the Debug menu and choose Delete All Breakpoints. When you are done, stop your project.

ERROR HANDLING

Error handling is an essential part of any good code. In Visual Basic 2015, the error mechanism is based on the concept of *exceptions* that can be *thrown* to raise an error and *caught* when the error is handled. If you do not provide any type of error handling and an error occurs, your user receives a message about an unhandled exception, which is provided by the CLR, and then the program may terminate, depending on the type of error encountered. This is not a user-friendly message and does not inform the user about the true nature of the error or how to resolve it. The unhandled exception could also cause users to lose the data that they were working with or leave the user and the data in an unknown state.

Visual Studio 2015 provides *structured error-handling* statements that are common across all languages. Structured error handling is a way to organize blocks of code in a structure that handles errors. In this section, you examine structured error handling and how it can be incorporated into your programs with very little effort.

Structured error handling in Visual Basic 2015 is incorporated with the `Try. . .Catch. . .Finally` block. You execute the code that might throw an exception in the `Try` block, and you handle anticipated errors in the `Catch` block. The `Finally` block, which is optional, is always executed if present; it enables you to place any cleanup code there regardless of whether an error has occurred. If an error occurs that was not handled in the `Catch` block, the CLR displays its standard error message and terminates your program. Therefore, it is important to try to anticipate all possible errors for the code contained in the `Try` block.

Take a look at the syntax for the `Try. . .Catch. . .Finally` statement:

```
Try
    [try statements]
    [Exit Try]
Catch exceptionvariable As exceptiontype
    [catch statements]
    [Exit Try]
  [Additional Catch blocks]
Finally
    [finally statements]
End Try
```

➤ The `[try statements]` are the statements to be executed that may cause an error.

➤ The `exceptionvariable` can be any variable name. It will be set to contain the value of the error that is thrown.

➤ The `exceptiontype` specifies the exception class type to which the exception belongs. If this type is not supplied, your `Catch` block handles any exception defined in the

System.Exception class. This argument enables you to specify the type of exception that you may be looking for. An example of a specific exception is IOException, which is used when performing any type of I/O (input/output) against a file.

➤ The [catch statements] handle and process the error that has occurred.

➤ The [finally statements] are executed after all other processing has occurred. Finally is always executed even if an error occurs and is handled in the Catch block.

➤ The optional Exit Try statement enables you to completely break out of a Try...Catch...Finally block and resume execution of code immediately following the Try...Catch...Finally block. You can have multiple Catch blocks, meaning that you can test for multiple errors with different exception types within the same Try block. When an error occurs among the Try statements, control is passed to the appropriate Catch block for processing.

When you define a Catch block, you can specify a variable name for the exception and define the type of exception you want to catch, as shown in the following code fragment. This code defines an exception variable named IOExceptionErr, and the type of exception is an IOException. This example traps any type of I/O exception that may occur when processing files, and stores the error information in an object named IOExceptionErr:

```
Catch IOExceptionErr As IOException
  . .
    code to handle the exception goes here
  . .
```

When dealing with mathematical expressions, you can define and catch the various errors that you may encounter, such as a divide-by-zero exception. You can also catch errors such as overflow errors, which may occur when multiplying two numbers and trying to place the result in a variable too small for the result. However, in cases such as these it may be better to check for problems in advance—you should use exceptions only in exceptional circumstances.

When testing Try...Catch statements, you can cause an error by using the Throw keyword inside the Try statement. To throw a new error, use the following syntax:

```
Throw New FileNotFoundException()
```

Inside of Catch statements, you can raise an error that has occurred back up to the caller. To throw an error back up to the caller, use the following syntax, which allows the caller to handle the actual error:

```
Throw
```

USING STRUCTURED ERROR HANDLING

In the following Try It Out, you add some structured error handling to the sample program with which you have been working. When you first ran the Debugging project, you received the NullReferenceException that was shown in Figure 9-8 because you tried to access the properties of the `strData` string variable before it had been set. This code is a prime candidate for structured error handling. You temporarily bypassed the problem at that point by using an `If...Then...Else` statement to first see whether the variable had been initialized. Another way to handle such a case is in a `Try...Catch` block.

TRY IT OUT   **Structured Error Handling**

In this example, you will update your code to handle the `null` check with a `Try...Catch` statement versus an `If...Then` statement. All the code in this Try It Out is in the `Debugging` folder in the Zip file for this chapter.

Modify the code for the `strData` variable in the `btnStart_Click` procedure as shown:

```
lstData.Items.Add("String variable data:")
Try
    If strData.Length > 0 Then
        lstData.Items.Add(strData)
    End If
Catch NullReferenceExceptionErr As NullReferenceException
    strData = "String now initialized"
    lstData.Items.Add(strData)
End Try
```

How It Works

The code you entered contains a `Try` block and a `Catch` block. You opt not to use the `Finally` block in this error-handling routine because the `Catch` block performs the necessary code to set the `strData` variable, and have the contents of that variable added to the list box on your form:

```
Try
    If strData.Length > 0 Then
        lstData.Items.Add(strData)
    End If
Catch NullReferenceExceptionErr As NullReferenceException
    strData = "String now initialized"
    lstData.Items.Add(strData)
End Try
```

When you try to access the `Length` property of the `strData` variable in the `Try` block, a `NullReferenceException` exception is thrown because the variable has been declared but not set.

The error that you want to trap is a `NullReferenceException`, and that exception is specified in the `Catch` block. You defined the variable `NullReferenceExceptionErr` for the exception variable argument; the standard practice among most developers is to use the exception name along with a suffix of `Err`. You then defined the type of exception that you want to test for and trap.

You place your error-handling code within the `Catch` block, as you have done here. When a `NullReferenceException` occurs, you set the `strData` variable to a string constant and then add the contents of that variable to the list box on your form.

Testing Your Error Handler

In the final example for this chapter, you use the Watch Window to make sure your Try...Catch statement is working. All the code in this Try It Out is in the Debugging folder in the Zip file for this chapter.

1. Set a breakpoint on the Try statement and then run your project. Once the form appears, click the Start button.

2. Once the breakpoint is encountered, right-click the variable strData and add a Watch from the context menu. Click the Watch1 window so that you can view the contents of the variable.

3. At this point, the strData variable has a value of Nothing. Click the Step Into icon on the toolbar; you'll be taken to the first line of code in the Try block.

4. Click the Step Into icon again. A NullReferenceException is thrown, and you are taken to the Catch block.

5. Note the value of the variable in the Watch1 window, click the Step Into icon twice more, and note the value of the variable in the Watch1 window (see Figure 9-26).

6. Click the Continue icon on the toolbar to allow the rest of your code to run.

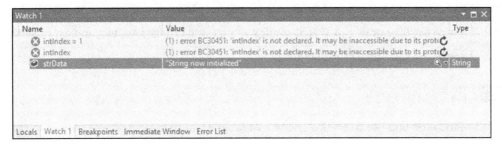

FIGURE 9-26

How It Works

As you become more familiar with the types of errors that can occur, you will be able to write more sophisticated structured error handlers. This comes only with experience and testing. You will discover more errors and will be able to handle them only by thoroughly testing your code. The online documentation for most methods that you use in Visual Studio 2015 will have Exceptions sections that list and explain the possible exceptions that could occur by using the method.

SUMMARY

This chapter covered some useful debugging tools that are built into the Visual Studio 2015 development environment. You saw how easy it is to debug your programs as you stepped through the various Try It Out sections.

In the discussion of breakpoints, you learned how to stop the execution of your program at any given point. As useful as this is, setting breakpoints with a hit counter in a loop is even more useful, because you can execute a loop several times before encountering a breakpoint in the loop.

You also examined some of the various windows available while debugging your program, such as the Watch window and the Locals window. These windows provide you with valuable information about the variables and expressions in your program. You can watch the values change and are able to change the values to control the execution of your code.

You should know what types of major errors you may encounter while developing and debugging your code, and you should be able to recognize syntax and execution errors, correcting them if possible. Although debugging a program for logic errors may be difficult at first, it does become easier with time and experience.

This chapter also covered structured error handling, and you should incorporate this knowledge into your programs at every opportunity. Structured error handling provides you with the opportunity to handle and correct errors at run time.

To summarize, you should know:

- How to recognize and correct major types of errors
- How to use breakpoints successfully to debug your program
- How to use the Locals and Watch windows to see and change variables and expressions
- How to use structured error handling

EXERCISES

1. What window do you use to track a specific variable while debugging?

2. How do you look at all of the variables in scope while debugging?

3. How do you best add error handling to your code?

4. Sometimes you need to cause errors to happen in your code. What keyword do you use to cause errors?

5. While debugging, how do you move to the very next statement?

▶ **WHAT YOU HAVE LEARNED IN THIS CHAPTER**

TOPIC	CONCEPTS
Major Types of Errors	Syntax, Execution, and Logic Errors
Error handling	Use `Try. . .Catch. . .Finally` statements to handle exceptions that are raised or thrown from your code. The `Finally` block always executes.
Breakpoints	Use breakpoints to stop execution of your code at a certain spot to debug.
Debugging	Step Into, Step Over, Step Out, Run, and Run To Cursor are common commands you will use to debug your program. You will use the Watch window, QuickWatch dialog, Locals window, and Autos window to aid your debugging.

10

Building Objects

WHAT YOU WILL LEARN IN THIS CHAPTER:

- ➤ Building a reusable object with methods and properties
- ➤ Inheriting the object that you build in another object
- ➤ Overriding methods and properties in your base object
- ➤ Creating your own namespace

WROX.COM CODE DOWNLOADS FOR THIS CHAPTER

The wrox.com code downloads for this chapter are found at www.wrox.com/ begvisualbasic2015 on the Download Code tab. The code is in the 092117 C10.zip download and individually named according to the names given throughout the chapter.

You may have heard the term *object-oriented* a lot since you first started using computers. You may also have heard that it is a scary and tricky subject to understand. In its early years it was, but today's modern tools and languages make object orientation (OO) a wonderfully easy-to-understand concept that brings massive benefits to software developers. This is mainly because languages such as Visual Basic and C# have matured to a point where they make creating objects and the programs that use them very easy indeed. With these languages, you will have no problem understanding even the most advanced object-oriented concepts and will be able to use them to build exciting object-based applications.

You have been using objects and classes throughout this book, but in this chapter you look at OO in detail and build on the foundations of the previous chapters to start producing some cool applications using Visual Basic 2015.

UNDERSTANDING OBJECTS

An object is almost anything you can think of. We work with physical objects all the time: televisions, cars, customers, reports, light bulbs—anything. In computer terms, an *object* is a representation of a thing that you want to manipulate in your application. Sometimes, the two definitions map exactly onto each other. So, if you have a physical car object sitting in your driveway and want to describe it in software terms, you build a software `Car` object that sits in your computer.

Likewise, if you need to write a piece of software that generates a bill for a customer, you may well have a `Bill` object and a `Customer` object. The `Customer` object represents the customer and may be capable of having a name and address, and also have the capability to generate the bill. The `Bill` object would represent an instance of a bill for a customer and would be able to impart the details of the bill and may also have the capability to print itself.

What is important here is the concept that the object has the intelligence to produce actions related to it—the `Customer` object can generate the bill. In effect, if you have a `Customer` object representing a customer, you can simply say to it: "Produce a bill for me." The `Customer` object would then go away and do all the hard work related to creating the bill. Likewise, when you have a `Bill` object, you can say to it: "Print yourself." What you have here are two examples of object *behavior*.

Objects are unbelievably useful because they turn software engineering into something conceptually similar to wooden building blocks. You arrange the blocks (the objects) to build something greater than the sum of the parts. The power of objects comes from the fact that, as someone using objects, you don't need to understand how they work behind the scenes. You're familiar with this concept with real-world objects, too. When you use a mobile phone, you don't need to understand how it works inside. Even if you do understand how a mobile phone works inside—even if you made it yourself—it's still much easier to use the mobile phone's simple interface. The interface can also prevent you from accidentally doing something that breaks the phone. The same is true with computer objects. Even if you build all the objects yourself, having the complicated workings hidden behind a simple interface can make your life much easier and safer.

OO is perhaps best explained by using a television metaphor. Look at the television in your home. There are several things you know how to do with it:

- ➤ Watch the image on the screen
- ➤ Change the channel
- ➤ Change the volume
- ➤ Switch it on or off

What you don't have to do is understand how everything works to allow you to carry out these activities. If asked, most people couldn't put together the components needed to make a modern television. We could, with a little research and patience, come up with something fairly basic, but nothing as complex as the one sitting in my home. However, we do understand how to use a television. We know how to change the channel, change the volume, switch it on and off, and so on.

Objects in software engineering work in basically the same way. When you have an object, you can use it and ask it do things without having to understand how the internals of it actually work. This is phenomenally powerful, as you'll see soon.

Software objects typically have the following characteristics:

> **Identity:** *User*: "What are you?" *TV*: "I'm a TV."

> **State:** *User*: "What channel am I watching?" *TV*: "You're watching Channel 4."

> **Behavior:** *User*: "Please turn up the volume to 50%." Then, we can use the State again. *User*: "How loud is the volume?" *TV*: "50%."

Encapsulation

The core concept behind object-oriented programming (OOP) is *encapsulation*. This is a big word, but it's very simple to understand. What this means is that the functionality is wrapped up in a self-contained manner and that you don't need to understand what it's actually doing when you ask it to do something.

If you remember from Chapter 3, you built a function that calculated the area of a circle. In that function, you encapsulated the logic of calculating the area so that anyone using the function could find the area without having to know how to perform the operation. This is the same concept but taken to the next level.

Methods and Properties

You interact with objects through methods and properties which can be defined as follows:

> *Methods* are ways of instructing an object to do something.

> *Properties* are things that describe features of an object.

A method was defined previously as a self-contained block of code that does something. This is true, but it is a rather simplistic definition. In fact, the strict definition of a method applies only to OO and is a way to manipulate an object—a way to instruct it to perform certain behaviors. In previous chapters, you created methods that instructed an object—in most cases a form—to do something. When you create a form in Visual Basic 2015, you are actually defining a new type of Form object.

So, if you need to turn on the TV, you need to find a method that does this because a method is something you get the object to do. When you invoke the method, the object is supposed to understand what to do to satisfy the request. To drive the point home, you don't care what it actually does; you just say, "Switch on." It's up to the TV to switch on relays to deliver power, boot up the circuitry, warm up the electron gun, and do all the other things that you don't need to understand!

> **NOTE** *On the other hand, if you need to change the channel, you might set the* Channel *property. If you want to tune into Channel 10, you set the* Channel *property to the value* **10**. *Again, the object is responsible for reacting to the request; you don't care about the technical hoops it has to go through to do that.*

Events

In Visual Basic 2015, you listen for events to determine when something has happened to a control on a form. You can consider an event as something that an object does. In effect, someone using an object can listen to events, like a `Click` event on a button or a `PowerOn` event on a TV. When the event is received, the developer can take some action. In OO terms, there is the `SwitchOn` method that gets invoked on the TV object; when the TV has warmed up (some old TVs take ages to warm up), it raises a `PowerOn` event. You could then respond to this event by adjusting the volume to the required level.

An event might also be used when the performer of an action is not the only entity interested in the action taking place. For example, when you have the TV on, you might go and get a drink during a commercial break. However, while you're in the kitchen, you keep your ears open for when the program starts again. Effectively, you are listening for a `ProgramResume` event. You do not cause the program to resume, but you do want to know when it does.

Visibility

To build decent objects you have to make them easy for other developers to use. For example, internally it might be really important for your TV object to know what frequency the tuner needs, but does the person using the TV care? More important, do you actually want the developer to be able to change this frequency directly? What you're trying to do is make the object more *abstract*.

Some parts of your object will be private, whereas other parts will be public. The public interface is available for others to use. The private parts are what you expect the object itself to use internally. The logic for the object exists in the private parts and may include methods and properties that are important but won't get called from outside the object. For example, a TV object might have methods for `ConnectPower`, `WarmUp`, and so on. These would be private and would all be called from the public `SwitchOn` method. Similarly, while there is a public `Channel` property, there will probably be a private `Frequency` property. The TV could not work without knowing the signal frequency it was receiving, but the users are interested only in the channel.

Now that you understand the basics of OO, take a look at how you can use objects within an application.

You'll notice that some of the code samples you saw in previous chapters included a line that looked similar to this:

```
lstData.Items.Add(strData)
```

That's a classic example of OO! `lstData` is, in fact, an object. `Items` is a property of the `lstData` object. The `Items` property is an object in its own right and has an `Add` method. The period (`.`) tells Visual Basic 2015 that the word to the right is a *member* of the word to the left. So, `Items` is a member of `lstData`, and `Add` is a member of `Items`. Members are either properties or methods of an object.

`lstData` is an instance of a class called `System.Windows.Forms.ListBox` (or just `ListBox`). This class is part of the .NET Framework you learned about in Chapter 2.

The ListBox class can display a list of items on the form and let a user choose a particular one. Again, here's the concept of encapsulation. As a user of ListBox, you don't need to know anything about the technologies involved in displaying the list or listening for input. You may not have even heard of GDI+, standard input, keyboard drivers, display drivers, or anything else that's part of the complex action of displaying a list on a form, yet you still have the capability to do it.

The ListBox is an example of an object that you can see. Users can look at a program running and know that a ListBox is involved. Most objects in OO programming are invisible and represent something in memory.

What Is a Class?

A *class* is the definition of a particular kind of object. The class is made up of the software code needed to store and retrieve the values of the properties, carry out the methods, and undergo the events pertaining to that kind of object. This is effectively the circuitry inside the black box. If you want to build a software object, you have to understand how the internals work. You express those internals with Visual Basic 2015 code. So, when the software developer using your object says, "Turn up the volume," you have to know how to instruct the amplifier to increase the output. (As a side note, remember that the amplifier is just another object. You don't necessarily need to know how it works inside. In OO programming, you will often find that one object is made up of other objects with some code to link them—just as a TV is made of standard components and a bit of custom circuitry.)

Each object belonging to a class is an *instance* of the class. So, if you have 50 TV objects, you have 50 instances of the TV class. The action of creating an instance is called *instantiation*. From now on, we won't say that you *create classes* but that you *instantiate objects*. The difference is used to reduce ambiguity. Creating a class is done at design time when you're building your software and involves writing the actual code. Instantiating an object is done at run time, when your program is being used.

A classic analogy is the cookie cutter. You can go out to your workshop and form a piece of metal into the shape of a Christmas tree. You do this once and put the cutter in a drawer in your kitchen. Whenever you need to create Christmas tree cookies, you roll some dough (the computer's memory) and stamp out however many you need. In effect you're instantiating cookies. You can reuse the cutter later to create more cookies, each the same shape as the ones before.

When you've instantiated the objects, you can manipulate each object's properties defined for the class, and you can invoke the methods defined for the class on the object. For example, suppose you build a class once at design time that represents a television. You can instantiate the class twice to make two objects from that class—say, one to represent the TV in the living room and one to represent the TV in the bedroom. Because both instances of the object share the same class, both instances have the same properties and methods. To turn on either TV, you invoke the SwitchOn method on it. To change the channel, you set its Channel property, and so on.

BUILDING CLASSES

You have already started building classes, particularly in Chapter 5. In general, when you design an algorithm, you will discover certain objects described. You need to abstract these real-world objects into a software representation. Here's an example:

1. Select a list of 10 customers from the database.

2. Go through each customer and prepare a bill for each.

3. When each bill has been prepared, print it.

For a pure object-oriented application (and with .NET you end up using objects to represent everything), every real-world object needs a software object. For example:

➤ **Customer:** An object that represents a customer.

➤ **Bill:** An object that represents a bill that is produced.

➤ **Printer:** An object that represents a hardware printer that can be used to print the bill.

When you write software in Visual Basic 2015, you are given a vast set of classes called the Microsoft .NET Framework classes. These classes describe virtually everything about the computing environment for which you're trying to write software. Writing object-oriented software for .NET is simply a matter of using objects that fit your needs and then creating new objects if required. Typically, while building an application, some of the classes you need are included in the .NET Framework, whereas you have to build others yourself.

For example, some objects in the .NET Framework provide printing functionality and database access functionality. Because your algorithm calls for both kinds of functionality, you don't need to write your own. If you need to print something, you create an object that understands how to print, tell it what you want to print, and then tell it to print it. Again, this is encapsulation—you don't care how to turn your document into PostScript commands and send it down the wire to the printer; the object knows how to do this for itself. In this example, there are classes that deal with printing that you can use to print bills, although there's no specific Printer object.

In some cases, objects that you need to represent do not exist in the .NET Framework. In this example, you need a Customer object and a Bill object.

REUSABILITY

Perhaps the hardest aspect of learning OOP is understanding how to divide responsibility for the work. One of the most beautiful aspects of OO is *code reuse*. Imagine that your company needs several different applications: one to display customer bills, one to register a new customer, and one to track customer complaints. In each of those applications, you need to have a Customer object.

To simplify the issue, those three projects are not going to be undertaken simultaneously. You start by doing the first; when finished, you move on to the second; when you've finished with that, you move on to the third. Do you want to build a new Customer class for each project, or do you want to build the class once and reuse it in each of the other two projects?

Reuse is typically regarded as something that's universally good, although there is a trade-off. Ideally, if you build a Customer class for one project, and another project you're working on calls for another Customer class, you should use the same one. However, it may well be that you can't just plug the class into another project for some reason. We say "for some reason" because there are no hard-and-fast rules when it comes to class design and reuse. It may also be easier or more cost-effective to build simple classes for each project rather than trying to create one complex object that does everything. This might sound like it requires a degree in clairvoyance, but luckily it comes with experience! As you develop more and more applications, you'll gain a better understanding of how to design great, reusable objects.

Each object should be responsible for activities involving itself and no more. We've discussed only two objects—Bill and Customer—so you'll look only at those.

The activity of printing a bill (say, for telephone charges) follows this algorithm:

- ➤ For a given customer, find the call details for the last period.
- ➤ Go through each call and calculate the price of each one.
- ➤ Aggregate the cost of each call into a total.
- ➤ Apply tax charges.
- ➤ Print out the bill with the customer's name, address, and bill summary on the first page and then the bill details on subsequent pages.

You have only two places in which you can code this algorithm: the Bill object or the Customer object. Which one do you choose?

The calls made are really a property of the Customer. Basically, you are using these details to create a bill. Most of the functionality would be placed in the Bill object. A Customer is responsible for representing a customer, not representing a bill. When you create a Bill object, you would associate it with a particular customer by using a Cust property, like this:

```
myBill.Cust = myCustomer
```

The Bill object would then know that it was a bill for a given customer (represented by the myCustomer object) and could use the customer's details when creating a bill. You might want to change some other properties of the Bill, such as where it will be mailed, whether it should contain a warning because it is overdue, and so on. Finally, the Bill would have a Print method:

```
myBill.Print()
```

The Bill object would then *use* a Printer object in order to print the bill. The Bill object would be said to be the user or *consumer* of the Printer object. It would even be said to consume the Printer object, even though (at least you hope) the printer is not used up or destroyed in printing the bill.

DESIGNING AN OBJECT

Contrary to what's been said so far, in this first project you're not going to define an algorithm and then build objects to support it. For this rather academic example, you're going to walk through some of the features of a typical object—in this case, a car.

There are certain facts you might want to know about the object:

➤ **What it looks like:** A car includes things like make, model, color, number of doors, and so on. These aspects of the car rarely change during the object's lifetime.

➤ **Its capabilities:** Horsepower, engine size, cylinder configuration, and so on.

➤ **What it's doing:** Whether it's stationary, moving forward or backward, and its speed and direction.

➤ **Where it is:** The Global Positioning System (GPS) coordinates of its current position. This is effectively its position relative to another object (the planet Earth).

> **NOTE** Controls on forms have coordinates that describe their location relative to the form (say, in pixels to the right of and below the top left corner).

You might also want to be able to control the object—for example, tell it to:

➤ Accelerate

➤ Decelerate

➤ Turn left

➤ Turn right

➤ Straighten out of a turn

➤ Do a three-point turn

➤ Stop completely

As described earlier, there are three concepts about objects that you need to be aware of: identity, state, and behavior. You should assume that identity is covered because you know what the class is, so the state and behavior are of interest here.

State

State describes facts about the object now. For example, a car's location and speed are part of its state. When designing objects, you need to think about what aspects of state you need to handle. It might not be useful to know a customer's speed, for example, but you might well want to know that customer's current address.

State tends to be implemented as values inside an object. Some of these values are publicly available through properties, and some are private. Also, some aspects of state might be publicly readable but not changeable. For example, cars have a speedometer that is readable to anybody using the car. But you can't change the car's speed by playing with the speedometer—you need to alter the car's behavior by using the brake or accelerator.

Behavior

Although a car might have a read-only Speed property, it would have methods to accelerate and decelerate. When you invoke an object's method, you are telling your object to do something—so behavior is usually associated with methods. Properties can also be associated with behavior. When you set a property to a particular value (such as by changing the setting of a control), you can trigger behavior.

Behavior is implemented as a set of Visual Basic 2015 statements that do something. This usually involves one or both of the following:

➤ **Changing its own state:** When you invoke the Accelerate method on a car, it should get faster if it is capable of doing so.

➤ **Somehow affecting the world outside the object:** This could be manipulating other objects in the application, displaying something to the user, saving something to a disk, or printing a document.

In this chapter, you won't build all the properties and methods discussed. Instead, you'll build a handful of the more interesting ones. You begin in the following Try It Out by creating a new class.

TRY IT OUT Creating a New Project and the Car Class

In this example, you will create a simple Car class. All the code for this Try It Out is in the Object folder in the Zip file for this chapter.

To learn how to add a class to a project, follow these simple steps:

1. Start Visual Basic 2015 and select File ➪ New Project from the menu.

2. When the Add New Project dialog appears, select the Console Application template and enter the name of the project as **Objects.** Click OK to create the project.

3. You now need to create a new class, which is done through the Solution Explorer, so right-click the Objects project and select Add ➪ Class. When prompted for a new class name, enter Car.vb and click Add. The new class is added to the Solution Explorer, and the editor now shows the code listing for it, albeit empty.

How It Works

In this example, you learned how to add a class to a project. This is the first step in creating your own custom objects.

Storing State

State describes what the object understands about itself, so if you give a Car object some state—for example, "You are blue"—you're giving the car object a fact, "The car I represent is blue."

How do you actually manage state in your classes? State is typically held in variables, and you define those variables within the class. You will see how to do this in a moment.

Usually, the methods and properties you build will either affect or use the state in some way. Imagine that you've built a property that changes the color of the car. When you *set* that property, the variable that's responsible for storing the state is changed to reflect the new value that it has been given. When you retrieve (*get*) that property, the variable responsible for storing the state is read, and the current value is returned to the caller.

In a way, then, properties *are* behaviors. Under the hood, a public property has two methods: a `Get` method and a `Set` method (defined by `Get. . .End Get` and `Set. . .End Set` blocks of code, as you already encountered in Chapter 5). A simple `Get` method for the `Color` property contains code to tell the caller the color of the car. A simple `Set` method for the `Color` property sets a value that represents the car's color. In a real application, though, `Color` would probably mean something more than just remembering a value. In a driving game, for example, the `Set` method of the `Color` property would need to make the screen change the color in which the car is shown on the screen.

When a property has no behavior at all, you can cheat. In the next Try It Out, you create a `Color` property by declaring a `Color` variable and making it public. When a property is implemented like this, it is also called a *field*. Although this can be a useful and very fast technique for adding properties, declaring a field instead of the `Property`, `Get`, and `Set` blocks is not actually recommended, but for this small example it is just fine.

TRY IT OUT   Creating an Object and Adding a Color Property

This example will teach you how to create a field or a property without a `Get` and `Set` block. Be sure to use the class you created in the preceding example. All the code in this Try It Out is in the code folder `Objects` in the Zip file for this chapter.

1. In the `Car` class, add this code below the `Public Car Class` statement:

    ```
    Public Color As String
    ```

2. That's it! However, you do need a way to consume the class so that you can see it working. Open `Module1.vb` and add this code:

    ```
    Sub Main()
            'Create a new car object
            Dim objCar As New Car

            'Set the Color property to Red
            objCar.Color = "Red"

            'Show what the value of the property is
            Console.WriteLine("My car is this color:")
            Console.WriteLine(objCar.Color)

            'Wait for input from the user
            Console.ReadLine()
    End Sub
    ```

3. Save your project by clicking the Save All button on the toolbar.

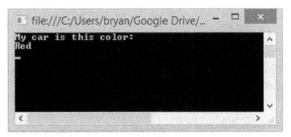

4. Now run the project. A new window similar to Figure 10-1 will appear.

5. Press Enter to end the program.

How It Works

FIGURE 10-1

This example illustrates that defining a field is easy. The following line of code tells the class that you want to create a variable called `Color` and you want the field to hold a string of text characters:

```
Public Color As String
```

The use of the `Public` keyword when you declare the `Color` variable tells the class that the variable is accessible to developers using the `Car` class, not only from within the class itself. Using the object is simple, and you do this from within `Module1.vb`. This process actually takes two steps:

1. Declare a variable to refer to an object for the class.

2. Instantiate the object. The following line of code creates an object variable called `objCar` and specifies that it will hold exclusively any objects created using the `Car` class:

```
Dim objCar As Car
```

When you define the variable, it doesn't yet have an object instance associated with it; you are simply identifying the type of object. It's a bit like telling the computer to give you a hook that you can hang a `Car` object on, and calling the hook `objCar`. You haven't hung anything on it yet—to do that you have to create an instance of the class. This is done using the `New` keyword:

```
Set objCar = New Car
```

But Visual Basic 2015 allows you to combine both steps into one line of code:

```
'Create a new car object
Dim objCar As New Car
```

What you're saying here is, "Let `objCar` refer to a newly created object instantiated from the class `Car`." In other words, "Create a new car and hang it on the hook called `objCar`." You now have a `Car` object and can refer to it with the name `objCar`.

After you have an object instance, you can set its properties and call its methods. Here is how you set the `Color` property:

```
'Set the Color property to Red
objCar.Color = "Red"
```

After the property has been set, it can be retrieved as many times as you want or its value can be changed at a later point. Here, retrieval is illustrated by passing the `Color` property to the `WriteLine` method on the `Console` class:

```
'Show what the value of the property is
Console.WriteLine("My car is this color:")
Console.WriteLine(objCar.Color)
```

The `Console.ReadLine` line means that the program does not continue until you press Enter. Basically, the console window is waiting for input from you:

```
'Wait for input from the user
Console.ReadLine()
```

Even though this is not really a property from the point of view of a developer using the class, it works just like one. In fact, real properties are methods that look like variables to users of the class. Whether you use a method or a property really depends on what the users of your class find easier. You'll start to see this in the next section.

Real Properties

Now that you've seen how to cheat (using a field), let's see how to do things properly. The property you saw can be set to pretty much anything. As long as it's a string, it will be accepted. Also, setting the property doesn't do anything except change the object's internal state. Often you want to control what values a property can be set to; for example, you might have a list of valid colors that a car can be. You might also want to associate a change to a property with a particular action. For example, when you change a channel on the TV, you want it to do a bit more than just change its mind about what channel it's displaying. You want the TV to show a different picture! Just changing the value of a variable won't help here.

Another reason to use real properties is that you want to prevent the user of the class from directly changing the value. This is called a *read-only property*. The car's speed is a good example of how a class that models a real-world object should behave like that real-world object. If you are going 60 mph, you cannot simply change the speed to a value you prefer. You can read the speed of a car from the speedometer, but you cannot change (write) the speed of the car by physically moving the needle around the dial with your finger. You have to control the car in another fashion, which you do by stepping on the gas pedal or the brake to either accelerate or decelerate, respectively. To model this feature in the `Car` class, you use methods (`Accelerate`, `Decelerate`) that affect the speed and keep a read-only property around called `Speed` that will report on the current speed of the vehicle.

You'll still need to keep the speed around in a member variable, but what you need is a member variable that can be seen or manipulated only by the class itself. You accomplish this by using the `Private` keyword:

```
Private intSpeed As Integer
```

The `intSpeed` variable is marked as `Private` and can, therefore, be accessed only by functions defined inside the class. Users of `Car` will not even be aware of its presence.

TRY IT OUT Adding a Speed Property

Now you'll see how you can build a property that gives the user of the object read-only access to the car's speed. All the code for this Try It Out is in the Object folder in the Zip file for this chapter.

1. To define a private variable, use the Private rather than the Public keyword. Add this statement to the Car class:

```
Public Color As String
Private intSpeed As Integer
```

2. To report the speed, you need to build a read-only property. Add this code to your Car class:

```
'Speed—read-only property to return the speed
Public ReadOnly Property Speed() As Integer
    Get
        Return intSpeed
    End Get
End Property
```

3. Now build a method called Accelerate that adjusts the speed of the car by however many miles per hour you specify. Add this code after the Speed property:

```
'Accelerate—add mph to the speed
Public Sub Accelerate(accelerateBy As Integer)
    'Adjust the speed
    intSpeed += accelerateBy
End Sub
```

4. To test the object, you need to make some changes to the Main procedure in Module1. Open the file and modify the code as shown:

```
Sub Main()
    'Create a new car object
    Dim objCar As New Car

    'Report the speed
    Console.WriteLine("The car's speed is:")
    Console.WriteLine(objCar.Speed)

    'Accelerate
    objCar.Accelerate(5)

    'Report the new speed
    Console.WriteLine("The car's speed is now:")
    Console.WriteLine(objCar.Speed)

    'Wait for input from the user
    Console.ReadLine()
End Sub
```

5. Now run the project. A new window similar to Figure 10-2 appears.

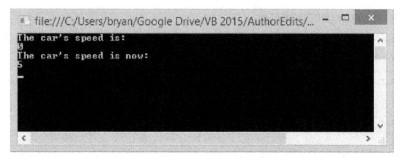

FIGURE 10-2

How It Works

The first thing you do in this example is define a private member variable called `intSpeed` in the `Car` class:

```
Private intSpeed As Integer
```

By default, when the object is created, `intSpeed` has a value of zero because this is the default value for the `Integer` data type.

You then define a read-only property that returns the current speed:

```
'Speed—readonly property to return the speed
Public ReadOnly Property Speed() As Integer
    Get
        Return intSpeed
    End Get
End Property
```

When you define properties, you can set them to be read-only (through the `ReadOnly` keyword), write-only (through the `WriteOnly` keyword), or both readable and writable (by using neither keyword). Reading a property is known as *getting* the value, whereas writing to a property is known as *setting* the value. The code between `Get` and `End Get` is executed when the property is read. In this case, the only thing you're doing is returning the value currently stored in `intSpeed`.

You also created a method called `Accelerate`. This method doesn't have to return a value, so you use the `Sub` keyword:

```
'Accelerate—add mph to the speed
Public Sub Accelerate(accelerateBy As Integer)
    'Adjust the speed
    intSpeed += accelerateBy
End Sub
```

The method takes a single parameter called `accelerateBy`, which you use to tell the method how much to increase the speed by. The only action of the method is to adjust the internal member `intSpeed`. In real life, the pressure on the accelerator pedal, along with factors such as wind speed and road surface, affect the speed. The speed is an outcome of several factors—not something you can just change. You need some complex code to simulate this. Here you are just keeping things simple and incrementing the intSpeed variable with the value passed to the method.

Accelerating a car is another example of encapsulation. To accelerate the car in a real-world implementation, you need an actuator of some kind to open the throttle further until the required speed is reached. As consumers of the object, you don't care how this is done. All you care about is how to tell the car to accelerate.

Consuming this new functionality is simple:

1. Create the variable and instantiate the object as you did in the previous exercise:

```
'Create a new car object
Dim objCar As New Car
```

2. Write the current speed:

```
'Report the speed
Console.WriteLine("The car's speed is:")
Console.WriteLine(objCar.Speed)
```

Notice that you're using the read-only Speed property to get the current speed of the car. When the object is first created, the internal intSpeed member will be set at 0.

3. Call Accelerate and use it to increase the speed of the car:

```
'Accelerate
objCar.Accelerate(5)
```

4. Write out the new speed:

```
'Report the new speed
Console.WriteLine("The car's speed is now:")
Console.WriteLine(objCar.Speed)
```

Read/Write Properties

Why would you need to use the Property keyword to define properties that are both readable and writable if you can achieve the same effect with a line like this?

```
Public Color As String
```

If you build the property manually using the Property keyword, you can write code that is executed whenever the property is set or read. This is extremely powerful!

For example, the Property keyword allows you to provide validation for new values. Imagine you had a property called NumberOfDoors. You wouldn't want this to be set to nonsense values like 0 or 23453. Instead, you would have a possible range. For modern cars, this will range from 2 to 5.

> **NOTE** This is an important consideration for developers building objects. It's imperative that you make life as easy as possible for a developer to consume your object. Dealing with problems such as making sure a car can't have 10 million doors is an important aspect of object design.

Likewise, you might not have the information to return to the consumer of your object when you are asked to return the property; you might have to retrieve the value from somewhere or otherwise calculate it. You might have a property that describes the total number of orders a customer has ever made or the total number of chew toys a dog has destroyed in its life. If you build this as a property, you can intercept the instruction to get the value and find the actual value you require on demand from some other data store, such as a database or a web service. You'll see this in later chapters.

For now, let's deal with the number of doors problem.

TRY IT OUT   Adding a NumberOfDoors Property

You have already seen how to add a property, and this example will help you reinforce that knowledge. All the code for this Try It Out is in the Objects folder in the Zip file for this chapter.

1. The first thing you need to do is build a private member that will hold the number of doors. You'll define this member as having a default of 5. Add this code in the Car class as bolded here:

    ```
    Public Color As String
    Private intSpeed As Integer
    Private intNumberOfDoors As Integer = 5
    ```

2. Now you can build a property that gets and sets the number of doors, provided the number of doors is always between 2 and 5. Add this code to your Car class directly beneath the Accelerate method:

    ```
    'NumberOfDoors—get/set the number of doors
    Public Property NumberOfDoors() As Integer
        'Called when the property is read
        Get
            Return intNumberOfDoors
        End Get
        'Called when the property is set
        Set(value As Integer)
            'Is the new value between two and five
            If value >= 2 And value <= 5 Then
                intNumberOfDoors = value
            End If
        End Set
    End Property
    ```

In this chapter, you'll ignore the problem of telling the developer if the user has provided an invalid value for a property. Ideally, whenever this happens, you need to throw an exception. The developer will be able to detect this exception and behave accordingly. (For example, if the user types the number of doors as 9999 into a text box, the program could display a message box indicating that an invalid value has been provided for the number of doors, because no car has that many.) You learned about exception handling in Chapter 9.

3. To test the property, you need to change the Main procedure in Module1 by modifying the code as indicated here:

```
Sub Main()
    'Create a new car object
    Dim objCar As New Car

    'Report the number of doors
    Console.WriteLine("The number of doors is:")
    Console.WriteLine(objCar.NumberOfDoors)

    'Try changing the number of doors to 1000
    objCar.NumberOfDoors = 1000

    'Report the number of doors
    Console.WriteLine("The number of doors is:")
    Console.WriteLine(objCar.NumberOfDoors)

    'Now try changing the number of doors to 2
    objCar.NumberOfDoors = 2

    'Report the number of doors
    Console.WriteLine("The number of doors is:")
    Console.WriteLine(objCar.NumberOfDoors)

    'Wait for input from the user
    Console.ReadLine()
End Sub
```

4. Now run the project. You should see a screen like the one in Figure 10-3.

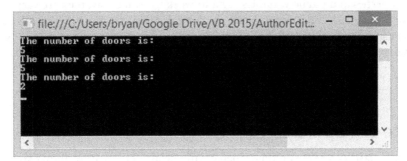

FIGURE 10-3

How It Works

In this example, you define a private member variable called intNumberOfDoors. You also assign the default value of 5 to this variable.

```
Private intNumberOfDoors As Integer = 5
```

The motivation behind setting a value at this point is simple: You want `intNumberOfDoors` to always be between 2 and 5. When the object is created, the `intNumberOfDoors` will be assigned a value of 5. Without this assignment, `intNumberOfDoors` would have a default value of 0. This would be inconsistent with the understanding that the number of doors must always be between 2 and 5, so you guard against it.

Next is the property itself. The `Get` portion is simple. Just return the value held in `intNumberOfDoors`. The `Set` is more complex; it involves a check to ensure that the new value is valid. The new value is passed in through a parameter called `value`:

```
'NumberOfDoors—get/set the number of doors
Public Property NumberOfDoors() As Integer
    'Called when the property is read
    Get
        Return intNumberOfDoors
    End Get
    'Called when the property is set
    Set(value As Integer)
        'Is the new value between two and five
        If value >= 2 And value <= 5 Then
            intNumberOfDoors = value
        End If
    End Set
End Property
```

The test code you add to Module1 is not very complex. You simply display the initial value of `intNumberOfDoors` and then try to change it to `1000`. The validation code in the `NumberOfDoors` property won't change the `intNumberOfDoors` member variable if an inconsistent number is used, so when you report the number of doors again, you'll find it hasn't changed from 5. Lastly, you try setting it to 2, which is a valid value; and this time, when you report the number of doors, you get an output of 2.

Even though read-write properties and public variables seem to work the same way, they are very different. When your Visual Basic 2015 code is compiled, the compiled code treats property calls as calls to a method. Always using properties instead of public variables makes your objects more flexible and extendable. Of course, using public variables is easier and quicker. You need to decide what is most important in each case.

Auto-Implemented Properties

A newer feature in Visual Basic can save you time when creating class. This feature allows you to create and set properties on one line of code. The code that follows is an example of how you would create an auto-implemented property named `Speed` with a default value of zero.

```
Public Property Speed As Integer = "0"
```

When using this new feature, a private field is created named `_Speed`. You will not be able to use a variable with the same name or you will see a compile error. This hidden field is called a backing field.

The IsMoving Method

When building objects, you should always have the following question in the back of your mind: "How can I make this object easier to use?" For example, if the consumer needs to know whether the car is moving, what would be the easiest way to determine this?

One way would be to look at the Speed property. If this is zero, it can be assumed that the car has stopped. (On most cars, the speed is not reported when the car is moving in reverse, so assume for now that you have only forward gears!) However, relying on the developers using the object to understand this relies on their having an understanding of whatever is being modeled. Common sense tells us that an object with a speed of "zero mph" is stationary, but should you assume anyone consuming the object shares your idea of common sense?

Instead, it's good practice to create methods that deal with these eventualities. One way you can solve this problem is by creating an IsMoving method, as shown in the next exercise.

TRY IT OUT   Adding an IsMoving Method

The IsMoving method will return a Boolean value. Either the car is moving or not. All the code for this Try It Out is in the Object folder in the Zip file for this chapter.

1. All the IsMoving method needs in order to work is a simple test to look at the speed of the car and make a True or False determination as to whether it's moving. Add this code to the Car class after the NumberOfDoors property:

```
'IsMoving—is the car moving?
Public Function IsMoving() As Boolean
    'Is the car's speed zero?
    If Speed = 0 Then
        Return False
    Else
        Return True
    End If
End Function
```

2. To test this method, make the following changes to the Main procedure in Module1 with this new code as indicated:

```
Sub Main()
    'Create a new car object
    Dim objCar As New Car

    'Accelerate the car to 25mph
    objCar.Accelerate(25)

    'Report whether or not the car is moving
    If objCar.IsMoving = True Then
        Console.WriteLine("The car is moving.")
    Else
```

```
        Console.WriteLine("The car is stopped.")
    End If

    'Wait for input from the user
    Console.ReadLine()
End Sub
```

3.   Now try running the project. A new window similar to Figure 10-4 will appear.

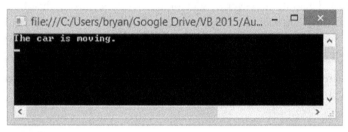

FIGURE 10-4

How It Works

In this example, you created a simple method that examines the value of the Speed property and returns True if the speed is not zero, or False if it is:

```
'IsMoving—is the car moving?
Public Function IsMoving() As Boolean
    'Is the car's speed zero?
    If Speed = 0 Then
        Return False
    Else
        Return True
    End If
End Function
```

Although this method is simple, it removes the conceptual leap required on the part of the consumer to understand whether the object is moving. There's no confusion as to whether the car is moving based on interpreting the value of one or more properties; one simple method returns a definitive answer.

Of course, before you go off and build hundreds of methods for every eventuality, remember that, ironically, the more methods and properties an object has, the harder it is to understand. Take care while designing the object and try to strike the right balance between too few and too many methods and properties.

You may be wondering why you used a method here when this is actually a property. All you are doing is reporting the object's state, without affecting its behavior. There is no reason for not using a property here. However, using a method does remind users of the object that this value is calculated and is not a simple report of an internal variable. It also adds a bit of variety to your examples and reminds you how easy it is to add a method!

CONSTRUCTORS

One of the most important aspects of object design is the concept of a *constructor*. As mentioned in Chapter 9, this is a piece of initialization code that runs whenever an object is instantiated. It's extremely useful when you need the object to be set up in a particular way before you use it. For example, it can be used to set up default values, just as you did for the number of doors earlier.

In this Try It Out, you take a look at a simple constructor.

TRY IT OUT Creating a Constructor

You need to set a few properties whenever the object is instantiated. You will set three properties with default values in this example. All the code for this Try It Out is in the Object folder in the Zip file for this chapter.

1. For the sake of this discussion, you're going to remove the default value of 5 from the intNumberOfDoors member. Make this change to the Car class:

```
Public Color As String
Private intSpeed As Integer

Private intNumberOfDoors As Integer
```

2. Add this method, which forms the constructor. Any code within this method is executed whenever an object is created from the Car class:

```
'Constructor
Public Sub New()
    'Set the default values
    Color = "White"
    intSpeed = 0
    intNumberOfDoors = 5
End Sub
```

3. To test the action of the constructor, you create a separate procedure that displays the car's details. Add the DisplayCarDetails procedure in Module1:

```
'DisplayCarDetails-procedure that displays a car's details
Sub DisplayCarDetails(theCar As Car)
    'Display the details of the car
    Console.WriteLine("Color: " & theCar.Color)
    Console.WriteLine("Number of doors: " & theCar.NumberOfDoors)
    Console.WriteLine("Current speed: " & theCar.Speed)
End Sub
```

4. Modify the Main procedure in Module1 to call the DisplayCarDetails procedure:

```
Sub Main()
    'Create a new car object
    Dim objCar As New Car

    'Display the details of the car
    DisplayCarDetails(objCar)

    'Wait for input from the user
    Console.ReadLine()
End Sub
```

5. Try running the project. You should see output similar to Figure 10-5.

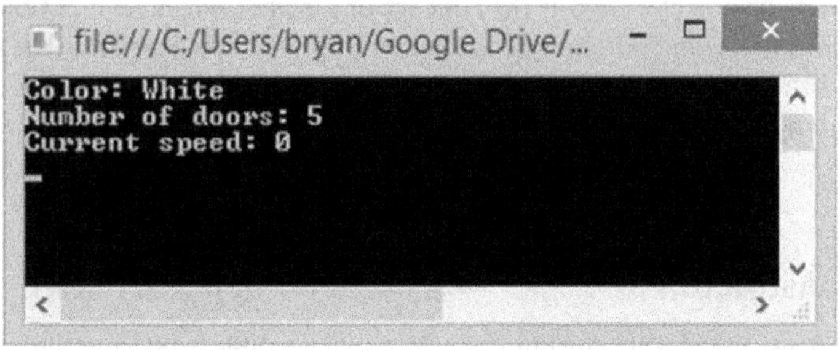

FIGURE 10-5

How It Works

In this example, the code in the constructor is called whenever an object is created. This is where you take an opportunity to set the default values for the members:

```
'Constructor
Public Sub New()
    'Set the default values
    Color = "White"
    intSpeed = 0
    intNumberOfDoors = 5
End Sub
```

You see the results of the changes made to the properties when you run the project and see the details of the car displayed in the window. A constructor must always be a subroutine (defined with the Sub keyword) and must always be called New. This provides consistency in the .NET Framework for all class constructors, and the .NET Framework will always execute this procedure when a class is instantiated.

When you test the object, you use a separate function called DisplayCarDetails in Module1. This is useful when you need to see the details of more than one Car object or want to see the details of the Car object multiple times in your code.

INHERITANCE

Although the subject of *inheritance* is quite an advanced OOP topic, it is really useful. In fact, the .NET Framework itself makes heavy use of it, and you have already created classes that inherit from another class—every Windows Form that you write is a new class inherited from a simple blank form (the starting point when you create a form).

Inheritance is used to create objects that have everything another object has, but also some of their own bits and pieces. It's used to extend the functionality of objects, but it doesn't require you to have an understanding of how the internals of the object work. This is in line with your quest of building and using objects without having to understand how the original programmers put them together.

Inheritance enables you to, in effect, take another class and bolt on your own functionality, either by adding new methods and properties or by replacing existing methods and properties. For example, you can move from a general car class to more specific variations—for example, sports car, SUV, van, and so on.

For example, if you wanted to model a sports car, you would likely want the default number of doors to be 2 rather than 5, and you might also like to have properties and methods that help you understand the performance of the car, such as `Weight` and `PowerToWeightRatio`, as shown in Figure 10-6.

One thing that you need to understand about inheritance is the way that access to public and private members is controlled. Any public member, such as `Color`, is accessible to inheriting classes. However, private members such as `intSpeed` are not. This means that if `SportsCar` has to change the speed of the car, it has to do so through the properties and methods provided in the `Car` class itself.

In other commonly encountered terminology, the inheriting class is called a *derived class*, and the class it inherits from is its *base class*. `Car` is the base class from which `SportsCar` is derived. The terms *subclass* and *superclass* are also used. `SportsCar` is a subclass of `Car`; `Car` is the superclass of `SportsCar`. The sub and super prefixes mean the same as they do when speaking of subsets and supersets in mathematics.

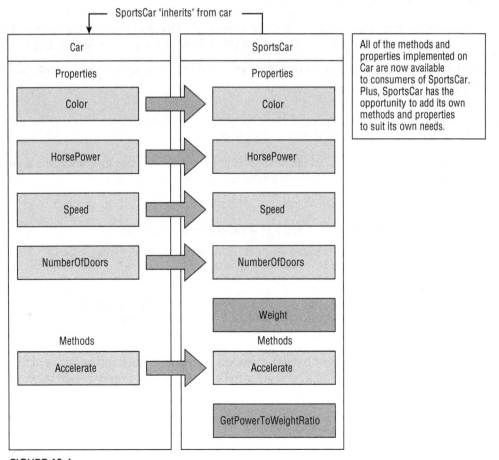

FIGURE 10-6

Adding New Methods and Properties

To illustrate inheritance, you will inherit from a base class next.

Inheriting from Car

In the next Try It Out, you create a new class called `SportsCar`, which inherits from `Car` and enables you to see the power-to-weight ratio of your sports car. All the code for this Try It Out is in the `Object` code folder in the Zip file for this chapter.

1. For this demonstration, you need to add an additional public variable to the `Car` class that represents the horsepower of the car. Of course, if you want to make it really robust, you would use a property and ensure a sensible range of values. But here, simplicity and speed win out. Open the `Car` class and add this line of code as indicated:

```
Public Color As String
Public HorsePower As Integer
Private intSpeed As Integer
Private intNumberOfDoors As Integer
```

2. Create a new class in the usual way by right-clicking the Objects project in the Solution Explorer and selecting Add ⇨ Class. Enter the name of the class as `SportsCar.vb` and click Add.

3. To tell `SportsCar` that it inherits from `Car`, you need to use the `Inherits` keyword. Add this code to `SportsCar`:

```
Public Class SportsCar
    Inherits Car
End Class
```

4. At this point, `SportsCar` has all the methods and properties that `Car` has. What you want to do now is add a new public variable called `Weight` to the `SportsCar` class:

```
Public Weight As Integer
```

5. To test the new class you need to add a new procedure to Module1:

```
'DisplaySportsCarDetails—procedure that displays a sports car's details
Sub DisplaySportsCarDetails(theCar As SportsCar)
    'Display the details of the sports car
    Console.WriteLine()
    Console.WriteLine("Sports Car Horsepower: " & theCar.HorsePower)
    Console.WriteLine("Sports Car Weight: " & theCar.Weight)
End Sub
```

6. Modify the `Main` procedure in Module1. Pay close attention to the fact that you need to create a `SportsCar` object, not a `Car` object, in order to get at the `Weight` property. Add the new code as indicated:

```
Sub Main()
    'Create a new sports car object
```

```
    Dim objCar As New SportsCar

    'Modify the number of doors
    objCar.NumberOfDoors = 2

    'Set the horsepower and weight(kg)
    objCar.HorsePower = 240
    objCar.Weight = 1085

    'Display the details of the car
    DisplayCarDetails(objCar)
    DisplaySportsCarDetails(objCar)

    'Wait for input from the user
    Console.ReadLine()
End Sub
```

7. Run the project. You should see output similar to that shown in Figure 10-7.

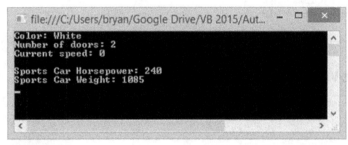

FIGURE 10-7

How It Works

The directive to make SportsCar inherit from Car is done with the Inherits keyword in this example:

```
Public Class SportsCar
    Inherits Car
```

At this point, the new SportsCar class contains all the methods and properties of the Car class, but it cannot see or modify the private member variables. When you add your new property:

```
Public Weight As Integer
```

You have a property that's available only when you create instances of SportsCar, and not available to you if you are creating plain instances of Car. This is an important point: If you don't create an instance of SportsCar, you'll get a compile error if you try to access the Weight property. Weight isn't, and never has been, a property of Car (refer to Figure 10-6 for a clarification of this).

The new DisplaySportsCarDetails procedure displays the Horsepower property from the Car class and the Weight property from the SportsCar class. Remember that because the SportsCar class inherits from the Car class, it contains all the methods and properties in the Car class:

```
'DisplaySportsCarDetails—procedure that displays a sports car's details
Sub DisplaySportsCarDetails(theCar As SportsCar)
    'Display the details of the sports car
```

```
        Console.WriteLine()
        Console.WriteLine("Sports Car Horsepower: " & theCar.HorsePower)
        Console.WriteLine("Sports Car Weight: " & theCar.Weight)
    End Sub
```

You instantiate a new `SportsCar` object in your `Main` procedure; this allows you to get and set the value for the `Weight` property:

```
'Create a new sports car object
        Dim objCar As New SportsCar
```

You can call the `DisplayCarDetails` procedure and pass it a `SportsCar` object because `SportsCar` is a subclass of `Car`—that is, every `SportsCar` is also a `Car`. The `DisplayCarDetails` procedure does not access any of the properties of the `SportsCar` class, so call this procedure, passing it the `SportsCar` object that you created. You then call the `DisplaySportsCarDetails` procedure to display the properties of both the `Car` class and the `SportsCar` class:

```
'Display the details of the car
        DisplayCarDetails(objCar)
        DisplaySportsCarDetails(objCar)
```

Adding a GetPowerToWeightRatio Method

The `GetPowerToWeightRatio` method will determine how much horsepower per pound is produced. You will add it next.

TRY IT OUT   Adding a GetPowerToWeightRatio Method

A `GetPowerToWeightRatio` method could be implemented as a read-only property (in which case you would probably call it `PowerToWeightRatio` instead), but for this discussion you'll add it as a method in the next Try It Out. All the code in this Try It Out is in the `Objects` folder in the Zip file for this chapter.

1. For this method, all you need to do is divide the horsepower by the weight. Add this code to the `SportsCar` class:

```
'GetPowerToWeightRatio—work out the power to weight
Public Function GetPowerToWeightRatio() As Double
    'Calculate the horsepower
    Return CType(HorsePower, Double) / CType(Weight, Double)
End Function
```

2. To see the results, add the bolded code to the `DisplaySportsCarDetails` procedure in Module1:

```
'DisplaySportsCarDetails—procedure that displays a sports car's details
Sub DisplaySportsCarDetails(theCar As SportsCar)
  'Display the details of the sports car
  Console.WriteLine()
  Console.WriteLine("Sports Car Horsepower: " & theCar.HorsePower)
  Console.WriteLine("Sports Car Weight: " & theCar.Weight)
  Console.WriteLine("Power to Weight Ratio: " & theCar.GetPowerToWeightRatio)
End Sub
```

3. Run the project and you'll see something similar to Figure 10-8.

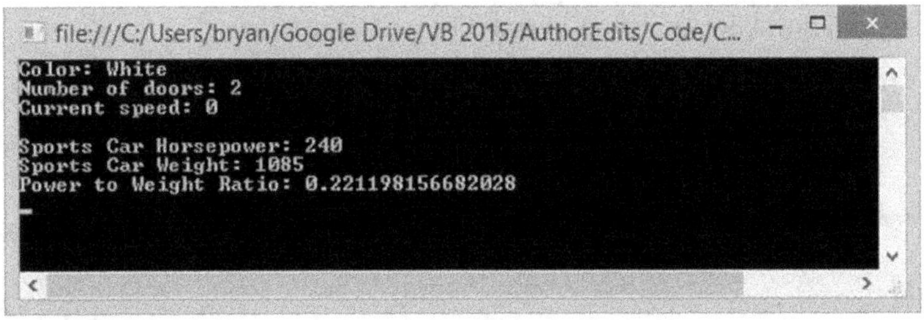

file:///C:/Users/bryan/Google Drive/VB 2015/AuthorEdits/Code/C...
Color: White
Number of doors: 2
Current speed: 0
Sports Car Horsepower: 240
Sports Car Weight: 1085
Power to Weight Ratio: 0.221198156682028

FIGURE 10-8

How It Works

Again, all you've done in this example is to add a new method to the new class called `GetPowerToWeightRatio`. This method then becomes available to anyone working with an instance of `SportsCar`, as shown in Figure 10-9.

SportsCar "inherits" from car
Car
Properties
Color
HorsePower
Speed
NumberOfDoors
Methods
Accelerate
SportsCar
Properties
Color
HorsePower
Speed
NumberOfDoors
Weight
Methods
Accelerate
GetPowerToWeightRatio
A new method is added and is only available to consumers of SportsCar, not consumers of Car.

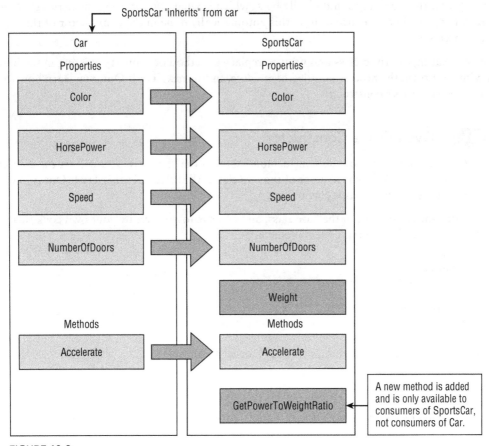

FIGURE 10-9

The only thing you have to be careful of is that if you divide an integer by an integer, you get an integer result, but what you actually want here is a floating-point number. You have to convert the integer `HorsePower` and `Weight` properties to `Double` values in order to see the results:

```
'Calculate the horsepower
Return CType(HorsePower, Double) / CType(Weight, Double)
```

Changing Defaults

In addition to adding new properties and methods, you might want to change the way an existing method or property works from that of the base class. To do this, you need to create your own implementation of the method or property.

Think back to the discussion on constructors. These are methods that are called whenever the object is created, and they enable you to get the object into a state where it can be used by a developer. In this constructor you set the default `intNumberOfDoors` value to be 5. However, in a sports car, this number should ideally be 2, which is what you set using the `NumberOfDoors` property. But wouldn't it be nice to have this automatically done in the constructor of the `SportsCar` class?

If you are creating a derived class and want to replace a method or property existing in the base class with your own, the process is called *overriding*. In this next Try It Out, you learn how to override the base class's constructor.

TRY IT OUT Overriding a Constructor

The `SportsCar` class does not need the same default values as the `Car` class. You will set the correct default values by overriding the constructor of the `Car` class. All the code in this Try It Out is in the `Objects` folder in the Zip file for this chapter.

1. To override the constructor in the base class, all you have to do is create your own constructor in the `SportsCar` class. Add this code to `SportsCar`:

    ```
    'Constructor
    Public Sub New()
        'Change the default values
        Color = "Green"
        NumberOfDoors = 2
    End Sub
    ```

2. Remove the following code from the `Main` procedure in Module1:

    ```
    'Modify the number of doors
    objCar.NumberOfDoors = 2
    ```

3. Run your project to test your constructor in the `SportsCar` class. You should see output similar to Figure 10-10.

How It Works

The new constructor that you added to SportsCar in this example runs after the existing one in Car. The .NET Framework knows that it's supposed to run the code in the constructor of the base class before running the new constructor in the class that inherits from it, so in effect it runs this code first:

```
'Constructor
Public Sub New()
    'Set the default values
    Color = "White"
    intSpeed = 0
    intNumberOfDoors = 5
End Sub
```

Then it runs this code:

```
'Constructor
Public Sub New()
    'Change the default values
    Color = "Green"
    NumberOfDoors = 2
End Sub
```

To summarize what happens:

1. The constructor on the base class Car is called.

2. Color is set to White.

3. intSpeed is set to 0.

4. intNumberOfDoors is set to 5.

5. The constructor on the new class SportsCar is called.

6. Color is set to Green.

7. NumberOfDoors is set to 2.

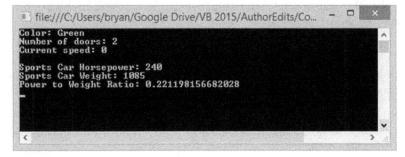

FIGURE 10-10

Because you defined intNumberOfDoors as a private member in Car, you cannot directly access it from inherited classes, just as you wouldn't be able to access it directly from a consumer of the class. Instead, you rely on being able to set an appropriate value through the NumberOfDoors property.

Polymorphism: Scary Word, Simple Concept

Another very common word mentioned when talking about OOP is *polymorphism* (defined in a little bit). This is perhaps the scariest term, but it is one of the easiest to understand! In fact, you have already done it in the previous example.

Look again at the code for `DisplayCarDetails`:

```
'DisplayCarDetails-procedure that displays a car's details
    Sub DisplayCarDetails(theCar As Car)
        'Display the details of the car
        Console.WriteLine("Color: " & theCar.Color)
        Console.WriteLine("Number of doors: " & theCar.NumberOfDoors)
        Console.WriteLine("Current speed: " & theCar.Speed)
    End Sub
```

The first line says that the parameter you want to accept is a `Car` object; but when you call the object, you're actually passing it a `SportsCar` object.

Look at how you create the object and call `DisplayCarDetails`:

```
'Create a new sportscar object
    Dim objCar As New SportsCar

    'Display the details of the car
    DisplayCarDetails(objCar)
```

How can it be that if the function takes a `Car` object, you're allowed to pass it as a `SportsCar` object?

Well, *polymorphism* (which comes from the Greek for *many forms*) means that an object can be treated as if it were a different kind of object, provided common sense prevails. In this case, you can treat a `SportsCar` object like a `Car` object because `SportsCar` inherits from `Car`. This act of inheritance dictates that what a `SportsCar` object can do must include everything that a `Car` object can do; therefore, you can treat the two objects in the same way. If you need to call a method on `Car`, `SportsCar` must also implement the method.

This does not hold true the other way around. Your `DisplaySportsCarDetails` function, defined like this, cannot accept a `Car` object:

```
    Sub DisplaySportsCarDetails(theCar As SportsCar)
```

`Car` is not guaranteed to be able to do everything a `SportsCar` can do because the extra methods and properties you add to `SportsCar` won't exist on `Car`. `SportsCar` is a more specific type of `Car`.

To summarize, when people talk about polymorphism, this is the action they are referring to—the principle that an object can behave as if it were another object without the developer having to go through too many hoops to make it happen.

Overriding More Methods

Although you've overridden `Car`'s constructor, for completeness you should look at how to override a normal method.

To override a method, you need to have the method in the base Car class. Because Accelerate shouldn't change depending on whether you have a sports car or a normal car, and IsMoving was added for ease of use—and hence doesn't really count in this instance, because it isn't a behavior of the object—you need to add a new method called CalculateAccelerationRate. Assume that on a normal car this is a constant, and on a sports car you change it so that it takes the power-to-weight ratio into consideration. In the following Try It Out, you add another method to override.

TRY IT OUT Adding and Overriding Another Method

This example will reinforce the concept of overriding. All the code for this Try It Out is in the Object folder in the Zip file for this chapter.

1. Add this method to the Car class:

```
'CalculateAccelerationRate—assume a constant for a normal car
Public Function CalculateAccelerationRate() As Double
    'If we assume a normal car goes from 0-60 in 14 seconds,
    'that's an average rate of 4.2 mph/s
    Return 4.2
End Function
```

2. To test the method, change the DisplayCarDetails procedure in Module1 to read like this:

```
'DisplayCarDetails—procedure that displays a car's details
Sub DisplayCarDetails(theCar As Car)
    'Display the details of the car
    Console.WriteLine("Color: " & theCar.Color)
    Console.WriteLine("Number of doors: " & theCar.NumberOfDoors)
    Console.WriteLine("Current speed: " & theCar.Speed)
    Console.WriteLine("Acceleration rate: " &
        theCar.CalculateAccelerationRate)
End Sub
```

3. Run the project. You should get output similar to Figure 10-11.

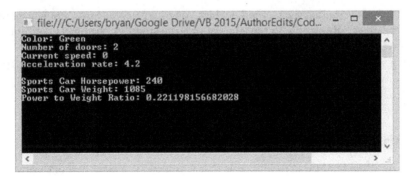

FIGURE 10-11

You've built a method on Car as normal. This method always returns a value of 4.2 mph/s for the acceleration rate.

4. To override the method, you just have to provide a new implementation in `SportsCar`. However, there's one thing you need to do first. To override a method, you have to mark it as `Overridable`. To do this, open the `Car` class again and add the `Overridable` keyword to the method:

```
Public Overridable Function CalculateAccelerationRate() As Double
```

5. Now you can create a method with the same name in the `SportsCar` class. To override the method in the base class, you must add the `Overrides` keyword before the method type (`Function` or `Procedure`):

```
'CalculateAccelerationRate—take the power/weight into consideration
Public Overrides Function CalculateAccelerationRate() As Double
    'You'll assume the same 4.2 value, but you'll multiply it
    'by the power/weight ratio
    Return 4.2 * GetPowerToWeightRatio()
End Function
```

6. Run the project; you get an adjusted acceleration rate, as shown in Figure 10-12.

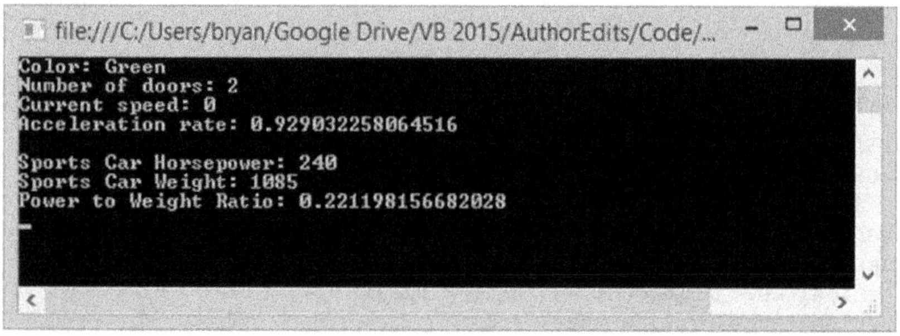

FIGURE 10-12

How It Works

In this example you learned that overriding the method enables you to create your own implementation of an existing method on the object. Returning to the concept of encapsulation, the object consumers don't have to know that anything is different about the object—they just call the method in the same way as they would for a normal `Car` object. This time, however, they get a result rather different from the constant value they always got on the normal `Car` object.

Inheriting from the Object Class

With respect to inheritance, the final thing to look at is that if you create a class without using the `Inherits` clause, then the class automatically inherits from a class called `Object`. This object provides you with a few methods that you can guarantee are supported by every object you'll ever have. Most of these methods are beyond the scope of this book, but the two most useful methods at this level are as follows:

➤ `ToString`: This method returns a string representation of the object. You can override this to provide a helpful string value for any object; for example, you might want a person object to return that person's name. If you do not override it, it will return the name of the class.

➤ `GetType`: This method returns a `Type` object that represents the data type of the object.

Remember, you do not have to inherit explicitly from `Object`. This happens automatically.

OBJECTS AND STRUCTURES

You created a structure in Chapter 5. Like a class, a structure provides a way to group several pieces of information together that all refer to one thing. A structure can even have methods and properties as well as member variables, just as a class can. Here are some of the differences between structures and classes.

In terms of semantics, structures are known as *value types*, and classes are known as *reference types*. That is, a variable representing a structure means the actual chunk of computer memory that stores the contents of the structure, whereas a variable representing a class instance is actually, as you have seen, a "hook" on which the object hangs.

This explains the difference in instantiation—you don't need to use the `New` keyword to instantiate a structure before you use it because it is a value type, just like an integer. You do have to use the `New` keyword with a form or other complex object because it is a class instance—a reference type.

You have seen that two different object variable hooks can be used to hang up the same object. If you set a property in the object using either of the hooks, both objects will have the same value:

```
Dim objMyCar As New Car     'objMyCar.Color is "White"
Set objThisCar = objMyCar   'same object, different hooks
objThisCar.Color = "Beige"  'now objMyCar.Color is also "Beige"
```

Two different structure variables, on the other hand, always refer to different groups of information:

```
Dim structMyCustomer As Customer, structThisCustomer As Customer
structMyCustomer.FirstName = "Victor"
structThisCustomer = structMyCustomer  'different structures
structThisCustomer.FirstName = "Victoria"
'structMyCustomer.FirstName is still "Victor"
```

Also, you cannot inherit from a structure—another important consideration when choosing whether to use a class or a structure.

THE FRAMEWORK CLASSES

Although Chapter 2 included a general discussion of the .NET Framework, a more in-depth look at some aspects of the .NET Framework's construction can help you when building objects. In particular, you want to take a look at namespaces and how you can create your own namespaces for use within your objects.

Namespaces

The .NET Framework is actually a vast collection of classes. There are more than 4,000 classes in the .NET Framework all told, so how are you, as a developer, supposed to find the ones that you want?

The .NET Framework is divided into a broad set of namespaces that group similar classes together. This limits the number of classes that you have to hunt through when you're looking for a specific piece of functionality.

These namespaces are also hierarchical in nature, meaning that a namespace can contain other namespaces that further group classes together. Each class must belong to exactly one namespace—it can't belong to multiple namespaces.

Most of the .NET Framework classes are lumped together in a namespace called `System`, or namespaces that are also contained within `System`. For example:

- ➤ `System.Data`: Contains classes related to accessing data stored in a database.
- ➤ `System.Xml`: Contains classes used to read and write XML documents.
- ➤ `System.Windows.Forms`: Contains classes for drawing windows on the screen.
- ➤ `System.Net`: Contains classes for communicating over a network.

The existence of namespaces means that all the objects you've been using actually have longer names than the ones used in your software code. Until this point, you've been using a shorthand notation to refer to classes.

In fact, when we said earlier that everything has to be derived from `Object`, we were stretching it a bit. Because `Object` is contained within the `System` namespace, its full name is `System.Object`. Likewise, `Console` is actually shorthand for `System.Console`, meaning the following two lines refer to the same thing:

```
Console.ReadLine()

System.Console.ReadLine()
```

> **NOTE** *This can get a little silly, especially when you end up with object names such as "System.Web.Services.Description.ServiceDescription."*

.NET automatically creates a shorthand version of all the classes within `System`, so you don't have to type `System` all the time. Later, you'll see how you can add shorthand references to other namespaces.

There is also the My namespace, which you've already seen in use in some of the earlier chapters. This namespace provides access to the common classes that you're most likely to need in your everyday programming tasks.

Like the System namespace, the My namespace contains a collection of other classes, which in turn contain classes of their own. At the top level, there is the My.Application class, which provides a wealth of information related to the currently executing application, such as the application's assembly name, the current path to the application's executable file, and so on. There is also the My.Computer class, which provides detailed information about the computer on which the application is executing, such as the amount of free space on the hard drive and the amount of available memory.

The My.Forms class provides access to the various forms in the application and allows you to manipulate those forms easily; for example, you can show, hide, and close them. There is also the My.Resources class, which provides quick and easy access to an application's resource files if it contains them. You can place localized text strings and images in a resource file and use the My.Resources class to gain access to these resources for use in your application.

The My.Settings class provides access to an application's configuration file if it has one and allows you to quickly read the settings needed by your application, such as startup settings or database connection information. It also allows you to create, persist, and save user settings for your application. Finally, there is the My.User class, which provides a wealth of information related to the current user of your application, such as login name and the domain name that the user is logged into.

TRY IT OUT   Finding the Name of the Current Namespace

Every class must be in exactly one namespace, but what about the classes we've made so far? Well, this project has a default namespace, and your new classes are placed into this namespace. In the next Try It Out, you discover a current namespace. All the code for this Try It Out is in the Object folder in the Zip file for this chapter.

1. To see the namespace that you're using, double-click My Project in the Solution Explorer.

2. The Root Namespace entry in the Objects Property Pages window gives the name of the namespace that will be used for new classes, as shown in Figure 10-13.

How It Works

What this means is that your classes have the text Objects prefixed to them, like this:

➤ The Car class is actually called Objects.Car.

➤ The SportsCar class is actually called Objects.SportsCar.

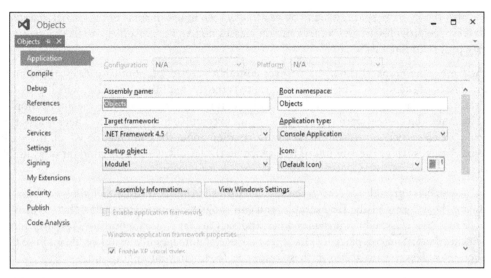

FIGURE 10-13

As you may have guessed, .NET automatically creates a shorthand version of your classes, too, so you can refer to SportsCar instead of having to type Objects.SportsCar.

The motivation behind using namespaces is to make life easier for developers using your classes. Imagine that you give this project to another developer for use and they have already built their own class called Car. How do they tell the difference between their class and your class?

Yours will actually be called Objects.Car, whereas theirs will have a name like MyOwnProject.Car or YaddaYadda.Car. Namespaces remove the ambiguity of class names. (Of course, we didn't choose a very good namespace because it doesn't really describe the classes that the namespace contains—we just chose a namespace that illustrates the purpose of the chapter.)

The Imports Statement

Now you know you don't need to prefix your classes with Car or System because .NET automatically creates a shorthand version, but how do you do this yourself? The answer is the Imports statement!

If you go back to Chapter 9, you might remember this code from the top of the Debug form:

```
Public Class Debug
```

You may recall this code as well:

```
'Using the List<T> class
    Private objCustomerList As New List(Of Customer)
```

You used the Imports statement to import the System.Collections.Generic namespace into your project. You needed to do this for access to the List<T> class. The full name of this class is System.Collections.Generic.List(Of T), but because you added a namespace import declaration, you could just write List (Of Customer) instead, substituting the Customer class in place of the T parameter.

All Imports statements must be written at the top of the code file in which you want to use them, before any other code, including the Class declaration.

However, if you import two namespaces that have an identically named class or child namespace, Visual Basic 2015 cannot tell what you are after (such as Car.Car and MyOwnProject.Car). If this happens, Visual Basic 2015 informs you that the name is ambiguous—in which case the quickest and easiest thing to do is to specify the full name.

Creating Your Own Namespace

Namespaces are defined by wrapping the Class...End Class definition in a Namespace...End Namespace definition. By default, classes created in Visual Basic 2015 are automatically assigned to a root namespace. Visual Studio 2015 automatically names this root namespace based on the project name.

TRY IT OUT Creating a Namespace

In the next Try It Out, you learn to create a namespace. All the code for this Try It Out is in the Object folder in the Zip file for this chapter.

1. Using the Solution Explorer, double-click My Project. The Root Namespace field tells you the name. In this case, the root namespace name is Objects.

2. It's often recommended that you build your namespaces so that the full names of the classes you develop are prefixed with the name of your company. For example, if your company were called MyCodeWidgets, ideally you would want the Car class called MyCodeWidgets.Car. To do this, change the Root Namespace field from Objects to **MyCodeWidgets** (see Figure 10-14). Then click the Save button on the toolbar to have this change applied to your project.

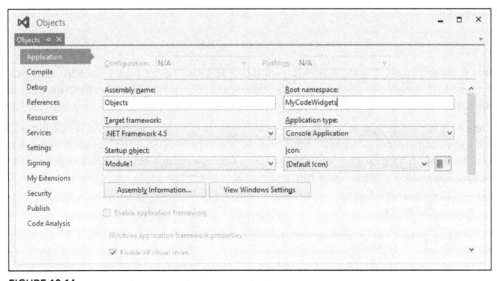

FIGURE 10-14

3. The Visual Studio 2015 Object Browser is a useful tool that enables you to see what classes are available in your project. You can find it by selecting View ➪ Object Browser from the menu bar or by pressing F2. Now, click My Solution in the Browse combo box and then navigate to find your Car class (see Figure 10-15).

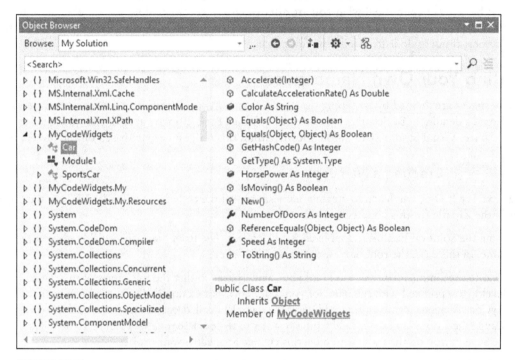

FIGURE 10-15

4. Note that you can also see the methods, properties, and member variables listed for the class. Pertinent to this discussion, however, is the namespace. This is immediately above the class and is indicated by the icon containing the open and close brace symbols ({ }).

    That's fine, but imagine now that you have two projects both containing a class called Car. You need to use namespaces to separate the Car class in one project from the Car class in the other. Open the Code Editor for Car, add **Namespace CarPerformance** before the class definition, and add **End Namespace** after it (I've omitted the code for brevity):

```
Namespace CarPerformance
    Public Class Car
    ...
    End Class
End Namespace
```

5. Open the Object Browser again and you'll see a screen like the one shown in Figure 10-16.

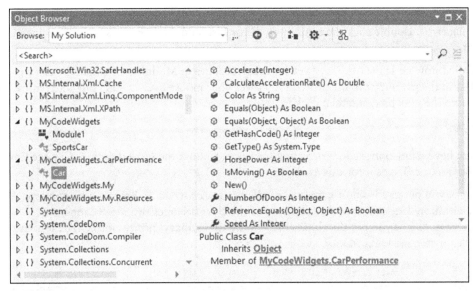

FIGURE 10-16

6. Because you added the CarPerformance namespace to the Car class, any code that references the Car class needs to import that namespace in order to access the shorthand methods of the Car class.

If you take a look at the SportsCar class, you'll notice that Visual Studio 2015 is reporting an error on the Inherits statement for Car. Hover your mouse over Car in your code and then move your mouse into the gray box and click it. This can be a little tricky to click in the right place.

As shown in Figure 10-17, you have two options: Import the namespace or prefix Car in the Inherits statement with the namespace. You want to choose the first option, so click Import MyCodeWidget .CarPerformance. This causes the Imports statement to be added to the top of the SportsCar class.

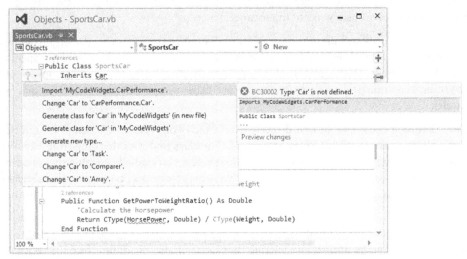

FIGURE 10.17

7. If you click the Error List tab at the bottom of the IDE, you'll notice that it is reporting one remaining error. Double-click the error in the Error List, and the IDE takes you to the line of code in error.

8. You should now be at the `DisplayCarDetails` procedure in Module1, in which the error is on the `Car` class in the parameter to the procedure. Hover your mouse over `Car` in your code, move your mouse into the gray box, and then click it.

How It Works

This time, you have many options for correcting the error. Choose the second option, Change Car to `CarPerformance.Car`. That's it for this example.

In this example, you put `Car` inside a namespace called `CarPerformance`. Because this namespace is contained within `MyCodeWidgets`, the full name of the class becomes `MyCodeWidgets`
`.CarPerformance.Car`. If you put the classes of the other (imaginary) project into `CarDiagnostics`, it would be called `MyCodeWidgets.CarDiagnostics.Car`.

> **NOTE** Module1 *still appears directly inside* MyCodeWidgets. *That's because you haven't wrapped the definition for* Module1 *in a namespace as you did with* Car. *Running your project at this point will produce the same results as before.*

Inheritance in the .NET Framework

Inheritance is an advanced object-oriented topic, but it's very important to include this here because the .NET Framework makes heavy use of inheritance.

One thing to understand about inheritance in .NET is that no class can inherit directly from more than one class. Because everything must inherit from `System.Object`, if a class does not specifically state that it inherits from another class, it inherits directly from `System.Object`. The upshot of this is that everything must inherit directly from exactly one class (everything, that is, except `System`
`.Object` itself).

When we say that each class must inherit directly from exactly one class, we mean that each class can mention only one class in its `Inherits` statement. The class that it's inheriting from can also inherit from another class. So, for example, you could create a class called `Porsche` that is inherited from `SportsCar`. You could then say that it *indirectly* inherits from `Car`, but it *directly* inherits from only one class—`SportsCar`. In fact, many classes indirectly inherit from many classes—but there is always a direct ancestry, in which each class has exactly one parent.

You may want to have some functionality in different classes that are not related to each other by inheritance. You can solve the problem by putting that functionality in an interface that both classes implement, such as the `IDisposable` interface you encountered in Chapter 9.

SUMMARY

In this chapter, you looked at how to start building your own objects. You kicked off by learning how to design an object in terms of the properties and methods that it should support and then built a class that represented a car. You then started adding properties and methods to that class and used it from within your application.

Before moving on to the subject of inheritance, you looked at how an object can be given a constructor: a block of code that's executed whenever an object is created. The discussion of inheritance demonstrated a number of key aspects of object-oriented design, including polymorphism and overriding.

To summarize, you should know:

➤ How to create properties and methods in a class

➤ How to provide a constructor for your class to initialize the state of your class

➤ How to inherit another class

➤ How to override properties and methods in the inheriting class

➤ How to create your own namespace for a class

EXERCISES

1. Modify your `Car` class to implement the `IDisposable` interface. In the `Main` procedure in `Module1`, add code to dispose of the `objCar` object after calling the `DisplaySportsCarDetails` procedure.

2. Modify the code in the `Main` procedure in `Module1` to encapsulate the declaration and usage of the `SportsCar` class in a `Using...End Using` statement. Remember that the `Using...End Using` statement automatically handles disposal of objects that implement the `IDisposable` interface.

▶ **WHAT YOU LEARNED IN THIS CHAPTER**

TOPIC	CONCEPTS
Creating classes	Use properties and methods to represent an object. You can use a Constructor to set up default values.
Inheritance	You can create a class with the same properties of another by inheriting it. When you inherit a class, you can change the way the new class works by overriding its properties and methods.
Polymorphism	Treating an object as another. So when you inherit a class, the new class can be treated as the inherited one.
Encapsulation	The complex code is hidden inside the class. To use the class, you do not need to understand how it does what it does.

11

Advanced Object-Oriented Techniques

WHAT YOU WILL LEARN IN THIS CHAPTER:

- ➤ How to create a favorite viewer
- ➤ How to create an alternative favorite viewer
- ➤ How to work with shared properties and methods
- ➤ Understanding object-oriented and memory management

WROX.COM CODE DOWNLOADS FOR THIS CHAPTER

The wrox.com code downloads for this chapter are found at www.wrox.com/begvisualbasic2015 on the Download Code tab. The code is in the 092117 C11.zip download and individually named according to the names given throughout the chapter.

In Chapter 10, you looked at how you can build your own objects. Prior to that, you had been mostly using objects that already existed in the .NET Framework to build your applications. In this chapter, you'll take a look at some more object-oriented software development techniques.

In the first half of this chapter, you create your own classes. You will create a single-tier application like the others discussed so far in this book. You then learn about creating your own shared properties and methods. These are very useful when you want a method or property to apply to a class as a whole, rather than a specific instance of that class. Finally, you look at memory management in Visual Studio 2015 and what you can do to clean up your objects properly.

BUILDING A FAVORITES VIEWER

In the first half of this chapter, you'll build a simple application that displays all your Internet Explorer favorites and provides a button that you can click to open the URL in Internet Explorer. This application illustrates a key point regarding code reuse and some of the reasons why building code in an object-oriented fashion is so powerful. Using other browsers may not work in this example because they do not all use this folder. If you don't normally use Internet Explorer, you should add a few shortcuts for this example.

Internet Shortcuts and Favorites

You're most likely familiar with the concept of favorites in Internet Explorer. What you may not know is how Internet Explorer stores those favorites. In fact, the Favorites list is available to all other applications—provided you know where to look.

Windows applications have the option of storing data in separate user folders within a main folder. On earlier Windows systems such as Windows XP, this folder is called `C:\Documents and Settings`. On Windows Vista and Windows 7, this folder is called `C:\Users`. In Figure 11-1 you can see that my computer has many user folders including: `Public`, `bryan`, and `Bryan.CHARLOTTE`.

> **NOTE** *Bryan is the default user who was specified on this computer when Windows 8 was set up. This will most likely be different for you. If you see a Default folder, it is a special folder that Windows uses whenever a new user logs onto the computer for the first time. The Public folder is where public documents, downloads, music, videos, and pictures are stored that are accessible to all users of that computer. Depending on your operating system (OS), view settings, and number of users on your machine, you may have more or fewer folders than this.*

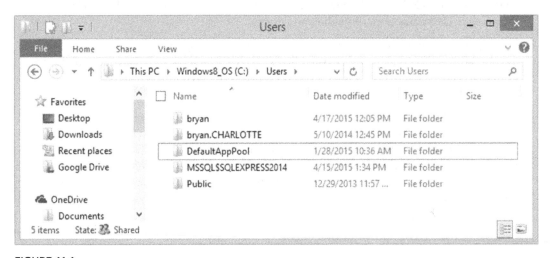

FIGURE 11-1

Depending on how the security of your computer is configured, you may not be able to access the C:\Users folder. If you can, open the folder whose name matches the name that you supply when you log on. In the screenshots throughout this chapter, I've used Bryan (the folder for my user is bryan.charlotte). (If you cannot consistently open the folder, ask your system administrator to help you log in as a different user or give you the appropriate permissions.) If you open this folder, you'll find another group of folders. You'll see something like what is shown in Figure 11-2 (though it may look different depending upon how your login is configured).

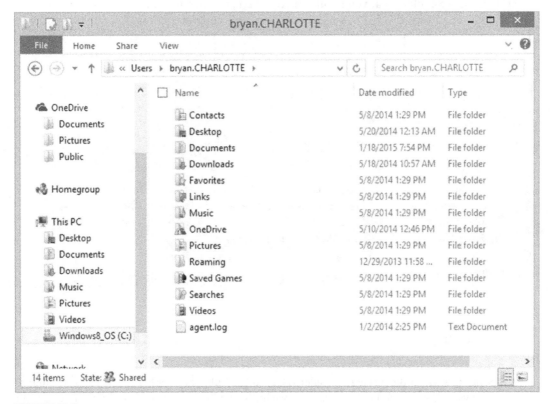

FIGURE 11-2

You may notice that some folder icons appear as faint icons, whereas others appear as normal folder icons on some computers. If the computer is configured to show all folders, so you may find that on your machine the faint folders do not appear because they are normally hidden. This doesn't matter because the one you're specifically looking for—Favorites—will appear whatever your system settings are.

This folder (Bryan on this computer) is where Windows stores a lot of folders related to the operation of your computer for your login account. Some of these may be hidden from your current view. Here are a few of the folders, for example:

➤   `AppData` stores application data related to the applications that you use.

➤   `Contacts` stores the Windows contacts, similar to the contacts stored in Microsoft Outlook.

➤   `Desktop` stores the folders and links that appear on your desktop.

➤   `My Documents` stores any folders or documents that you create.

➤   `Favorites` stores a list of Internet Explorer favorites.

It's the `Favorites` folder that you're interested in here, so open it. You'll see something like Figure 11-3 (obviously, this list will be different on your computer because you'll have different favorites).

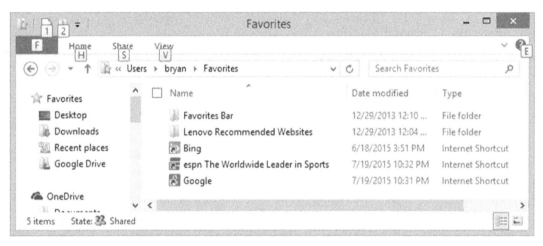

FIGURE 11-3

You'll notice that the links inside this folder relate to the links that appear in the Favorites menu in your browser. If you double-click one of those links, you'll see that Internet Explorer opens and navigates to the URL that the favorite points to.

You can be fairly confident at this stage that if you have a folder of links that appear to be favorites, you can create an application that opens this folder and can do something with the links—namely, iterate through all of them, add each of them to a list, find out what URL it belongs to, and provide a way to open that URL from your application. In the example that follows, you'll ignore the folders and just deal with the favorites that appear in the root Favorites folder.

Your final application will look like Figure 11-4.

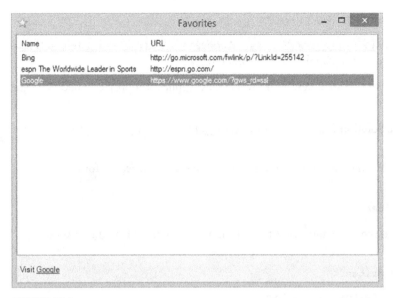

FIGURE 11-4

Using Classes

So far in this book, you've built basic applications that do something, but most functionality that they provide has been coded into the applications' forms. Here, you're about to build some functionality that can load a list of favorites from a user's computer and provide a way to open Internet Explorer to show the URL. However, you do it in a way that means you can use the *list of favorites* functionality elsewhere.

The best way to build this application is to create a set that includes the following classes:

➤ **WebFavorite**: Represents a single favorite and has member variables such as Name and Url

➤ **Favorites**: Can scan the Favorites list on the user's computer, creating a new WebFavorite object for each favorite

➤ **WebFavoriteCollection**: Contains a collection of WebFavorite objects

These three classes provide the *back-end* functionality of the application—in other words, all classes that do something but do not present the user with an interface. This isolates the code in the classes and allows you to reuse the code from different parts of the application: *code reuse*. You also need a *front end* to this application, which in this case will be a Windows form with a couple of controls on it.

In the following sections, you build your classes and Windows application and come up with the application shown in Figure 11-4.

TRY IT OUT Creating a Favorites Viewer

In the first Try It Out, you start by building the Windows Application project. All the code in this Try It Out is in the `Favorites` folder in the Zip file for this chapter.

1. Open Visual Studio 2015 and create a new Windows Forms Application project called **Favorites Viewer**.

2. Rename Form1.vb in the Solution Explorer to **Viewer.vb** and then modify the form properties as follows:

    ➤   Set `Icon` to **a Favorites.ico from the image library.** Just search for the word favorites.

    ➤   Set `Text` to **Favorites**.

3. Add a ListView control to the form and size it to look similar to Figure 11-5 and set these properties:

    ➤   Set `Name` to **lvwFavorites**.

    ➤   Set `Anchor` to **Top, Bottom, Left, Right**.

    ➤   Set `FullRowSelect` to **True**.

    ➤   Set `View` to **Details**.

4. Select the Columns property in the Properties window for the `lvwFavorites` control. Click the ellipsis (…) button to display the ColumnHeader Collection Editor dialog.

5. Click the Add button. Set these properties on the new column header:

    ➤   Set `Name` to **hdrName**.

    ➤   Set `Text` to **Name**.

    ➤   Set `Width` to **200**.

6. Click the Add button again to add a second column. Set these properties on the new column header:

    ➤   Set `Name` to **hdrUrl**.

    ➤   Set `Text` to **URL**.

    ➤   Set `Width` to **350**.

7. Click OK to close the editor.

8. Add a LinkLabel control to the bottom of the form and set these properties:

    ➤   Set `Name` to **lnkUrl**.

    ➤   Set `Anchor` to **Bottom, Left, Right**.

    ➤   Set `TextAlign` to **MiddleLeft**.

9. Your completed form should now look similar to the one shown in Figure 11-5.

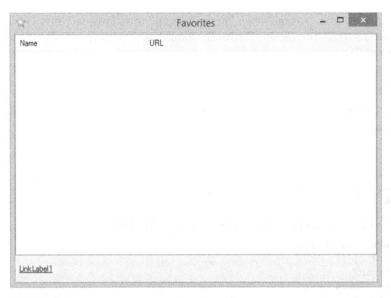

FIGURE 11-5

10. Save your project by clicking the Save All button on the toolbar.

How It Works

All that you've done here is to build the basic shell of the application, the form that will display the results of the processing. You started by modifying some basic properties of the form and then added two controls: a list view and a link label. The ListView control will be used to display the name and URL of each favorite in your Favorites folder. The LinkLabel control will be used to launch a browser with the selected favorite URL in the list.

That's the basics of the form put together.

TRY IT OUT Building WebFavorite

In the next Try It Out, you look at how you can add the back-end classes. In previous chapters, you learned how to add classes to a Visual Studio 2015 project, so you will use this knowledge to create the back end of your application. All the code in this Try It Out is in the Favorites folder in the Zip file for this chapter.

1. Using the Solution Explorer, right-click Favorites Viewer. Select Add ➪ Class from the menu to display the Add New Item-Favorites Viewer dialog. Enter a name of **WebFavorite.vb** and then click the Add button.

2. Add this namespace import declaration to the top of the code listing:

```
Imports System.IO

Public Class WebFavorite
```

3. This class will need to implement the `IDisposable` interface, so add this `Implements IDisposable` statement. When you press Enter, Visual Studio 2015 inserts the members and methods associated with the `IDisposable` interface:

```
Public Class WebFavorite
Implements IDisposable
```

4. Now add the following two members after the `IDisposable` interface code (`#End Region`) inserted by Visual Studio 2015:

```
#End Region

'Public Members
Public Name As String
Public Url As String
```

5. Now add the `Load` method, which loads the member variables in this class:

```
Public Sub Load(fileName As String)
    'Declare variables
    Dim strData As String
    Dim strLines() As String
    Dim strLine As String
    Dim objFileInfo As New FileInfo(fileName)

    'Set the Name member to the file name minus the extension
    Name = objFileInfo.Name.Substring(0,
        objFileInfo.Name.Length-objFileInfo.Extension.Length)

    Try
        'Read the entire contents of the file
        strData = My.Computer.FileSystem.ReadAllText(fileName)
        'Split the lines of data in the file
        strLines = strData.Split(New String() {ControlChars.CrLf},
            StringSplitOptions.RemoveEmptyEntries)

        'Process each line looking for the URL
        For Each strLine In strLines
            'Does the line of data start with URL=
            If strLine.StartsWith("URL=") Then
                'Yes, set the Url member to the actual URL
                Url = strLine.Substring(4)
                'Exit the For..Next loop
                Exit For
            End If
        Next
    Catch IOExceptionErr As IOException
        'Return the exception to the caller
        Throw New Exception(IOExceptionErr.Message)
    End Try
End Sub
```

How It Works

In this example, you created the `WebFavorite` class. It will be useful to examine how the `WebFavorite` class populates itself when the `Load` method is invoked.

The first thing you do is declare the variables needed by this method. The strData variable is used to receive the entire contents of the favorite's shortcut file. The strLines() variable is used to create an array containing each individual line of data from the strData variable, and the strLine variable is used to iterate through the array of lines. Finally, the objFileInfo object gets the file information from the full path and filename passed to this method:

```
Public Sub Load(fileName As String)
    'Declare variables
    Dim strData As String
    Dim strLines() As String
    Dim strLine As String
    Dim objFileInfo As New FileInfo(fileName)
```

Next, the Name member is set to just the filename of the favorite's shortcut file; for example, Google. This is the name of the favorite that shows up on the Favorites list in the browser. The fileName parameter passed to this method will contain the complete path to the file, the filename, and the file extension (for example, C:\Users\Bryan\Favorites\Google.url). What you have to do is extract only the filename from the complete path.

You do this by using the objFileInfo object, which has been initialized to an instance of the FileInfo class with the fileName variable passed to it. The FileInfo class provides several methods that return the various parts of the complete file path and name, such as only the filename and only the file extension.

You use the Name property of the objFileInfo object to get just the filename and extension of the file without the path, and you use the Substring method of the Name property to extract the filename minus the file extension. To supply the parameters to the Substring method, you also use the Length property of the Name property in the objFileInfo object to determine how long the filename is and use the Length property of the Extension property to determine how long the file extension is.

So basically what you're saying here is, "Take a substring, starting at the first character, and continue for the complete length of the string minus the length of the Extension property." This, in effect, removes the .url from the end. Remember that the array of characters that make up a string is zero-based; thus, you specify a starting position of 0 for the SubString method:

```
'Set the Name member to the file name minus the extension
Name = objFileInfo.Name.Substring(0,
    objFileInfo.Name.Length-objFileInfo.Extension.Length)
```

You read the entire contents of the file next into the strData. Because you are reading from a file, you'll want to encapsulate the logic in a Try...Catch block to handle any input/output (I/O) exceptions that might occur.

The first thing that you do in this Try...Catch block is read the entire contents of the file into the strData variable. This is done using the My.Computer namespace and the ReadAllText method of the FileSystem class. This method handles all the details of opening the file, reading the entire contents, closing the file, and releasing the resources used to perform these operations:

```
Try
    'Read the entire contents of the file
    strData = My.Computer.FileSystem.ReadAllText(fileName)
```

After the contents of the file have been read, the `strData` variable will contain something similar to the data shown here. This is the data from the `C:\Users\Bryan\Favorites\Google.url` shortcut file:

```
[DEFAULT]
BASEURL=http://www.google.com/
[InternetShortcut]
URL=http://www.google.com/
IDList=
IconFile=http://www.google.com/favicon.ico
IconIndex=1
[{000214A0-0000-0000-c120-000000000046}]
Prop3=19,2
```

Now that you have the entire contents of the favorite's shortcut file in a single string variable, you split the contents of the `strData` variable into separate lines. This is done using the `Split` method of the `String` class, from which the `strData` variable is derived. The `Split` method is an overloaded method, and the version that you are using here accepts an array of strings as the first parameter and the split options as the second parameter.

The data in the `strData` variable is separated with a carriage return and line feed character combination, and thus you provide a string array containing only one entry, `ControlChars.CrLf`, as the first parameter of the `Split` method. The split options parameter of the `Split` method is a value in the `StringSplitOptions` enumeration that lets you specify how empty elements are handled. Here you specify the `RemoveEmptyEntries` constant of that enumeration, to remove any empty entries in the array that are returned:

```
'Split the lines of data in the file
strLines = strData.Split(New String() {ControlChars.CrLf},
    StringSplitOptions.RemoveEmptyEntries)
```

Next you need to process each line of data in the `strLines` array using a `For...Next` loop. You are looking for the line of data that begins with `"URL="`. Using an `If...Then` statement, you check the `strLine` variable to see whether it begins with the specified text. The `StartsWith` method of the `String` class, the class from which the `strLine` variable is derived, returns a `Boolean` value of `True` if the string being tested contains the string that is passed to this method and a value of `False` if it does not.

If the line of data being tested starts with the text `"URL="`, it is the actual URL that you want to save in the `Url` member of the class. To do so, you use the `SubString` method to get the URL in the `strLine` variable minus the beginning text. In order to do this, you pass a starting position of 4 to the `SubString` method, telling it to start extracting data at position 4, because positions 0 - 3 contain the text `"URL="`. Once you find the data that you are looking for and set the `Url` member, there's no need to process the rest of the `strLines` array, so you exit the `For...Next` loop:

```
'Process each line looking for the URL
For Each strLine In strLines
    'Does the line of data start with URL=
    If strLine.StartsWith("URL=") Then
        'Yes, set the Url member to the actual URL
        Url = strLine.Substring(4)
        'Exit the For..Next loop
        Exit For
    End If
Next
```

The Catch block handles any I/O exception that might be thrown. Here you want to return the exception to the caller of this method, so you throw a new Exception and pass it the Message property of the IOExceptionErr variable. This gracefully handles any I/O exceptions in this class and returns the message of the exception to the caller:

```
Catch IOExceptionErr As IOException
        'Return the exception to the caller
        Throw New Exception(IOExceptionErr.Message)
    End Try
End Sub
```

Scanning Favorites

So that you can scan the favorites, in the next Try It Out you will add a couple of new classes to the project.

TRY IT OUT Scanning Favorites

Next, add two new classes. The first, WebFavoriteCollection, holds a collection of WebFavorite objects. The second, Favorites, physically scans the Favorites folder on the computer, creates new WebFavorite objects, and adds them to the collection. All the code in this Try It Out is in the Favorites folder in the Zip file for this chapter.

1. Using the Solution Explorer, create a new class called **WebFavoriteCollection**. This class will be instantiated to an object that can hold a number of WebFavorite objects.

2. Add the bolded code in your class:

```
Public Class WebFavoriteCollection
Inherits CollectionBase

Public Sub Add(Favorite As WebFavorite)
    'Add item to the collection
    List.Add(Favorite)
End Sub

Public Sub Remove(Index As Integer)
    'Remove item from collection
    If Index >= 0 And Index < Count Then
        List.Remove(Index)
    End If
End Sub

Public ReadOnly Property Item(Index As Integer) As WebFavorite
    Get
    'Get an item from the collection by its index
    Return CType(List.Item(Index), WebFavorite)
    End Get
End Property
End Class
```

3. Create another new class called **Favorites**. This will be used to scan the Favorites folder and return a WebFavoriteCollection containing a WebFavorite object for each favorite in the folder. Like the WebFavorite class, this class implements the IDisposable interface. Enter the following bolded code and press Enter to add the properties and methods of the IDisposable interface to your class:

```
Public Class Favorites
    Implements IDisposable
```

4. Add this member below the code for the IDisposable interface:

```
'Public member
Public FavoritesCollection As WebFavoriteCollection
```

5. You need a read-only property that can return the path to the user's Favorites folder. Add the following code to the Favorites class:

```
Public ReadOnly Property FavoritesFolder() As String
    Get
        'Return the path to the user's Favorites folder
        Return Environment.GetFolderPath( _
            Environment.SpecialFolder.Favorites)
    End Get
End Property
```

6. Finally, you need a method that's capable of scanning through the Favorites folder looking for files. When it finds one, it creates a WebFavorite object and adds it to the Favorites collection. You provide two versions of this method: one that automatically determines the path of the favorites by using the FavoritesFolder property, and one that scans through a given folder. To create this overloaded method, add the following code to the Favorites class:

```
Public Sub ScanFavorites()
    'Scan the Favorites folder
    ScanFavorites(FavoritesFolder)
End Sub

Public Sub ScanFavorites(folderName As String)
    'If the FavoritesCollection member has not been instantiated
    'then instantiate it
    If FavoritesCollection Is Nothing Then
        FavoritesCollection = New WebFavoriteCollection
    End If

    'Process each file in the Favorites folder
    For Each strFile As String In _
        My.Computer.FileSystem.GetFiles(folderName)

        'If the file has a url extension..
        If strFile.EndsWith(".url", True, Nothing) Then

            Try
                'Create and use a new instance of the
                'WebFavorite class
```

```
              Using objWebFavorite As New WebFavorite
                  'Load the file information
                  objWebFavorite.Load(strFile)
                  'Add the object to the collection
                  FavoritesCollection.Add(objWebFavorite)
              End Using
          Catch ExceptionErr As Exception
              'Return the exception to the caller
              Throw New Exception(ExceptionErr.Message)
          End Try

      End If

  Next
End Sub
```

To make this work, you need to have the Favorites Viewer project create an instance of a `Favorites` object, scan the favorites, and add each one it finds to the list. You do this in the next Try It Out.

How It Works

There's a lot to take in for this example, but a good starting point is the `WebFavoriteCollection` class, which illustrates an important best practice when working with lists of objects. As you saw in Chapter 5, you can hold lists of objects in one of two ways: in an array or in a collection.

When building classes that work with lists, the best practice is to use a collection. You should build collections that are also tied into using whatever types you're working with, so in this example you built a `WebFavoriteCollection` class that exclusively holds a collection of `WebFavorite` objects.

You derived `WebFavoriteCollection` from `CollectionBase`. This provides the basic list that the collection will use:

```
Public Class WebFavoriteCollection
    Inherits CollectionBase
```

To fit in with the .NET Framework's way of doing things, you need to define three methods on a collection that you build. The `Add` method adds an item to the collection:

```
Public Sub Add(Favorite As WebFavorite)
    'Add item to the collection
    List.Add(Favorite)
End Sub
```

The `List` property is a protected member of `CollectionBase` that only code within classes inheriting from `CollectionBase` can access. You access this property to add, remove, and find items in the list. You can see from the `Add` method here that you specified that the item must be a `WebFavorite` object. This is why you're supposed to build collections using this technique—because you can add objects only of type `WebFavorite`; anyone who has a `WebFavoriteCollection` object knows that it will contain objects only of type `WebFavorite`. This makes life much easier for users because they will not get nasty surprises when they discover it contains something else, and therefore it reduces the chance of errors. The `Remove` method that you built removes an item from the list:

```
Public Sub Remove(Index As Integer)
    'Remove item from collection
    If Index >= 0 And Index < Count Then
        List.Remove(Index)
    End If
End Sub
```

The Item method lets you get an item from the list when given a specific index:

```
Public ReadOnly Property Item(Index As Integer) As WebFavorite
    Get
        'Get an item from the collection by its index
        Return CType(List.Item(Index), WebFavorite)
    End Get
End Property
```

How do you populate this collection? Well, in the Favorites class you built an overloaded method called ScanFavorites. The second version of this method takes a folder and examines it for files that end in .url. But before you look at that, you need to look at the FavoritesFolder property.

Because the location of the Favorites folder can change depending on the currently logged-in user, you have to ask Windows where this folder actually is. To do this, you use the shared GetFolderPath method of the System.Environment class:

```
Public ReadOnly Property FavoritesFolder() As String
    Get
        'Return the path to the user's Favorites folder
        Return Environment.GetFolderPath(
            Environment.SpecialFolder.Favorites)
    End Get
End Property
```

The GetFolderPath method uses one of the constants from the Environment.SpecialFolder enumeration. This enumeration provides constants for many different special folders that you are likely to need access to when writing applications.

When the application asks this class to load in the favorites from the Favorites folder, it calls ScanFavorites. The first version of this method accepts no parameters. It looks up the location of the user's Favorites folder and passes that to the second version of this overloaded method:

```
Public Sub ScanFavorites()
    'Scan the Favorites folder
    ScanFavorites(FavoritesFolder)
End Sub
```

The first thing that the second version of this overloaded method does is check to ensure that the FavoritesCollection member has been instantiated using the WebFavoriteCollection class. If it hasn't, it instantiates this member using that class:

```
Public Sub ScanFavorites(folderName As String)
    'If the FavoritesCollection member has not been instantiated
    'then instantiate it
    If FavoritesCollection Is Nothing Then
        FavoritesCollection = New WebFavoriteCollection
    End If
```

Next, you want to get a list of files in the Favorites folder and process them. You do this by calling the GetFiles method in the FileSystem class and passing it the path and name of the Favorites folder. This class exists in the My.Computer namespace, as indicated by the following For Each code.

The GetFiles method returns an array of filenames, and you process this array using a For Each...Next loop. You declare the variable, strFile, inline in the For Each loop, as indicated in the following code, and this variable will be set to a filename in the Favorites folder for each iteration of the loop:

```
'Process each file in the Favorites folder
For Each strFile As String In _
    My.Computer.FileSystem.GetFiles(folderName)
```

Within the loop, you first test the filename to see whether it is a Favorites file by checking to see whether it contains a .url file extension. The strFile variable is derived from the String class; thus, you can use the EndsWith method to determine whether the filename ends with the .url file extension.

The EndsWith method is an overloaded method, and the version that you are using here accepts three parameters. The first parameter accepts the value to be compared to the end of the string, and here you supply the text .url. The next parameter accepts a Boolean value indicating whether the EndsWith method should ignore the case of the text when making the comparison. You do want to ignore the case when making the comparison, so you pass a value of True for this parameter. The final parameter accepts the culture information that will be used when making the comparison. Passing a value of Nothing here indicates that you want to use the current culture information defined on the user's computer:

```
'If the file has a url extension..
If strFile.EndsWith(".url", True, Nothing) Then
```

If the filename being processed does contain the .url file extension, you want to load the file information and have it added to the Favorites collection. Because you are using the WebFavorite class, and this class reads the file, the potential for an exception exists. Therefore, you need to encapsulate the next block of code in a Try...Catch block to handle any exceptions that might be thrown by the WebFavorite class.

The first thing that you do in the Try block is use a Using...End Using block to declare, instantiate, use, and destroy the WebFavorite class. Remember that you can use the Using statement only with a class that implements the IDisposable interface, which is why you added that interface to the WebFavorite class.

The first thing that you do in the Using...End Using block is call the Load method on the objWebFavorite object, passing it the filename of the favorite's shortcut file. Then you add the objWebFavorite to the Favorites collection:

```
Try
    'Create and use a new instance of the
    'WebFavorite class
    Using objWebFavorite As New WebFavorite
        'Load the file information
        objWebFavorite.Load(strFile)

        'Add the object to the collection
        FavoritesCollection.Add(objWebFavorite)
    End Using
```

The Catch block contains the necessary code to handle an exception that might be thrown by the WebFavorite class and to return that exception to the caller of this method. This is done by throwing a new Exception, passing it the message received in the ExceptionErr variable:

```
Catch ExceptionErr As Exception
    'Return the exception to the caller
    Throw New Exception(ExceptionErr.Message)
End Try
        End If

    Next
End Sub
```

In the following Try It Out, you implement the new functionality in your form.

TRY IT OUT Creating an Instance of a Favorites Object

In this Try It Out, you change the form to use the Favorites class to gather all your Internet Favorites and the WebFavorite class to load those shortcuts in the ListView control on your form. All the code in this Try It Out is in the Favorites folder in the Zip file for this chapter.

1. View the code for the Viewer form, select (Viewer Events) in the Class Name combo box, and then select Load in the Method Name combo box. Add the bolded code:

```
Private Sub Viewer_Load(sender As Object,
    e As EventArgs) Handles Me.Load

    Try
        'Create and use a new instance of the Favorites class
        Using objFavorites As New Favorites

            'Scan the Favorites folder
            objFavorites.ScanFavorites()

            'Process each objWebFavorite object in the
            'favorites collection
            For Each objWebFavorite As WebFavorite In
                objFavorites.FavoritesCollection

                'Declare a ListViewItem object
                Dim objListViewItem As New ListViewItem

                'Set the properties of the ListViewItem object
                objListViewItem.Text = objWebFavorite.Name
                objListViewItem.SubItems.Add(objWebFavorite.Url)

                'Add the ListViewItem object to the ListView
                lvwFavorites.Items.Add(objListViewItem)
            Next

        End Using
```

```
    Catch ExceptionErr As Exception
        'Display the error
        MessageBox.Show(ExceptionErr.Message, "Favorites Viewer",
            MessageBoxButtons.OK, MessageBoxIcon.Warning)

    End Try
End Sub
```

2. Run the project and you should see something similar to Figure 11-6.

FIGURE 11-6

How It Works

In this example, you hooked up the form with the classes you created earlier. Since both the `Favorites` and `WebFavorite` classes can throw an exception, you must handle any exceptions that might be thrown. Therefore, all your code is encapsulated in a `Try...Catch` block. You use a `Using...End Using` statement to declare, instantiate, and destroy the object created with the `Favorites` class. Regardless of whether this class throws an exception, the `Using` statement destroys the `objFavorites` object that it declares:

```
Private Sub Viewer_Load(sender As Object,
    e As EventArgs) Handles Me.Load

    Try
        'Create and use a new instance of the Favorites class
        Using objFavorites As New Favorites
```

Inside the `Using...End Using` block, the `objFavorites` object scans the user's Favorites folder by calling the `ScanFavorites` method. The effect here is that a new `WebFavoritesCollection` object is created and filled and will be accessible through the `FavoritesCollection` property:

```
'Scan the Favorites folder
objFavorites.ScanFavorites()
```

After the `ScanFavorites` method finishes, you take each `WebFavorite` in the `FavoritesCollection` and add it to the ListView control on your form. You do this by first declaring a `ListViewItem` and then setting the `Text` property to the Favorite name. Then you add the URL of the Favorite to the `SubItems` collection, and finally you add the `objListViewItem` to the `Items` collection of the ListView control:

```
'Process each objWebFavorite object in the
'favorites collection
For Each objWebFavorite As WebFavorite In
    objFavorites.FavoritesCollection

    'Declare a ListViewItem object
    Dim objListViewItem As New ListViewItem

    'Set the properties of the ListViewItem object
    objListViewItem.Text = objWebFavorite.Name
        objListViewItem.SubItems.Add(objWebFavorite.Url)
        'Add the ListViewItem object to the ListView
        lvwFavorites.Items.Add(objListViewItem)
    Next

End Using
```

You wrap up this code with the `Catch` block, which handles any exceptions thrown and displays the exception message in a message dialog:

```
Catch ExceptionErr As Exception
        'Display the error
        MessageBox.Show(ExceptionErr.Message, "Favorites Viewer",
            MessageBoxButtons.OK, MessageBoxIcon.Warning)
    End Try
End Sub
```

That's it! Now you can display a list of the favorites installed on the user's machine. However, you can't actually view favorites, so let's look at that now.

Viewing Favorites

You will add some code to view your favorite in the next Try It Out.

TRY IT OUT Viewing Favorites

Now that all your code is in place to retrieve and display a list of favorites, in this Try It Out you add some code to display the selected favorite in the LinkLabel control on your form and then add some code to the control to process the selected link in Internet Explorer. All the code in this Try It Out is in the Favorites folder in the Zip file for this chapter.

1. In the Code Editor for Viewer, click lvwFavorites in the Class Name combo box and the Click event in the Method Name combo box. Add the following bolded code to the Click event handler:

```
Private Sub lvwFavorites_Click(sender As Object,
e As EventArgs) Handles lvwFavorites.Click

'Update the link label control Text property
lnkUrl.Text = "Visit " & lvwFavorites.SelectedItems.Item(0).Text

'Clear the default hyperlink
lnkUrl.Links.Clear()

'Add the selected hyperlink to the LinkCollection
lnkUrl.Links.Add(6, lvwFavorites.SelectedItems.Item(0).Text.Length,
    lvwFavorites.SelectedItems.Item(0).SubItems(1).Text)
End Sub
```

2. Click lnkUrl in the Class Name combo box and select the LinkClicked event in the Method Name combo box. Add the following bolded code to the LinkClicked event:

```
Private Sub lnkUrl_LinkClicked(sender As Object,
e As LinkLabelLinkClickedEventArgs) Handles lnkUrl.LinkClicked

'Process the selected link
Process.Start(e.Link.LinkData)
End Sub
```

3. Run the project. You should now see that when a URL is selected from the list, the LinkLabel control changes to reflect the name of the selected item (refer to Figure 11-4). When you click the link, Internet Explorer opens the URL in the LinkLabel control's LinkCollection.

How It Works

Now that you have the application working in this example, let's look at how it works. When you click an item in the ListView control, the Click event is fired for that control. You add code to the Click event to load the LinkLabel control with the selected link. You start by first setting the Text property of the LinkLabel control. This is the text that will be displayed on the form as shown in Figure 11-4.

You set the Text property using the static text Visit followed by the actual favorite name. The favorite name is retrieved from the ListView control's Item collection. Each row in the ListView control is called an item, and the first column contains the text of the item. Each column past the first column in a row is a subitem of the item (the text in the first column). The text that gets displayed in the link label is taken from the Text property of the Item collection:

```
Private Sub lvwFavorites_Click(sender As Object,
    e As EventArgs) Handles lvwFavorites.Click

    'Update the link label control Text property
    lnkUrl.Text = "Visit " & lvwFavorites.SelectedItems.Item(0).Text
```

The `Links` property of the LinkLabel control contains a `LinkCollection` that contains a default hyperlink consisting of the text that is displayed in the LinkLabel control. You clear this collection and set it using the correct hyperlink for the selected Favorite. You do this by calling the `Clear` method on the `Links` property:

```
'Clear the default hyperlink
lnkUrl.Links.Clear()
```

Finally, you add your hyperlink using the subitem of the selected item in the ListView control. The `Add` method of the `Links` property is an overloaded method, and the method that you are using here expects three parameters: `start`, `length`, and `linkdata`. The `start` parameter specifies the starting position of the text in the `Text` property that you want as the hyperlink, and the `length` parameter specifies how long the hyperlink should be.

You do not want the word *Visit* to be part of the hyperlink, so you specify the starting position to be 6, which takes into account the space after the word Visit. Then you specify the `length` parameter using the `Length` property of the `Text` property of the selected item in the ListView control. Finally, you specify the `linkdata` parameter by specifying the selected subitem from the ListView control. This subitem contains the actual URL for the favorite.

```
'Add the selected hyperlink to the LinkCollection
    lnkUrl.Links.Add(6, lvwFavorites.SelectedItems.Item(0).Text.Length,
        lvwFavorites.SelectedItems.Item(0).SubItems(1).Text)
End Sub
```

When a hyperlink on the LinkLabel control is clicked, it fires the `LinkClicked` event, and this is where you place your code to process the hyperlink of the favorite being displayed in this control. The `LinkLabelLinkClickedEventArgs` class contains information about the link label and, in particular, the actual hyperlink in the `LinkCollection`.

To retrieve the hyperlink, you access the `LinkData` property of the `Link` property. Then you pass this data to the `Start` method of the `Process` class, which causes a browser to be open and display the selected hyperlink:

```
Private Sub lnkUrl_LinkClicked(sender As Object,
    e As LinkLabelLinkClickedEventArgs) Handles lnkUrl.LinkClicked

    'Process the selected link
    Process.Start(e.Link.LinkData)
End Sub
```

AN ALTERNATIVE FAVORITE VIEWER

You know that building separate classes promotes code reuse, but let's prove that. If code reuse is such a hot idea, without having to rewrite or change any of the code you should be able to build another application that can use the functionality in the classes to find and open favorites.

In this case, you might have given a colleague the `Favorites`, `WebFavorite`, and `WebFavoriteCollection` classes, and that colleague should be able to build a new application that uses this functionality without having to understand the internals of how Internet shortcuts work or how Windows stores users' favorites.

Building a Favorites Tray

In this section, you build an application that displays a small icon on the system tray. Clicking this icon opens a list of the user's favorites as a menu, as shown in Figure 11-7. Clicking a favorite automatically opens the URL in Internet Explorer or whatever browser the user has set to be the default.

Bing

espn The Worldwide Leader in Sports

Google

Exit

FIGURE 11-7

To demonstrate this principle of code reuse, you need to create a new Visual Basic 2015 project in this solution.

TRY IT OUT Building a Favorites Tray

In this example, you will add a new project. All the code in this Try It Out is in the Favorites folder in the Zip file for this chapter.

1. Using Visual Studio 2015, select File ⇨ Add ⇨ New Project from the menu and create a new Visual Basic 2015 Windows Forms Application project called **Favorites Tray**. Now, you will see two projects in the Solution Explorer.

2. When the Designer for Form1 appears, click the form in the Forms Designer and then change the WindowState property to Minimized and change the ShowInTaskbar property to False, which effectively prevents the form from being displayed.

3. Using the Toolbox, drag a NotifyIcon control onto the form. It will drop into the component tray at the bottom of the form. Set the Name property of the new control to **icnNotify**; and set the Text property to **Right-click me to view Favorites**; and set the Icon property to the same as before, the **Favorites.ico**.

4. Next, open the Code Editor for Form1. In the Class Name combo box at the top of the Code Editor, select (Form1 Events), and in the Method Name combo box select VisibleChanged. Add the following bolded code to the event handler:

```
Private Sub Form1_VisibleChanged(sender As Object,
e As EventArgs) Handles Me.VisibleChanged

'If the user can see us, hide us
If Me.Visible = True Then Me.Visible = False
End Sub
```

5. Right-click the Favorites Tray project in the Solution Explorer and select Set As Startup Project. Now try running the project. You should discover that the tray icon is added to your system tray, as shown in Figure 11-8, but no form window will appear. If you hover your mouse over the icon, you'll see the message that you set in the Text property of the NotifyIcon control.

6. Notice that there appears to be no way to stop the program! Flip back to Visual Studio 2015 and select Debug ➤ Stop Debugging from the menu.

7. When you do this, although the program stops, the icon remains in the tray. To get rid of it, hover the mouse over it and it should disappear. Windows redraws the icons in the system tray only when necessary (for example, when the mouse is passed over an icon).

FIGURE 11-8

How It Works

You learn that setting a form to appear minimized (WindowState = Minimized) and telling it not to appear in the taskbar (ShowInTaskbar = False) has the effect of creating a window that's hidden in this example. You need a form to support the tray icon, but you don't need the form for any other reason. However, this is only half the battle because the form could appear in the Alt+Tab application switching list, unless you add the following code, which you already did:

```
Private Sub Form1_VisibleChanged(sender As Object,
    e As EventArgs) Handles Me.VisibleChanged

    'If the user can see us, hide us
    If Me.Visible = True Then Me.Visible = False
End Sub
```

This event handler has a brute-force approach that says, "If the user can see me, hide me."

Displaying Favorites

In the next Try It Out, you look at how to display the favorites.

TRY IT OUT Displaying Favorites

In this example, the first thing you need to do is include the classes built in Favorites Viewer in this Favorites Tray solution. You can then use the Favorites object to get a list of favorites back and build a menu. All the code in this Try It Out is in the Favorites folder in the Zip file for this chapter.

1. To display favorites, you need to get hold of the classes defined in the Favorites Viewer project. To do this, you add the Favorites, WebFavorite, and WebFavoriteCollection classes to this project.

Using the Solution Explorer, right-click the Favorites Tray project and select Add ➪ Existing Item. Browse to the classes in your Favorites Viewer project and find the Favorites class. After clicking Add, the class appears in the Solution Explorer for this project. You can select multiple files simultaneously by holding down the Ctrl key.

2. Repeat this for the `WebFavorite` and `WebFavoriteCollection` classes.

3. Create a new class in the Favorites Tray by clicking the project once more and selecting Add ⇨ Class. Call the new class `WebFavoriteMenuItem.vb` and then click the Add button to add this class to the project.

4. Set the new class to inherit from `System.Windows.Forms.MenuItem` by adding this code:

```
Public Class WebFavoriteMenuItem
    Inherits MenuItem
```

5. Add this member and method to the class:

```
'Public member
Public Favorite As WebFavorite

'Constructor
Public Sub New(newFavorite As WebFavorite)
    'Set the property
    Favorite = newFavorite

    'Update the text
    Text = Favorite.Name
End Sub
```

6. Unlike `ListViewItem`, `MenuItem` objects can react to themselves being clicked by overloading the `Click` method. In the Class Name combo box at the top of the Code Editor, select (WebFavoriteMenuItem Events) and then select the `Click` event in the Method Name combo box. Add the following bolded code to the `Click` event handler:

```
Private Sub WebFavoriteMenuItem_Click(sender As Object,
    e As EventArgs) Handles Me.Click

'Open the favorite
If Not Favorite Is Nothing Then
    Process.Start(Favorite.Url)
End If
End Sub
```

7. You need to do a similar trick to add an Exit option to your pop-up menu. Using the Solution Explorer, create a new class called `ExitMenuItem.vb` in the Favorites Tray project. Add the following bolded code to this class:

```
Public Class ExitMenuItem
Inherits MenuItem

'Constructor
Public Sub New()
    Text = "Exit"
End Sub

Private Sub ExitMenuItem_Click(sender As Object,
    e As System.EventArgs) Handles Me.Click

    Application.Exit()
End Sub
End Class
```

8. Finally, you're in a position in which you can load the favorites and create a menu for use with the tray icon. Add these members to Form1:

```
Public Class Form1
'Public member
Public Favorites As New Favorites()

'Private member
Private blnLoadCalled As Boolean = False
```

9. In the Class Name combo box select (Form1 Events) and in the Method Name combo box, select the Load event. Then add the following bolded code to this event handler:

```
Private Sub Form1_Load(sender As Object,
    e As EventArgs) Handles Me.Load

'Load the favorites
Favorites.ScanFavorites()
'Create a new context menu
Dim objMenu As New ContextMenu()

'Process each favorite
For Each objWebFavorite As WebFavorite In Favorites.FavoritesCollection
    'Create a menu item
    Dim objItem As New WebFavoriteMenuItem(objWebFavorite)
        'Add it to the menu
        objMenu.MenuItems.Add(objItem)
    Next

    'Add a separator menu item
    objMenu.MenuItems.Add("-")

    'Now add the Exit menu item
    objMenu.MenuItems.Add(New ExitMenuItem())

    'Finally, tell the tray icon to use this menu
    icnNotify.ContextMenu = objMenu

    'Set the load flag and hide ourselves
    blnLoadCalled = True
    Me.Hide()
End Sub
```

10. Modify the Form1_VisibleChanged procedure as follows:

```
Private Sub Form1_VisibleChanged(sender As Object,
 e As System.EventArgs) Handles Me.VisibleChanged

'Don't set the Visible property until the Load event has
'been processed
If blnLoadCalled = False Then
    Return
```

```
End If

     'If the user can see us, hide us
    If Me.Visible = True Then Me.Visible = False
End Sub
```

11. Run the project, and the icon will appear on the system tray. Right-click the icon and you'll see the list of favorites shown in Figure 11-7. Clicking one opens Internet Explorer; clicking Exit closes the application. Depending on what applications you have open and your settings, the icon can be grouped in the hidden icon section on the taskbar.

How It Works

That completes this example. Note that because of the order of events that are fired for your form, you have to create a variable in Form1 called blnLoadCalled. This variable makes sure that your favorites get loaded in the form's Load event.

The WebFavoriteMenuItem class accepts a WebFavorite object in its constructor and it configures itself as a menu item using the class. However, this class provides a Click method that you can overload, so when the user selects the item from the menu, you can immediately open the URL:

```
Private Sub WebFavoriteMenuItem_Click(sender As Object,
     e As EventArgs) Handles Me.Click

    'Open the favorite
    If Not Favorite Is Nothing Then
        Process.Start(Favorite.Url)
    End If
End Sub
```

The ExitMenuItem class does a similar thing. When this item is clicked, you call the shared Application.Exit method to quit the program:

```
Private Sub ExitMenuItem_Click(sender As Object,
     e As EventArgs) Handles Me.Click

    Application.Exit()
End Sub
```

The important thing is not the construction of the application itself; you can reuse the functionality you built in a different project. This underlines the fundamental motive for reuse; it means you don't have to reinvent the wheel every time you want to do something.

The method of reuse described here was to add the existing classes to your new project, hence making a second copy of them. This isn't efficient because it takes double the amount of storage and maintenance needed for the classes; however, the classes are small, so the cost of memory is minimal. It did save you from having to create the classes from scratch, allowing you to reuse the existing code, and it was very easy to do.

An alternative way of reusing classes is to create them in a class library. This *class library* is a separate project that can be referenced by a number of different applications so that only one copy of the code is required.

USING SHARED PROPERTIES AND METHODS

On occasion, you might find it useful to access methods and properties that are not tied to an instance of an object but are still associated with a class.

Imagine that you have a class that stores the username and password of a user for a computer program. You might have something that looks like this:

```
Public Class User
    'Public members
    Public Username As String

    'Private members
    Private strPassword As String
End Class
```

Now imagine that the password for a user has to be of a minimum length. You create a separate member to store the length and implement a property like this:

```
Public Class User
    'Public members
    Public Username As String
    Public MinPasswordLength As Integer = 6

    'Private members
    Private strPassword As String

    'Password property
    Public Property Password() As String
        Get
            Return strPassword
        End Get
        Set(value As String)
            If value.Length >= MinPasswordLength Then
                strPassword = value
            End If
        End Set
    End Property
End Class
```

That seems fairly straightforward. But now imagine that you have 5,000 user objects in memory. Each MinPasswordLength variable takes up 4 bytes of memory, meaning that 20KB of memory is being used to store the same value. Although 20KB of memory isn't a lot for modern computer systems, it's extremely inefficient, and there is a better way.

Using Shared Properties

See how to use shared properties and understand them in the next example.

TRY IT OUT Using Shared Properties

Ideally, you want to store the value for the minimum password length in memory against a specific class once and share that memory between all the objects created from that class, as you'll do in the following Try It Out. All the code in this Try It Out is in the folder Shared Demo in the Zip file for this chapter.

1. Close the existing solution if it is still open and create a new Windows Forms Application project called **Shared Demo**.

2. When the Designer for Form1 appears, change the Text property of the form to **Shared Demo** and then drag a ListBox, a Label, and a NumericUpDown control from the Toolbox onto the form. Set the Text property of the Label to **Password Length**. Arrange the controls as shown in Figure 11-9.

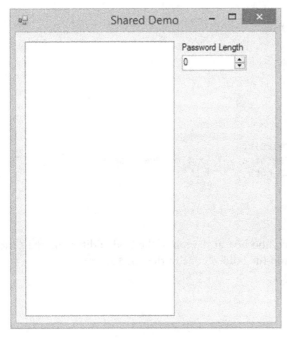

FIGURE 11-9

3. Set the Name property of the ListBox control to **lstUsers**.

4. Set the Name property of the NumericUpDown control to **nudMinPasswordLength,** set the Maximum property to **10**, and set the Value property to **6**.

5. Using the Solution Explorer, create a new class named **User**. Add the bolded code to the class:

```
Public Class User
    'Public members
    Public Username As String
    Public Shared MinPasswordLength As Integer = 6
    'Private members
    Private strPassword As String

    'Password property
    Public Property Password() As String
        Get
            Return strPassword
```

```
        End Get
    Set(value As String)
        If value.Length >= MinPasswordLength Then
            strPassword = value
        End If
      End Set
    End Property
    End Class
```

6. View the code for Form1 and add this highlighted member:

```
Public Class Form1
    'Private member
    Private arrUserList As New ArrayList()
```

7. Add this method to the Form1 class:

```
Private Sub UpdateDisplay()
    'Clear the list
    lstUsers.Items.Clear()

    'Add the users to the list box
    For Each objUser As User In arrUserList
        lstUsers.Items.Add(objUser.Username & ", " & objUser.Password &
            " (" & User.MinPasswordLength & ")")

    Next
End Sub
```

8. Select (Form1 Events) in the Class Name combo box at the top of the Code Editor and the Load event in the Method Name combo box. Add the bolded code to the Load event:

```
Private Sub Form1_Load(sender As Object,
    e As EventArgs) Handles Me.Load

    'Load 100 users
    For intIndex As Integer = 1 To 100
        'Create a new user
        Dim objUser As New User
        objUser.Username = "Stephanie" & intIndex
        objUser.Password = "password15"

        'Add the user to the array list
        arrUserList.Add(objUser)
    Next

    'Update the display
    UpdateDisplay()
End Sub
```

9. Select nudMinPasswordLength in the Class Name combo box at the top of the Code Editor and the ValueChanged event in the Method Name combo box. Add the bolded code to the ValueChanged event:

```
Private Sub nudMinPasswordLength_ValueChanged(sender As Object,
    e As EventArgs) Handles nudMinPasswordLength.ValueChanged

    'Set the minimum password length
    User.MinPasswordLength = nudMinPasswordLength.Value
    'Update the display
    UpdateDisplay()
End Sub
```

10. Save your project by clicking the Save All button on the toolbar.

11. Run the project. You should see a screen like the one shown in Figure 11-10.

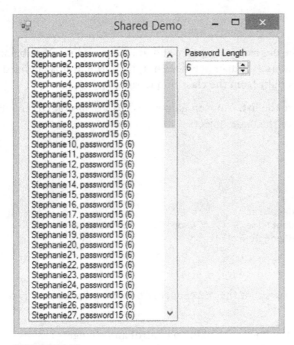

FIGURE 11-10

12. Scroll the NumericUpDown control up or down, and the list updates: The number in parentheses changes to correspond to the number shown in the NumericUpDown control.

How It Works

To create a member variable, property, or method on an object that is shared, you use the Shared keyword as you did in this example:

```
Public Shared MinPasswordLength As Integer = 6
```

This tells Visual Basic 2015 that the item should be available to all instances of the class.

Shared members can be accessed from within nonshared properties and methods as well as from shared properties and methods. For example, here's the `Password` property, which can access the shared `MinPasswordLength` member:

```
'Password property
Public Property Password() As String
    Get
        Return strPassword
    End Get
    Set(value As String)
        If value.Length >= MinPasswordLength Then
            strPassword = value
        End If
    End Set
End Property
```

What's important to realize is that although the `Password` property and `strPassword` member belong to the particular instance of the `User` class, `MinPasswordLength` does not; therefore, if it is changed the effect is felt throughout all the object instances built from the class in question.

In the form, `UpdateDisplay` is used to populate the list. You can gain access to `MinPasswordLength` as if it were a normal, nonshared public member of the `User` object:

```
Private Sub UpdateDisplay()
    'Clear the list
    lstUsers.Items.Clear()

    'Add the users to the list box
    For Each objUser As User In arrUserList
        lstUsers.Items.Add(objUser.Username & ", " & objUser.Password &
            " (" & User.MinPasswordLength & ")")
    Next
End Sub
```

At this point, you have a listing of users that shows that the `MinPasswordLength` value of each is set to 6 (refer to Figure 11-10).

Things start to get interesting when you scroll the NumericUpDown control and change `MinPasswordLength`. Because this is a shared member, you don't specifically *need* an instance of the class. Instead, you can set the property just by using the class name:

```
Private Sub nudMinPasswordLength_ValueChanged(sender As Object,
    e As EventArgs) Handles nudMinPasswordLength.ValueChanged

    'Set the minimum password length
    User.MinPasswordLength = nudMinPasswordLength.Value

    'Update the display
    UpdateDisplay()
End Sub
```

When building this method, you may notice that after you type **User**, Visual Studio 2015's IntelliSense pops up a list of members, including the `MinPasswordLength` property (see Figure 11-11).

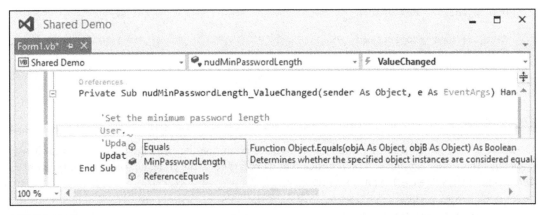

FIGURE 11-11

Shared members, properties, and methods can all be accessed through the class directly—you don't specifically need an instance of the class.

When you change this member with code in the ValueChanged event handler, you update the display, and this time you can see that the perceived value of MinPasswordLength has seemingly been changed for all instances of User, even though you changed it in only one place.

Using Shared Methods

Although you've seen how to make a public member variable shared, you haven't seen how to do this with a method. The main limitation with a shared method is that you can only access other shared methods and shared properties in the class in which it is defined.

> **NOTE** This is a hypothetical example of using a shared method, as you could do the same job here with a customized constructor.

TRY IT OUT Using a Shared Method

In this Try It Out, you look at an example of how to build a shared method that can create new instances of User. All the code in this Try It Out is in the folder Shared Demo in the Zip file for this chapter.

1. Open the Code Editor for User. Add the following code to the User class:

```
Public Shared Function CreateUser(userName As String,
    password As String) As User

    'Declare a new User object
```

```
        Dim objUser As New User()

        'Set the User properties
        objUser.Username = userName
        objUser.Password = password

        'Return the new user
        Return objUser
    End Function
```

2. Open the Code Editor for Form1 and locate the Load event handler. Change the code so that it looks like the following block. You'll notice that as you type in the code, as soon as you type User, IntelliSense offers CreateUser as an option:

```
Private Sub Form1_Load(sender As Object,
    e As EventArgs) Handles Me.Load

    'Load 100 users
    For intIndex As Integer = 1 To 100
        'Create a new user
        Dim objUser As New User
        objUser = User.CreateUser("Stephanie" & intIndex, "password15")

        'Add the user to the array list
        arrUserList.Add(objUser)
    Next

    'Update the display
    UpdateDisplay()
End Sub
```

3. If you run the project, you get the same results as the previous example.

How It Works

The important thing to look at in this example is the fact that CreateUser appears in the IntelliSense list after you type the class name. This is because it is shared and you do not need a specific instance of a class to access it. You create the method as a shared method by using the Shared keyword:

```
    Public Shared Function CreateUser(userName As String,
        password As String) As User
```

One thing to consider with shared methods is that you can access only members of the class that are also shared. You cannot access nonshared methods simply because you don't know what instance of the class you're actually running on. Likewise, you cannot access Me from within a shared method for the same reason.

UNDERSTANDING OBJECT-ORIENTED PROGRAMMING AND MEMORY MANAGEMENT

Object orientation has an impact on how memory is used in an operating system. .NET is heavily object-oriented, so it makes sense that .NET would have to optimize the way it uses memory to best suit the way objects are used.

Whenever you create an object, you're using memory. Most of the objects you use have *state*, which describes what an object knows. The methods and properties that an object has will either affect or work with that state. For example, an object that describes a file on disk will have state that describes its name, size, folder, and so on. Some of the state will be publicly accessible through properties. For example, a property called Size returns the size of the file. Some state is private to the object and is used to keep track of what the object has done or what it needs to do.

Objects use memory in two ways. First, something needs to keep track of the objects that exist on the system in memory. This is usually a task shared between you as an application developer and .NET's Common Language Runtime (CLR). If you create an object, you'll have to hold a reference to it in your program's memory so that you know where it is when you need to use its methods and properties. The CLR also needs to keep track of the object to determine when you no longer need it. Second, the CLR needs to allocate memory to the object so that the object can store its state. The more state an object has, the more memory it will need to use it.

The most expensive resource on a computer is the memory. *Expense,* here, means in terms of what you get for your money. You can buy a huge hard drive for the same amount of money that you can buy 4GB of memory. Retrieving data from memory is thousands of times faster than retrieving it from disk, so there's a trade-off—if you need fast access, you have to store it in memory, but there isn't as much memory available as there is hard-disk space.

When building an application, you want to use as little memory as possible, so there's an implication that you want to have as few objects as possible and that those objects should have as little state as possible. The upside is that today's computers have a lot more memory than they used to have, so your programs can use more memory than their predecessors of 10 years ago. However, you still need to be aware of your application's memory usage.

The CLR manages memory in several distinct ways. First, it's responsible for creating objects at the request of the application. With a heavily object-oriented programming platform like .NET, this will happen all the time, so Microsoft has spent an enormous amount of time making sure that the CLR creates objects in the most efficient way. The CLR, for example, can create objects far faster than its Component Object Model (COM) predecessor could. Second, the CLR is responsible for cleaning up memory when it's no longer needed. In the developer community, the manner in which the CLR cleans up objects is one of the most controversial.

Imagine that you're writing a routine that opens a file from disk and displays the contents on the screen. Well, with .NET you could use perhaps two .NET Framework objects to open the file and read its contents: System.IO.FileStream and System.IO.StreamReader. However, after the contents have been read, do you need these objects anymore? Probably not, so you remove your references to the objects and make the memory the objects were using available for creating more objects.

Imagine now that you don't remove your references to the objects. In this situation, the memory that the objects were using can't be used by anyone else. Now imagine that happening several thousand times. The amount of memory that's being wasted keeps growing. In extreme circumstances, the computer runs out of memory, meaning that other applications wouldn't ever be able to create any objects. This is a pretty catastrophic state of affairs.

We describe an object that is no longer needed but that holds onto memory as a *leak*. Memory leaks are one of the biggest causes of reliability problems on Windows because when a program is no longer able to obtain memory, it will crash.

With .NET this *should* never happen, or, at the very least, to leak memory you would have to go to some pretty extreme steps. This is because of a feature called *garbage collection*. When an object is no longer being used, the *garbage collector* (GC) automatically removes the object from memory and makes the memory it was using available to other programs.

Garbage Collection

The GC works by freeing the memory allocated to an object when it is no longer in use.

To understand this, think back to the discussion of scope in Chapter 3. Imagine that you create a method and you define a variable with local scope at the top of that method. That variable is used to store an object (it doesn't matter what kind of object is used for this discussion). At this point, one part of the program knows about the object's existence—that is, the variable is holding a reference to the object. When you return from the method, the variable goes out of scope, and therefore the variable forgets about the object's existence; in other words, the only reference to the object is lost. At this point, no one knows about the object, so it can be safely deleted.

For an example, look at the following code:

```
Dim objObject As New MyObject
Console.WriteLine(objObject.GetType().FullName)
objObject = Nothing
```

This code snippet creates a new object from the `MyObject` class, invokes a method on it, and then removes the reference to the object. In this case, when you create the object, the `objObject` variable is the only thing that holds a reference to it. In the last line, `objObject` is set to `Nothing`, hence removing the only reference to the object. The GC is then free to remove the reference to the object.

The GC does not run constantly. Instead, it runs periodically based on a complex algorithm that measures the amount of work the computer is doing and how many objects might need to be deleted. When the GC runs, it looks through the master list of all the objects the program has ever created for any that can be deleted at this point.

In old-school programming, programmers were responsible for deleting their own objects and had the freedom to say to an object, "You, now, clean yourself up and get out of memory." With .NET this ability is gone. Instead an object will be deleted at some *indeterminate* time in the future.

Exactly when this happens is nondeterministic—in other words, as a developer you don't know when the GC is going to run. This means that there is no immediate connection between the removal of the last reference to an object and the physical removal of that object from memory. This is known as *nondeterministic finalization*.

Releasing Resources

In some cases, objects that you build may need access to certain system and network resources, such as files and database connections. Using these resources requires a certain discipline to ensure that you don't inadvertently cause problems.

Here's an example. If you create a new file, write some data to it, but forget to close it, no one else will be able to read data from that file. This is because you have an *exclusive lock* on the file; it doesn't make sense for someone to be able to read from a file when it's still being written to. You must take care to release system resources should you open them.

When an object has access to scarce system or network resources like these, it's important that the caller tell the object that it can release those resources as soon as they're no longer needed. For example, here's some code that creates a file:

```
'Open a file
Dim objFileStream As New FileStream("c:\myfile.txt", FileMode.Create)
'Do something with the file
...
'Close the file
objFileStream.Close()
'Release your reference to the object
objFileStream = Nothing
```

As soon as you finish working with the file, you call Close, which tells .NET that the consumer is finished with the file, and Windows can make it available for other applications to use. This is known as *releasing the lock*. When you release the object reference in the next line by setting objFileStream = Nothing, this is an entirely separate action from calling Close.

The FileStream object releases the lock on the file when its Finalize method is called. However, as you've just learned, the time period between the instance of the FileStream object becoming a candidate for garbage collection (which happens when objFileStream = Nothing) and Finalize being called is nondeterministic. So, if you had not called Close, the file would have remained open for a period of time, which would have caused problems for anyone else who needed to use the file.

Another way to release resources within objects is to implement the IDisposable interface, which you did with the WebFavorite and Favorites classes. This interface provides a Dispose method for your objects, in which you can put code to clean up the resources used in that class.

Ideally, the consumer of these objects would call the Dispose methods on these objects when they are done using them; if they do not, the Finalize method in these objects will do so when the GC runs.

Defragmentation and Compaction

As the last item in its bag of tricks, the GC can defragment and compact memory. In much the same way that your computer's hard disk needs periodic defragmentation to make it run more efficiently, so does memory. Imagine that you create 10 small objects in memory, each about 1KB in size. Imagine that .NET allocates them all on top of each other, so you end up taking up one 10KB piece of memory. (In reality, you don't usually care where objects exist in memory, so this discussion is a bit academic.)

Next, imagine you want to create another object and this object is of medium size, say about 3KB. .NET has to create this object at the end of the 10KB block. This means that you'll have allocated 13KB in total.

Then imagine that you delete every other small object, so now your 10KB block of memory has holes in it. Not much of a problem, but imagine you want to create another 3KB object. Although there's 5KB of space in the original block, you can't put it there because no gap is big enough. Instead, it has to go on the end, meaning your application is now taking up 16KB of memory.

What the GC can do is defragment memory, which means that it removes the gaps when objects have been removed, as shown in Figure 11-12. The upshot of this is that your application uses memory more efficiently, so applications take up less memory.

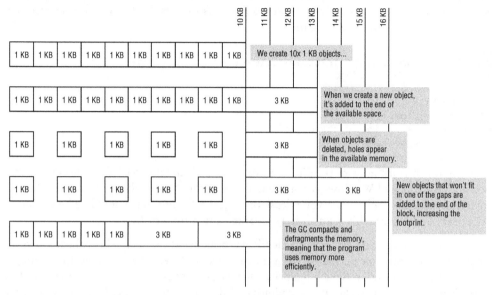

FIGURE 11-12

Although this might not seem like a big deal on a PC with 1GB of memory available, consider that .NET could potentially be running on much smaller devices where memory usage is a big deal—for example, a mobile device with 32MB of memory in total. Besides, imagine making three thousand 5KB savings in this example; you have saved more than 15MB of memory!

SUMMARY

In this chapter, you took a look at some more valuable techniques that you can use to assist the building of object-oriented software. Initially, you examined the idea of reuse. Specifically, you looked at classes that allow you to examine the Internet Explorer Favorites stored on the user's computer. You consumed these classes from two applications: one standard desktop application and an application that exists on the system tray.

You then examined the idea of shared members, properties, and methods. Sharing these kinds of items is a powerful way to make common functionality available to all classes in an application.

Finally, you examined how consumers of objects should ensure that scarce system resources are freed whenever an object is deleted by the GC using the `Dispose` and `Finalize` methods.

To summarize, you should know how to:

➤   Build a class that inherits from the `System.Collections.CollectionBase` namespace, add methods that allow you to add and remove objects from the collection, and provide a property that allows an application to query for the number of items in the collection.

➤ Use the Collections class in your own application to create objects and add them to the collection.

➤ Use shared properties and methods in a class that can be shared among all instantiated instances of the class.

➤ Properly dispose of resources to make efficient use of the GC.

EXERCISES

1. Modify the Favorites Viewer project to select the first favorite in the ListView control automatically after it has been loaded so that the LinkLabel control displays the first item when the form is displayed.

You also need to modify the Load event in Form1, and ensure that the ListView control contains one or more items before proceeding. You do this by querying the Count property of the Items property of the ListView control. Then you select the first item in the ListView control using the lstFavorites.Items(0).Selected property and call the Click event for the ListBox control to update the LinkLabel control.

▶ WHAT YOU LEARNED IN THIS CHAPTER

TOPIC	CONCEPTS
Code reuse	You can access your classes by more than one application.
Shared methods and properties	You can mark these as shared to have them associated with the class and not each instance of the class.
Memory management	Understand that garbage collection happens automatically and you should release expensive resources as soon as the program is finished using them.

12

Accessing Data Using Structured Query Language

WHAT YOU WILL LEARN IN THIS CHAPTER:

➤ What you need to know to complete this chapter's exercises

➤ What a database really is

➤ Using the SQL SELECT statement

➤ Examining the SQL JOIN statement

➤ Using the SQL UPDATE statement

➤ Examining the SQL DELETE statement

➤ Using the SQL INSERT statement

➤ Examining the SQL comment

➤ How to execute queries in SQL Server

WROX.COM CODE DOWNLOADS FOR THIS CHAPTER

The wrox.com code downloads for this chapter are found at www.wrox.com/begvisualbasic2015 on the Download Code tab. The code is in the 092117 C12.zip download and individually named according to the names given throughout the chapter.

Most applications manipulate data in some way. Visual Basic 2015 applications often manipulate data that comes from relational databases. To do this, your application needs to interface with relational database software such as Microsoft Access, Microsoft SQL Server, Oracle, or Sybase.

Visual Studio 2015 provides the data access tools and wizards to connect to these databases and retrieve and update their data. In this chapter, you will look at some of these tools and wizards and use them to retrieve data from a database.

The next chapter concentrates on writing code directly, which gives you more flexibility and control than relying on Visual Studio 2015 to create it for you. With practice, writing code will also take less time than working through a wizard.

WHAT YOU NEED TO COMPLETE THIS CHAPTER'S EXERCISES

To complete the exercises in this chapter, you need to have access to a version of SQL Server. The chapter is based on SQL Server 2014, but the code should work with other SQL Server versions with only minor adjustments, if any. As a beginner, it's easier for you to use SQL Server 2014 without the worry of minor changes. The database can reside in SQL Server 2014 on your local machine or in SQL Server on a network. This chapter has examples of SQL Server 2014 Express running locally. The database the examples use is the pubs database from Microsoft.

You can download SQL Server 2014 Express, without cost, from `www.microsoft.com/sql`. Select the version with tools. You can also enter the following URL directly: `www.microsoft.com/en-us/download/details.aspx?id=42299` and select the correct file. For a 32-bit operating system, download the file named `SQLEXPRWT_x86_ENU.exe`. For a 64-bit operating system download the file named `SQLEXPRWT_x64_ENU.exe`.

Here are some notes for installing SQL Server 2014 Express (Runtime with Management Tools):

➤   You should install a named instance of SQLEXPRESS to avoid having to customize the code. Be sure to use the name of **SQLEXPRESS** during the install. This should be the default value.

> **NOTE** *The code examples in this book use mixed mode authentication to allow a username and password to be passed into SQL Server. The book uses the sa login with a password of SQL2014wrox, which has system administrator rights. This is not normally how you would access SQL Server from code. For production, create a login that has as few rights as possible to use, or use Windows authentication mode, in which you can give rights to users or groups.*

➤   Select to install the database engine.

➤   Be sure to select mixed-mode authentication. The sa account will not be active unless mixed-mode authentication is selected.

➤   To use the examples in this chapter without changing the username and password, set the sa password to **SQL2014wrox**.

➤   When selecting user accounts for services, use the network service or local service account.

To locate a copy of the pubs database, go to the following resources:

➤ You can download SQL Server 2000 scripts and instructions from `www.microsoft.com/en-us/download/details.aspx?id=23654`. This script works with 2014 versions. And this website is the easiest place to get the database.

➤ If the links are a hassle to type, just go to `www.microsoft.com/downloads` and search for SQL Server Sample Databases. The search results will contain the preceding link.

➤ When you run the MSI package, it will install to `C:\SQL Server 2000 Sample Databases` (the drive may vary based on your configuration). You can then open the file `instpubs.sql` into SQL Management Studio by double-clicking it. Once open, execute the code by clicking F5 or the Execute button, and the pubs database will be created and loaded with data.

➤ When you execute the file `instpubs.sql` in SQL Server Management Studio for SQL Server 2014, there will be one error, which is a stored procedure that is no longer present; the error can safely be ignored.

```
Msg 2812, Level 16, State 62, Line 56
Could not find stored procedure 'sp_dboption'.
```

WHAT IS A DATABASE?

A *database* consists of one or more large, complex files that store data in a structured format. The database engine, in your case Microsoft SQL Server 2014, manages the file or files and the data within those files. The database format is known as a *relational database.* At its most basic level, data is stored in tables, rows, and columns similar to how you see data in a spreadsheet. The data in tables is related by special database keys, which allows for better storage and faster retrieval. To access the data, you will use *Structured Query Language (SQL).* After you complete this chapter, you'll understand all this information.

Database Tables

A table contains a collection of data, which is represented by one or more columns and one or more rows of data. Imagine the way data is stored in a spreadsheet in rows and columns. Each column in a table represents an attribute of the data stored in that table. For example, a column named First Name would represent the first name of an employee or customer. This column is an attribute of an employee or customer. A row in a table contains a collection of columns that form a complete set of attributes of one instance of the data stored in that table. For example, suppose a table contains two columns: First Name and Last Name. These two columns in a single record describe the name of that one person. This is illustrated in Figure 12-1.

TRY IT OUT Creating Tables

In this Try It Out, you use SQL Server Management Studio (SSMS) to create a database and add a table.

FIGURE 12-1

> **NOTE** *SQL Server Management Studio is a tool you use to help manage SQL Server Databases. As a developer, you may or may not have access to your company's SQL Server databases. If you are allowed to access them, this is the best tool to use. It enables you to create and change databases you are using in your applications, as well as to create and test SQL statements you will use in your application. There are many other features this application can do for you to help manage your databases that you will not use in this book. Just know that this is the tool to use to manage your SQL Server databases.*

1. When you installed SQL Server with tools, a program named SQL Server Management Studio was installed as well. Open this program and connect to your local database. For the server name, you must enter the server, followed by a forward slash (\), followed by the instance name. You may use localhost, (local), a period, the IP address, or your computer name for the server name. See Figure 12-2 for an example of the Connect to Server dialog.

2. When the program opens, you will see the Object Explorer on the left. Right-click the Databases folder and select New Database, as shown in Figure 12-3. If you cannot see the Object Explorer, just press F8 to show it.

3. In the New Database dialog, set the Database Name to **TestDB** and click OK. Leave all other default values.

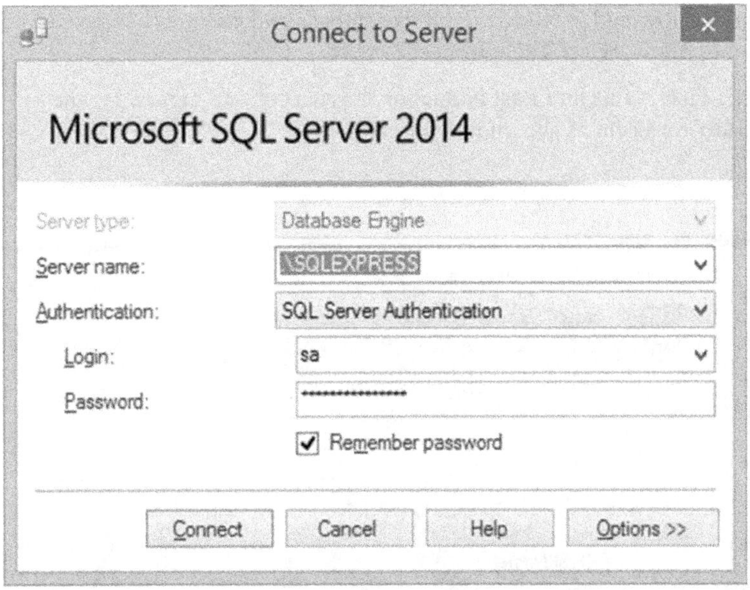

FIGURE 12-2

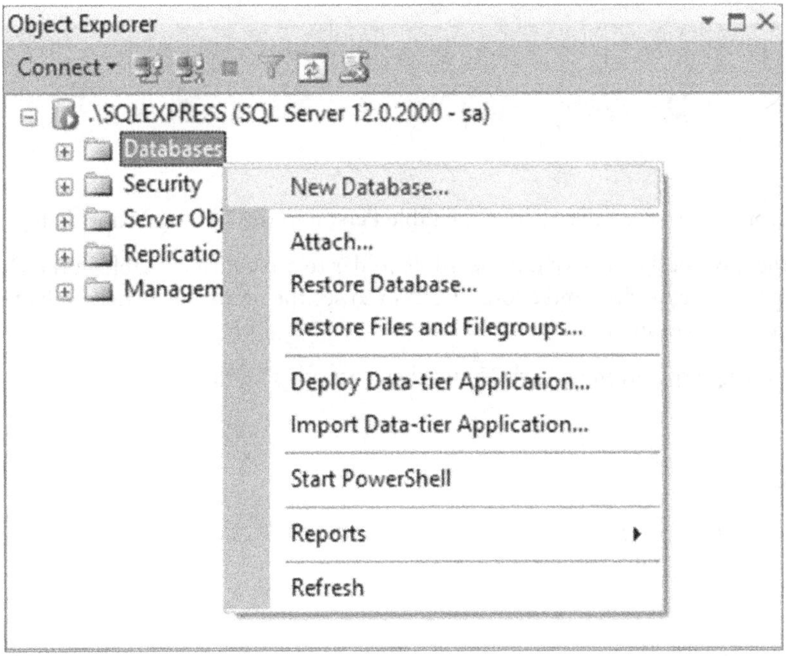

FIGURE 12-3

4. Expand the Databases folder now and locate the TestDB database and expand the tree view. Find the Tables folder and right-click it. Select Table from the menu.

5. In the table designer, enter **First Name** and **Last Name** for the two column names. Set the Data Type to **varchar(50)** for both, as shown in Figure 12-4.

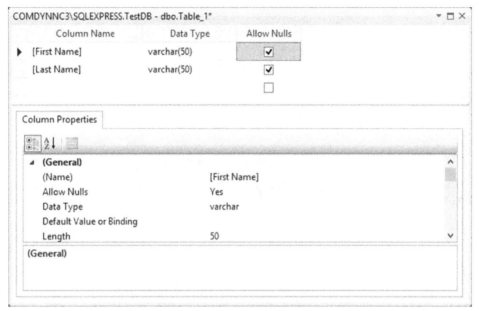

FIGURE 12-4

6. Now click the Save icon to save the table. Name the table **Person** in the Choose Name dialog.

7. You can now close the table designer. Expand the Table folder to see your new table in the Object Explorer. You may need to right-click and choose Refresh to see the new table. Alternately, you can create a table via a SQL command.

8. In SSMS, press the New Query button or Ctrl+N and then enter this SQL:

```
USE TestDB
GO
CREATE TABLE Person2
  (
  [First Name] varchar(50) NULL,
  [Last Name] varchar(50) NULL
  )
```

9. To execute the command, click the ! Execute button or press F5. To see the new table, right-click the Tables folder in the Object Explorer and choose Refresh. You will see the same tables, as shown in Figure 12-5.

FIGURE 12-5

How It Works

Using SSMS you can use simple wizards to create a new database and a new table. This is the quickest way to add new tables to a database.

A second way is to use a SQL command and execute the command using SSMS. The command started by telling SSMS which database the query or command should be run against. The USE keyword is followed by a database name. The USE keyword identifies what database to use for the statements that follow it. As a best practice, you should begin all your SQL scripts in SSMS with a USE statement followed by GO. GO ends the current batch of SQL and basically resets everything for the next statement:

```
USE TestDB
GO
```

In the SQL Editor toolbar, you also find a database drop-down list, in which you can select the database that SSMS should target for the query.

Next is the command to create a table:

```
CREATE TABLE Person2
  (
  [First Name] varchar(50) NULL,
  [Last Name] varchar(50) NULL
  )
```

The syntax for this command is:

```
CREATE TABLE table-name
  (
```

```
column-name data-type null-or-not-null,
column-name data-type null-or-not-null
)
```

The varchar data type you entered states that the column holds variable-length string data with a maximum length of 50 characters. Table 12-1 describes some of the common data types you can use for tables.

TABLE 12-1: SQL Server Common Data Types

DATA TYPE	DESCRIPTION
Bit	Holds a 1 or 0. Used for true/false data. True = 1, and False = 0.
Varchar(n)	1 – 8000 characters. Used to store string data. You set the length of the data like this. Varchar(50) for a string column that can hold 50 characters.
Varchar(MAX)	A special type of string data that can store up to 2GB of data.
Char(n)	1 – 8000 characters. Stores string data that is fixed length. Spaces are added to fill any missing characters. So a field of char(10) would store and return the string abc with 7 spaces appended to the end of the string.
TinyInt	0 – 255 Integer data.
SmallInt	+/– 32 thousand (approximately) Integer data.
Int	+/– 2 billion (approximately) Integer data.
BigInt	+/– 9 quintillion (approximately) Integer data.
Numeric(p,s) or Decimal(p,s)	+/– 10^38 numbers with fixed precision and scale. Precision is the number of digits to store and Scale is the number of digits to the right of the decimal. Numeric(10,2) would hold a number like 12345678.12. Precision can be set from 1 to 38, and Scale can be set as high as the Precision if all the numbers are to the right of the decimal point.
Float(n) or Real	+/– 100000000000000000000000000000000000000 (approximately) depending on the number of decimals. Real is equivalent to Float(24). Note: The numbers stored are not exact in all cases. Use decimal or numeric data types for storing exact numbers with defined precision.
Date	0001–01–01 through 9999–12–31. Only stores the date: month, day, and year.
Time	Stores the hours, minutes and seconds. Up to 7 decimal places on the seconds.
SmallDateTime	1900–01–01 through 2079–06–06. Stores time to the nearest minute.
DateTime	1753–01–01 through 1999–12–31. Stores time in fractional seconds to three digits.
Uniqueidentifier	Hexadecimal digits 0–9 or a–f. Guarantees uniqueness. These will not be duplicated from one machine to another. They are in this format: XXXXXXXX-XXXX-XXXX-XXXX-XXXXXXXXXXXX.

> **NOTE** *To get the exact data ranges and more detail, go to MSDN at the following link:* `http://msdn.microsoft.com/en-us/library/ms187752.aspx`.

Primary and Foreign Keys

In the world of relational databases, you need to understand primary and foreign keys because they are key concepts for relational database design.

Understanding Primary Keys

Each table you create should contain a unique key that makes each row unique. This key is a column or combination of columns called a *primary key*. You commonly see tables such as Customer with a primary key named `CustomerID`. There are two common ways to make sure this column guarantees that each row is unique in SQL Server.

Within SQL Server, you can set a primary key as an *identity* column; when set, SQL Server will automatically increase the ID by 1 for each row. To use an *identity* primary key, you normally set the `column` data type to `integer`. Because an integer can store a number up to just over 2 billion, you could have 2 billion rows in your table before you run out of key values. That should handle almost all your database scenarios.

There is one case to consider, though. By default, an *identity* column starts with a value of 1 and SQL Server increments it by 1 for each new row. What if you have databases in more than one location storing the same data? At some point, you'll need to put that data together in the same database. In each database, the same key values are used. If this happens, you cannot merge the data. However, you have a way to solve this: Use a *uniqueidentifier* as a primary key.

When you create a primary key that is a *uniqueidentifier*, they look like this: `3F9559FF-8B85 -D011-B42D-11C04BC864FF` and are unique across computers. This is important if you have data that is created in more than one place. For example, say you are creating a database to track sales for a chain of 1,000 stores. If you use an identity primary key at each location, you cannot merge the data of all stores into one table without manipulating the data at your corporate office. If you use a `uniqueidentifier`, they are unique even when you create them on different machines. By using `uniqueidentifiers`, you can put all your data into one table without any complex data manipulation.

Understanding Foreign Keys

You read earlier that Microsoft SQL Server is a *relational database management system* (RDMS). In a relational database, tables are related by what are known as *foreign keys*. To explain a foreign key, think about the data for a school or university. Some of the main objects are students, teachers, and classes, which would all be created as tables.

As you design a database for a school, you must think about how the data relates to each other. There are different types of relationships. This section focuses on two types (one-to-many relationships and many-to-many relationships).

Before you had access to an RDMS, you might have stored this data in a spreadsheet. The columns in the spreadsheet would be ClassName, ClassNumber, RoomNumber, TeacherFirstName, TeacherLastName, TeacherEmail, and TeacherPhone. In a spreadsheet, you would have one small problem. Because a teacher can teach more than one class, you would have to repeat the teacher's information on every row. The problem comes when the teacher gets a new phone number, and you must update every row in the spreadsheet for that teacher. This is where a foreign-key relationship comes into play.

In an RDMS, you have two tables versus one spreadsheet; this is where you can implement a foreign key. Let's look at the two tables: teacher and class. A teacher has attributes such as First Name, Last Name, Email, and Phone Number. A class can be described by its Name, Number, and Room Number. Also, you need to add a primary key to each table: ClassID and TeacherID. At this school, a class can have only one teacher, but the teacher can teach more than one class. That defines a one-to-many relationship between class and teacher.

To handle this in an RDMS, you use a *foreign key* that defines a relationship between two tables. In this case, a class can have one teacher, so you can store the teacher in the class table. To do this, you add a primary key of the teacher table to the class. The primary key is TeacherID. The key beside the column name denotes that the column is the primary key for the table. Figure 12-6 shows a layout of these tables. The line between the tables represents a foreign-key constraint between the TeacherID columns in both tables.

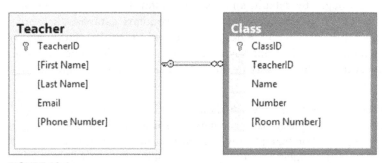

FIGURE 12-6

In the university example, a student can take one-to-many classes, and a class can have one-to-many students. To define this relationship in an RDMS, you create one table for student and one table for class. This relationship (student can take many classes and a class can have many students) is called a one-to-many relationship. To handle this properly, you must add a bridge table and convert the many-to-many relationship into one-to-many relationships. In this case, add a table to the database-named roster with two columns: ClassID and StudentID. Now you have two relationships, and they are both one-to-many. A student can have many rows in a roster, and each roster row can have one student. Also, a class can have more than one row in a roster, and a roster can have one class. See Figure 12-7 for the layout of these tables.

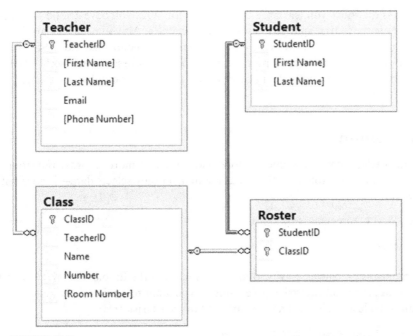

FIGURE 12-7

Queries

A *query* in a database is a group of *Structured Query Language* (*SQL*) statements that allow you to retrieve and update data in your tables or even change or create database objects like you saw earlier. You can use queries to select, insert, delete, or even update all the data or specific data in one or more tables.

In SQL Server, you can save queries as a stored procedure. A stored procedure is much like a function you use in Visual Studio. You call it, pass in parameters and get a return value from the database. Using stored procedures can make your Visual Basic 2015 code easier because you have fewer complex SQL queries included in your code. They can also make your programs faster because database engines can precompile execution plans for queries when you create them, whereas the SQL code in a Visual Basic 2015 program needs to be reinterpreted every time it's used. You will learn more about stored procedures in Chapter 13.

To really understand the implications of queries, you need to learn some SQL. Fortunately, compared with other programming languages, basic SQL is really simple.

UNDERSTANDING BASIC SQL SYNTAX

The *American National Standards Institute* (*ANSI*) defines the standards for ANSI SQL. Most database engines implement ANSI SQL to some extent and often add some features specific to the given database engine.

The benefit of ANSI SQL is that once you learn the basic syntax for SQL, you have a solid grounding from which you can code the SQL language in almost any database. All you need to learn is a new interface for the database that you are working in. Many database vendors extended SQL to use advanced features or optimizations for their particular database. It is best to stick with ANSI-standard SQL in your coding whenever possible, in case you want to change databases at some point.

Using SELECT Statement

The SQL SELECT statement selects data from one or more fields in one or more records, and from one or more tables in your database. Note that the SELECT statement only selects data—it does not modify the data in any way.

The simplest allowable SELECT statement is like this:

```
SELECT * FROM Employees
```

The preceding statement means "retrieve every field for every record in the Employees table." The * indicates "every field." Employees indicates the table name. If you want to retrieve only first names and last names, you can provide a list of field names rather than an asterisk (*):

```
SELECT [First Name], [Last Name] FROM Employees
```

You need to enclose these field names in square brackets because they contain spaces. The square brackets indicate to the SQL interpreter that even though there is a space in the name, it should treat First Name as one object name and Last Name as another object name. Otherwise, the interpreter cannot follow the syntax.

SQL is a lot like plain English—even a nonprogrammer could probably understand what it means. Now say you wanted to retrieve only the employees whose last names begin with D. To do this, you add a WHERE clause to your SELECT statement:

```
SELECT [First Name], [Last Name]
FROM Employees
WHERE [Last Name] LIKE 'D%'
```

A WHERE clause limits the selection of data to only those records that match the criteria in the WHERE clause. The preceding SELECT statement would cause the database to look at the Last Name column and select only those records in which the employee's last name begins with the letter D. The % character is a wildcard that means any other characters.

Last, if you want to retrieve these items in a particular order, you can, for example, order the results by first name. You just need to add an ORDER BY clause to the end:

```
SELECT [First Name], [Last Name]
FROM Employees
WHERE [Last Name] LIKE 'D%'
ORDER BY [First Name];
```

This means that if you have employees named Angela Dunn, Zebedee Dean, and David Dunstan, you will get the following result:

```
Angela    Dunn
David     Dunstan
Zebedee   Dean
```

You're specifying a specific command here, but the syntax is pretty simple—and very similar to how you describe what you want to an English speaker. Usually, when ordering by a name, you want to order in an ascending order so that A comes first, and Z comes last. If you were ordering by a number, though, you might want to have the bigger number at the top—for example, so that a product with the highest price appears first. Doing this is really simple—just add DESC (short for descending) to the ORDER BY clause, which causes the results to be ordered in descending order:

```
SELECT [First Name], [Last Name] FROM Employees
                    WHERE [Last Name] LIKE 'D%' ORDER BY [First Name] DESC;
```

The D% means "begins with a D followed by anything." If you had said %D%, it would mean, "anything followed by D followed by anything" (basically, "contains D"). The preceding command would return the following:

```
Zebedee   Dean
David     Dunstan
Angela    Dunn
```

You can summarize this syntax in the following way:

```
SELECT select-list
    FROM table-name
    [WHERE search-condition]
    [ORDER BY <i>order</i>-<i>by</i>-<i>expression</i> [ASC | DESC]]
```

This means that you must either provide a list of fields to include or use an * to select them all. You must provide a table name. Optionally, you can choose to provide a search condition. You can also choose to provide an order by expression and if you do, you can make it either ascending or descending.

Using the JOIN Statement

SQL joins allow you to put data that is in separate tables together to bring all the useful information back to the user or application. Let's think back to the school example. If you look at Figure 12-8, you'll see the Class table, in which there is a foreign key to the Teacher table. The TeacherID field stores the primary key values in the Teacher table, and they would be integers such as 1 or 119. In a report, having teacher 119 might not mean much versus having the teacher's name, Bob Smith. Joining tables together can help.

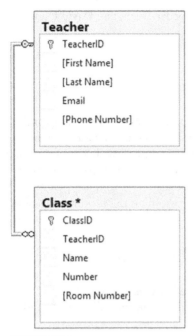

FIGURE 12-8

There are two main types of joins: INNER and OUTER. The difference is that an INNER JOIN returns rows that only match on tables. That may be hard to understand, so think about it this way. You have data in your Teacher table for all new, current, and past teachers. In your Class table, you have classes for only the most recent five semesters. This means that in your data you have new and past teachers that are not teaching classes. Those teachers have no data in the Class table. If you join the two tables with an INNER JOIN, you'll only get data for teachers that have classes. On the other hand, if you use an OUTER JOIN you get all teachers and the classes that they are teaching.

To join two tables together and return all columns, you would create statements like the following:

```
SELECT *
FROM Teacher
INNER JOIN Class
ON Teacher.TeacherID = Class.TeacherID
```

The previous code returns all rows in which the primary key in Teacher has a record or foreign key in Class. If the same TeacherID is in Class more than once, a row is returned for each occurrence. So, you will see all teachers that are teaching one or more classes with this statement.

To see all the data from Teacher, even if a teacher is not teaching a class, write an OUTER JOIN.

```
SELECT *
FROM Teacher
LEFT OUTER JOIN Class
ON Teacher.TeacherID = Class.TeacherID
```

The preceding returns all rows in Teacher regardless of the presence of a foreign key match in Class. If the same key is in Class more than once, a row is returned for each occurrence.

To limit the data returned to specific columns from each table, specify the list of columns after the SELECT keyword. You can append the table name to the column and separate it by a period, as you have done before. It is better to always append the table name because you may have the same column in each table, and your query will contain an error in this case.

For OUTER JOINs, you can use a LEFT OUTER JOIN or RIGHT OUTER JOIN. When writing outer joins, you do not have to use the keyword OUTER; you can just write LEFT JOIN or RIGHT JOIN. This is the most common syntax for OUTER JOINs and the rest of this book focuses on this join syntax. To convert what you do here to a RIGHT JOIN, just change the order of the tables. You can basically use them both in any occasion, and it is a matter of preference. In my experience, you rarely see developers use a RIGHT JOIN.

Using the UPDATE Statement

To update data in the database, you use the SQL UPDATE statement. The basic UPDATE statement looks like this:

```
UPDATE Table
SET Name = 'Bryan'
```

This updates the Name column to Bryan in every row in the table. You may want to update just one row or maybe only certain rows. In this case, you add the WHERE:

```
UPDATE Teacher
SET Name = 'Bryan'
WHERE TeacherID = 4
```

This updates the Name column for one row that has the ID of 4 to Bryan. You can use all the same options that you saw earlier for the WHERE clause.

You can summarize the basic UPDATE syntax in the following way:

```
UPDATE table-name
   SET column = value
     [,column = value
     ,column = value]
   [WHERE search-condition]
```

Using the DELETE Statement

To delete data in the database, you use the SQL DELETE statement. The basic DELETE statement looks like this:

```
DELETE FROM Teacher
```

Or this:

```
DELETE Teacher
```

This statement deletes every row in the table. You may want to delete just one row or maybe only certain rows. In this case, you just add the WHERE clause—the same statement that you learned using the SELECT statement. The FROM keyword is optional; use it if you think the SQL is more readable.

```
DELETE FROM Teacher
WHERE TeacherID = 4
```

The previous code deletes the row that has the TeacherID of 4 from the table.

You can summarize the basic DELETE syntax in the following way:

```
DELETE [FROM] table-name
   [WHERE search-condition]
```

Using the INSERT Statement

To insert data in the database, you use the SQL INSERT statement. The basic INSERT statement looks like this:

```
INSERT INTO Teacher(Name, Address, Zip)
VALUES ('Bryan', '123 Main Street', '20211')
```

Or this:

```
INSERT Teacher(Name, Address, Zip)
VALUES ('Bryan', '123 Main Street', '20211')
```

This statement inserts one row in the table. As you can see, the INTO keyword is optional, and you should use it when it makes your code more readable. Sometimes, you need to insert more than one row at a time. You do this a lot when loading data into a temp. To load data like this, you can SELECT data from another table and INSERT it into a table:

```
INSERT INTO Teacher_Temp(Name, Address, Zip)
   (SELECT Name, Address, Zip from Teacher
   WHERE Zip = '20211')
```

The previous code inserts all rows that have a Zip of 20211 from Teacher into Teacher_temp.

You may find that you need to enter data that already exists in a table, but one column must be changed to a new value.

```
INSERT INTO Teacher(ID, Name, Address, Zip, InsertUser)
   (SELECT 'AX0001', Name, Address, Zip, 'Bryan' from Teacher_Temp
   WHERE ID = 'QX1278')
```

The previous SQL code inserts a row into Teacher and copies data from the row with ID QX1278. The difference is that you assign a new ID of AX0001 and the InsertUser of Bryan.

You can also leave off the column list for the inserting table, and SQL Server inserts the data into the columns in order like this. You have to make sure of the column order.

```
INSERT INTO Teacher_Temp
   (SELECT Name, Address, Zip from Teacher
   WHERE Zip = '20211')
```

These shortcuts are never a good practice because the table definition may change. Your SQL will either fail or worse, it may insert data into the wrong columns.

You can summarize the basic INSERT syntax in the following way:

```
INSERT [INTO] table-name (Column-List)
   Values(Data to insert)
```

Or this:

```
INSERT [INTO] table-name (Column-List)
   (SELECT Column-List FROM table-name [WHERE search-condition])
```

Using the SQL Comment

When you write SQL, you need to put in comments for complex areas of your code or to stop a line from running. You can do this in two main ways.

To comment a single line of code, use two dashes:--. To comment a group of lines, begin a multiline comment with a slash and asterisk: /* and end the comment with an asterisk and a slash: */. See the following examples:

```
-This is a single line comment
```

Or this:

```
/*
This is a multi-line comment
Where you need to comment
More than one line of SQL
*/
```

EXECUTING QUERIES IN SQL SERVER

SQL is really a basic programming language, and if you are a programmer who accesses databases, you'll need to use it. The best way to learn SQL is to do it. In this next Try It Out, you see all the statements discussed in the last section in action.

TRY IT OUT Create, Manipulate, and Retrieve Data

In this Try It Out, you use SSMS and the pubs database to learn SQL. The final code for this Try It Out is in the code file Chapter12_Queries.sql in the Zip file for this chapter.

1. Open SSMS and open a new query pressing Ctrl+N.

2. At the top of the query window, type the following code and then press F5 to execute it:

```
USE pubs
GO
SELECT * FROM authors
SELECT * FROM titleauthor
SELECT * FROM titles
```

The results window will display all the data in the three tables.

3. Scroll up and down to see all three recordsets that are displaying the data. Then add two authors using the INSERT statement. The code in the book wraps on more than one line based on page margins. In SQL you can wrap the lines anywhere you want, so make your code as readable as possible. Be sure to use the same values for au_ids and au_fnames as shown here. The data in the other columns will not matter.

```
INSERT INTO authors
(au_id,au_lname,au_fname,phone,address,city,state,zip,contract)
VALUES
('111-22-3333','Smitty','Brianna','555 123-1234','123 Main St',
'Clemmons', 'NC', '27222',1)

INSERT INTO authors
(au_id,au_lname,au_fname,phone,address,city,state,zip,contract)
VALUES
('222-22-3333','Smitty','Bobby','555 123-1234','123 Main St',
'Clemmons', 'NC', '27222',1)
```

4. Add a title and connect the title with the first author you added to the database. To run just these two statements, highlight them in SSMS before pressing F5 or the Execute button. Only highlighted statements are executed if any statements are highlighted.

```
INSERT INTO TITLES
(title_id,title,type,pub_id,price,advance,royalty,ytd_sales,notes,pubdate)
SELECT 'WX1111',title,type,pub_id,price,advance,royalty,ytd_sales,notes,pubdate
FROM titles
WHERE title_id = 'BU1032'

INSERT INTO titleauthor(au_id,title_id,au_ord,royaltyper)
VALUES('111-22-3333','WX1111',1,100)
```

5. Finally, add a title and connect the title with the first author you added to the database. Be sure to highlight these two SELECT statements and then press F5. You will see different results in the two recordsets, as shown in Figure 12-9.

```
SELECT *
FROM authors
LEFT JOIN titleauthor
    ON authors.au_id = titleauthor.au_id
LEFT JOIN titles
    ON titles.title_id = titleauthor.title_id
WHERE authors.au_id = '111-22-3333' OR authors.au_id = '222-22-3333'

SELECT *
FROM authors
INNER JOIN titleauthor
    ON authors.au_id = titleauthor.au_id
INNER JOIN titles
    ON titles.title_id = titleauthor.title_id
WHERE authors.au_id = '111-22-3333' OR authors.au_id = '222-22-3333'
```

FIGURE 12-9

How It Works

To begin, you added a USE statement followed by GO to tell SSMS that you were using the pubs data-base. You then selected the data using the SELECT statement from the three tables that you were going to work into the example so you could see the column in the tables as well as the data in each column. It's good to have an idea of what you're working with, so look at the data in your database before you start making changes, if you can.

```
USE pubs
GO
SELECT * FROM authors
SELECT * FROM titleauthor
SELECT * FROM titles
```

You then used INSERT statements to add two new authors to the author table. In these INSERT state-ments, you specified the exact data to add one new row into the table in each command:

```
INSERT INTO authors(au_id,au_lname,au_fname,phone,address,city,state,zip,contract)
VALUES('111-22-3333','Smitty','Brianna','555 123-1234','123 Main St',
```

```
'Clemmons', 'NC', '27222',1)

INSERT INTO authors(au_id,au_lname,au_fname,phone,address,city,state,zip,contract)
VALUES('222-22-3333','Smitty','Bobby','555 123-1234','123 Main St',
'Clemmons', 'NC', '27222',1)
```

Again you used INSERT statements to add two rows of data to the database. In the first query, you selected data from the TITLES table and changed the title_id to be WX1111. In the second query, you added a new row to the titleauthor table:

```
INSERT INTO TITLES
(title_id,title,type,pub_id,price,advance,royalty,ytd_sales,notes,pubdate)
SELECT 'WX1111',title,type,pub_id,price,advance,royalty,ytd_sales,notes,pubdate
FROM titles
WHERE title_id = 'BU1032'

INSERT INTO titleauthor(au_id,title_id,au_ord,royaltyper)
VALUES('111-22-3333','WX1111',1,100)
```

Finally, you wrote two similar JOIN queries to see the data you just added. In the first query, you used LEFT JOINs to SELECT the data. LEFT JOINs return all the data from the table of the left side of the JOIN. In this case, that is the authors table, which means that you'll see all authors, even if they do not have a title. If you look back at your results or Figure 12-9, you'll see that starting with column 10, au_id (from left to right), Bobby Smitty has null values. These columns are from the titleauthor and titles tables where Bobby does not have any data.

If you have a hard time determining the left and right table, write your JOIN on the same line beginning with the FROM keyword. Then you can easily see that the authors table is to the left of LEFT JOIN.

```
SELECT *
FROM authors
LEFT JOIN titleauthor
    ON authors.au_id = titleauthor.au_id
LEFT JOIN titles
    ON titles.title_id = titleauthor.title_id
WHERE authors.au_id = '111-22-3333' OR authors.au_id = '222-22-3333'
```

In the final query, you used INNER JOINs to SELECT the data. INNER JOINs return only the data where there is a match in every table. Because you added data only to the titleauthor and titles table for Brianna, you saw only one row returned.

```
SELECT *
FROM authors
INNER JOIN titleauthor
    ON authors.au_id = titleauthor.au_id
INNER JOIN titles
    ON titles.title_id = titleauthor.title_id
WHERE authors.au_id = '111-22-3333' OR authors.au_id = '222-22-3333'
```

SUMMARY

You started this chapter by exploring what a database actually is and then looked at the `table` object. To retrieve data, you used the SQL `SELECT` and `JOIN` statements. You then learned other ways to manipulate data using the `INSERT`, `UPDATE`, and `DELETE` statements. To add information that makes your code easier to understand, you saw how to add SQL comments to your queries. You put this knowledge to use by creating queries in the pubs.

You have seen how to access and change data in a database using SQL and SSMS. Chapter 13 shows you how to use Visual Studio 2015 to create programs that programmatically bind data to controls on a form to deliver business applications to manage your data. You'll also explore the data access components in detail and learn how to set their properties and execute their methods from your code.

EXERCISES

1. How would you write a query to retrieve the `Name`, `Description`, and `Price` fields from a table called `Product`?

2. What would you add to the query to retrieve only items with `DVD` in their description?

3. How would you order the results so that the most expensive item comes first?

4. What do you put around column names that have spaces in them?

5. In SSMS, what function key do you press to execute SQL statements?

6. In SSMS, how do you execute only certain statements on a query window?

▶ **WHAT YOU LEARNED IN THIS CHAPTER**

TOPIC	CONCEPTS
Using SSMS to execute SQL queries	Connect to a SQL Server and execute statements for a query window.
Reading data from a database	Use the SQL SELECT statement to read data. Filter data with a WHERE clause. Sort data using ORDER BY.
Joining data from a database	Use the SQL JOIN statement to join related tables together in queries to provide clear data output.
Manipulating data from a database	Use the SQL INSERT, UPDATE, and DELETE statements to change data. Filter data with a WHERE clause.

13

Database Programming with SQL Server and ADO.NET

WHAT YOU WILL LEARN IN THIS CHAPTER:

➤ About ADO.NET objects

➤ Binding data to controls

➤ Searching for and sorting in-memory data using ADO.NET DataView objects

➤ Selecting, inserting, updating, and deleting data in a database using ADO.NET

WROX.COM CODE DOWNLOADS FOR THIS CHAPTER

The wrox.com code downloads for this chapter are found at www.wrox.com/ begvisualbasic2015 on the Download Code tab. The code is in the 092117 C13.zip download and individually named according to the names given throughout the chapter.

Chapter 12 introduced SQL. You obtained data from a single table and multiple tables in a SQL Server database. You learned how to use queries to manipulate data.

This chapter dives much deeper into the topic of database programming. In this chapter, you explore how you can use the built-in capabilities of ADO.NET to retrieve and update data from databases. You will also learn to manipulate, filter, and edit data held in memory by the DataSet.

The data you extract will be bound to controls on your form, so you also need to explore binding. You will see how you can use controls to view one record at a time (for example, using text boxes) and how to navigate between records by using the CurrencyManager object.

You will also learn how to access SQL Server databases using the `SqlClient` data provider. `SqlClient` is significantly faster than `OleDb`, but it works only with SQL Server databases. To complete the exercises in this chapter, you need to have access to a version of SQL Server 2014. The chapter is based on SQL Server 2014, but the code should work with SQL Server 2005 and up with only minor adjustments, if any. As a beginner, it will be easier for you to use SQL Server 2014 without the worry of minor changes. The database can reside in SQL Server 2014 on your local machine or in SQL Server on a network. This chapter has examples of SQL Server 2014 Express running locally. The database the examples use is the pubs database from Microsoft.

If you need help installing SQL Server or the pubs database, refer to the installation instructions in Chapter 12.

ADO.NET

ADO stands for *ActiveX Data Objects* and goes back to before the .NET framework was born. ADO.NET is the version you use today to access databases. ADO.NET is designed to provide a *disconnected architecture*. This means that applications connect to the database to retrieve a load of data and store it in memory. They then disconnect from the database and manipulate the in-memory copy of the data. If the database needs to be updated with changes made to the in-memory copy, a new connection is made, and the database is updated. The main in-memory data store is the `DataSet`, which contains other in-memory data stores, such as `DataTable`, `DataColumn`, and `DataRow` objects. You can filter and sort data in a `DataSet` using `DataView` objects, as you will see later in the chapter.

Using a disconnected architecture provides many benefits; most important is that it allows your application to *scale up*. This means that your database will perform just as well supporting hundreds of users as it does supporting ten users. This is possible because the application connects to the database only long enough to retrieve or update data, thereby freeing available database connections for other instances of your application or other applications using the same database.

ADO.NET DATA NAMESPACES

The core ADO.NET classes exist in the `System.Data` namespace. This namespace, in turn, contains some child namespaces. The most important of these namespaces are `System.Data.SqlClient` and `System.Data.OleDb`, which provide classes for accessing SQL Server databases and OLE (Object Linking and Embedding) DB-compliant databases, respectively. In this chapter, you use `System.Data.SqlClient` with its equivalent classes, including `SqlConnection` and `SqlDataAdapter`.

Classes from the `System.Data.OleDb` namespace include `OleDbConnection` and `OleDbDataAdapter`. You use the `System.Data.OleDb` namespace to connect to data stores from something as simple as text files or spreadsheets to something as complex as databases.

Another child namespace also exists in the `System.Data` namespace: `System.Data.Odbc`. The `System.Data.Odbc` namespace provides access to older Open Database Connectivity (ODBC) data sources that do not support the `OleDb` technology.

`System.Data.SqlClient`, `System.Data.OleDb`, and `System.Data.Odbc` are known as *data providers* in ADO.NET. Although other data providers are available, this book concentrates on only the first two.

In this chapter, you access SQL Server databases using the `SqlClient` namespace. However, in ADO.NET, the different data providers work in a very similar way, so the techniques you use here can be easily transferred to the `OleDb` classes. With ADO.NET, you use the data provider that best fits your data source—you do not need to learn a whole new interface because all data providers work in a very similar way.

As you start working with ADO.NET, you will soon learn how the pieces fit together, and this chapter helps you in reaching that goal.

Because the space here is limited, you will focus on the specific classes that are relevant to the example programs in this chapter. The following list contains the ADO.NET classes, from the `System .Data.SqlClient` namespace, that you will be using:

➤ `SqlConnection`

➤ `SqlDataAdapter`

➤ `SqlCommand`

➤ `SqlParameter`

Remember that they are specifically `SqlClient` classes, but that the `OleDb` namespace has very close equivalents.

You can use the `Imports` keyword so you do not have to fully qualify members of the `SqlClient` namespace in your code, as shown in the following fragment:

```
Imports System.Data.SqlClient
```

If you want to use the core ADO.NET classes, such as `DataSet` and `DataView`, without typing the full name, you must import the `System.Data` namespace, as shown here:

```
Imports System.Data
```

You should already be familiar with importing different namespaces in your project. However, to be thorough, you also cover this when you go through the hands-on exercises.

Next, we'll take a look at the main classes in the `System.Data.SqlClient` namespace.

The SqlConnection Class

The `SqlConnection` class is at the heart of the classes discussed in this section because it provides a connection to a SQL Server database. When you construct a `SqlConnection` object, you can choose to specify a *connection string* as a parameter. The connection string contains all the information required to open a connection to your database. If you don't specify one in the constructor, you can set it using the `SqlConnection.ConnectionString` property. In the previous chapter, Visual Studio .NET built a connection string for you from the details you specified in the Data Link Properties dialog. However, it is often more useful or quicker to write a connection string manually—so let's take a look at how connection strings work.

Working with the Connection String Parameters

The way the connection string is constructed depends on what data provider you are using. When accessing SQL Server, you usually provide a `Server` and a `Database` parameter, as shown in Table 13-1.

TABLE 13-1: Server and Database Parameters

PARAMETER	DESCRIPTION
Server	The name of the SQL Server that you want to access, which is usually the name of the computer running SQL Server. You can use (local) or localhost if SQL Server is on the same machine as the one running the application. If you are using named instances of SQL Server, this parameter would contain the computer name, followed by a backslash, and then followed by the named instance of SQL Server.
Database	The name of the database to which you want to connect.

You also need some form of authentication information, which you can provide in two ways: by using a username and password in the connection string or by connecting to SQL Server using the NT account under which the application is running. If you want to connect to the server by specifying a username and password, you need to include additional parameters in your connection string, as shown in Table 13-2.

TABLE 13-2: Additional Parameters When Connecting with a Username

PARAMETER	DESCRIPTION
User ID	The username for connecting to the database. An account with this user ID needs to exist in SQL Server and have permission to access the specified database.
Password	The password for the specified user.

However, SQL Server can be set up to use the Windows NT account of the user who is running the program to open the connection. In this case, you don't need to specify a username and password. You just need to specify that you are using *integrated security*. (The method is called integrated security because SQL Server is integrating with the Windows NT security system, providing the most secure connection because the `User ID` and `Password` parameters need not be specified in the code.) You do this by using the `Integrated Security` parameter, which you set to `True` when you want the application to connect to SQL Server using the current user's NT account.

Of course, for this to work, the user of the application must have permission to use the SQL Server database. This is granted using the SQL Server Management Studio (SSMS).

To see how these parameters function in a connection string to initialize a connection object, consider the following code fragment. It uses the `SqlConnection` class to initialize a connection object that uses a specific user ID and password in the connection string:

```
Dim objConnection As SqlConnection = New SqlConnection("Server=localhost" &
    "\WROX;Database=pubs;" & "User ID=sa;Password=wrox;")
```

This connection string connects to a SQL Server database. The `Server` parameter specifies that the database resides on the local machine. The `Database` parameter specifies the database that you want to access—in this case, it is the pubs database. Finally, the `User ID` and `Password` parameters specify the User ID and password of the user defined in the database. As you can see, each parameter has a value assigned to it using `=`, and each parameter-value pair is separated by a semicolon.

A great resource for help with just about any kind of connection string is www.connectionstrings.com.

Opening and Closing the Connection

After you initialize a connection object with a connection string, as shown previously, you can invoke the methods of the `SqlConnection` object such as `Open` and `Close`, which actually open and close a connection to the database specified in the connection string. An example of this is shown in the following code fragment:

```
' Open the database connection.
objConnection.Open()

' .. Use the connection

' Close the database connection.
objConnection.Close()
```

Although many more properties and methods are available in the `SqlConnection` class, the ones mentioned so far are all you really need to complete the hands-on exercises, and they should be enough to get you started.

The SqlCommand Class

The `SqlCommand` class represents a SQL command to execute against a data store. The command is usually a select, insert, update, or delete query, and can be a SQL string or a call to a stored procedure. The query being executed may or may not contain parameters.

For the moment, you'll look at command objects alone. You learn how they relate to data adapters in the next section.

The constructor for the `SqlCommand` class has several variations, but the simplest method is to initialize a `SqlCommand` object with no parameters. Then, after the object has been initialized, you can set the properties you need to perform the task at hand. The following code fragment shows how to initialize a `SqlCommand` object:

```
Dim objCommand As SqlCommand = New SqlCommand()
```

When using data adapters and datasets, there isn't much call for using command objects on their own. They are mainly used for executing a particular select, delete, insert, or update, so that is what you do in this chapter. You can also use command objects with a data reader. A *data reader* is an alternative to a `DataSet` that uses fewer system resources but provides far less flexibility. In this book, you concentrate on using the `DataSet` because it is the more common and useful of the two.

The Connection Property

Certain properties must be set on the SqlCommand object before you can execute the query. The first of these properties is Connection. This property is set to a SqlConnection object, as shown in the next code fragment:

```
objCommand.Connection = objConnection
```

For the command to execute successfully, the connection must be open at the time of execution.

The CommandText Property

The next property that must be set is the CommandText property. This property specifies the SQL string or stored procedure to be executed. Most databases require that you place all string values in single quote marks, as shown here in bold:

```
Dim objConnection As SqlConnection =
    New SqlConnection("server=(local);database=pubs;user id=sa;password=")
Dim objCommand As SqlCommand = New SqlCommand()
objCommand.Connection = objConnection
objCommand.CommandText = "INSERT INTO authors " &
                    "(au_id, au_lname, au_fname, contract) " &
                    "VALUES('123-45-6789', 'Barnes', 'David', 1)"
```

The INSERT statement is a very simple one that means, "Insert a new row into the authors table. In the au_id column, put '123-45-6789'; in the au_lname column, put 'Barnes'; in the au_fname column, put 'David'; and in the contract column, put '1'."

This assumes that you know the values to insert when you are writing the program, which is unlikely in most cases. Fortunately, you can create commands with parameters and then set the values of these parameters separately.

The Parameters Collection

Placeholders are variables prefixed with an at (@) sign in the SQL statement; they get filled in by parameters. For example, if you wanted to update the authors table, as discussed in the previous section, but didn't know the values at design time, you would do this:

```
Dim objConnection As SqlConnection =
    New SqlConnection("server=(local);database=pubs;user id=sa;password=")
Dim objCommand As SqlCommand = New SqlCommand()
objCommand.Connection = objConnection
objCommand.CommandText = "INSERT INTO authors " &
                    "(au_id, au_lname, au_fname, contract) " &
                    "VALUES(@au_id,@au_lname,@au_fname,@au_contract)"
```

Here, instead of providing values, you provide placeholders. Placeholders, as mentioned, always start with an @ symbol. They do not need to be named after the database column that they represent, but it is often easier if they are, and it helps to self-document your code.

Next, you need to create parameters that will be used to insert the values into the placeholders when the SQL statement is executed. You create and add parameters to the Parameters collection of the

`SqlCommand` object. The term *parameters* here refers to the parameters required to provide data to your SQL statement or stored procedure, *not* to the parameters that are required to be passed to a Visual Basic 2015 method.

You can access the `Parameters` collection of the `SqlCommand` object by specifying the `Parameters` property. After you access the `Parameters` collection, you can use its properties and methods to create one or more parameters in the collection. The easiest way to add a parameter to a command is demonstrated in the following example:

```
Dim objConnection As SqlConnection =
    New SqlConnection("server=(local);database=pubs;user id=sa;password=")
Dim objCommand As SqlCommand = New SqlCommand()
objCommand.Connection = objConnection
objCommand.CommandText = "INSERT INTO authors " &
                        "(au_id, au_lname, au_fname, contract) " &
                        "VALUES(@au_id,@au_lname,@au_fname,@au_contract)"
objCommand.Parameters.AddWithValue("@au_id", txtAuId.Text)
objCommand.Parameters.AddWithValue("@au_lname", txtLastName.Text)
objCommand.Parameters.AddWithValue("@au_fname", txtFirstName.Text)
objCommand.Parameters.AddWithValue("@au_contract", chkContract.Checked)
```

The `AddWithValue` method here accepts the name of the parameter and the object that you want to add. In this case, you are using the `Text` property of various `TextBox` objects on a (fictitious) form for most of the columns. For the `Contract` column, you use the `Checked` property of a `CheckBox` on the same form. In previous versions of ADO.NET, you could use the `Add` method to add a parameter with a value. That overload is now obsolete.

The ExecuteNonQuery Method

Finally, you can execute the command. To do this, the connection needs to be opened. You can invoke the `ExecuteNonQuery` method of the `SqlCommand` object. This method executes the SQL statement and causes the data to be inserted into the database. It then returns the number of rows that were affected by the query, which can be a useful way to check that the command worked as expected. To complete your code fragment, you need to open the connection, execute the query, and close the connection again:

```
Dim objConnection As SqlConnection =
    New SqlConnection("server=(local);database=pubs;user id=sa;password=")
Dim objCommand As SqlCommand = New SqlCommand()
objCommand.Connection = objConnection
objCommand.CommandText = "INSERT INTO authors " &
    "(au_id, au_lname, au_fname, contract) " &
    "VALUES(@au_id,@au_lname,@au_fname,@au_contract)"
objCommand.Parameters.AddWithValue("@au_id", txtAuId.Text)
objCommand.Parameters.AddWithValue("@au_lname", txtLastName.Text)
objCommand.Parameters.AddWithValue("@au_fname", txtFirstName.Text)
objCommand.Parameters.AddWithValue("@au_contract ", chkContract.Checked)
objConnection.Open()
objCommand.ExecuteNonQuery()
objConnection.Close()
```

The SqlDataAdapter Class

The `SqlDataAdapter` supports only SQL Server databases. You can configure a `SqlDataAdapter` using wizards or in code. This chapter explains how to configure and use a `SqlDataAdapter` in code.

Data adapters act as bridges between your data source and in-memory data objects such as the `DataSet`. To access the data source, they use the *command objects* you've just looked at. These command objects are associated with connections, so the data adapter relies on command and connection objects to access and manipulate the data source.

The `SqlDataAdapter` class's `SelectCommand` property is used to hold a `SqlCommand` that retrieves data from the data source. The data adapter then places the result of the query into a `DataSet` or `DataTable`. The `SqlDataAdapter` also has `UpdateCommand`, `DeleteCommand`, and `InsertCommand` properties. These are also `SqlCommand` objects, used to write changes made to a `DataSet` or `DataTable` back to the data source. This may all seem complicated, but the tools are really easy to use, in fact. You learned enough SQL in the previous chapter to write a `SelectCommand`, and there are tools called *command builders* that you can use to automatically create the other commands based on this.

The following section takes a look at the `SelectCommand` property and then examines how you can create commands for updating, deleting, and inserting records.

The SelectCommand Property

The `SqlDataAdapter` class's `SelectCommand` property is used to fill a `DataSet` with data from a SQL Server database, as shown in Figure 13-1.

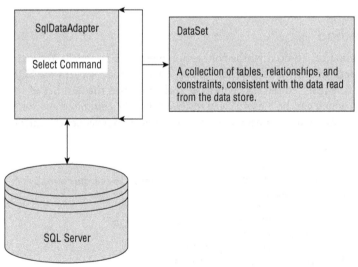

FIGURE 13-1

When you want to read data from the data store, you must set the `SelectCommand` property of the `SqlDataAdapter` class first. This property is a `SqlCommand` object and is used to specify what data to select and how to select that data. Therefore, the `SelectCommand` property has properties of its own, and you need to set them just as you would set properties on a normal SQLCommand. You've already seen the following properties of the SqlCommand object:

- ➤ **Connection:** Sets the SqlConnection object to be used to access the data store.
- ➤ **CommandText:** Sets the SQL statements or stored procedure name to be used to select the data.

In the previous examples of SqlCommand objects, you used straight SQL statements. If you want to use stored procedures, you need to be aware of an additional property, CommandType, which sets a value that determines how the CommandText property is interpreted.

This chapter concentrates on SQL statements, but stored procedures are often useful, too, particularly if they already exist in the database. If you want to use one, set the CommandText property to the name of the stored procedure (remember to enclose it in quote marks because the compiler treats this as a string) and set the CommandType property to **CommandType.StoredProcedure**.

Setting SelectCommand to SQL Text

Take a look at how you set these properties in code. The code fragment that follows shows the typical settings for these properties when executing SQL text:

```
' Declare SqlDataAdapter object..
Dim objDataAdapter As New SqlDataAdapter()

' Assign a new SqlCommand to the SelectCommand property
objDataAdapter.SelectCommand = New SqlCommand()

' Set the SelectCommand properties..
objDataAdapter.SelectCommand.Connection = objConnection
objDataAdapter.SelectCommand.CommandText =
    "SELECT au_lname, au_fname FROM authors " &
    "ORDER BY au_lname, au_fname"
```

The first thing that this code fragment does is declare the SqlDataAdapter object. This object has a SelectCommand property set to a new SqlCommand; you just need to set that command's properties. You set the properties by first setting the Connection property to a valid connection object, one that will already have been created before the code that you see here. Next, you set the CommandText property to your SQL SELECT statement.

Setting SelectCommand to a Stored Procedure

This next code fragment shows how you could set these properties when you want to execute a *stored procedure*. A stored procedure is a group of SQL statements that are stored in the database under a unique name and are executed as a unit. The stored procedure in this example (usp_select_author_titles) uses the same SQL statement that you used in the previous code fragment:

```
' Declare SqlDataAdapter object..
Dim objDataAdapter As New SqlDataAdapter()

' Assign a new SqlCommand to the SelectCommand property
```

```
objDataAdapter.SelectCommand = New SqlCommand()

' Set the SelectCommand properties..
objDataAdapter.SelectCommand.Connection = objConnection
objDataAdapter.SelectCommand.CommandText = "usp_select_author_titles"
objDataAdapter.SelectCommand.CommandType = CommandType.StoredProcedure
```

The `CommandText` property now specifies the name of the stored procedure that you want to execute rather than the SQL string that was specified in the previous example. Also notice the `CommandType` property. In the first example, you did not change this property because its default value is `CommandType.Text`, which is what you need to execute SQL statements. In this example, it is set to a value of `CommandType.StoredProcedure`, which indicates that the `CommandText` property contains the name of a stored procedure to be executed.

Using Command Builders to Create the Other Commands

The `SelectCommand` is all you need to transfer data from the database into your `DataSet`. After you let your users make changes to the `DataSet`, you will want to write the changes back to the database. You can do this by setting up command objects with the SQL for inserting, deleting, and updating. Alternatively, you can use stored procedures. Both of these solutions require knowledge of SQL outside the scope of this book. Fortunately, there is an easier way; you can use *command builders* to create these commands. It takes only one more line:

```
' Declare SqlDataAdapter object..
Dim objDataAdapter As New SqlDataAdapter()

' Assign a new SqlCommand to the SelectCommand property
objDataAdapter.SelectCommand = New SqlCommand()

' Set the SelectCommand properties..
objDataAdapter.SelectCommand.Connection = objConnection
objDataAdapter.SelectCommand.CommandText = "usp_select_author_titles"
objDataAdapter.SelectCommand.CommandType = CommandType.StoredProcedure
' automatically create update/delete/insert commands
Dim objCommandBuilder As SqlCommandBuilder = New SqlCommandBuilder
(objDataAdapter)
```

Now you can use this `SqlDataAdapter` to write changes back to a database. You look more at this later in the chapter. For now, look at the method that gets data from the database to the `DataSet` in the first place: the `Fill` method.

The Fill Method

You use the `Fill` method to populate a `DataSet` object with the data that the `SqlDataAdapter` object retrieves from the data store using its `SelectCommand`. However, before you do this you must first initialize a `DataSet` object:

```
' Declare SqlDataAdapter object..
Dim objDataAdapter As New SqlDataAdapter()

' Assign a new SqlCommand to the SelectCommand property
objDataAdapter.SelectCommand = New SqlCommand()

' Set the SelectCommand properties..
```

```
objDataAdapter.SelectCommand.Connection = objConnection
objDataAdapter.SelectCommand.CommandText = "usp_select_author_titles"
objDataAdapter.SelectCommand.CommandType = CommandType.StoredProcedure

' Create the DataSet
Dim objDataSet as DataSet = New DataSet()
```

Now that you have a `DataSet` and `SqlDataAdapter`, you can fill your `DataSet` with data. The `Fill` method has several overloaded versions, but this chapter discusses the one most commonly used. The syntax for the `Fill` method is shown here:

```
SqlDataAdapter.Fill(DataSet, string)
```

The `DataSet` argument specifies a valid `DataSet` object that will be populated with data. The `string` argument gives the name you want the table to have in the `DataSet`. Remember that one `DataSet` can contain many tables. You can use any name you like, but usually it's best to use the name of the table from which the data in the database has come. This helps you self-document your code and makes the code easier to maintain.

The following code fragment shows how you invoke the `Fill` method. The string `"authors"` is specified as the `string` argument. This is the name you want to use when manipulating the in-memory version of the table; it is also the name of the table in the data source.

```
' Declare SqlDataAdapter object..
Dim objDataAdapter As New SqlDataAdapter()

'Create an instance of a new select command object
objDataAdapter.SelectCommand = New SqlCommand

' Set the SelectCommand properties..
objDataAdapter.SelectCommand.Connection = objConnection
objDataAdapter.SelectCommand.CommandText = "usp_select_author_titles"
objDataAdapter.SelectCommand.CommandType = CommandType.StoredProcedure

' Create the DataSet
Dim objDataSet as DataSet = New DataSet()

' Fill the DataSet object with data..
objDataAdapter.Fill(objDataSet, "authors")
```

The `Fill` method uses the `SelectCommand.Connection` property to connect to the database. If the connection is already open, the data adapter will use it to execute the `SelectCommand` and leave it open after it's finished. If the connection is closed, the data adapter will open it, execute the `SelectCommand`, and then close it again.

You now have data in memory and can start manipulating it independently of the data source. Notice that the `DataSet` class does not have `Sql` at the start of its class name. This is because `DataSet` is not in the `System.Data.SqlClient` namespace; it is in the parent `System.Data` namespace. The classes in this namespace are primarily concerned with manipulating data in memory rather than obtaining data from any particular data source. Once you have the data loaded into a `DataSet`, it no longer matters what data source it came from (unless you need to write it back). Let's have a look at two of the classes in this namespace: `DataSet` and the `DataView`.

The DataSet Class

The DataSet class is used to store data retrieved from a data store and stores that data in memory on the client. The DataSet object contains a collection of tables, relationships, and constraints that are consistent with the data read from the data store. It acts as a lightweight database engine all by itself, enabling you to store tables, edit data, and run queries against it using a DataView object.

The data in a DataSet is disconnected from the data store, and you can operate on the data independently from the data store. You can manipulate the data in a DataSet object by adding, updating, and deleting the records. You can apply these changes back to the original data store afterward by using a data adapter.

The data in a DataSet object supports Extensible Markup Language (XML), meaning that you can save a DataSet as a file or easily pass it over a network. The XML is shielded from you as a developer, and you should never need to edit the XML directly. All editing of the XML is done through the properties and methods of the DataSet class. Many developers like using XML and will sometimes choose to manipulate the XML representation of a DataSet directly, but this is not essential.

Because the DataSet contains the actual data retrieved from a data store, you can bind the DataSet to a control or controls to have them display (and allow editing of) the data in the DataSet. You will see more of this later in this chapter.

DataView

The DataView class is typically used for sorting, filtering, searching, editing, and navigating the data from a DataSet. A DataView is *bindable*, meaning it can be bound to controls in the same way that the DataSet can be bound to controls. Again, you learn more about data binding in code later in this chapter.

A DataSet can contain a number of DataTable objects; when you use the SqlDataAdapter class's Fill method to add data to a DataSet, you are actually creating a DataTable object inside the DataSet. The DataView provides a custom view of a DataTable; you can sort or filter the rows, for example, as you can in a SQL query.

You can create a DataView from the data contained in a DataTable that contains only the data that you want to display. For example, if the data in a DataTable contains all authors sorted by last name and first name, you can create a DataView that contains all authors sorted by first name and then last name. Or you can create a DataView that contains only last names or certain names.

Although you can view the data in a DataView in ways different from the underlying DataTable, it is still the same data. Changes made to a DataView affect the underlying DataTable automatically, and changes made to the underlying DataTable automatically affect any DataView objects that are viewing that DataTable.

The constructor for the DataView class initializes a new instance of the DataView class and accepts the DataTable as an argument. The following code fragment declares a DataView object and initializes it using the authors table from the DataSet named objDataSet. Notice that the code accesses the Tables collection of the DataSet object by specifying the Tables property and the table name:

```
' Set the DataView object to the DataSet object..
Dim objDataView = New DataView(objDataSet.Tables("authors"))
```

The Sort Property

Once a `DataView` has been initialized and contains data, you can alter the view of that data. For example, suppose you want to sort the data in a different order from that in the `DataSet`. To sort the data in a `DataView`, you set the `Sort` property and specify the column or columns that you want sorted. The following code fragment sorts the data in a `DataView` by author's first name and then last name:

```
objDataView.Sort = "au_fname, au_lname"
```

Note that this is the same syntax as the ORDER BY clause in a SQL SELECT statement. As in the SQL ORDER BY clause, sorting operations on a `DataView` are always performed in an ascending order by default. If you wanted to perform the sort in descending order, you would need to specify the DESC keyword, as shown here:

```
objDataView.Sort = "au_fname, au_lname DESC"
```

The RowFilter Property

When you have an initialized `DataView`, you can filter the rows of data that it will contain. This is similar to specifying a WHERE clause in a SQL SELECT statement; only rows that match the criteria will remain in the view. The underlying data is not affected, though. The `RowFilter` property specifies the criteria that should be applied on the `DataView`. The syntax is similar to the SQL WHERE clause. It contains at least a column name followed by an operator and the value. If the value is a string, it must be enclosed in single quote marks, as shown in the following code fragment, which retrieves only the authors whose last names are Green:

```
' Set the DataView object to the DataSet object..
objDataView = New DataView(objDataSet.Tables("authors"))
objDataView.RowFilter = "au_lname = 'Green'"
```

If you want to retrieve all rows of authors except those with the last name of Green, you would specify the not-equal-to operator (<>) as shown in this example:

```
' Set the DataView object to the DataSet object..
objDataView = New DataView(objDataSet.Tables("authors"))
objDataView.RowFilter = "au_lname <> 'Green'"
```

You can also specify more complex filters, as you could in SQL. For example, you can combine several criteria using an AND operator:

```
objDataView.RowFilter = "au_lname <> 'Green' AND au_fname LIKE 'D*'"
```

This returns authors whose last names are not Green and whose first names begin with D.

The Find Method

If you want to search for a specific row of data in a `DataView`, you invoke the `Find` method. The `Find` method searches for data in the sort key column of the `DataView`. Therefore, before invoking the `Find` method, you first need to sort the `DataView` on the column that contains the data that you want to find. The column that the `DataView` is sorted on becomes the sort key column in a `DataView` object.

For example, suppose you want to find the author who has a first name of Ann. You would need to sort the DataView by first name to set this column as the sort key column in the DataView and then invoke the Find method, as shown in the following code fragment:

```
Dim intPosition as Integer
objDataView.Sort = "au_fname"
intPosition = objDataView.Find("Ann")
```

If it finds a match, the Find method returns the position of the record within the DataView. Otherwise, the DataView returns a -1, indicating that no match was found. If the Find method finds a match, it stops looking and returns only the position of the first match. If you know there is more than one match in your data store, you could filter the data in the DataView, a subject that is covered shortly.

The Find method is not case sensitive, meaning that to find the author who has a first name of Ann, you could enter either Ann or ann.

The Find method looks for an exact case-insensitive match, so you must enter the whole word or words of the text that you are looking for. For example, suppose you are looking for the author who has the first name Ann. You cannot enter An and expect to find a match; you must enter all the characters or words that make up the author's name. Notice that the following example specifies all lowercase letters, which is perfectly fine:

```
Dim intPosition as Integer
objDataView.Sort = "au_fname"
intPosition = objDataView.Find("ann")
```

You have seen that a DataView can be sorted on more than one column at a time. To do so, you need to supply an array of values to the Find method rather than just a single value. For example, you may want to find where Simon Watts appears in the DataView, if at all:

```
Dim intPosition As Integer
Dim arrValues(1) As Object
objDataView.Sort = "au_fname, au_lname"

' Find the author named "Simon Watts".
arrValues(0)= "Simon"
arrValues(1) = "Watts"
intPosition = objDataView.Find(arrValues)
```

THE ADO.NET CLASSES IN ACTION

You've now looked at the basics of the ADO.NET classes and how they enable you to retrieve and insert data into SQL Server. No doubt your head is spinning from information overload at this point, so the best way to ensure that you understand how to use all the objects, methods, and properties that you have been looking at is to actually use them. In the next two Try It Outs, you'll see how to exploit the power of the DataSet object to expose data to your users. You may find that you want to come back and reread the previous section after you've completed the Try It Outs; this will help to clarify ADO.NET in your mind.

The first Try It Out implements the `SqlConnection`, `SqlDataAdapter`, and `DataSet` classes. You will see firsthand how to use these classes in a simple example in which you need to retrieve read-only data and display that data in a data grid.

> **NOTE** When writing your programs, you can often use a combination of wizards and coding to create powerful programs quickly and easily. The components you will create in this chapter can be created by drag-and-drop wizards. This chapter concentrates on code.

Before you dive into the details of creating the program, take a look at the data and the relationships of the data that you want to display. The data that you want comes from the pubs database in SQL Server. If you are using SQL Server 2000, SQL Server 2005, or SQL Server 2008, you should be seeing the exact same data. Newer versions SQL Server do not come with the pubs database. The link to get the database is at the beginning of Chapter 12.

You want to display a list of authors, their book titles, and the price of their books. Figure 13-2 shows the tables that this data resides in and also the relationship of the tables.

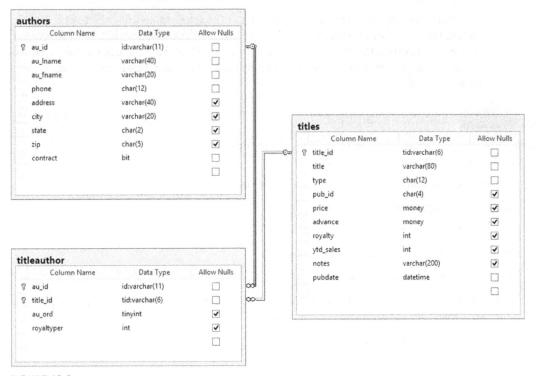

FIGURE 13-2

You want to display the author's first and last names, which reside in the `authors` table, and the title and price of the book, which reside in the `titles` table. Because an author can have one or more books, and a book can have one or more authors, the `titles` table is joined to the `authors` table via a *relationship table* called `titleauthor`. This table contains the many-to-many relationship of authors to books.

Having looked at the table relationships and knowing what data you want, consider the SQL SELECT statement that you need to create to get this data:

```
SELECT au_lname, au_fname, title, price
FROM authors
JOIN titleauthor ON authors.au_id = titleauthor.au_id
JOIN titles ON titleauthor.title_id = titles.title_id
ORDER BY au_lname, au_fname
```

Note the following about the previous code:

➤   The first line of the SELECT statement shows the columns that you want to select.

➤   The second line shows the main table from which you are selecting data, which is `authors`.

➤   The third line *joins* the `titleauthor` table to the `authors` table using the au_id column. Therefore, when you select a row of data from the `authors` table, you also get every row in the `titleauthor` table that matches the au_id in the selected row of the `authors` table. This join returns only authors who have a record in the `titleauthor` table.

➤   The fourth line joins the `titles` table to the `titleauthor` table using the title_id column. Hence, for every row of data that is selected from the `titleauthor` table, you select the corresponding row of data (having the same title_id value) from the `titles` table. The last line of the SELECT statement sorts the data by the author's last name and first name using the ORDER BY clause.

TRY IT OUT   DataSet Example

Now, you'll create a project in this Try It Out. All the code in this Try it Out is in the folder DatasetExample in the Zip file for this chapter.

1.   Create a new Windows Forms application called **DatasetExample**.

2.   Set the following properties of the form:

➤   Set Size to **600, 230**.

➤   Set StartPosition to **CenterScreen**.

➤   Set Text to **Bound DataSet**.

3.   From the Toolbox, locate the DataGridView control under the Windows Forms tab and drag it onto your form. Set the properties of the DataGridView as follows:

➤   Set Name to **grdAuthorTitles**.

➤   Set Dock to **Fill**.

4.   Add the Imports statements for the namespaces you will use. Open the code window for your form and add the namespaces in bold at the very top of your code:

```
' Import Data and SqlClient namespaces..
Imports System.Data
```

```
Imports System.Data.SqlClient

Public Class Form1

End Class
```

5. You need to declare the objects necessary to retrieve the data from the database, so add the following bold code. Ensure that you use a user ID and password that have been defined in your installation of SQL Server. If you need help, go to your SQL Server Management Studio (SSMS) and connect from the Object Explorer. You will see the Connect to Server dialog, as shown in Figure 13-3, which has most of the information you need here.

```
Public Class Form1
    Dim objConnection As New SqlConnection _
        ("server=localhost\SQLExpress;database=pubs;user
            id=sa;password=SQL2014wrox")

    Dim objDataAdapter As New SqlDataAdapter()
    Dim objDataSet As New DataSet()
```

FIGURE 13-3: End Class

6. To add a handler for the form's Load event, select (Form1 Events) in the first combo box (General) and then select Load in the second combo box (Declarations). Insert the following bold code:

```
Private Sub Form1_Load(sender As Object, e As EventArgs) _
        Handles Me.Load
    ' Set the SelectCommand properties..
    objDataAdapter.SelectCommand = New SqlCommand()
    objDataAdapter.SelectCommand.Connection = objConnection
    objDataAdapter.SelectCommand.CommandText =
        "SELECT au_lname, au_fname, title, price " &
        "FROM authors " &
```

```
              "JOIN titleauthor ON authors.au_id = titleauthor.au_id " &
              "JOIN titles ON titleauthor.title_id = titles.title_id " &
              "ORDER BY au_lname, au_fname"
       objDataAdapter.SelectCommand.CommandType = CommandType.Text

       ' Open the database connection..
       objConnection.Open()

       ' Fill the DataSet object with data..
       objDataAdapter.Fill(objDataSet, "authors")

       ' Close the database connection..
       objConnection.Close()

       ' Set the DataGridView properties to bind it to our data..
       grdAuthorTitles.AutoGenerateColumns = True
       grdAuthorTitles.DataSource = objDataSet
       grdAuthorTitles.DataMember = "authors"

       ' Clean up
       objDataAdapter = Nothing
       objConnection = Nothing
   End Sub
```

7. Run the project. You should see results similar to what is shown in Figure 13-4.

8. Note that the DataGridView control has built-in sorting capabilities. If you click a column header, the data in the grid will be sorted by that column in ascending order. If you click the same column again, the data will be sorted in descending order.

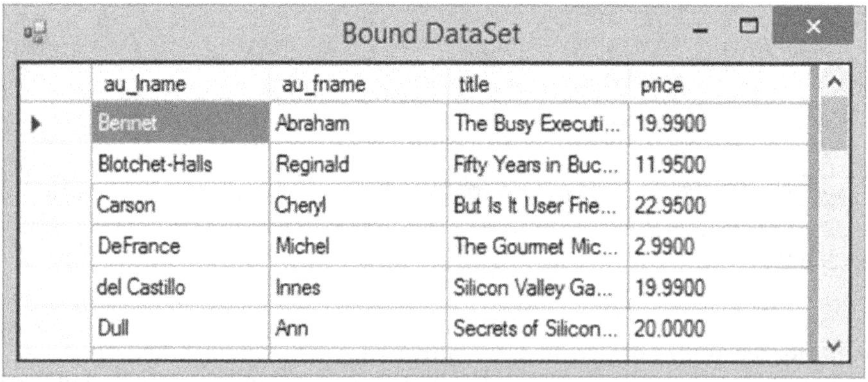

au_lname	au_fname	title	price
Bennet	Abraham	The Busy Executi...	19.9900
Blotchet-Halls	Reginald	Fifty Years in Buc...	11.9500
Carson	Cheryl	But Is It User Frie...	22.9500
DeFrance	Michel	The Gourmet Mic...	2.9900
del Castillo	Innes	Silicon Valley Ga...	19.9900
Dull	Ann	Secrets of Silicon...	20.0000

FIGURE 13-4

> **NOTE** *Error handling has been omitted from the exercise to preserve space. You should always add the appropriate error handling to your code. Review Chapter 9 for error-handling techniques.*

How It Works

To begin, you first imported the following namespaces:

```
' Import Data and SqlClient namespaces..
Imports System.Data
Imports System.Data.SqlClient
```

Remember that the System.Data namespace is required for the DataSet and DataView classes; and the System.Data.SqlClient namespace is required for the SqlConnection, SqlDataAdapter, SqlCommand, and SqlParameter classes. In this example, you'll only use a subset of the classes just mentioned, but you do require both namespaces.

Then you declared the objects that were necessary to retrieve the data from the database. These objects were declared with class-level scope, so you placed those declarations just inside the class:

```
Public Class Form1
    Inherits System.Windows.Forms.Form

    Dim objConnection As New SqlConnection _
        ("server=localhost\SQLEXPRESS;database=pubs;" &
        "user id=sa;password=SQL2014wrox")

    Dim objDataAdapter As New SqlDataAdapter()
    Dim objDataSet As DataSet = New DataSet()
```

The first object that you declared was a SqlConnection object. Remember that this object establishes a connection to your data store, which in this case is SQL Server.

The next object that you declared was a SqlDataAdapter object. This object reads data from the database and populates the DataSet object.

The last object in your declarations was the DataSet object, which serves as the container for your data. Remember that this object stores all data in memory and is not connected to the data store.

> **NOTE** *In this particular example, there was no need to give these objects class-level scope. You use them in only one method, and you could have declared them there. However, if your application enabled users to write changes back to the database, you want to use the same connection and data adapter objects for reading and writing to the database. In that case, having class-level scope is very useful.*

With your objects defined, you placed some code to populate the DataSet object in the initialization section of the form. Your SqlDataAdapter object is responsible for retrieving the data from the database. Therefore, you set the SelectCommand property of this object. This property is a SqlCommand object, so the SelectCommand has all the properties of an independent SqlCommand object:

```
' Set the SelectCommand properties..
objDataAdapter.SelectCommand = New SqlCommand()
objDataAdapter.SelectCommand.Connection = objConnection
objDataAdapter.SelectCommand.CommandText = _
```

```
"SELECT au_lname, au_fname, title, price " &
"FROM authors " &
"JOIN titleauthor ON authors.au_id = titleauthor.au_id " &
"JOIN titles ON titleauthor.title_id = titles.title_id " &
"ORDER BY au_lname, au_fname"
```

First, you initialize the SelectCommand by initializing an instance of the SqlCommand class and assigning it to the SelectCommand property.

Then you set the Connection property to your connection object. This property sets the connection to be used to communicate with your data store.

The CommandText property is then set to the SQL string that you wanted to execute. This property contains the SQL string, or stored procedure, that will execute and retrieve your data. In this case, you used a SQL string, which was explained in detail earlier.

After all the properties are set, you open your connection, fill the dataset, and then close the connection again. You open the connection by executing the Open method of your SqlConnection object:

```
' Open the database connection..
objConnection.Open()
```

You then invoke the Fill method of the SqlDataAdapter object to retrieve the data and fill your DataSet object. In the parameters for the Fill method, you specify the DataSet object to use and the table name. You set the table name to authors, even though you are actually retrieving data from several tables in the data store:

```
' Fill the DataSet object with data..
objDataAdapter.Fill(objDataSet, "authors")
```

After you fill your DataSet object with data, you need to close the database connection. You do that by invoking the Close method of the SqlConnection object:

```
' Close the database connection..
objConnection.Close()
```

As you learned earlier, you do not have to open and close the connection explicitly. The Fill method of the SqlDataAdapter executes the SelectCommand and leaves the connection in the same state as when the method was invoked. In this case, the Fill method left the connection open. If you did not explicitly write code to open and close the connection, the SqlDataAdapter.Fill method opens and closes the connection for you.

Then you set some properties of the DataGridView to bind your data to it. The first of these properties is the AutoGenerateColumns property. Here you let the control create all the columns you needed by setting the AutoGenerateColumns property to True. The next property is the DataSource property, which tells the DataGridView where to get its data:

```
' Set the DataGridView properties to bind it to our data..
grdAuthorTitles.AutoGenerateColumns = True
grdAuthorTitles.DataSource = objDataSet
grdAuthorTitles.DataMember = "authors"
```

The DataMember property selects the table in the data source, and here you set it to authors, which is the table used in your DataSet object.

Then, to free memory, you clean up the objects that are no longer being used:

```
' Clean up
objDataAdapter = Nothing
objConnection = Nothing
```

When you ran the example, the `DataGridView` control read the schema information from the `DataSet` object (which the `DataSet` object created when it was filled) and created the correct number of columns for your data in the `DataGridView` control. It also used the column names in the schema as the column names for the grid with each column having the same default width. The `DataGridView` also read the entire `DataSet` object and placed the contents into the grid.

TRY IT OUT   Changing the DataGridView Properties

In this Try It Out, you use some of the DataGridView properties to make this a more user-friendly display of data. All the code for this Try It Out is in the folder `DataExample` in the Zip file for this chapter.

1.   Here are some changes you can make to make your `DataGridView` more user-friendly:

➤   Add your own column header names.

➤   Adjust the width of the column that contains the book titles so that you can easily see the full title.

➤   Change the color of every other row so that the data in each one stands out.

➤   Make the last column in the grid (which contains the price of the books) right-aligned.

You can do all this by making the following modifications in bold to your code in the `Form1_Load` method:

```
' Set the DataGridView properties to bind it to our data..
    grdAuthorTitles.DataSource = objDataSet
    grdAuthorTitles.DataMember = "authors"

    ' Declare and set the currency header alignment property..
    Dim objAlignRightCellStyle As New DataGridViewCellStyle
        objAlignRightCellStyle.Alignment =
        DataGridViewContentAlignment.MiddleRight

    ' Declare and set the alternating rows style..
    Dim objAlternatingCellStyle As New DataGridViewCellStyle()
    objAlternatingCellStyle.BackColor = Color.WhiteSmoke
        grdAuthorTitles.AlternatingRowsDefaultCellStyle =
        objAlternatingCellStyle

    ' Declare and set the style for currency cells ..
    Dim objCurrencyCellStyle As New DataGridViewCellStyle()
    objCurrencyCellStyle.Format = "c"
```

```
        objCurrencyCellStyle.Alignment =
        DataGridViewContentAlignment.MiddleRight

    ' Change column names and styles using the column index
    grdAuthorTitles.Columns(0).HeaderText = "Last Name"
    grdAuthorTitles.Columns(1).HeaderText = "First Name"
    grdAuthorTitles.Columns(2).HeaderText = "Book Title"
    grdAuthorTitles.Columns(2).Width = 225

    ' Change column names and styles using the column name
    grdAuthorTitles.Columns("price").HeaderCell.Value ="Retail Price"
        grdAuthorTitles.Columns("price").HeaderCell.Style =
        objAlignRightCellStyle
        grdAuthorTitles.Columns("price").
        DefaultCellStyle = objCurrencyCellStyle

    ' Clean up
    objDataAdapter = Nothing
    objConnection = Nothing
    objCurrencyCellStyle = Nothing
    objAlternatingCellStyle = Nothing
    objAlignRightCellStyle = Nothing
End Sub
```

2. Run your project again. You should now see results similar to what is shown in Figure 13-5. You can compare this figure to Figure 13-4 and see a world of difference. It's amazing what setting a few properties will do to create a more user-friendly display.

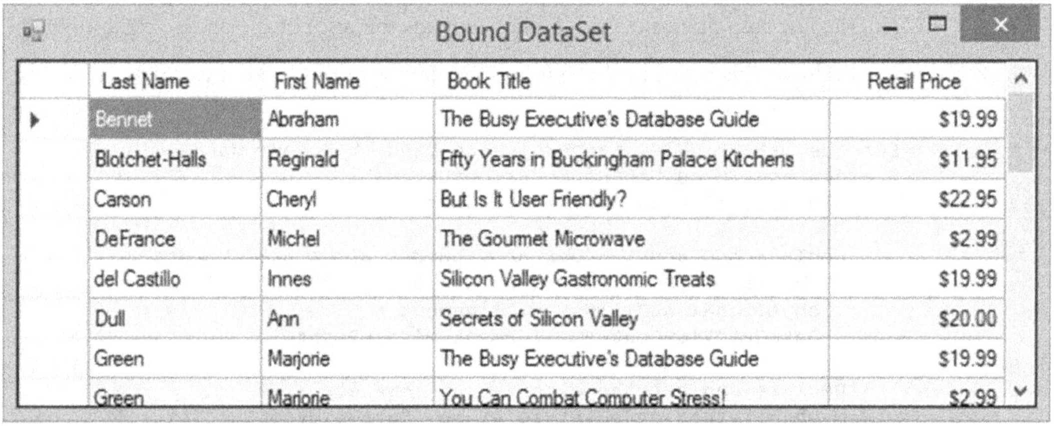

	Last Name	First Name	Book Title	Retail Price	
▶	Bennet	Abraham	The Busy Executive's Database Guide	$19.99	
	Blotchet-Halls	Reginald	Fifty Years in Buckingham Palace Kitchens	$11.95	
	Carson	Cheryl	But Is It User Friendly?	$22.95	
	DeFrance	Michel	The Gourmet Microwave	$2.99	
	del Castillo	Innes	Silicon Valley Gastronomic Treats	$19.99	
	Dull	Ann	Secrets of Silicon Valley	$20.00	
	Green	Marjorie	The Busy Executive's Database Guide	$19.99	
	Green	Marjorie	You Can Combat Computer Stress!	$2.99	

FIGURE 13-5

How It Works

The DataGridView uses inherited styles to format the output table the users see. Style inheritance enables you to apply default styles that cascade to all cells, rows, columns, or headers under the parent style. Then, you can change only individual items that do not match the default styles. The architecture of styles is very powerful. You can set individual style properties or create your own DataGridViewCellStyle objects to set multiple style properties and reuse them.

To start, you declare a `DataGridViewCellStyle` object. Then you change the alignment to middle-right, which enables you to align the price column later:

```
' Declare and set the currency header alignment property..

Dim objAlignRightCellStyle As New DataGridViewCellStyle
    objAlignRightCellStyle.Alignment = DataGridViewContentAlignment.MiddleRight
```

The first thing that you do here is alternate the background color of each row of data. This helps each row of data stand out and makes it easier to see the data in each column for a single row. The `Color` structure provides a large list of color constants, as well as a few methods that can be called to generate colors:

```
' Declare and set the alternating rows style..
Dim objAlternatingCellStyle As New DataGridViewCellStyle()
objAlternatingCellStyle.BackColor = Color.WhiteSmoke
grdAuthorTitles.AlternatingRowsDefaultCellStyle = objAlternatingCellStyle
```

Next, changes to the currency cells for Retail Price are set up. You change the format to currency and right-align the column:

```
' Declare and set the style for currency cells ..
Dim objCurrencyCellStyle As New DataGridViewCellStyle()
objCurrencyCellStyle.Format = "c"
objCurrencyCellStyle.Alignment = DataGridViewContentAlignment.MiddleRight
```

Some changes to the format of the DataGridView are easy to make at the property level. Column titles can simply be changed by accessing the column and setting `HeaderText` or `HeaderCell.Value` properties. You set both properties in the code that follows.

You changed the book Title column width to 225 to display the title in a more readable format.

```
' Change column names and styles using the column index
grdAuthorTitles.Columns(0).HeaderText = "Last Name"
grdAuthorTitles.Columns(1).HeaderText = "First Name"
grdAuthorTitles.Columns(2).HeaderText = "Book Title"
grdAuthorTitles.Columns(2).Width = 225
```

Next, you set the styles on the Price column based on the style objects above. What is great about using style objects is you can apply the same styles to multiple objects. For example, if you have three columns that hold dollar amounts, you can set up one style object and reuse this style on all three columns.

```
' Change column names and styles using the column name
grdAuthorTitles.Columns("price").HeaderCell.Value = "Retail Price"
grdAuthorTitles.Columns("price").HeaderCell.Style = objAlignRightCellStyle
grdAuthorTitles.Columns("price").DefaultCellStyle = objCurrencyCellStyle
```

You have now seen how to bind the `DataSet` object to a control, in this case a DataGridView control. In the next Try It Out, you expand on this knowledge by binding several controls to a `DataView` object and by using the `CurrencyManager` object to navigate the data in the `DataView` object. However, before you get to that point, the following section describes data binding and how you can bind data to simple controls, such as the TextBox control, and how to navigate the records.

DATA BINDING

The *DataGridView* control is a great tool for displaying all your data at one time. You can also use it for editing, deleting, and inserting rows, provided you have the logic to write changes back to the data source. However, you will often want to use a control to display a single column value from one record at a time. In cases like these, you need to bind individual pieces of data to simple controls, such as a TextBox, and display only a single row of data at a time. This type of data binding gives you more control over the data, but it also increases the complexity of your programs because you must write the code both to bind the data to the controls and to navigate between records. This section takes a look at what is involved in binding data to simple controls and how to manage the data bindings.

In this discussion, the term *simple controls* refers to controls that can display only one item of data at a time, such as a TextBox, a Button, a CheckBox, or a RadioButton. Controls such as ComboBox, ListBox, and DataGridView can contain more than one item of data and are not considered simple controls when it comes to data binding. Generally speaking, nonsimple controls have particular properties intended for binding to a data object such as a `DataTable` or `Array`. When binding to simple controls, you are actually binding a particular item of data to a particular property.

BindingContext and CurrencyManager

Each form has a built-in `BindingContext` object that manages the bindings of the controls on the form. Because the `BindingContext` object is already built into each form, you don't need to do anything to set it up.

The `BindingContext` object manages a collection of `CurrencyManager` objects. The `CurrencyManager` is responsible for keeping the data-bound controls in sync with their data source and with other data-bound controls that use the same data source. This ensures that all controls on the form are showing data from the same record. The `CurrencyManager` manages data from a variety of objects, such as `DataSet`, `DataView`, `DataTable`, and `DataSetView`. Whenever you add a data source to a form, a new `CurrencyManager` is automatically created. This makes working with data-bound controls very convenient and simple.

> **NOTE** *The* `CurrencyManager` *gets its name because it keeps the controls current with respect to the data in the data source. The controls do not represent currency (monetary amounts).*

If you have multiple data sources in your form, you can declare a `CurrencyManager` variable and set it to refer to the appropriate `CurrencyManager` object for a given data source in the collection managed by the `BindingContext` object. You then have the capability to manage the data in the data-bound controls explicitly.

The following code fragment, using the `DataSet` object that you have been using in the previous example, defines and sets a reference to the `CurrencyManager` that manages the data source containing the local `authors` table. First, the code declares a variable using the `CurrencyManager` class.

Then it sets this CurrencyManager variable to the currency manager for the DataSet object (objDataSet) contained in the BindingContext object. The CType function is used to return an object that is explicitly converted. The CType function accepts two arguments: the expression to be converted and the type to which the expression is to be converted. Because the expression is to evaluate to a CurrencyManager object, CurrencyManager is specified for the type argument:

```
Dim objCurrencyManager As CurrencyManager
objCurrencyManager = _
    CType(Me.BindingContext(objDataSet), CurrencyManager)
```

After you have a reference to the data source object, you can manage the position of the records using the Position property, as shown in the following example. This example advances the current record position in the objDataSet object by one record:

```
objCurrencyManager.Position += 1
```

If you wanted to move backward one record, you would use this code:

```
objCurrencyManager.Position - = 1
```

To move to the first record contained in the DataSet object, you would use the following:

```
objCurrencyManager.Position = 0
```

The Count property of the CurrencyManager contains the number of records in the DataSet object managed by the CurrencyManager. Therefore, to move to the very last record, you would use the following code:

```
objCurrencyManager.Position = objCurrencyManager.Count - 1
```

Note that this code specifies the Count value minus one. Because the Count property contains the actual number of records and the DataSet object has a base index of zero, you must subtract one from the Count value to get the index to the last record.

Binding Controls

When you want to bind a data source to a control, you set the DataBindings property for that control. This property accesses the ControlBindingsCollection class. This class manages the bindings for each control, and it has many properties and methods. The method of interest here is Add.

The Add method creates a binding for the control and adds it to the ControlBindingsCollection. The Add method has three arguments, and its syntax is shown here:

```
object.DataBindings.Add(propertyname, datasource, datamember)
```

In this syntax, note the following:

➤ The *object* represents a valid control on your form.

➤ The *propertyname* argument represents the property of the control to be bound.

➤ The *datasource* argument represents the data source to be bound and can be any valid object, such as a DataSet, DataView, or DataTable, that contains data.

➤ The *datamember* argument represents the data field in the data source to be bound to this control.

An example of how the Add method works is shown in the following code. This example binds the column name au_fname in the objDataView object to the Text property of a text box named txtFirstName:

```
txtFirstName.DataBindings.Add("Text", objDataView, "au_fname")
```

Sometimes, after a control has been bound, you may want to change the bindings for that control. To do this, you can use the Clear method of the ControlBindingsCollection. The Clear method clears the collection of all bindings for this control. Then you can make the change you need. An example of this method is shown in the following code fragment:

```
txtFirstName.DataBindings.Clear()
```

Now that you have had a look at the BindingContext, CurrencyManager, and ControlBindings Collection objects, learn how all these pieces fit and work together in a practical hands-on exercise.

Binding Examples

The following Try It Out demonstrates not only how to use the BindingContext, CurrencyManager, and ControlBindingsCollection objects, but also how to use the DataView, SqlCommand, and SqlParameter classes.

> **NOTE** For this Try It Out, you'll use the query from the previous example as the base for your new query, and you'll again display all the authors' first and last names, as well as their book titles and prices. However, this example differs from the last one in that it displays only one record at a time.

You use the CurrencyManager object to navigate the records in the DataView object and provide the functionality to move forward and backward, as well as to the first and last records.

The other Try It Outs in this section then show you how to add sorting functionality and how to add the functionality to add, update, and delete records. Finally, you code the btnUpdate_Click and btnDelete_Click procedures in the last two Try It Outs.

TRY IT OUT Binding Simple Controls

All the code for this Try It Out is in the folder BindingExample in the Zip file for this chapter. To build this example, follow these steps:

1. Create a new Windows Forms application project called **BindingExample**. Set the various form properties as follows:

   ➤ Set FormBorderStyle to **FixedDialog**.

   ➤ Set MaximizeBox to **False**.

➤ Set MinimizeBox to **False**.

➤ Set Size to **430, 360**.

➤ Set StartPosition to **CenterScreen**.

➤ Set Text to **Binding Controls**.

2. Drag a ToolTip control from the Toolbox and drop it on your form to add it to the designer.

3. Add objects to the form so that the form ends up looking like Figure 13-6.

> **NOTE** *The steps that follow provide the controls you need, but do not specify the exact layout. The cosmetic properties are not as important; you can approximate the layout visually based on Figure 13-6.*

FIGURE 13-6

4. Add a GroupBox control to the form. You can find the GroupBox controls under the Containers node in the Toolbox. Set the GroupBox1 Text property to **Authors && Titles**.

5. Using this list, add the required controls to GroupBox1 and set their properties:

➤ Add a Label control. Set Text to **Last Name**.

➤ Add a Label control. Set Text to **First Name**.

➤ Add a Label control. Set Text to **Book Title**.

➤ Add a Label control. Set Text to **Price**.

➤ Add a TextBox control. Name it **txtLastName** and set ReadOnly to **True**.

➤ Add a TextBox control. Name it **txtFirstName** and set ReadOnly to **True.**

➤ Add a TextBox control. Name it **txtBookTitle.**

➤ Add a TextBox control. Name it **txtPrice.**

6. Now add a second GroupBox and set Text to **Navigation.**

7. In GroupBox2, add the following controls:

➤ Add a Label control. Set Text to **Field.**

➤ Add a Label control. Set Text to **Search Criteria.**

➤ Add a ComboBox control. Name it **cboField** and set DropDownStyle to **DropDownList.**

➤ Add a TextBox control. Name it **txtSearchCriteria.**

➤ Add a TextBox control. Name it **txtRecordPosition** and set TabStop to **False;** TextAlign to **Center.**

➤ Add a Button control. Name it **btnPerformSort** and set Text to **Perform Sort.**

➤ Add a Button control. Name it **btnPerformSearch** and set Text to **Perform Search.**

➤ Add a Button control. Name it **btnNew** and set Text to **New.**

➤ Add a Button control. Name it **btnAdd** and set Text to **Add.**

➤ Add a Button control. Name it **btnUpdate** and set Text to **Update.**

➤ Add a Button control. Name it **btnDelete** and set Text to **Delete.**

➤ Add a Button control. Name it **btnMoveFirst** and set Text to |<; ToolTip on ToolTip1 to **Move First.**

➤ Add a Button control. Name it **btnMovePrevious** and set Text to <; ToolTip on ToolTip1 to **Move Previous.**

➤ Add a Button control. Name it **btnMoveNext** and set Text to >; ToolTip on ToolTip1 to **Move Next.**

➤ Add a Button control. Name it **btnMoveLast** and set Text to >|; ToolTip on ToolTip1 to **Move Last.**

8. Finally, add a StatusStrip control. Leave its name as the default StatusStrip1, and its default location and size. Click the new StatusStrip1 control on the form; you have an option to add a StatusLabel control in the menu. Select StatusLabel from the menu and leave the default settings.

9. When you are done, your completed form should look like the one shown in Figure 13-6.

10. Again, you need to add imports to the namespaces needed. To do this, switch to Code Editor view and then insert the following lines of code at the very top:

```
' Import Data and SqlClient namespaces..
Imports System.Data
Imports System.Data.SqlClient
```

11. Declare the objects that are global in scope to this form, so add the following bold code:

```
Public Class Form1
    ' Declare objects..
```

```
Dim objConnection As New SqlConnection _
    ("server=localhost\SQLEXPRESS;database=pubs;" &
      "user id=sa;password=SQL2014wrox;")
Dim objDataAdapter As New SqlDataAdapter( _
    "SELECT authors.au_id, au_lname, au_fname, " &
    "titles.title_id, title, price " &
    "FROM authors " &
    "JOIN titleauthor ON authors.au_id = " &
      "titleauthor.au_id " &
    "JOIN titles ON titleauthor.title_id = " &
      "titles.title_id " &
    "ORDER BY au_lname, au_fname", objConnection)
Dim objDataSet As DataSet
Dim objDataView As DataView
Dim objCurrencyManager As CurrencyManager
```

> **NOTE** Be sure to update the connection string to match your settings for
> the user ID and password, and also set the Server to the machine where SQL
> Server is running if it is not your local machine.

12. The first procedure you need to create is the FillDataSetAndView procedure. This procedure,
    along with the following procedures, is called in your initialization code. Add the following code to
    the form's class, just below your object declarations:

```
Private Sub FillDataSetAndView()
    ' Initialize a new instance of the DataSet object.
    objDataSet = New DataSet()

    ' Fill the DataSet object with data.
    objDataAdapter.Fill(objDataSet, "authors")

    ' Set the DataView object to the DataSet object.
    objDataView = New DataView(objDataSet.Tables("authors"))

    ' Set our CurrencyManager object to the DataView object.
    objCurrencyManager = _
      CType(Me.BindingContext(objDataView), CurrencyManager)
End Sub
```

13. The next procedure you need to create actually binds the controls on your form to your DataView
    object:

```
' Clear any previous bindings..
  txtLastName.DataBindings.Clear()
  txtFirstName.DataBindings.Clear()
  txtBookTitle.DataBindings.Clear()
  txtPrice.DataBindings.Clear()

  ' Add new bindings to the DataView object..
  txtLastName.DataBindings.Add("Text", objDataView,
  "au_lname")
```

```
txtFirstName.DataBindings.Add("Text", objDataView,
  "au_fname")
txtBookTitle.DataBindings.Add("Text", objDataView,
  "title")
txtPrice.DataBindings.Add("Text", objDataView, "price")

  ' Display a ready status..
  ToolStripLabel1.Text = "Ready"
End Sub
```

14. Now you need a procedure that displays the current record position on your form:

```
Private Sub ShowPosition()
  'Format number in the txtPrice field to include cents
  Try
    txtPrice.Text=Format(CType(txtPrice.Text,
Decimal), "##0.00")
  Catch e As System.Exception
      txtPrice.Text = "0"
    txtPrice.Text=Format(CType(txtPrice.Text,
Decimal), "##0.00")
  End Try

  ' Display the current position and the number of records
  txtRecordPosition.Text = objCurrencyManager.Position + 1 &
    " of " & objCurrencyManager.Count()
End Sub
```

15. You've added some powerful procedures to your form, but currently there is no code to call them. You want these procedures, as well as some other code, to execute every time the form loads. Therefore, return to the Form Designer, double-click the Form Designer, and add the following bold code to the Form_Load method (note that you must click an area outside of the GroupBox controls):

```
Private Sub Form1_Load(sender As Object,
              e As EventArgs) Handles MyBase.Load
  ' Add items to the combo box..
  cboField.Items.Add("Last Name")
  cboField.Items.Add("First Name")
  cboField.Items.Add("Book Title")
  cboField.Items.Add("Price")

  ' Make the first item selected..
  cboField.SelectedIndex = 0

  ' Fill the DataSet and bind the fields..
  FillDataSetAndView()
  BindFields()

  ' Show the current record position..
  ShowPosition()
End Sub
```

16. To add the code for your navigation buttons, you need to switch back and forth between the Design and Code views by double-clicking each button and then adding the code. Alternatively, you can select the buttons in the Class Name combo box and then select the Click event in the Method Name combo box. Add the following code in bold to the procedure for the btnMoveFirst button first:

```
Private Sub btnMoveFirst_Click(Sender As Object,
            E As EventArgs) Handles btnMoveFirst.Click
    ' Set the record position to the first record..
    objCurrencyManager.Position = 0

    ' Show the current record position..
    ShowPosition()
End Sub
```

17. Add the code in bold to the btnMovePrevious button next:

```
Private Sub btnMovePrevious_Click(Sender As Object,
            E As EventArgs) Handles btnMovePrevious.Click
    ' Move to the previous record..
    objCurrencyManager.Position -= 1

    ' Show the current record position..
    ShowPosition()
End Sub
```

18. The next procedure you want to add code to is the btnMoveNext procedure:

```
Private Sub btnMoveNext_Click(Sender As Object,
            E As EventArgs) Handles btnMoveNext.Click
    ' Move to the next record..
    objCurrencyManager.Position += 1

    ' Show the current record position..
    ShowPosition()
End Sub
```

19. The final navigation procedure that you need to code is the btnMoveLast procedure:

```
Private Sub btnMoveLast_Click(Sender As Object,
            E As EventArgs) Handles btnMoveLast.Click
    ' Set the record position to the last record..
    objCurrencyManager.Position = objCurrencyManager.Count-1

    ' Show the current record position..
    ShowPosition()
End Sub
```

20. At this point, you have entered a lot of code and are probably anxious to see the results of your work. Run the project to see how your DataView object gets bound to the controls on the form and to see the CurrencyManager object at work as you navigate through the records.

After your form appears, you should see results similar to Figure 13-7. The only buttons that work are the navigation buttons, which change the current record position. Test your form by navigating to the next and previous records and by moving to the last record and the first record. Each time you move to a new record, the text box between the navigation buttons will be updated to display the current record.

FIGURE 13-7

While you are on the first record, you can try to move to the previous record but nothing will happen because you are already on the first record. Likewise, you can move to the last record and try to navigate to the next record and nothing will happen because you are already on the last record.

If you hover your mouse pointer over the navigation buttons, you will see a ToolTip indicating what each button is for. This just provides a nicer interface for your users.

> **NOTE** *Error handling has been omitted from the exercise to preserve space. You should always add the appropriate error handling to your code. Please review Chapter 9 for error-handling techniques.*

How It Works: Namespaces and Object Declaration

As usual, you import the `System.Data` and `System.Data.SqlClient` namespaces. Next, you declare the objects on your form. The first three objects should be familiar to you because you used them in your last project.

Take a closer look at the initialization of the `SqlDataAdapter` object. You use a constructor that initializes this object with a string value for the `SelectCommand` property and an object that represents a connection to the database. This constructor saves you from writing code to manipulate the `SqlDataAdapter` properties; it's already set up.

The SELECT statement that you use here is basically the same as in the previous project, except that you add a couple more columns in the *select list* (the list of columns directly following the word SELECT).

The au_id column in the select list is prefixed with the table name authors because this column also exists in the titleauthor table. Therefore, you must tell the database which table to get the data from for this column. Likewise for the title_id column, except that this column exists in the titles and titleauthor tables:

```
Dim objConnection As New SqlConnection _
    ("server=localhost\SQLEXPRESS;database=pubs;" &
        "user id=sa;password=wrox;")
Dim objDataAdapter As New SqlDataAdapter( _
    "SELECT authors.au_id, au_lname, au_fname, " &
    "titles.title_id, title, price " &
    "FROM authors " &
    "JOIN titleauthor ON authors.au_id = titleauthor.au_id " &
    "JOIN titles ON titleauthor.title_id = titles.title_id " &
    "ORDER BY au_lname, au_fname", objConnection)
Dim objDataSet As DataSet
Dim objDataView As DataView
Dim objCurrencyManager As CurrencyManager
```

You use the DataView to customize your view of the records returned from the database and stored in the DataSet. The CurrencyManager object controls the movement of your bound data, as shown in the previous section.

How It Works: FillDataSetAndView

The first procedure you create is the FillDataSetAndView procedure. This procedure, which will be called in your code, will get the latest data from the database and populate your DataView object.

First, you need to initialize a new instance of the DataSet object. You do this here because this procedure might be called more than once during the lifetime of the form. If it is, you do not want to add new records to the records already in the DataSet; you always want to start afresh:

```
Private Sub FillDataSetAndView()
    ' Initialize a new instance of the DataSet object..
    objDataSet = New DataSet()
```

Next, you invoke the Fill method on objDataAdapter to populate the objDataSet object. Then you specify that your DataView object will be viewing data from the authors table in the DataSet object. Remember that the DataView object allows you to sort, search, and navigate through the records in the DataSet:

```
' Fill the DataSet object with data..
objDataAdapter.Fill(objDataSet, "authors")

' Set the DataView object to the DataSet object..
objDataView = New DataView(objDataSet.Tables("authors"))
```

After you initialize your DataView object, you want to initialize the CurrencyManager object. Remember that the BindingContext object is built into every Windows form and contains a collection of CurrencyManagers. The collection contains the available data sources, and you choose the DataView object:

```
' Set our CurrencyManager object to the DataView object..
objCurrencyManager = _
    CType(Me.BindingContext(objDataView), CurrencyManager)
```

How It Works: BindFields

The next procedure that you create (BindFields) binds the controls on your form to your DataView object. This procedure first clears any previous bindings for the controls and then sets them to your DataView object.

> **NOTE** It is important to clear the bindings first because after you modify the DataView object by adding, updating, or deleting a row of data, the DataView object will show only the changed data. Therefore, after you update the database with your changes, you must repopulate your DataView object and rebind your controls. If you didn't do this, the data that would actually be in the database and the data in the DataView may not be the same.

Using the DataBindings property of the controls on your form, you execute the Clear method of the ControlBindingsCollection class to remove the bindings from them. Notice that the controls that you bound are all the text boxes on your form that will contain data from the DataView object:

```
Private Sub BindFields()
    ' Clear any previous bindings to the DataView object..
    txtLastName.DataBindings.Clear()
    txtFirstName.DataBindings.Clear()
    txtBookTitle.DataBindings.Clear()
    txtPrice.DataBindings.Clear()
```

After you clear the previous bindings, you can set the new bindings back to the same data source: the DataView object. You do this by executing the Add method of the ControlBindingsCollection object returned by the DataBindings property. As described earlier, the Add method has three arguments, shown in the code that follows:

➤   The first argument is *propertyname* and specifies the property of the control to be bound. Because you want to bind your data to the Text property of the text boxes, you have specified "Text" for this argument.

➤   The next argument is the *datasource* argument, which specifies the data source to be bound. Remember that this can be any valid object, such as a DataSet, DataView, or DataTable, that contains data. In this case, you are using a DataView object.

➤   The last argument specifies the *datamember*. This is the data field in the data source that contains the data to be bound to this control. Note that you have specified the various column names from the SELECT statement that you executed in the previous procedure.

```
    ' Add new bindings to the DataView object..
    txtLastName.DataBindings.Add("Text",
        objDataView, "au_lname")
    txtFirstName.DataBindings.Add("Text",
        objDataView, "au_fname")
    txtBookTitle.DataBindings.Add("Text", objDataView, "title")
    txtPrice.DataBindings.Add("Text", objDataView, "price")
```

The last thing you do in this procedure is set a message in the status bar using the Text property of ToolStripLabel1:

```
' Display a ready status..
    ToolStripLabel1.Text = "Ready"
End Sub
```

How It Works: ShowPosition

The CurrencyManager object keeps track of the current record position within the DataView object.

The price column in the titles table in pubs is defined as a Currency data type. Therefore, if a book is priced at $40.00, the number that you get is 40; the decimal portion is dropped. The ShowPosition procedure seems like a good place to format the data in the txtPrice text box, because this procedure is called whenever you move to a new record:

```
Private Sub ShowPosition()
   'format the number in the txtPrice field to include cents
   Try
     txtPrice.Text=Format(CType(txtPrice.Text, Decimal), "##0.00")
   Catch e As System.Exception
     txtPrice.Text = "0"
     txtPrice.Text=Format(CType(txtPrice.Text, Decimal), "##0.00")
   End Try

   ' Display the current position and the number of records
   txtRecordPosition.Text = objCurrencyManager.Position + 1 &
     " of " & objCurrencyManager.Count()
End Sub
```

This part of the function is enclosed in a Try...Catch block in case the txtPrice is empty. If txtPrice is empty, the Format function throws a handled exception, and the exception handler defaults the price to 0. The second line of code in this procedure uses the Format function to format the price in the txtPrice text box. This function accepts the numeric data to be formatted as the first argument and a format string as the second argument. For the format function to work correctly, you need to convert the string value in the txtPrice field to a decimal value using the CType function.

The last line of code displays the current record position, and the total number of records that you have. Using the Position property of the CurrencyManager object, you can determine which record you are on. The Position property uses a zero-based index, so the first record is always 0. Therefore, you specified the Position property plus 1 to display the true number.

The CurrencyManager class's Count property returns the actual number of items in the list, and you are using this property to display the total number of records in the DataView object.

How It Works: Form_Load

Now that you've looked at the code for the main procedures, you need to go back and look at your initialization code.

You have a combo box on your form that will be used when sorting or searching for data. This combo box needs to be populated with data representing the columns in the DataView object. You specify the Add method of the Items property of the combo box to add items to it. Here you are specifying text that represents the columns in the `DataView` object in the same order that they appear in the `DataView` object:

```
'Add any initialization after the InitializeComponent() call

' Add items to the combo box..
cboField.Items.Add("Last Name")
cboField.Items.Add("First Name")
cboField.Items.Add("Book Title")
cboField.Items.Add("Price")
```

After you have loaded all the items into your combo box, you want to select the first item. You do this by setting the `SelectedIndex` property to `0`. The `SelectedIndex` property is zero-based, so the first item in the list is item `0`:

```
' Make the first item selected..
cboField.SelectedIndex = 0
```

Next, you call the `FillDataSetAndView` procedure to retrieve the data and then call the `BindFields` procedure to bind the controls on your form to your `DataView` object. Finally, you call the `ShowPosition` procedure to display the current record position and the total number of records contained in your `DataView` object:

```
' Fill the DataSet and bind the fields..
FillDataSetAndView()
BindFields()

' Show the current record position..
ShowPosition()
```

How It Works: Navigation Buttons

The procedure for the `btnMoveFirst` button causes the first record in the `DataView` object to be displayed. This is accomplished using the `Position` property of the `CurrencyManager` object. Here you set the `Position` property to `0`, indicating that the `CurrencyManager` should move to the first record:

```
' Set the record position to the first record..
objCurrencyManager.Position = 0
```

Because your controls are bound to the `DataView` object, they always stay in sync with the current record in the `DataView` object and display the appropriate data.

After you reposition the current record, you need to call the `ShowPosition` procedure to update the display of the current record on your form:

```
' Show the current record position..
ShowPosition()
```

Next, you add the code for the `btnMovePrevious` button. You move to the prior record by subtracting 1 from the `Position` property. The `CurrencyManager` object automatically detects and handles the beginning position of the `DataView` object. It will not let you move to a position prior to the first record; it just quietly keeps its position at `0`:

```
' Move to the previous record..
objCurrencyManager.Position -= 1
```

Again, after you have repositioned the current record being displayed, you need to call the ShowPosition procedure to display the current position on the form.

In the btnMoveNext procedure, you want to increment the Position property by 1. Again, the CurrencyManager automatically detects the last record in the DataView object and will not let you move past it:

```
' Move to the next record..
   objCurrencyManager.Position += 1
```

You call the ShowPosition procedure to display the current record position.

When the btnMoveLast procedure is called, you want to move to the last record in the DataView object. You accomplish this by setting the Position property equal to the Count property minus one. Then you call the ShowPosition procedure to display the current record:

```
' Set the record position to the last record..
objCurrencyManager.Position = objCurrencyManager.Count-1

' Show the current record position..
ShowPosition()
```

TRY IT OUT Including Sorting Functionality

Now that you have built the navigation, you move on to add sorting functionality to this project in this Try It Out. All the code for this Try It Out is in the folder BindingExample in the Zip file for this chapter.

1. Double-click the Perform Sort button on the form in design mode to have the empty procedure added to the form class, or select the button in the Class Name combo box and then select the Click event in the Method Name combo box. Insert the following bold code in the btnPerformSort_Click event procedure:

```
Private Sub btnPerformSort_Click(Sender As Object,
        E As EventArgs) Handles btnPerformSort.Click
    ' Determine the appropriate item selected and set the
    ' Sort property of the DataView object..
    Select Case cboField.SelectedIndex
        Case 0 'Last Name
            objDataView.Sort = "au_lname"
        Case 1 'First Name
            objDataView.Sort = "au_fname"
        Case 2 'Book Title
            objDataView.Sort = "title"
        Case 3 'Price
            objDataView.Sort = "price"
    End Select

    ' Call the click event for the MoveFirst button..
    btnMoveFirst_Click(Nothing, Nothing)

    ' Display a message that the records have been sorted..
    ToolStripLabel1.Text = "Records Sorted"
End Sub
```

2. Test the new functionality by running it; click the Start button to compile and run it. Select a column to sort and then click the Perform Sort button. You should see the data sorted by the column that you have chosen. Figure 13-8 shows the data sorted by author last name.

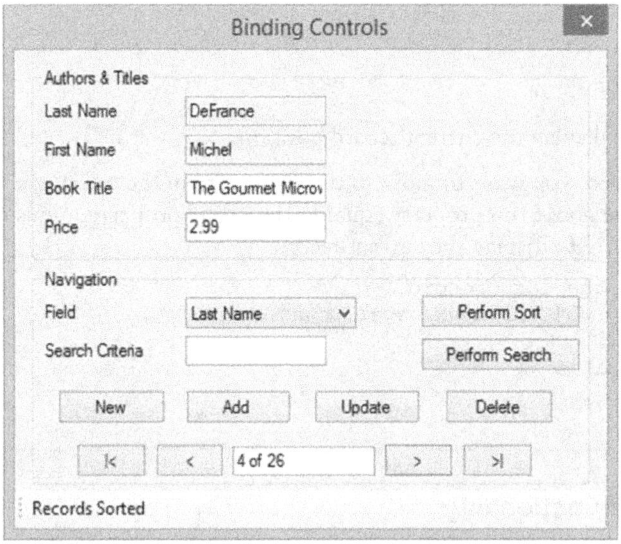

FIGURE 13.8

How It Works

First, you determine which field you should sort on. This information is contained in the cboField combo box:

```
' Determine the appropriate item selected and set the
' Sort property of the DataView object..
Select Case cboField.SelectedIndex
    Case 0 'Last Name
        objDataView.Sort = "au_lname"
    Case 1 'First Name
        objDataView.Sort = "au_fname"
    Case 2 'Book Title
        objDataView.Sort = "title"
    Case 3 'Price
        objDataView.Sort = "price"
End Select
```

Using a Select Case statement to examine the SelectedIndex property of the combo box, you can determine which field the user has chosen. After you have determined the correct entry in the combo box, you can set the Sort property of the DataView object using the column name of the column that you want sorted. After the Sort property has been set, the data is sorted.

After the data has been sorted, you want to move to the first record, and there are a couple of ways you can do this. You can set the Position property of the CurrencyManager object and then call the `ShowPosition` procedure, or you can simply call the `btnMoveFirst_Click` procedure, passing it `Nothing` for both arguments. This is the procedure that would be executed had you actually clicked the Move First button on the form.

The `btnMoveFirst_Click` procedure has two arguments: `ByVal sender As Object` and `E As EventArgs`. Because these arguments are required (even though they're not actually used in the procedure), you need to pass something to them, so you pass the `Nothing` keyword. The `Nothing` keyword is used to disassociate an object variable from an object. Thus, by using the `Nothing` keyword, you satisfy the requirement of passing an argument to the procedure, but have not passed any actual value:

```
' Call the click event for the MoveFirst button..
btnMoveFirst_Click(Nothing, Nothing)
```

After the first record has been displayed, you want to display a message in the status bar indicating that the records have been sorted. You did this by setting the `Text` property of the status bar as you have done before.

Note that another way to accomplish this is to have a procedure called `MoveFirst`, and to call that from here *and* from the `btnMoveFirst_Click` procedure. Some developers would opt for this method instead of passing `Nothing` to a procedure.

TRY IT OUT Including Searching Functionality

In this Try It Out, you take a look at what's involved in searching for a record. All the code for this Try It Out is in the `BindingExample` folder in the Zip file for this chapter.

1. Double-click the Perform Search button or select the button in the `Class Name` combo box and then select the `Click` event in the `Method Name` combo box, and add the following bold code to the `btnPerformSearch_Click` event procedure:

```
Private Sub btnPerformSearch_Click(Sender As Object,
        E As EventArgs) Handles btnPerformSearch.Click
    ' Declare local variables..
    Dim intPosition As Integer

    ' Determine the appropriate item selected and set the
    ' Sort property of the DataView object..
    Select Case cboField.SelectedIndex
        Case 0 'Last Name
            objDataView.Sort = "au_lname"
        Case 1 'First Name
            objDataView.Sort = "au_fname"
        Case 2 'Book Title
            objDataView.Sort = "title"
        Case 3 'Price
            objDataView.Sort = "price"
    End Select

    ' If the search field is not price then..
    If cboField.SelectedIndex < 3 Then
        ' Find the last name, first name, or title..
        intPosition = objDataView.Find(txtSearchCriteria.Text)
```

```
        Else
            ' otherwise find the price..
            intPosition = objDataView.Find(CType(txtSearchCriteria.Text, Decimal))
        End If
        If intPosition = -1 Then
            ' Display a message that the record was not found..
            ToolStripLabel1.Text = "Record Not Found"
        Else
            ' Otherwise display a message that the record was
            ' found and reposition the CurrencyManager to that
            ' record..
            ToolStripLabel1.Text = "Record Found"
            objCurrencyManager.Position = intPosition
        End If

        ' Show the current record position..
        ShowPosition()
    End Sub
```

2. Test the searching functionality that you added. Run the project and select a field in the `Field` combo box that you want to search on, and then enter the search criteria in the Search Criteria text box. Finally, click the Perform Search button.

If a match is found, you see the first matched record displayed, along with a message in the status bar indicating that the record was found, as shown at the bottom of Figure 13-9. If no record was found, you see a message in the status bar indicating the record was not found.

FIGURE 13.9

How It Works

This is a little more involved than previous Try It Outs because there are multiple conditions that you must test for and handle, such as a record that was not found. The first thing that you do in this procedure is declare a variable that will receive the record position of the record that has been found or not found:

```
' Declare local variables..
Dim intPosition As Integer
```

Next, you sort the data based on the column used in the search. The Find method searches for data in the sort key. Therefore, by setting the Sort property, the column that is sorted on becomes the sort key in the DataView object. You use a Select Case statement, just as you did in the previous procedure:

```
' Determine the appropriate item selected and set the
' Sort property of the DataView object..
Select Case cboField.SelectedIndex
    Case 0 'Last Name
        objDataView.Sort = "au_lname"
    Case 1 'First Name
        objDataView.Sort = "au_fname"
    Case 2 'Book Title
        objDataView.Sort = "title"
    Case 3 'Price
        objDataView.Sort = "price"
End Select
```

The columns for the authors' first and last names, as well as the column for the book titles, all contain text data. However, the column for the book price contains data that is in a currency format. Therefore, you need to determine which column you are searching on; and if that column is the price column, you need to format the data in the txtSearchCriteria text box to a decimal value.

Again, you use the SelectedIndex property of the cboField combo box to determine which item has been selected. If the SelectedIndex property is less than 3, you know that you want to search on a column that contains text data.

You then set the intPosition variable to the results returned by the Find method of the DataView object. The Find method accepts the data to search for as the only argument. Here you pass it the data contained in the Text property of the txtSearchCriteria text box.

If the SelectedIndex equals 3, you are searching for a book with a specific price, and this requires you to convert the value contained in the txtSearchCriteria text box to a decimal value. The CType function accepts an expression and the data type that you want to convert that expression to and returns a value—in this case, a decimal value. This value is then used as the search criterion by the Find method:

```
' If the search field is not price then..
If cboField.SelectedIndex < 3 Then
    ' Find the last name, first name or title..
    intPosition = objDataView.Find(txtSearchCriteria.Text)
Else
    ' otherwise find the price..
    intPosition = objDataView.Find(CType(txtSearchCriteria.Text, Decimal))
End If
```

After you execute the Find method of the DataView object, you need to check the value contained in the intPosition variable. If this variable contains a value of -1, no match was found. Any value other than -1 points to the record position of the record that contains the data. Therefore, if the value in this variable is -1, you want to display a message in the status bar indicating that no record was found.

If the value is greater than -1, you want to display a message that the record was found and position the DataView object to that record using the Position property of the CurrencyManager object:

```
ToolStripLabel1.Text = "Record Found"
objCurrencyManager.Position = intPosition
```

> **NOTE** The Find method of the DataView object performs a search, looking for an exact match of characters. There is no wildcard search method here, so you must enter the entire text string that you want to search for. The case, however, does not matter, so the name "Ann" is the same as "ann"; you do not need to be concerned with entering proper case when you enter your search criteria.

Last, you want to show the current record position, which you do by calling the ShowPosition procedure.

TRY IT OUT Adding Records

Now all that is left is to add the functionality to add, update, and delete records. Take a look at what is required to add a record first. All the code in this Try It Out is in the code file BindingExample in the Zip file for this chapter.

1. Add just two lines of code to the btnNew_Click procedure:

```
Private Sub btnNew_Click(Sender As Object,
                E As EventArgs) Handles btnNew.Click
    ' Clear the book title and price fields..
    txtBookTitle.Text = ""
    txtPrice.Text = ""
End Sub
```

2. Add code to the btnAdd_Click procedure. This procedure, which is responsible for adding a new record, has the largest amount of code by far of any of the procedures you have coded or will code in this project. That's because of the relationship of book titles to authors and the primary key used for book titles:

```
Private Sub btnAdd_Click(Sender As Object,
                E As EventArgs) Handles btnAdd.Click
    ' Declare local variables and objects..
    Dim intPosition As Integer, intMaxID As Integer
    Dim strID As String
    Dim objCommand As SqlCommand = New SqlCommand()

    ' Save the current record position..
    intPosition = objCurrencyManager.Position

    ' Create a new SqlCommand object..
    Dim maxIdCommand As SqlCommand = New SqlCommand _
```

```vbnet
                ("SELECT MAX(title_id) AS MaxID " & _
                "FROM titles WHERE title_id LIKE 'DM%'", objConnection)

    ' Open the connection, execute the command
    objConnection.Open()
    Dim maxId As Object = maxIdCommand.ExecuteScalar()
    ' If the MaxID column is null..
    If maxId Is DBNull.Value Then
        ' Set a default value of 1000..
        intMaxID = 1000
    Else
        ' otherwise set the strID variable to the value in MaxID..
        strID = CType(maxId, String)

        ' Get the integer part of the string..
        intMaxID = CType(strID.Remove(0, 2), Integer)

        ' Increment the value..
        intMaxID += 1
    End If

    ' Finally, set the new ID..
    strID = "DM" & intMaxID.ToString

    ' Set the SqlCommand object properties..
    objCommand.Connection = objConnection
    objCommand.CommandText = "INSERT INTO titles " & _
        "(title_id, title, type, price, pubdate) " & _
        "VALUES(@title_id,@title,@type,@price,@pubdate);" & _
        "INSERT INTO titleauthor (au_id, title_id) VALUES(@au_id,@title_id)"

    ' Add parameters for the placeholders in the SQL in the
    ' CommandText property..

    ' Parameter for the title_id column..
    objCommand.Parameters.AddWithValue("@title_id", strID)

    ' Parameter for the title column..
    objCommand.Parameters.AddWithValue("@title", txtBookTitle.Text)

    ' Parameter for the type column
    objCommand.Parameters.AddWithValue("@type", "Demo")

    ' Parameter for the price column..
    objCommand.Parameters.AddWithValue("@price", txtPrice.Text).DbType _
                            = DbType.Currency

    ' Parameter for the pubdate column
    objCommand.Parameters.AddWithValue("@pubdate", Date.Now)

    ' Parameter for the au_id column..
    objCommand.Parameters.AddWithValue _
                ("@au_id", BindingContext(objDataView).Current("au_id"))

    ' Execute the SqlCommand object to insert the new data..
    Try
```

```
        objCommand.ExecuteNonQuery()
    Catch SqlExceptionErr As SqlException
        MessageBox.Show(SqlExceptionErr.Message)
    End Try

    ' Close the connection..
    objConnection.Close()

    ' Fill the dataset and bind the fields..
    FillDataSetAndView()
    BindFields()

    ' Set the record position to the one that you saved..
    objCurrencyManager.Position = intPosition

    ' Show the current record position..
    ShowPosition()

    ' Display a message that the record was added..
    ToolStripLabel1.Text = "Record Added"
End Sub
```

3. Run your project. Choose an author for whom you want to add a new title and then click the New button. The Book Title and Price fields will be cleared, and you are ready to enter new data to be added, as shown in Figure 13-10. Take note of the number of records in the DataView (26 in Figure 13-10).

FIGURE 13-10

4. Enter a title and price for the new book and click the Add button. You will see a message in the status bar indicating that the record has been added, and you will see that the number of records has changed (to 27), as shown in Figure 13-11.

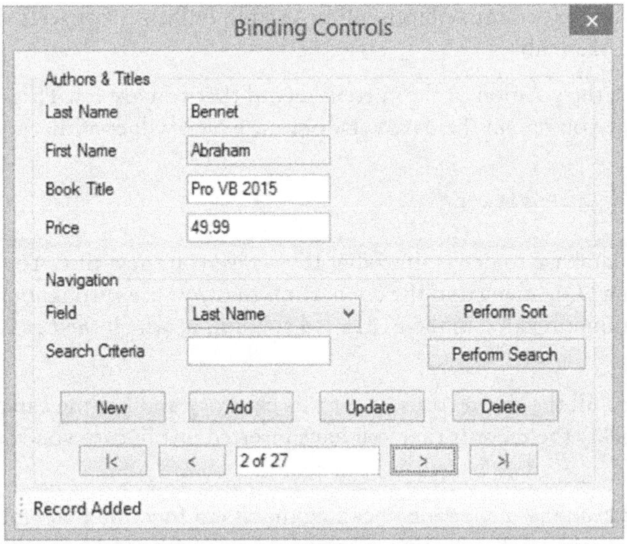

FIGURE 13-11

Now that you have added a record, examine what you actually did.

How It Works

Remember that the only data you can add is a new book title and its price, so instead of selecting the data in each of these fields, deleting it, and then entering the new data, you want to be able to simply click the New button. The job of the New button is to clear the Book Title and Price fields for you. All you need to do is set the Text properties of these text boxes to an empty string as shown here:

```
' Clear the book title and price fields..
txtBookTitle.Text = ""
txtPrice.Text = ""
```

When you click the New button, the fields are cleared. If you are updating or editing a record, those changes are lost. You would normally put logic into your application to prevent that problem, but for this example that type of validation was left out.

The primary key used in the titles table is not the database's Identity column. Identity columns use a sequential number and automatically increment the number for you when a new row is inserted. Instead of an Identity column, the primary key is made up of a category prefix and a sequential number. This means that you must first determine the maximum number used in a category and then increment that number by 1 and use the new number and category prefix for the new key.

The first thing that you want to do in the btnAdd_Click event procedure is declare your local variables and objects that will be used here. The intPosition variable will be used to save the current record position, and the intMaxID variable will be used to set and increment the maximum sequential number for a category. The strID will be used to store the primary key from the authors table and to set the new key for the `authors` table. Finally, the `objCommand` object will be used to build a query to insert a new record into the `titleauthor` and `titles` tables.

Before you do anything, you want to save the position of the current record that you are on. This enables you to go back to this record once you reload the `DataView` object, which will contain the new record that you add in this procedure:

```
intPosition = objCurrencyManager.Position
```

You need to execute a command on the database to determine what ID to give your new title. You use a `SqlCommand` object to do this, passing in a SQL string and the connection that you use throughout your program. This SQL string selects the maximum value in the `title_id` column, in which the `title_id` value begins with the prefix of `DM`.

There is no category for demo, so you add all the test records under this category and use the category prefix of `DM`, enabling you to identify quickly the records that you have inserted just in case you want to get rid of them manually later.

Because the `MAX` function you use is an *aggregate function* (meaning that it is a function that works on groups of data), the data is returned without a column name. Therefore, you use the `AS` keyword in the `SELECT` statement and tell SQL Server to assign a column name to the value—in this case, `MaxID`. You use a `LIKE` clause in the `SELECT` statement to tell SQL Server to search for all values that begin with `DM`:

```
Dim maxIdCommand As SqlCommand = New SqlCommand( _
    "SELECT MAX(title_id) AS MaxID " &
    "FROM titles WHERE title_id LIKE 'DM%'", objConnection)
```

This sets up your command object but doesn't execute it. To execute it, you need to open the connection and then call one of the `SqlCommand` execute methods. In this case, you use `ExecuteScalar`:

```
' Open the connection, execute the command
objConnection.Open()
Dim maxId As Object = maxIdCommand.ExecuteScalar()
```

`ExecuteScalar` is a useful method when you have a database command that returns a single value. Other commands you've used so far have returned a whole table of values (you have used these as the `SelectCommand` of a data adapter) or no values at all (you have executed these with `ExecuteNonQuery`). In this case, you are interested in only one number, so you can use `ExecuteScalar`. This returns the first column of the first row in the result set. In this case, there is only one column and one row, so that is what you get.

You want to check for a `Null` value returned from the command, so you compare the resulting `Object` against the `Value` property of the `DBNull` class:

```
' If the MaxID column is null..
If maxId Is DBNull.Value Then
```

If the expression evaluates to `True`, you have no primary key in the `titles` table that begins with `DM`, so you set the initial value of the `intMaxID` variable to a value of `1000`. You choose `1000` because all the other primary keys contain a numeric value of less than `1000`:

```
' Set a default value of 1000..
intMaxID = 1000
```

If the column value evaluates to `False`, you have at least one primary key in the `titles` table that begins with `DM`. In this case, you need to obtain the integer portion of this ID to work out which integer to use for your ID. To do this, you must convert your `maxId` object to a `String`:

```
Else
    ' otherwise set the strID variable to the value in MaxID..
    strID = CType(maxId, String)
```

Then you can extract the integer portion of the key by using the `Remove` method of the string variable, `strID`. The `Remove` method removes the specified number of characters from a string. You specify the offset at which to begin removing characters and the number of characters to be removed. This method returns a new string with the removed characters. In this line of code, you are removing the prefix of `DM` from the string so that all you end up with is the integer portion of the string. You then use the `CType` function to convert the string value, which contains a number, to an `Integer` value, which you place in the `intMaxID` variable. Finally, you increment it by one to get the integer portion of the ID that you will use:

```
' Get the integer part of the string..
    intMaxID = CType(strID.Remove(0, 2), Integer)
    ' Increment the value..
    intMaxID += 1
End If
```

After you get the integer part, you build a new primary key in the `strID` variable by concatenating the numeric value contained in the `intMaxID` variable with the prefix `DM`:

```
' Finally, set the new ID..
strID = "DM" & intMaxID.ToString
```

Next, you build the SQL statements to insert a new row of data into the `titles` and `titleauthor` tables. If you look closely, there are two separate `INSERT` statements in the `CommandText` property of your `objCommand` object. The two `INSERT` statements are separated by a semicolon, which enables you to concatenate multiple SQL statements. The SQL statements that you build use placeholders that are filled in by the `SqlParameter` objects.

> **NOTE** Because of the relationship between the `titles` table and the `authors` table, you must first insert a new title for an author into the `titles` table and then insert the relationship between the title and the author in the `titleauthor` table. Your `INSERT` statements are specifying the columns that you want to insert data into and then the values that are to be inserted, some of which are represented by placeholders.

You have seen the properties of the `SqlCommand` object before. This time, however, you are using properties rather than the constructor. You set the `Connection` property to a `SqlConnection` object and then set the `CommandText` property to the SQL string that you want executed—in this case, the two separate `INSERT` statements:

```
objCommand.Connection = objConnection
objCommand.CommandText = "INSERT INTO titles " &
```

```
"(title_id, title, type, price, pubdate) " &
"VALUES(@title_id,@title,@type,@price,@pubdate);" &
"INSERT INTO titleauthor (au_id, title_id) " &
"VALUES(@au_id,@title_id)"
```

You then add entries to the `Parameters` collection property for each of your placeholders in the preceding SQL statements. Where the same parameter name is used twice in the `CommandText` property—as `title_id` is here—you need only one `SqlParameter` object:

```
' Add parameters for the placeholders in the SQL in the
' CommandText property..

' Parameter for the title_id column..
objCommand.Parameters.AddWithValue ("@title_id", strID)

' Parameter for the title column..
objCommand.Parameters.AddWithValue ("@title", txtBookTitle.Text)

' Parameter for the type column
objCommand.Parameters.AddWithValue ("@type", "Demo")

' Parameter for the price column..
objCommand.Parameters.AddWithValue _
    ("@price", txtPrice.Text).DbType = DbType.Currency

' Parameter for the pubdate column
objCommand.Parameters.AddWithValue ("@pubdate", Date.Now)

' Parameter for the au_id column..
objCommand.Parameters.AddWithValue ("@au_id", BindingContext _
    (objDataView).Current("au_id"))
```

For the `@title_id` parameter, you use the `strID` variable that you created and set earlier in this method. For the `@title` parameter, you use the text in the Book Title text box entered by the user. For the `@price` parameter, you use the text in the Price text box. However, the `Text` property is a `String`. SQL Server cannot automatically convert between a `String` and a `Currency` data type, so you specify that the parameter is of the `DbType.Currency` data type.

For `@au_id`, you need to use the ID of the currently selected author. There are no bound controls for the au_id column, so you need to use some code to obtain the value. Take a close look at that particular statement:

```
BindingContext(objDataView).Current("au_id")
```

Here you are getting the form's `BindingContext` for the `objDataView` data source, which is the one you're using for all your bound controls. When you're accessing a `DataView` through `BindingContext`, the `Current` property returns a `DataRowView` object. This object represents the view of the particular row that the user is currently looking at. You are then able to select a particular column from that row, thus giving you a specific value. Here, of course, you are obtaining the au_id column.

The remaining parameters indicate that the new record is a `Demo` record and timestamp the record with the current date and time:

```
' Parameter for the type column
objCommand.Parameters.AddWithValue ("@type", "Demo")

' Parameter for the pubdate column
```

```
objCommand.Parameters.AddWithValue ("@pubdate", Date.Now)
```

After you add all your parameters, you execute the command using the `ExecuteNonQuery` method. This causes your SQL statements to be executed and the data inserted. After your new data is inserted, you close the database connection.

This is the one spot in your code that is really subject to failure, so very basic error handling is included here. You execute your `INSERT` statement inside the `Try` block of your error handler, and if an error is encountered, the code in the `Catch` block is executed. The code there simply displays a message box that shows the error encountered:

```
' Execute the SqlCommand object to insert the new data..
Try
    objCommand.ExecuteNonQuery()
Catch SqlExceptionErr As SqlException
    MessageBox.Show(SqlExceptionErr.Message)
Finally
    ' Close the connection..
    objConnection.Close()
End Try
```

Then the `FillDataSetAndView` and `BindFields` procedures are called to reload the `DataView` object and to clear and rebind your controls. This ensures that all new data is added, updated, or deleted in the tables in SQL Server.

You then reposition the `DataView` object back to the record that was being displayed by setting the `Position` property of the `CurrencyManager` using the `intPosition` variable. This variable was set using the current record position at the beginning of this procedure.

> **NOTE** The position that you set here is only approximate. It does not take into account any records that have been inserted or deleted by someone else or you. It is possible that the title you just inserted for a specific author could be returned prior to the title that was displayed before. If you need more detailed control over the actual record position, you need to add more code to handle finding and displaying the exact record that was displayed; however, this is a topic beyond the scope of this book.
>
> After you reposition the record that is being displayed, you call the `ShowPosition` procedure to show the current record position.
>
> Finally, you display a message in the status bar indicating that the record has been added.

TRY IT OUT   Updating Records

In this Try It Out, you code the `btnUpdate_Click` procedure. This procedure is a little simpler because all you need to do is update existing records in the `titles` table. You do not have to add any new records, so you do not have to select any data to build a primary key.

1. To the `btnUpdate_Click` event procedure, add the following bold code:

```
Private Sub btnUpdate_Click(Sender As Object,
            E As EventArgs) Handles btnUpdate.Click
    ' Declare local variables and objects..
    Dim intPosition As Integer
    Dim objCommand As SqlCommand = New SqlCommand()

    ' Save the current record position..
    intPosition = objCurrencyManager.Position

    ' Set the SqlCommand object properties..
    objCommand.Connection = objConnection
    objCommand.CommandText = "UPDATE titles " &
        "SET title = @title, price = @price WHERE title_id = @title_id"
    objCommand.CommandType = CommandType.Text

    ' Add parameters for the placeholders in the SQL in the
    ' CommandText property..

    ' Parameter for the title field..
    objCommand.Parameters.AddWithValue ("@title", txtBookTitle.Text)

    ' Parameter for the price field..
    objCommand.Parameters.AddWithValue ("@price", txtPrice.Text).DbType _
        = DbType.Currency

    ' Parameter for the title_id field..
    objCommand.Parameters.AddWithValue _
        ("@title_id", BindingContext(objDataView).Current("title_id"))

    ' Open the connection..
    objConnection.Open()

    ' Execute the SqlCommand object to update the data..
    objCommand.ExecuteNonQuery()

    ' Close the connection..
    objConnection.Close()

    ' Fill the DataSet and bind the fields..
    FillDataSetAndView()
    BindFields()

    ' Set the record position to the one that you saved..
    objCurrencyManager.Position = intPosition

    ' Show the current record position..
    ShowPosition()

    ' Display a message that the record was updated..
    ToolStripLabel1.Text = "Record Updated"
End Sub
```

2. Run your project. You can update the price of the book that you have just added, or you can update the price of another book. Choose a book, change the price in the Price field, and then click the Update button.

When the record has been updated, you see the appropriate message in the status bar, and the record will still be the current record, as shown in Figure 13-12.

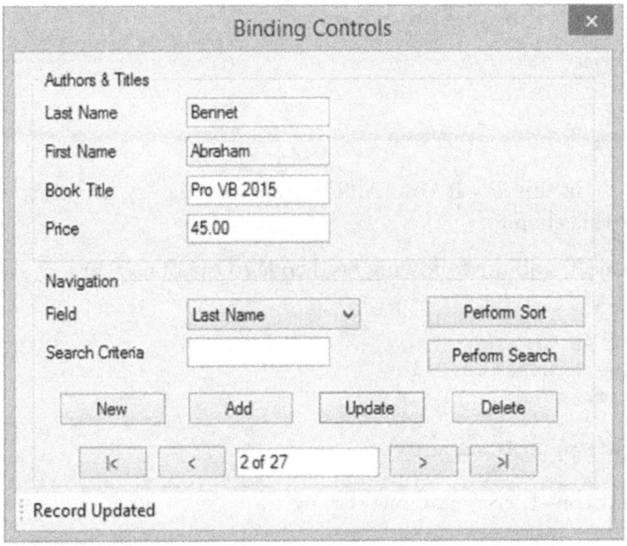

FIGURE 13-12

How It Works

As always, the first thing that you want to do is declare your variables and objects. You need one variable to save the current record position and one object for the SqlCommand object. Next, you save the current record position just as you did in the last procedure.

By adding the following code, you set the Connection property of the SqlCommand object using your objConnection object. Then you set the CommandText property using a SQL string. The SQL string here contains an UPDATE statement to update the Title and Price columns in the titles table. Note that there are three placeholders in this UPDATE statement: Two placeholders are for the title and price, and one is for the title_id in the WHERE clause:

```
' Set the SqlCommand object properties..
objCommand.Connection = objConnection
objCommand.CommandText = "UPDATE titles " &
    "SET title = @title, price = @price WHERE title_id = @title_id"
objCommand.CommandType = CommandType.Text
```

After you set the CommandText property, you set the CommandType property to indicate that this is a SQL string.

You need to add the appropriate parameters to the Parameters collection. The first parameter that you add is for the title column in your UPDATE statement. The title of the book is coming from the Text property of the txtBookTitle text box on your form.

The second parameter is for the price in your UPDATE statement. This parameter is used to update the price of a book, and the data is coming from the txtPrice text box on your form. You again need to set the DbType explicitly for this parameter.

This last parameter was for your WHERE clause in the UPDATE statement. The data for the Value property comes directly from the form's BindingContext, as the au_id did in the Adding Records example.

The rest of the procedure is similar to the btnAdd_Click event procedure.

TRY IT OUT Deleting Records

You code the final procedure, btnDelete_Click, in this Try It Out. All the code for this Try It Out is in the code file BindExample in the Zip file for this chapter.

1. To include delete functionality in your project, add the following bold code to the btnDelete_ Click event procedure:

```
Private Sub btnDelete_Click(Sender As Object,
                E As EventArgs) Handles btnDelete.Click
    ' Declare local variables and objects..
    Dim intPosition As Integer
    Dim objCommand As SqlCommand = New SqlCommand()

    ' Save the current record position–1 for the one to be
    ' deleted..
    intPosition = Me.BindingContext(objDataView).Position–1

    ' If the position is less than 0 set it to 0..
    If intPosition < 0 Then
        intPosition = 0
    End If

    ' Set the Command object properties..
    objCommand.Connection = objConnection
    objCommand.CommandText = "DELETE FROM titleauthor " &
            "WHERE title_id = @title_id;" &
            "DELETE FROM titles WHERE title_id = @title_id"

    ' Parameter for the title_id field..
    objCommand.Parameters.AddWithValue _
        ("@title_id", BindingContext(objDataView).Current("title_id"))

    ' Open the database connection..
    objConnection.Open()

    ' Execute the SqlCommand object to update the data..
    objCommand.ExecuteNonQuery()

    ' Close the connection..
    objConnection.Close()

    ' Fill the DataSet and bind the fields..
    FillDataSetAndView()
    BindFields()

    ' Set the record position to the one that you saved..
```

```
    Me.BindingContext(objDataView).Position = intPosition

    ' Show the current record position..
    ShowPosition()

    ' Display a message that the record was deleted..
    ToolStripLabel1.Text = "Record Deleted"
End Sub
```

2. To test this functionality, run your project, choose any book that you want to delete, and then click the Delete button. Before you delete a book, however, take note of the record count that appears on the form (see Figure 13-13). You may see an error because of a constraint in the database. This is because there is sales data for this book. Find the book you added; it will not have sales data associated with it.

FIGURE 13-13

After the delete has been performed, you will see one fewer record in the record count on the form.

How It Works

This procedure is a little more involved than the btnUpdate_Click procedure because of the relationship of titles to authors. Remember that there is a relationship table to join authors and titles. You must delete the row in the titleauthor relationship table before you can delete the row of data in the titles table. Therefore, you need two DELETE statements in your SQL string.

Note that this time after you declare your variables, you specify the Position property minus 1. This allows the user to be on the last record and delete it. You also allow the user to be on the first record as you check the value of the intPosition variable. If it is less than 0, you know that the user was on the first record, so you set it to 0; this means that when you restore the record position later, it is again on the first record.

Note also that you did not use the `CurrencyManager` object this time. Instead, you used the `BindingContext` object and specified the `objDataView` object as the object to be manipulated. Remember that the `BindingContext` object is automatically part of the form; there is nothing you need to do to add it. The `BindingContext` object is used here to demonstrate how to use it and so that you know that you do not have to use the `CurrencyManager` object to navigate the records contained in the `objDataView`:

```
' Declare local variables and objects..
Dim intPosition As Integer
Dim objCommand As SqlCommand = New SqlCommand()

' Save the current record position-1 for the one to be
' deleted..
intPosition = Me.BindingContext(objDataView).Position-1

' If the position is less than 0 set it to 0..
If intPosition < 0 Then
    intPosition = 0
End If
```

When you set the properties of your `SqlCommand` object, the SQL string specified in the `CommandText` property contains two `DELETE` statements separated by a semicolon. The first `DELETE` statement deletes the relationship between the `titles` and `authors` tables for the book being deleted. The second `DELETE` statement deletes the book from the `titles` table:

```
' Set the Command object properties..
objCommand.Connection = objConnection
objCommand.CommandText = "DELETE FROM titleauthor " &
    "WHERE title_id = @title_id;" &
    "DELETE FROM titles WHERE title_id = @title_id"
```

Again, you use a placeholder for the primary keys in `WHERE` clauses of your `DELETE` statements.

This statement uses only one placeholder. The next line sets it up in the normal way:

```
' Parameter for the title_id field..
 objCommand.Parameters.AddWithValue ("@title_id", _
     BindingContext(objDataView).Current("title_id"))
```

The rest of the code is the same as the code for the previous two methods, and should be familiar by now. That wraps up this project. It is hoped that you have gained some valuable knowledge about data binding and how to perform inserts, updates, and deletes using SQL to access a database.

Remember that error handling is a major part of any project. Except for one place in your code, it was omitted to conserve space. You also omitted data validation, so trying to insert a new record with no values could cause unexpected results and errors.

SUMMARY

This chapter covers a few very important ADO.NET classes, particularly the `SqlConnection`, `SqlDataAdapter`, `SqlCommand`, and `SqlParameter` classes. You saw firsthand how valuable these classes can be when selecting, inserting, updating, and deleting data. These particular classes are specifically for accessing SQL Server.

You also saw the DataSet and DataView classes from the System.Data namespace put to use, and you used both of these classes to create objects that were bound to the controls on your forms. Of particular interest to this discussion is the DataView object because it provides the functionality to sort and search data. The DataView class provides the most flexibility between the two classes because you can also present a subset of data from the DataSet in the DataView.

You saw how easy it is to bind the controls on your form to the data contained in either the DataSet or the DataView. You also learned how to manage the navigation of the data in these objects with the CurrencyManager class. This class provides quick and easy control over navigation.

This chapter has demonstrated using manual control over the navigation of data on the form and manual control over the insertion, update, and deletion of data in a data store. You should use the techniques that you learned in this chapter when you need finer control of the data, especially when dealing with complex table relationships such as you have dealt with here.

To summarize, after reading this chapter you should:

➤ Feel comfortable using the ADO.NET classes discussed in this chapter.

➤ Know when to use the DataSet class and when to use the DataView class.

➤ Know how to bind controls on your form manually to either a DataSet or a DataView object.

➤ Know how to use the CurrencyManager class to navigate the data in a DataSet or DataView object.

➤ Know how to sort and search for data in a DataView object.

EXERCISES

1. What properties do you need to set for a SQL Server connection string when passing a username and password?

2. Which method do you execute when updating data using a SQLCommand object?

3. Why would you use Integrated Security in your connection string?

4. If you do not need to create update/delete/insert commands, how do you have them created automatically?

5. What method do you use to populate a dataset with data?

▶ **WHAT YOU LEARNED IN THIS CHAPTER**

TOPIC	CONCEPTS
Installing SQL Server	Where to find a version of SQL Server to download and install.
Using `SQLConnection`, `SQLDataAdapter`, `SQLCommand`, `SQLParameter` **classes**	Use these common ADO.NET classes to insert, update, read, and delete data.
Working with `DataSet` **and** `DataView` **classes**	Getting data from the database. Binding to controls and sorting data.
Navigating and updating data on a form	Using the `CurrencyManager` and `BindingContext` to navigate through bound data on a form. Within the same example, use the controls along with ADO.NET classes to add, update, and delete data.

14

ASP.NET

WHAT YOU WILL LEARN IN THIS CHAPTER:

➤ A basic overview of web applications (thin-client applications), including the advantages of Web Forms versus Windows Forms

➤ Understanding web servers, browsers, HTML, JavaScript, and CSS

➤ Understanding the benefits of ASP.NET web pages, special web-site files, development, and the control Toolbox

➤ Gaining an understanding of tools for data validation, navigation, security, data entry, and look and feel

WROX.COM CODE DOWNLOADS FOR THIS CHAPTER

The wrox.com code downloads for this chapter are found at www.wrox.com/ begvisualbasic2015 on the Download Code tab. The code is in the 092117 C14.zip download and individually named according to the names given throughout the chapter.

As we look to the future, the Internet is sure to increase its presence in business, so it follows that developers need to gain knowledge of building robust, dynamic websites. In this chapter, you will learn about building Web Forms applications. You will focus on the basics for website development and moving to database-driven applications. With Visual Studio 2015, you will be building data-driven sites in no time.

Visual Studio 2015 is the best tool for creating ASP.NET sites on the market today. It provides you with the best IntelliSense, debugging, and control library to create websites written in Visual Basic. You can build ASP.NET websites (sometimes referred to as Web Forms applications), web services, and even sites targeted for mobile devices in Visual Studio 2015. In addition, you do not need IIS or any web server to host your site with Visual Studio 2015; ASP .NET Development Server is a tool included with Visual Studio that you can use to host your sites while developing them.

> **NOTE** *Before you get your first look at the code, you will have a short lesson on the building blocks developers use to create web applications.*

THIN-CLIENT ARCHITECTURE

In previous chapters, you have seen thick-client applications in the form of Windows Forms applications. Most of the processing is completed by the client application you built earlier, and many of the applications stood on their own and needed no other applications or servers. In web development, conversely, most of the processing is completed on the server and then the result is sent to the browser.

When you develop Web Forms applications, you do not have to distribute anything to the user. Any user who can access your web server and has a web browser can be a user. You must be careful with the amount of processing you place on the client. When you design a thin-client system, you must be aware that your users or customers will use different clients to access your application. If you try to use too much processing on the client, it may cause problems for some users. This is one of the major differences between Windows and Web Forms applications. You will learn about the major difference between these two types of Visual Studio 2015 applications later in this chapter.

When dealing with a Windows Forms application, you have a compiled program that must be distributed to the users' desktop before they can use it. Depending upon the application, there may also be one or more supporting dynamic link libraries (DLLs) or other executables that also need to be distributed along with the application.

In thin-client architecture, there is typically no program or DLL to be distributed. Users merely need to start their browsers and enter the URL of the application website. The server hosting the website is responsible for allocating all resources that the web application requires. The client is a navigation tool that displays the results the server returns.

All code required in a thin-client application stays in one central location: the server hosting the website. Any updates to the code are immediately available the next time a user requests a web page.

Thin-client architecture provides several key benefits. First and foremost is the cost of initial distribution of the application—there is none. In traditional client/server architecture, the program would have to be distributed to every client who wanted to use it, which could be quite a time-consuming task if the application is used in offices throughout the world.

Another major benefit is the cost of distributing updates to the application—again, there is none. All updates to the website and its components are distributed to the web server. Once an update is made, it is immediately available to all users the next time they access the updated web page. In traditional client/server architecture, the updated program would have to be distributed to every client, and the updates could take days or weeks to roll out. Thin-client architecture allows a new version of an application to be distributed instantly to all the users without having to touch a single desktop.

Another major benefit is that you can make changes to the back-end architecture and not have to worry about the client. Suppose, for example, that you want to change the location of the database from a low-end server to a new high-end server. The new server would typically have a new machine name. In a traditional client/server application, the machine name of the database server is stored in the code or Registry setting. You would need to modify either the code or the Registry setting for every person who uses the application. In thin-client architecture, you simply need to update the setting of the web server to point to the new database server and you are in business, and so are all of the clients.

You can see that in a thin-client architecture model, any client with a browser can access your website and immediately have access to updates. In fact, if your changes were transparent to the user, the client wouldn't even know that changes had been made.

Now that you have a basic understanding of thin-client architecture, let's look at how Web Forms work.

WEB FORMS VERSUS WINDOWS FORMS

In this section, you will get an overview of the advantages of both Windows Forms and Web Forms. This will give you an idea of when you build each type of application to solve a customer's problem. You will almost always have to choose between these two types of architecture when building solutions, so it is important to understand some of the advantages of both.

Windows Forms Advantages

Windows Forms applications have advantages in some types of systems. Typically, applications that require a responsive interface, such as a point-of-sale system at a retail store, are Windows Forms applications. Also, in most cases, processor-intensive applications such as games or graphics programs are better suited to a Windows Forms program.

A major advantage of Windows Forms is trust. When a user installs the application, it is given trust in the current zone. With this high-enough level of trust, you can store data and state about the current session on the local computer. The user can run the application, and it can interact with the local file system or Registry seamlessly. To avoid things like DOS (Denial of Service) attacks, trust is very limited, however, for an Internet application.

Another advantage is having control over the client application. This allows you to build a very powerful, rich user interface. As you will see, numerous controls are not available to a Web Form (although this is becoming less of a difference) to permit the developer to create user-friendly applications. Windows Forms allow for a more ample user interface.

Also, application responsiveness is an advantage with Windows Forms. With most or all of the processing being done on the client, the need to send data over the wire can be reduced. Any amount of data sent to servers can cause latency. For an application running locally on a computer, the normal events are handled more quickly. In addition, the speed of data transmission over a local network is much faster than the typical Internet connection. This speed enables data to move across the wire faster and create less of a bottleneck for the user.

Web Forms Advantages

Although the advantages of Web Forms may seem to be greater than the advantages of Windows Forms, don't permit this to transform you into a full-time web developer for every project. There will always be times when Windows Forms are a better solution.

The greatest advantage of a web application is distribution. To distribute a Web Forms application, just install it on the web server. That's it. There's no need to create an installation for every version of Windows, or ship CDs. When you make a change, just publish the change to the web server; and the next time customers access the site, they will use the latest application.

Version control, or change control, is another advantage. With all your application code at the same location, making changes is a breeze. You never have to worry about one user on version 8 and another on version 10; all users access the same application. As soon as you publish a change, all users see the update—with no user intervention necessary.

You may be familiar with the term *platform independence*. Web applications have it. It doesn't matter what type of computer the user has—as long as there is a browser and a connection to your web server, the user can access your application. There is no need to build application versions for different operating systems.

These advantages can add up to many thousands of dollars of savings compared with a Windows application. Being able to make quick changes and maintain one code base are great advantages. Still, there are times when a web application will not provide an adequate user experience. Make sure you evaluate both options for every project. Now, let's look more closely at Web Forms development.

WEB APPLICATIONS: THE BASIC PIECES

In its simplest form, a web application is just a number of web pages. In order for the user to access the web pages, there must be a web server and browser. A request is made by the browser for the page on the server. The server then processes the web page and returns the output to the browser. The user sees the page inside the browser window. The pages that the users see may contain *HyperText Markup Language (HTML)*, *Cascading Style Sheets (CSS)*, and client-side script. Finally, the page displays in the browser for the user. This section presents a basic overview of each piece of the system.

Web Servers

There are many web servers on the market today. The most well-known web servers in use today are Microsoft *Internet Information Services (IIS)* and Apache. For this book, you will focus exclusively on IIS.

Browsers

Every user of a Web Forms application must have a browser. The most popular browsers are Microsoft Internet Explorer (IE), Firefox, and Chrome. Microsoft is bringing an end to IE with Windows 10, and the new Edge browser is sure to be a player for web applications soon. When you develop public websites, you must be aware that the site may render differently in each browser. You will find that IE is the most lenient when it comes to valid HTML; and we will focus on IE10 for this book. The controls you use in Visual Studio will render browser-specific code to make your applications appear correctly in each browser. You still need to test each version your users will use to access your application.

Recently, the use of mobile phones and tablets has created more concerns for web developers; developers may find it hard to create a site that is user friendly for desktop users as well as mobile users. You need to determine whether you will support these mobile devices with small screens, remembering that you can build separate sites that provide the best user experience or just let mobile users see the main web application on a small screen.

HyperText Markup Language

Also known as *HTML*, *HyperText Markup Language* is the presentation, or design layout, of the web page. HTML is a tag-based language that allows you to change the presentation of information. For example, to make text bold in HTML, just place the `<strong>` tag around the text. The following text is an example of HTML:

```
<p>This is <strong>bold</strong> in HTML.</p>
```

If the previous text is then rendered by a browser, it would be displayed like this:

This is **bold** in HTML.

Browsers will interpret HTML and should conform to the standards from the World Wide Web Consortium (W3C). The W3C was created to develop common protocols for the web in the 1990s. You can read more about the W3C at its website: www.w3.org.

Although VS 2015 allows you to design ASP.NET websites without firsthand knowledge of HTML, you gain experience with hands-on exercises creating web pages with HTML later in the chapter.

JavaScript

A major part of web development is client-side script. If you are creating an application for the public that uses client-side script, you need to use JavaScript for support in all browsers. VBScript is a Microsoft-centric language that is more like Visual Basic syntax and slowly going away. You may see it in old code. Just know that it is supported only by Internet Explorer. You will probably never create new code using VBScript for client-side scripting.

Client-side scripting is typically used for data validation and dynamic HTML (DHTML). Validation scripts enforce rules that may require the user to complete a field on the screen before continuing. DHTML scripts allow the page to change programmatically after it is in memory on the browser. Expanding menus is an example of DHTML. Currently, IE supports more DHTML than is required by the W3C, so you may have to create DHTML for each target browser.

One of the great features of Visual Studio 2015 is the validation and navigation controls. You can drag these controls onto your web page without writing any client-side script. In most instances, you can manage with these controls, but for others you will need to be self-sufficient in the creation of client-side script. For this reason, you will write some of your own scripts later in this chapter.

Cascading Style Sheets

Cascading style sheets (CSS) allow for the separation of layout and style from the content of a web page. You can use CSS to change fonts, colors, alignment, and many other aspects of web page presentation. The best thing about CSS is that it can be applied to an entire site. By using a master CSS page, you can easily maintain and quickly change the look and feel of the entire website by changing one page. You will learn more about CSS in this chapter.

ACTIVE SERVER PAGES

With Visual Studio 2015, you create websites using Active Server Pages (ASP) or ASP.NET. This makes it easy to create dynamic, data-driven websites. This section explains the features and benefits of ASPX or Web Forms.

Benefits of ASP.NET Web Pages

When you create web applications, you could use many solutions. The most common types of pages are Active Server Pages (`.asp` and `.aspx`), JavaServer Pages (`.jsp`), Cold Fusion Pages (`.cfm`), Hypertext Preprocessor (`.php`), and basic HTML (`.htm` or `.html`). This book mainly focuses on ASPX, but you will also see some HTML.

Execution time is one benefit for which ASP.NET stands out above the rest. When an ASP.NET page is requested the first time, a compiled copy is placed into memory on the server for the next request. This offers great performance gains over interpreted languages.

Using Visual Studio 2015 to design your applications also makes a big difference in productivity. The .NET Framework supplies thousands of namespaces, objects, and controls for use in developing Web Forms applications. In addition, ASP.NET also supports all .NET-compatible languages. By default, Visual Basic and C# are available in Visual Studio 2015.

Special Website Files

When you work with ASP.NET, you will see many special files. These files are very important, and each could have an entire chapter written about it. The two files discussed here, `global.asax` and `web.config`, enable you to make site-wide changes from one location. There is much more to learn about them than we can present in a single chapter, and you can do research at `http://www.msdn.com`.

Global.asax

The `global.asax` file allows you to add code to certain application-level events. The most common events are `Application_Start`, `Application_End`, `Session_Start`, `Session_End`, and `Application_Error`. The application start and end events fire when the actual web application inside of IIS changes state. The application start event will fire with the first request to a website after the server or IIS is restarted. The session events fire on a per-user/browser session on the web server. When you save data to the user's session, you must be careful. This data will be saved for every user/browser who is browsing the application, which can create an extra load on the server. You can use the final event, `Application_Error`, to log all unhandled exceptions in one common place. Make sure to redirect users to a friendly error page after logging the error.

Web.config

`Web.config` is exactly what it appears to be—a configuration file for the web application; it is an XML document. You can update many application settings for security, errors, and much, much more. In most production apps, you store your connection string to the database here.

Development

As you build Web Forms applications in Visual Studio 2015, you will work in the integrated development environment (IDE) that you are familiar with from Windows Forms applications. As you work with web pages, you have the option to use what is known as a *code-behind page*. This enables you to keep your application logic separate from the presentation code. You have three views to work from: Design, Source, and Code view, the common ways to build applications. Design and Source view are for the `.aspx` page that contains the user interface and data validation. Code view is the `.vb` file that is the code-behind page. Visual Studio 2015 makes creating websites an easy task.

Controls: The Toolbox

The default controls you will use to build web applications are all in the Toolbox. If you do not see the Toolbox, press Ctrl+Alt+X to view it. The controls are organized by category. The standard category, along with its controls, is shown in Figure 14-1.

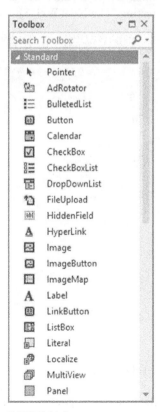

FIGURE 14-1

BUILDING WEBSITES

In this section, you will create a small web application demonstrating different aspects of web development. In accomplishing this, you will see how the basics of Web Forms applications work.

Creating a Web Form for Client- and Server-Side Processing

The Web Form in this Try It Out contains HTML and server controls. The HTML controls have client-side processing, and the server controls process the code on the server.

TRY IT OUT Server- and Client-Side Processing

This example will introduce you to your first custom website. All the code for this Try It Out is in the `Client_ServerProcessing` folder in the Zip file for this chapter.

1. Start this project by choosing File ➪ New Web Site. Make sure that Visual Basic is the language and select ASP.NET Web Forms Site. For the Web Location, be sure the drop-down box is set to File System and enter *[The default path for VS 2015]* `\Client_ServerProcessing`. A default path for Windows 8 will look like `C:\Users\bryan\Documents\`
`Visual Studio 2015\WebSites\Client_ServerProcessing`. Click OK to create a file system site that will use the built-in development web server for testing. The New Web Site dialog will look like Figure 14-2.

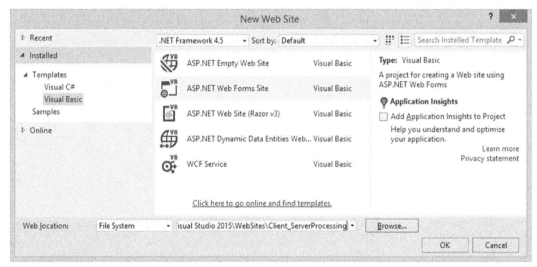

FIGURE 14-2

2. Visual Studio will create the default folders and files for the website. Take a look at the `Default.aspx`, shown in Figure 14-3. The `Default.aspx` page will be open in the IDE. The page already has a master page and default design created. You will learn more about master pages later in this chapter.

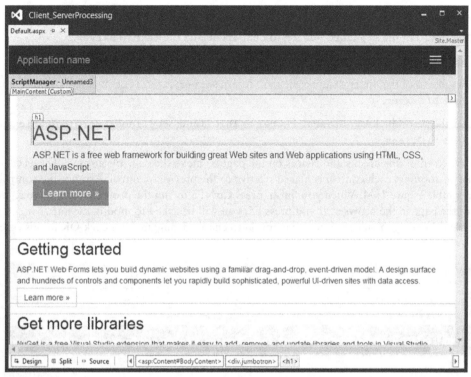

FIGURE 14-3

3. Remove the content inside the Content control. This is the control named MainContent. Click inside of the content, press Ctrl+A, and then click Delete. Next, you will add controls to MainContent while in Design mode. (To get to Design mode, while viewing the .aspx page, click the Design option on the lower left corner of the pane, or simply press Shift+F7.) You are only allowed to add controls inside of the content only because the page has a master page. Do not worry about the position of the controls for now, but make sure you use controls from the Standard and HTML tabs on the Toolbox.

> **NOTE** *The area at the bottom of the* Default.aspx *page that has Design, Split, Source, and may have other HTML tags on the right is known as the* tag navigator.

When adding the following controls to the form, you can arrange them in any order you want for now. To make designing the layout easier, put your cursor inside MainContent and press your Enter key five or six times. This will add space to your work area. This is a basic way to lay out your pages, and normally you would use either CSS layout or table layout for your websites. You will learn more about layout later in this chapter.

➤ From the Standard controls tab, add one Button and two Label controls.

➤ From the HTML controls tab, add one Input (Button) control.

4.   Change the properties of the controls as follows (see Figure 14-4 as a guide):

➤   Set the ID of the Standard:Button to **btnServer** and the Text to **Server**.

➤   Set the ID of the HTML:Input (Button) to **btnClient** and the value to **Client**.

➤   Set the ID of the upper Standard:Label to **lblServer**; set ClientIDMode to **Static** and the Text to **Server**.

➤   Set the ID of the lower Standard:Label to **lblClient**; set ClientIDMode to **Static** and the Text to **Client**.

5.   You have to enter line breaks and spaces on the page to move the controls around. This is called *relative positioning*; each control is placed relative to the previous control. Arrange the controls so they resemble Figure 14-4. When you finish, press Ctrl+F5 to run the project without debugging and see the page in the browser. If you press F5, you will be asked to modify the web.config page to enable debugging. You can choose the option to enable debugging and click OK in this case.

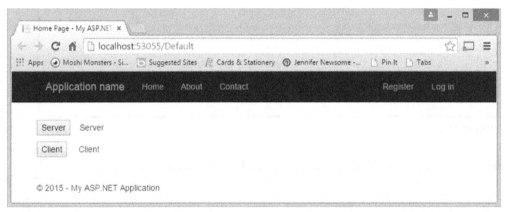

FIGURE 14-4

6.   Close the browser and go back to Visual Studio 2015. Double-click btnServer to jump to the btnServer_Click event handler. Depending on your settings, you will be either on the code-behind page or working in the source of the .aspx page. Add the following bolded code to the event:

```
Protected Sub btnServer_Click(sender As Object,
    e As EventArgs) Handles btnServer.Click
    lblServer.Text = "Changed"
End Sub
```

Run the program again and test the button's Click event. The label will display Changed after you click the Server button.

7.   Close the browser and go back to Visual Studio 2015. Create an event handler for the HTML Input (Button) and add a title to the page. (Make sure you have the Default.aspx page open in the IDE and that the Properties window has DOCUMENT selected.) To add a title, find the Title property

and set it to **My First Page**. On the tag navigator, click Source to change to HTML view. Add the following code below the page directive at the top of the page. This will start as the second line of code on the page. Note that JavaScript is case sensitive:

```
<asp:Content runat="server" ID="HeadContent"
    ContentPlaceHolderID="HeadContent">
    <script lang="javascript" type="text/javascript">
        function btnClient_onclick() {
            document.getElementById("lblClient").innerText =
                "Changed";
            document.getElementById("lblServer").innerText =
                "Server";
        }
    </script>
<</asp:Content>
```

You will see an error now. To resolve the error, open the Site.Master page and add the following code just above the `</head>`.

```
<asp:ContentPlaceHolder runat="server" ID="HeadContent" />
```

8. Next, find the HTML for `btnClient` and add the `onclick` event as shown in bold.

```
<input id="btnClient" type="button" value="Client"
    onclick="return btnClient_onclick();" />
```

9. Run the project again by pressing Ctrl+F5. Test both buttons.

How It Works

Now you can see that Web Forms development is very similar to Windows Forms development. This is one of the benefits of .NET development and Visual Studio 2015. Microsoft has made it easy for any developer to switch from client server to Web to Windows development with only a small learning curve.

First, consider the HTML source. The first line of code is the `Page` directive:

```
<%@ Page Title="My First Page" Language="VB"
    MasterPageFile="~/Site.Master" AutoEventWireup="true"
    CodeFile="Default.aspx.vb" Inherits="_Default" %>
```

Depending on the mode you develop in, you may see different default attributes set by Visual Studio 2015.

The `Page` directive has more than 30 attributes that can be set. Only the default attributes are discussed here, but if you want to explore the rest, search for **@Page** in the help files for VS 2015 or on the web.

Take a look at the default attributes in the `Default.aspx` page. First is `Title`. This is the title of the page displayed in the browser. Then you see the `Language` attribute, which is set to the language that all server code will compile into. Then there is `MasterPageFile`. This is the master page file used by the web page (you'll learn more about master pages later in the chapter). `AutoEventWireup` is the next attribute. Visual Studio 2015 sets this attribute to `true`. If you leave this attribute out of the `Page` directive, the default value is `true`. If you set this to `false` you have to manually hook up events like page load, and the code is more complex. Next is the `CodeFile` attribute. This is the page that contains the code when using a separate code file or the code-behind page. Finally, there is the `Inherits` attribute, which is simply the class name from which the page will inherit.

The JavaScript for client button click is next. The only event is the `OnClick` event of the `btnClient` control. Client side code is added to the HeadContent based on the master page. When you click the client button, this procedure executes. The first line of the subroutine uses the `getElementById` function to find the object in the document that has an `ID` of `lblClient`. Once it is found, the `innerText` is set to `Changed`. The same function is used to find the `lblServer` object on the next line. The `innerText` is then changed to `Server`. This is added to reset the Server button's label.

```
<asp:Content runat="server" ID="HeadContent"
    ContentPlaceHolderID="HeadContent">
    <script lang="javascript" type="text/javascript">
        function btnClient_onclick() {
            document.getElementById("lblClient").innerText =
                "Changed";
            document.getElementById("lblServer").innerText =
                "Server";
        }
    </script>
</asp:Content>
```

You added a placeholder to the master page to clear an error and allow the code to run. Without a placeholder, you are not allowed to add code to a page that is using a master page.

What you may not notice is the difference in the way each button performs event handling. It is hard to notice when running locally, but go back to the web page and watch the status bar of the browser while you click each button. When you click the Server button, the page actually calls the web server to process the event.

The Client button did not call back to the server; the browser handled the event itself. `ClientIDMode` is where you can set the behavior of the ID you will use in your script. Using `Static` will force the control's ID to be the client ID. You should be careful not to duplicate names in controls when using `Static`.

Now move to the `BodyContent` tag. This is where you added the controls:

```
<asp:Content ID="BodyContent" runat="server"
    ContentPlaceHolderID="MainContent">
```

When you click the Server button, the contents of the form are actually submitted to the server.

> **NOTE** You can look at the HTML source sent to the browser by choosing View ⇨ Source from the IE menu.

btnServer is a submit button. The function of a submit button is to pass form-data back to a web server.

The final portion of the code on the Default.aspx page is the markup for the controls. These are the controls you placed onto the design area of the form:

```
<br />
    <asp:Button ID="btnServer" runat="server" Text="Server" />
      
    <asp:Label ID="lblServer" runat="server" Text="Server"
        ClientIDMode="Static">
    </asp:Label>
    <br />
    <br />
    <input id="btnClient" type="button" value="Client"
        onclick="return btnClient_onclick()" />   
    <asp:Label ID="lblClient"
        runat="server" Text="Client" ClientIDMode="Static">
        </asp:Label>
    <br />
    <br />
</asp:Content>
```

Finally, look at the Default.aspx.vb page. In the code for the OnClick event of the btnServer control, you set the text of the label to Changed:

```
Partial Class _Default
    Inherits Page

    Protected Sub btnServer_Click(sender As Object,
        e As EventArgs) Handles btnServer.Click
        lblServer.Text = "Changed"
    End Sub

End Class
```

You have completed your first ASP.NET page. In this exercise, you saw a few basic controls and learned that client and server code are handled differently. In the next section, you will learn where you can host websites with Visual Studio 2015.

Website Locations with VS 2015

When you create a new site, you have a choice of locations for the site. The example in this chapter uses the File System location for the website, as shown in Figure 14-5. One advantage of this location is that the web server is not accessible to external users.

There are other ways to work with website projects, as you can see in the left panel of the Choose Location window. The first is using Local IIS (see Figure 14-6).

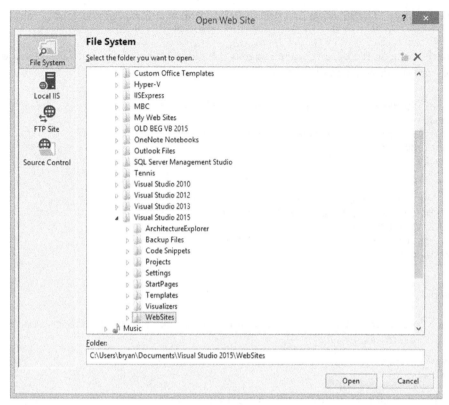

FIGURE 14-5

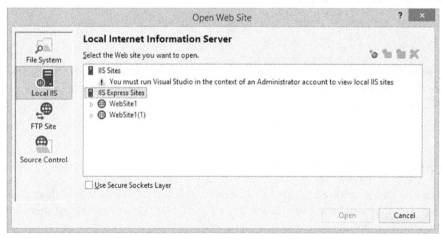

FIGURE 14-6

If you have a local web server, you can host your application there. This allows others to see the site and test it. The second option is to use an FTP site. In this case, you are most likely using a hosting company. All you have to do is add the location and authentication information, and you can code your application on the production server. You can see the setup screen for an FTP site in Figure 14-7.

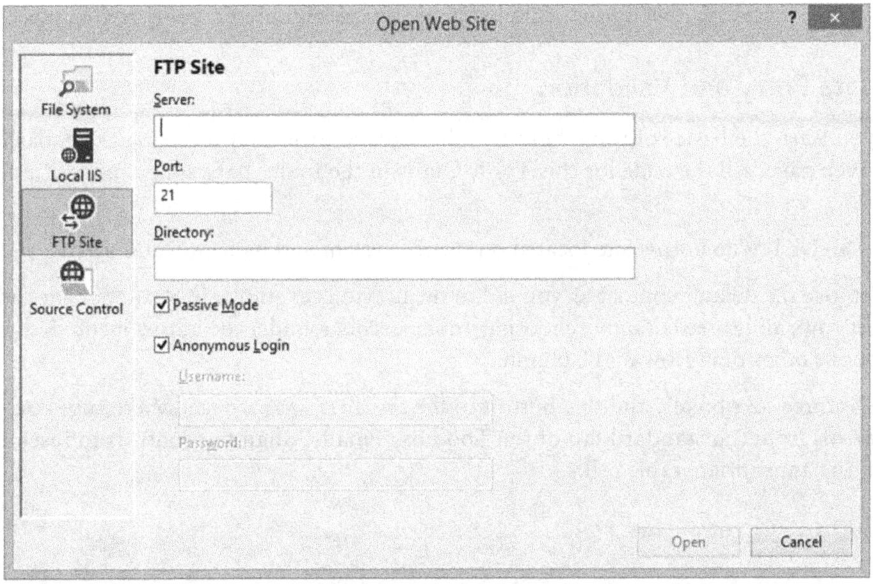

FIGURE 14-7

The final option is a source control. In a large development shop, you will likely work out of a source control, Team Foundation Server. In this case, you can open a website from Team Foundation Server directly. Also, with Visual Studio Online you can have free source control for a small development team now. You just have to add the connection info to your server so you can use this option, as shown in Figure 14-8.

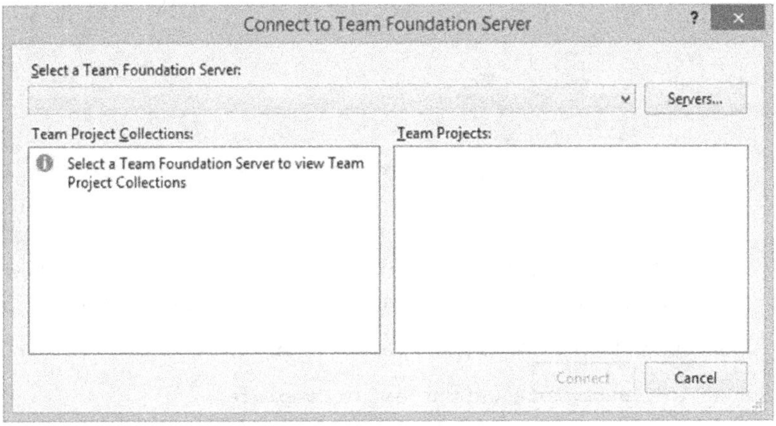

FIGURE 14-8

Performing Data Entry and Validation

One of the basic functions of almost every website is to gather some kind of information from the user. You have undoubtedly seen screens that have links such as Contact Us or Create an Account. Anywhere you see a text box on a web page, data entry and validation are probably taking place.

TRY IT OUT Data Entry and Validation

In this Try It Out, you learn the basics of using built-in validation controls and accessing the data the user enters into the web page. All the code for this Try It Out is in the folder `DataEntry` in the Zip file for this chapter.

1. Create a new ASP.NET Web Forms Site located on the file system and name it **DataEntry**.

2. You need to remove the default content as you did in the previous example. In `MainContent`, add a table with eight rows and three columns, choosing `Insert Table` under the `Table` menu. Keep all the default options other than Row and Column.

3. Add four labels, three text boxes, and one button to the `Default.aspx` page. Make sure you use server controls from the Standard tab of the Toolbox. Finally, align the controls to resemble Figure 14-9 in the appropriate table cell.

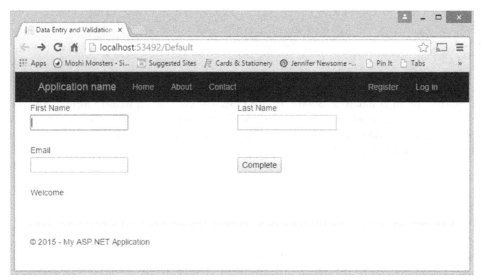

FIGURE 14-9

4. Set the properties of the eight controls and the document. You may want to use the Source view to make the changes to the control properties, because it is easier to make changes in this mode.

> Set the `Title` of the `Document` to **Data Entry** and **Validation**.

> Set the `ID` of the `Button` to **btnComplete** and the `Text` to **Complete**.

> Set the `ID` of the upper left `TextBox` to **txtFirstName**.

➤ Set the ID of the upper right TextBox to **txtLastName**.

➤ Set the ID of the lower TextBox to **txtEmail**.

➤ Set the Text of the upper left Label to **First Name**.

➤ Set the Text of the upper right Label to **Last Name**.

➤ Set the Text of the middle Label to **Email**.

➤ Set the Text of the lower Label to **Welcome** and the ID to **lblWelcome**.

5. Test the page by pressing Ctrl+F5. When the page opens, you will test three items. First, enter your name and email address and then click the Complete button. The page will post back to the server, and the HTML returned will still have your data in the text boxes. This is default behavior known as *view state*. Second, type the text **<SCRIPT>alert "Hi"</SCRIPT>** into the First Name text box and click Complete. You will see the error message shown in Figure 14-10. ASP.NET has a feature called *request validation* that checks for any dangerous input from the user unless you explicitly turn it off.

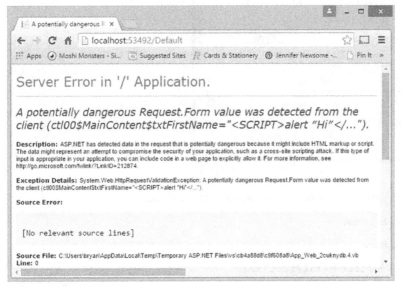

FIGURE 14-10

6. It is time to do something with the data the user enters. First, you need to open the code-behind page. The easiest way to do this is to press F7. Next, add an event handler for page load. To do this, select (Page Events) from the Objects combo box on the left and Load from the Events combo box. Add the following bolded code to update lblWelcome with the data input:

```
Protected Sub Page_Load(sender As Object,
        e As EventArgs) Handles Me.Load
    If Page.IsPostBack Then
        'If this is a postback and not the initial page load
```

```
              'Display the data to the user
              Me.lblWelcome.Text = "Hello" + Me.txtFirstName.Text + " " +
              Me.txtLastName.Text + "<BR>" + "Your email address is" +
              Me.txtEmail.Text
      End If
End Sub
```

7. Add validation to the input. Visual Studio has built-in controls just for this. To see the controls, switch to `Default.aspx`. From the Toolbox, select the Validation tab, which includes pre-built controls to assist with data validation. Add two RequiredFieldValidator controls and one ValidationSummary control to the form. Align the controls similar to Figure 14-11.

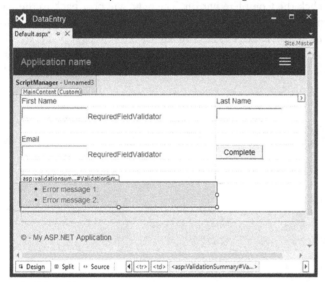

FIGURE 14-11

8. Set the following properties for the first `RequiredFieldValidator`:

   ➤ Set ID to **rfvFirstName**.

   ➤ Set Display to **None**.

   ➤ Set ControlToValidate to **txtFirstName**.

   ➤ Set ErrorMessage to **First name is required**.

9. Set the following properties for the second `RequiredFieldValidator`:

   ➤ Set ID to **rfvEmail**.

   ➤ Set Display to **None**.

   ➤ Set ControlToValidate to **txtEmail**.

   ➤ Set ErrorMessage to **Email is required**.

   ➤ Set ValidationSummary's ID to **ValidationSummary**.

      Your page should look like Figure 14-11 when you finish.

10. Run your project and try to submit blank entries for first name and email. You will see two error messages similar to those displayed in Figure 14-12.

> **NOTE** *This quick example explains how easy data validation is in ASP .NET. Other controls are available for enforcing data validation. The CompareValidator control tests a control to ensure that it matches a value. This value can be a constant, another control, or even a value from a data store. RangeValidator tests whether a value is within a specified range. For example, you can test to ensure that a person is between 18 and 35 years old.*

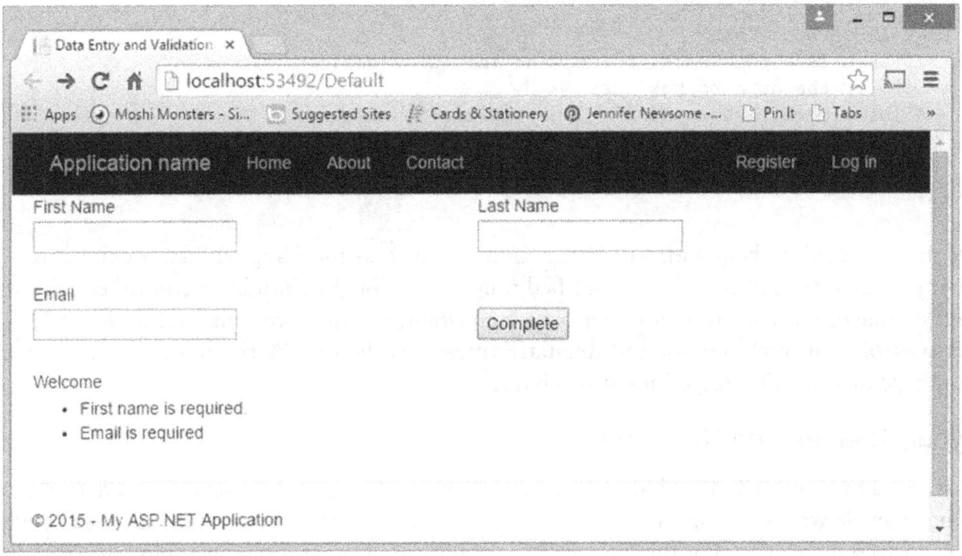

FIGURE 14-12

How It Works

Without writing any code, you can require that data entry fields are completed on a web page. You take advantage of controls already created for quick and hearty data validation.

You use the RequiredFieldValidator control to make sure the user entered data. You set a couple of properties on the control. You set the `ErrorMessage` to a string that displays in the ValidationSummary control. Setting `Display="None"` causes the error message not to be shown inside of the RequiredFieldValidator control. The required property, `ControlToValidate`, is set to the ID of the control that was required.

```
<asp:RequiredFieldValidator ID="rfvFirstName" runat="server"
    ControlToValidate="txtFirstName" Display="None"
    ErrorMessage="First name is required.">
</asp:RequiredFieldValidator>
```

You use the ValidationSummary control as a central location for displaying all error messages. If you decide not to use a summary object, you could set the `Display` property of the individual validation controls to `Static` or `Dynamic`. That way, the error messages are displayed within the validation control. No property changes are needed to use the ValidationSummary control. You just add it to the form at the location you want to display validation messages.

```
<asp:ValidationSummary ID="ValidationSummary" runat="server" />
```

The only code you write is added to the `Page_Load` event. Here, you tested for a postback using the `IsPostBack` property of the `Page` object. A *postback* is when a server control is used to send data back to the server. If it was a postback, you display the name and email entered by the user. You can still use the `Page_Load` event in VS 2015. To insert the event automatically, go into Design view on the ASPX page and double-click the page (not on any controls). The event will be generated, and you will be brought to the new event in the code-behind.

```
If Page.IsPostBack Then
    'If this is a post back and not the initial page load
    'Display the data to the user
    Me.lblWelcome.Text = "Hello" + Me.txtFirstName.Text + " " +
    Me.txtLastName.Text + "<BR>" + "Your email address is" +
    Me.txtEmail.Text
End If
```

There are more controls to help with validation. Controls such as the RangeValidator can be used to ensure that the value entered is within a specified range. The CompareValidator control enables you to compare the value of one control to another or to a constant. For more complex validation, there are two other controls: CustomValidator and RegularExpressionValidator. With these, you can basically handle any type of validation requirement you have.

Site Layout, Themes, and Navigation

In the past, a major drawback of web development was maintaining a consistent design across an entire site in a manageable way. Developers created user controls and inserted server-side includes in every page to try to accomplish this. For the most part, this worked. The hard part was ensuring that the opening tags that were in certain include files were closed in the pages that included them. Another cause of frustration for the designer was making sure that all user controls or include files appeared in the same location. This took time, and with every changed page, someone had to make sure the entire site looked okay. Today, Visual Studio provides the tools you need to maintain a consistent layout for design, navigation, and security.

TRY IT OUT   Understanding the Default ASP.NET Website

Login controls, navigation controls, and master pages are the tools to accomplish a consistent website. You will learn about all three in this Try It Out. All the code for this Try It Out is in the folder `DefaultSite` in the Zip file for this chapter.

1. Create a new site and name the project **DefaultSite**. When the site is created, it is set up with most if not all of your basic needs. If you take a look at the site features when you view it in the browser, you will see login capability and a common design theme. This basic site is all you need to have your own site ready in no time.

2. Run the site and click the links, register, and log in. That's a lot of functionality; let's go through the highlights.

How It Works

As you have seen in other parts of Visual Studio, you can do a lot with built-in tools. When you create a new ASP.NET site, the site includes the most common functionality, such as a menu, a login module, and master pages. All you have to do is go in and modify them to work the way you want them to. First, let's look at the master page and what it contains.

Master pages are the key to a consistent look and feel for your websites. By defining a common look and feel, developers of other pages will not be able to change their appearance when creating the new pages (they will inherit your specified look and feel). When creating a new page, you have access to update the ContentPlaceHolders. This makes it easy to add pages and just focus on their content, not worry about other areas of the website being affected.

Take a look at the site.master page created by default. This example focuses on a couple of important items in the source. At the top, you will see some required HTML. As a developer, you will be able to leave most of this alone. Let's go through each part of the basic HTML briefly.

The next line in the source code is the !DOCTYPE element. This tells the browser that it is an HTML document:

```
<!DOCTYPE html >
```

The actual HTML root element is next. You will see this element with no attributes set in many instances. lang="en" tells the browser the content is in English:

```
<html lang="en">
```

After the root html element is the head element. Children of this element are items that are not rendered, but they may affect how the page is displayed. You place elements, such as script, meta, title, link, and style here to define the page's look and feel. The following is what was placed in the example:

➤ **meta:** This sets the default character set used by the page.

➤ **Another meta tag:** This sets the view for mobile browsers to be the same width as the mobile screen.

➤ **title:** This is the title the browser displays for the page.

➤ **link:** A few of these tags tell the browser that there is a CSS related to this document and give its location. Also, the link tag sets the site's favorite icon, which you will see in the browser.

➤ **PlaceHolder:** Used to hold other controls.

➤ **Webopt:bundlereference:** Signals ASP.NET to minify the content at the path. This is used to improve performance.

```
<!DOCTYPE html>
<html lang="en">
  <head runat="server">
    <meta charset="utf-8" />
    <meta name="viewport" content="width=device-width, initial-scale=1.0" />
    <title><%: Page.Title %>—My ASP.NET Application</title>

    <asp:PlaceHolder runat="server">
        <%: Scripts.Render("~/bundles/modernizr") %>
    </asp:PlaceHolder>
    <webopt:bundlereference runat="server" path="~/Content/css" />
    <link href="~/favicon.ico" rel="shortcut icon" type="image/x-icon" />
  </head>
```

➤ **body, form, div and h1 elements or tags:** Both body and form tags are required. The body tag contains all HTML content, and all your ASPX controls need to be inside of the form tag. These tags are typically not changed except for applying styles. The div and h1 are HTML elements for content and are used for layout, along with many other HTML elements. This example does not go into detail about the HTML elements because it's more than we can cover in a chapter. As a developer, you just need to focus on learning the code for this chapter; you can work on the layout as you learn more.

Some controls of interest appear on the master page:

➤ **asp:LoginView:** This control is used with other login controls that implement .NET membership for authentication. When a page is rendered, you can display different views to authenticated users versus anonymous users using templates (AnonymousTemplate and LoggedInTemplate). As shown in the default site, a login link or welcome message with logout is a typical use of this control.

➤ **asp:ContentPlaceHolder:** This control is for developers to add content to new pages.

TRY IT OUT   Master Pages

In this exercise, you will see how quickly you can change the look and feel of a site with CSS, master pages, and themes. The code in this Try It Out is in the DefaultSite folder in the Zip file for this chapter.

1. In the default site, open the Default.aspx page in a browser and in Visual Studio. The easy way to view a web page in your solution is to right-click it in Solution Explorer and then choose View in Browser.

2. Change the footer contents from My ASP.NET Application to **Master Pages are easy**. Do this in the Site.master file. Refresh your web page and you will see what is shown in Figure 14-13. Browse other pages of the site and you will see your new message on all of them. You may have to hit Ctrl+F5 to force a full refresh if your browser caches web pages.

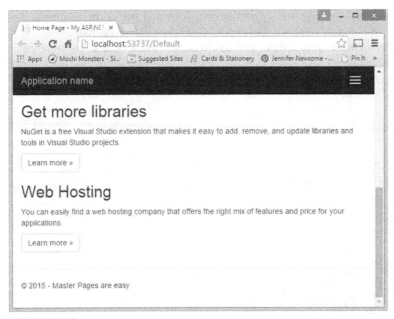

FIGURE 14-13

3.   That was a simple demonstration of the power of master pages. Now you will change the look and feel of the footer for the entire site. To accomplish this, go back to Visual Studio. Open `bootstrap.css` under the Content menu and locate the block for body with font-size. Once you find it, change the `font-size` attribute from `14px` to `44px`. Go back to your browser and press Ctrl+F5 to force a refresh in Internet Explorer (IE) because the browser may cache the CSS pages and it may be hard to get the latest changes to show in your browser. If you don't see the font increase (see Figure 14-14), it is almost always a caching issue. If you check other pages in your browser, you will see the same change to all pages. After you see how it works, change it back to `14px`.

```
font-size: 44px;
```

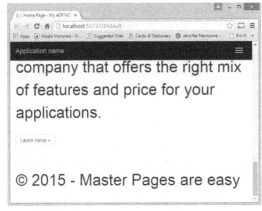

FIGURE 14-14

4. Next, you will add a new content page and apply the same look and feel as the entire site. Right-click the website name in Solution Explorer and choose Add, then Add New Item. Select Web Form and give it a name of **News.aspx**. Make sure to check the "Place code in separate file" and "Select master page" check boxes, as shown in Figure 14-15. When prompted to select a master page, choose Site.master. You should see that the site design is on the new page already.

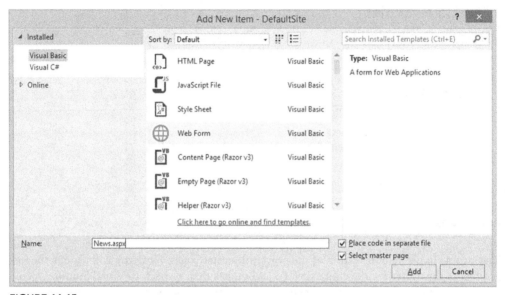

FIGURE 14-15

5. Add a Button to the ContentPlaceHolder and set its text to **Click Here**. Take a look at your new page in the browser and you will see your changes. Your new page has all the menus and design of the rest of the site with no extra effort.

How It Works

To see how quick it is to change a master page and have it affect the entire site, you updated the page footer to Master Pages are easy. Every page on the site that uses that master page will immediately display the change to the end users. This can be a very powerful tool when you set up applications this way for long-term success. Maintaining applications over a few years can be very difficult. Without the use of features like this, a simple change might require a change to every page on the site, which could take days or even weeks. Be sure to take advantage of master pages in your websites.

Next, you used CSS to alter the display properties of the login link. Because it was on the master page, it was changed on every other page also. CSS is very powerful and you can do much more than this with it. Almost any property that affects how an object looks in a browser can be changed via CSS; even a global change such as changing all the text in every div tag can be done using a simple block of CSS. Here, you used a tag that defined the scope of the CSS. You could have used div, and all div tags would have been affected.

You can apply the master page to any new page to instantly give it the look and feel of the site. In this case, you applied the Site.master to the News.aspx page you added.

Using the GridView to Build a Data-Driven Web Form

The data controls in ASP.NET have the ability to program *declaratively*. This no-code architecture allows you to look at the source of the Web Form and see your layout and design along with attributes that allow for data access and data manipulation.

In this Try It Out, you will see two of the best controls in ASP.NET for data access: the SqlDataSource control and the GridView control. You will set properties and attributes of these controls and also their child elements. Without writing any server-side or client-side code, you will create a web application to display data in the pubs database and update it.

TRY IT OUT No-Code Data Viewing and Updating

This Try It Out requires access to SQL Server with the pubs database installed. The code for this Try It Out is in the folder DataGridView in the Zip file for this chapter.

1. Create a new ASP.NET Empty Website and name it **DataGridView**. Add a Default.aspx Web Form.

2. Use the Source view and add the following changes highlighted in bold to the Default.aspx page. Be sure to change the values of the ConnectionString to match your development environment:

```
<<%@ Page Language="VB" %>
<!DOCTYPE html>
<html <url>xmlns="http://www.w3.org/1999/xhtml"></url>
  <head runat="server">
    <title>Grid View</title>
  </head>
<body>
<form id="form1" runat="server">
<div>
    <asp:SqlDataSource ID="sdsAuthors" Runat="server"
            ProviderName = "System.Data.SqlClient"
            ConnectionString = "Server=localhost\sqlexpress; User ID=sa;
            Password=wrox;Database=pubs;"
            SelectCommand = "SELECT au_id, au_lname,
            au_fname, phone,
            address, city, state, zip FROM authors"
            UpdateCommand = "UPDATE authors
            SET au_lname = @au_lname,
            au_fname = @au_fname, phone = @phone,
            address = @address,
            city = @city, state = @state, zip = @zip
            WHERE au_id = @au_id" >
    </asp:SqlDataSource>

    <asp:GridView ID="gdvAuthors" Runat="server"
     DataSourceID="sdsAuthors" AllowPaging="True" AllowSorting="True"
     AutoGenerateColumns="false" DataKeyNames="au_id" >
        <PagerStyle BackColor="Gray" ForeColor="White"
          HorizontalAlign="Center" />
        <HeaderStyle BackColor="Black" ForeColor="White" />
        <AlternatingRowStyle BackColor="LightGray" />
        <Columns>
          <asp:CommandField ButtonType="Button" ShowEditButton="true" />
```

```
            <asp:BoundField Visible="false" HeaderText="au_id"
                            DataField="au_id" SortExpression="au_id">
                            </asp:BoundField>
            <asp:BoundField HeaderText="Last Name" DataField="au_lname"
                            SortExpression="au_lname"></asp:BoundField>
             <asp:BoundField HeaderText="First Name" DataField="au_fname"
                            SortExpression="au_fname"></asp:BoundField>
             <asp:BoundField HeaderText="Phone" DataField="phone"
                            SortExpression="phone"></asp:BoundField>
             <asp:BoundField HeaderText="Address" DataField="address"
                            SortExpression="address"></asp:BoundField>
             <asp:BoundField HeaderText="City" DataField="city"
                            SortExpression="city"></asp:BoundField>
             <asp:BoundField HeaderText="State" DataField="state"
                            SortExpression="state"></asp:BoundField>
             <asp:BoundField HeaderText="Zip Code" DataField="zip"
                            SortExpression="zip"></asp:BoundField>
          </Columns>
       </asp:GridView>
    </div>
    </form>
    </body>
    </html>
```

3. Run the application without debugging by pressing Ctrl+F5. You will see a data grid appear similar to the one shown in Figure 14-16.

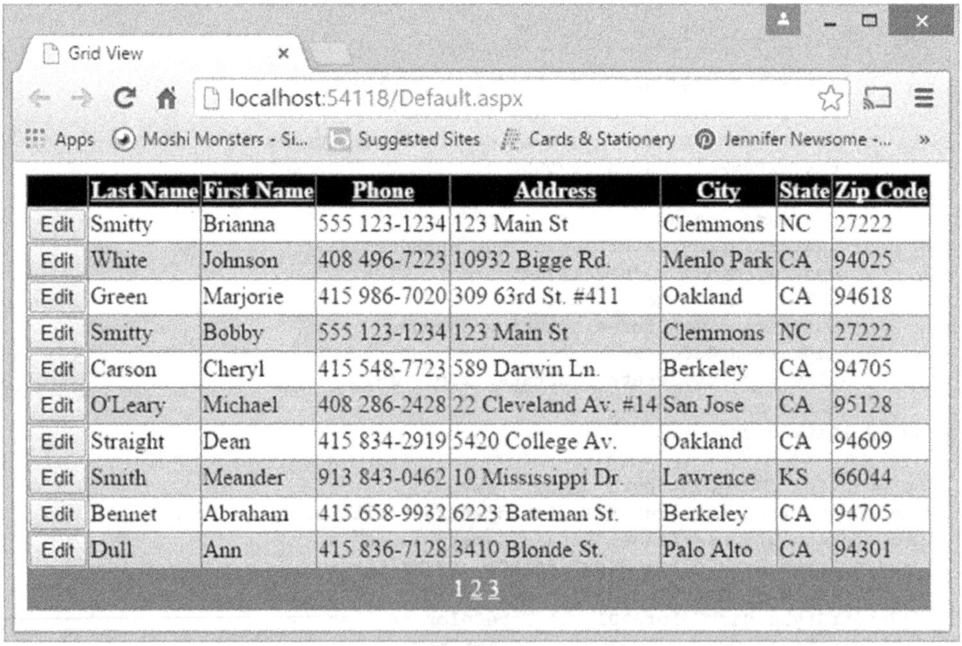
Grid View
localhost:54118/Default.aspx
Apps
Moshi Monsters - Si...
Suggested Sites
Cards & Stationery
Jennifer Newsome -...
Last Name First Name Phone Address City State Zip Code
Edit Smitty Brianna 555 123-1234 123 Main St Clemmons NC 27222
Edit White Johnson 408 496-7223 10932 Bigge Rd. Menlo Park CA 94025
Edit Green Marjorie 415 986-7020 309 63rd St. #411 Oakland CA 94618
Edit Smitty Bobby 555 123-1234 123 Main St Clemmons NC 27222
Edit Carson Cheryl 415 548-7723 589 Darwin Ln. Berkeley CA 94705
Edit O'Leary Michael 408 286-2428 22 Cleveland Av. #14 San Jose CA 95128
Edit Straight Dean 415 834-2919 5420 College Av. Oakland CA 94609
Edit Smith Meander 913 843-0462 10 Mississippi Dr. Lawrence KS 66044
Edit Bennet Abraham 415 658-9932 6223 Bateman St. Berkeley CA 94705
Edit Dull Ann 415 836-7128 3410 Blonde St. Palo Alto CA 94301
1 2 3

FIGURE 14-16

4. Test the functions of the grid. At the bottom, you can move to any page of the data. In addition, sorting is available by clicking any of the column headers. After trying both of these, update a row. To edit an author's data, click the Edit button on the left of the author's row. The screen refreshes, and you will see a new grid that looks like the one in Figure 14-17.

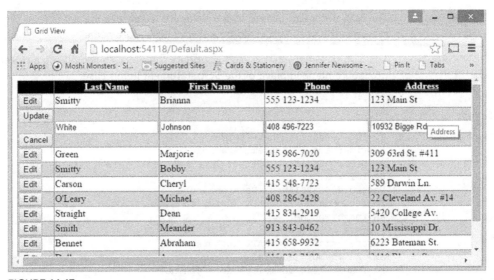

FIGURE 14-17

Change any field and click the Update button to make the change permanent. You can cancel a change by clicking any link or button other than the Update button.

How It Works

Now that was easy. By adding two controls, you created a fairly robust data access page. We'll explain how this happened.

First, you create the SqlDataSource control. Table 14-1 explains each attribute you add or change for the SqlDataSource control.

TABLE 14-1: SqlDataSource Controls

ATTRIBUTE OR ELEMENT	DESCRIPTION
ID	The control's identifier.
Runat	Specifies that the code for the control is run at the server before the page is sent to the browser.
ProviderName	Used to set the provider to access the data store. In this case, it is System.Data.SqlClient, the managed provider for SQL Server.

continues

TABLE 14-1 *(continued)*

ATTRIBUTE OR ELEMENT	DESCRIPTION
ConnectionString	This string value is used to gain access to the database resource, pubs.
SelectCommand	The SQL statement passed to the database to retrieve the data that is displayed in the grid. This could be a stored procedure name.
UpdateCommand	The SQL statement that is used to update the data. You could use a stored procedure name in place of the SQL statement in this case.

The code follows:

```
<asp:SqlDataSource ID="sdsAuthors" Runat="server"
                   ProviderName = "System.Data.SqlClient"
                   ConnectionString = "Server=localhost\sqlexpress;
                   User ID=sa;
                   Password=SQL2014wrox;Database=pubs;"
                   SelectCommand = "SELECT au_id, au_lname,
                   au_fname, phone,
                   address, city, state, zip FROM authors"
                   UpdateCommand = "UPDATE authors
                   SET au_lname = @au_lname,
                   au_fname = @au_fname, phone = @phone,
                   address = @address,
                   city = @city, state = @state, zip = @zip
                   WHERE au_id = @au_id" >
</asp:SqlDataSource>
```

The second control you add to the form is the GridView. Its attributes are described in Table 14-2.

TABLE 14-2: GridView Attributes

ATTRIBUTE OR ELEMENT	DESCRIPTION
ID	The control's identifier.
Runat	Defines that the code for the control is run at the server before the page is sent to the browser.
DataSourceID	The ID of the SqlDataSource object is used here.
AllowPaging	Can be set to True or False. Turns on paging features of the grid.
AllowSorting	Can be set to True or False. Turns on sorting features of the grid.
AutoGenerateColumns	Can be set to True or False. Determines how the GridView creates the columns automatically.
DataKeyNames	This element is the primary key used by the database table.

continues

TABLE 14-2 *(continued)*

ATTRIBUTE OR ELEMENT	DESCRIPTION
PagerStyle	This element defines the style of the paging area of the grid.
HeaderStyle	This element defines the style of the header row area of the grid.
AlternatingRowStyle	This element defines the style of every other row of the grid.
Columns	A collection of column objects.
asp:CommandField	Two properties of this object are used. The first is ButtonType, which is set to a type of button. You can insert a button, image, or link as a value. If left blank, the default is link. Next, is ShowEditButton. As you would guess, this shows or hides the edit button.
BoundField	This element allows for the binding of the data to the grid. For a better user interface, you use the Visible property to hide the primary key column. Also, you set the SortExpression of each column. This converts every column header to a link. When clicked, the data is sorted by that column. Next, you change the column headers with the HeaderText property. If this is blank, the column names are used as headers. Finally, the field to bind to is set using the DataField property.

The GridView control code is as follows:

```
<asp:GridView ID="gdvAuthors" Runat="server"
 DataSourceID="sdsAuthors" AllowPaging="True"
 AllowSorting="True"
 AutoGenerateColumns="false" DataKeyNames="au_id" >
    <PagerStyle BackColor="Gray" ForeColor="White"
      HorizontalAlign="Center" />
    <HeaderStyle BackColor="Black" ForeColor="White" />
    <AlternatingRowStyle BackColor="LightGray" />
    <Columns>
      <asp:CommandField ButtonType="Button"
          ShowEditButton="true" />
      <asp:BoundField Visible="false" HeaderText="au_id"
          DataField="au_id" SortExpression="au_id">
          </asp:BoundField>
      <asp:BoundField HeaderText="Last Name"
          DataField="au_lname"
          SortExpression="au_lname"></asp:BoundField>
      <asp:BoundField HeaderText="First Name"
          DataField="au_fname"
          SortExpression="au_fname"></asp:BoundField>
      <asp:BoundField HeaderText="Phone" DataField="phone"
          SortExpression="phone"></asp:BoundField>
      <asp:BoundField HeaderText="Address" DataField="address"
          SortExpression="address"></asp:BoundField>
      <asp:BoundField HeaderText="City" DataField="city"
          SortExpression="city"></asp:BoundField>
      <asp:BoundField HeaderText="State" DataField="state"
```

```
        SortExpression="state"></asp:BoundField>
      <asp:BoundField HeaderText="Zip Code" DataField="zip"
        SortExpression="zip"></asp:BoundField>
  </Columns>
</asp:GridView>
```

SUMMARY

In this chapter, you learned what thin-client development is. You saw the advantages of Web Forms and Windows Forms and why you would choose one type of application over the other. Maybe the low distribution cost of web applications is a major factor in your decision to create a web application over a Windows application, for example.

You also learned about the basic pieces that constitute a typical web application. From layout and formatting to database integration, you gained knowledge of the best features of ASP.NET and how they are implemented. Finally, you designed a code-free page that updated data in a database.

If you like web development, there is much more to learn than can be explained in one chapter. To continue learning, we recommend navigating to www.Wrox.com and clicking the ASP.NET link to find more resources to take you to the next level of web development.

You should now know how to:

➤   Choose between Web Forms and Windows Forms applications to suit your purpose

➤   Use the Toolbox for ASP.NET

➤   Create a website project in Visual Studio 2015

➤   Handle client and server Web Form events

➤   Use built-in controls for data validation

➤   Choose between the possible locations for websites in Visual Studio 2015

➤   Use master pages and CSS

➤   Use a GridView and a SqlDataSource to read and update data in a SQL database

EXERCISES

1. If you want to build a design and layout that can be inherited by Web Form pages, how do you build it?

2. To change the way elements of the page appear, you have two good options when designing web pages. What are they?

3. What property do you set to have static client IDs for server controls?

4. Name one control you can use to help validate form data.

▶ WHAT YOU LEARNED IN THIS CHAPTER

TOPIC	CONCEPTS
Client and server events	Some events (client) are handled by the browser, whereas others (server) are handled by the web server.
Data validation	In ASP.NET, you can use built-in validation controls to ensure your user input is valid.
Website layout and design	Use master pages and CSS to design your site.
Accessing data on the web	You can use the GridView control to bring your data to the web.

15

Deploying Your Application

WHAT YOU WILL LEARN IN THIS CHAPTER:

> ➤ Deployment concepts and terminology

> ➤ How to deploy a ClickOnce Application with Visual Studio 2015

> ➤ How to create a setup program with Visual Studio 2015

> ➤ How to edit the Installer user interface

Deploying an application can be a complicated process, especially when dealing with large, complex applications. A wealth of knowledge is required about nearly every aspect of a deployment. A large software installation for Windows requires knowledge ranging from Registry settings, MIME types, and configuration files to database creation and manipulation. Companies tend to rely on dedicated deployment software for these large installations, together with key people who understand the processes involved. However, Visual Studio 2015 provides deployment functionality, which is tremendously helpful for the standard developer and smaller installations.

Under the Visual Studio 2015 banner, you can create many different types of applications, from desktop to web applications and services. All of them have varying degrees of complexity when it comes installation time.

Since this is a beginner's guide, this chapter provides an overview of deployment.

WHAT IS DEPLOYMENT?

Deployment is the activity of delivering copies of an application to other machines so that the application runs in the new environment. It is the larger architectural view for what you may know as installation or setup. There is a subtle difference between deployment and installation.

Deployment is the art of distribution. In other words, deployment is the way in which software is delivered. Installation or setup is a process whereby you load, configure, and install the software. In other words, an *installation* is what you do to configure the software, and *deployment* is how you get it where you want it.

With this terminology, a CD/DVD is a deployment mechanism, as is the Internet. The two deployment mechanisms may have different installation requirements. For example, if an installation is on a CD/DVD, you may have all the additional dependent software on that CD/DVD. Delivery of the same application via the Internet might require users to visit additional sites to gather all the dependent software. Another example that may affect the installation option is one in which you may have written an installation in JavaScript. This may work fine when executed on a machine by a user who has the correct Windows user rights, but would not work through Internet Explorer. These kinds of considerations are important when deciding upon your best deployment option. The type of installations you require could also vary per application.

Now that you have an understanding of the terminology, it's time to learn how to deploy applications using Visual Studio 2015.

ClickOnce Deployment

ClickOnce deployment is the concept of sending an application or its referenced assemblies to the client in a way that allows self-updating applications. You have three distribution options for a ClickOnce application: file share, web page, or external media (CD, DVD, and so on). ClickOnce deployment has both benefits and limitations. It is a useful deployment option for small- to medium-size applications.

The benefits of ClickOnce deployment include three major factors. First, using this deployment option allows for self-updating Windows applications. You can post the latest version of the application at the original location, and it will install the latest version and run it the next time the user runs the application. Next, any user can install most ClickOnce applications with only basic user security. With other technologies, administrator privileges are required. Finally, the installation has little impact on the user's computer. The application can run from a secure per-user cache and add entries only to the Start menu and the Add/Remove Programs list. For programs that can run in the Internet or intranet zones that do not need to access the Global Assembly Cache (GAC), this is a terrific deployment solution for distribution via the web or a file share. If you distribute the ClickOnce application through external media, the installation will be run with higher trust and have access to the GAC.

TRY IT OUT   **Deploying a ClickOnce Application from the Web**

In this Try It Out, you learn how to deploy a ClickOnce application from the web. All the code in this Try It Out is in the ClickOnce folder in the Zip file for this chapter.

1. Create a new Windows Forms Application named **ClickOnce**.

2. On Form1, add a button and label. Change the button's Name property to **btnVersion** and the Text property to **Version**. Change the label Name to **lblVersion** and clear the Text property.

3. Add the following bolded code to the Click event for btnVersion:

```
Private Sub btnVersion_Click(sender As System. Object,
        e As EventArgs) Handles btnVersion.Click
    lblVersion.Text = "Version 1.0"
End sub
```

4. Test the form. When the user clicks the button, the label should display Version 1.0. Your form should look like Figure 15-1.

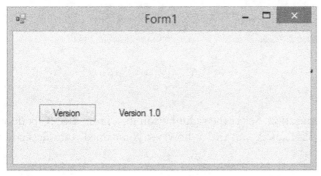

FIGURE 15-1

5. Prepare to publish the assembly to the web.

> **NOTE** *You can publish the file to a local or network drive, to a website, or to an FTP server. Just remember how you chose to publish the assembly. You may need to be running Visual Studio with elevated privileges to complete this. You may need to close Visual Studio: Right-click the shortcut and choose Run as Administrator to launch the software.*

6. Right-click the ClickOnce project in the Solution Explorer and choose Publish from the context menu. The Publish Wizard opens (see Figure 15-2). Choose a location to publish the file. In this example, choose a directory on the local computer like C:\Publish.

> **NOTE** *You will need to share this folder. Here the folder is shared as Publish. To share a folder in Windows 10 with other users on the network or this computer, navigate to the folder in Windows Explorer and right-click the folder to open the context menu. Choose Share With and then Specific People. At your work, you would choose a group of users who could access the shared folder or network share. For this example, just select or enter Everyone and then click Add. Next, click Share and then click Done to share the folder.*

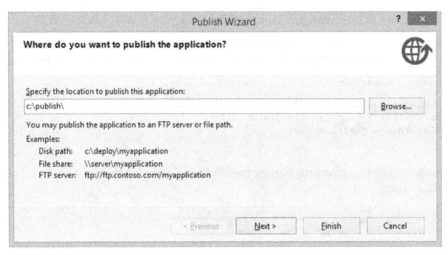

FIGURE 15-2

7. After setting the location, click Next.

8. Specify how users will install the application. Select the radio button for "From a UNC path or file share." Enter the UNC path as \\localhost\Publish or however you named your file share in step 6 (see Figure 15-3).

FIGURE 15-3

9. Click Next. In this step, you can choose whether to install a shortcut on the Start menu and add a listing in Add/Remove Programs. Select Yes, as shown in Figure 15-4, and then click Next. You will see the summary of your choices.

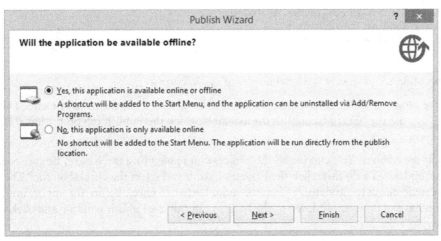

FIGURE 15-4

10. Click Finish to complete the wizard. The setup files will be copied to the file share.

11. When you run the install from the share, you may see a few security warnings, such as the one shown in Figure 15-5. If you see any, just click the button to continue. The form you created will open. Click the Version button and you will see Version 1.0. You can close the form. Check the Program Files directory; you will see firsthand that no files were added for the ClickOnce application, and a new shortcut has been added to the Start menu.

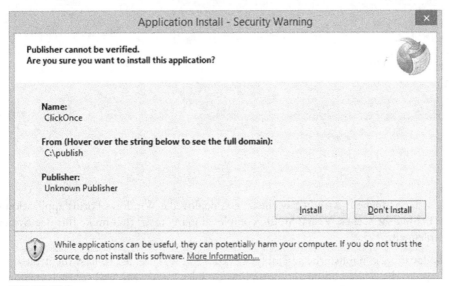

FIGURE 15-5

12. To update the application and see the self-updating capabilities in action, go back to the ClickOnce Windows application in Visual Studio and change the button `Click` event to update the label to `Version 1.1`. Your `Click` event handler should look like this:

```
Private Sub btnVersion_Click(sender As Object,  e As _
    EventArgs) Handles btnVersion.Click
    lblVersion.Text = "Version 1.1"
End Sub
```

13. Test the application to make sure the label now displays Version 1.1.

14. Right-click the project in Solution Explorer and choose Properties from the context menu. This time you will not use the wizard to publish the assembly. Click the Publish tab on the left side of the main window.

15. Take a look at the options. You can see all the choices you made using the wizard. Be sure to set the action for updates. To do this, click the Updates button and select the check box for "The application should check for updates." Click the radio button to check before the application starts. All you have to do is scroll down to the bottom right of the Publish window and click Publish Now.

16. Notice at the bottom of Visual Studio that it notes that Publish succeeded.

17. Run the application using the shortcut on the Start menu. You will be prompted to update the application. After the form opens, click the Version button; the text of the label indicates that the application is updated to Version 1.1. Click OK (see Figure 15-6).

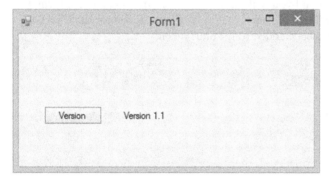

FIGURE 15-6

How It Works

That was easy, but what happened? After a few clicks, you deployed a Windows Forms application that was self-updating. Behind the scenes, Visual Studio completed many tasks that make this deployment strategy easy to implement.

First, you chose the location to publish the assembly: C:\Publish was created to host the deployment files for you. If you go to the folder and open the Application Files folder, you will see each version you have published. Your folder will look like Figure 15-7. Note that each version of the assembly has its own directory. By default, the .NET Framework is installed if the user does not have the correct version of the Framework. The Installer would download it from Microsoft. Feel free to browse around the directory. We will discuss the other files later.

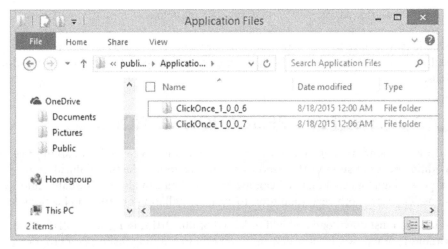

FIGURE 15-7

Next, you choose how the users will install the application. Here you tell the wizard how to deliver the application to the users' computers.

The next step of the wizard enables you to specify whether offline access is allowed. If you decide to allow offline access, a shortcut is added to Add/Remove Program files and the Start menu. The application is also installed to a secure cache on your computer. If you decide not to allow offline access, the user must return to the publishing location to launch the application on each use. In this case, the user would be required to have access to the share to launch the application for each use.

That's it. When you click Finish, Visual Studio 2015 goes to work. What happens behind the scenes is not magic. Actually, you could manually complete everything without Visual Studio if you ever needed to do so.

Referring to Figure 15-7, take another look at the files. Here's what happened: First, the application was deployed. Then a subdirectory was created for the current version's files. Also, required manifest files were generated and placed under the root and version subdirectory. Finally, a `setup.exe` file for deployment was created.

To install the application, you navigated to the share and ran Setup. Each time you launch the installed application, a check is made to see whether a newer version is available. When a new version is available, you are notified and presented with the option to install the update. ClickOnce deployment has a large number of deployment options. This exercise only scratched the surface.

XCOPY Deployment

XCOPY deployment gets its name from the MS-DOS XCOPY command. XCOPY is a copy procedure that simply copies a directory and all files, including subfolders. This is commonly associated with web applications, but with Visual Studio 2015 it can also apply to a desktop application. Since a standard .NET assembly does not need any form of registration, it fully supports this option.

XCOPY does not work with shared assemblies because they require installation (if they are used from the GAC). You learn more about shared assemblies later in this chapter. When you use XCOPY for desktop applications, you have to create any shortcuts or menu items via a script or manually. You would typically use XCOPY for website deployment and for testing and prototypes of Windows Forms applications.

VISUAL STUDIO 2015 SETUP APPLICATION OPTIONS

Visual Studio 2015 Professional version and above supports two other types of installation projects. The community edition does not support these more complicated tools. The InstallShield Limited Edition Project type is a high-end tool that you can use for free. You can also use Visual Studio Installer Extensions. These are both very good tools to create installation or setup applications.

InstallShield, which you must download and add to Visual Studio 2015, is a general platform for installing applications in Windows. It's a widely used solution to building installation programs and information, providing a lot of functionality, such as uninstall capabilities and transactional installation options (the ability to roll back if something fails) as well as other general features. Many of these features are either built-in (so that you do not have to do anything) or are configurable, extensible, or both. In addition, help is readily available online for even the most complex problems.

The Visual Studio 2015 InstallShield support has made it easier to create a simple installation. In addition, an Installer assistant is included to guide you through all the important information.

When you are creating setup applications, always be aware of the end user. By default, all the applications you will create with Visual Studio 2015 require, at a minimum, version 4.5 of the .NET Framework on the installation system. For internal applications, you will know what prerequisites are installed on each computer, but in many cases you will deliver your application to users with no idea of the target system configuration. When you are not sure of the user's configuration, it is up to you to make all required components available.

Visual Studio 2015 Installer Extensions are not as robust as the InstallShield project. You can handle most scenarios, and the tool may be easier to set up because you have less options and configurations for some. You can use this tool to quickly create a simple and customizable installation project. This was the only built-in tool in Visual Studio until 2012, when InstallShield was added. This extension can be added to the appropriate versions of Visual Studio.

DEPLOYING DIFFERENT SOLUTIONS

Deploying applications is actually a large and complex task, made easier by various tools. However, if you consider a large suite of applications such as Microsoft Office, you will notice that there can be a vast number of files. All these files require explicit locations or Registry entries. They all tie together to make the application work. In addition to size, there can also be many other complexities, such as database creation: What happens if the database already exists? What happens with the data that is already there? This kind of activity, commonly referred to as *migration*, could potentially mean a lot of work for an installation expert.

Having multiple application types can also make an installation complex, and detailed knowledge of the different applications is required for a successful installation. The following sections discuss some items related to different deployment scenarios surrounding the different types of applications that can be created with Visual Studio 2015.

Private Assemblies

Private assemblies are installed in a directory named `bin` located under the application directory. These files are private to the application. There are a few benefits to using private assemblies:

➤ No versioning is required as long as it is the same version as the one with which the application was built.

➤ The private assembly is not a shared assembly, and therefore it cannot be updated by another application (at least it is not meant to be).

➤ You can manually replace the assembly as long as it is the same version.

➤ It enables XCOPY deployment (the ability simply to copy and paste files to a location and have it work).

➤ You can make changes to the assembly, and if two different applications use it, you can update one independently from the other. This may be hard to maintain, so use this benefit only in special occasions that need it.

➤ No configuration or signing (see the following section) is necessary. It just works.

➤ It is great for small utility assemblies or application-specific code.

Private assemblies have the following negatives:

➤ When you have multiple applications using one assembly, you have to deploy the assembly to the `bin` directory of each application.

➤ You would normally have to include the assembly in each setup project in which it is used.

➤ Versioning is not enforced as it is in a shared assembly.

➤ It is not strongly named, which means someone could spoof your assembly.

> **NOTE** Spoofing an assembly is when someone creates an assembly that looks identical to yours and replaces yours with the spoofed copy. This spoofed copy could behave in malicious ways.

Shared Assemblies

Shared assemblies are actually more stable than private assemblies, and they have a thorough approach to assembly deployment. A shared assembly can also behave like a private assembly, so all the benefits of that approach apply here, too. The traditional shared assembly is different because of the extra work you need to do and the extra capabilities it then gains.

A shared assembly is like going back in time. In Windows 3.1, the main deployment location for these kinds of dynamic-link libraries (DLLs) was the `Windows\System` directory. Then you were advised to have these files in the local application path, which enabled easier installation and uninstallation. Today, the `System` directory concept returns in a new guise named the Global Assembly Cache (GAC). However, the strong naming of assemblies is a definite step up.

> **NOTE** *Any project type can use a shared assembly, including a web application.*

A shared assembly offers the following main benefits:

- ➤ It is signed and cannot be spoofed.
- ➤ It has strong versioning support and configuration options.
- ➤ It is stored in one central location and does not need to be copied to the `bin` directory of every application that uses it.
- ➤ Many different versions can be running side by side.

Shared assemblies have the following negatives:

- ➤ You have to sign the assembly.
- ➤ You have to be careful not to break compatibility with existing applications; otherwise, you have to configure different versions.
- ➤ Configuration can be a challenge, depending on the requirements.

Deploying Desktop Applications

In other editions of Visual Studio 2015, you can install setup projects that you can use to create setup files to deploy you applications. These include InstallShield Limited Edition tools as well as Visual Studio Installer.

Deploying Web Applications

Most websites are deployed using XCOPY or by publishing the project to the web server. You would normally set up the web server with all the requirements needed beforehand, thereby making deployment simpler.

Deploying XML Web Services

A web service is deployed in much the same way as a web application. It also has a virtual directory. The files that it requires are somewhat different, though. You need to deploy the `asmx` and `discovery` files together with the assembly.

Useful Tools

This section describes a few tools that either come with .NET or are in Windows ready for you to use. When creating an installation, you need to test it by installing it on various machines. Sometimes, when things do not go according to plan, you may need to do some or all the tasks manually to see which one was the cause of the problem.

For example, perhaps you suspect that the ASPNET_WP.dll process has become unstable or broken in some fashion and has affected the installation. In this scenario, you may want to restart Internet Information Server (IIS) before you run the install. In a similar vein, perhaps an assembly that was supposed to be registered in the GAC was not because a shared assembly cannot be found by the client; you may want to register it manually to check whether there was a problem with the registration. The following list briefly describes the tools you may need to use:

> ➤ **ASPNET_RegIIS:** The aspnet_regiis.exe command-line tool can be found in the `<sysdir>\Microsoft.NET\Framework\<version>` directory. This tool makes it an easy task to reinstall various aspects of the ASP.NET run time and change settings for ASP .NET in IIS.

> ➤ **IISReset:** IISReset simply restarts IIS without requiring you to open the IIS management console. Simply open a DOS prompt and type **IISReset**; it will immediately restart IIS.

> ➤ **ILDasm:** If you want to inspect the metadata of an assembly, MSIL Disassembler is the tool for the job. With this tool, you can inspect everything from the namespaces to the version. Start MSIL Disassembler by typing **ildasm** at a Visual Studio Developer command prompt.

> ➤ **GACUtil:** This is a Visual Studio command-line tool for registering/unregistering assemblies from the Global Assembly Cache. The /I option is for registering the assembly, and the /u option is for unregistering.

> ➤ **RegAsm:** This Visual Studio command-line utility is used for creating the necessary Component Object Model (COM) information from an assembly. This is used when you need to expose an assembly for COM Interop. The regasm tool includes switches for registering/unregistering type libraries.

> ➤ **MageUI (Manifest Generation and Editing Tool):** This is a graphical tool for generating, editing, and signing the application and deployment manifest for ClickOnce applications. Run MageUI from a Visual Studio command prompt to start the tool. A command-line version of this tool, Mage.exe, is available if you prefer to not have the user interface.

SUMMARY

We hope you enjoyed looking at some general aspects of deployment. In the first section of this chapter, you were introduced to some terminology, and then you learned how to create a ClickOnce application and a simple Setup application inside Visual Studio. You also learned the positives and negatives of private versus shared assemblies. Ultimately, we hope you learned that there is potentially a lot to learn in this area, from getting to know more about the features of the Windows Installer templates to learning how to do more with ClickOnce deployment.

To summarize, you should know:

➤ How to create a ClickOnce deployment application

➤ Visual Studio 2015 setup application options

➤ How to use general deployment terms such as XCOPY and understand the differences between shared versus private assemblies

EXERCISES

1. Where are shared assemblies stored?

2. How are updates handled when using ClickOnce deployment?

3. Describe a reason to not use XCOPY deployment.

▶ WHAT YOU LEARNED IN THIS CHAPTER

TOPIC	CONCEPTS
ClickOnce deployment	Applications will update when a new version is released. Windows applications can be released from a remote location such as a website or file share. You can choose whether to allow the user to run the application when not connected to the network or website. This is a very easy way to manage application installs to users in remote locations and keep them updated.
XCOPY deployment	A simple copy process. No shortcuts are created.
Useful tools	Many tools are available to assist you as a developer outside of the Visual Studio UI.

16

Windows 8 Apps

WROX.COM CODE DOWNLOADS FOR THIS CHAPTER

The wrox.com code downloads for this chapter are found at www.wrox.com/ begvisualbasic2015 on the Download Code tab. The code is in the 092117 C16.zip download and individually named according to the names given throughout the chapter.

With the release of Windows 8 comes Windows 8 apps. Developers using Visual Studio 2015 can build these next-generation applications and release them to the Windows Store to sell to users around the globe. Sound familiar? Google and Apple have been working with developers building and releasing apps to Google Play and Apple's App Store. In the July 2015, Apple totals more than 1,200,000 apps in its App Store. Google's Play housed over 1,300,000 apps and has now surpassed Apple. In its shorter life, the Windows Store has over 300,000 apps. As you can see from the numbers, there is a lot more room for Windows 8 apps.

Windows 8 applications are built to be touch friendly and run on many devices. These new types of applications move away from the normal design of mouse-clicking driving the interface design for actions. Now, developers must think of the use of fingers, pens, and yes, a mouse, too, to use and navigate applications. Think about using a tablet rather than a desktop for Windows 8 design (although your app can still run on a desktop with a mouse).

Throughout this chapter, the term Windows 8 relates to the latest version of Windows 8, which is 8.1. Microsoft made many changes to app design for the store with the release of 8.1, and this code is targeting Windows 8.1.

WINDOWS 8 APPLICATION DESIGN PRINCIPLES

The key to creating a great Windows 8 application is the user interface. Make sure that you prepare your application interface for many devices and keep touch in mind as a key form of interaction. Remember, users will download apps and expect them to have similar principles in place.

Using Touch

While you are building new Windows 8 apps, touch just may be the most important design principle. People today are used to touch interfaces on all kinds of phone and tablet devices. Be aware that there is a language that most people already use to interact with touchscreens. You are probably also familiar with this language, so that will help you with the touch design. Here are some of the common touch interactions you need to be aware of in your apps:

- ➤ **Check boxes:** Fingers are not good at selecting small targets such as check boxes. Avoid these small targets in your design.

- ➤ **Tap:** Allow the user to select or tap an entire item to navigate to a new view, see details, or perform an action versus selecting an item and then clicking a button.

- ➤ **Zoom:** Users are familiar with pinching and stretching for zooming in or out, so be sure to use this if your application supports zooming.

- ➤ **Rotate:** To rotate an item, the user places more than one finger on the device and rotates his or her fingers.

- ➤ **Move, Slide, and Pan:** No need to put arrows on the interface; the user will just move items and the screen by placing a finger on the screen and sliding up, down, left, or right.

- ➤ **Right Side:** Most people are right-handed and will hold the device in their left hand. This makes it easier to interact with the right side of the screen. The best placements for interactive elements of your app are on the right side.

- ➤ **Touch and Hold:** To show a context menu, the user can touch and hold. Used for commands such as cut, copy, and paste.

Application Commands

You learned about menus for commands in desktop applications in Chapter 8. In Windows 8 applications, these commands and menus are generally in one of four places: on the canvas, on the Appbar, as a Charm, or in a context menu.

➤ **Appbar:** The *Appbar* (see Figure 16-1) has commands such as Sort, Refresh, or Print, and is located at the top or bottom of the screen.

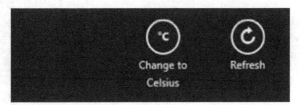

FIGURE 16-1

The user can swipe these areas or right-click the mouse to see the Appbar menus. By default, the Appbars are hidden from view and the commands can activate or show menus. For commands that are grouped together, you may want a menu to activate when the user taps the command. If your app has five ways to filter data, you could have five different filter commands or one filter command that has a menu with the options for filtering.

Placing commands on the Appbar is more of a science than an art. You should adhere to these common rules in your command placement when working out your design:

➤ **Always place commands that are based on the current selection to the far left.** Commands such as Select All or Show on Map should be shown to the far left.

➤ **Hide commands that are not currently valid.** If the user has all the text selected on the current element, hide the Select All command.

➤ **Manage Items using the New and Delete commands.** Place the New command to the right of the Appbar; it should have a plus sign and describe the new item with a descriptive label such as New Message. The Delete command, which appears as a trash can, always appears to the left of the New command.

➤ **To manage a list, use the Add and Remove commands.** The Add command, like the New command, is a plus sign and a label. You should place the Remove command to the left of Add and make it a minus sign.

➤ **To clear an element, use the Clear command.** The command is to the left of New or Add and represented by an X. Add a descriptive label such as Clear History.

➤ **Charms:** These are located on the right side of the screen with the system commands. Normal charms are Settings, Search, Share, and Devices. Figure 16-2 shows some of the common charms.

➤ **Canvas:** The canvas is what your user sees on the screen and basically is what you know as your form. Commands located on the canvas are how your user interacts with your application. You may have buttons or content, which the user can tap on the application canvas. Also, the canvas may contain other touch gestures, such as pinch or stretch, which allow the user to zoom in and out.

➤ **Context Menu:** Just as you learned in Chapter 8, context menus have a place in Windows 8 apps; with a context menu, users can select, copy, or paste text. Users will be familiar with touch and hold to show a context menu.

Windows 8 Controls

Visual Studio 2015 comes with a basketful of controls, which make building Windows 8 applications easier to create. You're probably familiar with most of these already. Table 16-1 describes some of the controls you will use in your Windows 8 apps.

FIGURE 16-2

TABLE 16-1: Windows 8 Controls

CONTROL	DESCRIPTION
AppBar	This is the toolbar in Windows 8 apps. There are top and bottom app bars.
Top AppBar	The app bar at the top of the screen. Normally it is used for navigation.
Bottom AppBar	The app bar at the bottom of the screen. This is used for commands and tools. You may see buttons such as Edit, New, Add, Refresh, and Help in the bottom app bar.
Border	Draws a border and/or background around an object.
Button	Similar to a button on form applications, it raises a `click` event that your app can handle to perform an action.
CheckBox	A control the user can check/select or uncheck.
ComboBox	This control is a drop-down list of items.
FlipView	Displays a collection of items the user can flip through like a photo slideshow.

CONTROL	DESCRIPTION
Grid	Displays a collection of items in a grid layout (rows and columns).
GridView	Displays a collection of items in a grid layout (rows and columns). This pans horizontally.
HyperlinkButton	Inserts a hyperlink in a text block.
Image	Displays an image.
ListView	Displays a collection of items in rows. This control pans vertically.
RadioButton	A group of controls from which the user can select one.
StackPanel	Groups controls into a single row or single column.
TextBlock	Displays text.
TextBox	A text field for a single or multiline entry.

Coding Windows 8 Apps with XAML

XAML is an Extensible Application Markup Language. But what exactly does this mean? Wikipedia (www.wikipedia.org) defines XAML as a declarative XML-based language used to initialize structured values and objects. Others define XAML as a declarative XML-based language that defines objects and their properties.

Given these definitions, you can begin to understand how the acronym for this new language was formed. You can see that this new language is based on XML, which has become the industry standard for sharing structured data between applications. The *A* in XAML is the application part of the acronym, and the declarative part of the definition refers to the language's ability to declare objects that represent controls on a form.

So you can start to visualize that this new language defines an application's UI in an XML-type language by defining the controls on a form. The controls that XAML defines map to classes in the .NET Framework. Keep in mind that XAML is an application markup language used to define a user interface and should not be confused with a programming language such as Visual Basic 2015.

To illustrate this point, here is a basic Windows application defined in XAML:

```
<Window x:Class="MainWindow"
    xmlns="http://schemas.microsoft.com/winfx/2006/xaml/presentation"
    xmlns:x="http://schemas.microsoft.com/winfx/2006/xaml"
    Title="Window1" Height="164" Width="207">
</Window>
```

You can see that XAML looks a lot like XML because it is an XML-based language and adheres to the XML standard. You can also see that the controls are defined in the sample map to classes in the .NET Framework, and that the output looks like a standard Windows application that you've already created in previous chapters.

Given the nature of XAML and the output it produces, you can start to visualize how XAML can more completely separate the duties of the UI designer from the developer. The UI designer would typically create the XAML code, using a tool such as Expression Blend, Expression Design, or Aurora XAML Designer, by visually creating the Windows form and having the tool create the XAML.

The next step would be for the UI designer to give the developer the XAML, which is stored in a file with a .xaml extension. The developer would import that XAML file into Visual Studio 2015 and then write the code to make the form have functional meaning, so that when the user clicks the button something useful happens.

This should give you the bigger picture and illustrate the concept behind XAML and what role you might play in this picture in the future. In larger organizations that have a person or team dedicated to creating user interfaces, this scenario may soon become a reality. Your job in that organization might then be to write the code to make these user interfaces functional.

Creating Your First Windows 8 App

So, now you have the basics of Windows 8 apps. In the next Try It Out, you will create your first app as well as acquire a developer's license.

TRY IT OUT   Tic Tac Toe

This application will allow you to play Tic Tac Toe against an opponent or the computer. If you play against the computer, it uses a random play algorithm and is a fair opponent only for a young child. All the code for this Try It Out is in the code file Tic Tac Toe.zip. You will likely need to run a clean under the build menu if you load and run the project in the Zip file.

1.   Open Visual Studio 2015 and select File ➪ New Project. In the New Project dialog, select Visual Basic and Windows 8 from the Project Types list. For a default installation, you will need to click to install the Windows 8 and Windows Phone Tools first as shown in Figure 16-3. In the Templates list, select Blank App (Windows 8.1). Enter **Tic Tac Toe** in the Name field and click OK.

2.   To create Windows 8 apps, you need a developer's license. You should be asked to obtain one if you do not have one. If you are not directed to get a license automatically, follow these instructions. In the menu, choose Project ➪ Store ➪ Acquire Developers License. Your license will work on a per machine basis and will need to be renewed each month. You may be prompted with the UAC where you have to allow Visual Studio to make changes to your computer. You must agree to this to acquire or renew your license. Figures 16-4 through 16-6 show the steps in the process, along with the outcome for a new license and a renewal.

3.   The first step is to delete the MainPage.xaml and add a new page based on a Windows 8 template. After deleting the MainPage.xaml, go to Project ➪ Add New Item. In the Add New Item dialog, select the Basic Page Template. There are many page templates available, as you see in Figure 16-7.

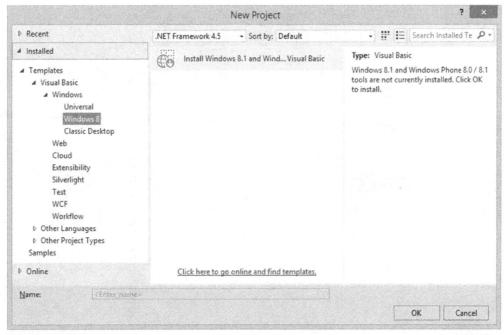

FIGURE 16-3

FIGURE 16-4

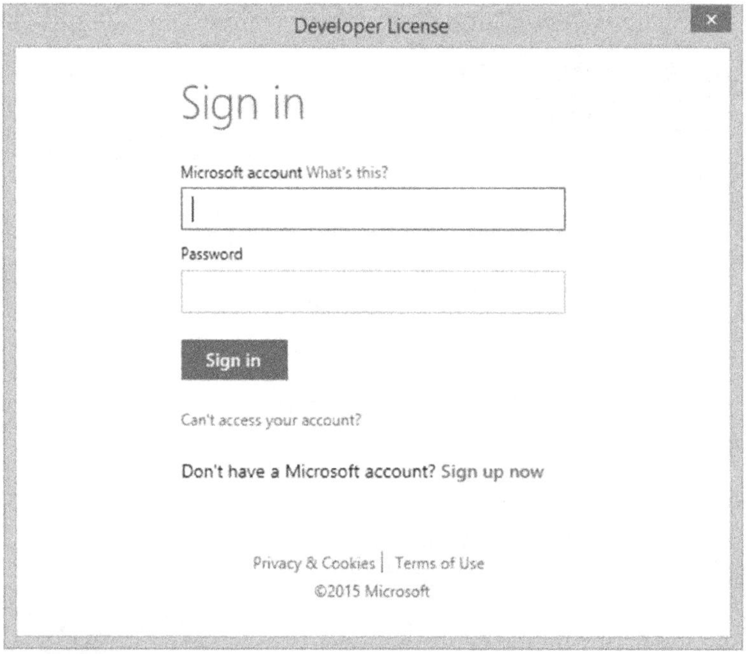

FIGURE 16-5

FIGURE 16-6

4.   Name the new page the same as the page you deleted: **MainPage.xaml**. You may see an alert that says items are missing from the project. Allow Visual Studio to add these files for you.

5.   View the XAML code in the new MainPage you added and change the AppName value to Tic Tac Toe, as shown in the bold code.

```
<Page.Resources>
  <!—TODO: Delete this line if the key AppName is declared in App.xaml—>
  <x:String x:Key="AppName">Tic Tac Toe</x:String>
</Page.Resources>
```

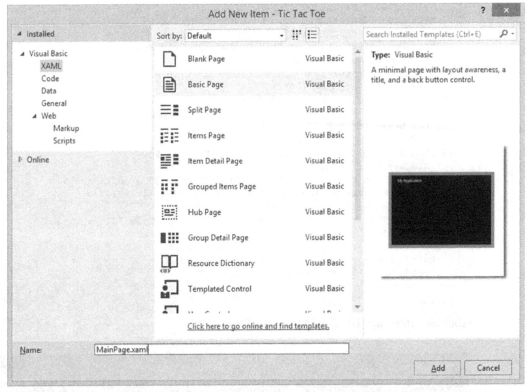

FIGURE 16-7

6. Next, add the following code between the two ending Grid tags at the bottom of the XAML code:

```
    </Grid>
    </Grid>
    Grid Grid.Row="1" Name="MainGrid">
      <Grid.RowDefinitions>
        <RowDefinition Height="100"/>
        <RowDefinition Height="100"/>
        <RowDefinition Height="100"/>
        <RowDefinition Height="Auto"/>
        <RowDefinition Height="Auto"/>
      </Grid.RowDefinitions>
      <Grid.ColumnDefinitions>
        <ColumnDefinition Width="100"/>
        <ColumnDefinition Width="100"/>
        <ColumnDefinition Width="100"/>
        <ColumnDefinition Width="*"/>
      </Grid.ColumnDefinitions>
      <Button Name="TopLeft" Grid.Column="0" Grid.Row="0"
          Width="100" Height="100"/>
      <Button Name="TopMiddle" Grid.Column="1" Grid.Row="0"
          Width="100" Height="100"/>
      <Button Name="TopRight" Grid.Column="2" Grid.Row="0"
```

```
        Width="100" Height="100"/>
    <Button Name="CenterLeft" Grid.Column="0" Grid.Row="1"
        Width="100" Height="100"/>
    <Button Name="CenterMiddle" Grid.Column="1" Grid.Row="1"
        Width="100" Height="100"/>
    <Button Name="CenterRight" Grid.Column="2" Grid.Row="1"
        Width="100" Height="100"/>
    <Button Name="BottomLeft" Grid.Column="0" Grid.Row="2"
        Width="100" Height="100"/>
    <Button Name="BottomMiddle" Grid.Column="1" Grid.Row="2"
        Width="100" Height="100"/>
    <Button Name="BottomRight" Grid.Column="2" Grid.Row="2"
        Width="100" Height="100"/>
    <StackPanel Orientation="Vertical" Grid.Column="3" Grid.Row="0">
      <TextBlock Name="Title" Text="Tic Tic Toe" FontSize="16"/>
      <TextBlock Name="Status" TextWrapping="Wrap"
        Text="The status of the game goes here" FontSize="12"/>
    </StackPanel>
    <StackPanel Orientation="Horizontal" Grid.Column="3" Grid.Row="1">
      <Button Name="NewGame" Content="New Game" />
      <Button Name="Random" Content="Random Play" />
    </StackPanel>
  </Grid>
```

Your user interface (UI) should look like Figure 16-8.

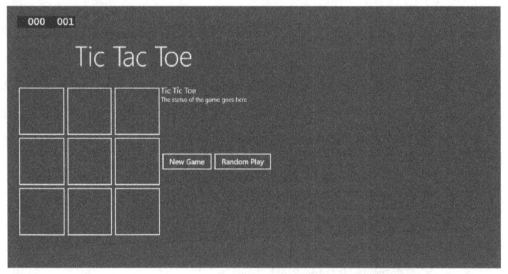

FIGURE 16-8

7. Now, add the code to make it work. Open the code behind for `MainPage.xaml`. Place the following code in the `MainPage` class after the current code and before `End Class`. The code you are creating here is all code you have created before, and no new concepts are shown. You may want to just copy the code-behind code from the download code if you have any issues.

```
Private _CurrentPlayer As String
  Public Property CurrentPlayer() As String
```

```vb
    Get
      Return _CurrentPlayer
    End Get
    Set(ByVal value As String)
      _CurrentPlayer = value
    End Set
End Property
Private _isWinnerFound As Boolean
Public Property isWinnerFound() As Boolean
  Get
    Return _isWinnerFound
  End Get
  Set(ByVal value As Boolean)
    _isWinnerFound = value
  End Set
End Property
Public Sub ChangePlayer()
  If CurrentPlayer.ToUpper = "X" Then
    CurrentPlayer = "O"
  Else
    CurrentPlayer = "X"
  End If
End Sub
Private Sub GameBoard_Click(sender As Object,
  e As RoutedEventArgs) Handles TopLeft.Click,
  TopMiddle.Click, TopRight.Click,
  CenterLeft.Click, CenterMiddle.Click,
  CenterRight.Click, BottomLeft.Click,
  BottomMiddle.Click, BottomRight.Click

  MakePlay(sender)
End Sub
Sub MakePlay(ByRef ButtonToPlay As Button)
  ButtonToPlay.Content = CurrentPlayer
  CheckForWinner(TopLeft.Content, TopMiddle.Content,
    TopRight.Content, CenterLeft.Content,
    CenterMiddle.Content, CenterRight.Content,
    BottomLeft.Content, BottomMiddle.Content,
    BottomRight.Content)
  ButtonToPlay.IsEnabled = False
  If isWinnerFound Then Exit Sub
  If GameIsTie() Then Exit Sub
  ChangePlayer()
  Status.Text = "Play " + CurrentPlayer.ToString
End Sub
Sub Winner(strPlayer)
  Status.Text = CurrentPlayer.ToString + " is the winner."
End Sub
Sub CheckForWinner(strTopLeft As String, strTopMid As String,
    strTopRight As String, strCenterLeft As String,
    strCenterMid As String, strCenterRight As String,
    strBottomLeft As String, strBottomMid As String,
    strBottomRight As String)
  If isRowWinner(strTopLeft, strTopMid,
    strTopRight) Then Exit Sub
  If isRowWinner(strCenterLeft,
```

```
        strCenterMid, strCenterRight) Then Exit Sub
    If isRowWinner(strBottomLeft,
        strBottomMid, strBottomRight) Then Exit Sub
    If isRowWinner(strTopLeft,
        strCenterLeft, strBottomLeft) Then Exit Sub
    If isRowWinner(strTopMid,
        strCenterMid, strBottomMid) Then Exit Sub
    If isRowWinner(strTopRight,
        strCenterRight, strBottomRight) Then Exit Sub
    If isRowWinner(strTopLeft,
        strCenterMid, strBottomRight) Then Exit Sub
    If isRowWinner(strTopRight,
        strCenterMid, strBottomLeft) Then Exit Sub
End Sub
Function isRowWinner(Square1 As String, Square2 As String,
            Square3 As String) As Boolean
    If Square1 <> " " And Square1 = Square2 And Square2 = Square3 Then
        Winner(CurrentPlayer)
        _isWinnerFound = True
        Return True
    End If
    Return False
End Function
Sub RandomPlay()
    If isWinnerFound Then Exit Sub
    If GameIsTie() Then Exit Sub

    Dim RandomGenerator As New Random()
    Dim blnIsComputersTurn As Boolean = True
    While blnIsComputersTurn
        Select Case RandomGenerator.Next(1, 10)
            Case 1
                If TopLeft.IsEnabled Then
                    MakePlay(TopLeft)
                    blnIsComputersTurn = False
                End If
            Case 2
                If TopMiddle.IsEnabled Then
                    MakePlay(TopMiddle)
                    blnIsComputersTurn = False
                End If
            Case 3
                If TopRight.IsEnabled Then
                    MakePlay(TopRight)
                    blnIsComputersTurn = False
                End If
            Case 4
                If CenterLeft.IsEnabled Then
                    MakePlay(CenterLeft)
                    blnIsComputersTurn = False
                End If
            Case 5
                If CenterMiddle.IsEnabled Then
                    MakePlay(CenterMiddle)
                    blnIsComputersTurn = False
```

```vb
        End If
      Case 6
        If CenterRight.IsEnabled Then
          MakePlay(CenterRight)
          blnIsComputersTurn = False
        End If
      Case 7
        If BottomLeft.IsEnabled Then
          MakePlay(BottomLeft)
          blnIsComputersTurn = False
        End If
      Case 8
        If BottomMiddle.IsEnabled Then
          MakePlay(BottomMiddle)
          blnIsComputersTurn = False
        End If
      Case 9
        If BottomRight.IsEnabled Then
          MakePlay(BottomRight)
          blnIsComputersTurn = False
        End If
    End Select
  End While
End Sub
Function GameIsTie() As Boolean
  'if any game board buttons are enabled
  'the game is a tie if no winner was found
  Dim GameButton As Button
  For Each ctrl In MainGrid.Children
    If TypeOf (ctrl) Is Button Then
      GameButton = ctrl
      If GameButton.Name <> "NewGame" And
        GameButton.Name <> "Random" Then
        If GameButton.IsEnabled Then
          Return False
        End If
      End If
    End If
  Next
  Status.Text = "The game is a tie."
  Return True
End Function
Sub Reset()
  Dim GameButton As Button
  For Each ctrl In MainGrid.Children
    If TypeOf (ctrl) Is Button Then
      GameButton = ctrl
      With GameButton
        If .Name <> "NewGame" And
          .Name <> "Random" Then .Content = " "
        .IsEnabled = True
      End With
    End If
  Next
  Status.Text = "Start the game by selecting" &
```

```
        " a square to play."
    CurrentPlayer = "X"
    isWinnerFound = False
End Sub
Private Sub MainPage_Loaded(sender As Object,
      e As RoutedEventArgs) Handles Me.Loaded
  Reset()
End Sub
Private Sub NewGame_Click(sender As Object,
      e As RoutedEventArgs) Handles NewGame.Click
  Reset()
End Sub
Private Sub Random_Click(sender As Object,
      e As RoutedEventArgs) Handles Random.Click
  RandomPlay()
End Sub
```

8.   Now run the app to be sure it is working. Your first Windows 8 app is complete. Notice that you can now choose to run the application locally or in a Simulator. In the Simulator, you can simulate more gestures while testing. Figure 16-9 shows the options for running the application.

FIGURE 16-9

How It Works

To start your application you have to obtain your developer's license from Microsoft. That is accomplished by following the on-screen prompts and using your Live ID.

After you got your license created or renewed, you created a new project. The first step was to delete the default main page and add a new one based on the Basic Page template, which contains layout-aware pages that have events that can handle vertical and horizontal alignment as well as snapping events. Common items such as styles and even controls are added to your project with these templates. You will see more of this later in the chapter.

Next, you changed the application name to Tic Tac Toe:

```
<Page.Resources>
  <!-TODO: Delete this line if the key AppName is declared in App.xaml->
  <x:String x:Key="AppName">Tic Tac Toe</x:String>
</Page.Resources>
```

To begin your design, you added the layout of the Tic Tac Toe grid. The grid has a layout of five rows and four columns. To keep the board in squares, the height and width for the game squares are set to 100 pixels each:

```
<Grid Grid.Row="1" Name="MainGrid">
  <Grid.RowDefinitions>
    <RowDefinition Height="100"/>
    <RowDefinition Height="100"/>
    <RowDefinition Height="100"/>
    <RowDefinition Height="Auto"/>
    <RowDefinition Height="Auto"/>
  </Grid.RowDefinitions>
  <Grid.ColumnDefinitions>
    <ColumnDefinition Width="100"/>
    <ColumnDefinition Width="100"/>
    <ColumnDefinition Width="100"/>
    <ColumnDefinition Width="*"/>
  </Grid.ColumnDefinitions>
</Grid.ColumnDefinitions>
```

To make the game playable, you added nine buttons. One button was added to each of the first three columns in the first three rows. You assigned each button to the correct cell on the grid by setting the Grid.Column and Grid.Row properties:

```
<Button Name="TopLeft" Grid.Column="0" Grid.Row ="0"
        Width="100" Height="100"/>
  <Button Name="TopMiddle" Grid.Column="1" Grid.Row="0"
        Width="100" Height="100"/>
  <Button Name="TopRight" Grid.Column="2" Grid.Row="0"
        Width="100" Height="100"/>
  <Button Name="CenterLeft" Grid.Column="0" Grid.Row="1"
        Width="100" Height="100"/>
  <Button Name="CenterMiddle" Grid.Column="1" Grid.Row="1"
        Width="100" Height="100"/>
  <Button Name="CenterRight" Grid.Column="2" Grid.Row="1"
        Width="100" Height="100"/>
  <Button Name="BottomLeft" Grid.Column="0" Grid.Row="2"
        Width="100" Height="100"/>
  <Button Name="BottomMiddle" Grid.Column="1" Grid.Row="2"
        Width="100" Height="100"/>
  <Button Name="BottomRight" Grid.Column="2" Grid.Row="2"
        Width="100" Height="100"/>
```

To lay out the text on the screen and the game play buttons, you used StackPanel controls. These controls allow you to orient other controls horizontally or vertically. Again, these controls were assigned to the appropriate cell in the grid:

```
<StackPanel Orientation="Vertical" Grid.Column="3" Grid.Row="0">
    <TextBlock Name="Title" Text="Tic Tic Toe" FontSize="16"/>
    <TextBlock Name="Status" TextWrapping="Wrap"
        Text="The status of the game goes here" FontSize="12"/>
  </StackPanel>
  <StackPanel Orientation="Horizontal" Grid.Column="3" Grid.Row="1">
    <Button Name="NewGame" Content="New Game" />
```

```
      <Button Name="Random" Content="Random Play" />
    </StackPanel>
  </Grid>
```

Finally you added the code behind to make the program function as a Tic Tac Toe game would. To begin, some properties used to maintain the application state were added:

```
Private _CurrentPlayer As String
  Public Property CurrentPlayer() As String
    Get
      Return _CurrentPlayer
    End Get
    Set(ByVal value As String)
      _CurrentPlayer = value
    End Set
  End Property
  Private _isWinnerFound As Boolean
  Public Property isWinnerFound() As Boolean
    Get
      Return _isWinnerFound
    End Get
    Set(ByVal value As Boolean)
      _isWinnerFound = value
    End Set
  End Property
  Public Sub ChangePlayer()
    If CurrentPlayer.ToUpper = "X" Then
      CurrentPlayer = "O"
    Else
      CurrentPlayer = "X"
    End If
  End Sub
```

To make the buttons work on the game board, you added one event handler to handle the click on any of the nine game squares. By adding more than one control, separated by commas, this one event works for every game square:

```
Private Sub GameBoard_Click(sender As Object,
    e As RoutedEventArgs) Handles TopLeft.Click,
    TopMiddle.Click, TopRight.Click,
    CenterLeft.Click, CenterMiddle.Click,
    CenterRight.Click, BottomLeft.Click,
    BottomMiddle.Click, BottomRight.Click

    MakePlay(sender)
End Sub
```

The MakePlay procedure defines how the game play works. First, it sets the square to X or O. After that, a check is made to see whether a winning row can be found. Next, the square is disabled, and the game is over if a winner or a tie is declared. If not, the player is changed, and directions are given that it is the new player's turn.

```
Sub MakePlay(ByRef ButtonToPlay As Button)
    ButtonToPlay.Content = CurrentPlayer
```

```
    CheckForWinner(TopLeft.Content, TopMiddle.Content,
      TopRight.Content, CenterLeft.Content,
      CenterMiddle.Content, CenterRight.Content,
      BottomLeft.Content, BottomMiddle.Content,
      BottomRight.Content)
    ButtonToPlay.IsEnabled = False
    If isWinnerFound Then Exit Sub
    If GameIsTie() Then Exit Sub
    ChangePlayer()
    Status.Text = "Play " + CurrentPlayer.ToString
  End Sub
```

To check for a winner, you created a function, isRowWinner, to test whether each square is the same. Then you called it for each vertical, horizontal, or diagonal row. When you found a winner, you displayed text to declare the winning player:

```
Sub CheckForWinner(strTopLeft As String, strTopMid As String,
      strTopRight As String, strCenterLeft As String,
      strCenterMid As String, strCenterRight As String,
      strBottomLeft As String, strBottomMid As String,
      strBottomRight As String)
  If isRowWinner(strTopLeft, strTopMid,
    strTopRight) Then Exit Sub
  If isRowWinner(strCenterLeft,
    strCenterMid, strCenterRight) Then Exit Sub
  If isRowWinner(strBottomLeft,
    strBottomMid, strBottomRight) Then Exit Sub
  If isRowWinner(strTopLeft,
    strCenterLeft, strBottomLeft) Then Exit Sub
  If isRowWinner(strTopMid,
    strCenterMid, strBottomMid) Then Exit Sub
  If isRowWinner(strTopRight,
    strCenterRight, strBottomRight) Then Exit Sub
  If isRowWinner(strTopLeft,
    strCenterMid, strBottomRight) Then Exit Sub
  If isRowWinner(strTopRight,
    strCenterMid, strBottomLeft) Then Exit Sub
End Sub
Function isRowWinner(Square1 As String, Square2 As String,
          Square3 As String) As Boolean
  If Square1 <> " " And Square1 = Square2 And Square2 = Square3 Then
    Winner(CurrentPlayer)
    _isWinnerFound = True
    Return True
  End If
  Return False
End Function
Sub Winner(strPlayer)
  Status.Text = CurrentPlayer.ToString + " is the winner."
End Sub
```

To allow for single play, you created the RandomPlay procedure. This code makes a random play on any open square. To do this, a random number greater than or equal to 1 and less than 10 is generated. That random number is assigned to a square, and if that square is open, the play is made on that square by calling `MakePlay`. If the square is not open, another try is made until an open square is found:

```
Sub RandomPlay()
    If isWinnerFound Then Exit Sub
    If GameIsTie() Then Exit Sub

    Dim RandomGenerator As New Random()
    Dim blnIsComputersTurn As Boolean = True
    While blnIsComputersTurn
        Select Case RandomGenerator.Next(1, 10)
            Case 1
                If TopLeft.IsEnabled Then
                    MakePlay(TopLeft)
                    blnIsComputersTurn = False
                End If
            Case 2
                If TopMiddle.IsEnabled Then
                    MakePlay(TopMiddle)
                    blnIsComputersTurn = False
                End If
            Case 3
                If TopRight.IsEnabled Then
                    MakePlay(TopRight)
                    blnIsComputersTurn = False
                End If
            Case 4
                If CenterLeft.IsEnabled Then
                    MakePlay(CenterLeft)
                    blnIsComputersTurn = False
                End If
            Case 5
                If CenterMiddle.IsEnabled Then
                    MakePlay(CenterMiddle)
                    blnIsComputersTurn = False
                End If
            Case 6
                If CenterRight.IsEnabled Then
                    MakePlay(CenterRight)
                    blnIsComputersTurn = False
                End If
            Case 7
                If BottomLeft.IsEnabled Then
                    MakePlay(BottomLeft)
                    blnIsComputersTurn = False
                End If
            Case 8
                If BottomMiddle.IsEnabled Then
                    MakePlay(BottomMiddle)
                    blnIsComputersTurn = False
                End If
            Case 9
                If BottomRight.IsEnabled Then
                    MakePlay(BottomRight)
```

```
            blnIsComputersTurn = False
        End If
    End Select
End While
End Sub
```

To check for a tie, you iterate through a collection of button controls on the grid. This code goes through the game squares (excluding the NewGame and Random buttons) and tests whether the button is enabled. If all buttons are disabled, the game is a tie:

```
Function GameIsTie() As Boolean
    'if any game board buttons are enabled
    'the game is a tie if no winner was found
    Dim GameButton As Button
    For Each ctrl In MainGrid.Children
        If TypeOf (ctrl) Is Button Then
            GameButton = ctrl
            If GameButton.Name <> "NewGame" And
                GameButton.Name <> "Random" Then
                If GameButton.IsEnabled Then
                    Return False
                End If
            End If
        End If
    Next
    Status.Text = "The game is a tie."
    Return True
End Function
```

To clear the board and start over, the Reset procedure enables each square, clears the last play, and directs the player to begin:

```
Sub Reset()
    Dim GameButton As Button
    For Each ctrl In MainGrid.Children
        If TypeOf (ctrl) Is Button Then
            GameButton = ctrl
            With GameButton
                If .Name <> "NewGame" And
                    .Name <> "Random" Then .Content = " "
                    .IsEnabled = True
            End With
        End If
    Next
    Status.Text = "Start the game by selecting" &
        " a square to play."
    CurrentPlayer = "X"
    isWinnerFound = False
End Sub
```

Your first Windows 8 application seems a lot like other applications you have created. In the next section, you will look at coding your application using styles to handle layout changes.

APPLICATION LAYOUT

When you start using your Windows 8 applications, you will notice that the screen size can change quickly. Just imagine that users are on a 10" tablet and trying to enjoy your new Tic Tac Toe game. They may snap your application to the left side while checking an email, and you'll realize that your application must handle such differences in screen size. This section shows you how to program for changing screens.

Application Views

When you build Windows Forms applications or Windows 8 applications, they both have views (states for the forms app). In a Windows form, the states are Minimized, Maximized, or Normal. For Windows 8 applications, the views are Snapped, Filled, FullScreenLandscape, or FullScreenPortrait.

Unlike the normal Windows Forms app, there is no control box to change the state of the form in a Windows 8 application. To change the application view, a user will touch and drag the app to the right or left to snap the application.

One of the key concepts to Windows 8 application design is to fill the screen area. For a snapped view, the width is 320 px, and the application pans vertically. If your app is in Filled view, it should fill 100 percent of the height and width and pan horizontally. In FullScreenLandscape or FullScreenPortrait views, your app would fill the screen and pan accordingly.

Screen Sizes and Orientation

Windows 8 apps center around two main design layouts:

- ➤ **Fixed layout:** The Tic Tac Toe game is a fixed layout; the screen size is not a concern for most games and many applications. Your program in this case will use fixed elements like a grid with three rows and three columns, no matter how wide the user's screen is. Even in a fixed layout, you may want to have your controls scale to fit. To accomplish this, you can add the controls to a ViewBox control. A ViewBox control can scale up and down to make your app fill the screen for larger screens. To use this control, set the width and height to 100 percent and then set your baseline size properties to the appropriate layout on which you are basing your design.

- ➤ **Adaptive layout:** To design applications such as a news reader or content app, you might choose this layout, which can have a header, navigation, footer, and content area. The content area would dynamically show more content based on orientation and screen size. To accomplish this, you might use a ListView control, which can dynamically change the number of rows and columns to adapt to the screen of the user as well as to changes in orientation.

Windows 8 apps also have two main resolutions for you to consider when designing your Windows 8 apps:

➤ **1024 × 768:** With this baseline resolution, you ensure your controls are not clipped on most screens. You can consider 1024 × 768 as the minimum resolution for your users.

➤ **1366 × 768:** This is the optimal resolution and it ensures the least amount of blank space for your user. To create an app that fills the screen best, design your applications at this resolution.

To show this all in action, in the following Try It Out, you will make some adjustments to the tic-tac-toe game to handle the user switch from `Snapped` view to `Filled` view.

TRY IT OUT Tic Tac Toe

For the Tic Tac Toe game you are creating, you will allow the game to adjust to fit the screen size better. Basically, you allow the application to scale for a better user interface. All the code for this Try It Out is in code file `Tic Tac Toe.zip`.

1. Go back to Visual Studio 2015 and the **Tic Tac Toe** project.

2. View the XAML code in the new `MainPage.xaml` you added in the previous Try It Out and change the `StackPanels` by adding a `Name` attribute and removing the `Grid.Column` and `Grid.Row` attributes:

```
<StackPanel Name="TextSP" Orientation="Vertical">
<StackPanel Name="ButtonSP" Orientation="Horizontal">
```

3. Now, change the application based on view state. To do this, add the following code to the `MainPage.xaml.vb`:

```
Private Sub MainPage_SizeChanged(sender As Object,
   e As SizeChangedEventArgs) Handles Me.SizeChanged

   If Window.Current.Bounds.Width <= 1000 Then
     Grid.SetColumn(TextSP, 0)
     Grid.SetColumn(ButtonSP, 0)
     Grid.SetColumnSpan(TextSP, 3)
     Grid.SetColumnSpan(ButtonSP, 3)
     Grid.SetRow(TextSP, 3)
     Grid.SetRow(ButtonSP, 4)
   Else
     Grid.SetColumn(TextSP, 3)
     Grid.SetColumn(ButtonSP, 3)
     Grid.SetRow(TextSP, 0)
     Grid.SetRow(ButtonSP, 1)
     Grid.SetColumnSpan(TextSP, 1)
     Grid.SetColumnSpan(ButtonSP, 1)
   End If
End Sub
```

4. Save your application, run it in the Simulator, and test the orientation and view states. To snap the application, place the mouse at the top of the Simulator screen, and then click the

mouse and drag the application down and to the left. The application will look like Figure 16-10.

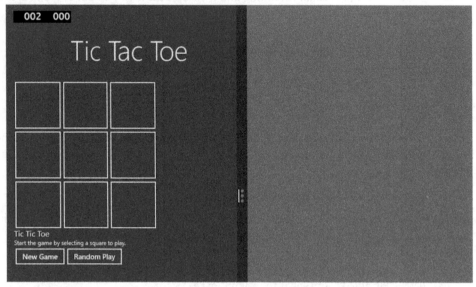

FIGURE 16-10

5. Drag the application back to the center. On the right of the Simulator, click the rotate icon to change the orientation. Your application will look like Figure 16-11.

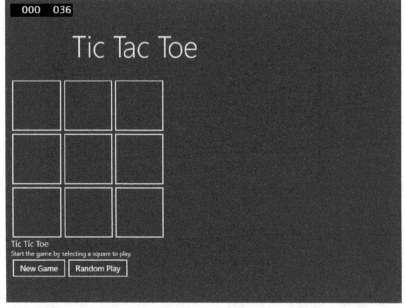

FIGURE 16-11

6. Add an `AppBar` to the application. Stop the application if it is running and go back to `MainPage`.`xaml`. Add the following XAML after the `</Page.Resources>` closing element:

```
<Page.TopAppBar>
 <AppBar x:Name="topBar">
  <Grid>
   <StackPanel Orientation="Horizontal"
      HorizontalAlignment="Left">
    <AppBarButton Icon="Save" Label="Save"
      Click="AppBar_Click" />
    <AppBarButton Icon="Upload" Label="Upload"
      Click="AppBar_Click" />
    <AppBarButton Icon="Delete" Label="Delete"
      Click="AppBar_Click" />
   </StackPanel>
  </Grid>
 </AppBar>
</Page.TopAppBar>
<Page.BottomAppBar>
 <AppBar x:Name="bottomBar">
  <Grid>
   <StackPanel Orientation="Horizontal"
      HorizontalAlignment="Left">
    <AppBarButton Icon="Edit" Label="Edit"
      Click="AppBar_Click" />
    <AppBarButton Icon="Add" Label="Add"
      Click="AppBar_Click" />
    <AppBarButton Icon="Remove" Label="Remove"
      Click="AppBar_Click" />
   </StackPanel>
   <StackPanel Orientation="Horizontal"
      HorizontalAlignment="Right">
    <AppBarButton Icon="Redo" Label="Redo"
      Click="AppBar_Click" />
    <AppBarButton Icon="Help" Label="Help"
      Click="AppBar_Click" />
   </StackPanel>
  </Grid>
 </AppBar>
</Page.BottomAppBar>
```

7. Add the following subroutine to the code behind:

```
Private Sub AppBar_Click(sender As Object,
        e As RoutedEventArgs)
End Sub
```

8. Test the application again. This time, right-click to open the new `AppBar` controls and to see what you added.

How It Works

First, you added a name to both `StackPanel` controls, allowing for easy programmatic control at run time. You also removed the design time code that set the `Grid` position for the controls:

```
<StackPanel Name="TextSP" Orientation="Vertical">
<StackPanel Name="ButtonSP" Orientation="Horizontal">
```

Next, you added the code to handle the snapping of the application. The `SizeChanged` event fires when the application's view changes. This is where you added code to customize the layout of the game:

```
Private Sub MainPage_SizeChanged(sender As Object,
    e As SizeChangedEventArgs) Handles Me.SizeChanged
```

To update the layout, you needed to test for the current width. As the developer, you get to decide how to handle the orientation options and snap options:

```
If Window.Current.Bounds.Width <= 1000 Then
```

Once you knew that the state was changed to `Snapped`, you had to move the `StackPanels` to avoid having them clipped off the screen. To do this, you moved the controls by calling `Grid.SetRow`, `Grid.SetColumn` and `Grid.SetColumnSpan`. These methods were used to position the text and buttons below the game board squares. If the case was that the view was not `Snapped`, you just moved that back to the original position:

```
Grid.SetColumn(TextSP, 0)
    Grid.SetColumn(ButtonSP, 0)
    Grid.SetColumnSpan(TextSP, 3)
    Grid.SetColumnSpan(ButtonSP, 3)
    Grid.SetRow(TextSP, 3)
    Grid.SetRow(ButtonSP, 4)
Else
    Grid.SetColumn(TextSP, 3)
    Grid.SetColumn(ButtonSP, 3)
    Grid.SetRow(TextSP, 0)
    Grid.SetRow(ButtonSP, 1)
    Grid.SetColumnSpan(TextSP, 1)
    Grid.SetColumnSpan(ButtonSP, 1)
```

To add new `AppBars`, you added the button controls within the `TopAppBar` Page element. To keep a consistent style across applications, Visual Studio includes icons. Icons available include the most common commands you would use: `Play`, `Rewind`, `Upload`, `Save`, `Add`, `Refresh`, and many more.

The `Click` property was set to an empty subroutine to avoid errors in the code. You would normally have unique events for each `Button` that would perform the actions for the button:

```
<Page.TopAppBar>
 <AppBar x:Name="topBar">
  <Grid>
   <StackPanel Orientation="Horizontal"
      HorizontalAlignment="Left">
      <AppBarButton Icon="Save" Label="Save"
        Click="AppBar_Click" />
      <AppBarButton Icon="Upload" Label="Upload"
        Click="AppBar_Click" />
      <AppBarButton Icon="Delete" Label="Delete"
        Click="AppBar_Click" />   </StackPanel>
  </Grid>
 </AppBar>
</Page.TopAppBar>
<Page.BottomAppBar>
```

```
<AppBar x:Name="bottomBar">
 <Grid>
  <StackPanel Orientation="Horizontal"
     HorizontalAlignment="Left">
     <AppBarButton Icon="Edit" Label="Edit"
       Click="AppBar_Click" />
     <AppBarButton Icon="Add" Label="Add"
       Click="AppBar_Click" />
     <AppBarButton Icon="Remove" Label="Remove"
       Click="AppBar_Click" />
    <Button Style="{StaticResource EditAppBarButtonStyle}"
      Click="AppBar_Click"/>
    <Button Style="{StaticResource AddAppBarButtonStyle}"
      Click="AppBar_Click"/>
    <Button Style="{StaticResource RemoveAppBarButtonStyle}"
      Click="AppBar_Click"/>
  </StackPanel>
  <StackPanel Orientation="Horizontal"
     HorizontalAlignment="Right">
     <AppBarButton Icon="Redo" Label="Redo"
       Click="AppBar_Click" />
     <AppBarButton Icon="Help" Label="Help"
       Click="AppBar_Click" />
  </StackPanel>
 </Grid>
</AppBar>
</Page.BottomAppBar>

Private Sub AppBar_Click(sender As Object,
        e As RoutedEventArgs)
End Sub
```

SUMMARY

In this chapter, you learned what Windows 8 applications are and how to create them in Visual Studio 2015. While building your first Windows 8 application, you learned about basic design principles for touchscreen applications. Also, you learned that your Windows 8 applications should handle changes to view state as well as orientation. You used many of the programming tools you learned throughout the book to build a random-play mechanism and game status logic. Remember that as a developer you must stay on top of new technologies. You will be able to leverage your previous knowledge to make the learning curve less steep.

To summarize, you should now know the following:

- ➤ What Windows 8 applications are
- ➤ What the common controls in Windows 8 applications are
- ➤ How to test Windows 8 applications using the Simulator
- ➤ How to use code to handle changes in Application view and orientation

EXERCISES

1. What are the two types of layout you learned about? Which one would you use most for content applications?

2. What is the most important consideration in Windows 8 design?

3. How do Windows 8 applications' design considerations differ from Windows applications?

4. What is the minimum screen resolution to use to design Windows 8 applications?

▶ **WHAT YOU LEARNED IN THIS CHAPTER**

TOPIC	CONCEPTS
Windows 8 design	For Windows 8 applications, be sure to consider the user interface and fill the screen when possible.
Touch	Windows 8 applications need to be designed with a touch interface in mind.
Windows 8 controls	`Appbar`, `FlipView`, and `StackPanel` are some of the new controls you learned about.

APPENDIX

Exercise Solutions

CHAPTER 1

The code for the following exercise is found in the code file `Chapter 1/Exercise1.zip`.

1. Create a Windows application with a Textbox control and a Button control that displays whatever is typed in the text box when the user clicks the button.

A. To display the text from a text box on a form when the user clicks the button, you add the following bolded code to the button's `Click` event handler:

```
Private Sub btnDisplay_Click(sender As Object, _
e As EventArgs) Handles btnDisplay.Click

    'Display the contents of the text box
    MessageBox.Show(txtInput.Text, "Exercise 1")
End Sub
```

CHAPTER 2

No exercises for Chapter 2.

CHAPTER 3

1. Create a Windows application with two button controls. In the `Click` event for the first button, declare two `Integer` variables and set their values to any number that you want. Perform any math operation on these variables and display the results in a message box. In the `Click` event for the second button, declare two `String` variables and set their values to anything that you like. Perform a string concatenation on these variables and display the results in a message box.

A. The first part of this exercise requires you to declare two Integer variables and set their values, and then to perform a math operation of these variables and display the results in a message box. The variables can be declared and set as:

```
'Declare variables and set their values
Dim intX As Integer = 5
Dim intY As Integer = 10
```

➤ To perform a math operation and display the results, you could write code such as:

```
'Multiply the numbers and display the results
MessageBox.Show("The total of " & intX.ToString & " * " &
intY.ToString & " = " & intX * intY, "Exercise 1")
```

➤ The second part of this exercise requires you to declare two String variables and set their values, and then to concatenate the variables and display the results in a message box. The String variables can be declared and set as:

```
'Declare variables and set their values
Dim strOne As String = "Visual Basic "
Dim strTwo As String = "2010"
```

➤ To concatenate the variables and display the results, you could write code such as:

```
'Concatenate the strings and display the results
MessageBox.Show(strOne & strTwo, "Exercise 1")
```

2. Create a Windows application with a text box and a button control. In the button's Click event, display three message boxes. The first message box should display the length of the string that was entered into the text box. The second message box should display the first half of the string, and the third message box should display the last half of the string.

A. This exercise requires you to display the length of the string entered into a text box, and then display the first half of the string and the last half of the string. To display the length of the string, you can use the Length property of the Text property of the text box, as shown here:

```
'Display the length of the string from the TextBox
MessageBox.Show("The length of the string in the TextBox is " &
txtInput.Text.Length, "Exercise 2")
```

➤ To display the first half of the string, you need to use the Substring method with a starting index of 0; and for the length you use the length of the string divided by 2, as shown here. Don't forget that with the Option Strict option turned on, you must convert the results of a division operation to an Integer data type for use in the SubString method:

```
'Display the first half of the string from the TextBox
MessageBox.Show(txtInput.Text.Substring(0,
CType(txtInput.Text.Length / 2, Integer)), "Exercise 2")
```

➤ To display the last half of the string, you again use the Substring method, but this time you simply give it a starting index of the length of the string divided by 2, as shown here:

```
'Display the last half of the string from the TextBox
MessageBox.Show(txtInput.Text.Substring(
CType(txtInput.Text.Length / 2, Integer)), "Exercise 2")
```

CHAPTER 4

1. When using a `Select Case` statement, how do you allow for multiple items in the `Case` statement?

A. Separate the items with commas.

2. What is the difference between a `Do Until` and a `Loop Until Do` loop?

A. With a `Loop Until` statement, it will always run the code one time.

3. Is "Bryan" and "BRYAN" the same string as Visual Basic sees it?

A. No. These strings are different. You can have your code run case-insensitive comparisons so they look the same when you want your code to see them as equal.

4. When you use the `String.Compare` method, what is the last parameter (a Boolean parameter) used for?

A. It indicates whether or not to use a case-sensitive comparison.

5. In a `Select Case` statement, how do you put in a catch all case for items that do not have a match?

A. `Case Else`

6. When writing a `For Each` loop, how do you have the loop iterate backward?

A. Use the `Step` keyword and give it a negative value.

7. What keyword do you use to exit a loop early?

A. `Exit`

CHAPTER 5

1. What keyword do you use to keep the values in an array that you `ReDim`? Where do you insert it?

A. `Preserve`. Insert it in the statement to redimension (after `ReDim`) the array.

2. How do you order an array?

A. By using the `Sort` method

5. Are arrays zero-based or one-based?

A. Arrays are zero-based.

4. Why would you use an enumeration in code?

A. To provide clarity and prevent invalid values from being submitted

5. When initializing an array with values, what characters do you use to enclose the values?

A. Brackets { }

6. How does a constant differ from a normal variable?

A. It cannot be changed during run time.

7. Structures are simpler and similar to what?

A. A class

8. `Hashtables` provide a fast mechanism for what?

A. Lookups. Hashtables are very fast at looking up key/value pairs.

CHAPTER 6

1. Name two controls you can use when adding a toolbar to your form.

A. You can use the following controls when adding a toolbar to your form: `ToolStrip`, `ToolStripButton, ToolStripSeparator, ToolStripProgressBar, ToolStripTextBox, ToolStripContainer, ToolStripDropDownButton,` and `ToolStripComboBox`.

2. What property do you set to display text to users when they hover over a button on a toolbar?

A. You set `ToolTipText` to display text to users when they hover over a button on the toolbar.

3. To work with a text box so a user can add many lines of text, what property must be set to `True` in a Windows Forms application?

A. `Multiline` must be set to `True`.

4. Why would you want to show a form using the `ShowDialog` method?

A. To show a form modally, you would open it using `ShowDialog`. This forces the user to act on the form. Normally, they act on the form by answering the question or clicking OK.

CHAPTER 7

1. To display a dialog to the user, what method do you use?

A. Use the `ShowDialog` method to display a dialog to the user.

2. What method do you call to display a message box?

A. Use the `Show` method to display a message box to the user.

3. Name the five different ways to change the display of an icon to the user on a message box.

A. The five different ways to show an icon are as follows:

    a. No icon

    b. Information icon

    c. Error icon

    d.   Exclamation icon

    e.   Question mark icon

4. How do you determine which button was pressed on a message box?

A. Use the `DialogResult` enumeration to determine which button was pressed.

5. If you need to write basic code, where should you look for a simple example inside of Visual Studio?

A. Simple code examples can be found by inserting snippets inside of Visual Studio.

CHAPTER 8

1. How do you add the commonly used menus and toolbars to either a `MenuStrip` or `ToolStrip` control?

A. To add commonly used items, you can choose Insert Standard Items from the control's context menu.

2. How do you add a custom context menu to a `TextBox` control?

A. First you create a `ContextMenuStrip` control and then you set the control's `ContextMenuStrip` property to the new menu you added.

3. How do you add a shortcut or accelerator to a menu item, such as Alt+F?

A. To provide an access key such as Alt+F for the File menu, you add & before the shortcut character.

4. How do you add a shortcut to a menu item, such as Ctrl+C?

A. To add a shortcut to a menu, use the `ShortcutKeys` property.

CHAPTER 9

1. What window do you use to track a specific variable while debugging?

A. To track specific variables, use the Watch window.

2. How do you look at all the variables in scope while debugging?

A. You can see variables in scope by using the Locals windows.

3. How do you best add error handling to your code?

A. The best way to add error handling is by using the `Try...Catch` block. You can also use `Finally` to always run code whether an error occurs or not.

4. Sometimes you need to cause errors to happen in your code. What keyword do you use to cause errors?

A. To cause an error, use the `Throw` keyword.

5. While debugging, how do you move to the very next statement?

A. Step Into enables you to move to the next statement.

CHAPTER 10

1. Modify your Car class to implement the IDisposable interface. In the Main procedure in Module1, add code to dispose of the objCar object after calling the DisplaySportsCarDetails procedure.

A. The code should now look like this for the Main procedure in Module1:

```
Sub Main()
  'Create a new sports car object
  Dim objCar As New SportsCar

  'Set the horsepower and weight(kg)
  objCar.HorsePower = 240
  objCar.Weight = 1085

  'Display the details of the car
  DisplayCarDetails(objCar)
  DisplaySportsCarDetails(objCar)

  'Dispose of the object
  objCar.Dispose()
  objCar = Nothing
  'Wait for input from the user
  Console.ReadLine()
End Sub
```

The Car class should look like this:

```
Namespace CarPerformance
  Public Class Car
      Implements IDisposable

      Public Color As String
      Public HorsePower As Integer

      Private intSpeed As Integer
      Private intNumberOfDoors As Integer

      'Speed - read-only property to return the speed
      Public ReadOnly Property Speed() As Integer
          Get
              Return intSpeed
          End Get
      End Property

      'Accelerate - add mph to the speed
      Public Sub Accelerate(accelerateBy As Integer)
          'Adjust the speed
```

```
        intSpeed += accelerateBy
End Sub

'NumberOfDoors - get/set the number of doors
Public Property NumberOfDoors() As Integer
    'Called when the property is read
    Get
        Return intNumberOfDoors
    End Get
    'Called when the property is set
    Set(value As Integer)
        'Is the new value between two and five
        If value >= 2 And value <= 5 Then
            intNumberOfDoors = value
        End If
    End Set
End Property

'IsMoving - is the car moving?
Public Function IsMoving() As Boolean
    'Is the car's speed zero?
    If Speed = 0 Then
        Return False
    Else
        Return True
    End If
End Function

'Constructor
Public Sub New()
    'Set the default values
    Color = "White"
    intSpeed = 0
    intNumberOfDoors = 5
End Sub

'CalculateAccelerationRate - assume a constant for a normal car
Public Overridable Function CalculateAccelerationRate() As Double
    'If we assume a normal car goes from 0-60 in 14 seconds,
    'that's an average rate of 4.2 mph/s
    Return 4.2
End Function

Private disposedValue As Boolean = False ' To detect redundant calls

' IDisposable
Protected Overridable Sub Dispose(disposing As Boolean)
    If Not Me.disposedValue Then
        If disposing Then
            ' TODO: free other state (managed objects).
        End If

        ' TODO: free your own state (unmanaged objects).
        ' TODO: set large fields to null.
    End If
```

```
        Me.disposedValue = True
    End Sub

#Region " IDisposable Support "
    ' This code added by Visual Basic to correctly implement disposable
pattern.
    Public Sub Dispose() Implements IDisposable.Dispose
        ' Do not change this code.  Put cleanup code in Dispose(ByVal
disposing As Boolean) above.
        Dispose(True)
        GC.SuppressFinalize(Me)
    End Sub

#End Region

  End Class
End Namespace
```

2. Modify the code in the Main procedure in Module1 to encapsulate the declaration and usage of the SportsCar class in a Using...End Using statement. Remember that the Using... End Using statement automatically handles the disposal of objects that implement the IDisposable interface.

A. The code should now look like this for the Main procedure in Module1:

```
Sub Main()
  'Create a new sports car object
  Using objCar As New SportsCar
    'Set the horsepower and weight(kg)
    objCar.HorsePower = 240
    objCar.Weight = 1085

    'Display the details of the car
    DisplayCarDetails(objCar)
    DisplaySportsCarDetails(objCar)
  End Using

  'Wait for input from the user
  Console.ReadLine()
End Sub
```

CHAPTER 11

1. Modify the Favorites Viewer project to select the first favorite in the ListView control automatically after it has been loaded so that the LinkLabel control displays the first item when the form is displayed.

   You also need to modify the Load event in Form1, and ensure that the ListView control contains one or more items before proceeding. You do this by querying the Count property of the Items property of the ListView control. Then you select the first item in the ListView control using the lstFavorites.Items(0).Selected property and call the Click event for the ListBox control to update the LinkLabel control.

A. The code should look like this:

```
Private Sub Viewer_Load(sender As Object,
        e As EventArgs) Handles Me.Load

    Try
        'Create and use a new instance of the Favorites class
        Using objFavorites As New Favorites

            'Scan the Favorites folder
            objFavorites.ScanFavorites()

            'Process each objWebFavorite object in the
            'favorites collection
            For Each objWebFavorite As WebFavorite In _
                objFavorites.FavoritesCollection

                'Declare a ListViewItem object
                Dim objListViewItem As New ListViewItem

                'Set the properties of the ListViewItem object
                objListViewItem.Text = objWebFavorite.Name
                objListViewItem.SubItems.Add(objWebFavorite.Url)

                'Add the ListViewItem object to the ListView
                lvwFavorites.Items.Add(objListViewItem)
            Next

        End Using
    Catch ExceptionErr As Exception
        'Display the error
        MessageBox.Show(ExceptionErr.Message, "Favorites Viewer", _
            MessageBoxButtons.OK, MessageBoxIcon.Warning)
    End Try

    'If one or more items exist...
    If lvwFavorites.Items.Count > 1 Then
        'Select the first item
        lvwFavorites.Items(0).Selected = True
        lvwFavorites_Click(Nothing, Nothing)
    End If

End Sub
```

CHAPTER 12

1. How would you write a query to retrieve the Name, Description, and Price fields from a table called Product?

A. `SELECT Name, Description, Price FROM Product`

2. What would you add to the query to retrieve only items with DVD in their description?

A. `WHERE Description LIKE "%DVD%"`

3. How would you order the results so that the most expensive item comes first?

A. `ORDER BY Price DESC`

4. What do you put around column names that have spaces in them?

A. Square brackets are used for column names with spaces, such as `[First Name]`.

5. In SSMS, what function key do you press to execute SQL statements?

A. Press F5.

6. In SSMS, how do you execute only certain statements on a query window?

A. By highlighting parts of your query; only the highlighted lines will be executed.

CHAPTER 13

1. What properties do you need to set for a SQL Server connection string when passing a user name and password?

A. You need to set `Server`, `User ID`, `Password`, and `Database`.

2. Which method do you execute when updating data using a `SQLCommand` object?

A. `ExecuteNonQuery` is the method to use to run update queries.

3. Why would you use Integrated Security in your connection string?

A. You would use Integrated Security when you want to access the database and have the security of the current application user.

4. If you do not need to create `update/delete/insert` commands, how do you have them created automatically?

A. Use a `SqlCommandBuilder` to create `update/delete/insert` commands.

5. What method do you use to populate a dataset with data?

A. Use the `Fill` method to populate a `DataSet`.

CHAPTER 14

1. If you want to build a design and layout that can be inherited by Web Form pages, how do you build it?

A. To create a design that other Web Forms can inherit, you should implement master pages.

2. To change the way elements of the page appear, you have two good options when designing web pages. What are they?

A. When creating Web Forms, you can use themes and skins or cascading style sheets to update the appearance of elements.

3. What property do you set to have static client IDs for server controls?

A. Set the `ClientIDMode` property to `Static` to force a static client ID.

4. Name one control you can use to help validate form data.

A. You can use a `RequiredFieldValidator` to force users to enter data when submitting a form. Other controls are `CompareValidator`, `CustomValidator`, `RangeValidator`, and `RegularExpressionValidator`.

CHAPTER 15

1. Where are shared assemblies stored?

A. Shared assemblies are stored in the GAC.

2. How are updates handled when using ClickOnce deployment?

A. Updates are handled automatically when using ClickOnce.

3. Describe a reason to not use XCOPY deployment?

A. When you need to install other requirements XCOPY deployment should not be used.

CHAPTER 16

1. What are the two types of layouts you learned about? Which one would you use most for content applications?

A. Fixed layout and adaptive layout. For a content application, use an adaptive layout.

2. What is the most important consideration in Windows 8 style design?

A. Touch

3. How do Windows 8 applications' design considerations differ from Windows applications?

A. The main differences you learned are the desire to fill the screen and support touch.

4. What is the minimum screen resolution to use to design Windows 8 applications?

A. The minimum resolution is 1024 × 768.

INDEX

INDEX

Connect with Wrox.

Participate

Take an active role online by participating in our P2P forums @ **p2p.wrox.com**

Wrox Blox

Download short informational pieces and code to keep you up to date and out of trouble

Join the Community

Sign up for our free monthly newsletter at **newsletter.wrox.com**

Wrox.com

Browse the vast selection of Wrox titles, e-books, and blogs and find exactly what you need

User Group Program

Become a member and take advantage of all the benefits

Wrox on twitter

Follow @wrox on Twitter and be in the know on the latest news in the world of Wrox

Wrox on facebook

Join the Wrox Facebook page at **facebook.com/wroxpress** and get updates on new books and publications as well as upcoming programmer conferences and user group events

Contact Us.

We love feedback! Have a book idea? Need community support?
Let us know by emailing wrox-partnerwithus@wrox.com

CPSIA information can be obtained
at www.ICGtesting.com
Printed in the USA
LVHW101523100220
646416LV00021BA/1449

9 781119 092117